Workers and Canadian History

Workers and Canadian History is a collection of twelve previously published essays by Gregory Kealey. Over the last twenty years Kealey's work
has inspired a rethinking of the history of workers in Canada and
elsewhere. Available for the first time in a single volume, the essays
provide an extensive study of various trends and themes in Canadian
labour and working-class history, covering major developments in
historiography, debates, and key events in the nineteenth and twentieth
centuries.

Kealey provides an overview of the study of workers in Canada as well
as in-depth studies of two of Canada's leading scholars in the field,
political economist Clare Pentland and Marxist historian Stanley Bréhaut
Ryerson. He analyses the development of Canadian labour history in
particular and of social history in general, and provides detailed empirical
studies of the Orange Order in Toronto, printers and their unions, the
Knights of Labor, and the Canadian labour revolt of 1919. The collection
concludes with three synthetic views of Canadian working-class history,
focusing on the labour movement, the role of strikes, and attempts by the
state to manage class conflict.

Workers and Canadian History will be of great interest to students and
scholars of Canadian history, labour history, Marxist and socialist theory
and history, and political science.

GREGORY S. KEALEY is professor of history and university research
professor, Memorial University, and the editor of *Labour/Le Travail*.

Workers and Canadian History

GREGORY S. KEALEY

McGill-Queen's University Press
Montreal and Kingston • Buffalo • London

© McGill-Queen's University Press 1995
ISBN 0-7735-1352-3 (cloth)
ISBN 0-7735-1355-8 (paper)

Legal deposit fourth quarter 1995
Bibliothèque nationale du Québec

Printed in Canada on acid-free paper

McGill-Queen's University Press is grateful
to the Canada Council for support of its
publishing program.

Canadian Cataloguing in Publication Data

Kealey, Gregory S., 1948–
   Workers and Canadian history

   Includes bibliographical references and index.
   ISBN 0-7735-1352-3 (bound)
   ISBN 0-7735-1355-8 (pbk.)

   I. Working class – Canada – History. 2. Labor
   movement – Canada – History. I. Title.

HD8104.K43 1995   331'.0971'09   C95-900594-3

To the memories of
Herbert Gutman (1928–1985) and
Christopher Lasch (1932–1994),
distinguished historians, mentors, and friends.

Contents

Tables, Figures, and Maps

Preface

The rise to prominence in Canadian historical writing of labour history or, as I and most labour historians prefer, working-class history has been one of the major historiographic themes of the past twenty-five years. A simple quantitative measure of this development is the space devoted to it in the series of bibliographic guides which have appeared sporadically since 1974 as guides for students and researchers of Canadian history. In 1974, when the first such guide appeared, "Labour and Industrial Relations" merited about two and one-half pages of Michael Bliss's chapter on "Business and Economic History."[1] Three years later, Bliss divided his identically titled chapter into two sections and devoted four and one-half pages to labour, with subsections on unions and working-class life. Most significantly, however, he noted in his conclusion that "I have suggested that working class and trade union history be given a separate chapter in the next edition of this guide."[2] When a new publisher produced a two-volume *Readers' Guide to Canadian History* five years later, the editors of the post-Confederation volume made good on Bliss's promise and commissioned Irving Abella to produce a chapter on "Labour and Working Class History." Abella's twenty-three-page chapter enthusiastically greeted this breakthrough: "Canadian labour history has finally arrived!"[3] Recently, a new editor commissioned Craig Heron to produce an unambiguously titled chapter on "Working-Class History." In response, Heron devoted thirty-seven pages (an exponential increase over Bliss's early efforts) to works organized under sections on "family and household," "neighbourhood and community," "wage-earners' struggles," "industry and union studies," "workers and politics," and "biographies." By way of introduction to the field, Heron alludes to the new debates that continue to fuel controversy in this area of historical study: "having established the legitimacy of using class as a category of historical analysis, historians are becoming more aware of the need to integrate gender and ethnicity/race as crucial factors in shaping the Canadian working-class experience. The field thus continues to evolve dynamically in innovative directions."[4]

A different measure of the development of the field is found in the history of the journal *Labour/Le Travail*.[5] The fledgling Committee on Canadian Labour History,[6] founded in 1971, decided at its meeting during the Learned Societies Conference at Queen's University in 1973 to strike a committee to investigate the possibility of founding a journal. Three years later the first issue of *Labour* appeared under the joint editorship of myself and James Thwaites. (I was then at Dalhousie and Thwaites was at the Rimouski campus of the University of Quebec.) The journal appeared as an annual under my editorship alone from 1977 to 1980 when it began to appear semi-annually. *Labour* moved from Dalhousie to Memorial with its editor the following year and has continued to expand and prosper. While an objective assessment can hardly come from the journal's editor, it seems fair to say that *Labour/Le Travail* enjoys a reputation as one of Canada's most vibrant historical journals.

This volume brings together my contributions to the development of the field of working-class history over the past fifteen years. These essays were previously scattered throughout various collections of conference proceedings, essays, and national and international journals, and while some were easily accessible, many were unfortunately in somewhat obscure places. This collection is intended to make this work more readily available, especially for students. In addition, however, I hope that their related themes and developing arguments justify their appearance in one volume on grounds firmer than simple convenience.

I first became interested in the study of Canadian labour and working-class history in the mid to late 1960s while a student at the University of Toronto. The intersection of my political commitments and my intellectual curiosity, both very much the product of that much-maligned decade, propelled me south of the border to pursue doctoral studies at the University of Rochester. I went there to work with the late Herbert G. Gutman, the American pioneer of the new working-class history. I did so despite nationalist opposition because I felt strongly that the available graduate programs in Canadian history had little to offer me in the area of working-class history. This decision I have never regretted, although I think it explains a hostility to my work that has on occasion surfaced in certain quarters.

While at Rochester, I benefitted not only from Gutman's mentoring but also from working with the late Christopher Lasch and from exposure to Eugene Genovese, then chair of the department. Perhaps above all else, I learned an immense amount from the remarkable group of graduate students that had gathered there to write American and European social history. Leon Fink, Russell Jacoby, William Leach, Bruce Levine, and David Noble, to mention only the best known, all contributed to an enormously stimulating intellectual climate that had much to do with the times. For those of us who experienced the intellectual ferment of the late 1960s and early 1970s, the subsequent decades have seemed but pale imitations. Some may regard this as mere nostalgia, but I look forward to a reoccurrence of such an exciting intellectual moment in North American and European universities.

The late 1960s and early 1970s were crucial years in my intellectual development. I returned to Toronto in 1972 to pursue the research for my doctoral dissertation, which formed the core of my *Toronto Workers Respond to Industrial Capitalism, 1867–1892*.[7] In 1974 I had the good fortune to receive an appointment in the Department of History at Dalhousie University, where for the next seven years I joined an impressive group of Canadian social historians and worked with an even more inspiring cadre of doctoral students. This move from Central Canada to Nova Scotia also proved crucial to my development as a Canadian social historian. Exposure to the import and impact of region in Canadian history combined with my intellectual commitment to the study of class and gender to complete a trilogy of historical interests that have proven increasingly unpopular with Central Canadian historians as the 1980s progressed into the current decade. My final career move to Memorial University in 1981 has only further deepened my exposure to the problems of Atlantic Canada and to the necessity for Canadian historiography to keep such questions at the forefront of debate.

This collection is divided into four sections, each of which illustrates separate but connected chapters in my intellectual biography of the past decades. Part I, "Antecedents," reviews the historiography of the Canadian working class. It begins with an overview and then provides an analysis of the contributions of two important Canadian scholars: Clare Pentland, whose work received attention largely posthumously, and Stanley Ryerson, whose work had its greatest impact in Quebec.

Part II, "Debates," brings together two somewhat different pieces. The first, "Labour and Working-Class History: Prospects for the 1980s," was my contribution to a symposium on Class and Community: Perspectives on Canada's Labour Past organized by Bryan Palmer and held at McGill University in March 1980. At this conference my paper was paired with one by David Bercuson, who used the occasion to launch a vigorous assault on those of us who he argued had created a mythology of working-class solidarity and class conflict in Canadian history through an appeal to a concept which he firmly rejected – working-class culture.[8] My paper attempts to place the development of the debate about working-class culture in a broader international historiographic context. In that sense, it is closely related to the other paper in this section, an attempt to introduce English Canadian social history to a British audience.

Part III, "Studies of Class and Class Conflict," contains samples of my work in various aspects of Canadian working-class history as opposed to the historiographic essays of Parts I and II. "Toronto Orangemen and the Corporation" is a retrospective look at the social and political origins of the Toronto working-class community of the late nineteenth century that was the subject of my monograph *Toronto Workers*.[9] It argues that class analysis is a useful analytic tool even in periods preceding the advent of industrial capitalism. (The irony of its inclusion in a collection of essays entitled *Forging a Consensus* seems to have been lost on everyone but me.[10])

Harry Braverman's work on the labour process in monopoly capitalism, published in 1974, heavily influenced the writing of North American working-class history.[11] My essay on Canadian printers and work control is drawn from the important collection of Canadian essays on the labour process, *On the Job*.[12] Again building on my earlier work on Toronto printers, I mount broader arguments about the success of Canadian typographers in the 1890s in neutralizing the introduction of typesetting machinery through their successful imposition of union rules and control.

"The Bonds of Unity" is a synthetic essay, written with Bryan D. Palmer, that summarizes many of the main arguments of our *Dreaming of What Might Be: The Knights of Labor in Ontario, 1880–1900*.[13] Building on my monograph on Toronto and Bryan's on Hamilton workers, the study surveys the massive organizational successes of the Knights of Labor in Ontario in the 1880s.[14] It argues that for a relatively brief moment in the mid-1880s the Knights built a movement culture of resistance to industrial capitalist society that held out the notion of a different form of social organization, one built on cooperation, democracy, and producers' power.[15]

The last essay in this section represents more recent developments in my work, which moves forward in time into the early twentieth century and focuses on class conflict and the state. "1919: The

Canadian Labour Revolt" was written for a 1983 University of Winnipeg Symposium on the General Strike. This presentation again
clashed strongly with the views of David Bercuson, presented at that
conference and more recently in the reprint of his 1974 study of the
strike.[16] I shall let readers come to their own conclusions about this
exchange. The arguments here on 1919 and the labour revolt have led
to my new research on state repression of labour and the left.[17]

In Part IV I have brought together three essays that provide overviews of Canadian working-class history. The first is an attempt to offer a broad periodization of the development of the Canadian working
class. The second, derived from work for volume 3 of the *Historical
Atlas of Canada* and co-authored with Douglas Cruikshank, offers an
overview of Canadian strike activity from 1890–1950.[18] The third and
last essay provides a long-range look at the development of the federal
state's policies in the realm of labour relations. Written for a British
conference on comparative state social policies in Australia, Argentina, and Canada, it surveys fifty years of development to demarcate
broad trends.

These twelve essays cover considerable historiographic ground and
range over the better parts of two centuries of Canadian history.
While tracing only one historian's intellectual development over the
past twenty years, they also illustrate trends in the discipline. Many of
the major changes in Canadian historical writing that have occurred
in the past twenty years have recently come under sustained attack.
Constitutional, military, and political history are once again being
trumpeted as what history is *really* about.[19] As Jack Granatstein put it
so succinctly, "Really, who cares about the history of housemaid's
knee in Belleville in the 1890s?"[20] I hope that in these essays I have
answered that question clearly. I care, and, more importantly, all
historians should care because history, as written by Donald Creighton or by his putative reincarnations, neither captures the Canadian
past nor speaks to Canada's present. Invocation of that tradition of
Canadian historical writing are little more than a plea for a return to
simpler times. Like all nostalgia, its satisfaction is fleeting at best; the
present has a curious habit of dramatically reimposing reality. A
Canadian history which ignores native people, peasants, workers,
women, ethnicity, race, and region in an effort to re-establish and to
privilege history as made by the Canadian corporate elite in Ottawa,
Montreal, and Toronto simply will not satisfy the demands of the vast
majority of Canadians to understand their past in order to deal with
the conflicts of the present.

Today there is a second attack on working-class history; indeed, in
its more extreme forms, on history itself. The rise of post-structuralist

theory has had significant international impact and while historians, especially Canadian historians, have maintained a sceptical distance, the international debate is nevertheless making its presence felt.[21] I shall not try to respond here to the more scathing dismissals of the discipline of history penned by any number of so-called "critical theorists," who are usually embedded in either literature departments or interdisciplinary programs such as cultural studies or women's studies. Their dismissal of the possibilities of *any* history lies beyond this discussion.[22] More serious, however, are developments within historical writing that seem intended to negate advances in social history, represented at their best by the work of the British Marxists. To a considerable degree this debate has been fiercest in English-speaking countries among American historians of France, predictably influenced by current French intellectual fashion, among women's historians, affected by developments in post-structuralist feminist theory, and among certain historians of the English working class, apparently still working out a combination of generational conflicts with the British Marxist historians (especially E.P. Thompson) and reactions of the demoralizing rise of Thatcherism.[23]

For our purposes, the last group has the most direct significance, although arguably post-structuralist-feminist theory has been most influential in Canada. The recent work of Gareth Stedman Jones and Patrick Joyce has generated whirls of historiographical controversy. It is my view that the criticisms of Jones's work on Chartism by an impressive array of scholars of the English working class have easily turned back his critique, which, while allegedly an important part of the so-called "linguistic turn" in social history, in reality reads more like a return to the formal history of political thought.[24] Similarly, although more adventuresome and polemical, the most recent work of Patrick Joyce is strongest in the empirical detail found in the middle chapters of his books and weakest in positing great theoretical ruptures with the work of the British Marxist historians. I would argue that the best work of historical materialism has been sensitive to what is sensible in these historians' new concern for language, emotion, and subjectivity. Meanwhile, the excessive claims of post-structuralist theory tend either to invalidate history completely or to entrap historians into what Charles Tilly has aptly termed "softcore solipsism."[25]

None of this should be taken as a denial of the significant contributions of women's history and of much of feminist theory. Recent work in Canadian history by scholars such as Bettina Bradbury, Karen Dubinsky, Franca Iacovetta, Joy Parr, Joan Sangster, and Mariana Valverde, to name only a few, have demonstrated the ever-increasing richness of our understanding of the working-class world when our framework of analysis is expanded to include sex and gender.[26] To choose but one specific example, Christina Burr's work on women in the Toronto printing trades has augmented significantly my earlier work on late-nineteenth-century typographers.[27] Hence, while women and gender do not play a prominent role in the essays that follow, if I were to rewrite them, they would. Having said that, I think it equally important to note that certain developments in post-structuralist feminist theory are antithetical to the core of historical materialism to which I still hold. Needless to say, serious criticism of such theory within women's history continues to make this clear.[28]

Thus in 1994 social history, historical materialism, and even history itself are all under attack from a variety of sources, ranging from Canada's old historical establishment of political and military historians to post-structuralist theorists. While the essays included in this collection undoubtedly will prove unacceptable to everyone within that range of critics, I can only hope that they will still find an audience among scholars, students, and other citizens who believe that the past can still tell us much about the present, that the past is indeed knowable, and that historical materialism is still a vital tool for accomplishing the task of writing history.

NOTES

1 J.L. Granatstein and Paul Stevens, eds., *Canada since 1867: A Bibliographical Guide* (Toronto: Hakkert 1974), 67–70.
2 J.l. Granatstein and Paul Stevens, eds., *Canada since 1867*, 2nd ed. (Toronto: Hakkert 1977), 80–4, quotation at 84.
3 J.L. Granatstein and Paul Stevens, eds, *A Readers' Guide to Canadian History* Vol. 2: *Confederation to the Present* (Toronto: University of Toronto Press 1982), 114–36, quotation at 114.
4 Doug Owram, ed., *Canadian History: A Reader's Guide.* Vol. 2: *Confederation to the Present* (Toronto: University of Toronto Press 1994), 114–36, quotation at 114.
5 The journal was originally titled *Labour/Le Travailleur* but was changed to its present *Labour/Le Travail* in 1983 to remove the sexist connotations of its original French title.
6 The Committee on Canadian Labour History was renamed the Canadian Committee on Labour History in 1991 to reflect its interest in the history of the international working class.
7 Gregory S. Kealey, *Toronto Workers Respond to Industrial Capitalism* (Toronto: University of Toronto Press 1980; rev. ed. 1991).
8 David J. Bercuson, "Through the Looking Glass of Culture: An Essay

on the New Labour History and Working-Class Culture in Recent Canadian Historical Writing," *Labour/Le Travailleur* 7 (1981): 85–112. Also available in David J. Bercuson, ed., *Canadian Labour History: Selected Readings* (Toronto: Copp Clark Pitman 1987), 257–72.

9 Kealey, *Toronto Workers*, esp. chap. 7–9.

10 Victor L. Russell, ed., *Forging a Consensus: Historical Essays on Toronto* (Toronto: University of Toronto Press 1984).

11 Harry Braverman, *Labor and Monopoly Capital: The Degradation of Work in the Twentieth Century* (New York: Monthly Review Press 1974).

12 Craig Heron and Robert Storey, eds, *On the Job: Confronting the Labour Process in Canada* (Montreal and Kingston: McGill-Queen's University Press 1986).

13 (New York: Cambridge University Press 1982) and (Toronto: New Hogtown Press 1987).

14 Kealey, *Toronto Workers*, and Bryan D. Palmer, *A Culture in Conflict: Skilled Workers and Industrial Capitalism in Hamilton, Ontario, 1860–1914* (Montreal and Kingston: McGill-Queen's University Press 1979).

15 Our arguments proved highly controversial. For one critique and our response, see Michael Piva, "'The Bonds of Unity': A Comment" and Kealey and Palmer, "'The Bonds of Unity': Some Further Reflections," *Histoire sociale/Social History* 31 (1983): 169–74, 175–89.

16 David J. Bercuson, *Confrontation at Winnipeg: Labour, Industrial Relations, and the General Strike* (Montreal and Kingston: McGill-Queen's University Press 1974; 2nd ed., 1990). See especially his new "A Longer View," 196–205. See also David J. Bercuson and David Bright, eds, *Canadian Labour History: Selected Readings*, 2nd ed. (Toronto: Copp Clark Pitman 1994), 163–239.

17 Examples of this work include Gregory S. Kealey and Reg Whitaker, eds, *RCMP Security Bulletins* (St John's: Canadian Committee on Labour History 1989–), 5 vols to date; "State Repression of Labour and the Left in Canada, 1914–20: The Impact of World War I," *Canadian Historical Review* 73 (1992): 281–314; "The Surveillance State: The Origins of Domestic Intelligence and Counter-Subversion in Canada, 1914–1920," *Intelligence and National Security* 7 (1992): 179–210; "The Early Years of State Surveillance of Labour and the Left in Canada: The Institutional Framework of the RCMP Security and Intelligence Apparatus, 1918–1926," *Intelligence and National Security* 8 (1993): 129–48.

18 See Plate 28, "Organized Labour, 1891–1929"; Plate 39, "Strikes, 1891–1929"; Plate 45, "Workers' Response to the Great Depression"; and Plate 62, "Organized Labour, Strikes and Politics, 1940–60"; in *Historical Atlas of Canada*, vol. 3 (Toronto: University of Toronto Press 1990), with Douglas Cruikshank.

19 See Michael Bliss, "Privatizing the Mind: The Sundering of Canadian

History, the Sundering of Canada," *Journal of Canadian Studies* 26, 4 (Winter, 1991–92: 5–17. For my response, see "Class in English-Canadian Historical Writing: Neither Privatizing, Nor Sundering," *Journal of Canadian Studies* 27, 2 (Summer, 1992): 123–9. For another response see Veronica Strong-Boag's CHA Presidential Address, "Contested Space: The Politics of Canadian Memory," 13 June 1994, CHA, Calgary, to appear in *Journal of the Canadian Historical Association*, NS no. 5 (1994): forthcoming; and Bryan D. Palmer, "On Second Thoughts: Canadian Controversies," *History Today*, forthcoming.

20 Christopher Moore, "The Organized Man," *Beaver* (April–May, 1991): 57–60, quotation at 59.

21 For helpful overviews of the phenomenon with which I am generally in agreement see Bryan D. Palmer, *Descent into Discourse: The Reification of Language and the Writing of Social History* (Philadelphia: Temple University Press 1990); Joyce Appleby, Lynn Hunt, and Margaret Jacob, *Telling the Truth about History* (New York: Norton 1994); and Lutz Niethammer, *Posthistoire: Has History Come to an End?* (London: Verso 1992).

22 For one, extreme example: Sande Cohen, *Historical Culture: On the Recording of Academic Discipline* (Berkeley: University of California Press 1986).

23 Among prominent proponents, the first category would include recent work by Joan Scott and William Sewell, the second Joan Scott again and many others, the third Gareth Stedman Jones and Patrick Joyce.

24 Gareth Stedman Jones, *Languages of Class: Studies in English Working Class History, 1832–1982* (Cambridge: Cambridge University Press 1983) and Patrick Joyce, *Visions of the People: Industrial England and the Question of Class, 1848–1914* (Cambridge: Cambridge University Press 1991). In the latter case, care must be taken with the dates of the study as the dust jacket refers to 1840, while the title page uses 1848. Ironically, the text is vague enough about such things that either date would do!

25 For only a few of these critiques see: Palmer, *Descent*, 128–33, 141–3; Palmer, "The Poverty of Theory Revisited: Or, Critical Theory, Historical Materialism, and the Ostensible End of Marxism," *left history* 1, 1 (Spring, 1993): 67–101 (also available in a slightly modified form in *International Review of Social History* 38 (1993): 133–62); Ellen Meiksins Wood, *The Retreat from Class: New "True" Socialism* (London: Verso 1986), 102–15; Neville Kirk, "In Defence of Class: A Critique of Recent Revisionist Writing on the Nineteenth-Century Working Class," *International Review of Social History* 32 (1987): 2–47; Kirk, "History, Language, Ideas and Post-modernism: A Materialist View," *Social History* 19 (1994): 221–40; Robert Gray, "The Deconstructing of the English Working Class," *Social History* 11 (1986): 363–73; James Epstein, "Re-

thinking the Categories of Working-Class History," *Labour/Le Travail* 18 (1986): 195–208; Nicholas Rogers, "Chartism and Class Struggle," *Labour/Le Travail* 19 (1987): 143–52; Charles Tilly, "Softcore Solipsism," *Labour/Le Travail* 34 (1994): 259–68, and many, many others.

26 Single examples of the important work of these authors includes: Bettina Bradbury, *Working Families: Age, Gender and Daily Survival in Industrializing Montreal* (Toronto: University of Toronto Press 1993); Karen Dubinsky, *Improper Advances: Rape and Heterosexual Conflict in Ontario, 1880–1929* (Chicago: University of Chicago Press 1993); Franca Iacovetta, *Such Hardworking People: Italian Immigrants in Postwar Toronto* (Montreal and Kingston: McGill-Queen's University Press 1992); Joy Parr, *The Gender of Breadwinners: Women, Men, and Change in Two Industrial Towns, 1880–1950* (Toronto: University of Toronto Press 1990); Joan Sangster, *Dreams of Equality: Women on the Canadian Left, 1920–1950* (Toronto: University of Toronto Press 1989); and, Mariana Valverde, *The Age of Light, Soap and Water* (Toronto: McClelland and Stewart 1991).

27 Christina A. Burr, "'Defending the Art Preservative': Class and Gender Relations in the Printing Trades Unions, 1850–1914," *Labour/Le Travail* 31 (1993): 47–73 and her "'That Coming Curse – The Incompetent Compositress': Class and Gender Relations in the Toronto Typographical Union During the Late Nineteenth Century," *Canadian Historical Review* 73 (1993): 344–66.

28 Interesting recent contributions are Joan Hoff, "Gender as Postmodern Category of Paralysis," *Women's History Review* 3 (1994): 149–68; Carolyn Steedman, "The Price of Experience: Women and the Making of the English Working Class," *Radical History Review* 59 (1994): 108–19; and her "Bimbos from Hell," *Social History* 19 (1994): 57–67.

Acknowledgments

The chapters in this book have appeared previously in whole or in part. The versions here have been only modestly revised for publication. I am happy to thank the following editors and publishers for permission to reprint my essays. I also acknowledge the support of a number of Social Sciences and Humanities Research Council of Canada grants which funded much of this research over the years.

I would also like to thank Philip Cercone of McGill-Queen's University Press for his enthusiastic support of this project, and Irene Whitfield and Joan Butler, the staff of the Canadian Committee on Labour History, for their talents and encouragement over the years.

PART ONE: ANTECEDENTS

Chapter 1   Prentice-Hall Canada. From John Schulz, ed., *Writing About Canada* (Toronto, 1990), 145–74.
Chapter 2   *Canadian Journal of Political and Social Theory* 3 (1979): 79–94.
Chapter 3   *Studies in Political Economy* 9 (1982): 103–71.

PART TWO: DEBATES

Chapter 4   Canadian Committee on Labour History. From *Labour/Le Travailleur* 7 (1981): 67–94.
Chapter 5   *Social History* 10 (1985): 347–65.

PART THREE: STUDIES OF CLASS
AND CONFLICT

Chapter 6   University of Toronto Press. From Victor L. Russell, ed., *Forging a Consensus: Historical Essays on Toronto* (Toronto 1984), 41–86.

Chapter 7   McGill-Queen's University Press. From Craig Heron and Robert Storey, eds, *On the Job* (Montreal and Kingston 1986), 75–101.

Chapter 8   Bryan D. Palmer and Gregory S. Kealey, *Histoire sociale/Social History* 28 (1981): 369–411.

Chapter 9   Canadian Committee on Labour History. From *Labour/Le Travail* 13 (1984): 11–44.

PART FOUR: OVERVIEWS

Chapter 10   Canadian Committee on Labour History. From W.J.C. Cherwinski and G.S. Kealey, eds, *Lectures in Canadian Labour and Working-Class History* (St John's 1985), 23–36.

Chapter 11   Canadian Committee on Labour History and Douglas Cruikshank. From *Labour/Le Travail* 20 (1987): 85–145.

Chapter 12   Macmillan. From D.C.M. Platt, ed., *Social Welfare, 1850–1950: Australia, Argentina and Canada Compared* (London 1989), 125–47.

PART ONE

Antecedents

1 Writing about Labour

By international standards, Canada has arrived on the labour history scene relatively late in the day. Our sister societies and publications all date from at least a decade before the creation of the Committee on Canadian Labour History in 1971 and the initial appearance of *Labour/Le Travail* in 1976.[1] *Labour History* (the United States) commenced publishing in 1960, the *Bulletin of the Society for the Study of Labour History* (England) in 1960, and *Labour History* (Australia) in 1961. Canada's relatively late start simultaneously generated advantages and problems for the writing of Canadian labour and working-class history. The advantage lay in the fact that almost from its genesis practitioners situated the field resolutely in the orbit of social history, avoiding to some degree the narrowness of institutional labour history. The difficulty arose from the relative paucity of prior work upon which to build. The plethora of studies available to British and American historians for the construction of new interpretations quite simply did not exist in Canada.

To understand that absence, we must turn to the history of the Canadian working class itself. Even the briefest account of Canadian labour must immediately identify three themes which, when taken together, account for the national uniqueness of the historical experience of our working class. The three are first, the geographic reality of sharing the North American continent with the United States of America, second, the deep national and regional identities which fracture the Canadian nation state, and third, the impact of the Canadian federal system which itself reflects those tensions. Taken together, all three have led to the historical fragmentation of both the

Canadian working class and its labour movement. Fragmentation, however, is but part of the story. The ebb and flow of working-class development and of class conflict, in turn, affected scholarly interest. Thus waves of industrial militancy and working-class self-assertiveness produced periods of academic notice. Among these, the most important were the "progressive" era from the 1880s up to the climactic strikes of 1919, the late Depression and World War II years, and the late 1960s to the present (although some might argue pessimistically that this period has also ended). In discussing the study of the Canadian working class, a multidisciplinary perspective proves more useful than one restricted to the formal discipline of history.

Any attempt to review the product of Canadian academia must make some minimal effort to consider the history of Canadian higher education as well. Here we are most concerned with the development of the discipline of history, of the cognate social sciences, of graduate studies, and of a national research infrastructure.[2] In the colonial and early national period Canadian universities maintained a classical curriculum in which moral philosophy continued to hold pride of place well into the early twentieth century.[3] While the sciences came to play an increasingly larger role in the second half of the nineteenth century, especially at McGill, history and particularly the social sciences developed slowly.[4] By 1890, most Canadian universities had Chairs of History and many began to appoint Chairs of Economics and Political Science. Still, in the 1890s most Canadians seeking higher degrees turned south to the United States and attended the new German-influenced graduate schools at Johns Hopkins, Cornell, Harvard, and Chicago.[5]

Gradually history and political economy became well-established at all Canadian universities, but remained, until the 1920s, firmly entrenched in their humanities tradition. The orientation of curricula continued to reflect the British influence more than the American, as evidenced by a strong reluctance to allow students to choose larger numbers of electives. On the other hand, steps towards professionalization had been taken. The lead in history and the social sciences came from Toronto, McGill, and Queen's. At Toronto, George Wrong began the annual *Review of Historical Publications Relating to Canada* in 1897 and in 1901 a University Press was established. Wrong's annual became the *Canadian Historical Review* in 1920 and two years later the Canadian Historical Association was founded. After an abortive first attempt in 1913, a Canadian Political Science Association was created in 1929 and the *Canadian Journal of Economics and Political Science* began publishing in 1935.[6]

The birth, in the 1920s, of a Canadian nationalism based on Canada rather than the British Empire also led to an increased concern for the development of Canadian graduate schools. Again Toronto, Queen's, and McGill played leading roles. The first PHDs in history and the social sciences came in the 1920s with history again leading the way.[7] Nevertheless this development should not be exaggerated. Most Canadian students still went south or across the Atlantic to pursue graduate degrees. After World War II Canadian graduate schools grew rapidly, owing at least partially to an infusion of American money derived initially from the Carnegie, the Rockefeller, and later the Ford Foundations and administered through the new Social Research Council, which was founded in 1940 as a social science equivalent of the National Research Council (1916). The nearly twenty-five year gap between the founding of the bodies suggests the Canadian government's relative lack of interest in the social sciences. In 1957, with the creation of the Canada Council, the federal government finally commenced a full-fledged program of graduate and post-graduate research funding, which in 1978 evolved into the Social Sciences and Humanities Research Council of Canada.

One unusual feature that marked the evolution of Canadian higher education was the hegemony of political economy. With the exception of McGill, where Carl Dawson developed a strong Sociology and Anthropology Department in the 1920s, most Canadian universities maintained a Department of Political Economy encompassing Economics, Political Science, Sociology, and, sometimes, Anthropology, until the 1960s. Toronto, the final holdout, only split its Political Economy Department into its three component parts – Commerce, Economics, and Political Science – in 1983. The implications of this historical dominance of political economy have been much debated. Canadian nationalists and some critical scholars, unhappy with the artificiality of disciplinary divisions, lament its loss while others note that the tardy development left these fields ripe for Americanization, which came with a vengeance in the 1960s when Canadian universities grew so rapidly that the recruitment of foreign academics became necessary.[8]

I

A delineation of roughly six periods of Canadian working-class development can help identify and, to some extent, explain the historical and related social scientific work that came about as a result of that development.[9] The first three periods include a colonial period up to the 1840s typified by staples extraction, an early industrial period from the 1850s to the 1890s that encompassed the creation of the new political state in 1867, and a period of capitalist consolidation from the 1890s to the early 1920s. This set is followed by a second set of three periods: first, the time from the mid-1920s to the immediate post-war era; second, the years from the late 1940s to the early 1960s (years characterized by American world dominance); and third, the period that commenced in the 1960s when the post-war, cold-war "consensus" (up to the degree that it ever existed) broke down entirely.

During the first two periods, that is up to the early 1890s, there was almost no academic writing. The early labour press of the 1870s and 1880s showed little interest in the colonial past and tended to look across the Atlantic or to the south for its historical lessons. The minuscule academic/intellectual community hardly noticed the emergence of the labour movement until events such as the nine-hour movement (a movement to reduce the working day to nine hours) of 1872, the rise of the Knights of Labor, and the Canadian version of the Great Upheaval of 1886 set off alarm bells among the elite. Renegade intellectuals, such as Canadian Knights of Labor "brain worker" Phillips Thompson, who had been nurtured in the bohemian world of nineteenth-century journalism rather than in the effete halls of academe, found themselves barred from speaking at Canadian universities.[10] Indeed, within the span of about twenty years the University of Toronto banned speeches by Thompson, by labour leader and free thinker Alfred Jury, and Jane Addams; the university also, adding anti-semitism and provincialism to reaction, refused to hire Lewis Namier into its history department because he was Jewish.

The industrial crisis of the 1880s, along with the success of the Knights of Labor in central Canada and the west, and of the Provincial Workmen's Association in the east, brought the labour question prominently into federal and provincial politics for the first time. Such social and political realities found only pale reflections in the hallowed halls of Canadian universities but they did at least lead to the initial appointments of Chairs of History and Political Economy in this period.[11] From such appointments grew some of the earliest social scientific research on the "labour problem," as it was then called. Thus, at the University of Toronto, for example, William Ashley's short tenure in the Chair of Political Economy led to the publication of the *Toronto University Studies in Political Science*, which included among its initial offerings Jean Scott's pioneering, "The Conditions of Female Labour in Ontario."[12] Such work, expressing clearly the pressing concerns of moral and social reformers, illustrates the early appearance of a "social science" tied tightly to the social projects of the growing middle class and its emerging professions.

These concerns dominated the subsequent period, the 1890s to 1919, in which the "labour problem" transformed itself into the threat of Bolshevism. In the process the Canadian working class brought more attention to itself than in any previous period, and arguably helped to establish much of the legislative and repressive framework that still governs class relations in Canada. While the repressive framework, especially the Royal Canadian Mounted Police Security Service, was a uniquely Canadian solution, the legislative framework that emerged was a peculiar amalgam of a) the North American progressive interest in the Australian and New Zealand experiment with compulsory arbitration, and b) the voluntarism of the United States' system. The author of the Canadian legislation, the major component of which was the Industrial Disputes Investigation Act of 1907, was Canada's first Deputy Minister of Labour, subsequently Minister of Labour, ultimately the country's first Prime Minister to hold a PHD, and also its longest-serving, William Lyon Mackenzie King.

King merits our attention because he epitomized the new progressive intellectual of the early twentieth century. Educated at Toronto, Chicago, and Harvard, he rejected an academic career to become Canada's first labour relations expert, successfully transforming an initially minor appointment as editor of the *Labour Gazette* into a successful career as a civil servant, mediator, politician, industrial relations consultant, author, and then Prime Minister.[13] His major work, *Industry and Humanity*, was published in Toronto in 1918, completing his commitment to the Rockefellers for whom he worked in the aftermath of the Ludlow Massacre.[14] In it he encapsulated his almost twenty years of labour relations experience and promoted a generally liberal view that included industrial peace among the rights of an ill-defined "community." King's extreme fear of labour unrest led him to the remarkable conclusion that "In many particulars, the horrors in international war pale before the possibilities of civil conflicts begotten of class hatreds."[15] Throughout the volume, his fascination with and admiration for industry and especially for management were patently clear.

King, while undoubtedly the most prominent, was but one of a group of generally American-educated intellectuals who came to the fore as social reformers and sometime students of Canadian labour in this period. They embraced the notion put forward by King that "the poor down trodden have more to hope from men who, having a specialized training in the operation of social forces, apply themselves to the proper remedy, than from all the windy, ultra-radical demagogues."[16] Scholars sharing these assumptions included Queen's political economists Adam Shortt, a frequent mediator for King under the terms of the IDIA, and O.D. Skelton, Shortt's successor at Queen's, whose major early work, *Socialism: A Critical Analysis*, won North American acclaim.[17]

Perhaps more important, however, than the scholars who wrote in this period were a younger group of intellectuals who attended university in these years and were heavily influenced by the rise of the labour movement, especially in the period 1917–20. A more activist group, many of them ended up pursuing careers in the United States for a variety of reasons: Louis Aubrey Wood had serious difficulties with Canadian university authorities, Bryce Stewart experienced a lack of career opportunities in Canada, and Norman Ware simply saw more attractive options in the United States.[18] Of the three, only Stewart returned to Canada, when, in 1939, he accepted King's offer to become Deputy Minister of Labour to supervise the creation of a new National Employment Service and the Unemployment Insurance Commission.[19] Wood pursued a distinguished career at the University of Oregon, and Ware, of course, became America's leading labour historian between the wars. Unfortunately, he turned his attention to Canadian labour for only a fleeting moment in the 1930s when he authored one of two essays in *Labour in Canadian-American Relations* for the Carnegie series on the interaction of the two countries. This study, based almost solely on secondary sources, shows little of the insight of Ware's major American studies, *The Industrial Worker* and *The Labor Movement in the United States*. Ware made his scholarly position clear in his preface to *Labor in Modern Industrial Society* (1935): "This book is written from the standpoint of labor. The author believes that this is a necessary and legitimate point of view."[20]

In the 1920s this generation of scholars completed a series of doctoral dissertations at American universities. Bryce Stewart, for example, after a brief stint working for the Amalgamated Clothing Workers, completed a Columbia PHD published in 1926 as *Canadian Labor Laws and the Treaty*.[21] This volume, while primarily a thorough examination of the evolution of Canadian labour legislation to 1925, also contains the fullest description of the history of the Canadian labour movement published up to that date. A fellow Canadian at Columbia, Edmund Bradwin, published his thesis, *The Bunkhouse Man: A Study of Work and Pay in the Camps of Canada, 1903–1914*, two years later.[22] An active reformer, Bradwin succeeded Alfred Fitzpatrick as principal of Frontier College, an educational organization that aimed to reform conditions in the bush camps housing Canadian resource workers. Perhaps the most significant of these early efforts, however, was Harold Logan's 1925 Chicago thesis titled, "The Organized Labor Movement in Canada: A History of Trade Union Organization in Canada," published in 1928.[23] Although published after Stewart's work, it seems clear that Stewart had made use of Logan's thoroughly researched thesis.[24] Logan's work was largely chronological and descriptive. He attempted little analysis, although he did show considerable interest in the One Big Union and the events of 1919, especially the Winnipeg General Strike.

The 1920s also saw in Canadian universities the tentative initiation of research into labour; a handful of MAS on the subject were completed, most at McGill with a few at Toronto as well. Unlike prewar Masters' theses, which were often undocumented and extremely brief, the theses of the 1920s conform to recognizable scholarly canons. Particularly strong McGill examples, deemed to merit publication, were Eugene Forsey's study of the Nova Scotia coal industry and Allan Latham's work on the emergence of confessional unionism in Quebec.[25] There can be little question that the militancy of the Cape Breton miners in the 1920s and the rise of Quebec's Catholic unions (along with their uniqueness by North American standards) led to these particular studies.

With significant exceptions, such as the epic struggles of Cape Breton's coal miners and steel workers, the 1920s were a dismal decade for Canadian labour. The Depression, however, led to the re-emergence of working-class militancy and to the revival of the labour movement. Similarly, the social problems engendered by the economic dislocations of the decade led to a rapid growth of academic study of Canadian workers. Unemployment merited most attention, but the massive slowdown in immigration also created a demographic breathing space in which significant scholarly attention was directed to the nature of western Canadian settlement and to the ethnic diversity of the Canadian labour force. These later projects derived much of their impetus from American scholarly concerns which had emerged in the 1920s as part of the debate on immigration restriction. Those controversies had led American social scientists to identify immigration and settlement as a major area of concern and eventually to focus on Canada as the readily available social laboratory for such studies. Thus, the Canadian Frontiers of Settlement series was launched. While completely funded by the American Social Science Research Council, Canadians controlled the research agenda; eventually eight volumes were published, the most significant of which, for our purposes, were Harold Innis' study of the mining frontier, A.R.M. Lower's work on the lumber industry, and Carl Dawson's on immigration.[26]

American funds, specifically Carnegie Endowment for International Peace money, also financed a second major series in the 1930s on Canadian-American relations. Launched in 1934 under the direction of Canadian-born James T. Shotwell, this series eventually resulted in the publication of some twenty-five volumes. While resolutely internationalist and pacifist in conception, the volumes vary sharply in focus. While a number condemn nationalism in general as irrational and downplay Canadian-American differences, the series also contains significant nationalist statements such as Donald Creighton's *Commercial Empire of the St. Lawrence* and Innis' *The Cod Fisheries*. Moreover, even the explicit binational conception found no support in the series' summary volume, John Bartlett Brebner's *The North Atlantic Triangle*, the thesis of which is accurately reflected in the title. The only volume specifically devoted to labour contained the short study by Norman Ware discussed earlier.[27]

The most significant American academic funding, however, at least in terms of Canadian working-class studies, was the Rockefeller Foundation's support for McGill's Social Science Research Project which commenced in 1930. To find a director to address the dual study of unemployment and the city of Montreal itself, McGill turned to those who had done similar English studies. On the recommendation of Sir William Beveridge, the University hired Leonard Marsh, who had worked on Beveridge's project to update Charles Booth's London survey. Marsh immediately set out to coordinate within the various social science departments a series of research projects on a variety of topics related to unemployment. The Rockefeller money funded not only faculty research but, more importantly, allowed McGill to recruit almost forty social science graduate students in the 1930s, all of whom received fellowships and eventually MAS for their individual work on the project. Among these students was Stuart Jamieson. After his McGill degree he wrote a PHD thesis at Berkeley on agricultural labourers, worked as Research Director for the Co-operative Commonwealth Federation (the social democratic predecessor of the New Democratic Party), and proceeded to an academic career at the University of British Columbia.[28] His major works, *Industrial Relations in Canada* (1957) and *Times of Trouble* (1968), represented the major surveys of labour relations and of strike activity in Canada until the late 1970s.[29] Jamieson's contribution to the Social Science Research Project was a study of the French and English presence in Montreal's institutions. Documenting carefully the dominance of the Anglo-Canadian elite, he concluded that Quebec had been conquered twice, first militarily and then economically. Prominent Yale labour economist Lloyd Reynolds also began his graduate work as a team member of the McGill project, and his own volume in the series of project publications, *The British Immigrant in Canada,* simultaneously gained him his Harvard PHD and involved him in his first academic controversy.[30]

Indeed the entire project found itself in continuous political difficulty. Marsh himself and many of the students leaned significantly to the left, either aligning themselves with the CCF or, in fewer cases, the Communist Party. At a university where the Chancellor was the President of the Canadian Pacific Railway, a clash was predictable. Moreover, studies of unemployment, immigration, and French-English relations were bound to arouse controversy, and they did. McGill rid itself of Marsh in 1941, when he moved to Ottawa as Research Director for the Committee on Reconstruction.[31] The product of that assignment, *The Report on Social Security for Canada,* is often taken as the Canadian equivalent of the Beveridge Report and regarded by some as a blueprint for postwar social policy.[32]

The social science activities at McGill in the 1930s were quite exceptional. Among historians, for example, the staples approach of economists Mackintosh and Innis held pride of place. Although representing an improvement on the whiggish constitutional history it replaced, it spent little time considering the men and women who produced the commodities upon which it focused. Even CCF activists, such as historian Frank Underhill, made no attempt to trace the emergence and development of the Canadian working class or its labour movement. Instead Underhill became intellectually fascinated by nineteenth-century Canadian liberalism and politically suspicious of the labour movement. His historical pursuit of radical intellectual roots led him not to the "brainworkers" of the Knights of Labor, nor to the early twentieth-century socialist movement, but rather to liberal politicians/intellectuals such as George Brown, Edward Blake, and Goldwin Smith. His socialism, while it lasted, was of the top-down variety, in which intellectuals played the major role. The Fabian intellectuals with whom he had contact while at Oxford before World War I represented an ideal intellectual elite, which he tried to create in the Canadian context.[33]

Political scientist and CCF activist Eugene Forsey, on the other hand, after failing to receive tenure at McGill, joined the labour movement as Research Director of the Canadian Congress of Labour; later, after its 1956 merger with the Trades and Labour Congress, he held the same position in the new Canadian Labour Congress. In his years in the labour movement, Forsey published a number of articles on the legal/constitutional side of labour history and subsequently, when nearing retirement, undertook to write a general history of the

Canadian labour movement as the CLC's Centennial Project. While not completed in time for Canada's 100th birthday and limited to the years up to 1902, Forsey's *History of Trade Unions in Canada, 1812–1902* eventually appeared in 1982. Resolutely institutional in its focus, this is not a book to read from cover to cover. On the other hand, if you want to know the TLC's position on technical education, or on anything else for that matter, in each and every convention down to 1902, and you do not want to check the original proceedings, you will find the answer here. While Forsey's book was not published until 1982, his unedited manuscript and much of the documentary material upon which it was based had been available for a number of years at the National Archives and had been broadly consulted.[34]

The Communist Party of Canada also produced some historical writing in the 1930s. Major party intellectual Stanley Ryerson offered an interpretation of the Rebellions of 1837 on their 100th anniversary, and party journalist Bill Bennett offered a brief historical overview of Canada's most westerly province in his *Builders of British Columbia* (1937). In addition, a scattering of historical essays appeared in *New Frontier*, the party's cultural and theoretical magazine in the 1930s. The CPC's major effort, however, commenced in 1948 when it launched a People's History project. Not surprisingly, the exigencies of the Cold War and the Crises of 1956 led to massive delays in the appearance of the projected multiple volumes. Nevertheless, material generated from this undertaking appeared in the late 1940s and 1950s in CPC magazines such as the *National Affairs Monthly, New Frontier*, and later in the *Marxist Quarterly*. In the 1960s Stanley Ryerson published two volumes of this work as *The Founding of Canada: Beginnings to 1815* (1960) and *Unequal Union: Confederation and the Roots of Conflict on the Canadas, 1815–1873* (1968). Charles Lipton's *Trade Union Movement of Canada, 1927–1959* (1966) also grew out of the original 1948 CPC conception of a people's history, although by the time of its appearance Lipton had left the party. To a considerable degree then, Norman Penner's generalizations about the relatively feeble nature of the Canadian Marxist intellectual tradition are sustainable, although somewhat overstated.[35]

Returning to the period of the late 1930s and World War II, we find yet another American "contribution" to Canadian labour studies. Foundation money was crucial to the creation of Industrial Relations institutes and departments in Canadian universities. In North America, the formal study of Industrial Relations had originated at Princeton in 1922 and had been funded by Rockefeller money. The Princeton model spread, and in October 1937 Queen's became the first Canadian university to adopt it.[36] Laval and the University of

Montreal followed, setting up institutes in 1944; the following year Laval began publishing *Relations Industrielles*, which in 1964 became a bilingual journal. After World War II, Toronto and McGill also set up Industrial Relations centres.

The Queen's initiative received broad business and governmental support. Not surprisingly, labour maintained a considerable distance. J.C. Cameron, the first director of the Industrial Relations Section, fits easily into the industrial pluralist consensus emerging in the 1940s. In a 1941 paper, "Dealing with Organized Labour," he called for broader rights and recognition for unions in return for legislative restrictions to ensure "responsible" behaviour.[37]

In 1945 a group of Ontario industrialists offered a hundred thousand dollars to the University of Toronto to open an Industrial Relations Department or Centre, along the lines of the one established at Queen's. Initially Toronto resisted, owing to Innis' reluctance to set up a centre that was too clearly management-oriented. The resistance was intensified by the fact that Harold Logan, the obvious labour expert at Toronto was regarded as too pro-labour by the donors. Because the university was hungry for social science research funds, a middle way was found after visits from Harvard's John Dunlop and Chicago's Fred Harbison. On 1 April 1946, an Institute of Industrial Relations under the directorship of V.W. Bladen was created. Bladen and the Australian-born C.W.M. Hart (an important institute member before he moved to Wisconsin in 1948) had both developed considerable interest in the work of another Australian, Elton Mayo (famous for the Hawthorne study), and so the Toronto centre developed a human relations orientation, the details of which we shall not pursue here. With the creation of a new Institute of Business Administration in 1950 under Bladen, the Industrial Relations School ceased to have a separate existence and lost much of its focus.[38]

While it existed, however, the institute gave labour studies at Toronto an unprecedented importance. Perhaps its most important associations were with Logan, whose *Trade Unions in Canada* (1948) received its support, and with a number of graduate students who were engaged in historical research on labour, including R.L. Elliott,[39] J.T. Montague, Egil Schonning, William Martin, and especially H. Clare Pentland. Montague's doctoral dissertation on labour in meat packing, Schonning's on unionism in the pulp and paper industries, and Martin's on the history of labour legislation in the area of conflict resolution were all important contributions written in the vein of institutional labour economics.[40] The work of Clare Pentland, however, pushed beyond the limited nature of these studies. Pentland addressed directly the question of the role of labour in the colonial staples economy. His earliest published work surveyed strikes by Irish navvies and the role of labour in early capitalist development.[41] Although his doctoral thesis was not completed until 1960 and was published only posthumously in 1981, it significantly influenced scholars of the 1960s and 1970s who were seeking historical approaches outside of the Canadian mainstream.[42] More recently, some scholars have criticized Pentland's approach, focusing on his failure to come to grips with the pre-capitalist nature of the early Canadian economy and on his inability to describe adequately the transition to capitalism.[43]

In his memoirs, V.W. Bladen, Director of the Toronto institute, drew attention to the difficulty of developing relationships with unions as well as with management. One specific incident tells us much about such problems. The presence of UAW leader Victor Reuther as a speaker at the institute's Winter Union School in 1948 led to a vigorous protest from James Duncan, President of Massey-Harris and a member of the university's Board of Governors. In 1949 union members wanted to invite Reuther again; Bladen sought University of Toronto President Sidney Smith's approval. He did not receive it because, as Bladen recalled, Smith feared that if he took such a request to the board it would be refused and he would have to resign. As a compromise, Reuther received an informal invitation from the union students.[44]

While the mainstream of Canadian historical writing was dominated in the 1930s by the staples school and then in the 1940s and 1950s by politics and biography in reaction against such allegedly "bloodless" economic history, there were always a few notable, if relatively uninfluential, exceptions. Two examples must suffice here, although there were others in the so-called "provincial" universities. At the University of Western Ontario, Fred Landon, a doctoral student at the University of Michigan under U.B. Phillips (who collaborated with John R. Commons on the *Documentary History of American Labor*), developed an early interest in social history, including the history of working people.[45] In an appreciation of his mentor, Landon commended Phillips for his belief that "history had been written too much upon the basis of what great men said ... or wrote."[46] As Landon observed in 1944: "History has a way of disinterring the records of very humble folk. ... History does not relate to the great alone but to all men, and the humble folk are always the more numerous."[47] Landon's eclectic work explored various aspects of life in south-western Ontario, including abolitionism, Black history, and the Rebellion of 1837. Among his most important contributions are: "The Common Man in the Era of Rebellion," *Western Ontario and the*

American Frontier (1941), *An Exile from Canada to Van Dieman's Land* (1960), and his C.H.A. presidential address, "The Canadian Scene, 1880–1890."[48] In the latter, Landon tackled a decade and postulated that "the general pattern of Canadian affairs during the 1880's ... like many other accepted patterns in history is incomplete." Why? Because, Landon answered, "These memoirs are chiefly political in character and show little interest in other phases of national life." He then drew attention to three other important "phases" of national life; the first of these was labour's struggles, especially the rise of the Knights of Labor and the Great Upheaval of 1886–87.[49]

As part of his enthusiasm for local history, Landon played a major role in commemorating the Tolpuddle Martyrs, five of whom settled in Ontario after their pardons.[50] In addition, Landon directed students' attention to the Knights of Labor, after attempting to collect their records in the 1930s.[51] J.I. Cooper and later Douglas Kennedy wrote MA theses under his supervision; Cooper focused on the Knights' role in the 1887 federal election and Kennedy attempted a full narrative history of the order in Canada.[52]

Landon, however, made little impact on Canadian historical writing. Early rejection slips from W.S. Wallace, the editor of the *Canadian Historical Review* might serve as an epitaph: "the subject strikes me as perhaps a trifle narrow" and, in a second case, "its interest is too local."[53] Landon did influence his students, however, and one of them, J.I. Cooper, went on to a long career at McGill where he authored some of the few early accounts of Canadian labour by a professional historian. His interest no doubt was also influenced by his personal background:

The home I grew up in was working-class, c of e, and *very* conventional. My mother was an elementary school teacher; my father a railway-engine driver. He divided his time unevenly between bouts on the foot-plate and minor office jobs in *The Trainmen's Journal*, where he was a very humble associate of Eugene Debs, the American socialist.[54]

Despite Cooper's assertion, this background was quite unconventional among Canadian academics of his generation. Not a prolific author, his major contributions in the field of labour history lay in two articles, the first, on the Quebec Ship Labourers Benevolent Society, was published in 1949 and the second, on the social structure of Montreal in the mid-nineteenth century, was published seven years later.[55] In addition, he supervised early graduate work in the field including theses on the role of the Knights in Canada in the 1880s, and an analysis of the Grand Trunk Railway strike of 1877.[56]

Cooper, if anything, had even less impact than Landon on Canadian historical writing. In reflecting on his career in 1979, he credited Landon as being the major influence on him, noting that "implicit in [his] teaching were the economic and social forces that operate on people." By his example even more than by his teaching, Landon convinced Cooper "that no historian is worth his salt if he does not concern himself critically and productively in the area in which he lives."[57] Such ideas remained unpopular in the 1940s and 1950s and local history was most often dismissed as the domain of antiquarians.[58]

Those four, Cooper, Landon, Pentland, and Ryerson, represent exceptions to Canadian historiography's mainstream in the late 1940s, 1950s, and most of the 1960s. While never as overtly self-congratulatory as the United States consensus-school historians, Canadian historians similarly turned away from the economic focus of the 1930s and instead concentrated on biography and political history. Even the most influential social democratic historian of the period, Kenneth McNaught, offered a biography, albeit not of a Prime Minister but of CCF founder J.S. Woodsworth.[59]

One biographer, or rather a partially biographical study, that was even farther from the mainstream than McNaught's, was Harry Ferns and Bernard Ostry's critical *The Age of Mackenzie King* (1955). Ferns, a Canadian and former Communist, who had been red-baited out of the public service and then deprived of an academic career in his own country, joined forces with Ostry to produce a slashing attack on the image of King as a pro-labour social reformer. This volume so upset the Liberal orthodoxy that the carefully orchestrated official biography which was proceeding at an appropriately magisterial pace was regarded as an inadequate response and an additional study was produced by King loyalist F.A. Macgregor.[60] Former Liberal cabinet minister Brooke Claxton, in a letter to fellow Liberal politician and former historian Jack Pickersgill, described the Ferns and Ostry volume as "tiresome emissions of Communist venom."[61] Ostry later authored two useful articles on Canadian labour and politics in the 1870s and 1880s.[62]

One other scholar of the 1950s joined Pentland in having an important underground following in the late 1960s. Frank Watt's iconoclastic Toronto PHD thesis on "Radicalism in English Canadian Literature Since Confederation" and his article on proletarian ideas in late Victorian Canada enjoyed a wide New Left audience.[63] Watt's careful reading of the nineteenth-century labour press not only opened up a viable research source in ways previously unanticipated but also identified numerous important working-class thinkers, including Phillips Thompson, for further study.

II

By the mid-1960s considerable dissatisfaction with Canadian historical writing began to emerge within the profession itself. In the late
1960s events in Quebec and in English Canada provided an additional external challenge to the national historiographic consensus.[64] A
number of developments coincided to create numerous tensions within Canadian historical writing and from these tensions decisive new
directions emerged.[65] Among these developments were: Quebec's nationalist challenge to the existence of a unified Canadian state and a
simultaneous surge of regional sentiment from other aggrieved components of the artificial Confederation of 1867; a liberal challenge to
all nationalisms, best reflected in the historical writing by Ramsay
Cook and in the political stances of Pierre Elliott Trudeau, and, ironically, a coincident surge of English Canadian (especially Ontario-
based) neo-nationalism, which expressed itself most strongly as anti-
Americanism in both the economic and foreign policy realms; a resurgence of working-class militancy, which led to a series of Royal
Commissions to investigate, yet again, the state's labour relations
machinery and which eventually resulted in a state-imposed wage
freeze in the guise of an incomes policy; and, finally, the emergence
of a New Left, itself split along national (French-English), regional,
and gender lines, which displayed a second division between leftist
nationalists and those they referred to disparagingly as "Metropolitan
Marxists." From this confusion emerged a Canadian social history in
which class, region, and (somewhat belatedly) ethnicity and gender
finally began to receive the attention they merited. But attempts to
integrate these diverse elements into a coherent historical whole have
so far failed. As historical reality fractured, no new syntheses emerged
to replace the older, all-encompassing views – a problem with which
u.s. historians have also tried to grapple.[66]

Broadly defined, Canadian labour and working-class history began
to appear in significant amounts in the late 1960s and early 1970s.
By 1971, enough interest existed to create the Committee on Canadian
Labour History. The committee started a *Newsletter*, eventually up-
graded to a *Bulletin* (closely modelled on that of the British "Society
for the Study of Labour History") and finally to *Labour/Le Travail* in
1976. Within the committee and on the *Labour/Le Travail* editorial
board tension developed between two identifiable groups: on the one
hand, young professors who had either just published or were about
to publish their first books and, on the other hand, graduate students
who had emerged from the student movement of the 1960s. What
seems remarkable in retrospect was the gap which separated these

two groups from more senior colleagues: for reasons that should by now be only too clear, there existed no direct line of succession from previous generations of scholars in the field. To be fair, there was an advisory editorial board filled with international luminaries (Royden Harrison, Jean Maîtron, and David Montgomery) and a number of senior Canadian scholars previously mentioned in this paper (Stuart Jamieson, Kenneth McNaught, Clare Pentland, and Stanley Ryerson). Their presence, however, was primarily promotional and the advisory board was allowed to lapse in 1980, its members having played no substantive role in the life of the journal. The one partial exception was Michael S. Cross (whose work in the 1960s on the Ottawa Valley timber trade went beyond the historiographic parameters of its day), who provided considerable support to the journal as a Dalhousie colleague of its editor in its first four years.[67]

The conflict reached a climax in the early 1980s, with a series of review essays by Kenneth McNaught, Desmond Morton, and David Bercuson on the one hand, and myself and Bryan Palmer on the other. Carl Berger's summary of the debate as "captious, intemperate, and confusing" suggests its flavour, and his characterization of the two sides as "the upholders of the social democratic tradition and those who had embraced a humanistic Marxism" has the advantage of offering a non-participant's viewpoint of the ideological origins of the debate. There is little to argue with in his overall assessment:

These exchanges also obscured the very significant achievements of those who had penetrated beyond the political confines. They recovered copious and scarcely suspected details on social life in the Victorian period: they have helped move to the centre of attention the social conflict that accompanied the arrival of industrial society, and have accorded a place to ideas and attitudes in history that belied the commonplace image of Marxist scholarship as materialistic, and they have contributed far more to the ultimate clarification of class – and class in history – than the statisticians of social mobility.[68]

Indeed the debate has to a large degree quieted. Many of Bercuson's "generation" have either moved into academic administration (Ross McCormack) or into other fields of historical interest such as military (Terry Copp, Morton), diplomatic (Bercuson), public policy (Donald Avery), and immigration (Irving Abella).

The debate emerged once more in 1984, this time from an unexpected source; *Studies in Political Economy*, Canada's major socialist academic journal, published a challenge to the so-called "new labour history" by left-nationalist, political scientist Daniel Drache. Building on the critiques of Bercuson and McNaught, Drache constructed an eclectic amalgam of various labour market theories, Innis' staples model, neo-nationalism, a pinch of world system analysis, and some curiously chosen empirical facts about Canadian labour history. Identifying three crucial periods of labour market formation – canal building in the early 1830s, central Canadian industrialization in the late 1890s, and the opening of the west and growth of a resource proletariat from 1900 to 1920 – Drache argued that the "new labour history" had mistaken Toronto and Hamilton for the entire country, had misunderstood the centrality of the national question, and had insufficiently addressed colonial developments.[69] In a spirited rejoinder, Bryan Palmer reviewed the development of Canadian labour studies and especially the criticisms of Bercuson, McNaught, and others in a fashion reminiscent of his September 1981 commentary at the Australian-Canadian-British (termed by its organizers "Commonwealth") Labour History Conference at Warwick.[70] Defending historians and their methods, Palmer assailed Drache's argument. In perhaps the most interesting part of his response, Palmer rejected the notion that labour historians' work had been too theoretical and called instead for more theory. Then, further exploring territory he had tentatively traversed in *Working Class Experience*, he redefined the terms of new labour history. It must, he argued, be "premised on the essential tenets of historical materialism," now understood as conceiving

class not in this or that particular, but as a totality resting on the essential economic relations of production, yet emerging and making itself, and being made, in an integrated series of realms that, by the very nature of bourgeois society, are divorced from one another and carved up between the public and private arenas, of an atomized social existence.

Most importantly, he called for more attention "to the structural and determining features of economic life," to the "peculiarities of place," to the state, and "above all else, to the two-sidedness of working-class life." He went on to argue that the strength of the work to date had been the description of working-class struggle and resistance; what was necessary now was equal attention to questions of accommodation in all its forms.[71]

An assessment of the two most recent attempts at synthesis in the field, Desmond Morton, *Working People* and Bryan Palmer, *Working-Class Experience: The Rise and Reconstitution of Canadian Labour, 1800–1980* also illustrates the two contrasting approaches.[72] The two books serve as core texts for most Canadian labour and working-class history courses and they could not be more different. Palmer sets out to study "the totality of working-class experience":

It is *class*, as embedded in the structural, primarily economic context of specific social formations, that is at the conceptual root of this study, not labour as an interest group fighting its way into a pluralist society by way of its unions and its political platform. The development of distinct working and nonworking classes was a protracted and contradictory process. It grew out of the economic relations of production, but was also clarified and reproduced over time in other formal and informal ways; through ritual and revelry, culture and conflict, family and funeral and, of course, through the strengths, weaknesses, and character of the workers' movement itself. At times new initiatives – from *capital* and/or the state – drove it into retreat, but its potential was never relinquished entirely.[73]

Contrast this with Morton's assertion that his book "does not build on theories borrowed from the great English labour historian E.P. Thompson" and his sarcastic comment that "it is one of the virtues of modern social history that it gives due attention to those who say little and do nothing of historical significance."[74] Of Palmer's 300 pages almost half are devoted to the nineteenth century, while Morton devotes only 66 of 357 pages to what he clearly regards as pre-history, noting critically of Palmer's book that it devotes only one-third of its coverage to the period after 1919.[75] Moreover, Morton asserts unequivocally that

... the crucial decade in Canadian working class history is ... the Second World War and the post war years of prosperity, full employment and expanding social justice. ... For those with utopian visions of what life and labour might be and for those who find romantic fulfillment in defeat, the prosperous post-war years have little appeal.[76]

The field of debate should be clear by now.

III

Nevertheless, a brief consideration of the three major edited collections in the field suggests that the debate of the early 1980s may itself have passed into history. Bercuson's *Canadian Labour History* includes two of the core texts of the debate and discusses in its introduction the generational differences between "democratic socialists" and Marxists. But Bercuson now describes labour history as a component of social history, which he promotes as "*the* dominant area of specialization" in Canadian historical writing. "Most historians," he argues, "now recognize that the history of workers is part of the history of employers and political leaders, and vice versa." Clearly, some ground has been gained.[77] Meanwhile, Palmer, in his introduction to *The Character of Class Struggle: Essays in Canadian Working-Class History, 1850–1985*, concedes "that there has been more to history than class war," but proceeds to demonstrate through this collection of essays how "the character of class struggle within particular political economies" has changed in the last 135 years. He concludes, "If the changing and complex character of class struggle in Canada has not consumed all of our history, it has at least occupied the centre of one of the stages on which our past had been acted out."[78]

The third reader, Craig Heron and Bob Storey's *On the Job: Confronting the Labour Process in Canada*, turns to a series of workplaces in the period from 1850 to the present and shows how workers and bosses have struggled for control, with varying degrees of respective success. In their overview, the editors remind us:

There has not been a single, permanent shift in working-class consciousness that resulted in complete submission and deference to capitalist authority. ... Instead a pattern of ebbing and flowing, of surging and receding, is evident: in 1867, the dramatic rise of labour in 1872 and the mid 1880s would have seemed unimaginable; in 1905 no one would have predicted the phenomenal upheaval of 1919; in 1935, the explosion of 1946 militancy would have seemed laughable; and in the serenity of the 1950s, no one was anticipating the turbulence of the late 1960s and early 1970s.[79]

All three collections of essays demonstrate that historians have finally realized that the working class is composed of women as well as men. Heron and Storey's book contains essays on women's paid and unpaid work in the home, in the office, in garment factories, and in the newest of capitalism's "factories," the fast-food industry. Palmer's collection includes studies on textile workers and public sector workers, and an assessment of working-class feminism, while Bercuson has chosen essays on telephone operators and on the working-class family economy in nineteenth-century Montreal. Yet the integration of women's history and working-class history, as Bettina Bradbury has recently argued, still poses significant difficulties. Nevertheless Bradbury sees cause for hope in the attempt by some labour historians to recreate a total working-class experience. In order for this hope to be realized, Bradbury believes there will need to be: first, an emphasis on working-class reproduction, both ideological and material, to match the usual attention paid to production; second, a serious examination of all aspects of the working-class family economy; third, an analysis of the process of class reproduction itself, "including marriage, childbearing, childrearing, and socialization";

and fourth, an examination of how gender has been defined, transmitted, or altered within the working class.[80] The importance of these themes has been echoed recently in u.s. historical discussion as well. Among the most intriguing of the commentaries on the late Herbert Gutman's work were those of David Montgomery and Susan Levine. Montgomery reiterated Gutman's emphasis on the role of the family in class formation and Levine pushed for further examination of how the relationships of working-class men and women influenced their interpretation of their common world.[81]

The three Canadian collections of essays show little evidence of one of Gutman's major concerns in his final work, in which he raised basic questions about the specific ethno-cultural composition of the working class and its development over time. Just as his emphasis on class formation in his examination of African-American slaves led him to the family, Gutman had also begun before his death to analyze class development from 1840 to 1890 by asking who constituted the American working class in those years.[82] His focus on immigration, on immigrant families, and on ethnic communities in America began to reshape in a more rigorous fashion his earlier insights about the constitution and reconstitution of the American working class. These insights had been present, albeit in only a problematic postulation, in his justly famous "Work, Culture and Society in Industrializing America."[83] Gutman's work has influenced Canadian historical writing in two rather different ways. First, Canadian historians have attempted of late to eliminate the divide between immigration history and working-class history, a split that emerged (artificially to some degree) from the competition of new fields and, perhaps, from the suspicion generated by Canadian governmental enthusiasm for multiculturalism. Clearly, the work now being produced on nineteenth- and twentieth-century immigration and the role that transoceanic, continental, and regional population movements have played in fuelling capitalist transformation and growth is greatly influencing our images of Canadian working-class development. To take but one example, Bruno Ramirez's work, including his *On the Move: Agriculture, Industry, and Migrants in the North Atlantic Economy, 1860–1978*, forces us to reconsider much of Quebec history by linking a series of processes that to date have been treated as discrete – the colonization movement, migration to New England, Italian immigration, and urbanization.[84] Moreover, in the wake of this reconstruction come important insights into the nature of immigrant behaviour, insights that look far beyond the sterility of earlier conceptions of ethnic docility and ethnic radicalism (generally expressed as ethnic versus class consciousness).[85]

Ramirez's work, while focused on Quebec as simultaneous population donor and recipient, raises important questions about similar migrations elsewhere in Canada. The massive population outpouring from the Atlantic provinces to New England and to other parts of the United States is reasonably well-known, but its implications for regional working-class development remain unexplored.

Secondly, Gutman's notion of working-class constitution and reconstitution and his resolute insistence that the concept of American exceptionalism was not an appropriate historical question has led to more attention being paid in Canadian historical writing, as elsewhere, to what workers did as opposed to what they failed to do. As Gutman put it:

We need to put aside the English model, the French model, and the Cuban model, and then ask a set of very, very tough questions about what American workers actually thought and did – and why. Once we free ourselves of the notion that it should have happened in one particular way, then we stop looking for the reasons why it didn't happen that way.[86]

This revolt against a teleological view of the working class, perhaps partially a North American variant of *The Forward March of Labour Halted*, has many reflections and echoes in recent Canadian work.[87]

As the prominence in this discussion of Bettina Bradbury and Bruno Ramirez (both of the Université de Montréal), might suggest, another positive feature of the 1980s is the developing dialogue among Canadian historians of the working class. While *Labour/Le Travail* has always been bilingual and has attempted from its inception to publish as much Quebec material as possible, the realities of academic and national politics in the 1970s made that a highly problematic goal. The changed political realities of the 1980s have led to increasing success in this realm. Quebec labour historiography has been slighted in the pages of this essay, but its direction has closely paralleled the developments described herein. If anything, there has been among Quebec labour historians a more tenacious institutional focus with most attention being devoted to trade union development, labour politics, and the national question.[88] In Quebec as elsewhere, however, this started to change in the early 1970s. Among the most prolific of the new practitioners in Quebec have been Jacques Rouillard and Fernand Harvey. In the 1980s working-class history in French and English Canada is marked by a growing congruence – a process reflected in recent issues of *Labour/Le Travail*.

As the renewed interest in migration suggests, the focus of Canadian working-class history has also begun to turn outwards in the last few years. The Warwick Conference mentioned earlier, a Welsh-Canadian Labour History Conference held in 1987, and a number of other international symposia have involved Canadian scholars in the attempt to develop a broader comparative understanding of working-class development.[89] Works such as those recently published by Charles Bergquist, and Ira Katznelson and Aristide Zolberg, with their attempts at systematic comparative approaches to class formation and development, appear to be but a beginning.[90] The new project of the International Institute of Social History in Amsterdam on "Determinants of the Development of Working-Class Movements, 1870–1914: A Comparative Analysis," which at last count involves scholars from at least twenty-five countries, aims to produce a systematic comparison of national experiences. The world-wide phenomenon of capitalist development, which to date has not produced an international proletariat capable of superceding it, appears somewhat ironically to be producing a labour and working-class history attempting to comprehend it. Canadian scholars may have arrived at the study of our working class relatively late in the day, but in the last fifteen years we have made significant strides. Certainly there is no longer a vacuum waiting to be filled.

NOTES

1 Initially named *Labour/Le Travailleur*, the French title was changed in 1983 to correct the sexism of the original. *Labour/Le Travail* appeared as an annual until 1981 and has been published semi-annually since that date.

2 Robin Harris, *A History of Higher Education in Canada, 1663–1960* (Toronto 1976).

3 A.B. McKillop, *A Disciplined Intelligence: Critical Inquiry and Canadian Thought in the Victorian Era* (Montreal 1979).

4 Marlene Shore, *The Science of Social Redemption: McGill, the Chicago School, and the Origins of Social Research in Canada* (Toronto 1987).

5 Harris, *A History of Higher Education*, 190–1.

6 V.W. Bladen, "A Journal is Born: 1935," *Canadian Journal of Economics and Political Science* 26 (1960): 1–5.

7 There were exceptions, such as the PHD the University of Toronto awarded to James Mavor in 1912 in order, in the words of Ian Drummond, "to clothe his academic nakedness." See Drummond, *Political Economy at the University of Toronto: A History of the Department, 1888– 1982* (Toronto 1983), 27.

8 C.B. Macpherson, "After Strange Gods: Canadian Political Science,

1973" in *Perspectives on the Social Sciences in Canada*, eds Thomas N. Guinsberg and Grant L. Reuben (Toronto 1974), 51–76.

9 See my introduction to G.S. Kealey and Peter Warrian, eds, *Essays in Canadian Working-Class History* (Toronto 1976), and my "The Structures of Canadian Working-Class History," in *Lectures in Canadian Labour and Working-Class History*, eds W.J.C. Cherwinski and G.S. Kealey (St John's 1985), 23–6; Bryan D. Palmer, *Working-Class Experience: The Rise and Reconstitution of Canadian Labour, 1800–1980* (Toronto 1983); Craig Heron and Robert Storey, "On the Job in Canada," in their *On the Job: Confronting the Labour Process in Canada* (Montreal and Kingston: McGill-Queen's University Press 1986), 3–46.

10 Phillips Thompson, *Politics of Labor* (New York 1887, reprint Toronto 1975); and R.G. Hann, "Brainworkers and the Knights of Labor," in Kealey and Warrian, *Essays*.

11 For discussion of such developments see Carl Berger, *The Writing of Canadian History* (Toronto 1986); McKillop, *A Disciplined Intelligence*; S.E.D. Shortt, *The Search for an Ideal: Six Intellectuals in an Age of Transition* (Toronto 1976); Drummond, *Political Economy*; Shore, *The Science of Social Redemption*; Doug Owram, *The Government Generation: Canadian Intellectuals and the State, 1900–1945* (Toronto 1986); and Paul Craven, *"An Impartial Umpire": Industrial Relations and the Canadian State, 1900–1911* (Toronto 1980).

12 Jean Scott, "The Conditions of Female Labour in Ontario," *Toronto University Studies in Political Science* 1 (1892): 84–113.

13 The literature on W.L.M. King is immense. Among the most useful contributions are Craven, "An Impartial Umpire"; H. Ferns and B. Ostry, *The Age of Mackenzie King* (London 1955); and Reg Whitaker, "The Liberal Corporatist Ideas of Mackenzie King," *Labour/Le Travail* 2 (1977): 137–69.

14 On the Rockefeller connection, see Stephen Scheinberg, "Rockefeller and King: The Capitalist and the Reformer," in *Mackenzie King: Widening the Debate*, eds John English and John O. Stubbs (Toronto 1977), 89–104.

15 W.L.M. King, *Industry and Humanity* (Toronto 1918), 24.

16 W.L.M. King, *The Secret of Heroism* (Toronto 1906), 114, as quoted in Whitaker, "Liberal Corporatist Ideas," 140.

17 O.D. Skelton, *Socialism: A Critical Analysis* (Boston 1911). It was published as volume 6 of the Hart, Schaffner, and Marx Prize Economic Essays and won the first prize of $1,000.

18 For brief descriptions of their careers, see G.S. Kealey, "Looking Backward: Reflections on the Study of Class in Canada," *The History and Social Science Teacher* 16:4 (Summer 1981): 213–22. On Woods' troubles

at Western see N.S.B. Gras to Fred Landon, 2 August 1921, Landon Papers, University of Western Ontario Archives.

19 On Stewart and the demise of his original Employment Service of Canada, see James Struthers, *No Fault of Their Own: Unemployment and the Canadian Welfare State, 1914–1941* (Toronto 1983), esp. chap. 1.

20 Norman Ware: "The History of Labor Interaction," in *Labor in Canadian American Relations*, ed. H.A. Innis (Toronto 1937); *The Industrial Worker, 1840–1860* (Gloucester 1959); *The Labor Movement in the United States, 1860–1895* (New York 1964); *Labor in Modern Industrial Society* (New York 1935).

21 Bryce Stewart, *Canadian Labor Laws and the Treaty* (New York 1926).

22 Edmund Bradwin, *The Bunkhouse Man: A Study of Work and Pay in the Camps of Canada, 1903–1914* (Toronto 1928; reprint Toronto 1972).

23 Harold Logan, *History of Trade Union Organization in Canada* (Chicago 1928).

24 Stewart, *Canadian Labor Laws*, 8.

25 Eugene Forsey, *Economic and Social Aspects of the Nova Scotia Coal Industry* (Toronto 1926); and Allan Latham, *The Catholic and National Labour Unions of Canada* (Toronto 1930).

26 Shore, *Science of Social Redemption*, 162–94.

27 Donald Creighton, *Commercial Empire of the St. Lawrence* (Toronto 1937); Harold Innis, *The Cod Fisheries* (Toronto 1954); John Bartlett Brebner, *The North Atlantic Triangle* (Toronto 1966); Ware, "The History of Labor Interaction."

28 The thesis was subsequently published as *Labor Unionism in American Agriculture* (Washington 1945).

29 Stuart Jamieson: *Industrial Relations in Canada* (Toronto 1957); *Times of Trouble* (Ottawa 1968).

30 Lloyd G. Reynolds, *The British Immigrant In Canada: His Social and Economic Adjustment in Canada* (Toronto 1935).

31 The events at McGill in the 1930s illustrate the fragility of academic freedom in Canadian universities, a story that merits more attention than it has received. Two examples must suffice. Political scientist Eugene Forsey was denied tenure and theologian King Gordon was forced out of his position; both were prominent CCF intellectuals.

32 Leonard C. Marsh, *Report on Social Security for Canada* (Ottawa 1943; reprint Toronto 1975).

33 On Underhill, see R. Douglas Francis, *Frank H. Underhill: Intellectual Provocateur* (Toronto 1986); Michiel Horn, *The League for Social Reconstruction: Intellectual Origins of the Democratic Left in Canada, 1930–1942* (Toronto 1980); and Berger, *Writing*, chap. 3.

34 Eugene Forsey, *History of Trade Unions in Canada, 1812–1902* (Toronto 1982).

35 William Bennett, *Builders of British Columbia* (Vancouver 1937). Stanley Ryerson: *The Founding of Canada: Beginnings to 1815* (Toronto 1960); *Unequal Union: Confederation and the Roots of Conflict on the Canadas, 1815–1873* (New York 1968); Charles Lipton, *Trade Union Movement of Canada, 1927–1959* (Montreal 1966); Norman Penner, *The Canadian Left* (Toronto 1978). On Ryerson, see G.S. Kealey, "Stanley Bréhaut Ryerson: Canadian Revolutionary Intellectual"; and "Stanley Bréhaut Ryerson: Marxist Historian," *Studies in Political Economy* 9 (1982): 103–71.

36 Queen's University, Industrial Relations Section, School of Commerce and Administration, *Industrial Relations: Papers Presented at 5th Conference* (Kingston 1940), 18–21. See also Clarence J. Hicks, *My Life in Industrial Relations: Fifty Years in the Growth of A Profession* (New York 1941), 127, 146–7, 150.

37 J.C. Cameron, "Dealing with Organized Labour," in Queen's University, Industrial Relations Section, *Industrial Relations: Papers Presented at 6th Conference* (Kingston 1941), 39–50, esp. 49–50.

38 On the Toronto experience, see Vincent Bladen, "Economics and Human Relations," *Canadian Journal of Economics and Political Science* 14 (1948): 301–11; and his *Bladen on Bladen: Memoirs of a Political Economist* (Toronto 1978), 96–107; Drummond, *Political Economy*, 95–6, 105–6; and University of Toronto, Institute of Industrial Relations, *Annual Report of Director*, 1947–50. Elton Mayo, a Harvard social scientist, conducted a series of studies for Western Electric at their Hawthorne plant outside Chicago. On Hart's interest in these, see his "The Hawthorne Experiments," *Canadian Journal of Economics and Political Science* 9 (1943): 150–63; and "Industrial Relations Research and Social Theory," ibid. 15 (1949): 53–73.

39 Harold Logan, *Trade Unions In Canada* (Toronto 1948); R.L. Elliott, "The Canadian Labour Press from 1867," *Canadian Journal of Economics and Political Science* 14 (1948): 220–45, and 515.

40 J.T. Montague, "Trade Unionism in the Canadian Meat Packing Industry" (PHD diss., University of Toronto 1950); W.S.A. Martin, "A Study of Legislation Designed to Foster Industrial Peace in the Common Law Jurisdictions of Canada" (PHD diss., University of Toronto 1954); and E. Schonning, "Union-Management Relations in the Pulp and Paper Industry of Ontario and Quebec, 1914–1950" (PHD diss., University of Toronto 1955).

41 H.C. Pentland: "The Lachine Strike of 1843," *Canadian Historical Review* 29 (1948): 255–77; "The Role of Capital in Canadian Economic Development before 1875," *Canadian Journal of Economics and Political Science* 16 (1950): 457–74; and "The Development of a Capitalistic Labour Market in Canada," *Canadian Journal of Economics and Political Science* 25 (1959): 450–61.

42 H.C. Pentland: "Labour in Canada in the Early 19th Century" (PHD diss., University of Toronto 1961); and *Labour and Capital in Canada, 1650–1860* (Toronto 1981).

43 For commentaries on Pentland see Paul Phillips, "Introduction" in Pentland, *Labour and Capital*; G.S. Kealey, "H.C. Pentland and Working-Class History," *Canadian Journal of Political and Social Theory* 3 (1979): 79–94; Bryan Palmer, "Town, Port and Country: Speculations on the Capitalist Transformation of Canada," *Acadiensis* 12 (1983): 131–9; and Allan Greer, "Wage Labour and The Transition to Capitalism: A Critique of Pentland," *Labour/Le Travail* 15 (1985): 7–22.

44 Bladen, *Bladen*, 101–2.

45 John R. Commons, Ulrich B. Phillips, Eugene A. Gilmore, Helen L. Sumner, and John B. Andrews, eds, *A Documentary History of American Industrial Society* (New York 1958).

46 Fred Landon, "Ulrich Bonnell Phillips: Historian of the South," *Journal of Southern History* 5 (1939): 364–71. Quotation from p. 370.

47 Fred Landon, "Foreword," to his *Lake Huron* (Indianapolis 1944). See also Patricia G. Skidmore, "Mind and Manuscript: A Profile of Historian Fred Landon," unpublished manuscript, University of Western Ontario Archives; F.H. Armstrong, "Fred Landon, 1880–1969," *Ontario History* 62 (1970): 1–4; and Hilary Bates, "A Bibliography of Fred Landon," *Ontario History* 62 (1970): 5–16.

48 Fred Landon, "The Common Man in the Era of Rebellion," in *Aspects of Nineteenth-Century Ontario*, ed. F.H. Armstrong et al. (Toronto 1974); *Western Ontario and the American Frontier* (Toronto 1941); "The Canadian Scene, 1880–1890," in Canadian Historical Association, *Annual Report* (1942): 5–18.

49 Landon, "The Canadian Scene," 5.

50 Fred Landon Papers, University of Western Ontario Archives, Scrapbooks.

51 Fred Landon, "The Knights of Labor: Predecessors of the CIO," *Quarterly Review of Commerce* 1 (1937): 133–9.

52 J.I. Cooper, "The Canadian General Election of 1887" (MA thesis, University of Western Ontario 1933); and Douglas Kennedy, "The Knights of Labor in Canada" (MA thesis, University of Western Ontario 1945). This later work was published by Western after Kennedy's untimely death (London 1956).

53 W.S. Wallace to Fred Landon, 22 June 1920 and 30 December 1920, Landon Papers, University of Western Ontario Archives.

54 J.I. Cooper to Carmen Miller, 3 December 1979, in author's possession. Emphasis in original.

55 J.I. Cooper: "The Quebec Ship Labourers Benevolent Society," *Canadian Historical Review* 30 (1949): 336–44; and "The Social Structure of

Montreal in the 1850's," Canadian Historical Association, *Annual Report* (1956): 62–73.

56 Robert Cox, "The Quebec Provincial General Election of 1886" (MA thesis, McGill University 1948); V.O. Chan, "The Canadian Knights of Labor with Special Reference to the 1880s" (MA thesis, McGill University 1949); and Shirley Ayer, "The Locomotive Engineers' Strike on the Grand Trunk Railway in 1876–1877" (MA thesis, McGill University 1961).

57 Cooper to Miller, 3 December 1979, in author's possession.

58 When Cooper was invited in 1980 to attend a McGill conference on "Class and Community: Perspectives on Canada's Labour Past," he wrote modestly to decline: "I am flattered, I need hardly say, to be remembered in this connection. ... I don't even know the direction that labour history has taken. I should hope that it concerns itself with the men and women (and children) on the shop floor, rather than with organization and leaders." Cooper to Miller, 23 February 1980, in author's possession.

59 Kenneth McNaught, *A Prophet in Politics* (Toronto 1959).

60 Ferns and Ostry, *The Age of Mackenzie King*; F.A. McGregor, *The Fall and Rise of Mackenzie King, 1911–1919* (Toronto 1962). On Ferns, see his enjoyable *Reading from Left to Right* (Toronto 1983), and on his adventures with Bernard Ostry, see 297–310.

61 Ferns, *Reading*, 305.

62 B. Ostry, "Conservatives, Liberals, and Labour in the 1870s," *Canadian Historical Review* 41 (1960): 93–127; and "Conservatives, Liberals and Labour in the 1880s," *Canadian Journal of Economics and Political Science* 27 (1961): 141–61.

63 Frank Watt: "Radicalism in English Canadian Literature Since Confederation" (PHD diss., University of Toronto 1958); and "The National Policy, the Workingman and Proletarian Ideas in Victorian Canada," *Canadian Historical Review* 40 (1959): 1–26.

64 Gregory S. Kealey, "The Writing of Social History in English Canada, 1970–1984," *Social History* 10 (1985): 347–65.

65 In addition to the Kealey article cited above, the second edition of Carl Berger, *The Writing of Canadian History: Aspects of English Canadian Historical Writing Since 1900* (Toronto 1986), contains a new final chapter on "Tradition and the 'New' History." See also Carl Berger, ed., *Contemporary Approaches to Canadian History* (Toronto 1987); and Terry Crowley, ed., *Clio's Craft* (Toronto 1988).

66 Herbert G. Gutman, "Historical Consciousness in Contemporary America," in *Power and Culture: Essays on the American Working Class*, ed. Ira Berlin (New York 1987), 395–412. For Canadian versions see William Acheson, "Doctoral Theses and the Discipline of History in

Canada, 1967 and 1985," *Historical Papers* (1986): 1–10; John English, "The Second Time Around: Political Scientists Writing History," *Canadian Historical Review* 67 (1986): 1–16; and Berger, *Writing*, 317–20. The New Left arose in the 1960s and distinguished itself from both orthodox communist and social democratic parties. While taking particular shapes in different national contexts, it most often focused on civil rights, anti-Vietnam war movements, and nuclear disarmament.

67 I should note that Eugene Forsey (after helping gain our initial funding support from Labour Canada) decided not to join the Advisory Editorial Board. His early support was crucial to the launching of *L/LT* and the first issue was dedicated to him.

68 Carl Berger, *Writing*, 306–7. Berger's description of the sides conforms closely to Bercuson's own view in "Introduction," *Canadian Labour History: Selected Readings* (Toronto:Copp Clark Pitman 1987), 1–2.

69 Daniel Drache, "The Formation and Fragmentation of the Canadian Working Class: 1820–1920," *Studies in Political Economy* 15 (1984): 43–89.

70 Bryan Palmer, "Listening to History Rather than Historians," *Studies in Political Economy* 20 (1986): 47–84.

71 Ibid., 75–8.

72 Desmond Morton, *Working People* (Ottawa 1980; 2d ed. 1984); and Bryan Palmer, *Working-Class Experience: The Rise and Reconstitution of Canadian Labour, 1800–1980* (Toronto 1983).

73 Palmer, *Working-Class Experience*, 3.

74 Morton, "Preface," *Working People*.

75 Ibid., 326.

76 Ibid.

77 Bercuson, *Canadian Labour History*, 3 and 231.

78 Bryan Palmer, *The Character of Class Struggle: Essays in Canadian Working-Class History, 1850–1985* (Toronto 1986), 9–14.

79 Craig Heron and Bob Storey, *On the Job: Confronting the Labour Process in Canada* (Montreal and Kingston: McGill-Queen's University Press 1986), 31–2.

80 Bettina Bradbury, "Women's History and Working-Class History," *Labour/Le Travail* 19 (1987): 23–43.

81 David Montgomery, "Gutman's Agenda for Future Historical Research" and Susan Levine, "Class and Gender: Herbert Gutman and the Women of 'Shoe City,'" *Labour History* 29 (1988): 299–312, 344–55.

82 Herbert Gutman and Ira Berlin, "Class Composition and the Development of American Working Class, 1840–1890," in his *Power and Culture*, 380–94.

83 Herbert Gutman, "Work, Culture and Society in Industrializing

America," *American Historical Review* 78 (1973): 531–88; also available
in the book of the same title (New York 1976).

84 Bruno Ramirez, *On the Move: Agriculture, Industry and Migrants in the
North Atlantic Economy, 1860–1978* (Toronto 1990). Also see his brief
"Ethnic Studies and Working-Class History," *Labour/Le Travail* 19
(1987): 45–8.

85 For a useful, earlier exploration of these questions, albeit one posed in
just these terms, see Donald Avery, *"Dangerous Foreigners": European
Immigrant Workers and Labour Radicalism in Canada, 1896–1932*
(Toronto 1979).

86 "Interview with Herbert Gutman" in *Power and Culture*, 343. The
debate about American exceptionalism commenced in the early twentieth century with German sociologist Werner Sombart's *Why is there no
Socialism in the United States?*, which appeared in 1906 and is now
most readily available in a version edited by C.T. Husbands (White
Plains, NY 1976). Recent commentaries include Eric Foner, "Why is
there no Socialism in America?" *History Workshop* 17 (1984); and Sean
Wilentz, "Against Exceptionalism: Class Consciousness and the American Labour Movement," *International Labour and Working-Class History*
26 (1984): 1–36, and 28 (1985): 46–55.

87 Martin Jacques and Francis Mulhern, eds, *The Forward March of Labour
Halted* (London 1981); Palmer, *Working-Class Experience*; Heron and
Storey, *On the Job*; Kealey, "Structure."

88 These generalizations are derived from Kealey, Palmer, and Jacques
Ferland, "Labour Studies," in *Thematic Guide to Canadian Studies*, ed.
A. Artibise (Montreal forthcoming).

89 Deian Hopkin and G.S. Kealey, eds, *Class, Community and the Labour
Movement in Canada and Wales, 1890–1930* (Aberystwyth 1989); D.C.M.
Platt, ed., *Social Welfare 1850–1950: Australia, Argentina and Canada
Compared* (London 1989); C. Harzig and D. Hoerder, eds, *The Press of
Labour Migrants in Europe and North America, 1880s–1930s* (Bremen
1985).

90 Charles Bergquist, *Labor in Latin America. Comparative Essays on Chile,
Argentina, Venezuela and Colombia* (Stanford 1986); and Ira Katznelson
and Aristide Zolberg, eds, *Working-Class Formation: Nineteenth-Century
Patterns in Western Europe and the United States* (Princeton 1986).

2 H.C. Pentland and Working-Class Studies

Clare Pentland may well have written his own best obituary in 1972 when he noted "the unusual combination of respect and neglect" which Gustavus Myers' *History of Canadian Wealth* had received. He went on to award Myers an accolade that better described himself: "A historian's historian – his work valued by Canada's most knowledgeable scholars, academic and otherwise."[1]

After any intellectual's death, the scholarly autopsy of a life's work is a discomforting examination for us all. Always disconcerting for the survivors, the consideration becomes vastly more complicated when the subject's career mirrors the commentator's own intellectual interests and political predilections.

The task transcends easy eulogy, it rapidly evolves into a search for intellectual roots which, in this case, leads inexorably to an exploration of the Canadian academic environment of the 1940s and 1950s.

H. Clare Pentland was a scholar whose work I have always greatly admired but whom I only met on two occasions – once casually at the Learneds in 1974 and more recently at a 1977 Winnipeg seminar. I suspect that many readers will share my memory of the quest in the mid to late 1960s for critical writings in the Canadian historical and political economy traditions – an all-too-often futile hunt. There were, however,a few underground classics of an unassimilated radical tradition. The two which influenced me (and other historians of the Canadian working class) the most were Pentland's unpublished 1960 Toronto PHD thesis, "Labour and the Development of Industrial Capitalism in Canada," and Frank Watt's "Radicalism and English Canadian Literature Since Confederation."[2] What remains most striking about both theses is their complete and brilliant idiosyncrasy. Pentland's evident interest in class analysis and especially in the development of the Canadian working class stands out from its Toronto political economy heritage as fully as does Watt's consideration of radicalism in Canadian literature.[3]

Although Pentland's work stands apart starkly from the Toronto political economy tradition, there are no clear explanations for this in his intellectual biography. Born in Justice, Manitoba in 1914, Pentland attended the Brandon campus of the University of Manitoba and received his honours BA in economics from Manitoba in 1940.[4] After receiving his MA from the University of Oregon, Pentland registered in the School of Graduate Studies at the University of Toronto. In the academic years 1946 through 1948 he studied economic history (H.A. Innis), economic theory (G.A. Elliott), labour economics (H.A. Logan), sociology (S.D. Clark), and industrial relations (F. Toombs). In 1949 he accepted a position in the economics department at the University of Manitoba where he taught for the rest of his life. Pentland's dissertation, defended in 1960, which had been described originally in 1946 as "The History of Labour in Canada to 1867" and then narrowed to "The Irish Labourer on the Canadian Canals and Railroads, 1830–1860," was broadened again in its final form to "Labour and the Development of Industrial Capitalism in Canada."

The value of Pentland's work is located in its break with other existing North American schools of labour studies. Not only did his work depart significantly from the predominant staples interpretation of Canadian economic history by focusing on the development of industrial capitalism in Canada, but it also showed no affiliation with the predominant modes of labour studies. The American Common's school tradition imported to Canada partially through the later (non-academic) successes of Willy King but also by the Chicago-trained Harold Logan had little impact on Pentland's work. Indeed one can think of almost no relationship whatsoever between the Pentland approach first demonstrated in his 1948 "The Lachine Strike of 1843" and the institutional approach of Logan's *Trade Unions in Canada*, published ironically that same year.[5] By the same token, Pentland showed no interest in the emerging industrial relations field developing largely in the United States in conjunction with welfare capitalism.

"The Lachine Strike," Pentland's first publication, contained the seeds of much of his later work. Anthologized as late as 1974, this article today remains not only our best overall account of the role of Irish labourers, but also represents a pioneering effort in a style of cultural analysis in ethnic studies which has only recently become popular. In addition, Pentland gave notice of his forthcoming breakthrough analysis of the genesis of industrial capitalism in Canada, for here he describes the 1840s as "a decade of transition, marking the rise of wage-labour on a large scale, and of a milieu that would forge labour into a self-conscious force."[6] Perhaps even more important, it is in this article that Pentland develops the intellectual project which he consistently pursued thereafter – the rescuing of Canadian workers from the margins of history:

Historians have paid considerable attention to the English capital that made possible Canada's canal and railway building, in the eighteen-forties and fifties, and some attention too, to the Scottish contractors who supervised the work. But there has been almost complete neglect of the real builders of Canadian public works, the thousands of labouring men, mainly Irish, who toiled with pick and shovel.[7]

By placing the Irish labourer at the centre of his account, Pentland almost totally broke with both the Canadian historiographic and political economy traditions. Moreover he not only allowed the labourer to stride into the middle of the historical stage but he gave him a speaking part – the labourers here speak for themselves through their letters to other labourers as well as through the historian's careful reconstruction of their behaviour, not through the lens of the biased, class and race prejudiced observers, but rather through a sharply focused analysis of their Irish cultural heritage and their encounter with the Canadian environment.

Where did Pentland find his intellectual inspiration for such work? He appears to have turned to the English Marxist tradition of historical writing. Although his debts are at best made only partially clear, a decision which undoubtedly owed more to the academic climate of cold war Canada than to any lack of gratitude on his part, there is much evidence both in his citations and in the nature of his arguments to show his familiarity with the economic history of Maurice Dobb and with the labour studies of various British communist scholars. Indeed these citations run through not only his early historical work, but are present again and again even in the later, more general reflections on the nature of the Canadian industrial relations system.

Pentland, however, added another component to the English scholarship, namely American economic history which in the post-second world war period was enjoying a lively renaissance as scholars turned to the pre-Civil War period to consider the role of the state in the development of the u.s. economy. Studies such as Hartz on Pennsylvania and the Handlins on Massachusetts stimulated Pentland to consider the North American path to industrial capitalism which stood at some variance with the classic British transformation.[8] Thus Pentland's work was, from the beginning, built from a broad comparative base. He linked this to an impressive research skill which led him to utilize the Public Archives of Canada with considerable creativity. His work in pre-Confederation government collections turned up nuggets of real value in sources which had previously yielded only political and constitutional dross.

Nevertheless, Pentland must have been a rather lonely scholar in the late 1940s and especially throughout the 1950s. His two very important articles on "The Lachine Strike" and on "The Role of Capital in Canadian Economic Development Before 1875" were followed by almost ten years of silence.[9] This quiet was broken only by the necessity to respond to Hugh Aitken's critique of Pentland's estimates of levels of capital imports and by occasional pieces on contemporary labour relations.[10] The pressure to complete his thesis led to his next important article which in many ways summarizes its core argument. His "The Development of a Capitalistic Labour Market in Canada" (1959) is perhaps his seminal contribution to Canadian working class studies and constitutes a perfect companion piece for his earlier discussion of capital formation.[11]

These two essays considered together fully elaborate an alternative view to the pervasive staples version of Canadian economic development. Here the outlines of the transformation to an industrial capitalist society sketched in "The Lachine Strike" are fully drawn. Here Pentland argues persuasively that "about the middle of the nineteenth century the Province of Canada was transformed from a raw, staple-producing area to a rounded, integrated economy that might be called metropolitan"[12] and further that the canals and railways "by integrating the Canadian market, opened the way for Canadian manufacturers to conquer it."[13] Although not written in an explicitly Marxist framework, it is obvious that these two essays pursue the crucial questions in any Marxist understanding of the genesis of industrial capitalism: the nature of the capital accumulation which allows Mr Moneybags to seek labour in the marketplace; and the process by which workers are forced to enter that same marketplace with nothing but their labour power to offer in return for their sustenance.

"Labour and the Development of Industrial Capitalism in Canada" extends the analysis of those essays. Here Pentland has room to explain more fully the scope of his undertaking:

In primitive societies (and also, ideally in socialist societies) the potential labour force consists of all the members of society, and the methods of production are those that these members conceive to yield the greatest mutual benefit ... production in all other societies is complicated by the division of these societies into a ruling class, which organizes the labour force in its own interest, and the ruled or working group whose satisfactions are a matter of expediency and consistency with the demands of the rulers.[14]

His study traces the evolution of European society in Canada "up to the flowering of full industrial capitalism." This involves a discussion of changes in the organization of labour from various forms of forced labour (slavery, indenture, convict, and military) through what he terms "feudal" (paternalistic, pre-industrial) to the emergence, "shortly after 1850," of a "capitalistic labour market and a well-developed capitalistic economy."[15]

This discussion is so broad and his insights are so rich about early Canadian social and economic history that it is impossible to comment on them all. Let it simply be noted that the discussion ranges from the labour of native people in the fur trade, through the failure of slavery in New France, to an intensive consideration of labour at the St Maurice Forges. He then considers immigration to the Canadas in the first half of the nineteenth century chronicling the cultural backgrounds of the American, English, Scottish, and especially the Protestant and Catholic Irish. The Irish, however, receive the most attention. The discussion begins with Ireland as the colony "in which the English learned the art of subjecting other peoples."[16] There follows an extended consideration of the cultural attributes of the Ulster and Southern Irish migrants which traces their deep-rooted conflict which they carried to Canada. The chapter closes with an extended Appendix on the Orange Order in central Canada which places the order fully in its working-class context. This represents a particularly valuable example of Pentland's constant ability to transcend the usually narrow confines of either economic or labour history. Instead his sensitivity to social and cultural factors allows him to generate intriguing synthetic comments on all aspects of Canadian life. Thus:

Orangeism and the moderate political conservatism which it built, represented the artisan well at a time when capitalism had not advanced enough to subordinate all other divisions to the one between capitalist and proletarian. In that time, the conservatism of the workingman was a fixed point of Canadian politics and the Orange Order was its typical form of organization.[17]

The final two chapters of this brilliant thesis contain the most important contributions. "The Transformation of Canada's Economic Structure" and "The Transformation of Canadians" provide the first and perhaps still, the fullest account of Canada's industrial revolution – an economic transformation of the mid-nineteenth century:

A paramount fact about Canada is that it did develop a national economy of an industrial type in the nineteenth century. The Canada that existed up until 1820 needs to be described ... in terms of staple production. ... But this language will not do to describe the Canada of 1870: what is required for that is the terminology of advanced industrial societies.[18]

Pentland's analysis of Canadian industrialization shows far more concern for ideas, policies, and the role of the state than for the actual process of economic transformation from handicraft through manufacture to modern industry. Indeed his study focuses on the debates surrounding tariff policy and pinpoints two amazing men, Robert Baldwin Sullivan and Isaac Buchanan, as key figures in the politics of Canada's industrial revolution. Predictably Pentland also examined labour's role in the great policy debates of mid-century:

While there was a real national policy from 1850 until 1880, both manufacturers and their workmen believed that their livelihood depended upon protection, and that protection was always in danger from railroads and merchants. In consequence, employers and employees relied on each other for marked consideration.[19]

Although overplaying the extent to which this led to a lessening of class conflict, Pentland develops the above insight into its political corollary:

What labour gave in return was ... consistent support for protection and the Conservative Party. The wage-earners – not least through the Orange Order in Canada West – were a dependable and not insignificant partner in Macdonald's coalitions.[20]

Here again we can see Pentland's understanding that labour is an active social force that demands continual historical consideration. Labour's political role did not await the arrival of socialism.

His "Transformation of Canadians" examines "the moral conditions of economic growth," in Karl Helleiner's phrase.[21] Here, again developing insights which were very evident in British Marxist historiography, he concerns himself with the process by which pre-industrial labour ("slothful, immediate, anarchic and irregular in work habits, and too easily seduced by noneconomic goals and means to goals") was transformed into "suitable material for a modern society."[22] In suggesting the terms on which he would pursue this question, he wrote with a penetrating realization of the complexity of historical transformation:

To make the material [labour] suitable required a complex and unknowable educative process. ... Now was the means to success capable of reduction to a precise dose of new discipline and new ambition that could be injected, once for all, like a coin in a machine. Success was attained rather by an indistinct and never-completed process of interacting stimulation and response. Human transformation was bound to be partial, and mostly unplanned, because men were remaking themselves without much comprehension or consciousness of it, because deliberate changes sent out other ripples of subtle, unrecognized adjustments to preserve the tension and balance of existence, and because the inanimate machinery of production to which man had to fit himself could only itself be transformed bit by bit and year by year. The nature and extent of the changes in the ways men regarded themselves, conducted themselves, and dealt with each other, have therefore to be indicated rather than expounded; and the direction of causation suspected rather than proved.[23]

One wishes all social scientists were as sensitive and as humble before the reality of the past.

In describing man's "remaking," Pentland was concerned with the new "spirit of capitalism," a new cosmos, "built around concepts like progress, 'science,' and invention."[24] He drew his readers' attention to education and to temperance – topics which only recently in Canada have begun to be placed firmly in a social history framework. After an innovative discussion of the role of mechanics' institutes and of patents, he turned to "the new labour relations" of industrial capitalism. Here he recognized the crucial division of the working class into the skilled and the unskilled. The artisan, whose strength he recognized, was "the key man who held the new technology in his hands and brain, and it was nowhere else." Anticipating the recent historiography of work process, Pentland asserted clearly, "Only the craftsmen knew how the work should be done."[25] It was the unskilled, however, who interested him most. Returning to the subject of his first article, he again examined the Irish labourers in the Canadas. They could not depend on their skill, of course, but neither were they passive:

The final arbiter of the disputes was not abstract right but physical force, the power of the massed labourers to do violence against the similar power of the troops that employers were able to call to their assistance.[26]

After a long discussion of strike activity among canal labourers and of the state role in providing military assistance and later in devising new modes of police activity, Pentland concludes that by the 1850s, Irish labourers had learned "to be increasingly judicious in their use of violence" and now "acted less like tribesmen, and more like a nationality, or class."[27] In summary, then:

The Irish contributed much: they did the heavy work, and built the canals and railways, and made the well-supplied market in common labour that supported industrial capitalism. They taught much: that there was not, after all, an atomistic labour market; that beyond a certain point of exploitation labourers would combine and revolt; that it was sometimes necessary to negotiate terms rather than dictate them. They learned much: that the rules of capitalism allow some discussion of wages, but none of employment; that unity, to be very effective, had to encompass all labourers; that life in a capitalistic society demanded a more calculating, more informed and more disciplined behaviour than they had been used to.[28]

Pentland's thesis represents a remarkable excursion through the Canadian past – a trip all the more amazing for its quite unique point of origin and for the places where he takes us. If Pentland can be considered to be a part of the Toronto political economy school at all, as Daniel Drache has recently claimed, then it should be only for the penetrating insights generated by the interdisciplinary method that we associate with political economy. To describe his work only as some derivative part of the Innisian tradition is simultaneously to distort and to belittle it.[29]

In the 1960s Pentland's work appears to have focused on European economic history where he tried to apply some of his insights about "feudal" labour relations, which he had developed in the Canadian context, to Europe. Put simply, Pentland argued that the elaborate system of law and custom surrounding the nature of labour relations built up in the Middle Ages was based on a "perennial shortage of labour."[30] In 1965 Pentland attended the third International Conference of Economic History in Munich and delivered a paper on "Population and Labour Growth in Britain in the Eighteenth Century." Based on very recent demographic work, Pentland argued strongly that "English population growth in the eighteenth century was a response to economic conditions."[31] Debating simultaneously with those who saw demography as independent of the economy and with those who equated surplus population directly with economic growth, Pentland appears to have received a good reception. Certainly E.J. Hobsbawn was impressed and he cites Pentland's argument in *Industry and Empire*.[32]

Also in the 1960s, as the Canadian political climate began to quicken and dissent gained an audience again, Pentland began to make a few tentative, political interventions. Articles on guaranteed full employment, foreign ownership, the role of labour in Canadian economic planning, and the Freedman Report appeared in various journals.[33] His political perspective was always critical and he seemed as happy to penetrate social democratic myth-making regarding the possibilities of full employment with the NDP as to attack foreign ownership since "an economic colony will also be a political colony and Canada's frequent subservience to the United States follows largely from our status as an economic subsidiary."[34] While welcoming the Freedman Report as establishing a "great social principle," Pentland sensed, correctly, that the gains would be difficult for labour to hold and to spread beyond the railways. In his commendation of Freedman, however, Pentland encapsulated very well his view of the role of the Canadian courts in labour relations:

It is not only that most judges move in a circle dominated by employer attitudes, but that the law which they enunciate makes these attitudes their "natural" ones. And, except possibly in the highest court, they are expected to hew to precedent and dispense order, rather than justice, so that courts may march more or less in step, that lawyers may give their clients reasonable forecasts of what the courts will decide and that they will not be too often over-hauled at a cost to unhappy petitioners and their own reputations. The judges best equipped for their work, then, are those with so little imagination that a disposition different from the traditional one does not occur to them, and with so little sensitivity that they feel no qualms about the injustices they have wrought.[35]

It was also in the climate of the late 1960s and early 1970s that Pentland came to play two additional roles: one as a consultant in labour relations to both the Manitoba and federal governments and second, to a limited extent, as a newly recognized pioneer of the study of the Canadian working class movement. The former role led to various reports for the Manitoba government and his "Study of the Changing Social, Economic and Political Background of the Canadian System of Industrial Relations" for the 1968 federal Task Force on Labour Relations.[36] The second led him to assessments of the Winnipeg General Strike on its fiftieth anniversary, to an overall consideration of the western Canadian labour movement, and to review essays on the republication of Gustavus Myers' *History of Canadian Wealth* and Gary Teeple's New Left collection of essays on *Capitalism and the National Question in Canada*.[37]

On rereading this work, Pentland's important contribution to the recent resurgence of interest in the western Canadian labour movement is especially apparent. Again, due partially to the inaccessibility of much of his work, his role in defining many of the issues in this literature has been somewhat obscured. Yet his 1969 article on the Winnipeg General Strike, "one of the great class confrontations of capitalist history," anticipates much of the more recent literature.[38] For example, consider Pentland's conclusions about Winnipeg:

The confusion of ideology and tactics, indeed goes to the heart of the General Strike. Contrary to what the strikers imagined, a general strike (in itself) does not bring the capitalists to their knees; it only makes them close ranks and fight like jungle beasts for their class interests.[39]

Meighen and the Tory government understood this and acted accordingly. Thus "if western labour was far too militantly class-conscious from an employer's point of view, it was not nearly class-conscious enough from a syndicalist and Marxist point of view."[40] This failure resulted in the crushing of the strike which Pentland correctly viewed as a major defeat for Canadian labour. Although Pentland's analysis is couched throughout in language alien to David Bercuson's recent *Confrontation at Winnipeg*, the congruence of their arguments is clear.[41]

Equally, Pentland's unpublished, 1973 "The Western Canadian Labour Movement, 1897–1919" which he delivered at the Toronto Learneds in 1974, prefigures much of the very recent literature on "western labour exceptionalism." His account, like his successors', suffers from an over-emphasis on the distinctiveness of Western radicalism. This over-emphasis flows partially from the contemporary strength of western regional sentiment – a sentiment that Pentland's work displayed consistently in the 1960s and 1970s – and partially from the frequently articulated sentiments of the western radical leaders themselves. They firmly believed they were distinct from workers unfortunate enough to labour east of the Manitoba-Ontario border. It is not surprising, then, to find historians countenancing these claims. Yet the great danger in the comparative method is that it demands equivalent knowledge about both sides of the equation and neither Pentland, nor more recently, Bercuson and McCormack have sufficiently studied labour in the industrial heartland or in the East.[42] To identify all of eastern labour with Tom Moore and Gideon Robertson is an error that the western radical leaders began to recognize themselves in 1919, as Gerry Friesen has recently argued.[43] My argument with Pentland here, however, only demonstrates his importance to the field, and the consensus of western labour historians lies with his argument at the moment.

If Pentland's Manitoba loyalties were evident in his writings on western labour, his Canadian nationalism also emerges strongly in his last essays. Actually the strength of this nationalism contrasts somewhat with his earlier work. For example, in his response to Aitken's critique of his analysis of early capital accumulation, Pentland argued:

Most merchants eschewed fixed investment not from blindness, but as creatures of a commercial system. That they were not more like American merchants is a consequence rather than a cause of differences in economic structure. It is seldom useful to explain the flow of capital in terms of patriotism or its lack, though it is useful to explain patriotism in terms of the flow of capital.[44]

Moreover in his thesis Pentland had spent considerable time demonstrating the similar role the Canadian and American states had played in nineteenth-century economic development. Yet his analysis of Gustavus Myers' *History of Canadian Wealth* moved in the opposite direction. There he criticized Myers for "regarding Canada as a junior and retarded copy of the United States" and emphasized as one major difference the role of the Canadian state with its "pragmatic," "interventionist tradition." The Canadian bourgeoisie also had acted differently, although his example suggests a difference in degree only:

When Canadians were deliberately dishonest, they – unlike American promoters – were apt to be ridden by guilt and impelled to confine their venality to what their consciences could half-justify, rather than all that could be got.[45]

His stronger nationalism was also slightly evident in his review of Teeple's *Capitalism and the National Question*. He greeted this book generously as "an important addition to our historical resources, marking the debut of a new generation of Marxist scholars."[46] His general encouragement did not prevent him, however, from pointing out that often in the collection "the application of Marxist tools is rather limited and awkward."[47] Here he gave most consideration to Tom Naylor's controversial overview of Canadian economic history. After depicting Naylor as fitting his "image of the young Karl Marx," Pentland contented himself with a summary of the arguments which implies criticism but never offers it directly. His summary position is aggravating and perhaps slightly paternalistic:

This is stimulating stuff. The dogmatism and far-fetched generalizations are exasperating, but must be balanced against the promise that when this author gets his welter of ideas sorted out, and has chiselled them into congruence with the historical evidence his contribution to scholarship can be very great.[48]

I wish Pentland had addressed Naylor's work more systematically for there can be little question that the Pentland thesis (and Stanley Ryerson's elaboration of it in *Unequal Union*) provide a rather distinct, opposite view of Canada's nineteenth-century industrial capitalist development.[49]

The entire debate on the nature of Canadian industrialization has recently heated up considerably. Naylor's article and his subsequent two volume *History of Canadian Business* have generated much controversy.[50] It seems rather ironic, however, that Pentland's work is now receiving its due as it gets dragged into the controversy. Ironic not only because his views are often typified as "Ryersonian," despite the heavy debt of gratitude which Ryerson pays to Pentland's prior work, but also because he is drawn into the debate simply to have his views dismissed before the altar of Innis.[51] Thus, Mel Watkins, while recognizing that "We must enquire into the formation of the working class ... a critical matter neglected by Innis and thus far by Naylor,"[52] still warns us that Pentland "veered more to a Ryersonian than Naylorian view of industrialization, so we need to be on our guard."[53] It appears that it never occurs to Watkins that it is precisely Pentland's careful inquiry "into the formation of the working class" which inspires his so-called "Ryersonian" view of Canadian economic development. This "critical matter" is indeed crucial and Watkin's meanderings on a "dependent" working class after 1902 fails to speak to the previous sixty years of working class development in Canada. Watkins, like Drache, only pays lip service to the importance of Pentland's work while in effect, dismissing its most important insights.[54] On the other hand recent work in nineteenth century working class history and in social reconstitution has certainly tended to support Pentland's view of industrialization.[55]

The various controversies which now swirl around Pentland's work would no doubt delight him since they suggest an intellectual and political environment which has finally caught up with the impact, insight and import of his writing. I cannot help but wonder, however, if he too would not appreciate some of the irony of these debates. Unlike Gustavus Myers, at least his work will not have to wait fifty years for recognition.

NOTES

1 H.C. Pentland, "How the Wealth Was Won," *Canadian Forum* 52, September 1972: 6–9.

2 Both unpublished University of Toronto, PHD theses – Watt's completed in 1958, Pentland's in 1961.

3 Information as recorded in Judy Mills and Irene Dombra, comps,

University of Toronto Doctoral Theses, 1897–1967 (Toronto 1968). In 1958, Watt's was only the fifth Toronto English PHD on any aspect of Canadian letters.

4 This limited biographical information is drawn from conversations with W.T. Easterbrook, S.D. Clark, and C.B. Macpherson. The University of Toronto political economy department also kindly allowed me to consult Pentland's student file.

5 H.C. Pentland, "The Lachine Strike of 1843," *Canadian Historical Review*, 1948: 255–77; Harold Logan, *Trade Unions in Canada* (Toronto 1948). For brief discussions of the origins of labour studies in Canada see R.G. Hann et al, "Introduction," *Primary Sources in Canadian Working Class History* (Kitchener 1973), and Russell G. Hann and Gregory S. Kealey, "Documenting Working Class History: North American Traditions and New Approaches," *Archivaria* 4 (1977): 92–114.

6 Pentland, "Lachine Strike," 277.

7 Ibid., 255.

8 See Oscar and Mary Handlin, *Commonwealth: A Study of the Role of Governments in the American Economy: Massachusetts, 1774–1861* (New York 1974) and Louis Hartz, *Economic Policy and Democratic Thought: Pennsylvania, 1776–1860* (Cambridge 1948). For a useful discussion of this literature see Robert Lively, "The American System: A Review Article," *Business History Review* 29 (1955): 81–96.

9 H.C. Pentland, "The Role of Capital in Canadian Economic Development Before 1875," *Canadian Journal of Economics and Political Science* 16 (1950): 457–74.

10 H.C. Pentland, "Further Observations on Canadian Development," *Canadian Journal of Economics and Political Science* 19 (1953): 403–10.

11 H.C. Pentland, "The Development of a Capitalistic Labour Market in Canada," *Canadian Journal of Economics and Political Science* 25 (1959): 450–61.

12 Pentland, "The Role of Capital," 457.

13 Ibid., 463.

14 Pentland, "Labour and Industrial Capitalism," 1–2.

15 Ibid., 4. Pentland's use of "feudal" is unique. What he means by it is the "labour organization that preceded the free labour market of industrial capitalism, that was not slavery, nor a putting-out system, nor the share system of early capitalist commerce" (64). Thus it is a name he uses for a pre-industrial *but* capitalist form of labour organization and should not be confused with classic European feudalism.

16 Ibid., 208.

17 Ibid., 259.

18 Ibid., 283.

19 Ibid., 357–8.

20 Ibid.
21 Ibid., 384.
22 Ibid.
23 Ibid., 385.
24 Ibid., 392.
25 Ibid., 402–3.
26 Ibid., 406.
27 Ibid., 421–2.
28 Ibid., 424–5.
29 See Daniel Drache, "Rediscovering Canadian Political Economy,"
   Journal of Canadian Studies 11, 3 August 1976: 3–18. In this essay
   Drache describes Pentland as a "Post-Innisian" "in whose writing we
   find an elaboration of the Innis model in terms of superstructural
   relations" (3). Later he does describe Pentland's thesis as an "underground classic" (18) and credits him with "the first substantial Canadian investigation of the working class and the development of the
   modern industrial relations system" (11).
30 H.C. Pentland, "Feudal Europe: An Economy of Labour Scarcity,"
   Culture 21 (1960): 280–307, at 282.
31 H.C. Pentland, "Population and Labour Growth in Britain in the Eighteenth Century," in D.C. Eversley, ed, *Third International Conference of
   Economic History, Munich 1965*, vol. 4 (Paris 1972), 157–89, at 179.
32 E.J. Hobsbawn, *Industry and Empire* (Harmondsworth 1969), 44, 55.
33 H.C. Pentland, "Guaranteed Full Employment: A Critique of the New
   Democratic Party Program," *Canadian Dimension* (November–December 1964): 11–14; "Are Co-operatives the Answer to Foreign
   Ownership," *Canadian Dimension* (July 1965): 15, 25; "The Role of
   Labour in Economic Planning for Canada," *Journal of Liberal Thought* 2,
   no. 2 (Spring 1966): 85–96; "The Freedman Report," *Canadian Personnel and Industrial Relations Journal* 13 (1966): 10–24.
34 H.C. Pentland, "Foreign Ownership," 15.
35 H.C. Pentland, "The Freedman Report," 10–12.
36 H.C. Pentland, "Change in the Manitoba Economy," in *Automation and
   the Individual Proceedings of the Manitoba Conference on Technological
   Change* (Winnipeg 1968).
37 H.C. Pentland, "Fifty Years After," *Canadian Dimension* 6, no. 2 (July
   1969): 14–17; "How the Wealth was Won," *Canadian Forum* 52 (September 1972): 6–9; "Marx and the Canadian Question," *Canadian
   Forum* 54 (January 1974): 26–8; "The Western Canadian Labour Movement, 1897–1919," unpublished paper delivered at Canadian Economics Association meetings, Toronto 1974.
38 Pentland, "Fifty Years After," 14.
39 Ibid., 16.

40 Ibid.

41 David Bercuson, *Confrontation at Winnipeg: Labour, Industrial Relations, and the General Strike* (Montreal 1990), *passim*.

42 See Ross McCormack, *Reformers, Rebels and Revolutionaries: The Western Canadian Radical Movement, 1899–1919* (Toronto 1977) and David Bercuson, *Fools and Wise Men: The Rise and Fall of the One Big Union* (Toronto 1978).

43 Gerald Friesen, "'Yours in Revolt': Regionalism, Socialism and the Western Canadian Labour Movement," *Labour* 1 (1976): 139–57.

44 Pentland, "Further Observations," 409.

45 Pentland, "How the Wealth was Won," *passim*.

46 Pentland, "Marx and the Canadian Question," 26.

47 Ibid., 28.

48 Ibid., 27.

49 See Stanley Ryerson, *Unequal Union* (Toronto 1967) and Ryerson's review of Naylor, "Who's Looking After Business?" *This Magazine* 10, 5 and 6, (November–December 1976): 41–6. For an excellent similar critique of Naylor, see Larry MacDonald "Merchants against Industry: An Idea and its Origins," *Canadian Historical Review* 56 (1975): 263–81. It can be noted that MacDonald acknowledges Pentland's comments and suggestions on this paper (263).

50 Tom Naylor, *History of Canadian Business*, 2 vols (Toronto 1975). Much of this debate has been more amusing than enlightening. See especially the Bliss-Naylor exchange in *Social History* 18 (1976): 446–9 and 19 (1977): 152–63, which reached a vituperative level previously unmatched in Canadian scholarship.

51 For the "Ryersonian" typification and for a general example of this tendency, see Mel Watkins, "The Staple Theory Revisited," *Journal of Canadian Studies* 12, no. 5 (Winter 1977): 82–95.

52 Ibid., 90.

53 Ibid., 91.

54 Ibid., 88–92. Note especially "[Pentland's thesis] still – incredibly – unpublished. Pentland deserves great credit for working within the Marxist paradigm when it was distinctly unusual to do so, and the tendency for his work to be ignored by the mainstream of Canadian economic historians – including myself [Watkins] in the 1963 article – tells us much about the limitations of orthodox economics as it impinges on economic history." Indeed! (95 n. 49)

55 Bryan Palmer, "Most Uncommon Common Men: Craft, Culture and Conflict in a Canadian Community, 1860–1914," unpublished PHD thesis, State University of New York at Binghampton 1977 and Gregory S. Kealey, "The Working Class Response to Industrial Capitalism in Toronto, 1867–1892," unpublished PHD thesis, University of Rochester

1977. Both of these theses, on Hamilton and Toronto respectively, demonstrate the high level of industrialization attained by the early 1870s. They also are both more concerned with the details of that transformation of production than was Pentland. Another study supportive of Pentland's view is Stephen Langdon, *The Emergence of the Canadian Working Class Movement* (Toronto 1975). Finally, Michael Katz's Hamilton project has now generated very interesting material on industrialization and on the development of class.

3 Stanley Bréhaut Ryerson: Canadian Revolutionary and Marxist Historian

The problem of those who write the history of communist parties is therefore unusually difficult. They must recapture the unique and, among secular movements, unprecedented *temper* of bolshevism, equally remote from the liberalism of most historians and the permissive and self-indulgent activism of most contemporary ultras.   E.J. Hobsbawm

The problem in writing a book about the communists – in any country but surely in smaller ones where communism has had feeble roots – is to combine a charitable sense of sympathy for men and women who avowed commendable objectives with a rigorous analysis, a readiness to let hard facts rebut high intentions.   Joseph Starobin

Anyone who writes the history of the Communist Party from the outside, from legal evidence, documents, and first hand accounts, risks being hampered by his prejudices; in any event he lacks one irreplaceable experience. If he has left the party he chokes on his own rancor and dips his pen in bile. If he writes from the inside, in collaboration with the leaders, he becomes an official historiographer, and either lies or dodges questions according to the positions of the day.   Jean-Paul Sartre

Stanley Ryerson joined the Communist Party of Canada (CPC) in the early 1930s. This was an unusual but certainly not unique decision in those early depression years. The party was growing rapidly, especially after the Bennett governments' prosecution and conviction of the CPC leadership under section 98 of the Criminal Code. Engaged in Third Period militancy, the party gained members in its concerted trade-union work through the Workers Unity League, in its leadership of the unemployed movement, in its active civil liberties work through the Canadian Labour Defence League, and finally among some young artists and intellectuals through new institutions such as Workers' Theatre, the Progressive Arts Club, and journals such as *The Masses* and *New Frontier.*[1]

Ryerson, then, was not the only "traditional" intellectual[2] to join the CPC, but he was one of the first and undoubtedly was to become the most important. Most commentators on the CPC have noted its relative failure to recruit Canadian intellectuals.[3] An attempt to explain this peculiarity of Canadian scholarly life lies beyond the scope of these articles, but this problem had important implications for Ryerson's life. In the American and British communist parties, artists and intellectuals (and even, specifically, historians) were present in significant numbers from the 1930s on. In Canada, Ryerson was a relatively lonely figure. This accounts partially for his rapid rise in the party hierarchy and his continued presence on the Central Committee (CC) until 1969, when he did not run for the CC. (He did not leave the party until 1971.) Thus Ryerson played a role in the political history of Canadian communism unlike that of his American or British counterparts. Herbert Aptheker and Philip Foner, for example, go unmentioned in the major works on the history of the Communist Party of the United States of America (CPUSA). Eric Hobsbawm has noted that none of the members of the Historians Group of the Communist Party of Great Britain (CPGB), with the exception of E.P. Thompson, were "politically important enough to be elected to his District Party Committee."[4] (They were, however, to be rather more prominent during the events of 1956.)[5] Yet Ryerson, in contrast, was always at the centre of Canadian party life from the mid-1930s on.

Ryerson's political responsibilities left him little time for the task of writing history. Yet, he has managed nevertheless to produce a sizeable shelf of historical work. Indeed, one can only wonder how much he would have produced with the university scholar's rather different priorities. The onerous duties of party work did have their costs and, for example, prevented extensive archival research. Thus Ryerson's historical writing has always been that of a Marxist synthesizer. He took the work available to him and recast it in a historical materialist mould.

My article cannot evaluate Ryerson's political career. Yet any consideration of his intellectual work must be made in the context of his life as a leading member of the CPC. I have tried to do this in what follows by first providing a biographical/bibliographical sketch of

Ryerson's life and work and then turning to a more specific discussion of his historical writing.[6]

This article fails to credit sufficiently Ryerson's major contribution to both the "Old" and "New" Left as an important teacher of Marxism and as a living example of the possibilities of engaged Marxist intellectual work. In Canadian universities of the 1960s there were few such figures. Ryerson's availability and willingness to communicate with a new generation of students beginning their encounter with Marxism are less tangible than his books but certainly no less significant.

THE PARTY INTELLECTUAL

Stanley Ryerson was born in March 1911 in Toronto. The offspring of a successful professional family – his father, Dr Edward Stanley Ryerson was later assistant dean of the University of Toronto Medical School – he enjoyed the benefits of an elite Toronto upbringing, including attendance at Upper Canada College from 1919 to 1929.[7] While a student there, he encountered Spinoza, "some radical schoolmates," and began to challenge the assumptions of his High Anglican background.[8] His early interests included not only the arts and languages (inheritances from his Québécois mother, Tessie (Bréhaut) Devinge) but also a keen interest in science, especially geology. After enrolling initially at the University of Toronto in geology, he transferred midway through his first year to Modern Languages and was active in theatre, especially in the Players Guild, which in 1931 produced a play he wrote on Abélard. He took his third year abroad and studied at the Sorbonne in 1931–32. In his first summer in Paris, he had a number of Canadian companions – Felix and Dorothy Walter, Barker and Margaret Fairley, Otto Van der Sprenkel, and fellow Toronto students Jean "Jim" Watts and Dorothy Livesay, all spent the summer months there. While overseas, he travelled in Italy and Spain as well as in France and encountered the political turmoil of the early depression years in Europe. During this year in Europe he became a communist:

The realization that the cultural values of art and literature were being turned by capitalism into what I can only describe as spiritual onanism and the discovery that communism, by solving the material problems of society, was the only path to a future creative renaissance, was the first impulse.[9]

On returning to Toronto to finish his undergraduate work, he joined the Progressive Arts Club, which had been founded in the spring of 1932. Its three groups of writers, artists, and theatre workers published *Masses*, an organ of socialist realist art, and established the Canadian Workers' Theatre, which enjoyed considerable success in 1932 and 1933. Ryerson contributed actively, writing theoretical articles and a short play, "War in the East," on the Chinese resistance to the Japanese invasion of Manchuria. Simultaneously, he had joined the Young Communist League (YCL) and soon became its educational director and editor of *The Young Worker*. Also active in the nascent Student League of Canada, he attended a December 1932 anti-war congress in Chicago. Thus, even in his first year of communist activity, Ryerson's talents had become quickly apparent. A middle-class student from a privileged background in an overwhelmingly proletarian milieu, he possessed indispensable tools but at the same time generated considerable unease. Although such tension would abate over the years, it would never disappear completely. Hard work represented the best way to prove oneself and Ryerson threw himself into party activities.

In his year back in Toronto, Ryerson was also involved in various study groups. Based to some degree on friendships and personal relations, these groups involved university figures and dissident intellectuals such as the Walters, the Fairleys, J.F. White (the soon-to-resign editor of *Canadian Forum*), Otto Van der Sprenkel, Leo Warshaw, and many others. Here, as well as in YCL study groups with Bill Sparks (the pseudonym of George Rudas, a Yugoslavian communist on loan to the Canadian party from the CPUSA), Ryerson was learning his Marxism.

Returning to Paris for post-graduate work in modern languages at the Sorbonne in the fall of 1933, Ryerson involved himself in communist activities while writing a Diplômes d'Études Supérieures study of Sicilian peasant-realist novelist Giovanni Verga. Ryerson's political work in France included participation in the Association des Écrivains et Artistes révolutionnaires, and preparation of material for *L'Avant Garde*. Ryerson was deeply influenced by the turn to the Popular Front by the Communist Party of France (PCF).[10]

On his return to Canada, he took up active party work in August 1934 in Montreal where he taught French studies at Sir George Williams College for three years. The party had few inroads in Quebec and Ryerson's language skills made him an obvious choice for work there. Initially education director, he joined the CC in 1935 and was elected provincial secretary in 1936. In this period, he continued to contribute to *The Worker* and *New Frontier*, but spent most of his time writing for *Clarté*, which he edited.[11] Although he wrote under the pseudonym E. Roger to protect his job, his politics nevertheless led to his non-renewal at Sir George Williams in 1937. His journalism in this period covered the gamut from book and movie reviews to political commentary to popular history. As part of the shift to united front activities, the party had taken an increased interest in the Canadian past and Ryerson quickly established himself as the party's major historian. Pieces on Papineau and Riel prepared the groundwork for his first book, *1837: The Birth of Canadian Democracy*. Dedicated "To the men of the Mackenzie-Papineau Battalion Fighting on the Battle-Field of Democratic Spain," this volume celebrated the centennial of the rebellions ("shrouded in a conspiracy of silence by Canadian authorities") and in the process introduced many of the themes pursued in his later historical work. In his "Foreword," Ryerson warned that Canadian democracy in 1937 was "beset with danger," a premonition proven correct a few months later when, on Christmas Eve, the Quebec provincial police, under the terms of the infamous Padlock Law, raided Ryerson's home and confiscated some 40 books, 100 pamphlets, and his research notes – ironically including those from his "Birth of Canadian Democracy." On a lighter note in that same foreword, he commented on his illustrious great-grandfather, Egerton Ryerson, who had turned from revolution to education, while he had turned from education to revolution.[12] Under the pseudonym "E. Roger," he also published *Le Réveil du Canada Français* in 1937, "dedié à la mémoire de tous les héros de la liberté, combattants de 1837." A strong indictment of Quebec's oppression ("particulièrement intenses"), this small book nevertheless called for Canadian working-class unity "dans une lutte commune contre l'ennemi commun, qui est l'oppression capitaliste." Denouncing Groulx and other Quebec nationalists as fascists, Ryerson condemned separatist discussion.[13]

In the fall of 1939 after Canada's declaration of war, Ryerson and other party leaders went underground. Strongly opposed to the war after the Nazi-Soviet non-aggression pact, Ryerson and the Canadian party looked to French-Canadian nationalist opposition to an imperialist war as the cutting edge of resistance. At this particular juncture, Quebec nationalism came to be viewed in a more nuanced fashion, one which would survive with Ryerson, at least, beyond the return to full support for the war effort which followed the Nazi invasion of the Soviet Union.[14] With the brief flirtation with Quebec nationalist sentiment ended (see *La Voix du Peuple*), the party began to publish a new paper, *La Victoire*, on which Ryerson worked. In the campaign to regain legal status for the party, Ryerson and other communist leaders surrendered to the Royal Canadian Mounted Police in Toronto on 25 September 1942.[15] Eventually cleared after an inquiry, they founded the Labor Progressive Party (LPP), of which Ryerson became national education director in August 1943. Relocating in Toronto, Ryerson also became managing editor of the LPP's new theoretical journal, *National Affairs Monthly*, which was launched in April 1944.

In his new role as LPP education director and editor of *National Affairs*, Ryerson took up an even more frantic pace. In his inaugural editorial, Ryerson argued that the new monthly demonstrated "the growing influence and acceptance in Canadian life of a current of Marxist thought and action, broadly connected with the people's movements for social change." The magazine, as an organ "of the opinions of Canadian Marxists on vital issues in Canadian life – past, present, and future," would study "Canada's economic and political growth" and "past history as it bears upon our understanding of the present and future."[16] During the three years in which he edited *National Affairs* (April 1944–March 1947), Ryerson also contributed numerous editorials and articles. Succeeded by Charles Sims as editor, Ryerson subsequently took on yet heavier party responsibilities as the LPP's organizational secretary.

In 1943, his *French Canada* was published, appearing in translation in an extensively revised version two years later. Written while underground, this work received considerable media attention when it appeared and enjoyed brisk sales of nearly 10,000 copies in two years.[17] B.K. Sandwell, the editor of *Saturday Night*, used his "Front Page" to worry that such communist activities would "exert a considerable impact on the great mass of the French Canadian people." And another illustrious descendant of Canadian Reform in the 1830s, Prime Minister William Lyon Mackenzie King, wrote to Ryerson to congratulate him on his book, which King felt "rendered a splendid service in seeking ... to promote and broaden the understanding between French-speaking and English-speaking Canadians."[18] A continuation of the work commenced in *1837*, *French Canada* explored "the problem of the relations of French and English Canada." Discovering further heroes in the French Canadians' "passionately striving for survival as a people," Ryerson provided a historical overview of Quebec development organized around Papineau, Lafontaine, Dorion, Riel, and Laurier. In a more sociological vein he also analyzed the backwardness of Quebec agriculture, the rise of monopoly capital, and the oppression of French-Canadian workers. Although partially avoiding hard questions about Quebec nationalism (as Ryerson was later to recognize himself), this volume nevertheless must be assessed in the context of World War II conditions and French-English antagonisms. In that light it still reads well.[19]

While LPP education director, Ryerson published his *A World to Win: An Introduction to the Science of Socialism* (1946; rev. ed. 1950). Basically a beginner's guide to Marxism, the book is notable for its attempt to introduce Marxist concepts through examples drawn from Canadian history, such as the Royal Commission on the Relation of Labor and Capital of 1886–89. Also of considerable interest is the encouragement given to novices in Marxist study to return to the classics. For example, Ryerson says of *Capital*: "The idea that this great work is 'heavy,' and 'incomprehensible' to the general reader, is a fairy tale that's spread by the enemies of Marxism. It's a vivid, powerfully written, exciting masterpiece of science and history."[20] Also in 1946, Margaret Fairley's *Spirit of Canadian Democracy* was published. A collection of short excerpts from Canadian poets, novelists, political figures, and scholars, this work fit solidly the Popular Front's concern to develop the party's interest in the Canadian past.[21]

In late December 1946, Ryerson's LPP Education Committee sponsored a National Affairs Conference on Marxist Studies of Canadian Development. This conference, organized around presentations by Ryerson, Margaret Fairley, and Tim Buck, led to the establishment of a number of permanent committees under the overall direction of Ryerson (chairman) and Fairley (secretary). In addition, Fairley chaired the "People's History" committee, while Beckie Buhay and M. Freeman took charge respectively of the committees to study Canadian labour history and Canadian imperialism.[22] This organizational structure led to the party's first systematic study of Canada and preliminary results appeared in a special issue of *National Affairs*, edited by the LPP's National Education Department in early 1949, and in subsequent issues that year.[23] Here too lay the roots of later works by Fairley, Ryerson, Frank and Libbie Park, and Charles Lipton.

The publication of Tim Buck's *Canada: The Communist Viewpoint* in 1948 may be taken as the high point of the party's intellectual activities. Ryerson's eulogistic foreword to this work not only termed the book a "landmark in the history of the labour movement of this country" but also described its author as "a tribune of the people who embodies and expresses the struggles of the working people from sea to sea."[24] Despite that excess, the book is undoubtedly the most systematic statement of Communist Party analysis and program calling for "A People's National Policy." Buck effectively criticized the post-war destruction of the Canadian economy by the Liberals' ongoing sell-out to the Americans.

Yet the years from 1948 to 1956 were not kind to the Canadian party. Various estimates suggest that approximately one-fifth to one-third of the party's members left in this period.[25] These losses came not from significant theoretical differences but rather from a steady erosion owing to the pressures of the Cold War and to the increasing marginality of the party. This is not, of course, to suggest that the party's work on post-war inflation, in the peace movement, and in exposing the Americanization of the Canadian economy and culture were not important. Nevertheless, in reading *National Affairs*, one witnesses the increasing isolation of the party – an isolation which despite frequent self-critical reflections on the process, evidenced itself in a growing sectarianism. Not surprisingly, Ryerson, in his role as organizational secretary of the LPP, penned a number of essays exhorting party members to greater contributions to the cause which manifested these symptoms only too clearly.[26]

Ryerson, who had been troubled by serious migraine difficulties after 1937, spent a number of months in a Soviet hospital in 1951–52, seeking some relief. On this trip he travelled widely in Eastern Europe and attended a CPGB congress. Active after his return in the federal election campaign of 1953 as a LPP candidate in Hamilton, he was injured in a July car accident.[27] A little over a year later, he returned to Eastern Europe as the Canadian party's representative on the editorial board of *For a Lasting Peace, For a People's Democracy*. Here he came in contact with the various currents of communist thought which swirled around Bucharest – currents which, after Stalin, pointed increasingly to a less-monolithic, less-Soviet-dominated, world communist movement.

Still experiencing health difficulties related to the 1953 accident, Ryerson again sought Soviet medical treatment. Thus in 1956 he joined Tim Buck in Moscow as Canadian delegate to the Twentieth Congress of the Communist Party of the Soviet Union (CPSU).[28] Like all foreign delegates, the Canadians were not present for Kruschev's denunciation of Stalin and the revelations of the Stalinist atrocities. Buck apparently only became aware of the startling news when, on his return voyage to Canada, he stopped in London and was informed by CPGB leader Harry Pollitt.[29] Ryerson, meanwhile, remained in Moscow until November for health reasons. Thus, he missed both the incredible confusion with which the Canadian party greeted the events of 1956 and the bulk of the open debate which swept through the party that summer and fall. Instead, Ryerson returned at the height of the leadership crisis after the National Committee had intervened to restore the Buck leadership after a badly split National Executive Committee (NEC) had ousted him, supported Gomulka in the Polish crisis, and called the CPSU to task for its intervention there. After his return, Ryerson joined with Leslie Morris to write the crucial draft resolution for the December 1956 National Committee meeting which lay the foundation for the complete victory of the Buck forces at the sixth national convention in April 1957.

THE PARTY CRISIS OF 1956–57

The complex events of 1956–57 cannot be analyzed in full detail here, but it is important to establish Ryerson's role, as summarized above. Early reports of the February 1956 Twentieth Congress gave no hint to Canadian party members of what had transpired.[30] Not until late March did details of the secret Kruschev report begin to be mentioned and then the *Canadian Tribune*, speaking for the party leadership, could only weakly note that on Buck's return all would become clear, for "lacking authentic information and texts, we deem it unwise to indulge in speculation or the drawing of hasty conclusions."[31] This totally inadequate response was followed a week later by Leslie Morris's equivocal answers to press queries concerning the CPC's position.[32] A CPC mass membership meeting of 600 in Toronto on 28 March demanded answers from Morris, who stalled further, awaiting Buck's return.[33] Writing from Europe, Buck's pat response at this point – and he never actually wandered too far from it throughout – was the stock CPSU explanation of the degenerating influences of the cult of the individual. Yet Buck also felt called on to warn: "Let nobody assume, however, that the result will be the obliteration of the name of Stalin. Without any doubt it can be said that his contribution to the struggle for socialism, in peace and in war, assure him a firm and lasting place in history."[34] In this same tone, initial letters printed in the *Tribune* engaged in attempts to defend Stalin from Kruschev's so-far unspecified attacks.

Buck's return to Canada ended that process. He immediately began to shift the CPC into accord with the new Kruschev line. His May Day speeches in Hamilton and Toronto indicated that his earlier position no longer sufficed. He spoke of "shocking distortions of Soviet policy, socialist democracy, and crimes." Moreover, he added, the LPP too had been guilty of similar errors.[35]

The NEC met almost nightly through late April and into May to hear Buck's report of Kruschev's revelations and to consider what to do. NEC member and Quebec provincial leader, Gui Caron, remembered later in his moving resignation letter:

I was sickened by the ghoulish tale of mass arrests in the middle of the night, of barbaric torture, of confessions extracted for the purpose of incriminating other innocent people, of executions without trial, of repression against the families of accused people, of a terror directed not against the enemies of socialism but against its finest flower, its leading and most courageous political and cultural leaders.[36]

When the National Committee (NC) finally met on 17 May, Buck did not reveal his personal knowledge of the contents of the secret Kruschev report, claiming privately that since it had been provided to him as personal information by Harry Pollitt, it had no official standing. This was, of course, convenient, since Buck and some other NEC members felt that membership should be spared "the gory details."[37] The National Committee, on the basis of this incomplete information, still called for a "searching reexamination of LPP policy," announced that the LPP's sixth national convention would be held in Toronto in January, and criticized the CPSU for withholding crucial information from other communist parties. The NC also sent Buck on a nation-wide speaking tour to calm the increasingly aroused party membership.[38] Beginning in mid-May, the pages of the *Tribune* had been opened "to stimulate a wide and free debate" on the "shocking distortions of Soviet democracy." The response had been overwhelming and the flow of critical commentary showed signs of developing into a torrent.[39]

Helping to feed this flood came two additional revelations. First was the confirmation of serious anti-semitic practices in the Soviet Union. Published initially in Poland and New York, these admissions finally appeared in the *Tribune* along with notes of self-criticism.[40] This admission led to the May reinstatement of J.B. Salsberg to the NEC, from which he had been dismissed in 1953 for refusing "to accept and publicly defend the full position of the party on the question of the Soviet Jewish writers and Jewish cultural institutions in the Soviet Union."[41] Indeed, the NC criticized itself for "failing to raise the issue with our brother party, the CPSU."[42] The second revelation came with the U.S. State Department's early June release of the full text of Kruschev's secret speech to the closed session of the Twentieth Congress. All the CPC could do was publish the text as received from the United States, criticize the CPSU for not providing the text earlier, and brace itself for another flood of criticism.[43]

These criticisms did indeed follow and the NEC meeting of 23 to 25 June 1956 issued its sharpest ever rebuke to the CPSU. Terming the Kruschev speech "not adequate," they asserted that "the leaders of the CPSU owed to the world labour and socialist movement thoroughgoing explanations." Warming to their task, they noted critically that it was "not a Marxist explanation to say that Stalin's personal weaknesses and shortcomings alone were responsible, as was suggested by Kruschev's speech for that explains Joseph Stalin by Joseph Stalin." Finally, treading on dangerous ground indeed, they argued that "clearly responsibility fell on the shoulders of the leadership of the CPSU as a whole" and they "deplored the absence of any mention ... of the suppression of Jewish culture in the CPSU."[44] Slightly earlier, in June, the Quebec provincial committee of the LPP had begun the process of turning the criticism inward. They called for "sharp struggle against an entrenched dogmatism and intolerance; against the idea that divergencies from accepted party policy automatically flow from alien ideology; against the idea of the infallibility of party leaders; against the stifling of criticism; against a certain conceit on our part in relations with non-party people." In other words, they concluded, "we need to create a new atmosphere in our party which will permit the free exchange of ideas where the opinions of every party member will be valued and assured of consideration."[45] Brave and promising words!

Yet the process so bravely begun was already slowing down. In early July the CC of the CPSU issued a lengthy statement clarifying the Twentieth Congress revelations and indicating clearly what the terms of future critical comment would be. Togliatti, leader of the Communist Party of Italy (PCI) was, for example, singled out as having overstepped the limits of fraternal comment. The *Tribune*, in contrast, greeted the CPSU statement: "It adds greatly to understanding. It puts the whole terrible 'Stalin affair' in better perspective." Although still not dealing with the Jewish question nor explaining the rationale for Kruschev's initial secrecy, the *Tribune* pronounced the statement "on balance, however, forthright."[46] Thus, the NEC's political letter announced one week later, calling for "the freest, widest and most democratic party discussions ever to take place in our ranks," came just as acceptable debate appeared to be narrowing. The NEC's further claim that "not a single question ... any of the matters relating to our application of Marxism in Canada – should be excluded from the discussion" and their articulation of questions to be pursued as including socialist democracy, political pluralism under socialism, and the dictatorship of the proletariat, would emerge later as hollow rhetoric.[47]

The *Tribune*'s early indication of CPC endorsement of the CPSU statement was confirmed when the NEC met in late July. Basically ignoring their earlier critical demands, they simply capitulated and accepted it as a sufficient explanation of Stalinism.[48] Apparently the only dissident votes on the NEC came from Gui Caron and J.B. Salsberg.[49] In the August *National Affairs*, Buck went still further by repudiating the earlier NEC position and joining his voice to the chorus of Togliatti's critics.[50] Nevertheless, the NEC dispatched Buck, Salsberg, Leslie Morris, and Bill Kardash to the Soviet Union in late August to meet with CPSU leaders in order to gain additional information.[51] Granted an interview with Kruschev himself, the Canadian leaders no doubt had their faith in the importance in the international communist movement reconfirmed. Kruschev, however, did little to reassure Salsberg on the Jewish question by making anti-semitic remarks and warning Salsberg not to be misled by Zionists and the bourgeoisie. Ryerson, still in Moscow, was present at these meetings and confirms Salsberg's story of Kruschev's slur that "when a Jew sinks his anchor, there immediately springs up a synagogue."[52] Despite this and the CPSU leaders' refusal to indicate anything beyond their 30 June statement, the *Tribune* reported that "further clarity was achieved."[53] According to Caron, the Soviet leadership went so far as to insist that inner-party democracy had existed throughout the Stalin years except at the highest levels near Stalin.[54]

At the 12 October NEC meeting to hammer out an official report on the trip to the Soviet Union, Caron proposed that the NEC state publicly that "some leaders of the CPSU have a certain negative attitude to the Jewish people which is inconsistent with socialist democracy." This was rejected with only Caron and Salsberg supporting it. Instead the NEC adopted the delegates' favourable report, registering only Salsberg's "certain reservations," which were not specified.[55]

Meanwhile Salsberg's and Buck's differences had finally become public. At meetings with the discontented Montreal membership, they clashed openly. Buck, apparently in response to a query about the dictatorship of the proletariat, indicated that this was "proposing we reexamine whether or not we should be a Marxist-Leninist Party." This was not a debatable question, said Buck, thus confirming for many the growing idea that "free discussion" was limited. These events led to the dramatic resignation of five members of the Quebec provincial LPP committee, including NEC member Gui Caron. Caron's resignation letter is undoubtedly the most critical and perhaps the most moving document of the LPP crisis. He argued that it had become clear that the LPP was incapable of transforming itself owing to "the very deep resistance to change in the party." Discussion, even in the NEC, had "been stalemated on what type of questions could or could not be asked." Thus, faced with "the ever-diminishing moral and political stature of our party in this country, in too large a measure the consequence of our own actions," he decided the only course left was resignation.[56]

The subsequent NEC meeting broke down in crisis and deadlock. On 22 October the NEC voted five to three with one abstention to remove Buck from his position. On the following day, the NEC "greeted" Gomulka and sent a cable to the CPSU condemning "any attempts at interference" with events in Poland.[57] Although later rescinding its removal of Buck, the NEC refused to withdraw its cable to the CPSU despite almost immediate protests from the LPP's Ukraini-

an National Committee, which termed it "an unpardonable usurpa-
tion of party authority." In their anger, the Ukrainian leaders also
made only too clear their view of recent events in the LPP, arguing
that under the banner of free debate there had been "an opening of
the doors to attacks on the principles of Marxism-Leninism, directed
towards splitting and ultimately liquidating the Canadian workers'
party of scientific socialism and towards the destruction of the
internationalism of the proletarian movement."[58]

With this crisis in the LPP augmented by the events of the Hungar-
ian uprising, the NC met in a marathon session from 28 October to 9
November. The differences exposed at this meeting ran deep and the
NC was "unable to solve its problems in a definitive way." They did
withdraw, however, the cable to the CPSU on Poland by a vote of 18 to
11 with one abstention. The NC also offered sharp criticisms of Buck
and the NEC for Buck's prevarications in May and for the inability of
the leadership to clarify issues for the members. While asserting the
increasingly formula-like invocation that "it is the right and duty of all
members of the party to fully and unrestrictedly express their points
of view on all questions in the pre-convention discussion," they
nevertheless indicated their political direction in the election of a new
NEC. For a NEC of 13, 11 were clearly elected, with three tied for the
final two positions. Those three, including J.B. Salsberg and A.A.
MacLeod, then withdrew; this was followed quickly by the resignations of Harry Binder and Norman Penner. It was then decided to
function with a new NEC of only nine members. Binder and Penner
explained in lengthy letters that their resignations were to protest the
NC's attempt to resolve political disagreements through removing the
minority faction from positions on the NEC. Binder especially emphasized that what was at issue was internal party democracy since
Buck's entire strategy had revolved around attacking his critics on the
NEC as "revisionists and liquidators" and calling for a new NEC "to
fight the right deviationists." This attitude, Binder argued, shut down
debate and labelled those who raised questions as "rotten elements"
and "do gooders." As examples, he cited Buck's Montreal speech
(which Caron too had noted) and the Ukrainian National Committee's
demand that "Trotskyites" be rooted out of the party. Buck had never
carried any of this through the NC in political discussion, but only
through the NEC election. Thus, Binder concluded, there could not be
"free and unfettered debate" and, moreover, for him to stay on the
NEC would only have covered up "the disruptive line pursued by the
national leader of the party." Penner's shorter letter made the same
points, blaming the election result on "fantastic rumours and
charges" and comparing the process to a "witchhunt."[59]

The new NEC issued a 17 November plea for loyalty to the party. Claiming this as the party's most difficult moment, it called on members "to close ranks and rally to the cause for which we are working." Regretting the resignations from the NEC, it called for "free discussion" and announced that it was preparing a political resolution for a mid-December NC meeting which would in turn lay the ground-work for the national convention.[60]

Approximately at this point Ryerson returned from Moscow. Aside from his presence at the meeting with Kruschev, his only involvement had been a *Tribune* article on the thirty-ninth anniversary of the Revolution. This particular article, while generally innocuous, did go out of its way to find socialism "flourishing" in Russia and to note that "criticism is everywhere." This criticism, however, was "positive, creative – not negative, destructive with its edge turned against socialist society itself."[61] This hint at his position on the Canadian debate proved only too accurate.

On his return to Canada, Ryerson joined with Leslie Morris to prepare the NEC's political draft resolution for the December NC meeting. His position in the ensuing debates was unequivocal. He backed the Buck leadership totally and one dissident group termed the majority grouping "the Buck/Ryerson faction."[62] His major contribution to the pre-convention discussion, "Getting Our Bearings: And Correcting a Dangerous List to Starboard," was a vigorous attack on the Smith/Salsberg grouping which carried over to include the attempted Penner and Sims compromises. In this piece Ryerson argued uncompromisingly that "the disclosure of serious errors made in the Soviet Union under Stalin's leadership has led some people to very wrong conclusions. They fail to see that the errors, however grave, are secondary compared to the achievements recorded in building and defending socialism." Moreover these critics were "so obsessed with the errors, they can see nothing else" and "so bent are they on dissociating themselves from the mistakes, that they take on, consciously or not, the tones of outright anti-Sovietism."[63]

In addition to this somewhat condescending dismissal of those concerned with the Twentieth Congress exposé, he also bitterly criticized the *Tribune* for what he viewed as an exaggerated attempt at objectivity and unbiased presentation in its pre-convention summary of "The Great Debate in the LPP." Here he attacked their implication that the major issue concerned errors of the LPP and whether they could be overcome – a point of view he typified as the Smith/Salsberg position. Moreover, he asserted, the main point in debate is the exist-ence of Marxism-Leninism in Canada since the platform of each minority was its elimination by either (a) speedy self-dissolution, or

(b) gradual self-poisoning. The Smith/Salsberg position he denigrated as "a swamp of anti-Soviet hostility, rejection of revolutionary working-class leadership, and exchanging working-class solidarity for boss-class nationalism."[64]

Not surprisingly, an irate Norman Penner responded in the next issue. Ryerson's letter, Penner argued, exemplified "the intolerance, contempt, and hatred on the part of a section of the LPP leadership toward those members of the party who attempt to examine all questions critically." Criticism of the U.S.S.R. was not necessarily anti-Soviet, criticism of the LPP was not necessarily dissolutionist, and references to the Twentieth Congress, Hungary, and Poland were not all Ottawa-inspired. The existence of the LPP was not the question, Penner continued; its relevance in Canada was. In summation, he noted: "It is the Ryerson position of continued intolerance, of continued uncritical acceptance of every view of the Soviet party, of continued insistence that only the LPP has all the answers, of continued opposition to the Co-operative Commonwealth Federation, of continued obstruction to independent labour political action – all of this raises the big question about the party's future."[65]

A meek Ryerson rejoinder in the same issue as Penner's apologized for implying that the right-wing was "inspired by Ottawa directly." He "sincerely and seriously" regretted this slur on the honesty of those holding the right-wing position, but, he added, he could not apologize for his anger since the proposals added up to "an attempt on the very life of the LPP."[66]

The National Convention was an anti-climax. The Buck forces triumphed totally while the Smith/Salsberg group received almost insignificant support, losing 121 to 9 with 14 abstentions. In the elections for the NC, Salsberg received only 21 votes and Smith only 20 of a possible 167. The compromise amendments to the draft resolution proposed by Penner and Sims received only 15 and 12 votes respectively. On the new NEC the only member who had voiced any significant difference with the Buck leadership was Edna Ryerson. New NEC members included Alf Dewhurst, Nelson Clarke, and Sam Walsh, all of whom had sided with the Buck faction.[67]

During the following month, Salsberg, Smith, Binder, and Sam Lipshitz broke publicly with the party, issuing a ringing declaration which was published in the Toronto *Globe and Mail*.[68] Nor surprisingly, the NEC issued a drastic denunciation of the four for "flying false flags of 'democracy' and 'anti-Stalinism'" – the "banner of revisionism and the distortion of Marxism-Leninism."[69] Within a year a number of other opponents of Buck left, albeit more quietly. Thus Edna Ryerson, Norman Penner, A.A. MacLeod, and Steve Endicott joined the mounting list of important party leaders who left the LPP during or soon after the crisis of 1956–57. More significant were the countless rank-and-file members who had disappeared. Some estimates place this figure as high as 50 per cent.[70] The party had indeed become what some hardliners had called "better small, but better." However, many might question their self-evaluation.

FROM HUNGARY TO CZECHOSLOVAKIA

In the aftermath of the convention, Ryerson took a much less active role in the party. His health still precarious, he convalesced while working out-of-doors in Leslie Hancock's nursery. His parting contributions to party debate for a few years were a call for a "regrounding in Marxism" and a warning against what he viewed as the two errors over which the LPP had just triumphed: a rightist liberal nationalism and an ultra-leftist doctrinaire dogmatism which too often led to complacency. On this score he engaged in some self-criticism, "complacency" having been evident in "the painful slowness with which the 'People's History' is being completed."[71] Politically, the next few years saw the Canadian party return to its depressing pre-1956 subservience to the CPSU. In 1958, Buck engaged in ridiculous posturings, echoing the renewed Soviet critique of Tito and the Yugoslavian party. The LPP denounced the program of the Yugoslav League of Communists as "anti-Marxist-Leninist" and "disruptive of and an attack on the ideological unity of the world communist movement and the international struggle for peace." But Buck went even further. Not satisfied with simply abetting the Soviet line, he absurdly connected Tito with the Canadian debate:

In Canada as in Yugoslavia, there were glaring contradictions between the words of the revisionists and the reality of their political role. For example, while those pretended "Canadianizers" were urging the members of the party to repudiate proletarian internationalism, they themselves were in fact, the representatives in Canada of an international grouping organized around a political program of revisionism. ... But worse ... they were inspired by and definitely part of an international attempt to undermine the world communist movement and not at all by concern for Canada and the Canadian working-class movement.[72]

If this was not bad enough, the same issue of *Marxist Review* carried a lengthy letter asking that the party reexamine its attitude to Joseph Stalin since "injustice had been done to Stalin and we shouldn't hesitate to speak in defence of his policies which we are sure were right at the time." Arguing that Stalin had no real alternatives, this horrendous apologia concluded: "And the fact is that a man is yet to be born who could measure up to the triumphs achieved by workers, farmers, and the little man generally under the direction of Joseph Stalin."[73]

This resurgence of Stalinism represented one pole of party activity in these years. The other, which reflected more positive developments in world communism after the Twentieth Congress, came to the fore during the sixteenth CPC convention of October 1959. This convention, which restored the name Communist Party, also endorsed the creation of a marxist studies centre in Toronto.[74] Reflecting this opening, Leslie Morris, the editor of *Marxist Review*, issued a clarion call for that journal to enter "Into the Battle of Ideas." Noting Marx's motto, "Nothing that is human is alien to me," Morris called for the party to engage more openly in intellectual debates in Canada. Ryerson was deeply involved in these developments.[75] In a subsequent issue, Phyllis Clarke greeted this invocation and noted that it was the first time since the crisis of 1956–57 that work in the cultural and intellectual arena had received any priority.[76]

Ryerson, who had returned to full-time party work co-ordinating the Toronto edition of *World Marxist Review*, actively participated and initially chaired the historical committee of the Marxist Studies Centre. This committee also took responsibility for reviewing the progress of the People's History and maintaining communication with Charles Lipton's work in labour history. By 1960 Ryerson had become director of the centre and the following year it began to publish a bulletin which reported on the centre's work and the director's travels. In the fall of 1960, Ryerson attended the Stockholm International Congress of Historical Science, and in the summer of 1961, Ryerson attended a PCF conference on "The Future of Mankind," establishing contact with Roger Garaudy. He also participated in editorial board meetings of the *World Marxist Review* in Prague and visited the Gramsci Institute in Rome and the editorial offices of *Marxism Today* in London.[77] Late that year, the CPC, following through on their new more-open direction, announced the termination of *Marxist Review* and the birth of *Marxist Quarterly* with Ryerson as editor.[78] It was no coincidence that this change took place simultaneously with Leslie Morris's succession to Buck's position as party leader.

The early years of the 1960s represented, on some levels, a return to the happier days of the popular front – a period which had deeply influenced Ryerson's attitudes and which had been the period of the party's greatest attractiveness to intellectuals in general. Ryerson's first volume of the People's History, *The Founding of Canada*, appeared in 1960, and that same year, Margaret Fairley's edition of *The Selected*

Writings of William Lyon Mackenzie was also published. The promise of the 1946 National Affairs Conference had finally come to fruition.[79]

Marxist Quarterly (renamed *Horizons* in 1966) had a refreshing openness about it. Not limited to party-sanctioned views, the journal actively reached out in the 1960s to the rapidly growing community of dissidents – initially, especially among intellectuals. This was evident from the journal's first issue, which contained Ryerson's reflections on Canadian intellectual history. Although noting the prevalence of philosophical idealism, Ryerson nevertheless called on Marxists to come to grips with this material and implicitly issued a public rebuke by noting that "we are still at a most elementary stage in our 'schooling' in this respect."[80] Moreover, in that same issue, Ryerson commented favourably on "The Week of Marxist Thought," an immensely successful French communist party conference on "Humanism and Dialectics." What made this positive note strikingly independent was his echoing of Roger Garaudy's assertion that communists must avoid the narrow "cramped conception of Marxism-Leninism simply as a position to be defended, a fortress to be held, with every portcullis closed, while one peers out over the battlements at all who are not 'our people' wandering on the distant plain." Ryerson added to this critique "the failure or reluctance to study the *content* of the work of our adversaries, satisfying oneself with affixing political labels to them." From such "open dialogue (for which it takes two)," Ryerson concluded, comes a "developed, deepened and enriched Marxist interpretation of reality."[81]

For seven years *Marxist Quarterly/Horizons* published interesting and lively material ranging from current affairs through all academic disciplines.[82] Perhaps most important, for the first time since the 1940s there was engagement with life outside the party. This involvement included the Christian-Marxist dialogue, the systematic reviewing of important works of Canadian scholarship, and the recognition of other progressive ideas and political forces. A simple example of this new awareness was the attitude towards C.B. Macpherson, whose *Democracy in Alberta* had been dismissed as the work of a bourgeois scholar in the *National Affairs* of the 1950s, while his *Theory of Possessive Individualism* and *Real World of Democracy* were reviewed sympathetically and with some comprehension of his actual intellectual position in the *Marxist Quarterly* of the 1960s. What was true for Macpherson also held for John Porter, for Marcel Rioux, and for other Quebec scholars.

These changes, of course, related to the dramatically different political and intellectual climate of the 1960s, both in Canada and in the world communist movement. Ryerson was in his element, especially with the reemergence of Quebec as the major item on the political agenda. The Quebec question began to give him a new access to non-party journals as well. He contributed to *Cité Libre* in 1965 and to *Socialisme* in 1967. The emergence of a nationalist and socialist left in Quebec provided Ryerson with a receptive audience, but not one necessarily interested in the CPC. The relationship to the Quebec Left was important for Ryerson because it opened up avenues and potential alternatives which had simply not existed in 1956. But initially at least, broad possibilities also seemed to exist within the CPC, especially before the death of Leslie Morris in 1964. Morris, in the summer before his death, had made it clear that he viewed the path forward to Canadian socialism to involve the abandonment of many of the dogmas of 1956–57:

I believe that in defeating the assault ... to some extent we strengthened or took refuge in certain sectarian outlooks and practices. ... Now we are confronted ... with an even more dangerous, insidious, cunning, attack from the "Left." This attack ... will not be fought back, resisted and defeated by taking any kind of refuge in sectarianism.

Instead he called for reconsideration of coalition governments, of multi-party governments, of relations with the New Democratic Party, of general relations with the broader Left – in general, for "a new set of points of contact and not a whole number of rigid and almost insurmountable obstacles between us and socialist-minded people."[83] The other crucial aspect of the new Morris leadership lay in the rethinking of positions on the national question. Here Ryerson played a major role in moving the party to accept, at least nominally, Quebec's right to self-determination.[84]

Ryerson too gave evidence of serious reflection on the philosophical issues which accompanied the rise of an independent left in the 1960s. In addition to encouraging the Marxist-Christian dialogue in *Marxist Quarterly* and *Horizons*, he also expressed interest in the new Marxist philosophical work of figures such as Agnes Heller. Moreover in 1964 he openly questioned the nature of the transition of leadership in the Soviet Union and called for increased "open debate of public policy" and a more rapid pace of "socialist democratization."[85] This concern was the central question of his *The Open Society: Paradox and Challenge*, published in New York in 1965. Making substantial use of popular sociological critiques of North American society to prove that capitalist society was a great deal less free than it pretended, he went on to pose the more difficult question of a "socialism open to democracy." Although beginning his analysis of the problem of democracy in the Soviet Union with the customary nod to "the cult of the personality," he quickly added that the "disastrous aberration" of the "Stalin and Mao 'cults'" was an inadequate explanation. Moreover, he admitted that the problem of ensuring that "organizations or leaders" did not arrogate "excessive power and thus imperil democracy," had not been faced up to by the communist movement. Instead, "for a long time not a few adherents of Marxism (I among them) believed that 'changing the system' was all that was needed to ensure that democracy would flourish." The problem of democracy then remained and was manifest in the "tension between the exigencies of struggle and the imperatives of freedom." Ryerson's only answer to this serious question, honestly posed, was the very tentative call for the "consistent application of democracy by the unremitting pressure of the led upon the elected leaders."[86]

In general, throughout this period Ryerson made clear his anti-Stalinism and, in effect, at least implicitly suggested that the abortive debate in 1956–57 had not gone deeply enough into the question of Stalin and of socialist democracy. For example, as early as 1963 he wrote:

In the past, Canadian Marxists – the present writer included – often tended to oversimplify grossly what was involved. One element in the error was to take too largely for granted that fundamental change in the *base* necessarily brought with it a solution of problems in the *superstructure*. Since Stalin, that mistake is not made so readily; but there are still implications of our underestimation of the relative autonomy of aspects of the superstructure that have yet to be worked through. Also the fact that a mechanical approach to this problem, as to many others, was prevalent in the period of Stalin's leadership, in no way absolves us of responsibility for adopting it.

These problems, however, soon resurfaced.[87]

Marxist Quarterly/Horizons ceased publication in the winter of 1968–69. Although there was no public battle, Ryerson's parting editorial indicated the serious debates within the party which underlay this decision. The CPC's determination to publish *Communist Viewpoint*, an official organ, he wrote, reflected *Horizons*'s failure to satisfy the party's need for "up-to-date political commentary," its inability to reach a working-class audience, and confusion about its relationship to the party. He added, after enumerating with pride *Horizons*'s contributions, that a new, biannual *Horizons* would continue. Not surprisingly, this journal never appeared.[88] Ryerson's editorial reference to this "unforeseen metamorphosis" would seem to be only slightly veiled sarcasm.

One can readily surmise from a perusal of *Horizons* 27 (Autumn 1968) that these issues came to a head with the movement of Soviet and other Warsaw Pact troops into Czechoslovakia. *Horizons*, which had never previously been used as a vehicle for official party pronouncements, suddenly carried not only two statements of the Central Executive Committee (CEC), but also surrendered valuable pages to the lengthy and vituperative rationalization of the German Democratic Republic (GDR) for its participation in the invasion of Czechoslovakia. One might add that room was also made for the CPUSA's acquiescent statement. The decision to publish this material was made while Ryerson was in Europe attending the Vienna International Congress of Philosophy. On his return he was furious, for he had helped draft the initial CEC statement which had reflected grave concern about events in Czechoslovakia and had implicitly criticized the Warsaw Pact intervention by insisting that there were significant "unsolved problems of socialist development and socialist democracy," not simply the "intrigues of enemies of socialism." In addition it had noted that the Warsaw Pact explanation of the situation was "at variance with the estimation and declaration of leading bodies in Czechoslovakia." This guarded critical stance was obliterated, however, by the GDR and CPUSA statements.

When the Central Committee met in early October, the lines of battle had been drawn. Buck, Kashtan, and the majority disavowed the earlier CEC statement and instead described the Soviet intervention as "the defence of socialism" against "creeping counterrevolution." The Kashtan resolution was adopted by a vote of 28 to 14 with the opposition coming most vociferously from John Boyd and Stanley Ryerson. Although admitting that the whole CC should have been consulted before the August CEC statement, Ryerson nevertheless refused to back down from its contents. Instead he attacked the addition of the GDR and CPUSA materials to *Horizons*, made without consulting its editor. Worrying that "the suppression of facts" might "be the pattern for pre-convention discussion," he denied the claim that the majority of the Czech praesidium had requested the Soviet intervention, noting that this too was a basic question of "communist honesty." Finally, he criticized the invasion as a "high-handed paternalism that hinders socialism," and asked rhetorically if the correct answer to 2000 words was 7000 tanks. In closing, he indicated that he felt the program and principles of the CPC were at stake in this debate. William Beeching followed Ryerson, dismissing all such concern as "bourgeois nonsense." This view prevailed both in the Central Committee and subsequently in the 1969 convention of the CPC; Ryerson's active party life came to an end at that congress.[89]

The debate over Czechoslovakia and Ryerson's role may strike some as ironic. At the twentieth convention of the Canadian party, many of the issues of 1956 again came to the fore. The debate was especially bitter because elements of the Canadian party had been especially enthusiastic about the Prague Spring which had been reported on sympathetically and at great length in the *Tribune* by John Boyd who was in Czechoslovakia.[90] Thus in late April, the CC of the CPC had sent congratulations to the Czech party for "deepening and extending socialist democracy."[91] During the August crisis, the *Tribune* carried numerous critical letters attacking the Warsaw Pact intervention. Roscoe Fillmore, for example, a pioneer Nova Scotia communist whose history extended back to the Socialist Party of Canada before World War I, wrote: "At 81 years of age and after over 50 years of defending in general the actions of the Soviet Union, I find myself unable to defend her actions and policies in the occupation of Czechoslovakia."[92]

Ryerson in the pre-convention discussion had argued strongly for the continuation of the directions Leslie Morris had proposed before his death and which *Marxist Quarterly* had stood for. This included support for Quebec's right of national self-determination, "a realistic and practical view ... that we at best are no more than a barely marginal force," and "a much-needed turn outward." Critical of "persisting sectarian negativism" and "dogmatic disquiet about 'the threat of spontaneity,'" he argued that the party must open itself to the student movement and to separatists, not simply dismiss them as petit bourgeois. Then, turning to Czechoslovakia, he argued for "*pluralism* in socialist society," citing Santiago Carrillo and the PCI as authoritative supporters. Equating "multi-party coalition under socialism, multiplicity of paths and models, etc." with the Twentieth Congress and de-Stalinization, he attacked those who dismissed them as revisionist as being unable to come to grips with the crucial question of socialist democracy. In closing, he quoted from an August article on Czechoslovakia which he had suppressed under a CEC directive:

The de-Stalinization initiated by the CPSU Twentieth Congress was an historic part of that process [democratizing socialism]; but strong pressures for "re-Stalinization" have intermittently asserted themselves. Invariably – as now – they have reinforced the very adversary they were supposed to exorcise. ... The latest power move on the Vltava will prove to be a boon to reaction, and a corresponding deplorable retrogression of socialist world influence.

His demand that the party work out "programmatic-political positions on democracy and culture and national paths of development to socialism" went unanswered.[93]

Thus Ryerson, having joined the Communist Party in Paris, left it in Prague, and leaving 35 years of party leadership behind, a year later accepted a position in the history department at the Université du Québec à Montréal. At age 58, he commenced the academic career he had sacrificed in the 1930s.

Although he remained active in Montreal in the Centre for Marxist Studies and contributed to the *Horizons Research Newsletter*, his active party life was over.[94] He formally left the party in 1971. His departure led to the following statement:

Stanley Ryerson recently advised the CEC and the CP that he had decided to withdraw from the party. The decision arises from the fact that he continues to maintain the different views he held prior to the twentieth convention and which the twentieth convention declared to be erroneous. Stanley Ryerson asked for time to think out his differences. This was agreed to. However, his views have not changed. The CEC now declares that S.B. Ryerson is no longer a member of the CPC.[95]

Any assessment of Ryerson's career as Canada's leading communist intellectual poses sharply the historical problems raised in this essay's introductory quotations. Recent critiques have dismissed Ryerson as a party bureaucrat whose work continually failed to transcend the CPC's political line of the particular moment. Further these critics have argued that Ryerson's understanding of Marxism was limited by "Stalinist" distortions.[96] There is certainly no question that Ryerson's important role in party leadership affected his intellectual work. Equally the orthodox Marxism of the Stalinized Comintern was based at best on a selective reading of Marx. Yet, as I will argue in "Stanley Bréhaut Ryerson: Marxist Historian," these criticisms are partial and share an a-historical point of view which fails to appreciate the ambiguities of Ryerson's life and work. Ultimately this failure leads to an easy dismissal of Ryerson which by removing him from his intellectual context denies him recognition as the major pioneer of Marxist historical writing in Canada.

In "Stanley Bréhaut Ryerson: Canadian Revolutionary Intellectual," I presented a biographical sketch of Ryerson which situated him in his intellectual and political context.[97] In the process the ambiguity of

Ryerson's role as both major party intellectual and key member of the Central Committee emerged as a peculiarly Canadian phenomenon. Other communist parties recruited many more intellectuals and thus they seldom combined political and scholarly roles. Ryerson, of course, did not have the academic luxury of distance from the corridors of party power. Instead he was a major actor both in the often tortured debates of the Canadian party and in the increasingly antediluvian debates of Comintern and post-Comintern international communism. Yet Ryerson also initiated the attempt to write Marxist history in Canada. In this article, I will survey his career as a Marxist historian and attempt to assess his contribution to Canadian historical writing.

In the same year that Warsaw Pact troops entered Prague, beginning the process that would lead to Ryerson's departure from the Communist Party of Canada (CPC), *Unequal Union: Confederation and the Roots of Conflict in the Canadas, 1815–1873*, the second volume of the "People's History," appeared. Receiving far more attention from the Canadian academy than his earlier work, this volume represented the high point of Ryerson's historical writing. Although, as we shall see, his work as an historian and political activist through the 1970s to the present remains vibrant and productive, this simultaneous break with the party and the publication of *Unequal Union* may be taken as a convenient point to turn to a more detailed consideration of Stanley Ryerson's contribution to the writing of Canadian history.

Although trained academically in literature and concerned actively with philosophy, the bulk of Ryerson's published work has been historical. Obviously taken with the ambiguities and ironies of his own personal history, Ryerson from the start of his career as a communist intellectual wrote history. His first contributions to the party press and to left-wing journals concerned Papineau and the Rebellion of 1837.[98] As part of the party's discovery of Canadian history, a series of essays appeared in *The Worker* in the fall of 1935 and the winter of 1935–36.[99] History at its eulogistic best (or worst), these articles ran under titles such as "Heroes from Canada's Past" and "Communists, Bearers of Great Traditions."[100] In addition, the new cultural/theoretical journal *New Frontier* carried historical work in its eighteen-month existence. In addition to Ryerson on 1837, articles by Leo Warshaw and Betty Ratz, then University of Toronto graduate students, were particularly notable.[101] Despite their sometimes too-overt didacticism and their tendency towards hagiography, these initial attempts at historical writing quickly established the method and themes which would remain important and within which the party's, and especially Ryerson's, major contributions to Canadian historical writing developed.

The first and most obvious point about the project is that it was to be Marxist. What that would mean precisely, of course, was not at all obvious. The nature and methods of historical materialism were not well known, almost no Marxist historical writing was available in English, and European material was relatively inaccessible.[102] This, of necessity, meant a return to Marx, Engels, and Lenin, but even there much remained untranslated and even unpublished in the 1930s. In the Canadian context, there was very little to draw on. Earlier socialist movements had produced relatively little analysis of the Canadian context.[103] Agrarian radicalism, on the other hand, had produced a number of muckraking accounts in its wake, including the works of Gustavus Myers and Edward Porritt.[104] The former's *History of Canadian Wealth* undoubtedly influenced Canadian progressives more than any other work. Ryerson, both in his introduction to the reprint (1972)[105] and in earlier commentaries, has acknowledged his debt of gratitude to what he termed "the first major step towards a Marxist interpretation of Canadian development." Moreover, he continued, "It constitutes a landmark; I owe much to it, both in getting my initial bearings in this field over a quarter-century ago, and in projecting some of the lines of search pursued in the present study [*Founding of Canada*]."[106] Ryerson's early work shows Myers's strong influence.

Also developing in the 1930s was the "Toronto school" of economic history, vigorously led by Harold Innis. The writings of Innis on the great staple trades would contribute strongly to Ryerson's work but also created a curious dialectic in which the unfolding Marxist work constantly had to resist the temptations of what it viewed as Innis's degeneration into economic and geographic determinism. Ironically, if Maurice Dobb set the economic context for the unfolding work of the British Communist Party's Historians Group, then one could argue that Innis did the same in Canada.[107] Clearly, their relationship to Innis's work was always tense and highly charged, but it was nevertheless quite compelling.[108]

But, in addition to being Marxist, the historical work of the communists had another primary aim. It was to be popular, "people's history," writing not for an academic audience but rather for the Canadian people – an entity relatively undefined in the days of the Popular Front, but certainly wider than the historical profession.[109] These two problems then frame Ryerson's project as an historian. It should be quite evident at the outset that the task he faced was not identical to that encountered by his colleagues in the academy – not even to speak of the unpropitious circumstances in which his work would be carried on.

A third point also should be made. Ryerson's interest was in *Canadian* history. Other Canadian scholars (E.H. Norman, C.B. Macpherson) would make major contributions to Marxism in other realms, but Ryerson, surrendering his early pursuit of European literature, turned resolutely to the study of the Canadian past. As he put it in the foreword to his first book, he hoped to provide "a starting point for an enterprise long overdue: the analysis, from the standpoint of Marxism, of our country's history."

Few Canadian communists reflected on writing history other than Ryerson. John Weir did so in "Our History" in 1944 with rather disastrous effects. Proudly influenced by Earl Browder, then leader of the Communist Party of the United States of America (CPUSA), Weir called on the party "to deepen our study of Canadian history to uncover not only the 'stormy' but also the 'peaceful' pages." Mimicking Browder's views, Weir explained that "confederation, a class compromise, did open up the road to the 'peaceful' achievement of the main tasks which the unsuccessful revolution of 1837 had set for itself."[110] This article then is a blatant example of Penner's criticism of the party for "confounding" theory and tactics and for too often subordinating theory to "the needs of the day."[111] In that same article, however, Weir called on the party to place a premium on historical work, "a political task of major importance," and suggested the creation of a history committee of the Labour Progressive Party's education department.

Ryerson, on occasion, considered historical materialism in a more theoretical vein. His address to the 1946 National Affairs Conference on Marxist Studies of Canadian Development drew its inspiration from Marx's 1846 letter to Annenkov. This letter uses Proudhon as a foil to draw out the general lines of historical materialism in a fashion similar to that of the more-famous preface to *Contribution to the Critique of Political Economy* of 1859. Ryerson in this speech also drew on the Annenkov letter to criticize Innis, after easily dismissing Creighton, Brebner, Lower, et al. as idealists. Innis's problem, like Proudhon's, argued Ryerson, lay in his inability to perceive the social relations which accompanied the productive forces he described. Thus class disappeared from his writing.[112]

The emphasis on social relations necessitated by the encounter with Innis's materialism is evident in later reflections as well. Ryerson always went out of his way to deny the charge that equated Marxism and economic determinism: "Marxism holds that it is the people who make history – their labor and their struggles and their dreams; and that these are understandable and have meaning when seen in their real setting." Moreover, he added: "Labor, production, the real relationships of living society: this is the point of departure for historical materialism. ... Thought and feelings, ideas and passion and imagination have their being in a material world, are conditioned by it, work upon it."[13] This approach to writing history is evident in his major work where "the struggles and ideas of people are what makes history. They operate, not in a vacuum but in and upon a specific setting, a given social system." This overt recognition of the interplay of freedom and necessity is present in Ryerson's history as it is in the best Marxist historical writing.[14]

THE PEOPLE'S HISTORY

The 1946 National Affairs Conference led to the establishment of a series of committees under the general direction of Ryerson and Margaret Fairley.[115] The major initial success of this work lay in a vibrant group of Toronto researchers who began to lay a systematic research framework which would eventually support the edifice of "A People's History." Early results of this work were published in a special issue of *National Affairs Monthly* in 1949 and continued to appear throughout that year and, far less frequently, in the early 1950s. Ryerson in "Re-conquest," his introduction to the special *National Affairs Monthly* issue, explained the rationale of the project: "A people have to win back into their own possession their land and the fruits of their labor and also their culture, ideology, and history." Pursuing the military metaphor, he concluded: "To restore to the working people the history of the past struggle – the real history of their land – is a worthy engagement in the battle of ideas."[116] On this occasion, he also reminded readers of the difficulty of the project while unrealistically promising the People's History within a year. First, "We pay for past neglect," he explained, since "the poverty of previous output requires that we begin almost from scratch." Second, skills were in short supply, and third, "the pull of immediate practical work" was always great. Problems two and three, of course, would increase over the next few years as party strength declined markedly. Nevertheless, the work published from this project was of a noticeably higher quality than that which preceded it in party publications. Jacqueline Cahan's work on labour in politics, for example, was much stronger than the party's usual reflections on labour's past and I. Wilson's overview of the development of Toronto provided an interesting periodization of the stages of Canadian capitalist development.[117]

People's History, as developed by the Canadian party, was at its best in Ryerson's two volumes, *The Founding of Canada* and *Unequal Union*, published in 1960 and 1968 respectively. Both have already sold around 12,000 copies in four printings and continue to sell well. Two of the projected three volumes of People's History, they owe much to the collective work of the late 1940s, and especially to Margaret Fairley, J.F. White, and Clare Pentland, but they also provide ample evidence of Ryerson's gifts as a Marxist synthesizer. Like his earlier works, they are based primarily on published material which the author reshaped into a Marxist overview. Like all surveys, they have certain problems owing to the inadequacy or non-existence of work in important fields, but as stimulating Marxist syntheses of Canada to 1873 they still have no equals. Moreover, they demand to be evaluated on their own terms as "a preliminary breaking of ground, suggesting a line of approach to a reinterpretation of this country's history."[118]

Founding of Canada, especially, fits that description. Written very much as a popular Marxist introduction to Canadian history, it offers little new material, instead providing significant shifts of emphasis which make the whole enterprise quite different than the familiar narrative would suggest. Partially stemming from Ryerson's eclectic interest in prehistory and Soviet anthropology, we receive, for example, six chapters on pre-European-contact Canada. Discovery, exploration, and first settlement are then surveyed not in the customary terms of great men and the spirit of adventure but instead in the context of the decline of feudalism and the rise of capitalism. Throughout Ryerson attempts to include the lower classes of society, providing interesting material on slaves, fishermen, voyageurs, habitants, artisans, and the initial surfacings of class discontent and organization. Written before the blossoming of the renaissance in Quebec historical writing, parts of the New France material are now, however, dated.

Unequal Union is the more adventuresome of the two works. Partially because of its focus on 60 as opposed to over 300 years, it delves more deeply into the events between the end of the War of 1812 and the entry of Manitoba, British Columbia, and Prince Edward Island into Confederation. Organized in three parts, it is less of a narrative history than its predecessor, instead focusing on three major themes: colonial revolt, the rise of industrial capitalism, and the creation of the new nation state. "A series of studies," then, it fully lives up to its avowed aims to "incite further exploration" and to make "some contribution to the eventual production of a full-scale, 'three-dimensional' history."[119]

By way of evaluating the overall contribution of Ryerson's corpus to Canadian history, a closer analysis of his writing on 1837, Quebec, the industrial revolution, and class – the major themes of his work – would seem in order.

1837: FAILED BOURGEOIS REVOLUTION?

Ryerson's first major work was *1837: The Birth of Canadian Democracy*. As we have already noted, it was written quickly and in an unstable, not to say dangerous, setting. Somewhat self-consciously, Ryerson noted in his "Foreword" that it was not a work of original research. "Such a task," he wrote, "would be extremely tempting, all the more since the documentary material has been scarcely touched, and next to nothing written on the Rebellion period – a gap which can hardly be unintentional."[120] (For this confession of inadequate original research, he received an irritated dismissal from Donald Creighton.)[121] Yet despite Ryerson's apologia the work retains considerable interest and provides the basic outline for the story he tells with additional evidence in *Unequal Union*.

Surprisingly, the book begins not with economic structure, but with ideas. The first chapter, "The Spirit of Democracy," situates the Canadian events in the grand sweep of the development of bourgeois democracy and sees 1837 as a peculiar hybrid of the British, French, and American revolutions. Analyzing briefly the ideas, language, and even the symbolism of the rebels and the patriotes, he demonstrates the overt linkages to the earlier revolutions. Although arguing as he would in later works that "the 1837 Rebellion was in aim and content an anti-feudal, anti-colonial bourgeois democratic revolution," he warned his readers that such a revolution was "at no time, a simple, schematic process" – especially, he added, in the New World, "for there the relations with the metropolis and the 'transplanting' of Old World institutions into a new setting create new and peculiar problems."

Then, in attempting to trace the specificity of 1837, he turned to an analysis of land and land-holding. From a correct recognition of the importance of land to the colonial ruling class, he overextended his argument to claim that land-monopoly represented "a sort of commercialized feudalism" which "loomed as the dominating problem before the Canadas." Drawing on a classical Marxist formulation, he argued further that "potential production forces were stifled by dominant property relations; and as long as the latter couldn't be broken down progress remained illusory." Thus the rebellion was an effort to break the "rule of a landlord-merchant oligarchy," which owing to its reactionary stance, was blocking industrial capitalist development.[122]

In subsequent chapters, he recognized that in Lower Canada the demand for political independence was part of the national struggle of French Canadians and led naturally to a demand for national independence. This theme, however, received less attention than it deserved and suggests the difficulty that Quebec nationalism in the 1930s presented to Marxist analysis.

In a chapter entitled, "Class Forces in Conflict," probably the first such writing in Canadian historiography, Ryerson describes in more detail the ruling class: "a kind of commercial-landlord aristocracy," "doubly parasitic" since it toadied to the British, while simultaneously exploiting the Canadian people. On the other side of the class divide, he found "the democratic masses: a commercial and industrial middle class, professionals, farmers, and city workers." While not pretending that a proletariat could yet be identified, he did draw attention to the emergence of trade unions in York and Montreal and to the active support of British Chartist workers. Less successful was his attempt to differentiate the moderate reformers from the rebels in class terms, that is a moderate bourgeoisie versus a rebellious popular mass.[123]

The volume then turned to a narrative of the events of the Rebellion of 1837. In concluding, Ryerson argued that, while a military defeat, the rebellion was a historic victory since it paved the way for responsible government and industrial capitalist development. The military defeat he blamed on the moderate reformers, the defensive strategy in Lower Canada, and organizational weaknesses.[124]

In Donald Creighton's view of 1938, "the book, in short, is a kind of garbled translation in the Canadian vernacular of what Marx thought about the class struggle in Europe. There is little evidence in it that Mr. Ryerson has discovered anything of much value concerning the class struggle in the Canadas."[125] In another review, B.K. Sandwell, the editor of *Saturday Night*, scoffed:

The determination of the communists to make 1837 their own private property and to masquerade as the descendants of the "patriots" ... a determination for which Mr. Ryerson is probably responsible ... is one of the most illogical features of a monumentally illogical campaign. Its sole motive is to justify rebellion by establishing an honourable precedent and by presenting it as a defence of constitutional rights against unconditional tyranny.[126]

In honour of the first attempt at Marxist historical writing, then, came the first classic statements of anti-Marxism. Creighton's dismissal of it as an importation of foreign theory imposed on Canadian reality and Sandwell's imputation of political motives, both remain all-too-familiar responses to Marxist historical writing in this country. On the other hand, Frank Underhill responded much more favourably to *1837*.[127]

How does *1837* look from a perspective other than Creighton's? (Creighton, by the way, chose to celebrate the anniversary of the rebel-

lions by addressing "the Canadian Bankers' Association on the economic crisis of 1837 and its consequences.")[128] The book fits easily
into the emerging Marxist historiography of its time. As communist
intellectuals came to write history, their attention turned predictably
to revolution. Thus in Britain, for example, Raphael Samuel has noted
"that the heaviest concentration of Marxist historical work was in the
field of 16th and 17th century England ... [especially] left-wing democracy in the English civil war."[129] In the United States the same held
true for the American Revolution. One suspects that Christopher
Hill's retrospective notion that "the celebration of 1640 – and especially of 1649 – did something for the party in giving it confidence in
a non-gradualist tradition"[130] has its echo in Canada with Ryerson's
treatment of 1837. Equally there can be little doubt that Ryerson
found it natural to embrace elements of the old radical-democratic
view of the rebellions. In the nineteenth-century liberal tradition,
Mackenzie enjoyed a place of considerable importance as can be seen
by the polemical exchanges which greeted the publication of J.C.
Dent's work in the 1880s, the suppression of William LeSueur's biography in the pre-war period, or even in the ongoing visions of his
grandson, William Lyon Mackenzie King.[131] This liberal tradition had
many contradictory elements: it combined a democratic-radical justification of rebellion by the masses with an unapologetically Whig
view of the subsequent results of the rebellions. It also substituted
vituperation for analysis in dealing with the Family Compact. Ryerson, unfortunately, incorporated much of the Whig strain as well as
the more radical and he too tended only to caricature the compact.[132]
Nevertheless, when compared with the new historical hegemony of
Creighton, Craig, and Ouellet, which dismisses the rebellions as
reactionary farces, Ryerson's work still has considerable value. His
typification of the revolts as bourgeois-democratic, for example, still
stands. On the other hand, his discussion of the class forces involved
in the revolts while suggestive remains underdeveloped and somewhat schematic. The revolts did not have to be led by an industrial
bourgeoisie to justify their categorization as bourgeois-democratic.[133]
Nevertheless the ongoing importance of Ryerson's interpretation is
evident in the recent work of young Quebec Marxist scholars such as
Denis Monière and Roch Denis. Even more interesting is the sympathetic reading it has recently received from Fernand Ouellet.[134]

FRENCH CANADA OR QUEBEC?

Ryerson's 1937 treatment of the rebellion in Lower Canada sets his
work off from the rest of Canadian historians almost as totally as his

membership in the Communist Party. His view of the patriotes as engaged in a struggle for national independence, which was later reinforced in *Unequal Union*, stands out as a major contribution. Carl Berger's summary of the views of Ryerson's professional contemporaries indicates the latter's uniqueness: "The English-Canadian historian, like the community in which he wrote, did not fundamentally accept the French-Canadian groups as anything more than a minority with certain rights within the province of Quebec. The idea of two equalities was utterly foreign to his mind."[135] Moreover, Ryerson's view of the patriotes provides a striking contrast with Donald Creighton's nearly simultaneous dismissal of "the economic and cultural inferiority of the French Canadians," which was much more in keeping with prevalent English Canadian attitudes.[136] Ryerson, however, did not sufficiently credit nationalism as a force in the rebellion. If anything, in an attempt both to reassert the connections between Upper Canadian and Lower Canadian experiences and to avoid the dreaded "bourgeois nationalism" which communists mortally feared, he actually underplayed nationalist sentiment. This is especially evident in his more polemical writings both in *Clarté* and in his 1937 anti-nationalist tract, *Le réveil du Canada français*. Yet the other possibility was always present in Ryerson's work and *Clarté* not only carried critiques of right-wing nationalism but also published a special issue in honour of 1837 and began in the fall of 1937 to sell portraits of Papineau. Thus in acknowledging nationalism as a force and in increasingly perceiving its progressive potential, Ryerson was moving towards the more complex formulation of his second book, *French Canada: A Study in Canadian Democracy*.

Mainly written while underground, the book analyzes "the problem of the relations of French and English Canada ... by probing deep beneath the surface of our past and present history; by abandoning two-dimensional surface concepts, and laying bare, in depth, the actual unfolding of the social and economic forces on which rests the life of every national community." Quebec is here a "minority nation."[137] In the first part of the book Ryerson delineates a "democratic tradition" by analyzing the contributions of Papineau, Lafontaine, Dorion, Riel, and Laurier. Again in treating the rebellion he defends the rebels as "democratic, patriot and internationalist," and engages in an effective polemic against Groulx and Creighton.[138] In moving on to Lafontaine and Dorion, however, Ryerson argues that the coming of responsible government in 1848 and the subsequent Confederation of 1867 brought with them "political equality." In his self-critical preface to the new edition of *French Canada*, Ryerson now argues that here he succumbed "to the liberal whig interpretation of history." Further he draws out the obvious political implication which followed: that if the bourgeois-democratic revolution had been successful by 1867 in gaining "political equality" for Quebec, then any discussion of self-determination in the present could only be bourgeois nationalism and thus reactionary. He now points out that "what was wrong with this line of reasoning was both its counter-factual basis and its flawed theoretical approach."[139] This self criticism, which closely resembles his similar concern, expressed when *Unequal Union* was translated and published in Quebec,[140] to some degree underestimates Ryerson's own contribution. For example, there can be little question that it was the thrust of his work with its emphasis on the democratic struggles of the Quebec people and their economic inequality in Confederation which helped pave the way for the Communist Party's eventual recognition of Quebec's right to self-determination. Equally it should be noted that even in 1943 under the pressure of Anglo-French tensions regarding the war, the crypto-fascism of the Duplessis years, and the overt fascism of some Quebec nationalists, *French Canada* still asserted that "the democratic struggle of the French Canadian people during the whole of the preceding period (1763–1867) had been *a struggle for the right of national self-determination*, for their right as a nation to choose their own form of state." Further, he argued, "Insofar as Quebec is concerned, Dominion-Provincial relations have to do not simply with 'provincial rights' but with the deeper problem of English-French Canadian *national* relationships."[141]

Nevertheless, this same problem reoccurs in the first edition of *Unequal Union*, not in reference to 1867, but to 1848. In the original Ryerson argued, as he had in *French Canada*, that the coming of responsible government "marked a key stage in the bourgeois democratic revolution ... from which the peoples of the Canadas could advance toward wider self-government and a fuller national equality."[142] In the 1972 French version, Ryerson caught his interpretative error and added:

Mais cette présence même servait à masquer un aspect important de la realité: à savoir, le fait que cette nouvelle autonomie au sien de l'Empire (home rule, responsible government) comportait le refus de l'autodétermination, du droit de *self-government*, de la nation canadienne-française. ... Ce qui s'est affirmé en 1848 est la réalisation d'une mesure fort modeste de démocratie dans le cadre d'une suprématie anglo-capitaliste, étayée par la puissance de l'Empire.

In the slightly revised 1973 English version, he went even further:

Concession of self-government to the Anglo-Canadian colonial bourgeoisie was conditional on assurance of a "proper subordination of the French" – to whose numerical minority status was superimposed a political mechanism with built-in guarantees of British-imperial stability. Conceded "from above," the Canadian bourgeois revolution was, in its limited way, successful; the French-Canadian one was not.[143]

Again we see further movement on the national question and the historical interpretation of Quebec.

Although Ryerson's analysis of Quebec from 1937 to 1981 has changed considerably, his revisions seem minor compared with events in Quebec or with the almost total rewriting of English Canadian historical views and those within Quebec as well. By English Canadian historical standards, Ryerson has possessed a remarkable sensitivity to, and insight into, Quebec history. The rapid development of Quebec historical writing in the last two decades, and especially the arrival of serious Marxist scholarship has gone a long way both to corroborate some of Ryerson's early work and also to fulfil his invocation for "further exploration." We still await the "full-scale, 'three-dimensional' history" to "do justice to social structure and national realities," but there has been significant movement in that direction.[144]

CANADA'S INDUSTRIAL REVOLUTION

The "unequal union" of confederation has been one major theme of Ryerson's work and the rise of industrial capitalism has been the other. Part two of Unequal Union, "Capitalist Industrialism," and especially the chapters surveying the development of manufacturing in the 1840s (chap. 9), railroad development (chap. 12), and the further growth of industry in the 1850s (chap. 13), have undoubtedly helped redirect the attention of Canadian historians away from the staple trades. The second half of the nineteenth century had always been the period least considered by the staples school. The demise of fur, timber, and central Canadian wheat, and the advent of New Ontario, western wheat, and hydro-electricity, the staples of Toronto school writing, left an awkward fifty-year gap from responsible government to Laurier. The transition in Canadian historical writing which came after World War II partially filled this gap with heroes (Creighton's Macdonald, Careless's Brown), or with heroics (Berton's Canadian Pacific Railway), but told us little about economic development. Equally, economic historians offered little, skipping over the period as quickly as possible in order to come to the Laurier "industrialization" period as can be best seen in Easterbrook and Aitken's standard text.[145] Ryerson's work has helped fill that lacuna.

This contribution was especially important because in the 1950s anti-Marxist historians in England had made a frontal assault on the notion of an industrial revolution. There the influence of Dobb's *Studies in the Development of Capitalism* and the writings of the Historians Group of the Communist Party helped defeat the attack.[146] In Canada there was no ideological attack, simply a consensus that nothing of consequence had happened until the twentieth century. Here the work of Clare Pentland (unfortunately much of which remained unpublished during his lifetime),[147] and then the publication of *Unequal Union*, were crucial in establishing the existence of nineteenth-century industrialization.

The insights of Pentland and Ryerson in this area have been instrumental in the transformation, over the last fifteen years, of Canadian and Quebec historical writing on the second half of the nineteenth century. It should be noted, however, that here again Ryerson suggested only the initial outlines of approach, and his work could be criticized for not digging deeply enough to document the nature of Canada's industrialization. His later reflections on the theme of industrial transformation are contained in his telling critique of Tom Naylor's *History of Canadian Business*.[148] The key importance of Ryerson's emphasis on capitalist industrialization is two-fold: first, it helps us to understand the process of nation-building within a colonial context, a process which differentiates the settler-colonies from other colonial experiences; and, second, it directs our attention to the creation of a working class.[149] The recognition of this last historical process represents Ryerson's final major contribution.

Ryerson, curiously, has written less about the development of the nineteenth-century Canadian working class than one might expect. This failing stems partially from the 1873 terminal date of *Unequal Union*, but it also comes out of his lack of primary research. None of his predecessors, whose work he was able to recast in the political, national, and, to some degree, economic realms provided him with material on the working class. What there was he utilized – Ratz on 1872, Pentland on navvies, Cooper on ship labourers, Szöke on Szalatnay, Catherine Vance on the 1830s, and Lipton on the trade union movement – but all of this added up to relatively little.[150] I suspect that Ryerson's problem here may in part relate to the original *National Affairs Monthly* division of labour in 1946 when labour history was hived off from the People's History project. There may also have been an implicit avoidance on Ryerson's part, since in this realm the party, especially with reference to the twentieth century, had shown considerable interest – an interest, one hastens to add, that led to wooden, orthodox, and, most often, uncritical and self-congratulatory writing. In sum, party writing on Canadian workers led only to the CPC, and party writing on the CPC itself never rose above hagiography.[151]

Whatever the reason, Ryerson's work, while always sensitive to the presence of the common people, does not engage in any specific analysis of these groups in pre-industrial society, nor does it examine closely the emergence of a working class. In fact, in my estimation, his comments at the close of *Unequal Union* regarding the emergence of working-class political forces during the Nine-Hour Movement of 1872 and with the publication of *The Ontario Workman* tend, if anything, to underestimate the strength of the young working-class movement.[152] Nevertheless, his tentative suggestions have led to a growing body of literature both in Quebec and in Canada.[153]

But this is to stop at *Unequal Union*, and to omit Ryerson's direct contribution in the 1970s to the writing of working-class history. Without attempting to assess this more recent work, it must be noted that with a number of colleagues at the Université du Québec à Montréal, Ryerson involved himself in a collective project on the history of Quebec workers' political movements which resulted in the publication of a collection of documents and a chronological history in the mid-1970s, as well as numerous theses.[154] In addition, he served as chief editor of the collection, Histoire des Travailleurs Québécois, of the Regroupement de chercheurs en histoire des travailleurs québécois. No doubt this work contributed to the emergence of another collective effort in which Ryerson was involved, *150 Ans de Lutte: Histoire du mouvement ouvrier au Québec, 1825–1976*, a very successful popular history of Quebec workers sponsored by the CSN and CEQ and published in 1979.[155]

Some belated recognition of Ryerson's contribution to Canadian historical writing was forthcoming in the 1970s. Elected to the council of the Canadian Historical Association in 1974, he served a three-year term and then chaired a committee to organize Canada's participation in the 1980 World Historical Congress in Bucharest. In addition, the March 1980 McGill Conference on Class and Culture: Aspects of Canada's Labour Past, organized by Bryan Palmer, was dedicated to Ryerson and included tributes by David Frank and Alfred Dubuc.

Ryerson's other major contribution in the 1970s and 1980s, however, stemmed from his ongoing involvement in Quebec. As an established analyst of the Quebec Left for English Canadian and American journals,[156] and as a link to the older world of the Quebec Left which was part of Ryerson's youth, he played an important role in the Quebec of the 1970s. Moreover, he continued to make active political interventions.[157] Finally, of late, he commenced a process of re-evaluating his own personal history, the first elements of which are evident in his recollection, "Comrade Beth," for, after all, Bethune's Montreal was Ryerson's as well.[158]

CONCLUSION

Stanley Ryerson – revolutionary, intellectual, teacher. A conclusion can only be premature, for Ryerson's career is certainly anything but over. How does one assess, moreover, the contributions of revolutionary intellectuals in non-revolutionary periods? One cannot turn to the evaluations of the bourgeois historical profession, for one hardly awaits their acclaim for Marxism. Yet, as has been suggested earlier, Ryerson has managed of late to win grudging admiration and acceptance even there. Although fitting Carl Berger's profile of a Canadian historian born before World War I, Ryerson was not considered for systematic evaluation in *The Writing of Canadian History*. Yet in the brief notice he receives, Berger's comments suggest Ryerson's unusual sensitivity to French Canada and his willingness to consider the rebellion of 1837 as a serious social movement.[159] The only systematic published consideration of Ryerson by Norman Penner is, however, more critical. No doubt influenced by the battles of 1956–57, Penner unmercifully pillories the CPC for confounding "theory and tactics" and for subordinating theory "to the needs of the day."[160] That there is a large element of justifiable criticism here is unquestionable, yet Penner in his comments on Ryerson's writing on Quebec far too narrowly interprets its aim. Moreover he confuses the "use" the party made of the work with the work itself, going so far as to cite a Sam Carr review to prove "the subordination of theory to tactics."[161] Finally, there is an ahistoricism about Penner's critique which fails to recognize Ryerson's relative uniqueness among Canadian historians.[162]

This defence of Ryerson is not an apologia. As I have tried to point out, much of his historical work contains serious problems, but he and it must be regarded in their own historical context if we are ever to approach a Marxist understanding of the history of Canadian Marxism. Similarly, the political decisions he made – especially those of 1956–57 and 1968–69 – demand to be considered in a similar context of the history of the communist movement. The works of Fournier and of Comeau/Dionne have commenced that process in Quebec, but we need similar studies in English Canada.[163]

Ryerson appears to have begun such an examination. In 1973, in considering Starobin's remarkable analysis of the post-war CPUSA, Ryerson referred to his own "uncompleted process of *examen de conscience*." Dropping hints along the way, however, he alluded to "the international influence" of Browderism, to "the throwing into reverse of the processes that the 20th Congress had seemed to inaugurate," to "a tacitly institutionalized intellectual, political dependence on what was seen as a world revolutionary movement whose historic centre of gravity resided outside the country," and, finally, to "a self-righteous (and self-defeating) sectarianism." Yet he also noted that "a certain toughness of historical sinew" accompanied the "stubborn durability of problems, not the least of them, planetary."[164]

Five years later, in "Comrade Beth," he reflected again on his own experience which, of course, had roots similar to Bethune's. Here he pursued the question of democracy which, as we have seen, had concerned him increasingly throughout the 1960s. "The issue is democracy," he wrote, "not 'formal,' merely, but in substance and in depth," not something which can be shelved as an irrelevancy, "a matter of action now." Worrying the issue of socialist democracy further, he noted that "The 'sect' is but the power-structure 'writ exceedingly small'" and that "the ingrown arrogance of dogmatism ... was just as likely to rub out personal identities as it was to fabricate 'cults of personality.'" For Bethune, the solution lay in his committed and courageous efforts in Spain and China; for Ryerson, it lay in his battle against the continued subservience of the CPC to the Soviet Union as evidenced by its acceptance of the events of 1968. After the Twentieth Congress of the CPC, Ryerson withdrew to consider his differences with the party, and in 1971 formally severed his ties to the CPC.[165]

Recently, of course, there has been a political retreat from the gains of the 1960s and the re-emergence of a Marxist-Leninist movement seemingly intent on replicating the errors of the past. In addition, there has arisen a Marxist theory which Edward Thompson and others have argued reflects that politics.[166] Ryerson too has raised his voice in that fight, denouncing the "woodenly mechanistic pseudo-Marxism ... of not a few leftist intellectuals in Quebec." "The resulting variant of 'structuralist Marxism,'" he argued, "excludes the subject, consciousness, culture – all of which exist only in the realm of the imaginary" for these thinkers. Moreover, "a lordly contempt for 'the empirical' exempts the 'neo-Marxist' from study of the specifics."[167] Although not a "reasoner" of 1956, Ryerson has now joined his voice to theirs in the critique of certain forms of Marxism. In addition, in his 1980 contribution to the political economy session in honour of Brough Macpherson, Ryerson noted:

Not the least of C.B. Macpherson's massive and perceptive contribution to social theory is that he takes democracy seriously. What I mean by that, is that instead of yielding to the fashionable whim of those on the left for whom democracy is merely a formal, tactical-instrumental device in the class struggle, he holds firm to democracy-as-content, as a fundamental human value.[168]

Ryerson, engaged in an earlier *"examen de conscience"* in the 1960s, had endorsed enthusiastically Garaudy's call to end "the cramped conception of Marxist-Leninism simply as a position to be defended, a fortress to be held ... while one peers out over the battlements of all who are not 'our people.'" In that same period he had also issued a clarion call to Canadian Marxists to study "the main feature of Canadian reality" in order to "explain Canada, her past and present, her relation to the profound process of world transformation of our time." This study, of course, has been a significant part of Ryerson's life.[169]

Ryerson, as he wrote of Norman Bethune, has been "a committed communist," "a consistent antifascist, anti-imperialist, a Canadian democrat and internationalist." Like Bethune, he too recognized that "national equality and self-determination are the only possible direction for any socialist advance." And, finally, like Bethune, although he has made mistakes, he too "was not mistaken."[170]

NOTES

This chapter is a revised version of a paper originally given at the Canadian Political Science Association meeting in Halifax in May 1981. For research aid I would like to thank Doug Cruikshank, Dan Moore, and Phyllis Clarke. For critical comments, I am grateful to David Frank, Craig Heron, Bryan Palmer, and Bruce Tucker. Norman Penner and I have agreed to differ on a number of points pursued here. *Studies in Political Economy* readers Phyllis Clarke, Alfred Dubuc, Jane Jenson, Leo Panitch, and Reg Whitaker had numerous useful comments. Finally, I must thank Stanley Ryerson for interviews in Halifax in June and in Montreal in November 1981. These discussions helped considerably in the revision process. Needless to say, the views expressed here are my own.

Since the original drafting of this paper, two theses on Ryerson have been completed. The first – Vivian McCaffery, "Stanley B. Ryerson: Marxist Intellectual and the French-Canadian National Question" (MA thesis, University of Ottawa 1981) – focuses on Ryerson's evolving position on Quebec. The second – Brian McDougall, "Stanley Ryerson and the Materialist Conception of History: A Study in the Stalinist Distortion of Marxism" (MA thesis, Carleton University 1981) – is, as its title suggests, a somewhat polemical and certainly *parti pris* critique of Ryerson which, I should add, also criticizes the earlier version of this essay.

Editor's note: *Tribune* and *National Affairs* are the shortened references for *Canadian Tribune* and *National Affairs Monthly*.

1 The only survey history of the CPC is Ivan Avakumovic's, *The Communist Party in Canada* (Toronto 1975). A more useful scholarly work which covers only the first decade of the CPC's history is William Rodney, *Soldiers of the International* (Toronto 1968). Also useful on the early period is the recently published: Ian Angus, *Canadian Bolsheviks: The Early Years of the Communist Party of Canada* (Montreal 1981). Among various theses on the CPC, see: Colin D. Grimson, "The Communist Party of Canada, 1922–1946" (MA thesis, McGill University 1966); Douglas Charles Rowland, "Canadian Communism: The Post-Stalinist Phase" (MA thesis, University of Manitoba 1964); Melvyn L. Pelt, "The Communist Party of Canada, 1929–1942" (MA thesis, University of Toronto 1964). On communist cultural activities: Robin Endres and Richard Wrights, eds *Eight Men Speak and Other Plays from the Canadian Workers Theatre* (Toronto 1976); Donna Phillips, ed. *Voices of Discord* (Toronto 1979); and Dorothy Livesay, *Right Hand Left Hand* (Erin 1977).

2 For the concept "traditional intellectual," see Antonio Gramsci, *Selections from the Prison Notebooks*, ed. and trans. Quintin Hoare and Geoffrey Nowell Smith (New York 1971), pp. 5–23.

3 Among others, see: Norman Penner, *The Canadian Left: A Critical Analysis* (Scarborough 1977); Phyllis Clarke, "Application of Marxist Thought to Canada" (PHD diss., University of Toronto 1977); and Michiel Horn, *The League for Social Reconstruction: Intellectual Origins of the Democratic Left in Canada 1930–1942* (Toronto 1980), p. 179.

4 Eric Hobsbawm, "The Historians Group of the Communist Party" in *Rebels and Their Causes: Essays in honour of A.L. Morton*, ed. Maurice Cornforth (London 1978), p. 28.

5 See: ibid.; Bryan D. Palmer, *The Making of E.P. Thompson: Marxism, Humanism and History* (Toronto 1981); and John Saville, "The Twentieth Congress and the British Communist Party," in *Socialist Register, 1976*, ed. Ralph Miliband and John Saville (London 1976).

6 Perhaps a personal note would not be out of place here. As a Marxist historian of the Canadian working-class, I claim little expertise in the realm of the CPC, intellectual history, or even the twentieth century. What I bring to this paper instead is a deep admiration for Ryerson's life and work – work without which Marxist scholarship in this country would be much poorer.

7 For general biographical data see: Carolyn Cox, "Dutch and French strains blend in this Labor-Progressive Leader," *Saturday Night* 59 (4 March 1944): 2; Sidney Jordan, "Stanley B. Ryerson," *Daily Clarion*, 2 November 1937; biographical sketch of author in Ryerson, *A World to Win: An Introduction to the Science of Socialism* (Toronto 1946); and David Frank, "Stanley Ryerson – An Appreciation" (Paper delivered at the conference, Class and Culture: Dimensions of Canada's Labour

Past, McGill University 1980). Finally, for reflections on his father, see Ryerson, "Comrade Beth" in his *Bethune: The Montreal Years* (Toronto 1978), pp. 151–2. Also useful is Vivian McCaffery, "Stanley B. Ryerson: Marxist Intellectual and the French-Canadian National Question" (MA thesis, University of Ottawa 1981), esp. chap. 1.

8 Cox, "Dutch and French."

9 Jordan, "Stanley B. Ryerson." On that summer in Paris, see Livesay, *Right Hand Left Hand*, pp. 31–6.

10 Ryerson, "Henri Barbusse: Comrade, Writer, Soldier of the Revolution," *Worker*, 7 September 1935. On the French party during these years, see David Caute, *Communism and the French Intellectuals* (London 1964), pp. 93–136.

11 On the party in Quebec see: Marcel Fournier, *Communisme et Anticommunisme au Quebec (1920–1950)* (Laval 1979); Claude Larivière, *Albert Saint-Martin, Militant D'Avant Garde 1865–1947* (Laval 1979); and Robert Comeau and Bernard Dionne, *Les communistes au Quebec, 1936–1956* (Montreal 1980). See also Ryerson, "Comrade Beth," for a sense of Montreal and the CP of the 1930s. For fleeting views of Ryerson's role in Montreal, see Pat Sullivan, *Red Sails on the Great Lakes* (Toronto 1955), pp. 15, 39–40, 92. Finally, specifically on *Clarté*, see Marcel Fournier, *"Clarté* ou le rève d'un front populaire," in Fernand Dumont et al., eds, *Idéologies au Canada Français 1900–1939* (Quebec 1978), pp. 273–94.

12 On raids see: *Daily Clarion*, 11, 28 December 1937 and *Clarté*, 20 November 1937. For quotations, see Ryerson, *1837: The Birth of Canadian Democracy* (Toronto 1937), pp. 9, 11.

13 E. Roger (Ryerson), *Le Réveil du Canada français* (Montreal 1937), pp. 9, 15, 13, 29.

14 Ryerson, "French Canada: Thorn in the Side of Imperialism," *Monthly Review* 1, no. 1 (March 1940): 25–30. For an attempt to situate this later, see Ryerson, "Canadian Communists and the French-Canadian Nation," *Marxist Quarterly* 15 (1965): 30. On the general situation under the War Measures Act, see G. Ramsay Cook, "Canadian Liberalism in Wartime: A Study of the Defence of Canada Regulations and some Canadian Attitudes to Civil Liberties in Wartime, 1939–1945" (MA thesis, Queen's University 1955). For the party's initial position on the war, see E. Roger (Ryerson), *La Conscription, c'est L'esclavage* (Montreal 1940).

15 See Fournier, *Communisme et Anticommunisme*, chap. 4; and Comeau and Dionne, *Les communistes*, pp. 8–23. On the surrender to the RCMP see: Oscar Ryan, *Tim Buck: A Conscience for Canada* (Toronto 1975), pp. 219–22; and William Beeching and Phyllis Clarke, eds, *Yours in the Struggle: Reminiscences of Tim Buck* (Toronto 1977), pp. 305–19. Also see

Avakumovic, *Communist Party in Canada*, pp. 151–2 and Sullivan, *Red Sails*, p. 104.

16 Ryerson, "By Way of a Birth Certificate," *National Affairs*, 1 (April 1944).

17 Ryerson, *French Canada: A Study in Canadian Democracy* (Toronto 1943); and idem, *Le Canada français: sa tradition, son avenir* (Montreal 1945). For sales and an explanation of the new version, see "Avant-propos," in ibid., pp. vi, viii.

18 B.K. Sandwell, "The Front Page," *Saturday Night* 59 (30 October 1943): 1. See also his review in *Canadian Historical Review* 25 (1944): 200–1, where he attributes the following motivation to the book's publication: "The object is to undermine the faith of the Quebec habitant ... a necessary step if communism is ever to make any great strides in that province." The King quotation is from Ryerson, *French Canada*, p. 7n. This new edition contains the author's reflections on his earlier work.

19 Ryerson, *French Canada*, pp. 21, 27. For Ryerson's own assessment see his *Le Capitalisme et la Confederation Aux sources du conflit, Canada-Quebec, 1760–1873* (Montreal 1972), pp. 506–10, and the new preface to the recent reprint.

20 Ryerson, *A World to Win*, p. 136.

21 Margaret Fairley, ed., *Spirit of Canadian Democracy: A Collection of Canadian Writings from the Beginnings to the Present Day* (Toronto 1946).

22 For announcement of conference see *National Affairs* 3 (1946): 358; for Ryerson's address see "Marxism and the Writing of Canadian History," ibid. 4 (1947): 46–51; for decisions taken, see ibid., 4 (1947): 51.

23 *National Affairs* 6, no. 1 (January–February 1949).

24 Ryerson, "Foreword" to Tim Buck, *Canada: The Communist Viewpoint* (Toronto 1948), pp. 11–12.

25 Karen Levine, "The Labour Progressive Party in Crisis, 1956–1957," (Paper prepared for York University); and Clarke, "Application of Marxist Thought."

26 See, for example, articles by Ryerson in *National Affairs*: "Man of the Party of Communists," 6, no. 11 (December 1949): 377–9; "Problems of Communist Leadership," 7, no. 4 (April 1950): 13–23; "Making the Turn," 7, no. 6 (June 1950): 47–52; "Some Problems of Cadre Work," 8, no. 1 (January 1951): 34–41; "A Note about Work with the People," 9, no. 7 (July 1952): 51–4; and "What Kind of People are Fighters for our Program," 11, no. 10 (October 1954): 23–30.

27 On the election see *Tribune*, 12 April, 11 May 1953; on the accident see ibid. (27 July 1953).

28 See Ryerson, "Where Working People Rule," *Tribune*, 23 April 1956.

29 For this story and Buck's further brief reflections on 1956, see Beech-

ing and Clarke, *Yours in the Struggle*, pp. 393–4. The famous Kruschev
speech was delivered while the Canadian and other foreign communists were addressing Soviet workers. Buck's speech is carefully
recorded in Ryerson, "Where Working People Rule." The irony only
became clear later.

30 See articles by Sam Russell in *Tribune*: "The Majestic Vision of a New
World," 20 February 1956; "Soviet Leader calls for new study of capitalist trends," 27 February 1956; and "Flowers, Cheers, and Tears of Joy,"
5 March 1956.

31 Sam Russell, "The Soviet Discussion on Collective Leadership," *Tribune*, 25 March 1956. See also the editorial, "The Discussion on the
Cult of the Individual," in the same issue.

32 *Tribune*, 30 April, 7 May 1956.

33 Ibid., 29 October 1956.

34 "Lessons of the 20th CPSU Congress," *Tribune*, 16 April 1956.

35 Ibid., 20 April, 7 May 1956.

36 See *Tribune*, 29 October 1956.

37 Ibid.

38 See: Levine, "Labour Progressive Party," pp. 7–8; and *Tribune*, 28 May
1956. For the NC resolution on the Twentieth Congress, see *National
Affairs* (May–June–July 1956): 83–5.

39 See, for example, the 14 May 1956 issue of *Tribune*, which includes: a
Toronto letter asking why the *Tribune* contained no discussions equivalent to those going on in the CPUSA as evidenced by the *Daily Worker*; a
letter from Charles MacDonald of Verdun attacking the "ostrich-like
attitude of the *Tribune*," and the lack of leadership in the Canadian
party; a letter from G. Sydney Arthur in Winnipeg asserting that the
"river of truth is rising swiftly"; and one from A. Devers of Montreal
calling for debate in the Canadian party, attacking Buck's article of 16
April as shutting off debate, and indicting Buck, Morris, and Freed for
their lack of self-criticism. This was only one issue's letters! The debate
continued in the pages of the *Tribune* into the fall of 1956, although in
an increasingly muted fashion. One should also note that the *Daily
Worker* debate in the United States not only started earlier but continued until the February 1957 convention. For the U.S. debate, see:
Joseph Starobin, *American Communism in Crisis, 1943–1957* (Cambridge,
Mass. 1972), esp. chap. 10; and John Gates, *The Story of an American
Communist* (New York 1958).

40 *Tribune*, 23 April, 21 May 1956.

41 *National Affairs* (May–June–July 1956): 89.

42 Ibid., p. 84.

43 *Tribune*, 18, 25 June 1956.

44 Ibid., 2 July 1956; *National Affairs* (May–June–July 1956): 23–5.

45 *National Affairs* (May–June–July 1956): 26–8.

46 *Tribune*, 6 July 1956.

47 Ibid., 16 July 1956.

48 Ibid., 6 August 1956.

49 Ibid., 29 October 1956. This is Caron's claim and it was not denied by the *Tribune*.

50 *National Affairs* (August 1956). See also *Tribune*, 29 October 1956.

51 *Tribune*, 27 August 1956.

52 See: Levine, "Labour Progressive Party," pp. 12–13; and Avakumovic, *Communist Party in Canada*, p. 229. Both cite J.B. Salsberg, "What Nikita Kruschev Told Us," *Canadian Jewish Weekly*, 6 December 1956. Also Ryerson interview with author.

53 *Tribune*, 10 September 1956.

54 Ibid., 29 October 1956.

55 Ibid., 22 October 1956.

56 Ibid., 29 October 1956.

57 Ibid.; Levine, "Labour Progressive Party," pp. 13–14; Avakumovic, *Communist Party in Canada*, pp. 229–30.

58 *Tribune*, 29 October 1956. See also John Kolasky, *The Shattered Illusion: The History of Ukrainian Pro-Communist Organizations in Canada* (Toronto 1979), pp. 149–54.

59 *Tribune*, 19 November 1956.

60 Ibid., 26 November 1956.

61 Ryerson, "Thirty-nine Years After," *Tribune*, 12 November 1956.

62 See *The Advocate for a Democratic Left* (Toronto) 1, no. 1 (April 1957). This paper, edited by Harry Fistell (expelled from the LPP) was critical of all sides in the crisis. It dismissed "the Buck/Ryerson" and "Salsberg/Smith" factions as equally complicit in the LPP's sorry history and was critical of the Sims and Penner amendments as mere window-dressing which did not go to the root of the LPP's problems.

63 *National Affairs* (February 1957).

64 Ryerson, "Critical Report on Great LPP Debate," *Tribune*, 1 April 1957. For the original report, see *Tribune*, 18 March 1957.

65 *Tribune*, 8 April 1957.

66 Ibid.

67 *Tribune*, 29 April, 6 May 1957. See also Robert S. Kenny Papers, Manuscript Collection 179, University of Toronto Archives, Box 4, and Frank and Libbie Park Papers, MG 31 K9, National Archives of Canada, Files 203 and 208. The new NEC consisted of Buck, Morris, Kashtan, Weir, Dewhurst, S. Walsh, D. Dionne, E. Ryerson, J. Gershman, N. Clarke, and John Boyd. In the National Committee elections, results included: Morris (141), Buck (136), Harris (125), Kashtan (122), S. Ryerson (120), Weir (114), Buller (106), Boyd (101), E. Ryerson (97), N.

Penner (96), M. Frank (95), J. Gershman (95), N. Freed (94), Frank Park (94), Szöke (87), Cohen (85), Boychuck (84). Among those not elected were Sims (45), Salsberg (21), and Smith (20).

68 *Globe and Mail*, 16 May 1957. The *Globe and Mail* had been quite well informed about the crisis in the LPP. Staff writer Ralph Hyman had written a series in December, for example, which highlighted the differences in the party. See *Globe and Mail*, 12–20 December 1956.

69 *Tribune*, 27 May 1957.

70 For post-convention evidence, see Frank Rasky, "Canada's Communists Wither Away," *Saturday Night* (12 October 1957); and Ralph Hyman, "Comrades who toil for capitalism," *Globe Magazine* (19 October 1957).

71 Ryerson, "Our Program and Our Study of Marxism," *Marxist Review* 15, no. 6 (August–September 1957), 39–43.

72 See: Tim Buck, "Tito Exposes Canadian Revisionists," *Marxist Review* 17 (August–September 1958); and LPP Statement on Program of the Yugoslav League of Communists.

73 Paul Pawlowski, "Letter to the Editor," *Marxist Review* 17 (August–September 1958).

74 For the Marxist Studies Centre, see Park Papers, File 223; and *Marxist Review* 17 (February–March 1959). For the centre's activities see *Marxist Study Centre Bulletin* (1960–61).

75 *Marxist Review* 17 (December 1959); and Leslie Morris, "Into the Battle of Ideas," *Marxist Review* 17 (March–April 1960).

76 Phyllis Clarke, "Passivity in the Cultural Field," *Marxist Review* 17 (May–June 1960).

77 *Marxist Study Centre Bulletin* (1960–61) in Park Papers, File 223. For Stockholm, see Ryerson, "Historians Debate at Stockholm," *Marxist Review* 18 (January–February 1961).

78 *Marxist Review* 18 (November–December 1961).

79 Ryerson, *The Founding of Canada: Beginnings to 1815* (Toronto 1960); and Margaret Fairley, ed., *The Selected Writings of William Lyon Mackenzie* (Toronto 1960).

80 Ryerson, "Conflicting Approaches in the Social Sciences," *Marxist Quarterly* 1 (1962): 46–64. The initial editorial also made it clear that the journal's pages would be open to non-Marxists. Ryerson's "Conflicting Approaches" was written for the Soviet journal, *Questions of Philosophy* and appeared in draft form as "Some Trends in the Social Sciences in Canada" in *Marxist Study Centre Bulletin* (March 1961). For announcement of journal see Norman Freed, "A New Marxist Journal," *World Marxist Review* 5, no. 9 (September 1962): 84–5.

81 "In France: 'The Work of Marxist Thought,'" *Marxist Quarterly* 1 (1962): 93–4. For French discussions see *World Marxist Review* 4, no. 10 (October 1961): 58–74, and 4, no. 12 (December 1961): 72–90.

82 For Ryerson's summary of the journal's contribution see "Seven Years – And a New Start," *Horizons* 28 (1969): 1–3.

83 Leslie Morris, "Opening Remarks to National Committee" and "Closing Remarks," *Viewpoint* (August 1964): 9–29. An abridged version of these remarks is available in *Look on Canada Now, Selected Writings of Leslie Morris, 1923–1964* (Toronto 1970), pp. 197–202.

84 See Leslie Morris, "National and Democratic Revolution in French Canada," in *Look on Canada Now*, pp. 204–12.

85 Ryerson, "Parliaments, Personalities and Power," *Marxist Quarterly* 12 (1964): 52–8.

86 Ryerson, *The Open Society: Paradox and Challenge* (New York 1965), pp. 108–9, 114–15; see esp. chaps 9–10. See also Ryerson's "Communists and Democracy: Problem of Individual Freedom in the Present Ideological Struggle," *World Marxist Review* 6, no. 6 (June 1963): 58–61.

87 Ryerson, "Notes on Freedom and Social Structure," *Marxist Quarterly* 6 (1963): 23–33, quotation at 32. One might also note here that the Ukrainians had finally discovered their national question in these years and the furore was as great, if not greater, than that surrounding the Jewish question. See Kolasky, *Shattered Illusion*, pp. 155–76.

88 Ryerson, "Seven Years," pp. 1–3.

89 For a construction of these events see Park Papers, File 196; for CEC statement see *Horizons* 27 (Autumn 1968): 11–12; for official view see William Kashtan, "Twentieth Convention of the Communist Party of Canada," *World Marxist Review* 12, no. 7 (July 1969); esp. 73, 79.

90 For Boyd's articles see *Tribune*, 1, 22 April, 26 June, 14 August 1968. See also Kolasky, *Shattered Illusion*, pp. 173–6.

91 For CC letter, see *Tribune*, 29 April 1968.

92 *Tribune*, 4 September 1968.

93 Ryerson, "For Broader Approaches," *Convention '69* (Toronto 1969), pp. 18–21. See also Kenny Papers, Box 5.

94 *Horizons Research Newsletter* 4 (January 1970) and 6 (February 1971).

95 *Tribune*, 10 March 1971.

96 McDougall, "Stanley Ryerson"; Penner, *The Canadian Left*.

97 (This part of chapter 3 is the second part of a revised paper first delivered in May 1981. As usual, more material appeared before it was published.) The major recent addition is *Canada's Party of Socialism: History of the Communist Party of Canada 1921–1976* (Toronto 1982). This committee-written text, commenced by Tim Buck, then continued by John Weir and later Norman Freed, was completed by Gerry Van Houten. A rather predictable volume, it has little to offer on Ryerson other than a rebuttal of his position on Czechoslovakia and an acknowledgment of his contributions on the Quebec question.

98 Ryerson, "Our Fathers Fought for Our Freedom: Louis Joseph Papi-

neau and 1837," *Worker*, 28 September 1935; idem, "God be Thanked for These Rebels!" *New Frontier* 1, no. 2 (May 1936): 6–8.

99 For a brief discussion of the international context, see Norman Penner's "The Socialist Idea in Canadian Political Thought" (PHD diss., University of Toronto 1975), p. 219ff; and his *Canadian Left: A Critical Analysis* (Scarborough 1977), pp. 105–6. For a brief discussion of Canadian communist historiography see also Phyllis E. Clarke, "Application of Marxist Thought to Canada" (PHD diss., University of Toronto 1977), esp. chap. 7.

100 See the following articles in *Worker*: J.W., "Section 98 in 1817," 14 September 1935 (on Robert Gourlay); idem, "Communist Bearers of Great Tradition," 1, 3 October 1935 (on W.L. Mackenzie); C.H., "Heroes from Canada's Past," 1, 22 February, 14 March 1936 (on Pierre du Calvet, Thomas Walker, and Pierre Bedard); John Weir, "How They Stole Canada," 14 September 1935; Stephen Brandon, "Fifty years of the CPR," 9 December 1935; and C.H., "Maintaining Law and Order, 1837 and 1936," 24 March 1936. (J.W. may well have been J.F. White, formerly editor of *Canadian Forum*, who had moved to the left of the League for Social Reconstruction. C.H. is listed as Charles Huot in *Clarté* versions.)

101 Betty Ratz, "United Front in Toronto – 1872," *New Frontier* 1, no. 3 (June 1936): 18–20; Leo Warshaw, "Social Planning for Canada," *New Frontier* 1, no. 2 (May 1936): 20–3. Among the editors of *New Frontier* were Leo Kennedy, Dorothy Livesay, J.F. White, Betty Ratz, Felix Walter, A.J.M. Smith, and S.I. Hayakawa.

102 Eric Hobsbawm, "The Historians Group of the Communist Party," in *Rebels and their Causes: Essays in Honour of A.L. Morton*, ed. Maurice Cornford (London 1978), pp. 22–3. See also Raphael Samuel, "British Marxist Historians, 1880–1980: Part One," *New Left Review* 120 (1980): 21–96. For the French tradition see David Caute, *Communism and the French Intellectuals* (London 1964), pp. 276–99.

103 Penner, *Canadian Left*, chap. 3.

104 Carl Berger, *The Writing of Canadian History* (Toronto 1976), p. 63.

105 Gustavus Myers, *History of Canadian Wealth* (1914; reprint ed., Toronto 1972).

106 Ryerson, "Acknowledgements," in his *The Founding of Canada: Beginnings to 1815* (Toronto 1972), p. 330.

107 Mike Merrill, "Interview with E.P. Thompson," *Radical History Review* 3 (Fall 1976).

108 For a communist commentary on Innis, see Phyllis Cohen (Clarke), "On Dr. Harold A. Innis," *National Affairs* 10, no. 2 (February 1953): 29–30. In addition, see: Ryerson, "Marxism and the Writing of Canadian History," *National Affairs* 4, no. 2 (1947): 46–51; idem, "Post-

script," in his *Founding of Canada*, p. 328; idem, "Postscript," in his *Le Capitalisme et la Confédération: Aux sources du conflit, Canada-Québec, 1760–1873* (Montreal 1972), p. 513; and idem, "Conflicting Approaches to the Social Sciences," *Marxist Quarterly* 1 (1962): 46–64.

109 On People's History, a theme worthy of lengthier consideration than is possible here, see Raphael Samuel, "People's History," in his *People's History and Socialist Theory* (London 1981), pp. xiv–xxxviii. See also one of Ryerson's direct inspirations: A.L. Morton, *A People's History of England* (London 1938). Finally, see Peter Burke, "People's History or Total History," in Samuel, *People's History*, pp. 4–9.

110 John Weir, "Our History," *National Affairs* 1 (1944): 116–19.

111 Penner, *The Canadian Left*, pp. 168, 85; see also idem, "Socialist Idea," pp. 188–9.

112 Ryerson, "Writing of Canadian History."

113 Ryerson, "A Note on Marxism and Canadian Historiography," in *Founding of Canada*, p. 326.

114 See Ryerson's "Foreword" to his *Founding of Canada*, p. vii. See also David Frank, "Stanley Ryerson – An Appreciation" (Paper delivered at the conference, Class and Culture: Dimensions of Canada's Labour Past, McGill University 1980).

115 "Decisions of National Affairs Conference on Marxist Studies," *National Affairs* 4 (1947): 51. There are Margaret Fairley papers at the University of Toronto, but they are mainly cultural in focus.

116 Ryerson, "Re-conquest," *National Affairs* 6, no. 1 (January–February 1949): 3–5.

117 See *National Affairs* 6, no. 1 (January–February 1949), especially Jacqueline Cahan, "Labour in World War 1," pp. 35–40; and I. Wilson, "Bay Street Spreads Out," 11–15. Both Cahan and Wilson were University of Toronto graduate students at the time. The relationship of Clare Pentland's work to that of these *National Monthly* study groups remains unclear to me, but I am almost certain there was some interaction. Later contributions of interest included Joseph Levitt, "Aspects of Confederation," *National Affairs* 6 (1949): 215–20; Jim Henry, "The Development of the Catholic Syndicates," *National Affairs* 6 (1949): 196–200; and later, Ben Swankey's four-part series on Riel in *National Affairs* 9 (1952).

118 Ryerson, *Founding of Canada*, pp. vii–viii. Maggie Bizzell of Progress Books in Toronto has kindly provided the following production figures for Ryerson's books. *French Canada: A Study in Canadian Democracy* (1943; 1944; 1980): total of 3,000 copies; *Founding of Canada* (1960; 1963; 1972; 1975): total of 12,000 copies; *Unequal Union: Confederation and the Roots of Conflict in the Canadas, 1815–1873* (1968; 1973; 1975): total of 11,500 copies.

96 Antecedents

119 Ryerson, *Unequal Union*, p. vi.

120 Ryerson, *1837: The Birth of Canadian Democracy*, p. 10.

121 Donald Creighton, "Review," *Canadian Historical Review* 19 (1938): 73–4.

122 Ryerson, *1837*, pp. 26, 35, 27.

123 Ibid., pp. 63–4, 68, 76.

124 Ibid., p. 127.

125 Creighton, "Review."

126 B.K. Sandwell, "Review," *Saturday Night* 58 (15 January 1938): 3.

127 Frank Underhill, *Canadian Forum* 17 (December 1937): 296–7.

128 Berger, *Canadian History*, p. 217.

129 Samuel, "British Marxist Historians," pp. 26–7.

130 Hobsbawm, "Historians Group," p. 43.

131 On Dent, see Donald Swainson's introduction to J.C. Dent, *The Last Forty Years* (1881; reprint ed., Toronto 1972); on LeSueur, see A.B. McKillop, ed., *A Critical Spirit: The Thought of William Dawson LeSueur* (Toronto 1977) and his introduction to William LeSueur, *William Lyon Mackenzie: A Reinterpretation* (Toronto 1979), pp. vii–xxx.

132 This particular problematic, common to all "people's history" and especially prevalent in the popular front period, is explored in Samuel, "British Marxist Historians," pp. 39–42; and in Samuel, "People's History," pp. xxviii–xxx.

133 For a discussion of a very different type of bourgeois-democratic revolution, see, for example, Eugene Genovese, *From Rebellion to Revolution: American Slave Revolts in the Making of the Modern World* (Baton Rouge 1979).

134 Denis Monière, *Le développement des idéologies au Québec* (Montreal 1977); and Roch Denis, *Luttes de classes et question nationale au Quebec 1948–1968* (Montreal 1979). A recent translation of Monière is *Ideologies in Quebec: The Historical Development* (Toronto 1981). See also Fernand Ouellet, "La formation d'une société dans la vallée du Saint-Laurent: d'une société sans classes à une société de classes," *Canadian Historical Review* 62 (1981): 407–50, esp. 440–4.

135 Berger, *Canadian History*, p. 184.

136 Alfred Dubuc, "The influence of the *Annales* School in Quebec," *Review* 1 (Winter 1978): 123–45. For a slightly revised version in French see *Revue d'histoire de l'amérique français* 33 (1975): 357–86.

137 Ryerson, *French Canada*, pp. 21, 23.

138 Ibid., pp. 36–7.

139 Ryerson, "Preface," in his *French Canada*, pp. 5–7.

140 Ryerson, "Postscript," in his *Le Capitalisme et la Confédération*, pp. 508–9. "La racine de l'erreur théorique est à chercher, me semble-t-il, dans une sous-estimation radical de l'importance du facteur *national* dans le processus historique."

141 Ryerson, *French Canada*, pp. 63–4, 71 (emphasis added).

142 Ryerson, *Unequal Union*, pp. 168–9.

143 Ibid.; and idem, *Le Capitalisme et la Confédération*, pp. 226–7.

144 On Quebec history, see: Dubuc, "*Annales* School in Quebec"; and Gilles Paquet and Jean Pierre Wallot, "Pour une meso-histoire du xixe Siècle Canadien," *Revue d'histoire de l'amérique français* 33 (1979): 387–425. For important critiques of Fernand Ouellet, whose work stands strongly in opposition to Ryerson's, see: Pierre Tousignant, "*Le Bas-Canada*: Une étape importante dans l'oeuvre de Fernand Ouellet," *Revue d'histoire de l'amérique français* 34 (1980): 415–36; Phillipe Reid, "L'émergence du nationalisme canadien-français: l'idéologie du *Canadien* (1806–42)," *Recherches Sociographiques* 21 (1980): 11–53; and Nicole Gagnon, "Revue," *Recherches Sociographiques* 19 (1978): 408–11. See also Pierre Savard, "Un quart de siècle d'historiographie Québécoise, 1947–1972," *Recherches Sociographiques* 15 (1974): 77–96. Note, however, Ouellet's interesting new work – for example, his "La formation d'une société."

145 For a brief discussion of this see Gregory S. Kealey, "Looking Backward: Reflections on the Study of Class in Canada," *History and Social Science Teacher* 17 (May 1981).

146 Hobsbawm, "Historians Group," pp. 38–9.

147 See H.C. Pentland, *Labour and Capital in Canada, 1650–1850* (Toronto 1981). There are further plans to publish or republish the rest of his writings as well. On Pentland, see Gregory S. Kealey, "H.C. Pentland and the Writing of Canadian Working-Class History," *Canadian Journal of Political and Social Theory*, 3 (1979); and Paul Phillips, "Introduction," to Pentland, *Labour and Capital*, pp. v–xliii.

148 Ryerson, "Who's Looking After Business: A Review," *This Magazine* 10, nos 5–6 (1976): 41–6.

149 On attempts to place the settler colonies in a "world historical" setting, see: Philip McMichael, "Settlers and Primitive Accumulation: Foundations of Capitalism in Australia," *Review* 4 (1980): 307–34; and Glenn Williams, "Canadian Industrialization: We Ain't Growin' Nowhere," *This Magazine* 9, no. 1 (1975): 7–9; and idem, "Canada: The Case of the Wealthiest Colony," *This Magazine* 10, no. 1 (1976): 28–32.

150 Ratz, "United Front"; H.C. Pentland, "Labour and the Development of Industrial Capitalism," *Canadian Historical Review* 29 (1949), and idem, "The Lachine Strike of 1843," ibid., pp. 255–77; Istvan Szöke, *We are Canadians* (Toronto 1954); Catherine Vance, "1837: Labour and the Democratic Tradition," *Marxist Quarterly* 12 (1964): 29–42 and her "Early Trade Unionism in Quebec," *Marxist Quarterly* 3 (1962); Charles Lipton, *The Trade Union Movement of Canada, 1827–1959*, 3rd ed. (Toronto 1973).

151 I will not include all such work. The list would be too long. "Classics"
include Oscar Ryan, *Tim Buck: A Conscience for Canada* (Toronto 1975);
and Louise Watson, *She Fought for Us* (Toronto 1976). On the party
itself, see Tim Buck, *Lenin and Canada* (Toronto 1970) and his *Thirty
Years* (Toronto 1952). For a searing critique of Buck as historian, see
Ian Angus, *Canadian Bolsheviks: The Early Years of the Communist Party
of Canada* (Montreal 1981), esp. pp. 80–6, 217–24.

152 Ryerson, *Unequal Union*, pp. 420–3. See, for contrast: Gregory S.
Kealey, *Toronto Workers Respond to Industrial Capitalism* (Toronto 1980);
Bryan Palmer, *A Culture in Conflict* (Montreal 1979); and Gregory S.
Kealey and Bryan Palmer, *Dreaming of What Might Be: The Knights of
Labor in Ontario, 1880–1902* (New York 1982).

153 There have been many recent evaluations of this literature. For
examples, see: Bryan Palmer, "Working-Class Canada: Recent Historical Writing," *Queen's Quarterly* 86 (1979): 594–616; David Bercuson,
"Through the Looking Glass of Culture," *Labour/Le Travailleur* 7 (1981);
and Gregory S. Kealey, "Labour and Working-Class History in Canada:
Prospects in the 1980s," *Labour/Le Travailleur* 7 (1981).

154 *L'Action politique des ouvriers Québécois (Fin du xixe siècle à 1919)*
(Montreal 1976) and *Chronologie des mouvements politiques ouvriers au
Québec de la fin du 19e siècle jusqu'à 1919* (Montreal 1975).

155 Ryerson, et al. *150 Ans de Lutte: Histoire du mouvement ouvrier au Québec, 1825–1976* (Montreal 1979).

156 See bibliography in original for contributions to *Canadian Dimension,
This Magazine, Marxist Perspectives,* and *Studies in Political Economy.*

157 See Ryerson, "Nos débats difficiles," *Socialisme Québécois* 24 (1974): 79;
idem, "Mémoire à la commission parlementaire chargé d'étudier la
'Charte de la langue français' au Québec," in his *La Capitalisme et la
Confédération,* pp. 350–64; and his sharp criticisms of the Quebec "M-
L" left in *Canadian Dimension, This Magazine,* and *Marxist Perspectives.*

158 Ryerson, "Comrade Beth," in Ryerson, Wendell MacLeod, and Libbie
Park, *Bethune: The Montreal Years; An Informal Portrait* (Toronto 1978),
pp. 136–67.

159 Berger, *Canadian History,* pp. 183–217.

160 Penner, *Canadian Left,* p. 168.

161 Ibid., pp. 113–20; quotation at p. 120.

162 For a congruent critique of Penner, see Leo Panitch, "Canada's Socialist Legacy," *Canadian Dimension* 13, no. 3 (August–September 1978):
38–44. These comments apply with even more force to Brian McDougall, "Stanley Ryerson and the Materialist Conception of History: A
Study in the Stalinist Distortion of Marxism" (MA thesis, Carleton University 1981).

163 Marcel Fournier, *Communisme et Anticommunisme au Québec*

(1920–1950) (Laval 1979); Robert Comeau and Bernard Dionne, *Les Communistes au Québec, 1936–1956* (Montreal 1980). Compared to the American situation, work on and information about the Canadian party is not very developed. In the United States a number of ex-communists in the 1960s and 1970s have written excellent, critical reflections on the American party experience. Of these, see especially: Joseph A. Starobin, *American Communism in Crisis: 1943–1957* (Cambridge, Mass. 1972); George Charney, *A Long Journey* (Chicago 1968); Peggy Dennis, *The Autobiography of an American Communist: A Personal View of a Political Life 1925–1975* (Westport, Conn. 1977); Jessica Mitford, *A Fine Old Conflict* (New York 1977); Vera Buch Weisbord, *A Radical Life* (Bloomington 1977); Al Richmond, *A Long View from the Left, Memoirs of an American Revolutionary* (Boston 1973); Max Gordon, "The Communist Party of the 1930s and the New Left," *Socialist Revolution* 27 (1976): 11–66; Jon Wiener, "The Communist Party Today and Yesterday: An Interview with Dorothy Healey," *Radical America* 11, no. 3 (May–June 1977): 23–45; Peggy Dennis, "On Learning from History," *Socialist Revolution* 29 (1976): 125–43; and Peggy Dennis, "A Response to Trimberger," *Feminist Studies* 5, no. 3 (1979): 451–61. On 1956 and the American party see Maurice Isserman, "The 1956 Generation: An Alternative Approach to the History of American Communism," *Radical America* 14, no. 2 (1980): 43–51, and the excellent novel by Clancy Sigal, *Going Away, A Personal Memoir* (Boston 1962). For approaches to the study of communism, see "Communism in Advanced Capitalist Societies," special issue of *Radical History Review* 23 (1980), especially articles by Buhle, Waltzer, and Gordon and the interview with David Montgomery. In Canada, little activity has taken place and some of it has been farcical. See, for example, the party's behaviour over the Tim Buck memoirs. Compare Oscar Ryan, *Tim Buck: A Conscience for Canada* (Toronto 1975) with William Beeching and Phyllis Clarke, eds, *Yours in the Struggle*. Finally, a recent, excellent study of the CPUSA is Maurice Isserman, "Peat Bog Soldiers: The American Communist Party During World War II" (PHD diss., University of Rochester 1979).

164 Starobin, *American Communism*. Ryerson's review is in *Canadian Forum* (February 1973): 40–2.

165 Ryerson, "Comrade Beth," pp. 162–3. Ryerson in this passage is drawing heavily on Jean-Paul Sartre's remarkable essay, "The Socialism That Came in from the Cold," written by Sartre as an introduction to the translation of Antonín J. Liehm, *Generace* (Vienna 1968). The French version, published as *Trois Générations* (Paris 1970), is the one Ryerson cites. I have used the American edition, published as *The Politics of Culture* (New York 1973). This remarkable book is a series of interviews conducted by Liehm with leading Czech intellectuals and completed in

May 1968 – after the flowering of the Prague Spring, but before the intervention of the Soviet and Warsaw Pact troops. Sartre's introduction (and Joseph Skvorecky's response) are remarkable indictments of the Soviet Union and eastern bloc "socialism." Ryerson's reflections on and use of Sartre here are of considerable interest. It is worth noting, however, that he deletes from his quotation Sartre's sharpest indictment. See *Canadian Tribune*, 10 March 1971, for the terse announcement: "The CEC now declares that Stanley Ryerson is no longer a member of the Communist Party of Canada."

166 E.P. Thompson, *The Poverty of Theory* (London 1978). See also Bryan Palmer, *The Making of E.P. Thompson: Marxism, Humanism, and History* (Toronto 1981). For an interesting commentary on Stalinism which goes beyond easy dismissal, see Alexandre Adler, "Stalinism and the History of the Workers' Movement: It Was Not a Simple Deviation," *International Labor and Working-Class History* 20 (Fall 1981): 1–6.

167 Ryerson, "The Canada/Quebec Conundrum," *Marxist Perspectives* 10 (1980): 149–50. See also his earlier intervention in such debates, calling for openness "sans ce genre d'"exclusions' dont l'effet d'inhibition pourra nous coûter cher." Idem, "Nos Débats Difficiles," *Socialisme Québécois* 24 (1974): 79.

168 Ryerson, "Property and Some Limitations on Liberty," in *Papers Presented at the Fifty-second Annual Meeting of the Canadian Political Science Association* (1980), p. 12.

169 Ryerson, "In France: 'The Week of Marxist Thought,'" *Marxist Quarterly* 1 (Spring 1962): 93–4; and idem, "Conflicting Approaches to the Social Sciences." See also idem, "Our Work with Ideas," *Viewpoint* 3, no. 5 (June 1966): 57–62.

170 Ryerson, "Comrade Beth."

PART TWO

Debates

4 Labour and Working-Class History in Canada: Prospects in the 1980s

The moment for critical evaluations of the labour and working-class history of the 1960s and 1970s has arrived. This has been signalled in the British context by the controversy that has emerged from the confrontation of Althusserian structuralism and Thompsonian "culturalist" or "socialist-humanist" history.[1] In the United States the discussion has been less heated, but a number of significant general assessments of social history have appeared recently, as well as a more specific consideration of the work of Herbert Gutman arising from the publication of his collected essays.[2] More controversy will no doubt soon follow owing to the recent publication of essay collections by two other prominent historians of the American working class, David Montgomery and David Brody.[3] In Canada the argument about the nature of working-class history is just beginning. This essay and its counterpart by David Bercuson will undoubtedly provide fuel for the fire,[4] smouldering since the publication of Terry Morley's uninformed attack on the so-called "new" labour history and Bryan Palmer's response to Morley which went far beyond the original and assessed recent work in the field.[5] Recent reviews of Palmer's own book suggest that non-Marxist Canadian labour historians have risen to Palmer's critique.[6] Ken McNaught's forthcoming *Canadian Historical Review* article "E.P. Thompson vs. Harold Logan," a review essay on writings on labour and the left in the 1970s, will make only too clear the eminently political nature of the emerging debate.[7]

In addition to helping fan the flames of debate, this essay is intended as an assessment of critical problems which have emerged in the collective work of Canadian historians of the working class, both

Marxists and non-Marxists alike. Before proceeding to that discussion, it might be useful to clarify what a number of us have said in the past decade on a number of the issues addressed in the subsequent essay.

In our first collective statement, drafted by Russell Hann, we set out our conception of working-class history and provided Canadian researchers with a preliminary guide to available materials which would allow the reconstruction of Canadian history along the lines we were promoting. In rereading that "Introduction," I find that there is surprisingly little that any of us would modify. Indeed, in pausing "along the road to a more complete picture of the forgotten causes, the failed efforts, the obsolete skills, and the private strengths of the largely unknown men and women whose history is essential to an understanding of the world in which we live," I think it fair to assess the last decade as one of significant progress in our self-appointed task.[8]

A few years after *Primary Sources*, in the polemical introduction to *Essays in Canadian Working Class History*, we asked rhetorically, "What is the new social history?" Having noted that it included many fields other than working-class history, we limited ourselves to a discussion of that area:

The major contribution of the "new" history has been to redefine "labour history" as "working class history." Thus labour history ceases to be simply a category of political economy, a problem of industrial relations, a canon of saintly working class leaders, a chronicle of union locals or a chronology of militant strike actions. Instead it becomes part of the history of society. Workers are no longer seen as isolated figures engaged only in trade unions, strikes, and radical politics; instead they are studied in a totality that includes their cultural backgrounds and social relations, as well as their institutional memberships and economic and political behaviour. In addition they must be seen neither as a class in complete social segregation nor as an undifferentiated mass. A class exists only in relation to another class and the new social history studies these relationships. Moreover, the working class is a variegated grouping.

Again, although we might not still say this in precisely the same way, it should be evident that the totality of the historical project never excluded the study of unions and labour politics *per se*. Nor did it ever call for a history simply "written from the bottom up," since it always placed the relationship between classes at the centre of the story. In the conclusion of that introductory essay we suggested the need for studies of the material conditions of Canadian workers, of demographic processes, of social and geographic mobility, of the role of women at work and in the home, of religion, of forms of popular expression, and repeated our "need to know more about the pattern of trade unionism in the country, about the role of strikes and violence, and about working-class politics both radical and conventional."[9]

Two years later in a lengthy review essay I reiterated this position, although I also emphasized with renewed vigour the need for quantitative studies, for material on women and the family, and on working-class politics at the local level. In the conclusion to this essay I argued that "a class analysis" would "transcend the refreshing and liberating pluralism of the 1960s call for attention to region, ethnicity, and class." I added that, of course, class in Canadian historical writing had to incorporate ethnicity and place.[10] While calling for a new synthetic overview based on class analysis, it was never my intention to imply that such an achievement would complete the writing of Canadian history. The absurdity of such a claim is self-evident.

I have summarized previous arguments here to clarify what I and others have said in the past decade about working-class studies in Canada. That much of this has been misunderstood has become only too apparent of late.

But let us now move beyond what we have said in the past. If there have been significant achievements in the 1970s, it is equally clear that there have been pressing problems. Let us begin to confront some of these difficulties in the writing of Canadian working-class history. Focusing on periodization, region, ethnicity, and culture, in what follows I will address some of the issues currently facing the field.

PERIODIZATION

History is by definition pre-eminently concerned with time. Yet periodization has received almost no attention from Canadian historians of the working class. Instead, labour history has all too often adopted the obscure benchmarks of an antiquated national political history. In 1976 we tentatively suggested a new periodization based on Canadian economic development.[11] The economic context established the parameters of life for Canadian workers. Although capitalist throughout the period in which we are interested, this economic structure was never static; it developed, changed, and grew. Thus the context in which Canadian workers lived, worked, and struggled also changed.

There were four major periods of Canadian working-class history in the nineteenth and twentieth centuries. First is a period before 1850 about which we have until recently known very little. This period, which I have previously described as pre-industrial capitalism, can also be described as a period of primitive accumulation. In this period labour continued to be exploited in the staples trades and in the growing towns and cities of British North America. These new urban areas witnessed the rapid spread of wage-employment and the beginnings of a subdivision of labour in the old forms of handicraft production.[12] With this growing division of labour came the first trade unions and the first strikes.

The second period, which has been studied far more extensively, covered the years from the 1850s to the 1890s and included Canada's industrial revolution. During this time workers actively participated in the destruction of the old colonial system and helped to build a new nation oriented to American trade and increasingly to industrial development behind protective tariffs and a boosterish promotional climate. These new economic directions also led to Confederation and the creation of a national economic entity out of the previously disparate British American colonies. The inspiration for this creation came from Toronto and Montreal capitalists and their British allies who saw a brave future in the economic exploitation of the west and the integration into a national system of the eastern colonies. It should be added, however, that the east had its share of industrial capitalist visionaries as well, although they were less powerful in their local bailiwicks than their central Canadian counterparts.

The first twenty-five years of the nation's existence were troubled ones, but beneath the pessimism associated with population loss and economic recession a steady industrial growth was achieved which especially accelerated during the early 1880s after the inauguration of the National Policy tariffs.[13] The CPR was not the only economic achievement of these years as rapid growth took place in both con-sumer goods and producer goods segments of the new manufacturing sector. Moreover, while the CPR tied the slowly developing west into the new state, the completion of the Intercolonial also integrated the east into the new national economy.

In these years central Canadian workers actively built craft unions, city centrals, and took the first steps toward broader central organiza-tion. The realities of the continental labour market, however, dictated the creation of strong bi-national ties to American craft unions long before the creation of equivalent British American bodies. During the 1880s central Canadian workers created an ongoing central organiza-tion, the Trades and Labour Congress (TLC), but tangible eastern and western participation developed very slowly. In that same decade came the remarkable rise of the Knights of Labor, the first workers' move-ment in North America to envision and to attempt the organization of the working class in its entirety, transcending divisions of skill, sex, race, and ethnicity. Initially a huge success in central Canada and the still sparsely settled west, the Knights left the east virtually untouched. In the Maritimes, however, the Provincial Workmen's Association showed important similarities to the Knights of Labor.

During these years competitive capitalism was at its height. Despite recent capitalist rhetoric, the state played an active role in economic development. Laissez faire was a myth that applied only in the social realm of government activity. Canadian tariff policy was only one example where the models of German and American industrial development helped offset the ideological claims of Manchester liberalism. The state was a particularly active partner in Canadian industrial development, as to some degree was the working class itself which found itself embracing a "producer ideology," especially in the 1860s and 1870s.[14] Placing a high premium on industrial development as the necessary price for employment and national success, this producer ideology proved incapable of withstanding the pressure of class conflict as it emerged in the 1870s and especially in the 1880s. Moreover, producer ideology with its underlying notion of class harmony also faltered in the face of an increasing awareness that capital benefitted from protection in manufactures, while workers suffered from free trade in labour. Canadian immigration policy, which became organized labour's *bête noire* in the 1880s, functioned in the service of capital accumulation by providing a cheap labour force. This labour reserve proved useful for capital as a source of strikebreakers in emergencies or, in normal times, as a simple labour surplus which helped reduce the scope for workers' demands.

The particular importance of the free trade in labour became more evident in the subsequent third period of capitalist development in Canada from the 1890s to the 1920s. Monopoly capitalism replaced the older form of competitive capitalism in those decades and consciously created a national labour market to match the new national product market. In addition, capitalists recruited labour from a vast international pool and extended the concentration and centralization of capital which had begun to emerge in the 1890s. At the workplace they turned to scientific management and other managerial innovations to wrest control of the production process away from skilled labour. And, overseeing all of these developments, capital had a more mature partner – a state which was willing to conciliate and to moderate between capital and labour through new agencies such as the Department of Labour and new legislation such as the Industrial Disputes Investigation Act.[15] If these allegedly neutral activities failed, then capital's partner was also willing to play a harsher role. Staggering demonstrations of force, unprecedented in the nineteenth century, were used to intimidate workers in the coal fields of Nova Scotia and British Columbia and in industrial centres such as Winnipeg and Sydney.[16]

An understanding of working-class history in Canada must seriously face the differences which confronted the working-class movement as capital changed its nineteenth-century face into its modern twentieth-century countenance. For too long Canadian history has viewed this transformation in only quantitative terms. The rapid growth of the Canadian industrial economy and the arrival of American capital have been appreciated, but the complete revision of the "rules" under which capital and labour operated has been underestimated. Capital in its new phase did not play according to the old rules and it took the labour movement some time to learn the nature of the new contest. Moreover, workers faced an entirely new set of problems created by the vast resources that capital now had in its service. These ranged from the ability to recruit labour internationally with the active support of the Canadian government to the state's increasing willingness to support capital in its struggles with labour by providing military aid. Labour faced a new enemy and the proven nineteenth-century tactics of class struggle had to be modified accordingly. The new strategies were evident in the level of class conflict which prevailed in Canadian society throughout these years; that they failed was also quite evident by the 1920s. The strength of capital had been too great. Moreover, labour's ability to resist in a concerted, country-wide fashion was weakened by the relatively late national consolidation of the labour movement itself. Institutionally the TLC only became nation-wide at the turn of the century and even this centralization led to the loss of certain national and Quebec unions, as well as the remnants of the Knights of Labor.

Many contemporary Canadian historians draw implicitly and perhaps even unconsciously on their understanding of workers in the twentieth century for their insights into those of the previous century. Yet this borrowing can be quite damaging in the colouration it lends their views. The Canadian working class in the second half of the nineteenth century was not the same working class that these historians study in the twentieth century, nor, as Bryan Palmer has pointed out, are the sources even the same. Immigration patterns, for example, made for a different ethnic mix. The Irish were perhaps the most "foreign" element present, with the exception of the Chinese who prefigured later patterns in the nineteenth century. Even the Irish, however, were far removed from the vastly more variegated and exotic mix of southern and eastern Europeans which capital assembled in Canada in the first decades of the twentieth century. Concern for the ethnic divisions within the working class then is important and valid, but the extent of the difficulty was quantitatively (and consciously) transformed by capital in its monopoly phase.

Equally it can be argued that the ever-increasing division of labour in twentieth-century factories, which destroyed old skills, created in the wake of that destruction a labour force honeycombed with divisions more complex than the older skilled-unskilled distinction which had a centuries-long pedigree. The working class reduced to a universal proletariat, the fantasy of vulgar critics of Marx, does not exist in the factories of early monopoly capitalism any more than it did in the workshops of the nineteenth century. The point is a simple one. The periodization suggested here is one of sufficient importance that, when crossing the divide from one period to another, we should as historians be conscious of entering a territory foreign in its customs, language, and experience. Too often these boundaries have been ignored by those in search of easy and often self-serving generalizations.

Having successfully defeated labour in major conflicts after World War I in Winnipeg and in Cape Breton, capital proceeded throughout the 1920s to reign in a freer fashion than had been previously possible. A defeated labour movement retreated to reconsider its strategies and for a time found itself in a tight defensive box. All this of course changed during the depression which untrammelled capitalism had created. Out of this major crisis and the class conflict it engendered, grew yet a fourth stage of capitalist development which saw the creation and elaboration of a welfare state as its major symbol. About this stage of Canadian capitalist and working-class development we still know relatively little, although much current work is now pointing us towards a better understanding of this period. The establishment and later sophistication of a different structure of legal constraints surrounding the entire realm of class relations was one major innovation of this period. The creation of a new administrative system of labour law entrenched in federal and provincial labour boards once again transformed industrial relations and provided both capital and labour with another set of new rules intended to regulate and delimit their struggles.[17]

Thus I suggest the following periodization of Canadian working-class development: pre-industrial capitalism to 1850; industrial capitalism, 1850 to the mid-1890s; monopoly capitalism, 1890s to 1929; and crisis and reconstruction, 1930 to the present. Whether a new and distinct stage of development is now emerging remains to be seen. Parts of this periodization are at best tentative, but I offer it as a framework which might provide increased precision to our future discussion.

REGION

None can deny the importance of regional differences for an understanding of Canadian working-class history. Yet the increasing
emphasis placed on "region" as the crucial variable which explains
sundry problems of Canadian development seems increasingly mis-
placed. As William Westfall has recently argued, the term "region"
lacks any precision or theoretical vigour. Moreover, in popular use it
confuses a number of distinct notions employed by geographers who
are increasingly critical of its explanatory value. Westfall has also
suggested the curious inversion by which the regional interpretation
simply stands the old nationalist history on its head by placing the
emphasis on and attributing positive value to "the regional end of the
continuum."[18] In complementary articles Garth Stevenson and David
Alexander unearth some of the curious ideological roots of regionalism and draw out its continentalist implications.[19] Region then is a
concept which demands careful consideration.

Monopoly capital did not create a national labour market in Canada until the turn of the century. Before that period we must return
to the regions for our understanding of working-class development.
Too often in the past our generalizations have been drawn from the
central Canadian experience which has been assumed to apply
nationally. In the nineteenth century there was not one Canadian
working class but many. Preliminary work on industrialization in the
Maritimes, mainly focusing on Saint John and Halifax, suggests a
reasonably congruent, if smaller-scale, picture of the early stages of
industrial-capitalist development.[20] Later the National Policy tariffs
created a hot-house environment in which Maritime industry, especially textile production, rapidly expanded.[21] As we have already noted
the working-class movement in the Maritimes maintained a considerable degree of independence in this early period, although a number
of major international craft unions were present from the 1860s. The
major independent development was the Provincial Workmens' Association which survived a number of fierce wars with the United Mine
Workers of America well into the twentieth century, although by the
end it had become little more than a company union.[22] The major
development for Maritime workers, however, was the beginnings of
monopoly capitalism. With the creation of a national labour market
and with a rapidly increasing centralization and concentration of
capital, Maritime industrial workers were faced with an economic
climate that even before World War 1 showed hints of its underdeveloped future.[23] The years after the war established that fact, which
remains today the constant cloud on the horizon of the Maritime

working class whenever it engages in any form of self-assertion. The threat of shutdowns and the removal of capital from the region are the constant refrains under which all negotiation and even organization itself occur.[24]

Our understanding of the role of Maritime workers and their struggles within the framework first of industrialization and then of underdevelopment is a recent phenomenon. Western workers and the western regional economy have received far more attention from historians. Yet the focus of these discussions has been too greatly influenced by regional protest. Thus far too much of the region's economic history has focused only on the staples of the Laurentian thesis, namely on wheat and resource extraction. We have been told relatively little about the development of the western cities and about their working classes (with the notable exception of Winnipeg). Moreover, all accounts have been influenced by a strong sense of western exceptionalism which increasingly seems more suggestive of the chauvinist attitudes of both the western working class of the period and of historians today. We have little firm basis for regional comparisons of any level of Canadian working-class activity but it does seem clear that the rather easy assumptions of a unique western working-class militancy have been overstated.[25]

Canadian social history to date has had a very local focus. Much of the work has had a community focus, illustrating the influence of Herbert Gutman and of the urban biography approach. Indeed most of the vibrancy in historical writing recently has come from the discovery of region and the rejection of the old national synthesis where the actors moved on stages limited to Ottawa, Toronto, and Montreal. Yet this historiographic shift has not resulted in any more adventuresome analytical generalization. Canadian historians have come to believe everything was different everywhere – had different timings, elicited different responses, involved different protagonists. This celebration of region has fit very well with the general direction of Canadian political life in the last decade. Surely the time has come to begin to reflect on region in a critical way. All advanced capitalist countries are typified by regional variation and significant regional underdevelopment. To Marxists this notion will come as little surprise since it is a direct result of the concentration and centralization of capital which figures so prominently in capitalist development. Thus the United States has its Appalachia and it also has its south – regions that figured prominently in the nation's history and especially in terms of working-class history, as Alan Dawley has recently argued.[26] Equally England has not only its Cornwall and Devon as well as Lancashire but also has its Scotland, Wales, and Ireland. So what is it about this country that so befuddles Canadian historians before the historical difficulties of considering Quebec, the Maritimes, and the west as well as Ontario? These regions, of course, contain, even within them, considerable variation. For example, Ontario has its own eastern underdevelopment and it also has its own resource region in the north. What we need to reflect on then is what this regional variation has meant for Canadian workers. How has our particular experience of nation building and of uneven development affected the shape and behaviour of the Canadian working class? So far very little thought has been given to such questions. For too long the two solitudes, or more accurately the country's many solitudes, have separated those who work in labour history. Even if the country were to fracture on regional lines tomorrow, any historical understanding of the working class of the new nations would still need to consider carefully the previous regional relationships. Yet of these interactions we know next to nothing. There have been a few speculative attempts but to date they have been more adventuresome than fruitful.

What kind of analysis does this historiographical situation demand? A return to an old national history? No, of course not, but rather the consideration on a national scale of the particular class experiences of Canadian workers in local and regional contexts which adds up to something more than local and regional exceptionalism. After 1867 with the creation of a federal state and certainly after the 1890s with the rise of monopoly capital, business operated in a national (not to mention international) framework in Canada. To study workers only locally or even regionally will too often fail to recreate the adverse situations they faced. Monopoly capital possessed a limited local face at best as miners and textile workers knew from one end of the country to the other after their fierce encounters with distant, intransigent owners.

ETHNICITY

If region for historians has been a major factor dividing Canadian workers, then ethnicity has been another. As was noted earlier, we need to be very specific about periodization in this discussion for immigration did not serve the same purposes across the entire span of Canadian history. Moreover any such analysis also must pay close attention to the immigrants themselves, to their backgrounds as well as to their Canadian experiences. This is one of the major areas which demands a cultural analysis. Indeed what has most ethnic history of the Canadian working class been if not a careful attempt to reconstruct the class and cultural backgrounds of the new Canadians? Here close attention is generally paid to the specificity of the immigrants' origins, the motivation or cause of the migration, and finally to the experience of the immigrants in their new home. In all cases a sense of culture is a strong part of that historical analysis.

The role the immigrants played in North America and their relationship to the larger working-class movement has been the subject of lengthy debates in the more developed American literature. Both this writing and the smaller Canadian literature should warn us against easy generalization. A number of sensitively drawn accounts have shown how ethnic culture could be utilized by immigrant workers to sustain and fuel resistance to exploitation. The image of the immigrant strikebreaker, while not totally fictional, should not be allowed to predominate over that other portrait of the violent, foreign revolutionist. Both images were nativist and xenophobic in origin, but each had some basis in reality. This qualification is not meant to diminish the significance of ethnicity and of the potentially divisive nature of ethnic heterogeneity to the Canadian working class. We must, however, on occasion remind ourselves that some of those ethnic workers also made important contributions to the Canadian working-class movement. We seem to manage to remember this when considering British immigrants who, in both their Scots and English guises, provided many leaders and theoreticians to the Canadian labour and socialist movement, but this was also true of many of the European immigrants whose experiences were often much wider than those of their Canadian counterparts. The linguistic limitations of even many of the Canadian historians who have shown interest in immigrant workers or the ethnic socialist movement have too often disguised this important fact.

We need to look at more than first generation immigrants to understand the impact of ethnic diversity on the working class. The literature on ethnicity and immigration, even in "multicultural" Canada, too often ignores ethnicity as an ongoing factor in historical analysis. No longer can we blame the melting-pot assumptions of the old immigration history, since we now formally celebrate our diverse ethnic heritages. Instead one might question the official ethnic interpreters of their history where middle class bias and, all too often, cold war assumptions have come to dominate the quasi-official version of the past. This past, which celebrates the achievements of each ethnic community, has little room in its pages for the embarrassments of working-class militancy and radical politics.

Thus we know little about the continuing inter-generational importance of ethnic identity to Canadian workers. In cases with which we are familiar, it could lend itself as easily to radicalism as it could to less active forms of response. Thus Irish Catholic working-class culture, despite the conservatism of much of the Irish Catholic hierarchy, sustained an identification with Irish nationalism that led it to significant sympathies with the Georgeite Single Tax and with other forms of late nineteenth-century radical thought. This ideology coalesced around the Knights of Labor in which Irish Catholics were very prominent in leadership roles on both sides of the border. Irish activism occurred despite the short-lived official ban on membership stemming from the opposition of French Canadian bishops. A later and equally unlikely case emerges in the role of Scots in the Cape Breton labour movement where various facets of Scots culture – including religion itself – came to serve the unpredictable end of militant and red trade unionism.[27]

Ethnicity considered independent of class often obscures important issues. The Italian ethnic community, for example, contained thousands of itinerant labourers who worked on railway building and other forms of seasonal migrant labour. The community also contained "King" Cordasco and his equivalents.[28] Cordasco, perhaps the most extreme case, should remind us that there were important class divisions within the ethnic communities themselves and these determined much that occurred out of sight of the predominantly Anglo society. We know far too little about the internal structure of Canadian ethnic communities, especially about their occupational structures. Material stemming from reconstitution of the nineteenth-century social structure (data lacking for the twentieth century) suggests that the ethnic world was far more variegated than we had previously appreciated.[29] The likelihood of this being true for the twentieth century as well seems high. Here again class will prove more crucial than some ethnic historians have previously suggested.

Finally, it should be kept in mind that Canada enjoys a significant uniqueness in the western capitalist world as one of the few nations which allowed relatively easy access to its labour market for immigrants in the post-World War II period. Thus when we consider the impact of ethnicity in the Canadian working-class experience, we are discussing an ongoing process. For most industrial countries this is no longer true, unless we are analyzing the different cases of illegal immigration (as in the American southwest and California) or the case of "guest" workers (as in western Europe). Both speak to the reality of international labour markets but have different effects on the national labour movements of the host nations.

Ethnic workers then provide a significant challenge to Canadian labour historians. Much remains to be unearthed about these communities, for too long ignored by Canadian scholarship. But, as in the

case of region, we must not be interested solely in the solitary reconstructions. We must also ask how these communities fit together, or
did not? How did they fit into the larger society? Here too periodization must always be remembered for the twentieth-century divide
yawns large when we look at the demographic composition of the
Canadian population. Finally, cultural analysis will be central to this
project.

CULTURE

The word culture has been described by Raymond Williams as "one
of the two or three most complicated words in the English language."
After a useful description of the word's etymology and of its development in non-English language contexts (especially German), Williams
concludes:

In general it is the range and overlap of meanings that is significant. The
complex of senses indicates a complex argument about the relations between
general human development and a particular way of life, and between both
and the works and practices of art and intelligence. Within this complex
argument there are fundamentally opposed as well as effectively overlapping
positions; there are also, understandably, many unresolved questions and
confused answers. ... The complexity, that is to say, is not finally in the word
but in the problems which its variations of use significantly indicate.[30]

There can be little doubt that Williams' use of the term in his immensely influential *Culture and Society* (London 1958) bears some
responsibility for its extended use in historical writing about the
working class. Thus his most recent explanation of his choice is
worth considering. In explaining why he adopted the term "in full
consciousness of its accumulated semantic range, to denote a whole
way of life," he argued:

I suppose that I felt for all its difficulties culture more conveniently indicates
a total human order than society as it has come to be used. ... Historically
culture was cultivation of something – it was an activity; whereas society can
seem very static. I often liked the term for this reason.[31]

The debate on the utility of the term in historical writing concerning the working class has become a bitter one. Much of the virulence
is generated in the English context by serious political and theoretical
differences within Marxism. The irony in the North American context
is that the structuralist Marxist attacks on so-called "culturalist" inter-

pretations appear to be partially congruent with anti-Marxist critics. There may well be a double irony here: first, each side would immediately disavow the other if aware of the other's existence; secondly, one wonders if there is not an underlying ideological connection somewhere in these two apparently different modes of thought.

My commentary here will proceed on two levels. A simple discussion of the "culturalist" contribution to recent historical writing as evidence that the tradition already has been surprisingly fruitful will be followed by a brief consideration of the debates in English Marxism about culture and their pale reflection in Canada.

The major contribution of "culturalist" interpretations in English language historical writing has come in two related areas: the study of slavery and the study of the working class. In the United States the explosion of historical interest in the question of slavery that flourished in the 1960s and 1970s led to a profusion of studies of slavery which increasingly argued and eventually proved that the answer to age-old questions about the slave experience lay in the careful reconstruction of the slaves' world. There is not space here to trace this literature through its development but there can be little doubt that work in this vein represented a coming of age of American social history and for the first time moved American historians into world prominence. Obviously the key works in this genre – and, equally obviously, not compatible views – were Eugene Genovese's *Roll Jordan Roll: The World the Slaves Made* (New York 1974) and Herbert Gutman's *The Black Family in Slavery and Freedom 1750–1925* (New York 1976). Both worked in an explicitly "culturalist" vein, although again it should be noted that the differences in approach and argument outweighed their simple commonality which is of interest here. Pursuing similar themes, Lawrence Levine's *Black Culture and Black Consciousness: Afro-American Folk Thought from Slavery to Freedom* (New York 1977) was another notable addition to this literature. All this pathbreaking work demonstrated the rewards of a cultural analysis.

A cultural approach in American work on labour history also generated a significant breakthrough. Most notably associated with Herbert Gutman, this work has greatly enriched the study of the American working class. Studies by Gutman and others influenced by his work have helped to transform the writing of working-class history in the United States. The work has not lacked critics. Other major American historians of the working class have each commented at length on the Gutman corpus. David Brody, Melvyn Dubofsky, and David Montgomery all have passed considered and lengthy judgments on Gutman's achievements and limitations. Dubofsky and Montgomery worried especially about the failure to consider the political and economic context which helped defeat the struggles that Gutman so sensitively describes. Only partially a question of context, they also called for more attention to the hegemony that capital successfully established in this period in American history, despite the courageous struggles of American workers and their allies. Montgomery in addition argued that Gutman was overemphasizing the ethnic composition of the American working class, forgetting the native American workers who grew up in the industrial context of post Civil War America and who provided much of the leadership to the trade-union movement. Finally, Montgomery also correctly criticized Gutman's too easy adoption of language associated with American sociology of the modernization school. Brody, on the other hand, called much of the project into question by arguing that subtly Gutman had shifted the Thompsonian focus on class *and* culture into a focus solely on culture. Brody further suggested that the extremely fragmented nature of the American working class prevented the use of an abstraction such as working-class culture. Indeed, reflecting the important work of David Montgomery and of Harry Braverman, Brody called instead for a return to the workplace as the potential synthesizing locus for discussions of the American working class.[32]

Despite their criticisms, all three major assessments of Gutman's work accorded it the importance that it deserves.[33] None questioned the advantages of the cultural approach, although Brody could see no synthesis deriving from it in the American context.

If we return to England we find the roots of "culturalism" in the work of Edward Thompson. *The Making of the English Working Class* (1963) has probably been the most influential piece of historical writing in the English language published since 1960, if not since the war. The later work of Thompson – both the essays and *Whigs and Hunters* on the eighteenth century and the publication of his revised *William Morris* on the nineteenth – has been equally influential.[34] I will not engage in an analysis of this work here. Bryan Palmer's book, *The Making of E.P. Thompson*, takes these questions up at length. For our purposes, Thompson's influence is our concern and this has been amply evident in the mass of historical work that has appeared on the British working class in the 1960s and 1970s. All of this work is richer for its encounter with Thompson; not all neo-Thompsonians, however, agree completely with his findings or method. The work is too extensive to comment on, but in passing one might mention the valuable work of *History Workshop*, both in its original form as a series of pamphlets, (written by "first-time historians" as Raphael Samuel identified the authors) and later in valuable ongoing collections of essays edited by Samuel and in the journal *History Workshop* where much of the current debate about Marxist historical writing can be found.[35] Of equal importance has been the debate on the labour aristocracy, pro and con, including the works of John Foster, Robert Gray, Geoffrey Crossick, and, for a later period, James Hinton, and the series of critiques that followed.[36] All of this work, even at its most critical of Thompson, provides evidence of the impact his corpus has had on the writing of working-class history in England.

In both England and North America, however, the "culturalist" work has been subjected to considerable criticism recently. These critiques are difficult to elaborate because both the source and the target vary enormously. The critiques stem in the English context primarily from other Marxist scholars and are aimed primarily at Thompson, while in North America the critics are most often anti-Marxists attacking works which have associated themselves with Thompson's method. Despite this considerable difficulty I will try to discuss a number of these criticisms. These include charges of romanticism and voluntarism, of an inadequate definition of class, of the misuse of disciplines such as anthropology, of the importation of "foreign" models, of a failure to situate working-class culture in its larger social and political context, and of inadequate "theorization." We will be most interested here in the critiques which have the strongest resonance in Canada.

The charge of romanticism has been bandied about more than any other. Often signifying nothing more than political disagreement concerning the revolutionary potentialities of the working class, in this guise it is rather easily dismissed as ideological. In a slightly more sophisticated form it emerges as a critique of Thompson's admiration for the early nineteenth-century romantic critique of industrial capitalism represented in the works of Blake, Wordsworth, and later of William Morris. Thompson has successfully answered these charges and here, even Perry Anderson, his most persistent critic, now gives much ground.[37] The reconsideration of romanticism might also be usefully associated with the reassessment of utopianism currently under way. Most evident in the utopian's ongoing concern about questions of sexuality and the sexual division of labour, there is clearly much of value in this tradition as well.[38] In both romantic and utopian thought, the realization that other forms of social organization had existed in the past provided the tradition with the ability to dream of an alternative future. For those steeped in these traditions the social relations of industrial capitalism were neither natural nor foreordained. The nineteenth-century working-class movement was richer for the insights of the romantic critique and for its contact with the utopians; the easy and often snide attacks on such traditions from those who share in the "insight" of twentieth-century "common sense" or even in the scientific surety of certain forms of Marxism represent the famous condescension of posterity that Thompson has so often polemicized against.[39]

The charge that some of Thompson's followers concentrate too much on non-material elements of working-class life perhaps has some merit. There can be little doubt that certain forms of social history have wandered far from the Marxist insights in which Thompson's work is always based. In some of this work the economy is barely present. Interestingly, however, the so-called new social history has been far more guilty of this than working-class history, where the focus on work itself most often pre-empts extreme versions of this difficulty.[40] This has also been true of some American work which tries to blend new social history and working-class history approaches.[41] Nevertheless some of the new working-class history certainly has not resolved the tangible difficulties of trying to blend structural and cultural arguments. This difficulty, however, should not lead to a blind retreat from the cultural into the structural, but rather to increased efforts to maintain the interface between the two aspects. As for the non-question of which is a "more materialist" approach, I will certainly stand with scholars such as Thompson and Williams who have argued persuasively for the materiality of culture itself.[42]

Thompson's definition of class has recently drawn the fire of some very heavy British artillery. Both G.A. Cohen and Perry Anderson expend considerable effort to restore the notion of "class-in-itself," which they claim Thompson had dropped by equating class with relationships and with consciousness and by denying it any static existence.[43] There is not space to review the philosophical arguments here or even to do justice to Thompson's later considerations of this question.[44] I would simply echo the fact that class does have an "objective" side and call attention to Eric Hobsbawm's discussion of the question in his "Class Consciousness in History."[45] The point that needs to be made, however, is that once we have asserted that class does have an objective side and have established the broad objective parameters of the period, we then, as historians, proceed to Thompson's terrain. We do so because the questions which most interest us as historians of the working class are precisely the questions of how that class behaves and how its behaviour changes and develops over time. Much of this is the territory of the "subjective." "Class-for-itself," or the failure of the working class to develop such, is almost by definition what working-class history concerns itself with.

The importation of methods from other disciplines and of materials from other nation states are also critical refrains often heard about

Thompson-influenced working-class history. The first is a legitimate concern and one that demands careful scrutiny. Like history itself all disciplines have their own historical developments and their own debates. Too often the naive historian shopping for an organizing framework or an analytic device will enlist a concept or even a method fraught with difficulties of which he or she remains unaware. The historian's relationship to the social sciences is an important one and other disciplines must not be regarded as forbidden gardens which can be raided surreptitiously for tasty treats after dark. Historians know only too well how they regard other disciplines which use history in this way. We should come to recognize that this particular maze has two entrances.[46]

Much the same can be said of the insights of other national histories. In the Canadian context in which the working class is being recruited from abroad, obviously we must know the territory from which workers drew their initial experiences and much of the framework of their lives, but we also must observe this passage as a process in which the material and ideological surroundings of the new home also played a role. All of this seems only too apparent but sometimes the obvious demands reiteration in the face of critiques such as Michael Katz's which claims that certain "labour historians" are engaged in "making the North American working class fit a British model." John Weaver has raised a similar question elsewhere.[47] These critics, especially Katz, know little of the working-class world they are considering. One scholar who should know, however, David Bercuson, has made a similar charge, accusing "modern 'working-class' historians" of paying "due obeisance to E.P. Thompson, the guru" and of "shoehorning their subjects into a Thompsonian mould regardless of any violence done to history in the process."[48] The curious virulence of this attack aside, it does seem incumbent upon those of us who utilize the insights of British (or any other country's) social history to demonstrate convincingly that they apply to the Canadian context.

Another difficult question sometimes raised about notions of working-class culture is its relationship to the dominant culture of the society.[49] This problem is most often raised in the context of suggesting that the working class shared in the values of the capitalist society or, in its less vulgar form, that workers at least had a shared institutional life with other classes. These mediating institutions such as the church, education, fraternal societies, and the temperance movement, are then usually taken as proof that there was no separate working-class culture. Interestingly it has been the work on the labour aristocracy debate in England that has pushed these questions furthest. There the question has not focused on whether there was a separate working-class culture. Instead it has been a debate about the role of the upper stratum of the working class within the entire class and within the larger society. The findings in those discussions, however, bear directly on the question at hand. E.J. Hobsbawm, a proponent of the labour aristocracy theory, has summarized recent discussions as concluding that the entire concept of "respectability" and all that it suggested " did not imply a simple ideological 'embourgeoisement' of the artisans." Instead it is clear that artisans understood themselves to be "part of the 'working classes' or even the 'working class' and in some senses spokesmen for all of it." Moreover, the artisans' version of "respectability" was not identical to that of the middle class especially in its dependence on collective institutions including, of course, unions. When the labour aristocrats' way of life came under attack from the innovations of monopoly capital at the turn of the century, they moved politically to the left not only in their trade-union practice with the innovations of revolutionary industrial unionism but also in their political practice where Lib-Labism found itself on the wane.[50]

These findings conform very well to similar studies of late nineteenth-century Hamilton and Toronto skilled workers where moulders and printers, for example, played dominant roles in the trade union movement and in labour politics. Moreover, these same skilled workers were among the most active members of fraternal organizations, the temperance movement, and in some cases even the churches. The weight of the evidence from these case studies suggests that, while many of these institutions were intra-class in nature, workers perceived and used them in a distinctive fashion which did not conflict with their overall self-identification as working class.[51] In the years after their position was challenged by the arrival of monopoly capitalism, they continued to provide leadership to the working-class movement. The striking presence, for example, of machinists and other metal trades workers all over Canada in the vanguard of revolutionary unionism during and after World War I stemmed from their encounter with the new way of life and work dictated by monopoly capital.[52]

In general then the notion that Canadian workers were deeply implicated in the capitalist system, which so often parades as a given, appears increasingly for the late nineteenth and early twentieth centuries at least to be one of those conventional wisdoms which now demands demonstration not easy acceptance. We have much evidence of other working-class assumptions and behaviour; where is the proof of workers' acquiescence?

We do know, of course, that they were defeated, but that is a different question. The confusion of these questions, however, lies at the root of much of this debate. In the British context, Thompson's most reflective critics, Johnson and Anderson, are not calling for the jettisoning of culture as a conceptual device. Instead they seek a more variegated use of culture which incorporates splits within the working-class world.[53] The peculiar notion that culture is only useful as a device if there is total working-class unanimity and solidarity on all questions apparently is derived from David Brody's critique of Gutman.[54] It appears to be particularly attractive to some Canadian labour historians who, after studying the working class in its most militant stages (Bercuson: Winnipeg and the OBU; McCormack: western radicalism; Abella: The CIO drive),[55] now seem fascinated with questions concerning the failure of those movements. (Interestingly all have moved towards ethnicity as a crucial variable for further study.)

Another approach to the problem of the failure of the working-class movement to overthrow capitalism is to look to the internal stratification of the class. This Marxist explanation sometimes bases itself in some version of the labour aristocracy thesis which now ranges from the classic notion of an upper strata of the working class being bought off for a time by the higher rewards of imperialism through more recent versions which look to authority in the workplace and to the powerful hold of bourgeois hegemony. Other versions of this explanation overtly jettison the labour aristocracy and instead simply call our attention to the stratification of the working class and to craft exclusivism as variables militating against united working-class action. In Canadian work, articles by Ian McKay and Craig Heron have raised these questions in studies of Halifax bakers in the second half of the nineteenth century and of Hamilton metal trades workers in the early twentieth century.[56] In both cases their findings have been posed extremely tentatively.

Those of us who have worked on the late nineteenth century have not studied a working class which possessed an articulate revolutionary option. Equally struggles of the magnitude of Winnipeg or the early twentieth-century coal battles in Nova Scotia and British Columbia were not present. Yet what has emerged from this work has been an image of a class surprisingly united – one in which divisions of ethnicity, skill, religion, and even sex were recognized, debated, and for a few years in the 1880s, at least, were overcome.[57] Yet these achievements were admittedly brief and they were dissipated in the 1890s. A militant working-class movement re-emerged in the first 20 years of the new century, one which, as a world-wide phenomenon, possessed revolutionary industrial unionism as its cutting edge.[58] These dramatic conflicts, culminating in the events of 1919, were defeated by the combined forces of capital and the state. For the ensuing decade the trade-union movement was weaker than it had been since the 1890s or perhaps, arguably, since the 1860s. Yet in the 1930s the Canadian working class again entered the theatre of class struggle on a national scale. Surely given this history it is possible to speak historically of a Canadian working class. Indeed it is now necessary to locate class conflict and class struggle at the centre of modern Canadian history.[59] The complexity and heterogeneity of the Canadian working-class experience does not deny the existence of a working class. It may have limited that class's effectiveness in specific struggles with capital; moreover, it may have prevented it at times from mounting significant challenges to capital's hegemony; it has never, however, eliminated the class tensions that arise between the working-class's attempts to make capitalism less oppressive and capital's own needs. And this is precisely the utility of cultural analysis. Recognizing that the "degree of homogeneity and distinctiveness of class cultures is historically very variable,"[60] it directs our attention precisely to the terrain of analysis which is crucial in our examination of working-class history. It does not of necessity demand a militant, united, battling working class, although often that is what it finds. Indeed it must explain the elements of working-class life that hinder the emergence of stronger resistance to capitalist hegemony.[61]

The last charge against the "culturalists," inadequate "theorization," calls forth another obvious point; namely the structuralist critique which calls for a return to a "scientific" Marxism surely must not be confused with the anti-Marxist, North American critics of Thompson and of writers influenced by him. The North American critics, deeply enmeshed in positivistic historical traditions extremely suspicious of "theory," will certainly not embrace Perry Anderson's confidential dismissal of Thompson's assertion that history cannot be "anything more than proximate." Anderson instead declares: "Exact and positive knowledge has never been beyond the powers of history: its vocation, as with its sister disciplines, is to extend it." Even his more cautious afterthought that "the process, as Lenin noted, will always be asymptotic to its object," will hardly satisfy those for whom a "scientific history" smacks of earlier and unhappier days of vulgar Marxist inquiry.[62] Moreover, the debate which has swirled about Richard Johnson's recent criticisms of Thompson suggests the same difficulties. Johnson's position that "Culturalism, preferring 'authenticity' to 'theory,' renders its own theoretical project guilty, surreptitious and only partly explicit" and his further attack on its "embargo on abstractions" can hardly reassure those who find theory and theoretical language distasteful.[63] Or is there yet another irony lurking here just below the surface? Could it be that positivistic history à la Ranke is not so removed from the "science" of the structuralist Marxists?

Such theoretical niceties cannot be pursued here, but it does seem important to suggest that the Canadian historian's general predilection to assume that theory lies outside the domain of history does not serve them well when they are asked to confront works which are situated in debates which have a wider theoretical currency.[64] In addition the failure to assess much of this work on its own political and social terrain seems strangely akin to the aforementioned criticisms made of Thompson's followers who supposedly import indiscriminately. Excellent work has been written recently on the British Marxist historical tradition and Canadian historians of the working class would benefit from a familiarity with the context from which so much influential material in the field stemmed.[65]

BY WAY OF CONCLUSION

We have moved rather far afield from the Canadian worker by now. The digression, however, is appropriate. The methods, theories, or if one prefers, simply the questions which historians of the working class pose, should be developed in an international dialogue. We gain little from a proud parochialism; we learn much from comparative discourse. The disagreements and debates that we discover elsewhere, however, especially in Britain, have an overt political colouration that is seldom addressed directly in North America. Here the ideology of objective scholarship and of professionalism are upheld as pillars of professorial pride. There seems little reason to continue this pretence. Canadian working-class history from its inception has borne the weight of conflicting ideological discourse. One stream of analysis has always been directly concerned in the attempt to mediate class conflict. Finding its political inspiration as well as its intellectual roots in the progressivism of John R. Commons and his institutional school of labour economics, Canadian scholars from the young W.L.M. King to Bryce Stewart to Harold Logan were actively involved in the world of mediation and conciliation. They also, especially Logan, found time to lay much of the groundwork in the field of labour history. This tradition entrenched itself in labour relations when that discipline emerged in Canada following World War II. Partially distinct from this first group were social democratic scholars such as Eugene Forsey and Stuart Jamieson, or later Ken McNaught, Desmond Morton, and Walter Young. In addition there was also a subterranean Marxist undercurrent represented by scholars such as Clare Pentland, Stanley Ryerson, and Charles Lipton.[66] What is important to note about this early scholarship is that it was all politically engaged. One might also suggest that the results of this scholarship were relatively thin at least if compared to the material produced in the United States ranging from Commons through Perlman to Taft, or in England by the Webbs, the Hammonds, and the Coles. This is of some significance for Canadian scholarship because the feebleness of previous analyses of the working-class experience leaves us little to build on and much room for embracing as new ideas which should have been repudiated long ago.

In the 1960s as labour history became a respectable academic pursuit, a new group of scholars emerged that was unshaped by the older left-wing political context and instead came out of a new university environment with a wider definition of the range of historical scholarship and a larger horizon of academic possibility due to the rapid expansion of the academy. This group includes many of the scholars now most active in the field: Irving Abella, Don Avery, David Bercuson, and Ross McCormack. Proudly and professionally independent, their work is typified by its alleged distance from politics and the labour movement. Many of these historians would describe themselves as realists and some of them might even embrace pragmatism as a positive virtue – these values, of course, always being posed in contradiction to the "romantics."[67] Such scholars have made a significant contribution to the study of Canadian working-class history.

In the 1970s a subsequent set of Canadian scholars in working-class history emerged. This grouping, which obviously includes the author, was formed by a rather different set of experiences. Undergraduates in the late 1960s and in graduate schools in the early 1970s, many of these historians were active in the New Left and influenced by the rebirth of Marxist scholarship. There is no question that these experiences colour their work as they have been the first to acknowledge. Their political identification has caused serious difficulties for the social-democratic scholars who to a large degree actively opposed the New Left, are still fighting the battles of the cold war, and whose knowledge of Marxism is limited to an equation that reads Marx equals Lenin equals Stalin. Their response has been predictable. The more significant assessment is that of the "realists." Although deeply suspicious of anything that smacks of commitment or ideology (and for some of them the two are easily equated), nevertheless they must evaluate the work on its own terms. After a period of caution that consideration appears to be now underway. Politics necessarily plays an important role in these discussions. The "realists" will respond proudly that they have no politics which affects their scholarship; that is, of course, a political statement in itself. For as E.H. Carr usefully warned in the mid-1950s, "To denounce ideologies in general is to set up an ideology of one's own." In a similar vein he also reminded us that "the most suspect historian is the one who makes the loudest professions of impartiality."[68]

These political questions, whether acknowledged or not, cannot be allowed to replace the canons of historical scholarship as understood by both sides. The issues which separate the younger historians of the working class[69] from the "realists" must be articulated, considered, and subjected to empirical test. Ideally, in the process both groups would learn from each other. Time will tell if that openness will prevail. Clearly neither group has a corner on historical talent or truth. Moreover, we do not learn only from those with whom we share an ideological and political identification.

The next few years will undoubtedly see many assessments of the working-class history which has been written to date. More important than such considerations, however, is the need to get on with the task before us, namely writing the history of Canadian workers and moving towards new views of the Canadian past which are built on such class analysis. Central to any such project will be the discussion of culture.

Ironically culture will be crucial to this ongoing work for the very reason that leads some critics to want to eliminate it. That the working class has suffered defeats and setbacks does not militate against a cultural argument. It does place the necessity of accounting for these on the historical agenda, for as John Saville has recently commented in discussing the British working class:

It is, after all, a remarkable phenomenon that in the most proletarian country in the world, it was not until the closing years of the nineteenth century that an independent working class party was established; and an equally remarkable historical fact that it took two world wars and the most serious economic crisis that world capitalism has so far known before the party achieved a parliamentary majority.[70]

When we place the achievements and failures of the Canadian working class in this comparative arena, which also must include the United States, then perhaps the pessimistic conclusions reached continually by the "realist" historians, especially about the present, are not as obvious as they think. They certainly do not apply to all periods of the past.[71]

NOTES

1 See, among many others, E.P. Thompson, *The Poverty of Theory and Other Essays* (London 1978); Perry Anderson, *Arguments Within English*

Marxism (London 1980); John Clarke, Chas. Critcher and Richard Johnson, *Working-Class culture: Studies in History and Theory* (London 1979); and Bryan Palmer, *The Making of E.P. Thompson: Marxism, Humanism, and History* (Toronto 1981). Although I will use "culturalist" throughout this essay, this should not be read as an acceptance of the term. Based on Althusserian premises, the term itself has only descriptive utility. For a further critique, see: Keith Neild and John Seed, "Theoretical Poverty or the Poverty of Theory: British Marxist Historiography and the Althusserians," *Economy and Society* 8 (1979): 383–416.

2 Herbert G. Gutman, *Work, Culture, and Society in Industrializing America: Essays in American Working-Class and Social History* (New York 1976) and its major reviews: David Montgomery, "Gutman's Nineteenth-Century America," *Labor History* 19 (1978): 416–29; David Brody, "The Old Labor History and the New: In Search of an American Working Class," *Labor History* 20 (1979): 111–26; and Melvyn Dubofsky, "The 'New' Labor History: Achievements and Failures," *Reviews in American History* 5 (1977): 249–54. More recent contributions are: David Montgomery, "To Study the People: The American Working Class," *Labor History* 21 (1980): 485–512 and Robert Ozanne, "Trends in American Labor History," *Labor History* 21 (1980): 513–21. Finally, the more general works are: James Henretta, "Social History as Lived and Written," *American Historical Review* 84 (1979): 1293–322 and Michael Frisch, "American Urban History as an Example of Recent Historiography," *History and Theory* 18 (1979): 350–77.

3 David Montgomery, *Workers' Control in America: Studies in the History of Work, Technology, and Labor Struggles* (New York 1979) and David Brody, *Workers in Industrial America: Essays on the Twentieth Century Struggle* (New York 1980).

4 Both essays were delivered at the McGill Conference, "Class and Culture: Dimensions of Canada's Labour Past," 7–8 March 1980. See David Bercuson, "Through the Looking Glass of Culture," *Labour/Le Travailleur*, 7 (1981): 95–112.

5 Terry Morley, "Canada and the Romantic Left," *Queen's Quarterly* 86 (1979): 110–19 and Bryan D. Palmer, "Working-Class Canada: Recent Historical Writing," *Queen's Quarterly* 86 (1979): 594–616.

6 The reviews I have in mind here are David Bercuson in the *American Historical Review*; Ken McNaught in the *Journal of American History*; Christopher Armstrong in *Ontario History*; and Robert Cuff in *Business History Review*. More favourable views are Terry Copp in *Queen's Quarterly*; Frank Watt in *Labour/Le Travailleur*; and Bill Freeman in *Our Generation*.

7 My thanks to Professor McNaught for risking my wrath and showing his critical essay to me in pre-publication form.

8 Russell Hann, Gregory S. Kealey, Linda Kealey, Peter Warrian, comps, *Primary Sources in Canadian Working Class History, 1860–1930* (Kitchener 1973). For an extended discussion of how such sources can be used, see Russell Hann and Gregory S. Kealey, "Documenting Working-Class History: North American Traditions and New Approaches," *Archivaria* 4 (1977): 92–114. I would like to emphasize here the collective nature of the work that I have been associated with in the last ten years. The individualistic bias of North American scholarship and the nature of the rewards system within which we all function has too often obscured this fact. The work of the last decade was conceived collectively and much of it has been executed co-operatively.

9 Gregory S. Kealey and Peter Warrian, eds, *Essays in Canadian Working-Class History* (Toronto 1976), 7–8, 11.

10 Gregory S. Kealey, "The Working Class in Recent Historical Writing," *Acadiensis* 7 (1978): 133–5.

11 Kealey, *Essays*, 8–10.

12 On primitive accumulation, see Bryan D. Palmer, *A Culture in Conflict: Skilled Workers and Industrial Capitalism in Hamilton, Ontario, 1860–1914* (Montreal 1979), 6–12. For stimulating and suggestive discussions of this early period see H.C. Pentland, *Labour and the Development of Industrial Capitalism in Canada* (Toronto 1981) and T. Ruddel, "Colonial Capital and Labour: Principles and Practices in the Quebec District, 1760–1840," unpublished paper delivered at the McGill Conference on Class and Culture, March 1980.

13 Among others see Duncan M. McDougall, "Canadian Manufactured Commodity Output, 1870–1915," *Canadian Journal of Economics* 4 (1971): 21–36 and the earlier G.W. Bertram, "Economic Growth in Canadian Industry, 1870–1915," *Canadian Journal of Economics and Political Science* 29 (1963): 159–84.

14 On "producer ideology," see Palmer, *A Culture in Conflict*, chap. 4 and Gregory S. Kealey, *Toronto Workers Respond to Industrial Capitalism, 1867–1892* (Toronto 1980), chap. 8–9.

15 Paul Craven, *"An Impartial Umpire" Industrial Relations and the Canadian State 1900–1911* (Toronto 1980).

16 For an excellent overview of this period in the Maritimes see Ian McKay, "Strikes in the Maritimes, 1901–1914," unpublished paper, Dalhousie University, 1980. See also Craig Heron, "The Crisis of the Craftsman: Hamilton's Metal Workers in the Early Twentieth Century," *Labour/Le Travailleur* 6 (1980): 7–48, for a fine discussion of the encounter of skilled workers with monopoly capital.

17 Laurel Sefton MacDowell, "The Formation of the Canadian Industrial Relations System During World War II," *Labour/Le Travailleur* 3 (1978):

175–96 and also her "Remember Kirkland Lake," PHD thesis, University of Toronto, 1979. For a helpful discussion of American capitalist development see Michel Aglietta, *A Theory of Capitalist Regulation: The US Experience* (London 1979) and for a useful commentary on Aglietta see Mike Davis, "Fordism in Crisis," *Review* 2 (1978): 207–69. Suggestive Canadian work on this period is included in Leo Panitch, ed., *The Canadian State* (Toronto 1977), although one wishes on occasion in reading this collection for less "theorization" and more empirical analysis.
18 William Westfall, "On the Concept of Region in Canadian History and Literature," *Journal of Canadian Studies* 15, 2 (Summer 1980): 3–15.
19 Garth Stevenson, "Canadian Regionalism in Comparative Perspective" and David Alexander, "New Notions of Happiness: Nationalism, Regionalism, and Atlantic Canada," ibid., 16–28, 29–42.
20 Richard Rice, "The History of Organized Labour in Saint John, NB, 1813–1898," MA thesis, University of New Brunswick, 1968; Robert Babcock, "Economic Development in Portland, (Maine) and Saint John, NB During the Age of Iron and Steam, 1850–1914," *American Review of Canadian Studies* 9 (1979): 3–37; T.W. Acheson, "The Great Merchant and Economic Development in Saint John, 1820–1850," *Acadiensis* 8 (1979): 3–27; Larry McCann, "Staples and the New Industrialism in the Growth of Post-Confederation Halifax," *Acadiensis* 8 (1979): 47–79; Ian McKay, "The Working Class of Metropolitan Halifax," honours BA thesis, Dalhousie University, 1975.
21 Peter DeLottinville, "The St. Croix Cotton Manufacturing Company and its Influence on the St. Croix Community, 1880–1892," MA thesis, Dalhousie University, 1979.
22 Sharon M. Reilly, "The Provincial Workmen's Association of Nova Scotia, 1879–1898," MA thesis, Dalhousie University, 1979.
23 Nolan Reilly, "The General Strike in Amherst, Nova Scotia, 1919," *Acadiensis* 9 (1980); David Frank, "The Cape Breton Coal Industry and the Rise and Fall of the British Empire Steel Corporation," *Acadiensis* 7 (1977); Donald MacGillivray, "Henry Melville Whitney comes to Cape Breton: The Saga of a Gilded Age Entrepreneur," *Acadiensis* 9 (1979): 44–70; T.W. Acheson, "The National Policy and the Industrialization of the Maritimes, 1880–1910," *Acadiensis* 1 (1972): 3–28.
24 See David Frank and Greg Kealey, eds, "Report on Atlantic Canada," *Canadian Dimension* 13, 2 (1978) and "Report on Sydney Steel," *Canadian Dimension* 14, 4–5 (1980): 33–52.
25 David Bercuson has been most guilty of this, although it is reflected in nearly all the western work. See especially, however, David Bercuson, "Labour Radicalism and the Western Industrial Frontier: 1897–1919,"

Canadian Historical Review 58 (1977): 154–75. For a congruent critique of western economic history see W. Peter Ward, "Western Canada: Recent Historical Writing," *Queen's Quarterly* 85 (1978): 271–88.

26 Alan Dawley, "E.P. Thompson and the Peculiarities of the Americans," *Radical History Review* 19 (1978–1979): 33–59.

27 In general see Donald Avery, *"Dangerous Foreigners" European Immigrant Workers and Labour Radicalism in Canada, 1896–1932* (Toronto 1979); for the Irish see: Kealey, *Toronto Workers*, chap. 10, 12, 14. David Frank, "Traditional Elements in Cape Breton Mining Society in the 1920s," paper presented at the McGill Class and Culture Conference, March 1980; see also Allen Seager, "'A Forecast of the Parliament of Man': Aspects of the Alberta Miners Movement, 1905–1945," ibid.

28 Robert E. Harney, "Montreal's King of Italian Labour: A Case Study of Padronism," *Labour/Le Travailleur* 4 (1979): 57–84.

29 Gordon Darroch and Michael D. Ornstein, "Ethnicity and Occupational Structure in Canada in 1871: The Vertical Mosaic in Historical Perspective," *Canadian Historical Review* 61 (1980): 305–33.

30 Raymond Williams, *Keywords: A Vocabulary of Culture and Society* (London 1976), 76–82. See also the discussion in his *Marxism and Literature* (London 1977): 11–20.

31 Raymond Williams, *Politics and Letters: Interviews with New Left Review* (London 1979), 154–5.

32 Montgomery, *Workers' Control*; Harry Braverman, *Labor and Monopoly Capital: The Degradation of Work in the Twentieth Century* (New York 1974). See also the later Michael Burawoy, *Manufacturing Consent: Changes in the Labor Process under Monopoly Capitalism* (Chicago 1979) and Richard Edwards, *Contested Terrain: The Transformation of the Workplace in the Twentieth Century* (New York 1979). For the critiques of Gutman, see note 2 above.

33 Gutman's influence can be seen in numerous recent studies. In Canada see Palmer, *A Culture in Conflict* and Kealey, *Toronto Workers*. In the United States among others see: Alan Dawley, *Class and Community: The Industrial Revolution in Lynn* (Cambridge, MA 1976); Daniel J. Walkowitz, *Worker City, Company Town: Iron and Cotton-Workers Protest in Troy and Cohoes, New York, 1855–84* (Urbana, IL 1978); John T. Cumbler, *Working-Class Community in Industrial America: Work, Leisure, and Struggle in Two Industrial Cities, 1880–1930* (Westport, CT 1979); Thomas Dublin, *Women at Work: The Transformation of Work and Community in Lowell, Massachusetts, 1826–1860* (New York 1979); and in the articles in Milton Cantor and Bruce Laurie, eds, *Class, Sex and the Woman Worker* (Westport, CT 1977) and Milton Cantor, ed., *American Working-Class Culture: Explorations in American Labor and Social History* (Westport, CT 1979).

34 Edward Thompson, *Whigs and Hunters* (London 1975); "The Moral Economy of the English Crowd in the 18th Century," *Past and Present* 50 (1971): 76–136; "Patrician Society, Plebeian Culture," *Journal of Social History* 8 (1974): 382–405; "Eighteenth-Century English Society: Class Struggle Without Class?" *Social History* 3 (1978): 133–65. On the nineteenth century, *William Morris – Romantic to Revolutionary* (London, rev. ed. 1977).

35 In addition to *History Workshop: A Journal of Socialist Historians* 1 (1975), see Raphael Samuel, ed., *Miners, Quarrymen and Saltworkers* (London 1976) and *Village Life and Labour* (London 1975). For a brief introduction see the "History Workshop 1–6," a series in *New Statesman* 15 February–21 March 1980, especially Raphael Samuel, "History Workshop 1: Truth is Partisan," *New Statesman* 15 February 1980. Finally see Samuel's "History Workshop Methods," *History Workshop* 9 (1980): 162–76.

36 A very useful summary of this work is E.J. Hobsbawm, "The Aristocracy of Labour Reconsidered," in Michael Flinn, ed., *Proceedings of the 7th International Congress on Economic History* (Edinburgh 1979), 457–66. The works mentioned in the text are John Foster, *Class Struggle and the Industrial Revolution* (London 1974); Robert Gray, *The Labour Aristocracy in Victorian Edinburgh* (London 1976); Geoffrey Crossick, "The Labour Aristocracy and Its Values: A Study of Mid-Victorian Kentish London," *Victorian Studies* 19 (1976): 301–28; and James Hinton, *The First Shop Stewards Movement* (London 1973). Part of the debate is evident in: H.F. Moorhouse, "The Marxist Theory of the Labour Aristocracy," *Social History* 3 (1978): 61–82; the response by Alistair Reid, "Politics and Economics in the Formation of the British Working Class," ibid., 347–61; and the final exchange, H.F. Moorhouse, "History, Sociology and the Quiescence of the British Working Class," ibid., 4 (1979): 481–90; and Reid, "Response," ibid., 491–3. Finally, see the useful overview, J. Field, "British Historians and the Concept of Labour Aristocracy," *Radical History Review* 19 (1979).

37 Anderson, *Arguments*, 157–75.

38 Barbara Taylor, "History Workshop 4: Lords of Creation," *New Statesman* 7 March 1980, and her "The Men are as Bad as their Masters ...: Socialism, Feminism, and Sexual Antagonism in the London Tailoring Trade in the Early 1830s," *Feminist Studies* 5 (1979): 7–40. The former is reprinted in *Radical America* 14, 4 (July–August 1980): 41–6.

39 Kealey and Palmer, *"Dreaming of What Might Be": The Knights of Labor in Ontario* (New York 1982) argues this position at length.

40 For a lively critique along these lines see Tomy Judt, "A Clown in Regal Purple: Social History and the Historians," *History Workshop* 7 (1979): 55–94. The journals under fire in this piece suggest the focus

of the critique. *Annales: Économiques-Sociétés-Civilisations; Comparative Studies in Society; Journal of Interdisciplinary History;* and *Journal of Social History.* Judt adds, unfairly to my mind, *Past and Present* "occasionally," 90 n.3. A similar attack, albeit broader in its selections of targets, was E.F. and E.D. Genovese, "The Political Crisis of Social History," *Journal of Social History* 10 (1976): 205–21. Another Judt attack is "The Rules of the Game," *The Historical Journal* 23 (1980): 181–91. Not surprisingly these attacks have evoked a series of responses from some of the victims in "Problems in Social History: A Symposium," *Theory and Society* 9 (1980): 667–81. These range from the outrageous (Edward Shorter, 670–4) to the considered (David Levine, 677–8, and Charles Tilly, 679–81). Another type of response has been forthcoming in two recent defences of "modernization." See Raymond Grew, "More on Modernization," *Journal of Social History* 14 (1980): 179–87, and Peter Stearns, "Modernization and Social History: Some Suggestions, and a Muted Cheer," ibid., 189–209.

41 See, for example, Susan E. Hirsch, *The Roots of the American Working Class: The Industrialization of Crafts in Newark, 1800–1860* (Philadelphia 1978) and Daniel J. Walkowitz, *Worker City, Company Town.*

42 Williams, *Marxism and Literature*, passim.

43 Anderson, *Arguments*, 39–43; G.A. Cohen, *Karl Marx's Theory of History: A Defence* (Princeton 1978), 73–7. I would suggest readers see the following before following Anderson in regarding Cohen's reading as definitive: Walter L. Adamson, "Review Essay," *History and Theory* 19 (1980): 186–204; Andrew Levine and Erik Olin Wright, "Rationality and Class Struggle," *New Left Review* 123 (1980): 47–68; and Paul Breines, "Toward an Uncertain Marxism: A Review Essay," *Radical History Review* 22 (1979–80): 100–16.

44 See Thompson, "Eighteenth-Century English Society" and his "Folklore, Anthropology and Social History," *Indian Historical Review* 3 (1978): 247–66.

45 E.J. Hobsbawm, "Class and Class Consciousness in History," in I. Meszaros, ed., *Aspects of History and Class Consciousness* (London 1971).

46 The best discussion of this problem I know is Gareth Stedman Jones, "From Historical Sociology to Theoretical History," *British Journal of Sociology* 27 (1976): 295–305. But see also E.P. Thompson on sociology: "On History, Sociology, and Historical Relevance," *British Journal of Sociology* 27 (1976): 387–402; and on anthropology: "Anthropology and the Discipline of Historical Context," *Midland History* 1 (1972): 42–55 and "Folklore, Anthropology and Social History." A fine specific critique of unreflective borrowing is Gareth Stedman Jones, "Class Expression Versus Social Control? A Critique of Recent Trends in the Social History of 'Leisure,'" *History Workshop* 4 (1977): 163–70. For a

defence of social control, however, see H.F. Moorhouse, "History, Sociology and the Quiescence of the British Working Class." An ill-tempered critique is Genovese, "The Political Crisis of Social History."

47 Michael B. Katz, Michael J. Doucet, and Mark Stern, "Migration and the Social Order in Erie County, New York, 1855," *Journal of Interdisciplinary History* 7 (1978): 700; John Weaver, "Urban Canada: Recent Historical Writing," *Queen's Quarterly* 86 (1979): 75–97. See for a better-humoured, albeit similar, argument: John H. O'Rourke, Jr. and Michael S. Cross, "To the Dartmouth Station: A Worker's Eye View of Labour History," *Labour/Le Travailleur* 1 (1976): 193–208, esp. 194–5.

48 David Bercuson, "Recent Publications in Canadian Labour History," *History and Social Science Teacher* 14 (Spring 1979): 180.

49 Tom Traves, "Class and Culture: Dimensions of Canada's Labour Past," *Labour/Le Travailleur* 6 (1980): 171–7.

50 Hobsbawm, "Aristocracy of Labour Reconsidered," 461–4.

51 Palmer, *A Culture in Conflict*; Kealey, *Toronto Workers*; Wayne Roberts, "Studies in the Toronto Labour Movement, 1896–1914," PHD thesis, University of Toronto, 1978.

52 Montgomery, *Workers' Control*, passim.

53 Johnson, "Culture and the Historians," 67–71, "Histories of Culture," 74–7, and "Three Problematics," 234–47. For Anderson see *Arguments*, passim and also his recognizable role in Williams, *Politics and Letters*, esp. 113–56, 324–58.

54 Brody, "The Old Labour History and the New," esp. 123–6.

55 David Bercuson, *Confrontation at Winnipeg* (Montreal 1974) and *Fools and Wise Men* (Toronto 1978); A. Ross McCormack, *Reformers, Rebels, and Revolutionaries: The Western Canadian Radical Movement, 1899–1919* (Toronto 1977); Irving Abella, *Nationalism, Communism, and Canadian Labour: The CIO, the Communist Party and the Canadian Congress of Labour, 1935–1956* (Toronto 1973).

56 Craig Heron, "The Crisis of the Craftsman: Hamilton's Metal Workers in the Early Twentieth Century," *Labour/Le Travailleur* 6 (1980): 7–48 and Ian McKay, "Capital and Labour in the Halifax Baking and Confectionary Industry during the Last Half of the Nineteenth Century," *Labour/Le Travailleur* 3 (1978): 63–108. See also the British material listed in note 36, above.

57 On the Knights' experience see Kealey and Palmer, *"Dreaming."*

58 Larry Peterson, "The One Big Union in International Perspective: Revolutionary Industrial Unionism, 1900–1925," *Labour/Le Travailleur* 7 (1981).

59 For the distinction between class conflict and class struggle, see Williams, *Politics and Letters*, 134–6.

60 Richard Johnson, "Historians of Culture/Theories of Ideology: Notes on

an Impasse," in Michèle Barrett, Philip Corrigan, Annette Kuhn, and Janet Wolff, eds, *Ideology and Cultural Production* (New York 1979), 76.

61 Perceptive readers will no doubt recognize that I am on the verge of introducing yet another foreign-sounding word and another foreign thinker here. To spare Canadian historians this infliction, I will only suggest that they read Raymond Williams' discussion of Gramsci's conception of hegemony. See Williams, *Keywords*, 117–18 and *Marxism and Literature*, 108–14. Let me note, however, the following: "[Hegemony] has continually to be renewed, recreated, defended, and modified. It is also continually resisted, limited, altered, challenged by pressures not all its own. We have then to add to the concept of hegemony the concepts of counter-hegemony and alternative hegemony, which are real and persistent elements of practice," ibid., 112–13. A useful discussion of the relationship of "hegemony" as an analytic device in writing working-class history is: Geoff Eley and Keith Neild, "Why does social history ignore politics?" *Social History* 5 (1980): 249–71.

62 Thompson, *Poverty of Theory*, 262; Anderson, *Arguments*, 12–13. Although not a major point, it's worth pointing out that Anderson renders this quotation incorrectly, substituting "approximate" for "proximate." This alters the meaning slightly since "proximate" conveys a sense of "nearest" compared to "approximate's" "near but not exactly." Given the closeness of Anderson's reading and argument, this is a disconcerting error. For a fine critique of developments of this kind in contemporary Marxism, see Russell Jacoby, "What is Conformist Marxism?" *Telos* 45 (1980): 19–43.

63 Richard Johnson, "Edward Thompson, Eugene Genovese and Socialist-Humanist History," *History Workshop* 6 (1978): 97. See for a fuller development of his ideas his "Three Problematics: Elements of a Theory of Working-Class Culture" in Clarke, Critcher, and Johnson, eds, *Working Class Culture*, 201–37. The ensuing debate in *History Workshop* which followed Johnson's initial article is too lengthy to be reviewed here, but see Keith McClelland, "Some Comments on Richard Johnson," *History Workshop* 7 (1979): 101–15; Gavin Williams, "In Defence of History," ibid., 116–24; "Letters" of Tim Putnam, Robert Shenton, and Tim Mason, ibid., 220–5; Simon Clarke, "Socialist Humanism and the Critique of Economism," *History Workshop* 8 (1979): 138–56; Gregor McLennan, "Richard Johnson and his Critics: Towards a Constructive Debate," ibid., 157–66; and "Letters" of Richard Johnson and Gareth Stedman Jones, ibid., 196–202. On the North American distaste for theory see McNaught and Bercuson reviews of Palmer cited earlier. The most accessible (in language) of the Johnson commentaries is his "Historians of Culture/Theories of Ideology," 49–77. Here, for example, his criticism of structuralism is clearest. To my mind, one of

the most substantive critiques of Thompson and culturalism, and one which I benefitted from having to confront, unfortunately is unpublished. See Ian McKay, "Towards a Materialist Approach to Canadian Labour History," Dalhousie University, 1980.

64 For a useful discussion see Jones, "From Historical Sociology to Theoretical History," and for a fine example of how history does help formulate theory see Raphael Samuel's, "Workshop of the World: Steam Power and Hand Technology in Mid-Victorian Britain," *History Workshop* 3 (1977): 6–72. I would argue, others would not, that Edward Thompson's work also serves this task well.

65 See, for example, Thompson, *Poverty of Theory*; Anderson, *Arguments*; Raymond Williams, *Politics and Letters*, esp. Parts 1 and v; Chas Critcher, "Sociology, Cultural Studies, and the Post-War Working Class" and Richard Johnson, "Culture and the Historians," in Clark, Critcher, and Johnson, *Working Class Culture*, 13–40, 41–71; Raphael Samuel, "British Marxist Historians, 1880–1980: Part One," *New Left Review* 120 (1980): 21–96; Eric Hobsbawm, "The Historians' Group of the Communist Party," in Maurice Cornforth, ed., *Rebels and Their Causes: Essays in Honour of A.L. Morton* (London 1978): 21–47; Ralph Miliband, "John Saville: A Presentation," in David E. Martin and David Rubenstein, eds, *Ideology and the Labour Movement: Essays Presented to John Saville* (London 1979), 15–31; and Palmer, *The Making of E.P. Thompson*.

66 For a discussion of the early work see my "Looking Backward: Reflections on the Study of Class in Canada," Dalhousie University, 1979. An abridged version of this work will appear in 1981 in the *History and Social Science Teacher*.

67 This group has been described recently as "the first generation of labour historians." I have rejected this terminology since by ignoring pre-1960s scholars it tends to be somewhat confusing. The description of the two groups which are defined by the phrases first and second generation, however, I am in complete agreement with. See Bryan Palmer, "Working-Class Canada."

68 E.H. Carr, *The New Society* (London 1956), 16, 103.

69 I would gladly embrace the term "romantic" but I suspect some of my associates would not so I will refrain. Critics, however, are welcome to describe me as such.

70 John Saville, "The Radical Left Expects the Past to do its Duty," *Labor History* 18 (1977): 266–74.

71 For an interesting consideration of u.s. working-class history in this vein, see Mike David, "Why the u.s. Working Class Is Different," *New Left Review* 123 (1980): 3–44, and his "The Barren Marriage of American Labour and the Democratic Party," *New Left Review* 124 (1980): 43–84.

5 The Writing of Social History in English Canada, 1970–84

Canadian social history, not surprisingly, shares similar roots with other English-language social history. To a large degree a product of the social movements of the 1960s, it has come to fruition in the 1970s and 1980s, establishing a firm professional base of societies, journals, and prominent promoters. In this, it resembles American, British, and Australian patterns. Perhaps much more interesting, however, are the areas where Canadian social history departs from the general patterns – areas of national distinctiveness generated by the particularity of Canada's role in the world capitalist system.

Canadians spend much of their time reflecting and commenting on their anomalous position in the world. Originally settled as an outpost of the French empire and then conquered by England in the middle of the eighteenth century, the various British North American colonies evolved towards the creation of a nation largely in reaction to the revolutionary path chosen by their neighbouring colonists to the south. By the middle of the nineteenth century the dismantling of the old British Imperial system had combined with new industrial aspirations and huge railway debts to propel a largely unwilling colonial populace towards Confederation. Vigorously opposed in Quebec and the Maritimes, the new country, Canada, emerged not as a feat of popular nation building but rather as a shotgun wedding of reluctant partners with England playing the bride's father.

Popular or not, the new nation state quickly evolved a national policy consisting of a transcontinental railway, high protective tariffs, and a liberal immigration policy. Rapid indigenous industrialization occurred in the late nineteenth century but gave ground quickly before the massive penetration of American capital in the early twentieth century. The rapacious demands for capital and science of the industries of the second industrial revolution combined with Canada's high tariff wall and preferential access to the British empire markets to create the world's first major branch plant economy. Thoroughly penetrated by American multinational firms, Canada's fragile national economy increasingly displayed tell-tale signs of continental distortion. The Canadian banks and various nefarious railroad, hydroelectric, and street railway interests, however, successfully resisted total incorporation and created in the West Indies and South America elements of a minor Canadian imperialist presence. The fragility of the national economy was matched by a stunted nationalism which has spent most of the twentieth century worrying about a distinctive national identity. These nationalist concerns pre-eminently found expression in the industrial heartland of Ontario and found few echoes in the colonized east or west of the country. Meanwhile, Quebec developed its own very tangible nationalism which viewed the conquest, the defeated rebellions of 1837, and the Confederation settlement as traumatic incidents in an overall pattern of English and English-Canadian oppression.

Given that history, it should come as no surprise that the old Canadian "national" history became one of the first victims of the rise of social history. The years 1967 and 1968 must figure large in any attempt to describe the development of Canadian social history in the last two decades. The two years, while close in time, had very distinct symbolic meanings for Canadian social history. The first, 1967, Canada's centennial year as a nation state, implies much of the particularity of Canadian developments, while 1968, the year of revolt, suggests the impact of the international conjuncture.

In 1967 as part and parcel of an orgy of national celebration and self-congratulations (ironic given the divided state of the nation), two of Canada's most eminent historians took time to assess Canadian national historiography. In "Canadian centennial cerebrations," Ramsay Cook, English Canada's leading historian of Quebec nationalism, captured the undercurrent of national questioning:

Perhaps instead of constantly deploring our lack of identity, we should attempt to understand and explain the regional, ethnic, and class identities that we do have. It might just be that it is in these limited identities that "Canadianism" is found, and that except for our over-heated nationalist intellectuals, Canadians find the situation quite satisfactory.[1]

In an address to the American Historical Association, meeting in Toronto because of Canada's Centennial, J.M.S. Careless, undoubtedly then Dean of Canadian history, elaborated on Cook's curious phrase "limited identities" and in the process raised it into the pantheon of Canadian historiography's key phrases. Proceeding from a notion of "one nation, eminently divisible," Careless attacked the old nationalist and whig "from colony to nation" school of Canadian historical writing and instead argued for a confrontation with region, class, and ethnicity as the key themes of Canadian development.[2] All of this in most national historical discussions would seem unexceptionable, but it came in Canada only two years after a striking discussion in the *Canadian Historical Review* of the concept of social class in the interpretation of Canadian history which, after finding little evidence of class analysis, could still conclude rather smugly that this simply reflected reality.[3]

We stand to gain something by more attention to the concept of social class. Especially, we have neglected lower-class history and the structure of society. On the other hand, the main outlines of Canadian history are not going to be fundamentally changed by any pragmatic response to the idea of class. There is no case for urging Canadian historians to devote themselves to the question of class and, forsaking all others, to cleave only onto it. (218)

Thus it would at first blush appear that progress was being made in 1967, although the curious confusion of categories of analysis such as class, ethnicity, and region, all thrown together into a pluralist stew, already suggested that the chefs might later want to rewrite the menu.

And indeed they did. After only a decade the same two historians worried that the historiographical revolt had gone too far. Careless, for example, fretted:

Ten years after one might well ask if there is any positive balance of satisfaction with Canada now left at all ... there has been a massive out-pouring both in popular and scholarly writings on regional interests and inequities, on cultural discords and demands, on class disparities and stresses, and such things as national concerns are by and large passed over or discounted. In this situation I feel a little like the farmer in the midst of a flood when he declared, "Lord knows I prayed for rain but this is ridiculous."[4]

Cook, in a more considered piece, also appeared contrite in calling for a return to historical consideration of the *national* experience. In his final formulation, however, he avoided Careless' implicit rejection of conflict:

Canada is, after all, not made up of what I once carelessly called "limited identities," but rather of unlimited identities. It has been the competition and clash of those identities, regional, ethnic, class, and sexual, which gives our history its dynamic.[5]

Note, by the way, the new ingredient here – women.

What had happened in Canadian historical writing in the intervening decade that so distressed Careless and others? The answer to that question demands a consideration of 1968. Canada, like other advanced industrial nations, was profoundly affected by the experience of the 1960s. The expansion of higher education influenced the social composition and role of the professoriate and of the student body. A new generation of university students, drawn from further down the class ladder and including far more women and the children of previously excluded immigrant groups, played a major role in the transformation of the universities and, perhaps more important for our purposes here, also concomitantly of the nature of Canadian scholarship. The New Left in Canada, given the weaknesses of the indigenous old left, had a disproportionately strong impact. Certainly the New Left itself was not as strong in Canada as in the United States, France, or Germany, but in the latter two cases at least the national intellectual discourse included Marxism whereas in Canada its impact on the academy had been very weak. Even in the United States Marxism, both indigenous and emigré, undoubtedly played a more important role in intellectual life.

In Canada when New Left and student movement activists began to ask questions about their country's history and especially about the nature of its economic development and class formation, they encountered little previous work which provided hints at direction. While the Canadian marxist tradition had actually produced more work than was apparent to 1960s activists, its weakness was, nevertheless, glaring. Indeed the major historical work in that tradition, Stanley Ryerson's *Unequal Union*, did not appear until 1968. Ryerson himself proved an important mentor to the student left just as he had to earlier generations of activists within the Communist Party of Canada (CPC). His major contribution in the 1970s, however, came within the contours of the debate about the national question in Quebec, especially after his departure from the CPC and his appointment to the History Department at the Université du Québec à Montréal.[6] Ryerson, however, remained a lonely figure in the 1960s.

The other available body of work, and one that Canadian left nationalists embraced enthusiastically, derived from the political economy of Harold Innis and his followers. This so-called Toronto school emphasized the influence of the staples in Canadian economic development and focused much attention on the distorting effects of an export-based resource economy.[7] The Innisian tradition found strong supporters among young Canadian political economists, many of whom played prominent roles in the elaboration of a left national- ist position within the New Democratic Party (NDP).[8] The Waffle movement, as this movement was named, eventually found itself ex- pelled from the NDP but many of its proponents have remained active and provide a counterweight to the emergence of a more recognizably marxist scholarship in Canada, derisively termed by them "metropoli- tan Marxism."

For those activists who rejected Innis and found the nationalist politics of the Waffle wanting, a considerable intellectual void loomed before them. Without doubt this void came to be filled by the British marxist historical tradition and especially by the work of E.P. Thomp- son. Here again this historiographical enthusiasm was hardly unique to Canada but in some ways Canadians may have been better equip- ped to take advantage of it than many Americans.[9] The Thompsonian politic remained in the forefront in Canada where British politics retained a familiarity that certainly was not paralleled in the United States. Yet Canadians also found themselves well situated to take advantage of the intellectual ferment south of the border and, while some Canadians studied at Warwick with Thompson and his succes- sors, more probably availed themselves of U.S. graduate schools and of the renascent American social history. Needless to say, Thompson and Hobsbawm played equally influential roles in the genesis of U.S. social history as the clear debts of gratitude of Herbert Gutman and David Montgomery make clear.[10]

Thus, undoubtedly the most vexing development for the old Cana- dian historical synthesis and its proponents was that one of the new approaches vying for place was historical materialism. Almost equally disconcerting, however, was the nearly simultaneous arrival of wom- en's history. In both cases the political developments of the 1960s and early 1970s played key roles, and recent denigrations of the politics of the 1960s make it all the more important to continue to demonstrate the interaction of the politics of protest with the intellec- tual emergence of historical materialism and women's history.[11]

Two interacting forces then have been at work in the last twenty years of historical writing. The breakdown of the old centralist, nationalist history has been the more ambiguous politically and therefore was the more acceptable to a broad spectrum of Canadian intellectuals who, for the first time, found themselves living outside the metropolitan centres of Montreal and Toronto and who began to discover new perspectives on the country that derived from the hinter- land and held the provinces – not Ottawa, Toronto, or Montreal – as their focal point. The legitimation of local and community studies explicit in many social historical approaches coincided with a massive political reassertion of regional sentiment. Perhaps best represented by the creation of B.C. *Studies* in 1968 and *Acadiensis: Journal of the History of the Atlantic Region* in 1971, this trend also saw new professional standards increasingly applied to older local historical publications such as *Ontario History* and its western equivalents.[12] P.A. Buckner, the first editor of *Acadiensis*, at the outset established the nature of this regional historiographic revolt:

Perhaps it is a sign of our basic insecurity and of our immaturity as a nation that our historians are still obsessed with the great "national" themes and that local history, despite a recognition of its importance, is more talked about than written.[13]

The metropolitan approval that this development received from Cook and Careless helped legitimize this pursuit but more important in the long run was how well it matched the aims of the young new leftists who commenced to write social history, nearly all of it local in focus. This thrust also found institutional embodiment in the creation of subgroups of the Canadian Historical Association – the Urban History Committee, the Committee on Canadian Labour History, the Canadian Committee on Women's History, and others.

Indeed in two of those cases publication of new historical journals also resulted. The *Urban History Review* (*UHR*) commenced publication in 1972 and was followed by *Labour/Le Travail: Journal of Canadian Labour Studies* (*L/LT*) in 1976.[14] In both cases initial funding came from state agencies. The *UHR* received its original support from the National Museum of Man and *L/LT* gained funding for its first issue from the Federal Department of Labour and subsequently has been supported by the Social Sciences and Humanities Research Council of Canada (*SSHRCC*). Also both journals and committees represented broad cross-sections of researchers with no prevailing methodological or ideological agreement, although the New Left found representation in both. This is an important distinction to make because *L/LT*, for example, is not an equivalent publication to *History Workshop* nor to the *Radical History Review*. Indeed its genesis if not its practice make it far more akin to the American journal *Labor History* (1960), to Australian *Labour History* (1961), or even to the English *Bulletin of the Society for the Study of Labour History* (1960).

Yet perhaps ironically the late development of labour history as a recognized subset of Canadian historical writing meant that almost from the outset it incorporated approaches that owed far more to both the American "new" social history and to British marxist approaches. The old orthodoxy of institutional labour history was only one of the avenues of research and, while initially better established, it soon gave way to the newer approaches.

While institutional labour history on the American Commons-Perlman or Wisconsin school model had failed to establish a dominant presence in Canada, there were two distinct strains of pioneering work.[15] Strongest of these was an emerging Canadian social democratic school which achieved an academic hegemony on the left far more easily after World War II than its trade union partners were to enjoy in their efforts to establish their control over the labour movement itself. By no means limited to historians, a group of intellectuals associated with the League for Social Reconstruction, the Cooperative Commonwealth Federation's own Fabian Society, provided pioneering studies of class in Canada.[16] Perhaps not too surprisingly, these intellectuals, with the significant exception of Eugene Forsey, showed somewhat less interest in the history of Canadian workers. Indeed the most important historian in the group, Frank Underhill, devoted most of his scholarly attention to the history of Canadian liberalism.[17]

Forsey, a political scientist by training and ironically an expert on the parliamentary system, produced his most important work almost as a retirement project. As research director of the Canadian Labour Congress he undertook in the 1960s the task of writing a survey history of Canadian Labour to celebrate Canada's centennial. After performing yeoman service in identifying sources and preserving archival materials, Forsey eventually produced *Trade Unions in Canada, 1812–1902*, some fifteen years after the nation's 100th birthday. Resolutely empiricist, this volume eschews analysis like the plague, aiming instead at factual correctness of an encyclopedic nature.[18]

The Communist Party of Canada also aspired to write Canadian labour history as well as to make it. However, the major work in this tradition, Charles Lipton's *The Trade Union Movement in Canada*, appeared long after its initial conception in late 1940s party discussion and arrived on the scene with a strong nationalist orientation by then not shared by the moribund CPC.[19] Despite its strong nationalist overtones, this volume nevertheless was written in a classic, orthodox marxist fashion.

Needless to say, there were many such efforts to write labour history on both banks of socialism's Rubicon but by and large the works of Forsey and Lipton can serve as proxies for the entire corpus. Arriving so late in both Forsey's and Lipton's careers, these works show little influence of their day, reflecting instead the politics and scholarly approaches of the immediate post-war period.

The subsequent decade, the 1950s, witnessed in Canada as elsewhere an historiographical detour away from the economy and towards biography and politics. Thus, Kenneth McNaught, one of the few social democratic counterweights to the prevailing liberal hegemony of that decade, appeared trapped by this biographical mode. His monograph on Methodist minister and founder of the Cooperative Commonwealth Federation, J.S. Woodsworth, fits easily into the historiographical conventions of the 1950s, while standing marginally outside of the decade's ideological assumptions. "Prophets" and their biographers apparently found the Cold War climate chilly and inhibiting.[20]

Of far more historiographic interest was the emergence in the late 1960s and early 1970s of a professionally trained cadre of historians whose dissertations and subsequent first books addressed themselves to various aspects of the history of Canadian labour. Obviously influenced by the turmoil of the 1960s and the melting of the Cold War, but yet not quite a part of the new activism, these scholars were not bound by the ideological framework of either Canadian social democracy or communism. Thus, Irving Abella's *Nationalism, Communism, and Canadian Labour* (Toronto 1973) managed simultaneously to describe the rise of industrial unionism in Canada and to avoid the worst excesses of Cold War dismissals of the role of the CPC. Interestingly, nationalism not socialism contributed passion to this volume and its major political point was a critique of international unionism. Conventional in historiographic terms, the book quickly established a reputation for itself and its author. A similar volume arguing the nationalist case in an earlier period emerged one year later. Robert Babcock's *Gompers in Canada* (Toronto 1974) posited the thesis that the Canadian labour movement had suffered serious damage from the intrusions of the American Federation of Labor in the first decade of the twentieth century. These disruptions, Babcock argued, had seriously distorted the development of the Canadian labour movement. Writing from the United States, Babcock's views showed the powerful impress of early American revisionist historiography. The turbulence of the Vietnam period deeply influenced American diplomatic and foreign policy history and that passion is evident here. Babcock's original Duke PHD thesis termed Gompers' efforts in Canada "labor imperialism," although the Canadian published version softened this to "continentalism."

Two other major working-class studies emerged from the debates about region. David Bercuson's *Confrontation at Winnipeg* (Toronto 1974) reconsidered the events of the 1919 General Strike by focusing on the evolution of class relations in the city in the first two decades of the twentieth century. While thus providing a temporal perspective on the 1919 revolt, he viewed the events largely in a local and regional context. The event for Bercuson was profoundly local and regional, an argument which he has carried forward in articles and in a subsequent monograph on the One Big Union, *Fools and Wisemen* (Toronto 1978). Sharing this western particularist viewpoint, Ross McCormack's *Rebels, Reformers, and Revolutionaries* (Toronto 1978) studied more clearly the ideological underpinnings of the labour revolt. While resorting to an overly schematic characterization of labourist, syndicalist, and revolutionary socialist traditions, the volume nevertheless made a major contribution to the field by fixing our attention on the significant debates in the working-class movement in the early twentieth century.

In addition, it should be noted that Bercuson and McCormack commenced the process by which the focus of labour studies turned from the national scene to a more particular viewpoint be it local or regional. This particularism they shared with an emerging group of scholars whose first collective statement, penned by Russell Hann, came in the guise of an introduction to an archival guide. This "manifesto," as it came to be viewed by its critics, by way of explaining the basis of archival and bibliographic selection used in the compilation, issued a clarion call for a social history of the working class which transcended institutional approaches. Interestingly, this introduction also pursued the opening offered by Careless and Cook and endorsed efforts "to create a new local history" that would "focus new attention on features of Canadian society that previously appeared as mere dots in the firmament of the old imperial vision." At the time that remained a relatively safe proposition, although the critique of left nationalism that followed in the introduction was not. In the labour history community, however, what primarily caused distress was the characterization of two previous "schools" of Canadian writing, an "institutional" school inspired by John R. Commons and a "political" school which whiggishly saw little more than the rise of social democracy on the one hand or on the other could see only the workers through their relationship to the Communist Party of Canada.[21]

With the appearance in 1976 of the first issue of *Labour*, the journal of the Committee on Canadian Labor History, and also *Essays in Canadian Working-Class History*, edited by Gregory S. Kealey and Peter Warrian, the "second generation," in Bryan Palmer's terminology, began to make their presence felt.[22] The first issue of *Labour* contained a number of essays by this "second generation," as well as one of the first bibliographical/historiographical commentaries on the emerging field, albeit written in a satirical form by its author, Michael S. Cross, who set the discussion in a bar in Dartmouth, Nova Scotia, and had two workers debate the issues in labour and working-class history.[23] *Essays in Canadian Working-Class History*, and especially its introduction written by Kealey, upset many because of its call for "working-class history" to replace "labour history":

Thus, labour history ceases to be simply a category of political economy, a problem of industrial relations, a canon of saintly working-class leaders, a chronicle of union locals, or a chronology of militant strike actions. Instead it becomes part of the history of society. Workers are no longer seen as isolated figures engaged only in trade unions, strikes, and radical politics; instead they are studied in a totality that includes their cultural backgrounds and social relations, as well as their institutional memberships and economic and political behaviour.[24]

In retrospect, this seems rather unexceptionable but it has become the touchstone for all subsequent work. For the critics *any* subsequent discussion of strikes, unions, leaders, or politics somehow became a betrayal of this second "manifesto," as it came to be viewed. The patent absurdity of that reading has not slowed the critics one bit.

Before turning to that debate, however, other emerging currents of Canadian social history should be added to the stream. They too owe their genesis to their times and, while varying in overt political commitment, nevertheless possess strong roots in the debates of the 1960s. The first, and perhaps most important, has been the development of Canadian women's history. While receiving some early support within the academy, especially at the University of Toronto, where Jill Ker Conway and Natalie Zemon Davis played important roles in establishing women's history as part of the curriculum, early work in this field developed outside the universities and very much inside the political debates of the emerging women's movement. For example, the founding of the Canadian Women's Educational Press and its pioneering collective effort, *Women at Work in Ontario, 1850–1930*, might well be credited with helping set the early terms for historical discussion.[25] The dominance of women's movement activists from the outset contributed a class analysis to much of the early women's studies work in Canada and initially gave hegemonic position to the emerging marxist-feminist dialogue. In addition, the emphasis on subjective experience of feminist analysis made much of this early work quite congruent to the emerging school of working-class history which looked to Edward Thompson's work for guidance. Although not necessarily written by historians – women's studies in

Canada as elsewhere have been vigorously interdisciplinary – much excellent work emerged on women's wage work, on earlier phases of the women's movement itself, and on theoretical debates within the contemporary women's movement. More recently, considerable work on women's non-waged work and on the family economy has added to our knowledge of women's historical role.[26] Of late, however, the previously pre-eminent position of a class-based gender analysis seems threatened. This challenge, of course, reflects international developments in both the women's movement and women's studies and is in no way unique to Canada. Equally troubling, professionalization and the threat of cutbacks appear to be contributing to a new conservatism in the field which worries about issues such as "presentism."

Just as the women's movement emerged from the politics of the 1960s and helped to create women's history, so too did urban reform play a major role in generating urban history in Canada. The politics of the 1960s created in Canadian cities a significant and strong urban reform movement which developed a strong historical consciousness in its attempt to block some of the more egregious efforts of urban renewal and development. This historical thrust in urban studies combined nicely with the rather different emphasis of the American "new social history" which had entered Canada through the brief presence of Charles Tilly at the University of Toronto and the more significant and lengthier stay of Michael Katz at the Ontario Institute for Studies in Education (OISE) and later at York University. Katz's Canadian Social History Project created much controversy not only in the field of urban history but in social history in general. Katz came under fire from older urban-biography style historians who felt his studies of Hamilton, Ontario, conveyed nothing of locale and they continually criticized his claims of typicality. He also came under attack from working-class historians who, in the case of his first book, found his economic history questionable and his use of class problematic and who later, in the case of his second volume, found his dismissal of working-class self-activity as ludicrous.[27] The direction of much of the new urban history, including Katz, towards mobility studies following Stephen Thernstrom and Theodore Hershberg and later towards family reconstitution after Michael Anderson and the Cambridge School, soon ended the congruence between Katz and the urban historians.

City-oriented urban history in Canada has been piloted energetically by Gil Stelter of the University of Guelph and Alan Artibise of the University of Winnipeg. The latter edits the *Urban History Review* and is the author of *Winnipeg: A Social History of Urban Growth* (1975) and together they have edited the major bibliography in the field and numerous volumes of essays.[28] These historians have continued to work on cities in what Stelter and Artibise have typified as three separate methods – the city as entity, the city as process, and the city as setting.

Probably a more important legacy of the Katz project are the spinoffs and related projects in the area of family history, demography, and mobility studies. At OISE David Levine's ongoing work, although not Canadian, nevertheless influences Canadian historians.[29] At York the research of Gordon Darroch and Michael Ornstein involving a stratified, random sample of the 1871 manuscript Canadian census continues to generate important findings.[30] In addition Gérard Bouchard's ongoing study of the Saguenay region of Quebec, influenced as much by Annales as North American social history, has also proven quite valuable.[31]

A third area of social history which also had deep political roots, albeit by and large not in the New Left, is immigration or "ethnic" history as it is often termed. While most often initially not sharing the same political assumptions as working-class or women's history, there can be no doubt that this field derives from the 1960s experience. The rapid expansion of Canadian higher education in that decade meant that for the first time working-class immigrant children, most often second generation, found themselves within the walls of academe. Once there, they too began to demand a Canadian history that spoke to their and their parents' experience. The older, filiopietistic, middle-class version of immigration history with its emphasis on social mobility and North American success came increasingly under challenge. Ironically these developments met with an ever-increasing governmental interest in this realm. For political reasons, namely the Liberal Party's dependence on new immigrant votes, the state promoted "multiculturalism" as an official policy. Thus the interdisciplinary field of ethnic studies enjoyed rapid growth, and historical work in the area also benefited.

Heavily supported by the state during the Trudeau years, the area has its own society, the Canadian Ethnic Studies Association and its own journal, Canadian Ethnic Studies. In addition to the federal support that the field found owing to the importance of multiculturalism to the Trudeau response to Quebec nationalism, it also picked up significant provincial funding, especially in Ontario where the Multicultural History Society received millions of dollars to study and preserve Ontario's ethnic heritage. Through an extensive archival and oral history program, the Society has certainly accomplished its second goal. It has worked on the first through a series of conferences, books and pamphlets, and its journal, Polyphony.[32] The major force in MCHSO has been Robert Harney, a University of Toronto historian of Italy who later turned to immigration history. Work on the Italians and Finns has been especially rich and there has been fruitful interaction with American colleagues and internationally. Additional state funding has also led to two series of publications in this area. The "Generations: A History of Canada's Peoples" series published by McClelland & Stewart, a multi-volume series with either a monograph or a collection of essays on each Canadian immigrant group,[33] and a pamphlet series, "Canada's Ethnic Groups," published by the Canadian Historical Association, providing similar but shorter treatments.[34]

This confusing cacophony of social history subsets has led to numerous exercises in empire building and much of what passed as critique between the areas often looks like muscular expansionism. Nevertheless, the core question underlying much of the debate both between these unfortunately fragmented fields and within them can be reduced to a certain ideological basis. That shared debate, not surprisingly, has to do with class and the role of class analysis in historical writing.

This debate has probably been sharpest in the realm of working-class history where in the early 1980s a series of review essays considered the intellectual outcome of the 1970s and found the marxist variant wanting.[35]

Implicit in much of this criticism has always been a notion that those who write of class conflict and of a working class in the Canadian context are simply importing "foreign models." The fact that Hann, Kealey, and Palmer all attended American graduate schools furthered this argument with some. Kealey's association with Herbert Gutman at the University of Rochester and Palmer's with Melvyn Dubofsky at the State University of New York at Binghamton simply provided fuel for some nationalist fires. (The very titles of two of the major review articles in the field are revelatory – Kenneth McNaught's "E.P. Thompson v. Harold Logan" [Logan was an institutional labour economist who wrote the first overview history of Canadian labour][36] and Desmond Morton's "E.P. Thompson dans des arpents de neige.") It became clear, however, in the mid- to late-1970s that the choice of U.S. graduate schools proved only momentary for as soon as Canadian working-class history became established students found congenial programs and supervisors in Canada. This proved especially true at Dalhousie (Cross, Fingard, Kealey), at York (Abella), and latterly at Simon Fraser (Palmer, Seager), although McNaught also continued to supervise theses in the area at the University of Toronto until his recent retirement.

The second generation had made their presence felt in the late 1970s with their first books and these became the focus of considerable debate. Palmer's community study of the Hamilton working class from 1850 to 1914, *A Culture in Conflict* (1979), was the runner-up for the CHA's John A. Macdonald prize for the best book on Canadian history in 1979. Kealey's *Toronto Workers Respond to Industrial Capitalism, 1867–1892* (1980) won that prize the following year. The differences between the two volumes have to some degree influenced their reception. Palmer's more sweeping arguments and more specific focus on culture has won the book much attention and praise internationally, while generating serious criticisms in Canada.[37] Kealey's more detailed account of the Toronto economy and his lengthy (some have said turgid) rendition of Toronto labour politics has led to a more favourable Canadian response but a more critical international reading.[38] Their joint effort *"Dreaming of What Might Be": The Knights of Labor in Ontario, 1880–1900* (1982) has to date received mixed reviews and the Corey Prize of the AHA/CHA.[39] Palmer's attempt at a synthetic statement, *Working-Class Experience*, appeared in 1983 and again was chosen as a runner-up for the Macdonald Prize.[40]

At its heart, the challenge to working-class history has come from historians who deny the centrality of class analysis and who especially view any emphasis on the role of workers and class conflict in history as romantic and exaggerated. As already mentioned, the purported "foreignness" of these ideas – Thompson, Hobsbawm, Gutman, Montgomery, and worse still, Marx – is sometimes deemed a sufficient critique. In more considered assessments, however, the critique revolves around the concerted attempt to demonstrate that a plethora of divisions, most often implicitly viewed as unique to Canada or sometimes to North America, prevented the emergence of anything that might be termed a Canadian working class. The specific choice of divisive factors varies but region, ethnicity, and gender receive frequent emphasis. Indeed much of the criticism of a cultural approach to Canadian working-class history has had this at its core – there can be no working-class culture, not because of problems of cultural analysis, but because there was no Canadian working class. In these approaches class then simply becomes one of a plethora of epistemologically equivalent variables.

As a result of Kealey and Palmer's initial focus on the late nineteenth century much of this debate has revolved around the role of the Knights of Labor. Captive to a large degree of an older American labour historiography, there has been a profound refusal even to consider that the Knights' experience represented a significant moment in one specific phase of Canadian working-class formation.

This rejection of a Canadian "Great Upheaval" stems partially from outmoded but pervasive views of the Canadian economy as industrializing only in the early twentieth century and from a teleological view of working-class development which views the nineteenth-century experience as pre-history. In this view the crisis of 1919 can be taken seriously, although viewed only as a specifically western Canadian event, while the earlier crisis can only be trivialized.

The major contribution of the Kealey, Palmer, and Kealey-Palmer monographs and related work has been to recapture this significant phase of Canadian working-class development. The decline and defeat of the Knights, indeed the brevity of their moment, does not diminish their significance. The profound restructuring of capitalism that ensued in the wake of the great depression of the 1890s successfully created a new phase of capitalist development in which different working-class strategies emerged from a recomposed labour movement. And these new strategies, especially revolutionary industrial unionism, built towards the next great conflagration, namely 1919, but this emphatically new challenge in no way obliterates the earlier crisis. Indeed, the working-class failure, perhaps even defeat, in 1919 also severely damaged the labour movement, which only re-emerged more than a decade later in the crisis of depression and war to challenge capital anew. And again on this occasion, in the 1937 to 1946 period, the challenge took innovative forms based on new understandings and strategies. Such an argument suggests that the historians of the Canadian working class are not the "romantics," as they are so often disparagingly termed, for within this view of class development there is analytic scope for notions of composition, decomposition, and recomposition, all derived from the outcomes of specific struggles which profoundly influence the nature of capitalist development. Instead perhaps the "realists," who hold Canadian working-class experience against some implicit model of correct working-class behaviour and find it wanting, are the historians guilty of holding the past captive to projections of appropriate development, namely some implicit form of revolutionary class consciousness.[41] In effect, the historians of Winnipeg (Bercuson), the OBU (Bercuson), western radicalism (McCormack), and the rise of industrial unionism (Abella) appear to lose their patience before the complexities and ambiguities of Canadian working-class formation. For the new professional labour historians, the eventual rise of Canadian social democracy failed to offer the consolation that it had for their pioneering predecessors. Instead they were left with a confusing historical record which from a pragmatic perspective appeared ultimately as a history of failure. In many ways closer to their American historical colleagues of a pre-Gutman and pre-Montgomery variety, they held Canadian workers up to the litmus test of revolutionary class consciousness and found them wanting. Any subsequent interpretation which tried instead to take Canadian workers at face value and trace the peculiarities and particularities of their class development was found equally wanting.

The other major contribution of recent working-class history has been the restoration of Eastern Canada to national consideration. Traditionally dismissed as backward and reactionary, especially when compared with western radicals, the workers of the Maritime provinces found little place in Canadian historical writing, even that concerned with labour. The work of a generation of Dalhousie University graduate students has helped reverse those notions and placed a very different set of questions on the agenda. The work of David Frank and Ian McKay on Nova Scotia coalminers, of Nolan Reilly on industrial Amherst, of Frank and Reilly on regional socialist traditions, and of McKay on regional strike patterns has totally transformed the view of the Maritimes and has helped to explode the myth of a uniquely western regional radicalism.[42]

Indeed for the first time since the emergence of the new working-class history, attempts are now being made to transcend the particularism of the local studies and to build a synthetic, national account of Canadian working-class formation which respects regional variation. Palmer's general text in labour and working-class history, *Working-Class Experience*, is one such attempt, as are recent articles by Kealey on the labour revolt of 1919, by Craig Heron on labourism as a political tradition, Larry Peterson on revolutionary industrial unionism, and by Palmer on class formation in North America.[43]

While no definitive and systematic response has emerged to meet all critiques – although Palmer's *Working-Class Experience* is a valiant attempt – the key task then appears increasingly to revolve around writing an adequate overview of Canadian working-class development using a conceptualization that avoids the teleologies of old left analyses, be they social democratic or Stalinist, explicit or implicit. Moreover, this overview must escape simultaneously the cynicism of most contemporary bourgeois scholars and the burgeoning pessimism of many left-wing analysts. Clearly nowhere in the capitalist world has actual working-class history conformed to the foreordained old left models. The smug satisfaction of the triumphant Canadian social democrats who viewed the world as evolving correctly with the growth of the welfare state, and "free" collective bargaining has collided head-on with the contemporary assault on both by first Liberal and now Conservative governments. The carefully constructed post-war consensus which the social democratic intellectuals helped to design while in opposition is currently being dismantled and the labour movement finds itself under assault from all quarters. Yet this moment is hardly unique to Canada and indeed the Canadian labour movement takes some grim consolation in its relative strength in the face of adversity when compared with the current traumas of American labour.

The governmental assault on labour and the welfare state is also making its presence felt in the realm of scholarship, the arts, and higher education.

The advancement of Canadian scholarship in general and of Canadian social history in particular in the last twenty years has owed much to a greatly expanded system of governmental aid to scholarship. Originally funded through the Canada Council, in 1978 scholarly funding was transferred to the newly created Social Sciences and Humanities Research Council of Canada. The sshrcc funds doctoral studies, post-doctoral research, scholarly research, scholarly associations including the blanket organizations the Social Science Federation of Canada and its Humanities equivalent, international scholarly travel, and scholarly publication. For example, on this last point only, most Canadian scholarly journals receive a sshrcc subsidy based on a formula combining pages published and number of subscribers. Moreover, nearly all scholarly monographs published in Canada receive subsidization under the Grants-in-aid of Scholarly Publication program administered by the Federations with money provided by the sshrcc. Predictably for the last dozen years at least, the excuse of a large and growing Canadian federal budgetary deficit has led to cutbacks in these areas. While in current dollars the sshrcc appears to have grown and now receives almost $60,000,000 annually, when translated into constant dollars this amount represents a considerable decline. Indeed in recent years only uncharacteristically capable lobbying has prevented yet deeper cuts. With the election of a Conservative government in 1984, which contains elements that look to Thatcher and Reagan for ideological guidance, sshrcc budgetary prospects looked dim. Needless to say, the drive to cut the deficit will hit targets far more worrisome than academics, but nevertheless the recent transformation of Canadian academia and scholarship could easily be sadly damaged by Tory know-nothings.

Cutbacks in the sshrcc budget, for example, would undoubtedly seriously endanger two ongoing Canadian social history series. The first of these, "The Social History of Canada," was established by University of Toronto Press in the early 1970s and under the editorship of Michael Bliss issued both reprints with critical introductions and edited collections of documents. Later under the new editor, H.V.

Nelles, this series started to publish monographs and now runs to 37 volumes.[44] The second series, the McClelland & Stewart Canadian Social History series has published ten volumes since 1974 and has another six under contract.[45] This series includes both monographs and collections of essays and is currently edited by Gregory S. Kealey. The same publisher has a five-volume "Readings in Canadian Social History Series" intended for classroom use at the university level. Edited by Kealey and Michael Cross, it provides an overview of some of the best writing in Canadian social history, especially in the theme areas of economy, social structure, social control, labour, women, and violence. The five volumes cover: *The French Regime, Pre-Industrial Canada, Canada's Age of Industry, The Consolidation of Capitalism*, and *Modern Canada.*[46]

As the reader has probably already gathered, the two solitudes that have historically separated English and French Canada are still alive and well. Yet perhaps ironically the internationalism of social history helps to break this separation down. While meeting only occasionally on Canadian ground, Quebec and Canadian social historians are likely to meet in the pages if not on the terrain of the world of international social history. In addition, the great divide of language, while still a hindrance for many in terms of conversation, presents fewer problems for reading. Indeed it is worth noting that all the newer historical journals discussed – *L/LT, HS/SH, Atlantis*, etc. – publish in both languages. Nevertheless it remains true that Quebec historians, many of them nationalists and some of them separatists, also preserve their own institutions and journals. The Institut d'histoire de l'Amérique française and its journal, *Revue d'histoire de l'Amérique français* (*RHAF*), function as Quebec national equivalents to the Canadian Historical Association, which it should be pointed out in passing does not possess a national journal. (The *Canadian Historical Review* (*CHR*) is a publication wholly owned by the University of Toronto Press and with a self-perpetuating editorial board, which only recently has ceased to be drawn solely from the University of Toronto History Department.) *RHAF*, perhaps predictably given the influence of French historiography in Quebec, has published far more social history in the last twenty years than the *CHR*.

The discussion here has limited itself largely to English-language Canadian social history which minimizes the importance of not only French-language work but also social history writing in non-Canadian fields. There is not space enough here to do justice to the variety of non-Canadian work but it is undoubtedly worth calling attention to important Canadian work in British social history, especially in the eighteenth and nineteenth centuries. Canadian scholars such as

Douglas Hay, Nicholas Rogers, Robert Malcolmson, Donna Andrew, John Beattie, Peter Bailey, Fred Donnelly, Jeanette Neeson, and Canadian expatriates Michael Ignatieff and Barbara Taylor, all have made major contributions to English social history. While no other field is as rich in Canadian universities as English social history, there are individuals of similar quality in other fields as well.

Equally this quick overview has given rather short shrift to non-historical scholarship. The same influences which contributed to the emergence of significant marxist work in Canadian history also affected the other Canadian social sciences. The rallying point for much of this work has become the journal *Studies in Political Economy* (founded in 1979) which has quickly established itself as Canada's major scholarly journal of the Left. Here too certain tensions are evident. In this case the major rift lies between left nationalist scholars, who continue to tie themselves tightly to the mantle of Canadian political economist Harold Innis, and a group of scholars who define themselves more in terms of international marxist debate.

No doubt reflecting the political climate of the times, it has become popular of late in some Canadian academic circles to bemoan the state of the university and of the academy. Among these historians have taken a particularly prominent place. Ironically, celebrating some golden age of the Canadian university which is blatantly mythical, these historians implicitly call for a return to the institution of the 1950s. When they turn their attention to historical writing, they are equally atavistic. One thing seems certain, however: the historiographical clock will not be easily turned back to the 1950s; there is now considerable work to build on. Equally certain, indeed already in progress, is the attempt to do just that.

NOTES

1 Ramsay Cook, "Canadian centennial cerebrations," *International Journal* 22 (Autumn 1967): 663. Cook's major writings on Quebec nationalism include *Canada and the French-Canadian Question* (Toronto 1967); French-Canadian Nationalism: An Anthology (Toronto 1969); and *The Maple Leaf Forever* (Toronto 1971). The major work in Canadian historiography is undoubtedly Carl Berger, *The Writing of Canadian History* (Toronto 1976). Unfortunately, this volume considers in depth only those Canadian historians born before World War 1. Thus, while quite useful for tracing the roots of historical scholarship, it stops short of any treatment of the themes pursued here. The most useful, critical bibliography is the two-volume *A Reader's Guide to Canadian History* (Toronto 1982). Volume 1, *Beginnings to Confederation* is edited by D.A.

Muise and Volume II, *Confederation to the Present* by J.L. Granatstein and Paul Stevens.

2 J.M.S. Careless, "Limited Identities in Canada," *Canadian Historical Review* 50 (1969): 1–10. For a similar argument, see also his "Nationalism, pluralism, and Canadian history," *Culture* 30 (1969): 19–26.

3 S.R. Mealing, "The Concept of Social class and the Interpretation of Canadian History," *Canadian Historical Review* 45 (1965): 201–18.

4 J.M.S. Careless, "Limited Identities – Ten Years Later," *Manitoba History* 1, no. 1 (1980): 3.

5 Ramsay Cook, "The Golden Age of Canadian Historical Writing," *Historical Reflections* 5, no. 1 (1977): 137–49.

6 For material on Ryerson, see chapter 3.

7 Berger, *Writing*, 85–111.

8 On the Waffle see John Bullen, "The Ontario Waffle and the Struggle for an Independent Socialist Canada: Conflict Within the NDP," *Canadian Historical Review* 64 (1983): 188–215.

9 Bryan D. Palmer, *The Making of E.P. Thompson* (Toronto 1980).

10 Herbert G. Gutman, *Work, Culture and Society in Industrializing America* (New York 1976) and David Montgomery, *Workers' Control in America* (New York 1979).

11 For one such denigration written by Canadian historians see David Bercuson, Robert Bothwell, and J.L. Granatstein, *The Great Brain Robbery* (Toronto 1984).

12 For examples, see *Saskatchewan History* (1948 and following), *Alberta History* (1953 and following), and *Manitoba History* (1980 and following).

13 P.A. Buckner, "Acadiensis II," *Acadiensis* 1, no. 1 (autumn 1971): 3.

14 The journal was originally *Labour/Le Travailleur*. The name was changed in 1984 to remove the sexism of the French title.

15 For classic examples of the Wisconsin school, see John R. Commons, "The American Shoemakers, 1648–1895," in his *Labor and Administration* (New York 1913) and Selig Perlman, *A Theory of the Labor Movement* (New York 1928). Recent critiques include: David Brody, "The Old Labour History and the New: In Search of an American Working Class," *Labor History* 20 (1979): 111–26 and his "Philip Taft, Labor Scholar," *Labor History* 19 (1978): 9–22; Thomas Kruger, "American Labor Historiography: Old and New," *Journal of Social History* 4 (1971): 277–85; and David Montgomery, "To Study the People: The American Working class," *Labor History* 21 (1980): 483–512.

16 Michael Horn, *The League for Social Reconstruction: Intellectual Origins of the Democratic Left in Canada, 1930–1942* (Toronto 1980).

17 Berger, *Writing*, 54–84 and Douglas Francis, "Frank H. Underhill: Canadian Intellectual" (PHD diss., York University, 1976).

18 (Toronto 1982). It should be pointed out, however, that the manuscript and research materials were available much earlier and were widely used by other scholars.

19 (Montreal 1967).

20 Kenneth McNaught, *A Prophet in Politics* (Toronto 1959).

21 R.G. Hann et al. (comps), *Primary Sources in Canadian Working-Class History, 1860–1930* (Kitchener 1973), 9–20.

22 Bryan Palmer, "Working-class Canada: Recent Historical Writings," *Queen's Quarterly* 84 (1979): 594–616; and Gregory S. Kealey and Peter Warrian (eds), *Essays in Canadian Working Class History* (Toronto 1976).

23 Michael S. Cross, "To the Dartmouth Station: A Worker's Eye View of Labour History," *Labour/Le Travailleur* 1 (1976): 193–208.

24 Kealey, "Introduction," *Essays*, 7–8.

25 Janice Acton et al. (eds), *Women at Work in Ontario, 1850–1930* (Toronto 1974).

26 For examples, see Charnie Guettel, *Marxism and Feminism* (Toronto 1974); Dorothy Smith, *Feminism and Marxism* (Vancouver 1977); Pat and Hugh Armstrong, *The Double Ghetto* (Toronto 1978); Pat Connelly, *Last Hired, First Fired* (Toronto 1978); Meg Luxton, *More Than a Labour of Love* (Toronto 1980); Linda Kealey (ed.), *A Not Unreasonable Claim: Women and Reform in Canada, 1880s–1920s* (Toronto 1979); Carol Lee Bacchi, *Liberation Deferred: The Ideas of the English-Canadian Suffragists, 1877–1918* (Toronto 1982); Barbara Latham and Cathy Kess (eds), *In Her Own Right: Selected Essays on Women in B.C.* (Victoria 1980); Barbara Latham and Roberta Pazdro (eds), *Not Just Pin Money: Selected Essays on the History of Women's Work in British Columbia* (Victoria 1984); Linda Briskin and Lynda Yanz (eds), *Union Sisters* (Toronto 1983); Laura and Robert Johnson, *The Seam Allowance: Industrial Home Sewing in Canada* (Toronto 1982); Paul and Erin Phillips, *Women and Work* (Toronto 1983); Jennifer Penney (ed.), *Hard Earned Wages* (Toronto 1983); and Joy Parr (ed.), *Childhood and Family in Canadian History* (Toronto 1982). Also useful are the recent documentary studies published by New Hogtown Press: Beth Light and Alison Prentice (eds), *Pioneers and Gentlewomen of British North America* (Toronto 1980) and Beth Light and Joy Parr (eds), *Canadian Women on the Move, 1867–1920* (Toronto 1983).

27 Michael Katz, *The People of Hamilton, Canada West* (Cambridge, Mass. 1976) and Michael Katz, Michael Doucet, and Mark Stern, *The Social Organization of Early Industrial Capitalism* (Cambridge, Mass. 1983). For the early debate, see Bryan Palmer, "Modernizing history," *Bulletin of the Committee on Canadian Labour History* 2 (1976): 16–25; Michael Katz, "Reply," ibid., 25–8; and Palmer, "Response," ibid., 29–31. For

the second volume, see Gregory S. Kealey's review in *Canadian Historical Review* 63 (1982): 561–3 and Bryan Palmer, "Emperor Katz's new clothes; or with the Wizard in Oz," *Labour/Le Travail* 13 (1983): 190–7.

28 Stelter and Artibise (eds), *The Canadian City: Essays in Urban History* (Toronto, 1977); Artibise and Stelter (eds), *The Usable Urban Past* (Toronto 1979); Stelter and Artibise (eds), *Shaping the Urban Landscape* (Ottawa 1982) and *Canada's Urban Past: A Bibliography to 1980* (Vancouver 1981).

29 David Levine, *Family Formation in the Age of Nascent Capitalism* (New York 1977).

30 Gordon Darroch and Michael Ornstein, "Ethnicity and Occupational Structure in Canada in 1871: The Vertical Mosaic in Historical Perspective," *Canadian Historical Review* 61 (1980): 305–33; "Family Co-residence in Canada in 1871: Family Life-cycles, Occupations, and Networks of Mutual Aid," *Historical Papers* (1981): 30–55; and "Family and Household in Nineteenth-century Canada: Regional Patterns and Regional Economics," *Journal of Family History* 9 (1984): 158–77.

31 Gérard Bouchard, "L'histoire de la population et l'étude de la mobilité sociale au Saguenay, xixe–xxe siècle," *Recherches sociographiques* 17 (1976): 353–72, and copious other publications of the project "Recherches sur la société Saguenayenne."

32 Among the most important of these are: Betty Boyd Caroli et al. (eds), *The Italian Immigrant Woman in North America* (Toronto 1978); George E. Pozzetta (ed.), *Pane e Lavoro: The Italian American Working Class* (Toronto 1980); Robert Harney and J. Vincenza Scarpaci (eds), *Little Italies in North America* (Toronto 1981); Michael Karni (ed.), *The Finnish Diaspora*, 2 vols (Toronto 1981).

33 Volumes to date include W.S. Reid (ed.), *The Scottish Tradition in Canada* (Toronto 1976); G.M. Anderson and David Higgs, *A Future to Inherit: Portuguese Communities in Canada* (Toronto 1976); Peter D. Chimbos, *The Canadian Odyssey: The Greek Experience in Canada* (Toronto 1980); B. Abu-Labar, *An Olive Branch on the Family Tree: The Arabs in Canada* (Toronto 1980). For a devastating critique of this series and for a generally penetrating overview of the field see Roberto Perin, "Clio as an ethnic: the third force in Canadian historiography," *Canadian Historical Review* 64 (1983): 441–67.

34 The series includes: D.H. Avery, *The Poles in Canada* (Ottawa 1982); J.M. Bumsted, *The Scots in Canada* (Ottawa 1982); W. Peter Ward, *The Japanese in Canada* (Ottawa 1982); David Higgs, *The Portuguese in Canada* (Ottawa 1982).

35 For a sampling of this debate see: David Bercuson, "Through the Looking Glass of Culture: An Essay on the New Labour History and Working-class Culture in Recent Canadian Historical Writing,"

Labour/Le Travailleur 7 (1981): 95–112; Gregory S. Kealey, "Labour and Working-class History in Canada: Prospects in the 1980s," ibid., 67–94; Bryan Palmer, "Classifying Culture," *Labour/Le Travailleur* 8/9 (1981–2): 153–83; Ian McKay, "Historians, Anthropology, and the Concept of Culture," ibid., 185–241; Terry Morley, "Canada and the Romantic Left," *Queen's Quarterly* 86 (1979): 110–19; Bryan Palmer, "Working-class Canada: Recent Historical Writing," ibid., 594–616; Kenneth McNaught, "E.P. Thompson v. Harold Logan: Writing about Labour and the Left in the 1970s," *Canadian Historical Review* 63 (1981): 141–68; and Desmond Morton, "E.P. Thompson dans des arpents de neige: les historiens canadiens-anglais et la class ouvrière," *Revue d'histoire de l'amérique française* 37 (1983): 165–84.

36 Harold Logan, *History of Trade Union Organization in Canada* (Chicago 1928) and *Trade Unions in Canada* (Toronto 1948).

37 See, especially, McNaught and Bercuson articles cited in n. 35.

38 Critical reviews include David Brody in *Labour/Le Travailleur* 8/9 (1981–2): 361–4, and John Modell in *Histoire Sociale/Social History* 29 (1981): 283–5.

39 See, on the one hand, the review essay by Ramsay Cook, "The Making of Canadian Working-class History," *Historical Reflections* 10 (1983): 127–42 and, on the other, the review by David Bercuson in *Business History Review* 57 (1983): 589–91.

40 Palmer, *Working-Class Experience*.

41 For further development of this notion in the u.s. context, see Sean Wilentz, "Against Exceptionalism: Class Consciousness and the American Labor Movement," *International Labor and Working Class History* 26 (Fall 1984): 1–24 and Eric Foner, "Why is There No Socialism in the United States?" *History Workshop* 17 (Spring 1984): 57–80.

42 David Frank, "The Cape Breton Coal Miners, 1917–1926" (PHD diss., Dalhousie University, 1979); Frank, "Company Town/Labour Town: Local Government in the Cape Breton Coal Towns, 1917–1926," *Histoire Sociale/Social History* 27 (1981): 177–96; Ian McKay, "Industry, Work and Community in the Cumberland Coal Fields, 1848–1927" (PHD diss., Dalhousie University, 1983); Nolan Reilly, "The Emergence of Class Consciousness in Industrial Nova Scotia: A Study of Amherst, 1891–1925" (PHD diss., Dalhousie University, 1982); Reilly, "The General Strike in Amherst, Nova Scotia, 1919," *Acadiensis* 9 (1980): 56–77; Frank and Reilly, "The Emergence of the Socialist Movement in the Maritimes, 1899–1916," *Labour/Le Travailleur* 4 (1979): 84–114; and McKay, "Strikes in the Maritimes, 1900–1914," *Acadiensis* 13 (1983): 3–46.

43 Bryan Palmer, *Working-Class Experience: The Rise and Reconstitution of Canadian Labour, 1800–1980* (Toronto 1983); Gregory S. Kealey, "1919:

the Canadian Labour Revolt," *Labour/Le Travail* 13 (1984): 11–44; Craig
Heron, "Labourism and the Canadian Working Class," ibid., 45–76;
Larry Peterson, "The One Big Union in International Perspective:
Revolutionary Industrial Unionism, 1900–1925," *Labour/Le Travailleur*
7 (1981): 41–66; and Bryan D. Palmer, "Social Formation and Class
Formation in North America, 1800–1900," in David Levine (ed.),
Proletarianization and Family History (New York 1984), 229–309.
44 Some cited examples: L.M. Grayson and Michael Bliss (eds), *The
Wretched of Canada: Letters to R.B. Bennett, 1930–1935* (1971); Greg
Kealey (ed.), *Canada Investigates Industrialism* (1973); Alan Bowker (ed.),
The Social Criticism of Stephen Leacock (1973); Paul Rutherford (ed.),
Saving the Canadian City (1974); Veronica Strong-Boag (ed.), *A Woman
With a Purpose: The Diaries of Elizabeth Smith, 1872–1884* (1980).
Reprints include: E.W. Bradwin, *The Bunkhouse Man* (1972); W.L.
Mackenzie King, *Industry and Humanity* (1973); Catherine Cleverdon,
The Woman Suffrage Movement in Canada (1974); Leonard Marsh,
Report on Social Security in Canada (1975); League for Social Recon-
struction, *Social Planning for Canada* (1975); new monographs include
Geoffrey Bilson, *A Darkened House: Cholera in Nineteenth-Century
Canada* (1980); Judith Fingard, *Jack in Port* (1982); and Carol Lee
Bacchi, *Liberation Deferred? The Ideas of the English Canadian Suffragists,
1877–1918* (1983).
45 In order of publication: Terry Copp, *The Anatomy of Poverty: The Condition of the Working Class in Montreal 1892–1929* (1974); Michael Bliss, *A
Living Profit: Studies in the Social History of Canadian Business, 1883–
1911* (1974); Kealey and Warrian (eds), *Essays*; Susan Mann Trofimen-
koff and Alison Prentice (eds), *The Neglected Majority: Essays in Canadian Women's History* (1977); Alison Prentice, *The School Promoters:
Education and Social Class in Mid-Nineteenth-Century Upper Canada*
(1977); John Thompson, *The Harvest of War: The Prairie West, 1914–
1918* (1978); Avery, *"Dangerous Foreigners"* (1979); Howard Palmer,
Patterns of Prejudice: A History of Nativism in Alberta (1982); Joy Parr
(ed.), *Childhood and Family in Canadian History* (1982); and Tom
Traves (ed.), *Essays in Canadian Business History* (1984).
46 (Toronto 1982–4).

PART THREE

Studies of Class and Class Conflict

6 Orangemen and the Corporation: The Politics of Class in Toronto during the Union of the Canadas

Labour and politics in early Victorian Canada have received rather different treatments at the hands of historians. The former remained virtually ignored until the last decade, while the latter represented the major focus of historical writing. The rise of social history in Canada has commenced the process of investigating the lives of the common people, but has tended to ignore their roles in politics. Fortunately, the view that discussions of politics and the state, and hence of power, somehow belonged to an "old" history no longer prevails. A major task for historians has become the analysis of politics and political systems from a resolutely social perspective.[1] This analysis, especially a close scrutiny of the social basis of political cleavage, will make a contribution to our consideration of the interaction of class and politics.

In Victorian Toronto a major component of the political system was, of course, the Orange Order. An organization largely composed of plebeians and, later in the cities, proletarians, the order was a secret society with deep roots in the Irish struggle. Its proud trinity of crown, empire, and Protestantism provided its members with an ideological tradition, but one that had to be constantly reformulated in the Canadian context. While giving guidance in matters political, it promised no certainties as the bitter internal Orange conflicts of the period amply demonstrate.[2] Often viewed simply as a reactionary dogma, static and unchanging, the order has more often than not played the villain in liberal views of nineteenth-century Canadian history.

Attempts to study the Orange Order have proven controversial, and, more important, all have dismissed the utility of class analysis.

really?

In Barrie Dyster's thoughtful and sensitive study of pre-Confederation politics in Toronto,[3] it was proposed that there was a "relative absence of overt class associations or class politics in Toronto during the two decades between 1840 and 1860."[4] This thesis, combined with his argument that ethnic and religious identities substituted for those of class, fails to recognize the ways class was imbricated in these struggles. Indeed, it assumes that class is pre-eminently an economic category. Dyster, then, in his search for a recognizable "modern" version of class politics, fails to recognize what Przeworski did, that "classes are not given uniquely by any objective positions because they constitute effects of struggles, and these struggles are not determined uniquely by the relations of production. ... Class struggles are structured by the totality of economic, political, and ideological relations; and they have an autonomous effect on the process of class formation."

Simply, ethnicity and religion do not stand outside class. In this period of rapid class formation, class, even more than usual, cannot be found through the search for it as a determined sociological structure. Instead, class is to be discovered as a relationship, an effect of struggles, that is in constant motion as the process of class organization, disorganization, and reorganization continues. The search for the working class as a continuous, recognizable, historical subject in such a period is bound to fail, and yet class struggle was certainly not absent from Toronto or Canadian politics in this period.[5] As Dyster partially recognized, an older hegemonic system based on the gentry paternalism of the Family Compact was giving way to new forms of bourgeois hegemony. The class struggle involved battles between old and new segments of the Canadian élite, as well as the necessity of reintegrating the masses on some new basis as the older gentry/crowd relation dissolved.

The years of the Union of the Canadas were eventful ones, the story of responsible government and the genesis of Confederation being all too familiar. Yet when viewed from the perspectives of politically conscious Toronto Orangemen, these and the similar "great" political events of the period begin to take on an unfamiliar appearance. The order, though founded for many purposes, was a political machine that in Toronto was involved in some 29 riots over the thirty years from Durham to Confederation. No fewer than 16 of these had direct political inspiration. These 16 riots included 4 election poll battles, 4 altercations at public meetings, and 8 politically inspired effigy burnings and street demonstrations (see Table 6.1).

Table 6.1
Toronto Riots 1839–66

Date*	Occasion	Participants	Outcome
15 October	1839 Durham meeting	Orange, Corporation vs Reformers	Petition to Legislative Assembly
April	1840 Celebration of the Queen's marriage	Attack *Examiner* Orange, Corporation	
	1841 Election riot	Orange vs Reform: Election victory procession	Legislative Assembly investigation
	1841 Election riot (Streetsville)	Orange vs Reform	Controverted election
8 November	1843 Effigies of Baldwin and Hincks burned	Orange vs Party Processions Act	–
12 July	1844 Twelfth	Orange vs city magistrates	Trial
March	1849 Effigies of Mackenzie et al.	Orange vs Prominent Reform over Rebellion Losses	–
May	1849 Effigy of Elgin	As above	–
October	1849 Riot vs Elgin	As above	Trial
	1851 Attack Anti-Clergy Reserves meeting	Orange, Corporation vs Grits	–
	1851 As above	Orange, Corporation vs Grits	–
4 July	1853 Fight with Hibernians	Orange vs Green	–
27 July	1853 As above	Orange vs Green	–
3–4 January	1855 Municipal election poll riot	Orange	Trial and controverted election
29 June	1855 Fire riot	Police vs firemen	Trial
July	1855 Circus riot	Orange crowd vs circus	Trial
January	1857 Municipal election poll riot	–	–
12 July	1857 Attack on policemen	Orange vs Green	Trial
12 July	1857 Attack on Catholic cathedral	?	–
August	1857 Omnibus riot	Carters	–
17 March	1858 St. Patrick's Day procession	Orange vs Green	Trial
12 July	1858 Twelfth	Orange vs Green	Trial
August	1859 Agnes Street parkland	?	–
September	1860 Visit of Prince of Wales	Orange	–
October	1860 Melinda Street riot	Firemen vs rolling mill workers	

Table 6.1 (continued)

Date*	Occasion	Participants	Outcome
	1861 Fire department demonstration	Firemen vs police	–
	1863 Separate schools	Orange	–
May	1864 Corpus Christi procession	Orange	–
November	1864 Guy Fawkes Day	Hibernian	–

*This list is not necessarily comprehensive. It is based on the Toronto press and on Orange sources. It certainly does not include every incidence of assault or rowdyism at election time.

Toronto had gained incorporation as a city in 1834 with a population of around 9,000. By 1848 the city had grown to 23,000, and Irish famine immigrants swelled that to over 30,000 by the time of the 1850 census. The city had reached almost 45,000 by 1861. At the time of the first religious census of the city in 1841 the city was approximately 17 per cent Roman Catholic. The Catholic proportion of the population had grown to 25 per cent by 1848, and this held constant with minor 1 per cent increases in the two subsequent decennial censuses.[6] The city's steady growth and shifting demographic composition were more than matched by its economic transformation as industrialization marched forward. The coming of the railways, protective tariffs, and the impetus provided by the American Civil War all provided Toronto's nascent industrialists with significant opportunities of which they were quick to take advantage.[7]

With industrial transformation came a growing wage-earning class and significant growth in trade union activity. The 1850s saw perhaps the first and certainly the most sustained period of widespread labour militancy in Canada to that point.[8] In Toronto, there were at least fourteen strikes in the years 1852–54, a level of strike activity not to be matched again until the labour upsurge surrounding the shorter-hours movement of 1872.[9] When combined with the massive unrest on Canadian public works in the 1840s and 1850s, it becomes only too clear that these decades witnessed the emergence of overt class conflict on a scale previously unknown in Canada.[10] Trade unionism was, however, only one of the effective and growing working-class institutions of this period. Workers were active in others. While primarily organized on ethno-religious lines, these organizations nevertheless performed services of great import for their primarily working class members. In the Irish Roman Catholic community, there was the Hibernian Benevolent Society, in the Protestant and British community, the Orange Order.

ethno-religion groups.

The Orange Order was active in Toronto at least from the early
1820s, and some accounts put its arrival in the late 1810s. As early as
1823, Toronto Reformer William Warren Baldwin tried to introduce
legislation to ban the order. The formal history of Orangeism in
Canada, however, commences with Ogle Robert Gowan's creation of
a Canadian grand lodge in 1830.[11] Subsequently, 12 lodges were
founded in Toronto in the 1830s, 17 in the 1840s, and 15 in the
1850s,[12] the lodge structure in Toronto remaining stable in the 1860s
with some 20 functioning lodges. The membership in these lodges
fluctuated, but for the late 1850s and early 1860s there were approximately 1,100–1,200 full members of the order in Toronto.[13] In an
adult male non-Catholic population of around 8,000, this 15 per cent
obviously played a significant role. Indeed, when we remember that
many of the non-members probably had passed through lodges at
some point in their lives, one is struck by the pervasiveness of the
institution.

In Toronto there were two main theatres of organized politics after
1834. The first was the Corporation. Although ostensibly non-partisan
throughout the period, there was never any doubt about the Corporation's politics. Following the delegitimation of Reform after the
Rebellions were suppressed, the Corporation developed into a impene-
trable bastion of Orange-Tory strength. Toronto mayors throughout
this period, while drawn from various elements of both the dying
patrician order and the emerging bourgeois community, often shared
titular membership in the Orange Order and always found themselves
in an uneasy relationship to the order's plebeian demands. This tense
reciprocity held equally true for aldermen and councillors, two of
whom were elected from each of Toronto's wards (five until 1847,
when a sixth ward was added, and then a seventh in 1853). Until 1859
the elected members of council then chose the mayor. In 1859 popular election of the mayor was instituted, but it survived only until
1866, when the choice was returned to the elected council. Although
the Tory hold on the mayor's chair was broken briefly in 1859–60
with the election of Adam Wilson, Toronto voters quickly returned to
tried and true Tory politicians for the remainder of the period of
popular elections (see Table 6.2). John George "The 10,000 pound
job" Bowes and Francis Henry "Old Squaretoes" Medcalf restored the
Tory ascendancy by holding the mayor's office from 1861 to 1866.

Toronto's second political theatre was provincial. The city elected
two members to the legislative assembly of the Canadas. They were
elected at large for the entire city until 1861 when the city was split
into Toronto West and Toronto East, with one member for each constituency. The city remained predominantly Conservative throughout

Table 6.2
Mayors of Toronto 1840–66

Year	Mayor	Occupation	Political affiliation	Birthplace
1840	John Powell	Lawyer	Compact	Canada
1841	George Munro	Merchant	Tory	Scotland
1842–4	Henry Sherwood	Lawyer	Compact	Canada
1845–7	William Henry Boulton	Lawyer	Compact	Canada
1848–50	George Gurnett	Journalist	Conservative	England
1851–3	John George Bowes	Merchant	Conservative	Ireland
1854	Joshua George Beard	Merchant	Conservative	England
1855	George William Allan	Lawyer	Compact	Canada
1856	John Beverley Robinson, Jr	Lawyer	Compact	Canada
1857	John Hutchison	Merchant	Conservative	Scotland
1858*	William Henry Boulton	(see 1845)		
1859–60†	Sir Adam Wilson	Lawyer	Reformer	Scotland
1861–3	John George Bowes	(see 1851)		
1864–6	Francis Henry Medcalf	Foundry owner	Orange	Ireland

*Boulton resigned on 8 November 1858 and was succeeded for the two remaining months of his term by David Breakenridge Read, a lawyer.
†From 1859 to 1866 mayors were directly elected.
SOURCE: Victor L. Russell *Mayors of Toronto I: 1834–1899*

the period, returning Reformers only in 1841, with the extraordinary efforts of Lord Sydenham, in 1857 and 1858 when George Brown managed to win a seat, and in 1863 when the separate school issue led to the return of two Toronto Reformers. Thus of the nineteen provincial campaigns fought in Toronto in the Union period, Reformers won only six times (see Table 6.3).

What was the Corporation and what was its political hold on the loyalties of the Toronto Orangemen, who were universally recognized to have constituted its core and were continuously condemned as its enforcers? The elected council stood at the centre of the Corporation, but the Corporation's appointed officials also provided strength. In the 1840s and 1850s the number of positions under council patronage was limited, but they included the city clerk, the city treasurer, the city inspector, the deputy inspector of licences, the police force (initially consisting of the high bailiff and four constables), two assessors, and five tax collectors. (Chief constables and chief engineers 1840–66 are listed in Table 6.4.) Added to these offices, however, were the equally important patronage powers of licensing the city's inns and taverns and carters and cabmen, of hiring labourers for corporation work, and of appointing special constables in unusual circumstances such as for the supervision of elections.

Table 6.3
Legislative Assembly Election in 1841–66

Year	Type of election	Winning candidates	Losing candidates
1841	General	J.H. Dunn*	H. Sherwood
		Isaac Buchanan*	George Munro
1843	By-election	H. Sherwood	Captain J.S. Macaulay
1844	General	H. Sherwood	J.H. Dunn*
		W.H. Boulton	
1847	General	H. Sherwood	J. Beaty*
		W.H. Boulton	
1851	General	G.P. Ridout	H. Sherwood
		W.H. Boulton	T. O'Neill*
			F.C. Capreol
1853	By-election	H. Sherwood	O.R. Gowan
1854	General	J.H. Cameron	H. Sherwood
		J.G. Bowes	W.H. Boulton
			G.P. Ridout
1857	General	G. Brown*	W.H. Boulton
		J.B. Robinson, Jr	J.G. Bowes
1858	By-election	G. Brown*	J.H. Cameron
1861	General	J. Crawford	G. Brown*
		J.B. Robinson, Jr	A. Wilson*
1863	General	A.M. Smith*	J. Crawford
		J. MacDonald*	J.B. Robinson, Jr

*Reform candidates
SOURCE: Toronto press 1840–63

Table 6.4
Chief Constables and Chief Engineers of Toronto 1840–66

Chief constables 1840–66	
1837–46	George Kingsmill
1847–52	George L. Allen
1852–8	Samuel Sherwood
1859–73	Captain William S. Prince

Chief engineers 1840–66	
1838–41	Thomas D. Harris
1842–6	Robert Beard
1847	James Armstrong
1851–77	James Ashfield

SOURCE: J.E. Middleton, *The Municipality of Toronto* (Toronto 1923), 788–9

This combination of positions and favours endowed the council with an extraordinary network that touched plebeian life in numerous places.

Control of the publicans, for example, provided the Corporation with crucial support. The inroads of the temperance movement were still relatively weak, and the tavern was central to working-class life. As one critic of the system noted: "The power of licensing or rather deciding upon the qualifications of applicants for licenses ... will and must inevitably be abused if entrusted to the caprice of an elected magistracy. It will be prostituted to seduce the wavering, to reward the compliant, to punish the refractory. The influence exercised by tavern keepers at public elections is notorious, and we feel that the means which the existing corporation have employed for securing or coercing this influence are sufficient to justify the preceding observation." Our best description of the intricacies of this process comes from the report of the commissioners appointed to investigate the 1841 Toronto election riot.[14] No fewer than five tavern keepers or former tavern keepers testified that they had lost or now expected to lose their licences for having opposed the Corporation's candidates in the first legislative assembly elections of the United Canadas. Irish publican Peter Harkin, for example, explained that upon his arrival in Toronto in 1840 he was instructed to apply to an alderman for a tavern licence. In return for a small bribe (£2) he received a licence, and the same alderman later helped defend him against an earlier charge of unlicensed selling and had his fine remitted. Shortly thereafter, however, Harkin refused to support the Tory candidates in the coming election. He was then offered £30 or £5 a day to keep open house for Tory candidates. He again refused and later cast his vote for the Sydenham candidates. Following those events his old fine was executed and he was subsequently charged and fined for refusing to help fight a fire.[15]

This pattern of rewarding friends and punishing enemies was also described by John Lindsay, former city constable, Irish publican, and Orangeman. After a short stint as a city constable, Lindsay had become the proprietor of the North of Ireland Tavern. He attributed his successes in both positions to his prominence in the Orange Order. In 1839, however, he decided to attend the Durham meeting held on Yonge Street, north of Toronto. Before this meeting he was asked by City Inspector William Davis, acting on the behest of Clarke Gamble and the Corporation, to attend the Durham meeting to oppose the Reformers. His noncommittal response, and his later refusal to don a purple ribbon offered by Alderman Alexander Dixon who was riding in a wagon with Alderman John Armstrong and four city

[margin notes: "Importance of the tavern", "tavern & politics"]

constables, began his problems. Lindsay's indignation at the constables' subsequent attack on the Reformers, which was led by Sheriff William B. Jarvis, with obvious aldermanic approval, caused him to support the Reformers when the meeting divided. This was duly noted by the sheriff who indicated that he would pay later. And so Lindsay did. He was refused his licence renewal and then prosecuted when he continued to sell. During the 1841 election campaign both Tory candidates offered him a licence in return for his support, and later City Inspector Davis also indicated that money and an open house designation were his in return for abstaining, or at least splitting his vote. He again refused and after the election was again charged with selling without a licence. His frequent petitions for a licence also failed.[16]

The importance of taverns in plebeian life cannot be overestimated. At its incorporation in 1834, Toronto had approximately 78 taverns, or one for every 120 individuals.[17] According to testimony before the 1841 Riot Commission, the Reform council of Dr Thomas David Morrison had reduced this to 36 by 1836–37. The return of a Tory council to power had led to a massive growth in taverns (119) and the additional ubiquitous beer licences (21).[18] This total of 140 licensed drinking places provided a legal bar for approximately every 100 Torontonians, the largest numbers of the period. In addition, there were reputed to be many unlicensed houses. A quick perusal of the licences issued for 1841 turns up Corporation stalwarts such as John "Tory" Earls, City Inspector Davis, Deputy Inspector of Licences James Bell, and Constable Thomas Earls.[19]

The Tories in this period appear to have been manipulating their licensing control to allow the tavern to expand. This growth in licences would eventually work against them when respectable Torontonians, increasingly influenced by evangelical reform, began to demand stringent enforcement. Nevertheless customary plebeian culture, supported and extended by the Corporation in return for electoral aid, would later prove extremely resistant to attempts at regulation. The small riots and frequent attacks on licence inspectors that commenced in the 1850s became a familiar component of cultural struggle in late Victorian Toronto, despite the city's later familiar "dry" reputation.

One example of the Corporation's use of drinking places was Allen's Coleraine Tavern, which provided a home for a number of Orange lodges, an open house for the unsuccessful Monro-Sherwood party in the 1841 election campaign, and a launching pad for the subsequent riot. Further, Allen was identified by a number of witnesses as the man who had recruited the Orangemen from the outlying area who were the aggressors in the day's violence. There was also persuasive testimony that Sherwood's brother, Samuel, later Toronto's police chief, had put Allen up to this. The ostensible rationale for the riot was the rumour that the victorious Reform procession would carry two coffins labelled "The Corporation" and "The Family Compact." Clearly, as the riot demonstrated, the Corporation was far from dead, no matter what the election result.[20]

Tavern licences were but one part of the Corporation's elaborate system. Cartage and cab licences were used in a similar fashion. Perhaps more important, however, was the control that the Corporation enjoyed over the police force. The appointment of the high bailiff and the constables provided far more than jobs for loyal Orangemen. A monopoly of legal violence, and the power to choose when to enforce the law, were significant weapons. Again the 1841 commissioners noted:

A force thus constituted must be liable, in times of political excitement, to be employed as political instruments in behalf of those to whom the corporation may be friendly. The authority legally vested in these men, their habitual intercourse with the lower classes, the impression that they possess the ear of their employers, the favouritism they may be enabled to suggest, the petty and indirect tyranny they may be permitted to exercise, all combine to degrade a force of this nature into formidable engines of oppression; and when we find, as in the late election, that the Corporation has cast itself into the political arena as a hot partizan of one of its own party – the Mayor of the City – in a bitter and unsuccessful contest, we can hardly be surprised that a stringent and unscrupulous use has been made of the machinery at their disposal.[21]

The commissioners' call for a "well-regulated and efficient police force ... appointed, directed, and governed by authorities remote from, superior to, and independent of local bias or interference" found little initial support, although, as we shall see, by the late 1850s this view would become dominant. In the meantime Orange membership was the major credential for a position on the Toronto police, a force which, like other urban police forces, expanded rapidly in the 1840s and 1850s. Francis Hincks, for example, recounted on numerous occasions the story of the promotion of Constable Wallace to a permanent position on the Toronto police, after his attack on Hincks during the Yonge Street riot of 1839.[22]

At the centre of the informal Corporation world was City Inspector Davis. With responsibility for public works and therefore a labour force, he stood at the centre of the city's patronage network. Naturally, it was he who orchestrated the more vociferous support of the Corporation when it was needed. Davis has been termed the "marshall of the mob"[23] by one historian, and the *Globe* called him the man "who has bullied the inhabitants of the city for many years, who has ruled the corporation with a rod of iron, who knows all the corporation rascalities from the beginning to the end, who controls the town elections as he thinks proper, the bosom friend and pitcher of Mr. Henry Sherwood."[24] Not too surprisingly, when Davis finally was removed from office by Mayor William Henry Boulton in 1845, the *Globe* greeted the news with considerable enthusiasm. Other members of the Corporation remained less convinced, and the mayor faced a serious challenge to his prerogative to fire without consulting the council. The central issue raised by the firing of Davis was control of the police. Boulton had removed Constable George Earls from the force for drunkenness. Earls, the brother of infamous Orange innkeeper and carter John "Tory" Earls, found an avid supporter in Davis, who apparently spread the rumour that Boulton himself had been drinking on the evening in question.[25] This proved too much for Boulton who, while an alderman in 1841, had failed in an early attempt to get Davis fired. Davis meanwhile re-emerged shortly thereafter as an elected councillor and continued to play an important Corporation role.[26]

When William Coffin and Nicholas Fullam, the Toronto riot commissioners, summarized their 1841 investigation into the workings of the Corporation, they concluded with a full assault on Orangeism. "Spread extensively through the City of Toronto," the order's "evil influence" was "direct, obvious and tangible." Moreover, the order's "portentous influence aggravated the evils of political acrimony and revived feuds and feelings, religious prejudices and party animosities, which had almost ceased to exist." The commissioners concluded: "The existence of Orangeism in this Province is a great and growing evil, which should be discountenanced, denounced, and repressed by the exercise of every authority and influence at the disposal of the Government."[27]

The proposal was quickly acted on. In 1842 the ministry of Robert Baldwin successfully introduced electoral reforms that were primarily aimed at Orangeism. The new law, which proved ineffective and was seldom enforced, outlawed the exhibiting of party flags and colours, treating at public places, the carrying of firearms, assault and battery, and bribery during elections. It also introduced multiple polling stations to diffuse the potential for violence, separated the nomination process from the polling for the same reason, and limited the polling to two days.[28]

174 Studies of Class and Class Conflict

Equally ineffectual, as it turned out, but far more bitterly contested were two further Baldwin reforms, the Party Processions Act and the Secret Societies Act of 1843. Although Parliament passed both, only the first was enacted, because Governor-General Lord Metcalfe reserved the latter for British consideration and it was subsequently disallowed.

In Parliament the opposition to these measures was led by Toronto Orange spokesmen Henry Sherwood and George Duggan. Sherwood, scion of the Brockville élite, had transferred his political career to the metropolis, where he found himself dependent on Orange support. Duggan, in contrast, owed his very presence in politics to his prominence in the order. The debate itself was initially focused on the pseudo-issue of the right to appeal under the Party Processions Act, but the discussion heated up considerably when the true anti-Orange motives of the act were alluded to in Francis Hincks's attack on Duggan for his role in the 1839 Yonge Street riot and for Orange violence at the poll in his election victory in York county, which was later successfully challenged by the loser. Duggan responded by accusing the government of trying to outlaw its opposition; if the violent acts described by Hincks were so reprehensible, why had there been no indictments? And again invoking the straw man of the right of appeal, he closed: "They will not put down these evils by any moderate means; no it must be by the iron heel of power, and the victim must be imprisoned whether guilty or not."[29]

The debate on the outlawing of all secret societies except the Masons, which in effect meant only the Orange Order, was even more heated and ended in the expulsion of Tory leader Allan MacNab from the assembly by the Speaker. Here again Sherwood and Duggan were prominent, with the former wisely warning that such proscription would fuel the growth of the order and the latter defending Orangemen's loyalty. This bill was also opposed by some moderates who felt it went too far. Toronto Orangemen certainly thought so, and after the bills were passed they gathered in front of Baldwin's residence to burn him and Francis Hincks in effigy. The aim of Baldwin's bill was clear enough. Under its terms members of a secret society would be barred from jury service and holding office under the crown and any innkeeper or tavern keeper who allowed secret societies to meet on his premises would have his licence revoked. Duggan's argument that such a bill was aimed at breaking the back of the political opposition to Reform highlights the crucial Orange basis of Tory support.[30]

The Orange response too should be noted. Orangemen took to the streets, for, like other plebeian groups, they assumed that the streets were theirs for political purposes. Gathering between 11 p.m. and midnight, a large body of Orangemen paraded with a cart, on which was mounted a gallows bearing effigies of Baldwin and Hincks. The effigies wore the label "traitors," and the cart was decorated with Orange slogans including "No Surrender." With the accompaniment of "the most indecent ribaldry," the effigies were burned at the house of Dr W.W. Baldwin.[31] This resort to effigy burning, which would be common in Toronto for the next decade, was an established form of plebeian political protest. Needless to say, the attempt to deny them the streets for their marches only further entrenched the crucial importance of the 12 July processions. Those, like John Neilson, who predicted that such prohibitive legislation would increase the strength of the order proved correct.

Tory opposition mounted quickly. "Never will these societies, and the Orangemen of Canada in particular, forget the debt of hatred they owe to the party who have cast shame and obloquy upon them."[32] Moreover, the various 1843 pieces of Reform legislation and the breakdown of Sydenham's carefully constructed alliance certainly did not help John Henry Dunn, who was trounced by Henry Sherwood and W.H. Boulton in the 1844 parliamentary election in Toronto. Reformers unsuccessfully protested the result, alleging bribery, corruption, illegal oaths, and the "gross partiality of the Returning officer." Reform opinion rationalized the defeat by blaming "the corporation which has always been a political body supporting the Family Compact tyranny." The methods of the Corporation involved "spending immense sums of money every week in various buildings and improvements in the city, by which means they are able to secure the votes of hundreds and to intimidate many more. They have the control of licensing taverns, carters, and cabmen, and it is well known that these bodies are nearly in every individual case Orangemen."[33]

The attempt at banning the order proved ineffectual, not only because of Orange intransigence but also because Governor-General Metcalfe soon found himself fighting his Reform ministry and thus of necessity turning to the Tories and their Orange allies.[34] Ironically, Gowan, the Orange grand master, enjoyed perhaps his greatest political influence in the middle years of the decade as a trusted adviser to the new Tory ministry. These were relatively quiet years, partially, no doubt, because of the order's political prominence. Orange leaders initially tried to prevent any too overt testing of the Party Processions Act, although many of their followers refused to heed their advice. In Toronto, for example, the first 12 July after the ban saw the Orange leadership lead its members on an excursion to Niagara Falls. This intentional ploy to prevent a direct challenge to

the act almost backfired when some 1,500–2,000 Irish Catholic navvies employed on the Welland Canal turned out to prevent any procession. The timely intervention of Niagara magistrates prevented a
riot, when they managed to convince the outnumbered Toronto Orangemen that discretion was the better part of valour and that disarm-
ing and avoiding party tunes would maintain the peace. Meanwhile,
in Toronto itself, Orangemen from outside the city refused to obey
the injunction against demonstrations and instead marched into the
city. On this occasion, undoubtedly because this contravened the
Orange design as well as the law, the Toronto magistrates intervened.
Led by important Orange aldermen George Gurnett and Alexander
Dixon, a saddler, the Toronto constables met the procession and
ordered it to disband. The response was a donnybrook in which Gurnett was assaulted. Following the reading of the Riot Act, a number of
arrests were made. Not surprisingly, at least one of those arrested had
been involved in the 1841 election riot.[35]

The return to power of a Conservative ministry in late 1844 ended
such difficulties, and Toronto Orangemen proceeded to march on the
twelfth with regularity for the rest of the decade, blatantly repudiating
the law. These processions were relatively quiet, and, although they
were formally illegal, no action was taken against them, despite the
frequent complaints of the Reform papers.[36]

In this brief interlude of relative quiet the fights in Toronto
occurred within the Conservative forces and focused on the growing
tension between the rising plebeian elements of the party and the
older, declining patricians – the Compact Tories. Constantly acting as
mediators in these struggles were the "Corporation Beauties," as the
Globe termed the aldermanic corps. Prominent in this role were
figures such as George Gurnett and the Beard brothers, who acted as
a "sturdy bridge between the compact gentry and the mass of horny-
handed townsmen within that predominant caste of post-Rebellion
Torontonians who professed strident loyalism."[37] This tension was
manifest in the fight to remove City Inspector Davis; but the conflict
was also apparent before provincial elections, when it was necessary
to nominate Tory candidates for the city. In 1844, for example, an
initial attempt to place G.P. Ridout on the ballot was resisted by
Orangemen who felt Ridout was insufficiently loyal.[38] The Corporation's choice was former Mayor George Munro, but the nomination
instead went to William Henry Boulton, who was acceptable to both
patricians and aspiring bourgeoisie. Boulton, although a descendant
of the Compact, appears as an example of the transitional political
figures who, despite their patrician roots, were not too proud to play
the emerging democratic game. Returned in 1844 to the legislature,

he was to enjoy the faithful support of Toronto voters until his financial difficulties of the late 1840s and early 1850s publicly embarrassed him.[39] His patrician tendencies, however, remained evident in his remarkable propensity to resign public office when he failed to get his own way.

Other Irish and Orange political figures continued to encounter resistance. Ogle Gowan, for example, used these relatively quiet years to pursue his goal of Irish political unity and the conversion of the Tory party into a moderate political force prefiguring the Liberal Conservative party of Sir John A. Macdonald. He paid dearly, however, for his Orange connections and his battles with the Compact Tories. This combination of disabilities kept him out of the cabinet. Ironically, he also lost the leadership of the order in 1846 to Belleville's George Benjamin, who appears to have been a better administrator than Gowan and also a more traditional Tory in his attitudes, especially toward the Anglican church.[40] Other Irish politicians with close ties to the Orange Order also suffered from Gowan's disability. Former Orange District Master George Duggan, for example, made a determined try for the Toronto mayor's chair on numerous occasions and failed. He came closest in 1847 by opposing incumbent Boulton on avowedly national grounds. His narrow 12 to 11 defeat pitted Compact Tories and a few Reformers against his Orange supporters, although the alliances were also coloured by the ongoing war between the Denisons and the Boultons, the great families of St Patrick's Ward. With the exception of the patrician lawyer Robert Baldwin Sullivan in 1835, the only Irish-born, council-selected mayor in this period was successful merchant John George Bowes, 1851–53. When popular election arrived briefly in the late 1850s and early 1960s Toronto voters chose two Irishmen of the three mayors elected – Bowes again, 1861–63, and (more significantly) Orange leader, former machinist, and foundry-owner Francis Henry Metcalf, 1864–66, the first Toronto mayor who was not a lawyer, merchant, or journalist[41] (see Table 6.3). The 1847 provincial election disaster for the Tories was not reflected in Toronto, where Boulton and Sherwood easily won re-election. The sole Reform candidate, James Beaty, tried to make much of his mechanic background but to no avail. The *Globe* complained in the aftermath of the election that "Toronto was not ripe for freedom" and blamed "the retainers and toadies of the Corporation" for the defeat.[42]

The return to power of a new Reform ministry in 1848 and the crisis that ensued brought the few years of harmony to a rapid and violent close. Yet before analysing the series of savage conflicts surrounding the Rebellion Losses Act and the Annexation Manifesto, it is worth noting the democratic reforms undertaken by this Reform ministry. Baldwin's Municipal Corporations Act of 1849 completed the work commenced by Sydenham in 1841 of bringing elective government to the local level. Until 1842 the appointed justices of the peace meeting in the court of quarter sessions had held all responsibility in the area of local government. In the pre-rebellion period the Reformers and William Lyon Mackenzie had backed the popular election of the magistrates, but this reform had not been accomplished. The 1840 Sydenham legislation had provided the districts with their first elected councils, though limiting the franchise and office-holding to the successful and retaining a central government veto. Baldwin had tried to extend these actions with his 1843 Municipal Act, but though it passed the assembly it was not implemented after the Baldwin ministry resigned. The succeeding Tory government failed to act in the field with the exception of a moderate democratic extension in 1846, when the elected councils were allowed to choose their own warden from among the elected councillors and to appoint their own officials.

Every commentator on these acts has recognized them as an attack on the old Tory magistracy. The extension of democracy to the local level, while still limited, nevertheless incorporated a broader populace into the electoral process. Baldwin asserted this as a major rationale of the act, arguing that local institutions would have "the effect of creating a school of practical statesmen." The 1849 act also finally regularized the legislative framework for urban areas which until then had evolved through specific pieces of legislation for each newly incorporated town or city.[43]

But what of the crisis of 1849? How did Toronto Orangemen deal with the most significant challenge of this period to their ideology? Not too surprisingly, they reacted in the streets. In March, May, and again in October, Toronto Orangemen expressed their discontent in riotous gatherings. In March they greeted the news of the Rebellion Losses Act and the return to Toronto of William Lyon Mackenzie with a procession with effigies that visited the homes of prominent Toronto Reformers. In front of Robert Baldwin's house the effigies of Baldwin and Francis Hincks were burned, along with numerous tar barrels. The crowd then visited the house of John McIntosh, where Mackenzie had been staying, and threatened to wreck it. Instead they only broke windows and doors and then marched to the houses of Dr John Rolph and of George Brown, where similar actions ensued.

Predictably, Reform opinion was infuriated, especially when no charges were laid. A number of Torontonians petitioned Lord Elgin for an investigation, arguing that they were "at the mercy of a drunken, reckless mob, which may at any moment issue forth from the low taverns and brothels of the city and make the political opinions of their victims a pretext for violence and proceed to attack the dwellings and threaten the lives of those who may happen to have incurred their displeasure."[44] Moreover, as the *Globe* pointed out, apparently the only Torontonians who remained unaware of the crowd's plans before the attack were Mayor Gurnett and High Bailiff Allen. Two other members of the Corporation, Aldermen Dempsey and Denison, played prominent roles in leading the crowd. Thus, when Gurnett responded to press criticism by trying to set up an investigation, his council flatly refused. Alderman Denison argued that the government was at fault since it had first refused to hang Mackenzie and now allowed him to return to Toronto. He asserted: "If it were not for the law I would not scruple a minute to take his life." Alderman Duggan then attacked the mayor for calling out the troops on the following evening to prevent a recurrence of the rioting. Finally, rather than support the mayor's call for an investigation of the riot, the council instead endorsed the crowd's opposition to the Rebellion Losses Act.[45]

Approximately one month later, and following a week of riots in Montreal which included the burning of the Parliament buildings, the Toronto crowd also rallied to demonstrate its opposition to Elgin's signing of the Rebellion Losses Act. Some 100–150 Orangemen met in a Queen Street tavern and then marched to city hall. This procession had been formally announced early in the week, so on this occasion the mayor had called out the military. When the crowd carrying the effigy of Elgin reached city hall, it was met by the mayor, the council, and the troops. The soldiers were present, however, only to guarantee the safety of the citizenry's property, and they did not interfere with the effigy burning. Alderman Beard, the city's deputy sheriff, was accused by the *Globe* of having led the procession. His subsequent denial claimed that he had only appeared to be leading the crowd because in his official capacity he had convinced the crowd not to attack the homes of John McIntosh, John Rolph, and John Montgomery.[46]

There was, of course, considerable fear by officials of what 12 July would bring in 1849. Yet Elgin's and Russell's cool and confident predictions that "nothing of consequence" would occur proved accurate and Toronto remained relatively quiet.[47] In Hamilton Orangemen marched with arms[48] and in the St Catharines area there was a fatal encounter between Roman Catholic navvies and Orangemen celebrating the Battle of the Boyne in a tavern.[49] The relative quiet in Toronto led one local Reformer and secret Elgin informant to write dismissively of the "constant meetings and caballings of the Orange associations," which he was certain signified little. He assured Elgin that "the late attempt at a riot here, the effigy burning, and all the demonstrations of the same character, were the work of a few Tory aldermen" and that the "masses took no interest." Moreover, the 12 July procession had involved only 400 Orangemen, which suggested to him that "respectable Orangemen were ashamed of Annexation."[50]

There can be no question that the ranks were now indeed split. The extensive involvement of Ontario Orange leaders such as Gowan in the British American League eventually provided the institutional wherewithal to break openly with annexation, but it took them a considerable length of time to clarify their position. Meanwhile, anonymous broadside writers had a field-day as they tried to rally the forces of loyal Protestant Britons to the cause. In August, for example, Toronto citizens awakened to find emblazoned on their city's walls:

PROCLAMATION
"TO YOUR TENTS, O, ISRAEL"
BRITONS OF THE CITY OF TORONTO – BRITONS OF THE HOME DISTRICT

Shall the rank rebels be permitted to tell that they will drive the bloody Tories out of the country? Up to your duty and let us no more slumber! The Political Judas Iscariot [Elgin] ... is expected to arrive in Toronto ... Shall Elgin ... be permitted to be welcomed by a gang of sneaking radicals, in the good old loyal city of Toronto? No! No! Forbid it heaven! Forbid it every principle of honour! By the memory of our fathers, who filled bloody though honourable graves rather than surrender their civil and religious freedom to a tyrannical and bigoted sovereign ... we publicly and solemnly warn the individual who calls himself James Bruce [Elgin] and his rebel partizans, against any attempt to outrage and insult the feelings of the Loyalist of Toronto by making a party triumph of his visit to Toronto – that is if he or they should dare to come ... Think of that Britishers of Toronto. Consequently, let your eggs be stale and your gunpowder dry! Down with Elgin! – Down with the rebels![51]

This was matched by another broadside in the following month from "The Watcher":

AWAKE! TREACHERY! TREASON!

Men of 1837 and '38, the plot has leaked out. For the purpose of receiving Rebel-rewarding Elgin ... hundreds of armed cutthroats have been hired to pour into Toronto ... to massacre the loyal inhabitant and to destroy their houses and property ... therefore perfect your Organization. Arm! Arm! Arm! Forward from the country! Forward from the city![52]

Opposition of this kind made it essential that Elgin visit the city. As his secret adviser in Toronto noted: "The time has come when His Excellency must go everywhere he chooses without hesitation. To pass Toronto would be too marked in any case and particularly after all the press has said about it and would be trumpeted as a concession to fear. That sort of impression going abroad would be very unfortunate and would beget mobs."[53] So on 9 October 1849 Elgin arrived in Toronto. His proposed visit had set off great debates over the nature of the address to present him. Tory MP Henry Sherwood's was rejected as too favourable, especially by W.H. Boulton, while Alderman Denison's was rejected as too partisan. A compromise was reached by Alderman Samuel Thompson, whose address noted the great disagreements raging in Toronto but nevertheless pledged the city's loyalty to Britain and to the queen's representative.[54] The unity apparent in this compromise was not shared by all Torontonians. Although Elgin was guarded by Denison's cavalry company, a few eggs still managed to find the governor-general's carriage on his arrival. That evening a crowd of 200 gathered and marched, with torches and an effigy of Elgin, on Elijah's Hotel on King Street. After an initial skirmish with the police, who ordered the crowd to disperse, it regrouped at the hotel, where a larger body of constables and the mayor met them. Arrests were made and the crowd dispersed. With unusual alacrity, which left even the *Globe* and the *Examiner* praising the magistrates, thirteen men were charged with riotous assembly and assault and another three with ringing the fire-bell when there was no fire. The fire-bells, under the control of Orange fire companies, were the standard Orange call to arms. Among those arrested for bell ringing were a tailor and two young O'Briens, one the son of Colonel E.G. O'Brien, the proprietor of the *Patriot*, and the other his cousin, the son of Dr Lucius O'Brien, a professor at King's College and the editor of the *Patriot*. Among those charged with assault and riotous assembly were a tailor, a shoemaker, a labourer, a carter, a confectioner, a tinsmith, and an innkeeper, and two Orange council members, the infamous William Davis and John Carr, later Toronto Orange district master.[55]

These arrests continued the debate about whether effigy burning was illegal in itself. This debate came to a head when Chief Justice Robinson instructed a grand jury that the burning of effigies was definitely illegal. Robinson had argued:

There seems to be a growing disposition to manifest displeasure by burning in effigy. As the exhibitions are indecent and insulting and have a tendency to lead to tumult, it is proper that it should be understood that by the law of England, and the law of Upper Canada is the same, the burning or hanging of any person in effigy openly and publicly, even without a tumultuous assemblage, is a misdemeanour punishable with fine or imprisonment or both and is a kind of libel ... and where the object is to bring odium on the government and its measures, it becomes then seditious in its character and exposes those concerned in it to be punished for that offence.

Here we have the reigning monarch of the Compact's remnants making quite clear that plebeian violence could no longer be tolerated.[56] Orange crowds battling "Yankee republicans" in the guise of radicals in the 1830s or attacking the alleged disloyalty of the Reform alliance of the 1840s had served Compact Tory, and later Corporation, aims well. The arrival of responsible government, while still uncertain in 1849, would make such politics an embarrassing anachronism in the 1850s, especially when they threatened the Conservative alliance with the Lower Canadian *Bleus*.

The willingness of the Toronto magistracy to break up this riot, partially on this basis, was carried through at the following assizes, when the thirteen were actually tried and three were convicted. Defended by Orange Aldermen George Duggan and Richard Dempsey, the rioters continued to claim that they had done nothing illegal in trying to burn an effigy, that the police had had no rights to interfere, and that the defendants had thus only engaged in legitimate self-defence. Here we have a defence of traditional plebeian political practice against the new constraints of a redefined public order. Duggan politicized the proceedings by claiming this was not "a state prosecution but a state persecution." A few days after their conviction and sentencing, Elgin intervened to have the three rioters released from jail.[57]

Later that fall in Toronto the British American League held its second meeting. Dominated by Orange leaders such as George Benjamin and Ogle Gowan, as well as Toronto Orange politicians such as Mayor Bowes, councilmen John Carr and William Davis, and aldermen Duggan, Denison, and Dempsey, the meeting finally broke with annexation. Instead it promoted the series of reforms that would represent a significant part of the new Liberal-Conservative consensus of the next two decades. Among the reforms promoted were a protective tariff, the extension of democratic institutions, and a broader British American union.[58]

Two celebrated cases involving Orangemen arose in 1850. In the first, John Hillyard Cameron, a rising Orange legislature star, came to the defence of Orangeman and former London MP Thomas Dixon, who had been removed from his office of justice of the peace. While failing to gain Dixon's office back, the case did embarrass the Baldwin ministry.[59] The second and more serious case involved a Brantford prosecution of local Orangemen under the Party Processions Act of 1843. Although there could be no doubt as to the nature of the 12 July procession, which included the traditional King Billy on horseback, the jury nevertheless refused to convict. Thus, in what was claimed to be the first prosecution under the controversial act, it became clear that it was probably impossible to find a jury willing to convict, no matter what the evidence.[60]

This led to the repeal of the Party Processions Act in August 1851. A petition earlier that year by Orange Grand Master George Benjamin had put the matter before the house,[61] but it was a motion of Toronto Tory MP, W.H. Boulton that managed to work its way through the house with surprisingly little opposition. Boulton, following Benjamin, argued that the act was unjust and unequal, and that it should therefore be repealed. He pointed also to the speech of Reformer John Ross (Baldwin's son-in-law) upon introducing the petition into the legislative council, when he credited the Orangemen with having proven their loyalty in 1849 and further argued that the act was totally inoperative, citing Hamilton and Slabtown (St Catharines) cases where juries had refused to convict even in the face of very clear evidence. Boulton then argued that the original legislation had been vindictive because of Orange opposition to Sydenham in the election of 1841.

Francis Hincks, now premier, eventually intervened in the debate to indicate that he had intended to remain silent and had not even decided whether to divide the house on the motion, but that speeches defending the Slabtown Orangemen went too far. Henry Sherwood picked him up on this, drawing out the point that the government obviously did not regard this as a crucial question and further reminding the house of Lord Metcalfe's withholding of the second piece of legislation in 1843 which would have banned the order. This too drew a response from Hincks, who asserted ironically that Metcalfe had actually written that legislation before his falling out with the Reform ministry. Support for repeal was indicated by John Hillyard Cameron and, more surprisingly, by William Lyon Mackenzie, who remembered how the Toronto Orangemen had at first supported him because of their hatred for the Baldwins. Since then, Mackenzie assured his fellow MPs, he had been on the order's hit list, but he still felt that they should be allowed to march. When the house divided, it was clear that this was not a party vote and the revoking of the act passed easily. Even the *Globe* acclaimed this action.[62]

What had happened between 1843, or even 1849, and 1851 to make such a great difference in attitude? The first Baldwin government could not do enough to remove the threat of the Orange Order. Yet the new Hincks Reform ministry of the early 1850s was only too willing to accede quietly to the order's acceptance as part of Canadian public life. The basic answer would appear to be that a new and different political consensus had been growing in the Canadas in the intervening decade, one that increasing numbers of Orange leaders had helped form. This consensus, emerging in the Draper ministry, had come under severe strain in 1849, but one is struck by the speed with which annexation, the most radical of the contending positions, was forgotten after that crisis. Signing the Annexation Manifesto proved no political impediment in the new Canadian political scene of the 1850s. The Hincks ministry captured the new consensus nicely, for Hincks himself was the author of the two key pieces of legislation that underlay the capitalist expansion of the decade: the Railway Guarantee Act and the Municipal Loan Fund Act. The retirement of Baldwin and Lafontaine cleared the way for a series of ministries in the 1850s that increasingly agreed on most developmental questions.[63] In Toronto this emerging business consensus can be seen in the election of Irish merchant John George Bowes as mayor and in the minor judicial appointments of George Duggan and George Gurnett. The fact that a Reform ministry could bring itself to make such appointments suggests much about the new consensus of the 1850s. As the Reform *Examiner* suggested, "The lion and the lamb have lain down together."[64]

Orange politicians were central to the development of this new consensus. They moved the Conservative party in that direction, in terms of both electoral style and policy. Take, for example, Ogle Gowan himself, when he sought the nomination in Leeds in 1851; the *Examiner* noted the "curious mixture of radicalism and toryism," which included platform planks such as an elected legislative council, election of all local government officials, household suffrage, and increased representation for urban constituencies.[65] While never personally acceptable to the élite, Gowan certainly helped to move the Conservative party from its high Tory roots and transform it into a party with democratic appeal. Although Sir John A. Macdonald usually receives full credit for these achievements, his colleagues from his early years in the assembly, such as Gowan, undoubtedly influenced him. Macdonald's own Orangeism, generally viewed purely as political manipulation, brought him into constant contact with the Orange mass base of his emerging popular Conservatism. There are other examples of the new Orange Conservative political leader. Both John

Hillyard Cameron and William Henry Boulton, despite a Compact background, appear to be politicians of this type. Boulton, for example, introduced legislation in the 1851 assembly session to extend the democratic system and to make the legislative council elective.

The consensus did not extend over the entire spectrum of Canadian affairs, and July 1851 saw Toronto again disrupted by bitter sectarian wrangling. This time the issue was the clergy reserves, and on this issue not all Orangemen stood united.[66] Some, like Gowan, in the new consensus were willing to see the reserves eliminated with a division of the proceeds between the various denominations. This solution was anathema to High Church Tories such as Sherwood and Cameron. In the Orange Order itself this led to a later split. In July 1851 the immediate issue was a meeting in Toronto of the Anti-Clergy Reserves Association. A first attempt at a meeting was broken up when a Tory mob invaded the hall and took control of the stage. One leader of the crowd, Alderman Dixon, was thrown off the stage by the Reverend Mr Esson, one of the Anti-Clergy Reserve organizers. Orangeman Dixon pressed an assault charge against the minister, only to see Police Magistrate Gurnett rule that this was a private meeting at which Dixon had no right to be present.[67]

Approximately two weeks later, the antis again scheduled a meeting at St Lawrence Hall. The supporters of the reserves meanwhile scheduled a counter-demonstration for the rear of the new city hall. The call for this meeting came from Aldermen Robinson, Medcalf, and Dixon, among others. Speeches from Dixon, E.G. O'Brien, and MP Henry Sherwood were followed by a call to visit the antis. An attack was then made on St Lawrence Hall but the group failed to gain entrance. To quell the siege, the Riot Act was read and the military called into action. In the aftermath of this riot the *Globe* indignantly attacked the magistracy for its failure to make any arrests. The mayor himself had been assaulted, but no charges were laid. For three hours the city was in the "possession of the mob," screamed the *Globe*, yet none could identify the participants. Perhaps, implied the *Globe*, High Bailiff Allen's Orangeism was interfering with his effectiveness as a policeman.[68]

During the general election campaign at the end of 1851, the events of the preceding years made themselves only too evident when it came time for the selection of Conservative candidates. Initially four Conservative candidates entered the field. The two incumbents, Henry Sherwood and W.H. Boulton, were joined by G.P. Ridout and Samuel Thompson. Their quasi-Reform opponents were Terence J. O'Neill, a Roman Catholic, and Frederick C. Capreol. With the spectre of a split vote before the Conservatives, the Orange Order intervened, supported

Sherwood and Boulton, and then requested Thompson and Ridout to withdraw from the contest. The internal workings of the order here perhaps suggest nascent anti-Gowan sentiment, because Thompson was both an Orangeman and Gowan's partner at the *Patriot*. Moreover, Thompson had been very vocal in criticizing Sherwood for his attempt at peacekeeping in the Elgin 1849 visit to Toronto. Whatever the internal debate, Thompson agreed to withdraw, while Ridout refused to do so in an open letter to E.T. Dartnell, the Orange leader.[69]

In the subsequent election Ridout topped the poll, followed by Boulton and Sherwood, with the Reformers well behind.[70] Two years later, however, Boulton was unseated when he was found not to have satisfied the £500 property requirement for candidacy for the assembly.[71] In the resulting by-election Henry Sherwood faced Ogle Gowan in a clear fight between the opposing elements of Toronto Orangeism. Gowan, at a disadvantage in his new home, proposed a formal nominating meeting. Sherwood simply refused to compete and asserted he would run no matter what a nomination meeting decided. At his nomination meeting Gowan attacked the Compact lawyers as a "cod fish aristocracy." E.T. Dartnell and some other Orangemen then surprised many by endorsing and actively working for Sherwood. Dartnell differed with Gowan on the clergy reserves and on separate schools, where Gowan was willing to be moderate and allow Catholics their own schools. All this was part of Gowan's moderate Conservative attempt to build unity among all Irish and even to appease public opinion in Quebec, if this became necessary politically. With some of Toronto's diehards these policies did not go down easily, though Gowan had the support of Orange Corporation worthies such as Aldermen Armstrong and Dempsey.[72]

Despite his attempt to draw Sherwood into a real campaign and his continuous appeal to the working classes of the city, Gowan could not defeat Sherwood at the polls. He was defeated soundly, 833 to 423, carrying only St John's Ward.[73] No doubt the split in the order damaged Gowan's chances greatly. This realization may have helped convince him of the necessity of regaining control of the grand lodge, for in June 1853 he challenged the Benjamin leadership and regained the position of grand master. The Benjamin forces regrouped and, screaming foul, refused to accept the election result, instead organizing a counter grand lodge. This schism in the order lasted until 1856. Most Ontario lodges, especially Toronto lodges, sided with Gowan. In 1855 he reported that only about one-third of the lodges paid dues to the Benjamin Grand Lodge. The split, which had probably originated in policy differences, itself intensified those disputes. Gowan continued to support a moderate Conservative approach which included an alliance with Quebec *bleus*, while Benjamin moved into an open alliance with George Brown's voluntarism and found himself accused by Gowan of fostering nativist and know-nothing sentiments. This last accusation was probably only Gowan's spite, for after the reunion of the grand lodges in 1856, accomplished by the resignation of the two rival leaders from the grand mastership, and the election in their place of George Lyttleton Allen (the former high bailiff of Toronto) Benjamin returned to the Conservative fold. That the Gowan forces were clearly dominant in 1856 was illustrated by the prominence of Gowan's two sons in the new unified leadership. Their dominance was again evident in 1858, when Gowan's son Nassau defeated John Holland, a Brown supporter, to become grand lodge secretary.

In addition to the costly split in the order and Gowan's inability to defeat Sherwood in the Toronto by-election, Orangemen faced other serious difficulties in the early and mid-1850s. A Green assault on a 12 July procession in Hamilton in 1852 led to the death of one of the Green assailants.[74] Although a grand jury acquitted the Orange defendant of any wrongdoing on the grounds of self-defence against an unwarranted assault, bitter feelings grew between the two communities. Thus in 1853 Toronto Orangemen marched with their Hamilton comrades on the twelfth and they went prepared. Lodge records show that the lodges offset the cost of supplying the members who marched in Hamilton with arms for the occasion.[75] Although quiet prevailed, this incident was generally indicative of the new self-assertiveness of the Roman Catholic community in Ontario under Bishop Charbonnel, which was to manifest itself in ever-increasing pressure for separate schools.[76] This policy would continue under Charbonnel's successor, Bishop Lynch. This assertiveness also began to appear in the streets of Toronto where, on 4 July 1853, a march of the Hibernian Benevolent Society resulted in a fracas with an Orange carter. Later that month 40 to 50 Orangemen marched with arms and engaged in a skirmish with some Irish Catholics. They explained afterwards that they had mobilized to defend William Mack's Enniskillen Home Tavern, a major Orange meeting place. Rumours had circulated of an impending attack by Irish Catholic railway navvies from Georgetown.[77]

These political difficulties continued with the emergence of George Brown and the *Globe* as bitter anti-Catholics and strong proponents of a Protestant alliance. This is not the place for this story to be told fully other than to note that the standard biography of Brown significantly underplays the virulence of the *Globe* in this period.[78] One example must suffice. In defending the Orangemen's right to walk, the *Globe* described a Montreal "romish" procession: "The melancholy spectacle of crowds kneeling down on the street and worshipping an eye carried on the end of a stick, to represent the Almighty, and the host, or the alleged living reality of Our Saviour, carried in a box."[79] This was from 1852, before the *Globe* had enthusiastically and totally embraced anti-Catholicism.

Thus although the Toronto Conservative machine had held the city in 1854, returning John Hillyard Cameron and John George Bowes over their Conservative opponents Henry Sherwood and George Ridout, things did not go so well in December 1857. George Brown agreed to run in Toronto in response to a draft petition that was signed by nearly 2,000 individuals, including an alleged 200 Orange-men. His opponents were initially John George Bowes and rehabili-tated W.H. Boulton, who on his return to Toronto early in 1857 after a number of years on the continent had been greeted by Gowan and Toronto Orangemen as a returning hero.[80] When it became apparent that Bowes would not poll well he stood aside for Compact figure and former mayor John Beverley Robinson, Jr, the son of the chief justice. Brown was formally nominated by dissident Orange leader John Hol-land and by militant Protestant master mariner Captain Bob Moodie, an enemy of the Robinsons, who called on the voters to turn out like men and Protestants. Defections among Orange voters must have aided considerably, for Brown actually led the polls, with Robinson following closely and Boulton trailing behind. There was considerable poll violence, but the *Globe* complained less than usual, for it was clear that Reform forces were ready and willing to do battle them-selves on this occasion.[81]

The following year, in the by-election that followed from the intricacies of the "Double Shuffle," Brown found himself opposed by John Hillyard Cameron, who was to become grand master of the Orange Order the following year. A vigorous campaign ensued, as had become the norm in Toronto at the end of the 1850s, though in the 1840s Compact Tory candidates often did not deign to campaign, leaving that to their subalterns who simply arranged for free houses. The new campaigning included a full series of ward meetings for each side and even the occasional appearance at each other's meet-ings, although the latter was still often impeded by supporters' predilection to shout down the opposition – or worse. The election itself was reasonably peaceful, probably more so than the previous December's poll. There were still Reform complaints of Tory rowdy-ism and an assault charge against Tory Alderman (Captain Bob) Moodie for attacking a Reform supporter at a meeting. Nevertheless, Brown's easy majority, which included victory in five of the seven Toronto wards, made pursuit of the rowdyism issue unnecessary.

Brown, who in 1857 had led Robinson by only 51 votes and Boulton by 164, on this occasion beat Cameron by about 150.[82] No doubt the broad-based perception that Brown had been victimized by the double shuffle helped him. Equally, one suspects that the Orange Order's strenuous attempt to impose discipline on its members' voting may have backfired when it became a public issue later in the campaign.[83]

In August the Orange district lodge had passed a series of motions in support of Cameron, though it had taken two meetings to get them through. In addition, it had added resolutions threatening the expulsion of any member who did not vote accordingly or revealed the injunction. Needless to say, when this secret circular was made available to the *Globe*, the paper made ready propaganda gains by exposing the "tyranny" of the order. The public revelation and Cameron's subsequent defeat led to an investigation and then a trial in the district grand lodge. John Holland, prominent in Brown's 1857 campaign, and two other lodge masters were charged. Holland was eventually suspended for two years by an overwhelming 34 to 2 vote, with Gowan in the minority. Later that fall all other masters who had voted for Brown were also suspended for two years, although the vote was far closer on this motion, 18 to 9. While this fight continued for the rest of the year and for a time four lodges threatened to leave the order, the issue had run its course by early 1859 and the dissident lodges were back in the fold.[84]

The political problems of Toronto Orangemen continued in the late 1850s when George Brown's Municipal Reform Association also mounted a successful challenge to Tory control of the Corporation. While partially stemming simply from the growth of Reform sentiment in the city, this campaign also grew out of a series of specific issues that involved elements of the order and raised a serious threat to their power base in the police force and the fire brigades. This story had been unfolding throughout the period. On every occasion of street violence the *Globe* and other forces of order had condemned the city's police. Complaints went back as far as the Durham Club Riot of 1839 and had continued to mount throughout the following twenty years.

Reform of the local justice system had been under discussion for a number of years. Initially the Corporation had objected to what it viewed as blatant attempts to limit its patronage, especially its ability to grant tavern licences. In 1845, however, it acceded to similar legislation in return for a pledge that the appointment would be made only at its request. When in 1847 it requested such an appointment, it found itself asking the new Baldwin ministry to appoint its Orange comrade, the stalwart George Duggan. Not surprisingly, the Baldwin government proceeded slowly. Indeed, no appointment was made until after the new Municipal Corporations Act of 1849 which created a stipendiary police magistrate as well as a recorder's court. Both officers were to be appointed by the provincial government. This centralization of power was no doubt softened for the Corporation when in 1851 two Orange worthies – George Duggan and George Gurnett – became respectively the city's first recorder and first police magistrate. These reforms and the striking appointments of Orange partisans suggest that there was a new bourgeois consensus emerging in the 1850s. The judgments meted out over the next two decades by Gurnett and Duggan further demonstrate this fact. As their biographers note, both men shed their partisanship and were perceived by all to have administered the law "fairly."[85] The transformation of the local legal system, however, proceeded far more peacefully than the ensuing debate over the police.

While the police were always a controversial issue in Toronto, the problem became especially prominent after 1855. On two occasions in 1855, only weeks apart, the police force not only proved incapable of maintaining the peace but also demonstrated its unwillingness to prosecute members of crowds with whom it shared general sympathies and Orange associations. The first incident arose during a fire on Church Street. The city's fire department, like that of many cities in this period, was still based on volunteer companies which combined club and social functions with their more useful civic pursuit. Competition was often fierce between these companies, and on 29 June a fight broke out among the firemen attending the Church Street blaze. When the police intervened to break up the fight, they were in turn attacked and administered a sound thrashing, by all accounts. As the *Examiner* noted, there was "a want of water, a want of method, and the Maine Law was much wanted." In the heat of the moment, and no doubt smarting from their injuries, the police arrested four of their assailants. When the cases came to court the next week, however, the police constables almost had to be dragged into court to obtain their testimony which then turned out to be so vague that only one of the four defendants' cases was committed for later trial. This failure on the part of the police force was condemned, and the *Globe* reported that "it is plainly asserted by those who have access to the best information that during the days which have been allowed to elapse since the fire, a compromise has been effected between the constables and the firemen, who are too much birds of a feather long to differ." "Utterly disgraceful to the administration of civic justice," this case demanded the reconstruction of the force "which thus proves itself utterly corrupt." The *Examiner* echoed the *Globe's* demands.[86]

All of this was bad enough, but only ten days later the police force found itself again assailed for almost identical behaviour. The second riot stemmed from an incident at a house of ill fame on King Street, when a few Toronto rowdies attacked some members of the visiting Howe circus. The circus performers gained the upper hand in the battle and seriously injured a shoemaker and a carpenter, both members of the Hook and Ladder Company. Police sought the clown who had administered the beatings, but he disappeared. On the following Friday night, a large crowd attacked the circus, initially trying to pull down the tent. A battle ensued in which Joseph Bird, a tavern-keeper and one of the Church Street rioters of the 29 June altercation, was badly beaten by the circus men. Toronto fire bells then rang, summoning fire department cronies and a huge crowd as reinforcements. The new troops turned the tide of battle, especially when the Hook and Ladder Company's truck was immediately put to use to pull down the tent. The circus men fled for their lives and the crowd turned on their wagons, which were broken into, overturned, and burned. The mayor desperately tried to restore order and managed to rescue some of the injured circus men, but finally he had to call out the troops. The riot then ended before the military arrived. Police constables present throughout did little to restrain the crowd, and, when called on later to make charges, they again developed collective amnesia about who had participated in the riot. After extreme pressure was administered, 17 rioters were arraigned, of whom 13 were committed for later trial. This time the *Globe* editorialized about the "additional disgrace" of the firemen's further involvement and demanded that the city council act to reform both the police force and the fire department.[87]

The debates and actions that followed these riots are especially instructive in terms of the underlying class conflict at issue here. In the riots and their aftermath, police and firemen behaved in ways that drew on working-class solidarities. As one critic noted, "There are three classes in the city which thoroughly understand one another as hale fellows well met – the innkeeper, the firemen, and the police." "These Classes," he continued, "are fed by the Orange Lodges."[88] Moreover, the circus crowd clearly acted as a community enforcer acting on unwritten codes of moral economy. Not too surprisingly, police and firemen appeared to share the same assumptions as the crowd. While none of this seems at first sight out of the ordinary, given the preceding fifteen years of riots in Toronto, something quite new was contained in the press response, speaking of course for the respectable citizenry, and in the ultimate actions of the city council. From these riots stemmed the first significant reforms of both the police and fire departments of the city, and in both cases the operative assumption that underlay the reforms was the perceived necessity to end political control of the institutions and professionalize them, thus eliminating their plebeian roots.

The fire department received the *Globe*'s initial attention. Finding it in general "a disgrace to the civic administration" and based on "utterly unsound principles," the *Globe* reviewed the force's history. Organized initially as a volunteer force, in the old days it had provided excellent service and recruited first-rate men. In recent years, however, this had changed. The increase in insurance had led to less concern on the part of the properties, and "their places were filled by men of lower standing." This in turn led to a small stipend being attached to volunteer service (£3), which in turn attracted more of the "dissolute young fellows." Yet the basis of organization was never changed to reflect its different class reality. The 352 volunteers were still allowed to control their own company membership and to elect their own officers and even the chief engineer. This, according to the *Globe*, meant that the officers had no control over the men. (So much for democracy!) All this led to fire companies getting "into the hands of a few evil-disposed fellows who chose others as their colleagues, and elect whomever they please." There was only one possible reform, a paid fire department.[89] A few weeks later the *Globe* returned to the subject and made its assumptions even more transparent: "The Toronto system must now be put an end to. It has served its day ... It must pass away, and be replaced by a system suited to the times and to our rapidly increasing city ... Toronto has outgrown that system ... A paid company work in a totally opposite manner. It is a system of subordination, while that element is scarcely known under the voluntary arrangement."[90] Thus under the rubric of being up to date, traditions of voluntary control must be swept away. Why? Because they were insufficiently "subordinate." Capitalist relations extended their tentacles yet further.

These goals were accomplished, and in that year a professional fire brigade was created. Yet only five years later, under the financial constraints of the economic crisis of the late 1850s, the council reversed itself and tried to revert to a voluntary basis. It expected that the officers, however, would still be paid by the city and also insisted that a city council committee maintain supervisory power.[91] The firemen reacted strongly to this proposal, which held nothing for them, and in June 1861 they paraded in protest with an effigy of Alderman Sproat, the architect of this plan. After a heated confrontation with the mayor and Chief Constable W.S. Prince in front of Sproat's house, the firemen marched on without burning their effigy, which was destroyed by Prince.[92] Shortly thereafter the city again began to release funds to the volunteer companies, and, when the economy began to recover the next year, it began hiring permanent firemen.[93] Thus the workingmen of the fire companies had adjusted to their new situation and commenced to fight on a new terrain when the city tried to worsen their situation further. Even after all these reforms, the fire department remained an Orange bastion throughout the century and still provided the Corporation's shock troops in late Victorian Toronto.

The police received even more criticism than the firemen for the two 1855 riots. A special investigation by city council led to strong criticism of the chief, Samuel Sherwood. The key element in the emerging critical consensus on the police was the need to remove the force from politics. The chief constable should be "free of the contamination of our local politics," wrote the *Globe*. Moreover, hiring of the force should be removed from the hands of the city council and given instead to a board of police commissioners composed of the mayor, the police magistrate, and the chief constable.[94] The investigating committee endorsed most of these suggestions, emphasizing especially the need for a trained, experienced chief. While city council agreed to commence a search for a successor to Sherwood, no other practical reform was implemented and the issue soon died out.[95]

The police, never far from the public eye in these years, became a major issue again in 1858. A 16 March St Patrick's Society dinner at the National Hotel, owned by Irish nationalist leader Owen Cosgrove, had ended in a serious riot which included an attack on D'Arcy McGee. During the procession of the following day, an Orange carter drove his cart through the line of march, and in the ensuing mêlée an Irish Catholic received a mortal stab wound. The subsequent furore continued for almost a month and led to a vigorous denunciation of secret societies by Police Magistrate George Gurnett (a former Orangeman) and even by the Tory *Leader*. Directly criticized first for refusing to testify and later for appearing to be in collusion with the accused Orangemen was Chief of Police Samuel Sherwood. Gurnett inveighed against "other obligations than those which are due to the public and the laws of the land," while the *Leader* editorialized about "the dangerous state of society in which any considerable portion of its members enter into secret obligations which are liable to defeat the ends of public justice." Things did not improve for the police when more shooting and rioting occurred on 12 July as well.

The controversy became a major issue in the fall when Mayor W.H. Boulton tried but failed to unseat Chief Constable Sherwood. The specific issue revolved around Sherwood's release of a prisoner charged with bank robbery. The police committee of city council mildly censured him, but Boulton demanded his resignation. When the mayor failed to carry his council, he resigned instead. This created a complete breakdown in the Conservative ranks, which had been in the process of trying to find a mayoralty candidate to oppose the nominee of George Brown's Municipal Reform Association: Adam Wilson. A series of Tory convention meetings broke down in embarrassment as various choices declined nomination. Meanwhile Boulton defied the convention by declaring that he intended to run even without its support. It finally settled on former mayor John Beverley Robinson, Jr, but he too refused. The subsequent mayoralty race saw Wilson opposed by Boulton, who had lost his Conservative support, and J.G. Bowes, who was still suffering from his association with the "10,000 pound job." Wilson triumphed easily, gaining almost 2,000 votes to the combined 1,500 of his opponents. Reform had triumphed in Toronto.[97]

Police reform became a central task of the new Reform majority. Provincial legislation had created a Toronto Board of Police Commissioners which first met on 1 December 1858 and was composed of the mayor, the recorder (George Duggan), and the police magistrate (George Gurnett).[98] The new board's structure reflected proposals that Reformers had been pressing since the 1841 commission on the Toronto election riot.[99] The emerging bourgeois consensus on the need for law and order and a "professional" police force was evident even before Mayor Wilson joined the commission. At its first meeting the commission had decided that "the present police force in the city should be reorganized at as early a day as practicable after full enquiry and mature deliberation."[100] In its first month of activity it disciplined no fewer than eight constables and set out to revise all police rules "with the view of increasing the efficiency of the force."[101] With Wilson's arrival in mid-January it proceeded to fire the former deputy police chief in the name of "the efficiency of the force" and began to seek a replacement for Chief Sherwood. It sought authorization from the city council "to offer such a salary ... as would induce the most efficient person that the Metropolitan Police of England or elsewhere could afford to accept the office."[102] This by then familiar bourgeois rhetoric about "efficiency" was, however, only one innovation of the police commissioners. With Wilson's arrival, they proceeded to rule that no member of a secret society could join the force.[103] This led to a storm of Orange protest, because it was only too clear that such a prohibition was aimed directly at the order. A public meeting was held at St Lawrence Hall in which prominent Orangemen such as John Hillyard Cameron, Nassau Gowan, Francis H.

Medcalf, and others inveighed against this new measure as reprehensible and an infringement of their rights as freeborn Englishmen.[104] A subsequent city council motion to reconsider failed by one vote. The district lodge condemned Alderman Joseph Reed, an Orangeman, who had cast the deciding vote in favour of the prohibition.[105]

The new commission reconstructed the force totally, choosing, avowedly without regard for party or sect, 58 constables. The new force included only 24 constables from the old, and 45 Anglicans, 5 Presbyterians, and 8 Roman Catholics received positions as constables.[106]

In 1860, after the defeat of the Reform council, the returned Tories voted to overturn the police commission's decision. In response to an inquiry from Police Chief Prince, in which he indicated that his constables now felt that they were free to join secret societies, the police commission asserted its independence and power: "[The police] are appointed by and hold their office at the pleasure of the Board of Commissioners of Police and the Board is the only authority which can make rules for their government. These are powers which have been conferred by Act of Parliament upon the Board and neither the Council nor any other body or person has the slightest right to interfere with the force in any respect. Number 50 rule which relates to secret societies must be observed as strictly now as at any other time heretofore and any disobedience of it will be punished with instant dismissal."[107] Although a modus vivendi was eventually worked out, the formal rule was upheld, as was the commission's independence of council.[108] The clause preventing membership in secret societies was entrenched in 1866 as part of the police constable's oath of office. Prince, drawing on his British army background, introduced military discipline and recruited many members of the force from the Irish constabulary. In late Victorian commentaries on the Toronto police, he is personally credited with creating the force that was proudly held to be "equal to that of any city in the world."[109] Nevertheless, Prince proved to be a controversial figure and was involved in a series of battles with city council over the next decade, including a celebrated battle in 1863 when he requested arms for the police to enable them to protect themselves against the Orange-dominated, armed militia.[110] The equally Orange-dominated council refused to grant this request.

While the council refused to arm the police for riot duty, Prince's major contribution to law and order in Toronto was undoubtedly the new attitude to crowd violence. The daily order book initiated by Prince on his arrival in 1859 is filled not only with careful preparations for the policing of potentially explosive political and ritual events but also with new attitudes to popular disorder. In late February 1859 the whole force was mobilized to police a St Lawrence Hall meeting, with a conspicuous deployment of constables outside while a support- ing force was hidden in the hall's anterooms. Upon the meeting's end, Prince ordered "the streets will be patrolled by three parties from each section for an hour."[111] On St Patrick's Day, the whole force was placed on active duty "from 9:00 until it is deemed necessary to dismiss them."[112] Two weeks later officers received instructions to "prevent disturbances amongst the cabmen," traditional Corporation retainers.[113] A special force of twenty-four was instructed to keep all crowds well away from the militia during 24 May celebrations, while for the "Glorious Twelfth" the whole force was again called out and special plans were made to prevent crowds from gathering, to scruti- nize the various lodges after the procession, and to arrest anyone firing guns in the street, a customary accompaniment of 12 July merriment. In addition, "particular care must be taken to prevent cab- men or others driving through the procession," and if "any attempt of this kind [took] place ... the arrest of the party or parties must be the immediate result."[114] Popular disorders of a more mundane type received similar attention: "Young blackguards" disrupting "services or class meetings" at the Elizabeth Street Missionary Church; taverns open after hours; the arrival in town of the circus. No disruption of the new bourgeois order evaded Chief Prince's vigilance.[115]

The specifics of the transformation wrought by Prince aside, what had been accomplished by Wilson and the legislative assembly reforms was the distancing of the police from their working-class roots. The emphasis on experience, recruitment abroad, and commis- sion control all further removed police from the plebeian milieu of which the earlier policemen had been an integral part. Again here, as in the case of the fire department, the reforms had this intent but did not totally achieve their aims. The Toronto police would also continue to play ambiguous class roles. Nevertheless the general thrust of capital to create dependable class institutions had proceeded one step further in Toronto.

The Toronto voters' flirtation with Reform, which Brown had heralded in 1859 as the final demise of the corruptionists, did not last long. Wilson personally gained a second term, but with a minority of supporters on council, and in 1861 the voters turned to an old friend, John George Bowes. He held the mayor's chair for three terms and was replaced for three more by Francis Medcalf, former Orange district master. During Medcalf's last term in office the legislative assembly, reflecting concern for urban property values, removed the direct election of the mayor from the people and returned it to the city council. This same legislative assembly also increased the property requirements for the exercise of the franchise to $600 leasehold and for holding office to $4,000 freehold or $8,000 leasehold, both qualifications being double the 1858 level.

Adam Wilson was only one of the problems faced by Toronto Orangemen in 1860. During the royal visit of the Prince of Wales to Canada, his adviser and companion, the Catholic Duke of Newcastle, precipitated a major crisis in the colony by refusing to receive Orange addresses or to pass under Orange arches. The subsequent series of incidents, which involved the cancellation of visits to Kingston and Belleville when local Orangemen refused to concede, has been described elsewhere.[117] In Toronto there was a major debate within the Orange order. Toronto's Orangemen were urged by their Kingston brothers to maintain their rights as citizens to march. However, respectable Torontonians had been planning their celebrations for months. After heated and prolonged negotiations, Toronto Orangemen arrived at a face-saving compromise by which they decided to hold their own separate march. This motion finally carried in the district lodge by a vote of 50 to 29, but the minority were quite unhappy.[118] They continued to demand both "arch and march" and no doubt were responsible for the ensuing double-cross. While the separate Orange march was peaceable and then dispersed to allow the members to greet the prince as private citizens without party regalia, the arch that was supposedly stripped of party slogan in fact carried a figure of King Billy. Thus Newcastle and the prince actually passed under an arch with Orange symbols despite the earlier guarantees. The furious duke blamed Mayor Wilson and the city council and demanded an apology, which he received. An additional incident took place on the following Sunday, when the prince and the duke attended services at the Anglican cathedral. Newcastle ordered the carriage to take a longer route to avoid the Orange arch. An Orange crowd then gathered at the cathedral and prepared a display of banners, flags, and decorations and threatened "to cut the trace and drag the Prince through the arch" as he left the service. When the royal party escaped through a side door the crowd's fury mounted. Later, when the duke went out for a walk, he was hissed and booed by a crowd that then burned him in effigy.[119] Though Toronto authorities and Orange leaders had managed to escape without a major incident, it had not been easy. Or as one of the many journalistic accounts of the tour noted, "the Battle of Toronto" was narrowly avoided.[120]

The ingenuity of the Orangemen was not to be underestimated. Aurora's Loyal Orange Lodge (LOL) 693 won a final victory over Newcastle when it erected an arch over the Northern Railway line which the prince's party passed under on its way to Barrie.[121] Meanwhile one Toronto lodge, Nassau LOL 4, passed a motion of thanks to its comrades in the fire brigade who had marched in the formal procession for the royal party, "on which occasion we were proud to observe the Orange rosette on the left breast of each Orange fireman in the procession."[122] "Arch and march" had been gained.

The royal visit turned into a major political crisis for John A. Macdonald and his ministry. It took serious fence mending to repair the Conservatives' damaged relationship with their Orange allies, who blamed the government for Newcastle's insult to the order. Critical motions, for example, were passed at the provincial grand lodge of Canada West meeting in Hamilton in late October: "That the government of Canada ... were guilty of a gross dereliction of their duty as the responsible representatives of the people and are chargeable with the unfortunate occurrence which afterwards took place; and this right worshipful Grand Lodge feels it due to itself to declare that the Ministry have in consequence forfeited all claim to the confidence of the orangemen of Western Canada and that the proper constitutional mode of redress ... is by withdrawing from them the direct and indirect support of the Loyal Orange body."[123] This motion failed to carry at the grand lodge meeting in Kingston the following January and was then repudiated in February at the provincial grand lodge meeting in Barrie. Through hard work, Macdonald had managed to repair the alliance.[124]

The rise to prominence of the separate school issue in the politics of the 1860s, and the emergence of a radical Irish Catholic nationalist grouping, the Hibernian Benevolent Society, kept sectarian issues at the centre of Toronto political life in the pre-Confederation years. The Fenian threat represented a natural rallying point for the Orange order and would eventually join 1837 as one of the central historical incidents in the elaborate, developing Orange mythology. As tension mounted in Toronto in the early 1860s, the city prepared for war – the Fenians surreptitiously, the Orange militia openly. On the route that would lead to the Fenian Raid battlefields, there were a few Toronto skirmishes in 1863 and 1864. Such tensions were of considerable significance in the coming of the new Confederation. The degree to which tensions of this kind reinforced the fears of Reformers about urban order, however, remains an open question. Nevertheless, more may well have been at stake in the 1866 disfranchisement than simply a protest over property taxes. Many Irish workers would have lost their votes under the new schema. Equally notable, "Old Squaretoes" Medcalf, Toronto's first mechanic mayor and the people's choice in the preceding three years, lost office under the new system when the council chose his opponent. In 1874, when Toronto voters were once again given the right to elect the mayor directly, they suggestively chose Medcalf.[125]

"The Irish Protestants," Don Akenson has written recently, "were like a cocked gun, always ready to go off."[126] While the Orange order in Toronto successfully expanded beyond its basic ethno-religious constituency, the organization nevertheless epitomizes Akenson's suggestive simile. In Ontario's major city, the order provided rising bourgeois elements with their major antagonist. While the struggles of the 1840s and 1850s have generally been viewed by historians as purely religious and ethnic conflicts, they did not reduce so easily for the participants. Battles over the licensing of taverns, over the right to march, over the burning of effigies, over the nature and composition of the police force and the fire brigade, and even over schools and church lands may not at first sight appear to be class issues. Yet, as the Yeos have recently reminded us in writing about Victorian England, such conflicts involved "struggles over time and territory. They were about social initiative, and who was to have it. They were about expected notions of what it is to be human and normal. They were struggles of substance in themselves. They were also struggles about form, the forms that association would take. When put together, they may be seen as struggles about the dominant styles and contours, constraints and opportunities of whole periods."[127] They further exhort historians to penetrate beneath the results of appearances in developing capitalist society to discover the conflicts that often mask the class struggles of the period.

Applying such methods, what can we make of the Canada of the 1840s and 1850s? Perhaps three contemporary figures should be allowed to guide our conclusions. First, John Macaulay, one of the last active Compact members, observed in 1850 that "the most alarming symptom which I observe in the country is the decay of old-fashioned loyalty, and a general want of respect for authority and station which once prevailed among us ... when, whatever were the failings of the much abused 'Family Compact,' we had a Government of Gentlemen."[128] Macaulay spoke astutely. The new bourgeois hegemony did not aspire to the patrician values of his old Compact contemporaries, be they real or pretend.[129] Nor did it harness popular consent by authority and station.

Second, note George Brown's positive assessment of the achievements of Adam Wilson's first term as mayor of Toronto: "Prior to Mr. Wilson's Mayoralty, the police was a mixture of incapacity and ruffianism. Now it is respectable in character and conduct, and thoroughly efficient in all respects." "Respectability" was a major value of the new bourgeois order, as was "efficiency." In this same assessment, Brown argued that Wilson's second major accomplishment was the dramatic reduction of tavern licences from 460 to 267.[130] Order, efficiency, and temperance, a new trinity far removed from plebeian society, had become the touchstones of the new. And yet we need to proceed cautiously here, for plebeian society too was changing.

Our third speaker, Orange leader Ogle Robert Gowan, made the following observations at the celebration of the Battle of the Boyne in 1855, comparing the twelfth of old with the new: "Then a few coarse straw hats and a few orange ribbons might have been borne by some drunken men staggering through the streets. But now the procession has that uniformity and respectability which in the eyes of their fellow subjects give a character to Orangeism."[131] "Uniformity," "respectability" – have we here evidence of the final "incorporation" of the Orange order into the new bourgeois hegemony? The answer to that question is, of course, both yes and no. There can be no incorporation "without the incorporating host being altered, as well as the incorporated guest."[132] Orangemen, who had once been viewed as incorporated by the Compact, had ironically played a significant part in the bourgeois alliance that promoted the extension of democratic reforms and had articulated the demand for tariff protection as an industrial strategy for Canada. So, yes, they too had changed, but not totally and not without a process of struggle, of reciprocal gains and losses – a process of the composition, decomposition, and recomposition of class. Gowan, himself, to cite one final irony, ended his career as Toronto's inspector of licences from 1869 to 1874.[133]

Orangemen had enjoyed one certain privilege from the 1830s to the 1860s, which they shared with no other force in Canadian society. They had been universally condemned even by those whose policies came to depend on their support. Francis Bond Head, Arthur, Durham, Sydenham, Metcalfe, Russell, Elgin, Edmund Head, Newcastle, a list of British political figures who probably agreed on nothing else, all despised the Orange order. The Yeos have pointed to working people as recalcitrant, innovative, and intrusive.[134]

These adjectives convey much about the class significance of the Orange order in the 1840s and 1850s. For Orangemen, "No Surrender" had many meanings.

NOTES

My thanks for research assistance to Jessie Chisholm, Doug Cruikshank, and Peter Delottinville. Useful comments on the first draft were provided by Michael Cross, Michael Frisch, Bryan Palmer, Nick Rogers, and Paul

Romney. The latter saved me from a number of egregious errors and
shared with me his intimate knowledge of early Toronto.

1 For suggestive articles on these questions, see Geoff Eley, "Rethinking
   the Political: Society History and Political Culture in 18th and 19th
   Century Britain," *Archiv fur socialgeschichte* (1981): 426–57, and Geoff
   Eley and Keith Neild, "Why Does Social History Ignore Politics?" *Social
   History* 5 (1980): 249–71. A stimulating review essay, which raises
   important questions, is Bryan D. Palmer, "Classifying Culture,"
   Labour/Le Travailleur 8/9 (1981–82): 153–83, especially 181–3. Especially
   useful during the revision of this paper were Paul Romney, "Voters
   under the Miscroscope: A Quantitative Meditation on the Toronto
   Parliamentary Poll Book of 1836" paper presented to Canadian Historical Association, Vancouver, 1983, and his "A Man out of Place: The
   Life of Charles Fothergill, 1782–1840" unpublished PHD diss., University of Toronto, 1981.
2 The literature on the Orange order has been recently strengthened by
   Cecil J. Houston and William J. Smyth, *The Sash Canada Wore: A
   Historical Geography of the Orange Order in Canada* (Toronto 1980).
   While I have numerous points of disagreement with their analysis (and
   they with mine), they present much useful data, especially on the
   growth of the order in Ontario. A stimulating general view is G.F.A.
   Best, "Popular Protestantism in Victorian Britain" in Robert Robson,
   ed., *Ideas and Institutions of Victorian Britain* (New York 1967), 115–42.
3 Barrie Dyster, "Toronto 1840–1860: Making it in a British Protestant
   Town," PHD diss., University of Toronto, 1970.
4 Ibid., 40.
5 This analysis of class is indebted to E.P. Thompson, "Eighteenth-Century English Society: Class Struggle without Class?" *Social History* 3
   (1978): 133–66; to Adam Przeworski, "Proletariat into a Class: The
   Process of Class Formation from Karl Kautsky's *The Class Struggle* to
   Recent Controversies," *Politics and Society* 7 (1977): 343–401, quotation
   at 367; and to his "Material Bases of Consent: Economics and Politics
   in a Hegemonic System," *Political Power and Social Theory* 1 (1980):
   21–66. In the Canadian literature, useful attempts to begin the discussion of early class formation are: Bryan D. Palmer, "Kingston
   Mechanics and the Rise of the Penitentiary, 1833–1836," *Histoire sociale*
   25 (1980): 7–32; his "Discordant Music: Charivaris and Whitecapping
   in Nineteenth-Century North America," *Labour/Le Travailleur* 3 (1978):
   5–62; and his attempt at a synthesis, *Working-Class Experience: The Rise
   and Reconstitution of Canadian Labour, 1800–1980* (Toronto 1983), esp.
   chap. 1.
6 Data drawn from Canada *Census* for various years. For a stimulating
   revisionist look at Canadian Irish, see Donald H. Akenson, "Ontario:

Whatever Happened to the Irish?" *Canadian Papers in Rural History* 3 (1982): 204–56.

7 On Toronto's industrialization, see Gregory S. Kealey, *Toronto Workers Respond to Industrial Capitalism* (Toronto 1980), 3–34.

8 Paul C. Appleton, "The Sunshine and the Shade: Labour Activism in Central Canada, 1850–1860," MA diss., University of Calgary, 1974. Also see Palmer, *Working-Class Experience*, 67–71, 316–20.

9 Strike data are drawn from Toronto press. See also the list in Palmer, *Working-Class Experience*, 316–20.

10 Ruth Bleasdale, "Class Conflict on the Canals of Upper Canada in the 1840s," *Labour/Le Travailleur* 8 (1981): 9–39.

11 Houston and Smyth, *The Sash Canada Wore*, 8–37, and Hereward Senior, *Orangeism: The Canadian Phase* (Toronto 1972), 13–39. See also William Perkins Bull, *From the Boyne to Brampton* (Toronto 1936), 17–90. Two early, useful studies which provide much background on the order in politics are Violet Nelson, "The Orange Order in Canadian Politics," MA thesis, Queen's University, 1950, and W.J.S. Mood, "The Orange Order in Canadian Politics, 1841–1867," MA thesis, University of Toronto, 1950. Finally, for a stimulating re-examination of the Irish roots of Orangeism, see Peter Gibbon, "The Origins of the Orange Order and the United Irishmen: A Study in the Sociology of Revolution and Counter-revolution," *Economy and Society* 7 (1972): 134–63. A similarly useful study of the other side is Tom Garvin, "Defenders, Ribbonmen, and Others: Underground Political Networks in Pre-Famine Ireland," *Past and Present* 46 (1982): 133–55.

12 The warrant books and much other Orange archival material is held in the Loyal Orange Association Archives in Willowdale (henceforth LOAA).

13 Material drawn from Minute Book, Loyal Orange Lodge of British North America (LOLBNA), District 2, York County, 1858–84, in LOAA. This paper will not engage in further demographic analysis of the order. For such a discussion, see Kealey, *Toronto Workers*, 98–123. While Houston and Smyth, *The Sash*, 101–11 quibble with my findings, I would argue that their evidence actually further augments the notion of the order as a plebeian, and later a proletarian, organization. In addition, this paper will also assume the discussion of internal organization and ritual that can be found in the same pages of *Toronto Workers*.

14 United Province of Canada, Legislative Assembly *Journals*, 1841, Appendix s, "Report of the Commissioners appointed to investigate certain proceedings at Toronto, connected with the Election for that City." Unfortunately, this lengthy report is unpaginated (henceforth Toronto Election Commission). For manuscript material from this investigation see Toronto Election Riot, RG5B33, National Archives of Canada (hence-

forth NA). On the 1841 election in general, see Irving Martin Abella, "The 'Sydenham Election' of 1841," *Canadian Historical Review* 47 (1966): 326–43.

15 Toronto Election Commission, Testimony of Peter Harkin, Tavern Keeper. Specific denials of Harkins damning testimony are contained in *Journals*, 1841, Appendix oo.

16 Ibid., Testimony of No. 32, John Lindsay, boarding-house keeper.

17 Howard Angus Christie, "The Function of the Tavern in Toronto, 1834–1875," unpublished MPHE thesis, University of Windsor, 1974, 10. On the importance of the tavern in Toronto see also F.H. Armstrong, "Toronto in Transition, 1828–1838," PHD diss., University of Toronto, 1965, 337–40.

18 Toronto Election Commission, Testimony of No. 41, John Eastwood, paper maker.

19 Ibid., List of tavern licences, 1841.

20 Ibid., passim. For campaign details see the *Metropolitan* (Toronto) and the *Examiner*, 27 February–13 March 1841.

21 Toronto Election Commission *Report*.

22 Ibid. and Elizabeth Gibbs, ed., *Debates of the Legislative Assembly*, 1841, 1008–10 and *Debates*, 1843, 438–9, 442 (henceforth *Debates*). For the legislative committee's report on the riot, see *Examiner*, 27 October 1841.

23 Dyster, "Toronto," 64.

24 *Globe*, 9 December 1845.

25 Ibid.

26 *Examiner*, 24 November 1841. Boulton's failure led to his resignation. Without doubt he failed because he was then fighting with the Orangemen. He had led the opposition to George Gurnett's quest for the mayoralty in 1841 by challenging his qualifications. See *Examiner*, 20 January 1841.

27 Toronto Election Commission *Report*.

28 John Garner, *The Franchise and Politics in British North America, 1755–1867* (Toronto 1969), 100–2.

29 *Debates*, 1843, 210, 398–408, 438–47, 456–7, 460, 733; quotation at 443.

30 Ibid., 164, 409, 497–511, 546–8, 662–3, 733, 1210.

31 *Examiner*, 8 November 1843.

32 *Canadian Loyalist* (Kingston) 2 November 1843.

33 *Victoria Chronicle* (Belleville) 31 October 1844; *Examiner*, 16, 23 October 1844.

34 *Examiner*, 21 February, 17 July 1844.

35 *Globe*, 16 July 1844; *Examiner*, 17, 24 July 1844. See also Samuel Thompson, *Reminiscences of a Canadian Pioneer* (Toronto 1884), 183.

36 See, for example, *Globe*, 31 July 1847, 15 July 1848, 14 July 1849. For the complex political history of the period, see Paul G. Cornell, *The Alignment of Political Groups in Canada, 1841–1867* (Toronto 1962).

37 Dyster, "Toronto," 83.

38 *Examiner*, 23 October 1844. See also R.I.K. Davidson, "Monro, George," *Dictionary of Canadian Biography* x (henceforth DCB).

39 Hereward Senior, "Boulton, W.H.," DCB x.

40 Hereward Senior, "Benjamin, George," DCB IX.

41 *Examiner*, 20 January 1847. See also Dyster, "Toronto," chap. 2 and 213–15.

42 *Globe*, 29 December 1847; *Examiner*, 22 December 1847, 3 January 1848.

43 Useful accounts of the Baldwin act are Leo Johnson, *History of the County of Ontario* (Whitby 1973), 172–7; C.F.J. Whebell, "Robert Baldwin and Decentralization, 1841–9" in F.H. Armstrong et al., eds, *Aspects of Nineteenth-Century Ontario* (Toronto 1974), 48–64; and J.H. Aitchison, "The Municipal Corporations Act of 1849," *Canadian Historical Review* 30 (1949): 107–22.

44 NA Petition of Toronto Inhabitants to Lord Elgin, 2 May 1849, RG5 CI vol. 261, 1016.

45 *Globe*, 24, 28 March 1849; *Provincial Telegraph* (Toronto) 29 March 1849; *Examiner*, 28 March, 4 April 1849.

46 *Globe*, 5, 9 May 1849; *Examiner*, 2, 9 May 1849.

47 Sir Arthur C. Doughty, ed., *The Elgin-Grey Papers, 1846–1852* (Ottawa 1937), 410, 413.

48 *Globe*, 21 July 1849.

49 Ibid., 14, 19 July, 9 August 1849.

50 Doughty, ed., *Elgin-Grey Papers*, 415.

51 Ibid., 462.

52 Ibid., 475; *Examiner*, 12 September 1849.

53 Doughty, ed., *Elgin-Grey Papers*, 468.

54 Thompson, *Reminiscences* 268–73, and C.D. Allin and G.M. Jones, *Annexation, Preferential Trade and Reciprocity* (Toronto 1912), 208–12; *Examiner*, 19 September 1849.

55 *Globe*, 22, 24, 26 January 1850; *Examiner*, 10, 17 October 1849.

56 Globe, 12 May 1849

57 Ibid. 24 January 1850

58 British American League *Minutes of the Proceedings of the Second Convention of Delegates* (Toronto 1849).

59 *Debates*, 1850, 411–20.

60 *Globe*, 7, 9 November 1850.

61 NA RG 4CI, vol. 326, item 788, Petition.

62 *Debates*, 1851, 847, 1419, 1441–7, 1500. See also *Globe*, 19 August 1851.

63 Useful background is provided in J.M.S. Careless, ed., *The Pre-Confede-ration Premiers* (Toronto 1980).

64 Dyster, "Toronto," 230–3; *Examiner*, 16, 23 October, 6, 27 November 1850, 1 January 1851. See also F.H. Armstrong, "Gurnett, George" DCB x, 262–3.

65 For the story of this complicated issue see Alan Wilson, *The Clergy Reserves of Upper Canada* (Toronto 1968) and John Moir, *Church and State in Canada West* (Toronto 1959), 27–81.

67 *Globe*, 12 July 1851.

68 Ibid., 24, 26, 29 July, 2 August 1851.

69 Ibid., 27, 29 November, 2, 6, 9 December 1851; *Toronto Mirror* 12 December 1851.

70 *Globe*, 11, 13 December 1851.

71 *Debates*, 1853, 260, 2330–1.

72 *Globe*, 5, 12, 19, 23, 26 April 1852; *Weekly North American* (Toronto) 21 April 1853; *Toronto Mirror* 8, 22, 29 April 1853. See also Foster J.K. Griezic "An Uncommon Conservative: The Political Career of John Hillyard Cameron,1846–62" MA thesis, Carleton University, 1965, 62–8.

73 *Globe*, 28 April 1853.

74 Ibid., 17 July 1852.

75 Harry Lovelock, "Reminiscences of Toronto Orangeism" in *Official Orange Souvenir. In Honour of the 212th Anniversary of the Battle of the Boyne* (Toronto 1912), 17; *Examiner*, 14 July 1852.

76 On separate schools, see Franklin A. Walker, *Catholic Education and Politics in Upper Canada* (Toronto 1955), and Moir, *Church and State*, 129–80.

77 *Globe*, 12 July 1853; *Leader*, 27 July, 1 August 1853; *Mackenzie's Weekly Message* 28 July 1853. See also Robin Burns, "Thomas D'Arcy McGee: A Biography," PHD diss., McGill University, 1976; Edward J. Doherty, "An Analysis of Social and Political Thought in the Irish Catholic Press of Upper Canada, 1858–1867,' MA thesis, University of Waterloo, 1976; Murray Nicholson, "The Catholic Church and the Irish in Victorian Toronto" PHD diss., University of Guelph, 1981; Gerald Stortz, "John Joseph Lynch, Archbishop of Toronto: A Biographical Study of Reli-gious, Political and Social Commitment," PHD diss., University of Guelph, 1980; Peter Toner, "The Rise of Irish Nationalism in Canada," PHD diss., National University of Ireland, 1974; Daniel Colman Lyne, "The Irish in the Province of Canada in the Decade Leading to Confed-eration," PHD diss., McGill University, 1960; and Jacques Gibeault, "Les Relations entre Thomas D'Arcy McGee et James G. Moylan, 1858–1865," MA thesis, Université d'Ottawa, 1971.

78 J.M.S. Careless, *Brown of the Globe* 1 (Toronto 1959).

79 *Globe*, 17 July 1852.
80 *Leader*, 24 January 1857.
81 Careless, *Brown* I, 244–6; *Globe*, 4, 15 December 1857; *Mackenzie's Weekly Messenger*, 4, 11, 18 December 1857. For the full story of this election, see Barrie Dyster, "Captain Bob and the Noble Ward." For an excellent, detailed breakdown of the vote, see *Leader*, 29 December 1857.
82 *Globe*, August 1858.
83 Ibid., 26 August 1858; Minute Book, Toronto District Lodge, 10, 18 August 1858, Orange Archives, Willowdale, Ontario
84 Minute Book, Toronto District Lodge, 7, 16, 28 September, 15, 19 October, 1, 16 December 1858, 11 January 1859.
85 See note 65.
86 *Globe*, 5 July 1855. See also ibid., 2, 3, 46, 6, 7 July 1855; *Examiner*, 4, 11 July 1855.
87 *Globe*, 16, 19 July 1855; *Examiner*, 18 July 1855. For interesting American studies of volunteer fire companies, see Bruce Laurie, "Fire Companies and Gangs in Southwark: The 1840s" in Allen F. Davis and Mark H. Haller, eds, *The Peoples of Philadelphia* (Philadelphia 1973), 71–88, and Geoffrey Giglierano, "'A Creature of Law': Cincinnati's Paid Fire Department," *Cincinnati Historical Society Bulletin* XL (1982): 78–99. On the importance of fires in nineteenth-century Canadian cities see John C. Weaver and Peter DeLottinville, "The Conflagration and the City: Disaster and Progress in British North America during the Nineteenth Century," *Histoire sociale/Social History* XXVI (1980): 417–49. A more peaceable view is offered in Bradley Rudachyk, "'At the Mercy of the Devouring Element': The Equipment and Organization of the Halifax Fire Establishment, 1830–1850," *Collections of the Royal Nova Scotia Historical Society* XLI (1982): 165–84. For Toronto background, see Armstrong "Toronto in Transition," chap. 8.
88 *Globe*, 21 July 1855.
89 Ibid., 3 July 1855.
90 Ibid., 27 July 1855.
91 Jarvis, "Mid Victorian Toronto," 148–54.
94 *Globe*, 1 June 1861.
93 Jarvis, "Mid Victorian Toronto," 154.
94 *Globe*, 19 July 1855.
95 Ibid., 24, 27 July 1855.
96 Ibid., 23, 24, 25, 27 March, 1 April, 13 July 1858; *Leader*, 18, 22, 23, 24, 25, 27 March, 1, 2, 5, 6, 8 April, 13 July 1858. See also Toronto petition in NA RG5 CI, vol. 550, item 625.
97 *Globe*, October–December 1858. For more on the Boulton-Sherwood struggle, see Dyster, "Captain Bob and the Noble Ward."
98 Board of Police Commissioners, Minute Book 1858–1862, 1 December 1858, Toronto Police Museum. For a more detailed study of police

reform, see Nick Rogers "Serving Toronto the Good," in Russell, *Forging a Consensus*, 116–40.

99 For a mid-1840s example of Reform attitudes, see *Examiner*, 1, 8, 15 October 1845.
100 Board of Police Commissioners, Minutes, 1 December 1858.
101 Ibid., 1, 2, 3, 4, 6, 7, 11, 18, 23, 27 December 1858; quotation from 11 December.
102 Ibid., 15 January 1859.
103 *Globe*, 17 January 1859.
104 Minute Book, District Lodge, 4 February 1859; *Patriot*, 2 March 1859; *Globe*, 25 February 1859.
105 *Globe*, 28 June 1859; Minute Book, District Lodge, 29 June 1859.
106 Jarvis, "Mid Victorian Toronto," 71–5.
107 Board of Police Commissioners, Minutes, 24 January 1860.
108 Rogers, "Serving Toronto the Good."
109 Conyngham Crawford Taylor, *The Queen's Jubilee or Toronto "Called Back" From 1887 to 1847* (Toronto 1887), 74–5. For the equally interesting stories of police reform in Montreal, see Elinor Kyte Senior, "The Influence of the British Garrison on the Development of the Montreal Police, 1832–1853," *Military Affairs* XLIII (1979), 63–8, and in Saint John, M.G. Marquis, "The Police Force in Saint John, New Brunswick, 1860–1890," MA thesis, University of New Brunswick, 1980.
110 Jarvis, "Mid Victorian Toronto," 89–90.
111 Toronto Police Order Book, 1859–63, 24 February 1859, Toronto Police Museum.
112 Ibid., 16 March 1859.
113 Ibid., 30 March 1859.
114 Ibid., 23 May, 11 July 1859.
115 Ibid., 5 July, 21 March, 8, 9 August, and 12 November 1859.
116 Gerner, *The Franchise*, 116–17.
117 Recent accounts include: Sean Conway, "Upper Canadian Orangeism in the Nineteenth Century: Aspects of a Pattern of Disruption," MA thesis, Queen's University, 1977; Ann MacDermaid, "The Visit of the Prince of Wales to Kingston in 1860," *Historic Kingston* XXI (1973), 50–61; and J.D. Livermore, "The Orange Order and the Election of 1861 in Kingston" in Gerald Tulchinsky, ed., "To Preserve and Defend: Essays on Kingston in the Nineteenth Century (Montreal 1976), 245–60.
118 Minute Book, District Lodge, 9, 15, 22, 30 August, 3, 5, 27 September 1860; *Globe*, 30, 31 August, 1, 4, 5, 6, 8 September 1860.
119 The Toronto events are described in: A British Canadian [H.J. Morgan] *The Tour of H.R.H. The Prince of Wales Through British America* (Montreal 1860), 156–74, and J.G.D. Englehart, *Journal of the Progress of H.R.H. The Prince of Wales* (London 1860), 56–8. For Newcastle's own account, see John Martineau, *The Life of Henry Pelham, Fifth Duke of*

Newcastle 1811–1864 (London 1908), 297–9. See also Kinahan, Corn-
wallis *Royalty in the New World; or, The Prince of Wales in America* (New
York 1860), 127–8. For a full description of events in Kingston and
Belleville, see William Shannon, *Narrative of the Proceedings of the Loyal
Orangemen of Kingston and Belleville* (Belleville 1861). See also *Address
Presented to H.R.H. The Prince of Wales During His State Visit to British
North America, 1860* (London 1860). For a general view, see James A.
Gibson, "The Duke of Newcastle and British North American Affairs,
1855–64," *Canadian Historical Review* XLIV (1963), 142–56.
120 Cornwallis, *Royalty*, 128.
121 Conway, "Upper Canadian Orangeism," 119.
122 Lovelock, "Reminiscences," 19.
123 "Resolution Passed at a Meeting of the Provincial Grand Orange Lodge
of Canada West, Head at Hamilton, Wednesday, October 24, 1860,"
broadside, University of Western Ontario Archives, London, Ontario.
124 Conway, "Upper Canadian Orangeism," 134.
125 Jarvis, "Mid Victorian Toronto," 62–5. See also C.P. Stacey, "Confederation: The Atmosphere of Crisis" and Bruce W. Hodgins, "Democracy
and the Ontario Fathers of Confederation" in Ontario Historical
Society, *Profiles of a Province: Studies in the History of Ontario* (Toronto
1967), 59–72 and 83–91, respectively.
126 Akenson, "Ontario: Whatever Happened to the Irish?" 241.
127 Eileen and Stephen Yeo, "Ways of Seeing: Control and Leisure versus
Class and Struggle," 128–54 in Eileen and Stephen Yeo, eds, *Popular
Culture and Class Conflict 1590–1914: Explorations in the History of
Labour and Leisure* (Brighton 1981).
128 Robert L. Fraser, "Like Eden in Her Summer Dress: Gentry, Economy
and Society: Upper Canada 1812–1840," PHD diss., University of
Toronto, 1979, 222. See also S.F. Wise, "John Macaulay: Tory for All
Seasons" in Tulchinsky, ed., *To Preserve and Defend*, 185–202.
129 On the new hegemony, see A.W. Rasporich, "The Development of
Political and Social Ideas in the Province of Canada, 1848–1858," PHD
diss., University of Toronto, 1970, esp. 495–503.
130 *Globe*, 24 December 1859.
131 Ibid., 13 July 1855.
132 Eileen and Stephen Yeo, "Ways of Seeing," 141–2. Here they make use
of a most effective metaphor, namely blotting paper, arguing that the
"absorbents are affected by what they absorb ... eventually there's more
ink than blotting paper in which case a new medium is needed by
those who wish to mop up."
133 Senior, "Gowan," 313.
134 Eileen and Stephen Yeo, "Perceived Patterns: Competition and Licence
versus Class and Struggle" in Eileen and Stephen Yeo, eds, *Culture and
Class Conflict*, 271–305.

7 Work Control, the Labour Process, and Nineteenth-Century Canadian Printers

In the nineteenth- and early twentieth-century Canadian labour and socialist movement, printers held pride of place. From D.J. O'Donoghue, "father of the Canadian labour movement," through stalwart Canadian presidents of the International Typographical Union (ITU), John Armstrong and W.B. Prescott, to socialist leaders such as Toronto's Jimmy Simpson, Winnipeg's Arthur Puttee, and Vancouver's R.P. Pettipiece, printers played prominent roles in the Canadian working-class world.[1] And for every printer who became a labour leader, there were probably ten others who became successful in some other walk of life – journalism, publishing, and politics representing only three of the most popular paths. The printers, then, represent the ultimate respectable Victorian craftsman. Indeed, they can be studied as the extreme example of the successful skilled workers who to a large degree maintained their societal positions, despite the onslaught of the Industrial Revolution. By studying printers and their responses to the changing nature of both their work and their workplaces over the course of the century, we can begin to evaluate the role of the successful skilled worker in capitalist transformation.

Printers are a particularly suitable choice for study because rich primary sources exist that allow us to penetrate at least some of the "mysteries of the craft." As well, there is a large secondary literature on both sides of the Atlantic, beginning with the very earliest academic studies of labour. In Canada, the richest extant data cover Toronto – the centre of the English-Canadian publishing industry and a city that possessed a vibrant newspaper press. Much of the material in this paper is drawn from Toronto sources, but other Canadian cities are also considered.

The study of Canadian printers in the nineteenth and early twentieth century divides into three distinct periods of workplace struggles defined by the interaction of labour and capital. The first period, up to mid century, was typified by handicraft production and small combined newspaper and "job" (mixed printing) shops with low levels of capitalization. Relations within the printing industry closely resembled Richard Price's notion of "autonomous regulation."[2] A second period, from the 1850s to the early 1880s, was ushered in by the arrival of the daily paper, rotary presses, and a growing division of labour between pressmen and compositors. In this period, the union and its importance grew, capitalization rose, and competition intensified. This second period might be typified as one of "union regulation," as the typographical unions became ever more crucial to the process of workplace struggle. Finally, from the early 1890s, with the introduction of the linotype machine through to the eight-hour struggle of 1905–7, a third period emerged in which a binational system of collective bargaining commenced and the local unions became increasingly subservient to the international union. At the same time, capitalists began effectively to mass their forces in city-wide and national associations. While it would be anachronistic to see this as a full-fledged "modern industrial relations system," we can nevertheless assert that the constituent ingredients were by then present, including an ever-increasing state role.

HANDICRAFT AND AUTONOMY

A history of Canadian printers in the first half of the nineteenth century, the period of autonomous regulation, commences in the 1820s, when Canadian print shops began to grow beyond simple artisan shops in which a master printer might utilize an apprentice or a combination of a journeyman and an apprentice.[3] By the 1820s the combined newspaper and job shops of the emerging Canadian cities began to bring small numbers of journeymen together in one shop and increasingly to allow the master, now a proprietor, to spend most of his time on journalism and politics. Indeed, some of the new enterprises of the late 1820s and 1830s placed men in charge of shops who were not members of "the art preservative," as printers described themselves. In these cases, journeymen were hired as foremen to run the practical side of the business.

What work did printers perform in these early shops? Printing involved two separate processes that in these early years were both carried out by the same individual: typesetting and presswork. Setting type or composing had not changed since Gutenberg and would not until the early 1890s. Composition involved taking a single piece of type from the case, placing it in a composing stick, and thus – letter by letter – spelling words with the appropriate spacing and line justification (insuring equal line length by either spacing-out or spacing-in through the addition or deletion of various slugs and leads). When the composing stick was filled with a few lines, they were transferred to a galley. When the galley was completed, it was run on a proofing press to take a single impression. After proof-reading, corrections were made and the galley was ready for the press. This second process, presswork, involved two printers working jointly – one inking, while the other screwed and pulled. The latter job involved considerable strength and both jobs were dangerous in the period of wooden presses whose screws occasionally broke, injuring the printers.

Thus, in the early years of the nineteenth century, printing remained a handicraft. Yet changes were already under way that heralded the industrialization of printing. The iron press was in the process of re-placing wood, rollers instead of balls began to be used for inking, and experiments with horsepower and steam-power were commencing.[4]

In the smaller British North American towns, newspaper shops would change very slowly, but already by the 1830s in the growing cities, print shops were increasing in size and number. More import-ant, it was also becoming clear that not all journeymen could aspire to be masters. As non-printers began to take on employers' roles as newspaper editors and publishers, the older craft solidarity of master and journeyman weakened. By the 1830s, then, printers for the first time began to identify their interests as distinct from those of their masters and from the trade at large. As a result, the first printers' unions emerged in the British North American colonies.[5]

The language of these early unions' statements of principle suggest how tenuous was this break. In Quebec, for example, printers formed their first union in 1827 and in 1836 defined their intent largely in terms of the improvement of the craft and declared their commitment to "the welfare of employer and employed."[6] In Toronto, the printers' initial public announcement pinpointed many persistent themes of nineteenth-century printers' unionism:

Owing to the many innovations which have been made upon the long established wages of the professors of the art of printing, it was deemed expedient by the journeymen printers of York, that they should form them-selves into a body, similar to societies in other parts of the world, in order to maintain that honourable station and respectability that belongs to the profession.[7]

Drawing on the strengths of informal craft custom derived from both the Old World and colonial America and on the established practices of the previous thirty years of printers' unionism in England and the United States, Toronto printers quickly established a standard rate, an unemployment benefit, a tramping benefit for fellow craftsmen who chose to move on in search of work, sick benefits, a card system, rules governing apprenticeship, and apprenticeship limitation. They also initiated attempts to influence hiring by insisting on priority for unemployed union members. The major conflicts of the period revolved around apprenticeship; the Toronto Typographical Society (TTS) petitioned the legislature in 1836 "for the better regulation of apprentices in the art of printing."[8]

At first, Canadian publishers appeared to welcome the new unions and their rules. In most cases, practical printers themselves, they willingly accepted the printers' proud avowals that "the object of this society was for the interest of the employer as well as the employed." In October 1836, however, Toronto printers demanded a $1 increase on their scale and the strict enforcement of their apprenticeship limitation clause. Employer/employee unity broke down and, when the masters refused the increase, the union struck. The strike met vigorous employer opposition and the men were forced to return to work under a general amnesty without gaining their objectives, although some printers did receive the higher rate. In this case, employer solidarity, the defection of at least one union foreman, and the combined ability of masters, "rats" (the printers' term for scabs), and apprentices to continue to produce the weekly papers helped defeat the union.[9]

Although attempts were made at inter-union communication, these first printers' unions in Quebec (1827), Toronto (1832), Montreal and Hamilton (1833), and Halifax (1837) were intensely local[10] (see appendix 1). The Toronto Typographical Society's early years can thus be used as an example of this early phase of class struggle in the printing trade. After a seven-year hiatus, the Toronto union re-emerged in early 1844. In the interim, the old union scale "had in the main been upheld," thus suggesting that much of the early printers' strength lay in informal work groups. The impetus for reorganization came not from any immediate desire to press new demands, but from the arrival of George Brown who attempted to organize the Printing Employers Association with the general aim of reducing wages to the level of the provincial towns. Brown's interest in cost cutting apparently arose from the expense of importing Toronto's first cylinder press for the *Globe* office. The new machinery created initial financial difficulties for him, and, as an improving capitalist, he continued to try to reduce his labour costs. Brown's familiarity with the newest in machinery presses was evident in his position as Canadian agent of H. Roe & Co. of New York, the major producer of the machinery.[11]

Another ongoing dispute between masters and men continued to focus on apprenticeship, which apparently provided the more traditional masters with their major saving. "This growing evil," as the union described "the mania for taking boys" in 1845, confounded the printers, for "it is a matter where the right of capital is so nicely balanced against the interest of labour that it requires a delicate and skillful touch to turn the scale in our favour." This "delicate touch" continued to escape the union and the most frequent grievance arising throughout the 1840s revolved around the terms and limitations of apprenticeship.[12]

Brown and his fellow employers slowly but surely were transforming the old handicraft trade into a new industry. Printers took note of these alarming developments and reorganized. Soon after Brown's arrival, the printers noted that "when clouds appear, wise men put on their cloaks." Thus, under a new motto "United to support, not combined to injure," the TTS explained that "as far as the scale of prices is concerned, they believe in adhering, taking all things into view, to what had hitherto been considered the customary rates in the city for piecework and weekly wages." In the working of the union's statement, "everything calculated to give offence to the employers was studiously avoided." Brown's initial attempt at rate cutting failed because he was unable to carry the other Toronto employers with him. And a few months later, the union formally pre-empted another possible means of cutting labour costs by resolving that "when a compositor is employed by the piece he shall not allow the foreman, or other person, paid by the week, to make up his matter and take the 'fat' of the same." In this way, they prevented any master from reducing costs by taking the "fat" (in printers' parlance, the material most easily and thus quickly composed) "for the office," that is, to be set by a printer on a weekly wage as opposed to the more customary piece rate of the trade. In addition, for the first time, an overtime rate was demanded and won for night composition after 7:00 p.m. These gains led one year later to a renewed assault on the union by George Brown who, after filling his shop with boys, began to hire journeymen printers below scale. When the union expelled those working under the scale, Brown fired his union printers, including the TTS president, asserting, "I will not be dictated to by the Society as to what wages I must give men belonging to it. I will not be compelled to pay every man $7 a week." The union declared the *Banner* a rat office, and published "A Plain Statement of Facts," which made clear their continuing belief in the customary wage:

For a number of years a certain scale of prices has prevailed in this city which was considered perfectly fair and reasonable by all the employers ... and which continued in operation without exception until [Brown's arrival] ... who has ever since been unremitting in his liberal endeavours to reduce as low as possible that justly considered fair and equitable rate of remuneration due to the humble operative ... The printers of Toronto are but acting on the defensive and contending for no additional remuneration – nothing exorbitant or unreasonable – but, on the contrary, are only endeavouring to maintain that which is considered by all the respectable proprietors, as fair and just reward for their labour and toil. "The labourer is worthy of his hire."[13]

The Toronto union had other problems in the late 1840s. It experienced low attendance at meetings, probably owing to the continued relative autonomy of individual office work groups. This problem was overcome in three ways in the late 1840s, however, and did not recur subsequently. First, in 1848 the benevolent aspects of the society were consciously expanded to increase its stability. Second, the following year, foremen became full members instead of sustaining their previous honorary status – an extremely important development given the foreman's control over hiring. (This rule, later imbedded in the International Typographical Union's Book of Laws, proved central to union power.) Finally, Brown and the other master printers provided additional impetus for union growth in 1847 when, after a meeting with the journeymen to discuss craft matters, they presented a plan for a reduction in the wage scale that the printers successfully resisted.

By the late 1840s, then, handicraft printing had begun its slow evolution toward full-fledged industrial production. Clearly differentiated groups of workers and employers had emerged and confronted each other over the latter's attempts to cut their costs of skilled labour. But the labour process itself was still largely unchanged. With his agency for the most advanced technology, George Brown represented the future, but the new world of printing remained no more than a dim cloud on the printers' horizon. Symbolically, the Toronto printers greeted the new decade with one of their frequent dinners, which still involved masters and men united in a celebration of "the art preservative."

THE ROTARY PRESS, THE DAILY NEWSPAPER, AND LOCAL UNION RULE

In the years from 1850 to 1890, Canada experienced an industrial revolution. For printers, however, as for many groups of craftsmen, industrialization proceeded unevenly. By the late 1840s, an important component of the printing trades was about to join the ranks of industry. City newspaper production, based on growing urban markets, would be transformed in the following decades by steam-powered cylinder and rotary presses and the arrival in Canada of the daily paper.[14] Yet, only urban newspapers purchased the new machine presses, while in the book and job segments of the industry and in the country newspaper offices, the old presses would hold on for decades to come. At the same time, the evolution of the labour process within each sector was equally uneven. Typesetting remained unchanged in its reliance on skilled printers, and the stark contrast between the pressmen with his massive machines and the compositor with his case and composing stick demonstrates well the uneven transition from handicraft to industry within printing. The divisions between these two groups of workers continued to increase, and the "all-round" printer started his journey towards obsolescence.

For both employers and employees, the uneven development of the industry would make the achievement of unity difficult, and thus keep the battles between them surprisingly equal. Only later, as the division of labour advanced and the industry sorted itself out into trade segments, would capital unite. Equally, only after the workers themselves divided into the newly created component crafts would the possibility of a new unity present itself.

The cities led the way in these dramatic developments. In Toronto the first steam-powered press was introduced at the *Christian Guardian* office in 1851.[15] Two years later, George Brown continued his role as an innovator by bringing to the *Globe* Toronto's first rotary presses. The huge increase in the pace of production that resulted allowed newspaper publishers to produce dailies in place of the older tri-weeklies, semi-weeklies, and weeklies. In 1860, the *Globe* added a second large, double-cylinder press and new American folding machines. The increasing size of the firm was reflected in its incorporation a few years later as the Globe Printing Company on a limited liability basis. In 1868, a new building was purchased large enough to house the paper's two massive new Hoe Lightning four-feeder presses. The demands of the daily papers for quicker production led to the introduction of new improved web presses (roll fed, rather than sheet fed) at the Montreal *Star* in 1875, and at the Toronto

Globe, Mail, and *Telegram* in 1880. By 1881 the *Globe* had the most sophisticated plant available.[16]

These new presses and the daily papers they made possible transformed the scale of newspaper production and dramatically raised capitalization levels. Between the 1850s and the 1880s, these pressures brought about a "fierce struggle" to extend circulation and eliminate competition that culminated in numerous newspaper failures and mergers, especially in the depressions of the late 1850s and the 1870s. Historian Paul Rutherford has described the industry as reaching the status of "ruthless" form of "big business" by the 1860s. The increasingly separate book and job branch of the industry also faced a crisis in the 1870s owing to "ruinous competition," which led Theodore L. De Vinne, a leading New York employer, to express concern about "menacing aspects of the future" for the industry. In Ottawa in particular, the problem was cutthroat competitive bidding for government printing contracts.[17]

These developments in the printing industry after 1850 had profound implications for the work force. In the first place, they drove a wedge between the compositors, whose handicraft skills remained intact, and the pressmen, who had become machine-tenders. A printer told a royal commission in the 1880s that he was familiar with small presses, but knew nothing of the large rotaries, which he described as "out of the line of the usual printer's work."[18] Although this division had been developing for years, the crisis came to a head in the 1870s and led initially to separately chartered pressmen's locals of the ITU (Ottawa 1880; Toronto 1883; Montreal 1887). In 1889, however, after years of tension, the pressmen seceded to form the International Printing Pressmen's Union (IPPU). This split led to years of inter-trade wrangling, although a modicum of pease resulted from the so-called Tri-Partite Agreement of 1895, which conceded local jurisdiction over pressmen to the IPPU and of bookbinders to the International Brotherhood of Bookbinders. All pledged to work together in an Allied Printing Trades Council in each city that would control the union label.[19]

Second, the growing separation of the book and job sector of the industry from newspaper publishing grew more apparent in the 1870s, as newspapers increasingly abandoned their job shops. This separation carried serious implications for printers because the branches emphasized different skills. Most job shops demanded more varied skills that more closely resembled the talents of the old-time, all-round printer, whereas the urban daily newspapers were increasingly specialized. The built-in variation in pay scales, whereby newspapers paid by the piece and job shops by the week, led increasingly to quite separate negotiations and different scales for the two branches of the industry.

In the newspaper offices, rising capitalization and vigorous competition led publishers to pursue cost-cutting tactics, especially in the still labour-intensive typesetting work. In the labour/management strife that ensued, masters viewed the conflict specifically in terms of workplace control: "The simple truth of the matter is the journeymen insist upon ruling editors, publishers and anyone connected with the establishments, especially in the morning paper offices. The dictation has reached the point where it becomes intolerable; and the employers, one and all, have resolved to submit to it no longer, be consequence what it may."[20]

The printers fought back by strengthening their union organization. In the wake of the 1854 strikes in Toronto and Quebec, they first canvassed the idea of a broader, Canada-wide organization, but without any success.[21] Eventually, the continental labour market in which Canadian artisans worked led Canadian printers to join the National Typographical Union in the United States. Saint John led the way in 1865, and locals in Toronto, Montreal, Ottawa, Hamilton, Halifax, London, St Catharines, and Quebec followed in quick succession (see appendix 2). The new Canadian membership brought a change in the name of the central organization to the International Typographical Union. Not surprisingly, these centres of printers' unionism coincided almost completely with the urban areas where daily papers had caught on: Montreal had eight; Halifax, Saint John, Toronto, and Quebec four each; and Ottawa, Hamilton, London, and St Catharines three each. (The lone exception to this pattern was Kingston, which had two dailies in 1872, but no ITU local until 1886). After encountering difficulties in the economically depressed 1870s (the Saint John and Halifax locals lapsed briefly), the ITU's Canadian membership rebounded with new vigour in the 1880s, and new locals were added in Ontario and the West.

These local unions sought to consolidate and defend craft control of the labour process through carefully policed "laws." As a Toronto printer explained in the 1880s, all matter in union shops was distributed equally: "Whatever may be first on the hook is given to the first men calling for it." Foremen, who were union members, had complete control over hiring. A wage scale was not reached by bilateral negotiation: the union men would simply "discuss it in the union first and then change the scale," the Toronto printer noted.[22] In 1878, the Toronto local further developed its organization by empowering a three-man "Guardian Committee" to act as a secret body to deal with "unfair" shops and printers who violated union rules.[23]

These unions' power lay not only in their members' valuable skills, which could be withdrawn from any printing offices that refused to accept union standards of employment, but also in the newspapers' susceptibility to public pressure owing to their dependence on circulation revenue. In 1853, the Toronto printers initiated a provocative and innovative strategy by appealing for broad support in *An Address to the Working Classes of Canada*. This general indictment of the Brown family's labour policies over its ten years in Canada concluded with a warning:

WORKING MEN, OF WHATEVER CALLING! ... Beware of the *Globe* – put no faith in its proprietor: The oppressor of the Journeymen Printers is the oppressor of the journeymen of every other trade. It is necessary, then, to say that George Brown *is the enemy of the working classes generally.*[24]

This kind of appeal was particularly effective in the midst of the newspapers' competitive battles in the 1880s, when printers first introduced boycotts against Toronto and Halifax newspapers, a tactic imported from the Irish struggles and popularized by the Knights of Labor throughout North America.[25]

In their confrontation with the ITU locals, the publishers resisted not only new wage demands, but also any restrictions on their ability to make use of their employees' labour-power. The most famous episode of industrial conflict in the period involved the question of shorter hours of work, which the Toronto union first raised in 1869, partially echoing the militant American movement spearheaded by the National Labor Union, in which the ITU was active. In 1872, a major struggle pitted the Toronto printers against George Brown and a hastily organized Master Employers' Association. The issue was the nine-hour day, and Toronto printers provided the cutting edge for the larger movement. This strike is almost as famous as the Winnipeg General Strike in Canadian history and need not delay us here, except to note that the issue revolved around control and authority, not wages. The printers sought a 10 per cent increase on piece rates and a 10 per cent decrease in hours in book and job shops. The masters indicated their willingness to concede the former, but with Brown's leadership resisted shorter hours and "the tyrannical thraldom of the Typographical Society." The strike became a political cause célèbre, especially when Brown decided to prosecute the leadership of the union for conspiracy. Great political advantage accrued to the Conservatives owing to their major Toronto newspaper's support of the printers, and to the Macdonald Tory government's passage of a Trade Unions Act to legalize unions. The strike resulted in a split decision:

the printers won the nine-hour day in most Toronto job and book-shops, but the union temporarily lost its position in some of the Toronto newspaper offices.[26]

Often in the years after 1850, Canadian printers fought more defensive battles, as their employers resorted to a variety of managerial innovations to chip away at craft control. After an 1853 strike in Toronto, the workers' recriminations against the great innovator, the *Globe*, brought these practices to light. "Anything but full employment had been the order of the house," since piece hands were often kept standing idle and week hands were frequently laid off for half and even quarter days, "a practice unknown in any other office, probably in America," the printers complained. Compositors were often kept at work until 3:00 or 4:00 a.m., only to find that there was no work for them the next day, "thus impairing their health and turning the hours of repose into those of labour." The printers also warned that apprentices suffered "gross injustices" at the *Globe* since they were subject to arbitrary dismissal and, in addition were not instructed in the secrets of the craft. Finally, against Brown's vow not to pay men of unequal merit the same rate, the union requested that he convert his shop from weekly pay to piece rates, as was the norm in other Toronto newspaper offices, and provide them with sufficient work.[27] In a similar vein, Saint John printers lost a strike in 1859 over the limitation of apprenticeships,[28] and in 1873 the Ottawa Master Printers declared that foremen must leave the union, that the open shop must prevail, that departing journeymen must give two weeks notice, and that no printer could leave work without the consent of the employer.[29]

Newer managerial tactics were even more threatening. One major change was the development of night work in order to produce morning papers. Toronto printers denounced this "unnatural" system of work in 1853, and the struggle against it continued the following year, when their demands included another advance in the overtime rate and, for the first time, pay while standing idle. The newspaper proprietors protested that these demands were a hidden attempt to abolish night work, but their compromise offer, which was eventually accepted in the major print shops, conceded differential rates for night work, but not its abolition, as the union had demanded the year before. Employers offered small advances with higher pay for night work while abolishing charges for overtime. In effect they moved toward a clearly recognizable shift system that entrenched night work in the industry.[30]

Another innovation in the 1850s that had serious long-term implications was the recruitment of women as compositors in a strike-breaking role. Toronto publishers used them in the 1854 strike, as did

London employers in 1856.[31] Boys and country printers continued to be used as well; in fact, a Toronto printer argued in the 1880s that the steady influx of young, country printers who "go and come like swallows" and often were not properly trained constituted the biggest problem facing that city's printers. But unionized printers' ire singled out employers who resorted to using women as "rats." By the 1880s, women, nonetheless, had only a limited role in the industry, mostly performing recognizably inferior work owing to their lack of training and their usually short time at the case. While welcome to join the union and entitled to equal pay, they seldom fulfilled the five-year initiation requirement to demonstrate competency. There were, however, two women in the Toronto union by 1887.[32]

In the 1870s and 1880s, new attacks were launched on compositors' customary prerogatives. In most offices, for example, the "fat," especially advertisements, had been distributed in various ways devised by the printers themselves to preserve equitable pay. These devices were necessitated by the standard piece rates of the newspaper branch of the industry. Innovative cost-cutters continued to fight for the right to keep the fat "for the office," that is, to give it to less efficient compositors paid by the week. similar struggles occurred over the ITU's "matrix law," whereby the union demanded that either all material published in a newspaper had to be typeset on the premises, or else the compositors had to be paid as though it had been. This rule prevented publishers from using various kinds of pre-set plate matter to fill their pages while avoiding composition costs. In the 1880s, numerous agencies sprang up to provide precisely these services to newspapers in the form of so-called boilerplate. The ITU fought plate matter from its inception, while profit-conscious employers tried to introduce it continuously.[33] When the Royal Commission on the Relations of Capital and Labour visited Saint John in the late 1880s, it discovered an ongoing fight over fat and plate matter. "I do not agree that the printer is entitled to the fat matter," one proprietor explained. "I think that a man who has control of a business like a newspaper, who has all the care and responsibility of the concern, should have something to say in the matter." He frankly admitted that taking the fat was an economy measure caused by increasing competition, as was the use of plate matter, which he viewed as "a kind of improved machinery."[34] In 1887, the Saint John local lost a major strike against the city's three newspapers over the use of plate matter,[35] and the St Catharines printers' defeat in three unsuccessful strikes in an eighteen-month period in the late 1880s over the same issue led to the local's demise.[36] A similar issue emerged in an unsuccessful strike against the Toronto *World* in 1888, when its proprietor refused to abide by a union rule that any additional insertion of an ad, if it was changed at all, was to be paid for again in its entirety.[37]

The years between the 1850s and the 1880s, then, saw the struggles between the skilled printers and their employers intensify. On the one hand, the workers had tightened the bonds of unity by joining the ITU and adopting its increasingly rigid set of "laws" governing the trade; on the other, their bosses, caught in cutthroat competitive battles, relentlessly attacked craft control over the labour process. There was no final victory in this trench warfare. In 1884, the Toronto *Mail* was still blustering that it "purported to resume the control of the necessary and proper economies of our own business, which had largely passed into the hands of the Printers Union";[38] and three years later the manager of the Saint John *Sun* was still muttering about management's right of "using their own property as suits themselves" and refusing to "submit to dictation on the subject."[39] In some cities, the printers had suffered severe defeats, but in Toronto at least, they maintained much of the workplace control (which David Montgomery and others have associated with the autonomous workman) that was now increasingly centred in the union. Certainly their maintenance of craft control should belie any lurking romantic notions of conflict-free handicraft based on "customs" and "traditions." There were customs, but they were established in the rough-and-tumble of class conflict. None was safe from the encroachment of improving employers.

THE LINOTYPE AND THE TRIUMPH OF THE INTERNATIONAL UNION

Two related changes took place in the labour process and work relations of the Canadian printing industry at the close of the nineteenth century – mechanization and bureaucratization. One brought machinery into the composing room, the bane of the improving-employers' life, which Theodore De Vinne (the F.W. Taylor of printing) once described as "the great sinkhole" where "the profits of the house are lost."[40] The second drew Canadian printers and their unions into much more centralized structures of collective bargaining.

The industry, especially the newspaper sector, was reaching much larger proportions by the 1890s. The first step towards concentration of capital appeared when the Southams of the Hamilton *Spectator* purchased the Ottawa *Citizen*, which they combined with their huge job shops in Toronto and Montreal.[41] Monopoly capitalist strategies thus began to figure even in the newspaper business, formerly a bastion of competition in limited markets. This trend toward concentration was also evident in the founding in 1889 of the McKim advertising agency as a central clearing house for the placing of national and regional newspaper advertisements.[42] Even more important, however, was the growth of national and continental employers' associations.

Across North America two of these organizations emerged in the late 1880s. The United Typothetae of America (UTA), covering the book and job branches of the industry, met for the first time in 1887 "to resist the demands of the International Typographical Union for the nine-hour day." While often split between what Clarence Bonnett called "negotiatory" and "belligerent" factions, the UTA was generally at war with the ITU. Encouraged by an initial victory in 1887 in defeating the union's campaign for shorter hours, the UTA proceeded to refuse any conference with the ITU and planned further assaults on long-standing union rules – control of foremen, limitation of apprentices, the holding of union meetings during business hours, the closed shop, the matrix law, priority laws, and other examples of union power. The UTA dealt the ITU another strike defeat in Pittsburgh in 1891–93 and won smaller victories in a number of local struggles, including Montreal and Ottawa, where Theodore De Vinne's "Printers' Protective Fraternity" provided strikebreakers. The ITU's continental alliance with the bookbinders' and pressmen's unions in 1895, however, convinced the UTA of the need for compromise, and in 1898 the Syracuse Agreement was signed, covering both Canada and the United States. The other continental employers' association, the American Newspaper Publishers' Association (ANPA), also founded in 1887, tended towards a "negotiatory" position, and after 1900 entered into elaborate international arbitration agreements with the ITU and other printing trades' unions.[43]

Canadian publishers and printers joined both the UTA and the ANPA, but they also had an organization of their own that shared a similar history. The Canadian Press Association (CPA) had been founded in 1859, but through its first three decades it functioned primarily as a social club for small-town newspaper publishers. The Toronto press, for example, maintained its splendid isolation from the CPA for many years. By the late 1870s, however, more interest was being expressed in the business side of newspaper publishing, and the trend continued in the 1880s. By 1888, the CPA had established its aim as "the principle of improving the prosperity of the newspaper industry." Complaining of too much competition, of the growth of advertising agencies and their commissions, and of declining subscription rates, the publishers piously pronounced that "a newspaper, to be a power for good, must make money." Not surprisingly, then, topics at conventions in the early 1890s included typesetting machinery and myriad discussions of managerial strategy. These interests intensified early in the twentieth century and in 1905, a Daily Newspapers Section of the CPA was created. This body would be a major actor in the renewed struggle over shorter hours.[44]

Meanwhile, union centralization was growing as a result of the union's failure to implement shorter hours in the trade in 1887. The creation of the UTA as an employers' association with clear anti-union aims and its success in defeating the ITU shorter-hours strikes in 1887 created an impetus for union reform. These institutional changes, which had been proposed earlier but rejected by the membership, brought in full-time officers, an international strike fund, and executive control over the decision to strike. The appointment of district organizers led to the development of specialists in bargaining who travelled from city to city as union trouble-shooters. The much-vaunted local autonomy of the typographical unions, especially big-city locals like Toronto Local 91, was considerably eroded in this process. By the turn of the century, a pattern of large-scale binational negotiations was established, with provisions for international arbitration.[45]

The significance of these binational developments was accentuated for Toronto printers because of their almost unique status of already having won the nine-hour day in 1872. One of only three ITU locals on the continent with this contract provision, the Toronto local was understandably less than enthusiastic about an expensive struggle against the UTA, especially when in 1891 it was refused international sanction for a proposed struggle to increase the Toronto wage scale. The events of the 1880s and 1890s signalled a real decline in local union power that, in the Toronto case, would be damaging to its interests in the future. This conflict between the local and the International was mediated for Toronto printers by the presence of W.B. Prescott, (a stalwart of the Toronto local) as ITU president from 1891 to 1898.

After 1887, union/management negotiations in Toronto were qualitatively different. Instead of the unilateralism of the autonomous regulation period, or even the tentative consultation of the period of union regulation, this period witnessed the establishment of full-scale collective-bargaining procedure. The union appointed a scale committee that, in effect, became a bargaining team. The committee formulated its demands and communicated them to the newly formed Toronto Printing Employers' Association. Meetings took place in which the masters presented their counterproposals in a bargaining environment. The committee then consulted the union on the revised set of proposals. Details on the 1887 negotiations are scant, but in 1890–91, this process took a full eleven months before the International refused to sanction a strike – a far cry from the immediate strikes called earlier in the century.[46]

These new, more centralized structures of capital and labour were soon tested in two major confrontations, first over the introduction of typesetting machinery and then over the eight-hour day. The major technological innovation, which finally ended the remaining handicraft skill of typesetting, was Otto Mergenthaler's invention of the linotype machine. Extraordinary efforts at designing a mechanical device to set type had continued throughout the nineteenth century, but the increased flurry of experimentation in the 1870s and 1880s that culminated in the new machine enjoyed considerable attention and enthusiastic support from the increasingly profit-conscious employers. Especially crucial in the newspaper industry, above all at the big-city dailies, where speed was of the essence, the machine spread across Canada in the 1890s. Initially, it appeared to represent an answer to employers' major problems: the physical limitations on production resulting from hand composition and the union's ongoing control of the composing room. As it turned out, only the first problem was overcome, since the ITU locals won control over the operation of the machines. Guided by central ITU policy, union strategy was not to resist their introduction, but to insist that only practical printers should run them.

The challenge of the linotype came first in the large cities, and the Toronto experience illustrates the union's success in integrating the machinery into its shop-floor control patterns. The *Globe* bought the first typesetting machine in 1891, and the union immediately began to prepare a new scale of wages for machine operators, simultaneously pushed by the *Mail*'s complaint that the union was forcing it to acquire machines because union printers were working too cheaply on the *Globe*'s machines. The employers responded that new scales were premature, since they were still unsure of the machines' capacities. But the union proceeded unilaterally to declare a new wage rate, which would be a time rate rather than the customary payment by the piece. The men wanted to avoid the speedup that might result from piecework on the new machines. In September, the newspaper publishers eventually agreed to an acceptable scale. Only the *News*, and a few months later the *Presbyterian*, forced the printers out on successful strikes to resist the introduction of piece rates. Even the *Telegram*, the only non-union office remaining in Toronto, came to terms and became a strict union office after almost twenty years of resistance. All Toronto newspapers, in fact, were union shops, as were most book and job shops, and estimates of union organization in the 1890s ranged between 85 and 90 per cent of the industry. Union members were to learn on the machines at a rate of $12 a week for six weeks and then $14 a week after demonstrating their proficiency, which was set at a low level of 2,000 ems per hour or 100,000 ems per week. Thus, by the early 1890s, the union had achieved almost complete organization of the industry and had won control over the use of the new machines, thanks to the combination of the printers' shop-floor and union strength, the skill requirements of the new technology, and the employers' evident desire to stabilize costs in the industry.[47]

The other great struggle of the period, for the eight-hour day, was co-ordinated even more tightly from ITU headquarters and highlighted the change that had taken place from autonomous control through union power to the triumph of centralization. After the "armed truce" of the 1898 Syracuse Agreement, which brought the nine-hour day a year later, both sides spent the following years "preparing and hoarding for a great struggle over the eight-hour day and the closed shop." In 1902, the ITU set up an International Eight-Hour Committee, which called on all locals not to sign contracts dated beyond 1 October 1905 unless they contained eight-hour clauses. The UTA, meanwhile, refused all attempts at compromise and discussion, instead insisting that the ITU cease to control foremen, an ITU rule dating from the 1850s. When, in 1903, the pressmen's union accepted a Typothetae guarantee of union scale and union conditions in return for the open shop, the war became inevitable. The fight commenced in September 1905, when the ITU called out all locals without the eight-hour day and not under contract in support of its embattled Chicago, Detroit, and San Antonio locals. This call pulled out some 88 locals and 3,000 printers, and the number increased by January 1906, the original date proposed for the strike. Unlike many strikes where victory or defeat are quick and clear, the strikes dragged on for almost three years. The 1907 ITU convention dismissed its Eight-Hour Committee with victory in sight, but the various strike assessments, while diminished after October 1906, were not completely lifted until the end of February 1908. The magnitude of the strike may perhaps be illustrated by the total of $4,163,970.64 that the ITU estimated it spent in winning the eight-hour day. And win it did, although at great cost. Even the UTA conceded defeat when, in February 1908, it quietly dropped the 54-hour-a-week phrase from its official policy. By that date the association had shrunk to half its pre-strike size, since each city employer's group was forced to resign when it capitulated to the ITU.[48]

The major struggle in Canada had taken place in Winnipeg, but there had been battles in several other centres. Only in Winnipeg and Saint John did resistance amount to much. After the ITU walked out in September 1905, the Winnipeg branch of the Typothetae fought long and hard, and resorted to the importation of English printers. The fact that these compositors were induced to migrate without being given information of the strike in progress created a furore that eventually led to a polite condemnation from the Department of Labour, penned by the inimitable W.L.M. King. The department officially listed the strike as over in November when the Typothetae members filled their shops with the unwitting Brits, but the strike continued and in January most of the English printers left work and joined the ITU. By June 1906, the local labour press reported all union printers at work in eight-hour shops. The Typothetae's open-shop drive had failed in Winnipeg.[49]

The Saint John local pressed its demand for eight hours in early December 1905 and succeeded with the newspapers but not with the job shops. After a short strike, most of the employers conceded, one of them muttering that it was "outrageous that an employer can be held up by his workmen and forced to grant whatever they have in mind to ask whether he feels like doing so or not." By April the last holdout conceded defeat and Saint John, too, was an eight-hour city.[50]

The other Canadian eight-hour strikes were minor affrays. In Hamilton and Halifax, brief strikes took place to force small recalcitrant shops into line. In London, it took only a one-day strike to gain the shorter day in all but one shop, while in Regina, one week proved enough to muscle one newspaper into line. The strike in Guelph, however, was more interesting. There, an agreement had been reached in summer 1905 that the printers would receive the eight-hour day on 1 January 1906, as long as the ITU did not change its position. As it turned out, later representations from the Daily Newspaper Section of the CPA to the ITU executive in September 1905 led to an agreement for an 8½-hour day on 1 January 1906 and a further reduction to eight hours on 1 July 1907. This settlement prevailed in many Ontario localities, including Guelph. Guelph printers, however, who had won an eight-hour Saturday three years before, could not believe that this meant an increase in Saturday hours for them until July 1907, and when the employers tried to enforce this increase, they struck. The employers appealed to the ITU executive, which responded by ordering their Guelph members back to work. Centralized power clearly cut in both directions.[51] This was also apparent in other Canadian jurisdictions. In Hamilton, a revolt against the 10 per cent levy on the union membership to finance the eight-hour fight led to the suspension of the local's charter for three months in 1906, while in Ottawa, the relatively privileged Government Printing Bureau printers led a major secession movement away from the ITU in protest over the extra assessment.[52]

In Toronto the scene proved even more complicated. Because they were tied into a three-year contract that did not expire until 1 June 1907, the city's printers were on the sidelines of the initial struggle. When, in early summer 1907, they began to negotiate, they demanded both eight hours and wage increases. The talks soon deadlocked and International vice-president J.W. Hays arrived in Toronto to intercede. Hays met with the local's scale committee and was filled in on their negotiating stance and on the fact that any agreement had to be ratified by the membership. He proceeded to settle for far less than they sought and signed the contract. In the ensuing tumult, the International president backed Hays and asserted that the International must support such a contract signed in good faith. The infuriated Toronto union threatened mightily, but eventually backed down before the International, which two months later claimed with a straight face that the Toronto agreement was a great victory. Sanctity of contract, bureaucratic dirty tricks, refusal of membership ratification rights, all came with what American writers of the J.R. Commons school liked to term "the high-water mark of typical American unionism."[53]

Both union control of the linotype in the 1890s and the shorter-hours victories of 1898 and 1906–7 were at best ambiguous triumphs. In their wake came a vastly more centralized, bureaucratized ITU – a union that increasingly defied rank-and-file control. This conflict would come to a head in the major confrontation between the New York Typographical Union "Big Six" and the ITU leadership in 1919, when the New York local broke openly with the ITU and took their members out in the so-called Vacationist Movement, after refusing to accept an international arbitration agreement. While eventually defeated in 1919 with the active support of the ITU leadership, rank-and-file printers had had enough, and in 1920 the old leadership was thrown out and replaced with the more militant "Progressives" led by John McParland.[54]

Although wages varied throughout Canada printing centres, other general patterns appeared in the 1880s and 1890s, including the surrender of local control to the international union and successful control of the linotype. By this period the seeds of twentieth-century developments were evident for labour, capital, and, in a muted fashion, the state. In the years after the eight-hour struggle, the ITU would grow even more powerful; the UTA – created first to battle labour and then later to conciliate it – would struggle vigorously for the open shop in 1921; and the Canadian state would extend its experimentations with developing a legal structure to contain and mediate class conflict.

Although the periods of handicraft and of autonomous control were long gone, printers continued to hold considerable power at the workplace – a power that had been maintained despite extensive mechanization, an ever-increasing concentration and centralization of capital, and the emerging machinations of a far-from-neutral state.

Printers, the labour aristocrats of Victorian and Edwardian Canada, won many victories in their struggles with capital. In the first period of autonomous control, they benefitted greatly from their rare skill and from the deep divisions that kept their partisan employers from uniting against them. The industrialization of printing brought power presses into the system, and an increasing division of labour both within the structure of the industry (newspapers versus book and job work) and between two distinct groups of printers (compositors versus pressmen). Nevertheless, more formalized union control, derived partially from the traditions of autonomous control, was established through ever more frequent struggles between printers and their employers. The latter still laboured under significant divisions and it was only in the late 1880s that they created continent-wide associations to battle the international union. The following two decades of warfare saw two significantly different employer strategies emerge. The newspaper branch of printing, buoyed by the extraordinary expansion of the dailies made possible by the linotype and the new national advertising revenues of the emerging monopoly sector, largely pursued a policy of peace. After testing the ITU on the machine question, they settled into a "negotiatory" stance that led to a series of international arbitration agreements governing the major city dailies of the continent after 1900. Meanwhile, the United Typothetae of America, born in the struggle against shorter hours, pursued a holy war for the open shop. Engaged in an intensely competitive branch of printing, the Typothetae's members felt they could not afford the concessions that the newspaper publishers extended to the ITU. Without doubt the ITU benefitted from this divergent employer strategy, although they increasingly did so by winning victories for the elite of their members – newspaper compositors – at the expense of other printers. The result of these struggles in the printing industry was a set of work relations governed by a rigid bureaucratic code of rules and regulations consolidated in contracts and watched over by a more centralized union bureaucracy.

Printers, then, entered the twentieth century with much of their power and control intact. Canadian printers were not unique in this achievement; it was shared by printers internationally. How do we account for their relatively unusual success in withstanding the onslaught of capital, unleashed in the massive restructuring of labour processes and of the working class? No single explanation will suffice. Printers combined their old craft customs with a vigorous trade unionism to defend their position. They also achieved control of the new technology of the typesetting machine by cleverly acceding to a process of reskilling and demonstrating their willingness to work the new machines. In addition, their literacy, general standing in the community, and leadership in the broader trade-union movement all provided extra clout in bargaining. And finally, in the newspaper industry, the employers' dependence on intensely competitive local markets led to their placing a high premium on stability. In this, printers resembled building-trades workers who also maintained strong craft traditions during this period.

There can be little doubt of the necessity of viewing working-class history through the lens of changing work relations. The eminently historical character of contemporary work relations demonstrates in important ways that they are not "inevitable and eternal," as they too often appear. "Technological determinism" and "iron laws of bureaucratization" must be debunked through a historical understanding of capitalist decision making about machines and workplace arrangements. Most important, this history must emphasize the role played by working-class resistance in the evolution of the capitalist work process. As Jonathan Zeitlin has argued in his stimulating study of British compositors and engineers, changes in the labour process are "the outcome of a complex process of struggle and negotiation which cannot be deduced from a unilinear view of capitalist development."[55]

Late nineteenth-century labour militants like George McNeill understood this struggle. Writing at the height of the "Great Upheaval," he noted that printers were "pioneers in testing and enforcing 'usages and customs' in trade unionism."[56] Yet the firmament of McNeill's America was transformed in the two decades following 1886. For printers, the major symbol of monopoly capital's brave new world was undoubtedly the typesetting machine. For Hamilton printer-historian Frank Kidner, alias "Red-Ink," this new world called forth a compendium of printers' lore. Nostalgically he worried about the passing "the old order of things" with its "race of printers full of quaint conceits and eccentricities," and he despaired of the new technology:

Ye printers dear, what's this I hear: the news that's goin' round?
A grand machine, to take your place, has surely now been found.
It'll set the type quite neatly, at a most tremendous speed.
And the clever printer man, they say, we shall no longer need.

Nostalgia and despair, however, were not Red-Ink's final reflection, nor should they be ours:

> But the summer time will come again and winter's winds will blow,
> And many a harvest time will come again and go,
> Ere the thing of cranks and gearing takes the place of pen and ink,
> Or supplants the toiling typo, with his power to *work* and *think*.[57]

APPENDICES

Appendix 1
Preliminary List of Nineteenth-Century Local Printers Unions

Quebec	1827–; 1836–44; 1855–
Toronto	1832–7; 1844–
Montreal	1833–?
Hamilton	1833–?; 1846–?; 1852–3; 1854–
Halifax	1837–?
Kingston	1846–?
London	1850–?
Saint John	1856–9
Victoria	1863–?
St John's	1833–

Appendix 2
Canadian ITU Locals to 1908

Local number	City	Date initial organization	Subsequent organization
85	Saint John	1865	surrendered 1878; rechartered 1881
91	Toronto	1866	
97	Montreal	1867	see locals 145,176
102	Ottawa	1867	
129	Hamilton	1869	suspended 1906; reinstated 1906
130	Halifax	1869	surrendered 1879; rechartered 1883
133	London	1869	
145	Montreal (Jacques Cartier)	1871	
147	St Catharines	1870	surrendered 1875; rechartered 223, 1887; surrendered 1891; rechartered 1901
159	Quebec (French)	1872 ⎫	amalgamated as local 302, 1893
160	Quebec (English)	1872 ⎭	
176	Montreal (English)	1871	
191	Winnipeg	1881	
201	Victoria	1884	
204	Kingston	1886	suspended 1906

Appendix 2 (continued)

Local number	City	Date initial organization	Subsequent organization
51	Brantford	1886	surrendered 1889?; rechartered 273, 1890; surrendered 1898; rechartered 378, 1900
171	Calgary	1887	failed, 1888?; rechartered 449, 1902
226	Vancouver	1887	
227	Peterborough	1887	suspended 1891; rechartered 279, 1893; surrendered 1894; rechartered 248, 1902
253	New Westminster	1889	suspended 1894; rechartered 264, 1899; surrendered 1903; rechartered 632, 1908
258	Guelph	1893	suspended 1896; rechartered 391, 1901
143	Belleville	1896	suspended 1898; rechartered 257, 1901; suspended 1902
280	Sherbrooke	1896	suspended 1900
317	Nelson	1896	suspended 1898; rechartered 340, 1899
335	Rossland	1896	
257	Brandon	1896	suspended 1898; rechartered 656, 1905; surrendered 1906
317	Woodstock	1899	suspended 1900; rechartered 1902; surrendered 1906
337	Nanaimo	1899	surrendered 1905
358	Greenwood	1899	suspended 1906
366	Berlin	1899	surrendered 1905
139	Stratford	1901	
393	Brockville	1901	suspended 1906
411	Galt	1901	
157	Sydney	1901	suspended 1903
459	St Thomas	1901	suspended 1906; reorganized 1908
460	Chatham	1901	surrendered 1906
464	Charlottetown	1901	suspended 1903
467	Dawson	1901	surrendered 1906
296	Lindsay	1902	surrendered 1906
550	Windsor	1902	suspended 1907; rechartered 553, 1907
604	Edmonton	1903	surrendered 1906; rechartered 1907
421	Sarnia	1904	surrendered 1905
579	St Hyacinthe	1904	suspended 1906
539	Pt Arthur	1904	surrendered 1906; rechartered 575
647	Sault Ste Marie	1905	surrendered 1906
417	Ft william	1905	
627	Moose Jaw	1905	
657	Regina	1905	
664	Fredericton	1905	

Appendix 2 (continued)

Local number	City	Date initial organization	Subsequent organization	
666	Moncton	1905	suspended 1906	
663	Saskatoon	1906		
540	Cranbrook	1907		
541	Vernon	1907		
551	Lethbridge	1907		
5	Toronto (mailers)	1894		
27	Winnipeg (mailers)	1905		
6	Ottawa (newspaper writers)	1902	suspended 1903	
10	Montreal (newspaper writers)	1904	suspended 1906	
23	Winnipeg (German-American)	1906		
5	Ottawa (pressmen)	1880	surrendered 1890	
10	Toronto (pressmen)	1883	surrendered 1890	
30	Montreal (pressmen)	1887	suspended 1892	
7	Ottawa (pressfeeders)	1889		IPPU
7	Toronto (pressfeeders)		surrendered 1890	
1	Toronto (web pressmen)	1894		
4	Ottawa (bookbinders)	1889	surrendered 1893	IBB
21	Toronto (stereotypers)	1893		
33	Montreal (stereotypers)	1898		ISEU
50	Ottawa (stereotypers)	1901		
9	Montreal (photo-engravers)		suspended 1899; rechartered 1901; suspended 1903	IPEU
20	Toronto (photo-engravers)		suspended 1901	

IPPU   International Printing Pressmen's Union, 1889
IBB   International Brotherhood of Bookbinders, 1893
ISEU   International stereotypers and Electrotypers Union, 1902
IPEU   International Photo-Engravers Union, 1902
SOURCE: ITU, *Proceedings*

Appendix 3
Tentative List of Canadian Printers' Strikes to 1908

1836 Toronto	1869 Ottawa	1877 Ottawa
1853 Toronto	Montreal	1878 Toronto
1854 Toronto	1870 Ottawa	Montreal
Quebec	1872 Hamilton	1879 Stratford
1856 London	Montreal (2)	1880 London
1859 Saint John	Toronto	Montreal
1866 Quebec	1873 Ottawa	1881 Saint John

Appendix 3 (continued)

1882 Montreal	1888 Saint John	Vancouver
Winnipeg	Ottawa	1899 Toronto
1883 Toronto	Hamilton	Halifax
Montreal (2)	Quebec	London
Ottawa	St Catharines (2)	Ottawa
1884 Toronto	1889 Vancouver	Winnipeg
1885 Winnipeg	Halifax	1901 Montreal (3)
1887 Vancouver	1890 Toronto	1902 Toronto
	St Catharines	Halifax
	Montreal	1903 Montreal
	1891 Toronto	1904 Quebec
	1892 Vancouver	Montreal (2)
	Ottawa (2)	Winnipeg
	Toronto (2)	1905 Winnipeg (2)
	Saint John	Edmonton
	Halifax	Halifax
	1893 Toronto (2)	Saint John
	Vancouver	1906 Saint John
	1894 Winnipeg	Winnipeg (2)
	1895 St John's	Montreal
	Toronto	London
	1896 Toronto	Guelph
	Winnipeg	Regina
	Vancouver	Hamilton
	1897 Rossland	1908 Saint John
	Winnipeg	Winnipeg
	Calgary	Halifax
	1898 Winnipeg	Vancouver
	Brandon	

SOURCES: ITU, *Proceedings*; *Historical Atlas of Canada*, vol. 2, thanks to Bryan Palmer, *Historical Atlas of Canada*, vol. 3: research.

NOTES

My thanks to Doug Cruikshank for research assistance, and to Russell Hann whose insights into the transformation of the nineteenth-century newspaper industry have been particularly stimulating. In addition, I would like to thank Craig Heron and Robert Storey, the editors of *On the Job*, for their scrupulous and rigorous efforts. An even earlier version of this paper was presented at the Commonwealth Labour History conference, University of Warwick, 2–4 September 1981.

  1 On O'Donoghue, see Gregory S. Kealey, *Toronto Workers Respond to Industrial Capitalism* (Toronto: University of Toronto Press 1980; rev. ed. 1991), passim, and Gregory S. Kealey and Bryan D. Palmer, *Dreaming of What Might Be: The Knights of Labor in Ontario* (New York and Cambridge 1982), passim; on Armstrong, see Kealey, *Toronto Workers*;

on Simpson, see Gene Howard Homel, "James Simpson and the Origins of Canadian Social Democracy," (PHD dissertation, University of Toronto 1978); on Puttee, see A. Ross McCormack, "Arthur Puttee and the Liberal Party, 1899–1904," *Canadian Historical Review* (hereafter CHR) 51 (1970): 141–63, and his "British Working-Class Immigrants and Canadian Radicalism: The Case of Arthur Puttee," *Canadian Ethnic Studies* 10 (1978): 22–37; on Pettipiece, see McCormack, "The Emergence of the Socialist Movement in British Columbia," BC *Studies* 21 (1974): 3–27, and his letters to the *Typographical Journal* 24 (1904): 304–5, 646; 28 (1904): 292; 26 (1905): 576; International Typographical Union (hereafter ITU), *Proceedings*, 1908.

2 Richard Price, *Masters, Unions and Men* (Cambridge 1980); see also his "The Labour Process and Labour History," *Social History* 8 (1983): 57–76, and "Rethinking Labour History: The Importance of Work," in James E. Cronin and Jonathan Schneer, eds, *Social Conflict and the Political Order in Modern Britain* (New Brunswick, NJ 1982).

3 On early Canadian printing, see H. Pearson Gundy, *Early Printers and Printing in Canada* (Toronto 1957); Eric Haworth, *Imprint of a Nation* (Toronto 1969); Carl Benn, "The Upper Canadian Press, 1793–1815," *Ontario History* 70 (1978): 91–114; and similar literature for other Canadian regions.

4 Rollo G. Silver, *The American Printer, 1787–1825* (Charlottesville, Va. 1967), passim. See also Lawrence C. Wroth, *The Colonial Printer* (Charlottesville, Va. 1964).

5 Note, for example, the prominent treatment given printers in Eugene Forsey, *Trade Unions in Canada* (Toronto 1982), 9–31.

6 Ibid., 14–15.

7 On the early years, see John Armstrong's serialized history of the Toronto Typographical Union published in the *Toiler* (Toronto), and conveniently available in a scrapbook in the Robert Kenny Papers, University of Toronto Archives. See also Sally F. Zerker, *The Rise and Fall of the Toronto Typographical Union, 1832–1972* (Toronto 1982), chap. 2, and Forsey, *Trade Unions*, 18–28. Quotations as rendered by Armstrong from original minute book, 12 October 1832.

8 John Armstrong's serialized "history."

9 For a curious view of this strike, see F.H. Armstrong, "Reformer as Capitalist: William Lyon Mackenzie and the Printers' Strike of 1836," *Ontario History* 59 (1967): 187–96. For anyone who finds this persuasive, see also Paul Romney, "William Lyon Mackenzie as Mayor of Toronto," *Canadian Historical Review* 56 (1975): 416–36.

10 Forsey, *Trade Unions.*

11 John Armstrong's serialized "history"; Toronto Typographical Union (hereafter ITU), minutes, Ontario Archives; *Globe* (Toronto); Zerker,

Rise and Fall, chap. 3; Forsey, *Trade Unions*, chap. 1; on Brown, see J.M.S. Careless, *Brown of the Globe*, 2 vols (Toronto 1959–63), 1; on the press, see Paul Rutherford, *A Victorian Authority: The Daily Press in Late Nineteenth-Century Canada* (Toronto 1982).

12 On the pervasiveness of the apprenticeship question, see John R. Commons, ed., *A Documentary History of American Industrial Society* (Cleveland 1910–11), 7, 109–31.

13 TTU, minutes, 2 July 1845.

14 Rutherford, *Victorian Authority*, chap. 2–3.

15 Elizabeth Hulse, *A Dictionary of Toronto Printers, Publishers, Booksellers, and the Allied Trades, 1798–1900* (Toronto 1982), x–xi.

16 For details on the *Globe*, see Careless, *Brown*, passim. See also Rutherford, *Victorian Authority*.

17 Rutherford, *Victorian Authority* and idem, *The Making of the Canadian Media* (Toronto 1978), 9; ITU, *Proceedings*; *Printers' Circular* (Philadelphia) 4, no. 10 (December 1869): 373; 7, no. 7 (September 1872): 253–4; 8, no. 7 (September 1873): 248.

18 Canada, Royal Commission on the Relations of Capital and Labour, *Report* (hereafter RCRCLR): *Ontario Evidence* (Ottawa 1889), 36–51.

19 For an excellent history of the pressmen, see Elizabeth Faulkner Baker, *Printers and Technology: A History of the International Printing Pressmen and Assistants Union* (New York 1957).

20 *Globe*, 2 July 1853.

21 Hamilton Typographical Union, minutes, Special Collections, Hamilton Public Library.

22 RCRCLR, *Ontario Evidence*, 36–51.

23 TTU, minutes, 1878–80.

24 This pamphlet, partially damaged, is held in the pamphlet collection of the Ontario Archives.

25 Kealey and Palmer, *Dreaming of What Might Be*.

26 Despite the fame of the strike, Paul Craven's recent discovery of the court records in the Criminal Assize Clerk's Files at the Ontario Archives promises new insights.

27 *Address to the Working Classes in Canada*. On the many strikes of the 1850s, see Paul Appleton, "The Sunshine and the Shade: Labour Activism in Central Canada, 1850–60" (MA thesis, University of Calgary 1974); and Bryan D. Palmer, *The Working-Class Experience: The Rise and Reconstitution of Canadian Labour, 1800–1980* (Toronto 1983), chap. 2.

28 *Daily Sun* (Saint John), 23 February 1898, in Canada, Department of Labour, vertical file, RG 27 (3126), file 1, National Archives of Canada (NA).

29 *Printers' Circular* 4, no. 10 (December 1869): 373; 13, no. 7 (September 1873): 248.

30 *Globe*, 28 June, 2 July 1853; 2, 7, 8, 9, 12, 16, 23 June 1854.

31 Appleton, "Sunshine and Shade."

32 RCRCLR, *Ontario Evidence*, 36–51.

33 ITU, Executive Council, *A Study of the History of the International Typo-graphical Union, 1852–1963*, 2 vols (Colorado Springs 1964), 2, section 3 (hereafter ITU, *Study*).

34 RCRCLR, New Brunswick, 179–86.

35 Saint John Typographical Union, minutes, New Brunswick Museum; Richard Rice, "History of Organized Labour in Saint John, New Brunswick, 1813–90" (MA thesis, University of New Brunswick 1968), chap. 5.

36 ITU, *Proceedings*; Kealey and Palmer, *Dreaming of What Might Be*, 370–1.

37 *Globe*, 26, 27 July, 8, 15 August 1888; *Typographical Journal*, 15 September 1889; *Mail*, 17 August 1889.

38 For a full discussion of the Toronto context, see Kealey, *Toronto Workers*.

39 Quoted in Rice, "Organized Labour in Saint John," 152.

40 Quoted in Baker, *Printers and Technology*, 69.

41 Charles Bruce, *News and the Southams* (Toronto 1968).

42 H.E. Stephenson and Carlton McNaught, *The Story of Advertising in Canada* (Toronto 1940), 19.

43 On the employers' associations, see Clarence E. Bonnett, *Employers' Associations in the United States* (New York 1922), especially chaps 8–9; Leona M. Powell, *The History of the United Typothetae of America* (Chicago 1926); Charlotte E. Morgan, *The Origin and History of the New York Employing Printers' Association* (New York 1930); Selig Perlman and Philip Taft, *History of Labour in the United States, 1896–1932* (reprint, New York 1966), 51–60.

44 A.H.U. Calquhoun et al., *A History of Canadian Journalism ... 1859–1908* (Toronto 1908); W.A. Craick, *A History of Canadian Journalism, II: 1919–1959* (Toronto 1959).

45 ITU, *Study*, II, section III, chap. 3.

46 Zerker, *Rise and Fall*, chap. 6.

47 For a detailed discussion of these struggles, see Kealey, *Toronto Workers*, chap. 6.

48 ITU, *Proceedings*, 1905–8.

49 Ibid.; *Typographical Journal*, 1905–8; *Labour Gazette*, 1905–8, especially W.L.M. King, "Investigation of Alleged Fraudulent Practices in England to Induce Printers to Come to Canada," 4 (1905–6): 1122–30; *Clarion* (Winnipeg), 4 November 1905 (clipping in Russell Papers, Public Archives of Manitoba).

50 *Daily Sun* (Saint John), 1 January 1906. My thanks to Robert Babcock for this source.

237 Control, Labour, and Nineteenth-Century Printers

51 *Labour Gazette*, 6 (February 1906): 918–19.
52 ITU, *Proceedings*, 1907.
53 Perlman and Taft, *History*. On the strike, see ITU, *Minutes* and Zerker, *Rise and Fall*, chap. 8. While Zerker's account is factually correct, the attribution of the difficulty to the 49th parallel is indefensible. Needless to say, major American locals were also being victimized. The greatest conflict of this kind would come later in 1919, when the ITU turned its full power against New York's "Big Six" to destroy the so-called Vacationist Strike. Nationalism is too simple an answer. See my review in *Canadian Book Review Annual* (1982): 337–8.
54 ITU, *Study*, section III, chap. 4.
55 Jonathan Zeitlin, "Craft Control and the Division of Labour: Engineers and Compositors in Britain, 1890–1930," *Cambridge Journal of Economics* 3 (1979): 263–74, quotation at 272.
56 George McNeill, *The Labor Movement* (New York 1887), 189.
57 "Red-Ink" [Frank Kidner]. *"Pi": A Compilation of Odds and Ends Relating to Workers in Sanctum and Newsroom Culled From the Scrap-book of a Compositor* (Hamilton 1890), 215–16.

8 The Bonds of Unity: The Knights of Labor in Ontario, 1880–1900

WITH BRYAN D. PALMER

There has historically been no movement in the experience of North American labour that weighed so heavily on the collective mind of the working-class movement in the years 1900–30 as that of the Knights of Labor upsurge of the 1880s. Until the resurgence of labour in the 1930s, revealed most dramatically in the rise of the Congress of Industrial Organizations, workers recalled this past and drew upon its many and varied inspirations. Thus, when John L. Lewis consciously strove to create an image of himself as part of a long line of "tough people," "fighters," and class militants, he recalled (or fabricated) the story of his father's early involvement in the Knights of Labor in Lucas, Iowa, where Tom Lewis helped lead a bitter strike in 1882, an action supposedly earning him a place on the company's blacklist and exile from the town.[1] Clinton S. Golden, labour intellectual and founder of the United Steel Workers of America, first drank from the fountain of labour solidarity with "Big John" Powderly, brother of the Order's central figure, Terence V. Powderly. "Big John," whom Clint tended drill for at the tender age of twelve, preached the gospel of the Noble and Holy Order long after the Knights had succumbed to employer resistance, the economic crisis of the 1890s, and internal divisions and trade-union opposition. But even in the face of the Knights' ultimate defeat, Powderly's brother remained true to the cause of an all-embracing organization of the American wage earners. He imparted his enthusiasm to his young helper, and Golden recalled of the Knights that:

Their ritualism, the secrecy with which their meetings were conducted, the signs and symbols that gave notice to their members as to when and where meetings were to be held, fired my interest and imagination and in my own mind I resolved that henceforth my lot was cast with that of the wage earners. I began to see class lines and distinctions. I discovered that there were people in America besides those who lived their lives upon farms that were largely self-sufficient. People who worked long hours for low wages in hazardous employment, lived in miserable tenements and hovels, whose very life depended on having a job, earning money but rarely more than enough to provide for the bare necessities of life.[2]

John Peebles, a jeweller-watchmaker in Hamilton in the 1880s, and later mayor of that city in the difficult years 1930–33, remembered his early attachment to the Order, commenting in 1946:

I became a member of the Knights of Labor about sixty years ago, when I was quite a young chap. I thought its programme would revolutionize the world, not only because of its programme which included co-operation and State ownership of all public utilities ... and the purification of Politics and of all law and State Administration which also included the full belief in the honesty and sincerity of all members of the order. In short it was a crusade for purity in life generally.[3]

Gordon Bishop, active in the organization of steel workers in eastern Ontario, buttressed the assessments of Golden and Peebles, arguing that the ritualistic passwords and secrets of the Order insured large attendance at ordinary meetings, and riveted workers to a cause. Members of the Knights of Labor, he recalled, "did not forget their obligation easily."[4]

These individual statements were supplemented by a more general remembrance of the place and significance of the Knights of Labor. "Never since the palmiest days of the Knights of Labor," declared Toronto's *Citizen and Country* in the midst of the craft union boom of 1898–1904, "have trade unions taken such a firm hold of the toilers as today."[5] As these turn-of-the-century organizational gains were consolidated, however, some workers could still tar the American Federation of Labor with a brush dipped into the resentments of the 1880s and 1890s. In 1903 a Western Federation of Miners member from Slocan, British Columbia wrote to the *Miners' Magazine*: "Now there are thousands of old-line K of L's in the WFM and the unsavoury acts of the AFL officials have not been altogether forgotten."[6] Twenty years later many radicals and socialists saw this newly-arrived, and increasingly conservative, international craft unionism in terms even more antagonistic. When the One Big Union in Canada sought a glorious past to contrast with the dismal realities of AFL–TLC trade unionism in the 1920s, it was the fires of the Knights of Labor it chose to rekindle. "One of the great land-marks in the history of class struggle," the Knights were regarded as "a mass organization grouped in Geographical units" that prefigured the industrial unionism of the One Big Union. The Order, claimed these dissident workers, had been the very same "one big union" that they were trying to build and sustain.[7] For their part, as David J. Bercuson has noted, the AFL pure and simple unionists linked the OBU with the Knights of Labor, the American Railway Union of Eugene Debs, and the American Labor Union. It was the latest "subtle and pernicious plea again resorted to for the purpose of severing the wage earners from their orderly and practical course of action."[8] By 1929, the radical challenge of the post-war reconstruction years had been at least partially undermined, and in this context of "normalcy" the AFL met in Toronto in October. With southern textile workers urging the organization of their mill towns, observers at the convention reported "a pitch of enthusiasm not seen in labor gatherings since the spring tide of the Knights of Labor."[9]

For these, and many other, reasons, Norman J. Ware, perhaps the most perceptive student of the Knights of Labor, saw the Order as just that "sort of One Big Union of which Karl Marx would have approved, if – and this is a large 'if' – it could have been transformed into a political organization under socialist leadership." Given this kind of orientation, which rests on the argument that the Knights of Labor "more fully represented the wage-earners as a whole than any general labor organization either before or after its peak year, 1886,"[10] it is odd indeed that Gerald Grob's intellectual history of the Knights of Labor has gained such widespread acceptance, achieving something of an interpretive hegemony. Grob's focus is on the Knights' political activity, and he places them unambiguously in a late nineteenth-century utopian reform stream characterized by "a lack of mature class consciousness." Within this meandering current we find a confused swirl of politicians and professional reformers, inept leaders, and archaic thought, all drifting towards the *petit bourgeois* dream of re-establishing the relationships of an earlier era, "based on the dominance of the small producer." Only in the rare eddy does an actual worker rear his/her head, or a specific class action flow off into some small tributary: but they are all diverted, or sucked under by the visionaries and utopians who chart the course of the ultimate direction of the river.[11] It would not do to dismiss totally the Grob analysis, for there was much muddled thinking within the Order, and political activity was a realm highly charged with charlatanism; many less than admirable figures played out their roles, and not a few dealings and events were dirtied with the sordid business of self-interest or party serving. But the Ware interpretation will not stand the test of close scrutiny, for as Leon Fink has argued, it tends to distance the Knights too readily from electoral politics and established institutions.[12] Collapsing the Knights' so-called struggle for democracy into a "popular movement" without necessary and organic connections to the politics of late nineteenth-century America, Ware comes perilously close to anticipating Grob by associating the Order with a broad-based reformism "engrafted upon the movement by the farmers or the radical fringe of socialists and communists of one stripe of another." Ware is at least sensitive to the appeal and potential of such a reform thrust, while Grob is clearly antagonistic and sceptical. But if Ware thus sees the Order as a working-class movement, he regard its class content as resting outside the sphere of political engagement, traditionally defined, directed by forces peripheral rather than central to the movement's history and experience. In the Ware framework, then, the Knights rush, leaderless, and without coherence, into the political fray in the highly charged atmosphere of 1886–87, then abdicate totally in 1890–94, as the Order's national leadership suffers paralysis and the agrarian or "western" section takes over, highlighting the populist content of the Knights' world-view. Again, it is not that this depiction of the Order lacks value, but that it neglects important realities and compresses too much into a rather small package.

The Knights of Labor were not this kind of small package, in either the Grob or Ware sense, and we propose to interpret the experience differently. By examining the structural situation of the Order, where and when it organized in Ontario, and how many (in rough terms) it drew to its ranks, we believe that we can establish the class character and importance of the Knights of Labor. We shall argue that the Noble and Holy Order of the Knights of Labor represented a dramatic shift away from past practices within the history of Ontario workers. Although the Knights built very much on the accumulated experience of the working class, they channelled that experience in new directions. In the words of Raymond Williams they took a whole series of residual aspects of the class experience, built upon them, and erected a structural and intellectual apparatus that was the beginning of emergent purpose. In short, the Knights of Labor in Ontario created, for the first time, what Lawrence Goodwyn has called a movement culture of alternative, opposition, and potential. In the breadth of their vision, the scope of their organization, and the unique refusal to collapse the cause of workers into this reform or that amelioration or restrict entry to the movement to this stratum or that group, the Knights of Labor hinted at the potential and possibility that are at the foundation of the making of a class. Politically, the Order's efforts in the federal, provincial, and municipal fields testified to the movement's willingness and ability to transcend the economistic concerns of the workplace. At the same time, the Order's important place in the class struggles and confrontations of the last two decades of the nineteenth century points to problems inherent in viewing the Knights of Labor from the perspective of its leaders' anti-strike rhetoric. To be sure, both in the political sphere and at the workplace, the Knights found themselves caught in many ambiguities and contradictions, among the most important being their political relationship to the established Grit and Tory parties, and their capacity to defend the interests of their membership in the face of fierce employer resistance and a post-1886 trade-union opposition. Some, but not all, of these difficulties were of the Order's own making. But as the first expression of the social, cultural, and political emergence of a class, the Knights of Labor understandably groped for answers more than they marched forcefully towards solutions. The Order was itself inhibited by the context of late nineteenth-century Ontario which, aside from its own peculiar "regional" divisions, stood poised between an economy of competitive capitalism, but recently arrived, and the monopoly capitalism which stood literally around the corner with the Laurier boom years of the twentieth century. The Knights, in many ways, straddled each epoch, looking simultaneously forward and backward, longing for the rights they knew to be justly theirs, attacking the monopolists they saw controlling the business, politics, and culture of their society.[13]

Beyond this general interpretive thrust two final points need to be made, for they are as much a part of our purpose as any attempt to shift analysis of the Knights of Labor in new directions. First, we have attempted to work through the history of the Knights of Labor in ways which convey as adequately as is possible the human forces behind the doctrines, practices, and campaigns of the 1880s and 1890s. In this abbreviated statement, which is a severe compression of a larger, book-length manuscript, something of this orientation may well be lost, but we are nevertheless in agreement with one principled member of the Order, whose reminiscences are prefaced by this general statement:

When there is so much warmth in the making of labor's history it is strange that there has been so little in the writing of it. As a rule, it has been written by dry-as-dust economists who treat it as if it were the record of the advance of an economic doctrine. As well write the history of the religious movement as if it were the record of the advance of theological doctrine. Labor doctrines have never advanced except as they have been lived and loved by individuals.[14]

Second, we want to insist that the experience of the Knights of Labor be considered, not as some minor episode in labour history, but as an integral part of the late nineteenth-century Canadian past, in all its complexities. The rise of the Order was intimately related to the economic and political developments of the period, it was an implicit component of that "manufacturing condition" that came into prominence in the late nineteenth century, but that is so often written about with only a cursory view of the labouring class.[15] That historians of politics and business have been willing and able to do this is perhaps understandable, but it does not make for a history premised upon the need to comprehend totality and interrelationship. It is odd, for instance, that much of the political history of these years can be written with only a fleeting glance at the working-class constituency which was so consistently courted by John A. Macdonald, Edward Blake, and others. Even a source as unimpeachable as the *Journal of Commerce* noted in 1888 that "the future of the artizan fills the whole horizon of politics, and no other class is considered at all."[16] The Royal Commission on the Relations of Labor and Capital in Canada (1889) was likely the impetus behind such a caustic comment, and revealed how seriously the established political structure regarded the pressing question of labour.[17]

One cannot, then, divorce the experience of the Ontario Knights of Labor from all that has been considered as central to the history of Canada in these years.[18] Comprehension of the late nineteenth-century milieu demands a knowledge of the Order, and this in turn sheds new light on the history of economic, social, and political life. We start our journey towards this understanding with a brief discussion of the economic and social context of late nineteenth-century Ontario. We then close with particular attention to the structural features of the Knights of Labor presence, the movement culture created and generated by the Knights, and the political and social confrontations at the polls and in the workplace.

ECONOMIC BACKGROUND: LABOUR AND
INDUSTRIAL CAPITALISM TO 1890

The nineteenth century was the crucible from which Canada would emerge as a capitalist economy and society. Regardless of whether one looks towards a tradition of dissenting scholarship that begins with Myers, consolidates around Pentland and Ryerson, and continues with much recent work, or in the direction of an economic history erected upon aggregate data and estimates of real manufacturing output, it is indisputable that the latter half of the nineteenth century saw the creation of a sophisticated transportation network, the articulation of a strategy of industrial development that pinned the hopes of Canada's rising capitalists on political consolidation, tariff protections and settlement, and the evolution of a diversified manufacturing sector.[19] All this, to be sure, developed in the context of a social order wracked by major depressions and frequent recessionary downturns. Nevertheless, as early as the 1860s the transforming power of capital had become visible in the rise of the factory, the increasing use of steam-power, and the mechanization of important industries such as tailoring and boot and shoe production. For the People's Journal these were the hallmarks of momentous change, factors which had "set agoing an industrial revolution."[20]

Between 1870 and 1890 the industrial sector tasted the fruits, both bitter and sweet, of this great transformation: establishments capitalized at $50,000 and over increased by about 50 per cent; employment in manufacturing rose by 76 per cent and output in constant dollar terms by 138 per cent; railway mileage from 3,000 in 1873 to over 16,000 in 1896; manufacturing's place, in terms of value-added, rose from 19 per cent of the Gross National Product in 1870 to 23.5 per cent in 1890; the rate of real manufacturing output climbed from 4.4 per cent in the decade 1870–80 to 4.8 per cent in the 1880–90 period, slipping to 3.2 per cent in the 1890s, thus establishing the 1880s as an extremely significant moment in the historical rate of growth, surpassed only by the boom years 1900–10 and 1926–29. Indeed, it is the growth of manufacturing facilities in many industries during the cresting fortunes of the National Policy that is most striking. Between 1880 and 1890, for instance, the value of cotton cloth output rose by 125 per cent, but even this dramatic increase understated the gains of the decade's first five years: the number of mills, spindles, looms, and capital investment tripled in that short period.[21] Such developments took place, moreover, within the context of a general decline of prices which, using Michell's index, plummeted from roughly 100 in 1873 to a low of about 75 in 1886.[22]

Ontario stood at the very centre of this process of capitalist development. Aggregate data began to tell the story. Capital invested more than doubled in each decade between 1870 and 1890, while the number of hands employed increased 90 per cent over the twenty-year period. These aggregate data can give us an imprecise measure of the character of social and productive relations, the setting within which the Knights of Labor operated, and one which they must have influenced (Table 8.1).

Table 8.2 illuminates trends within the aggregate data for the years 1871–1911. However crude and unrefined the categories, they reveal

Table 8.1
Aggregate Ontario Data, 1871–1911

Year	Capital invested ($)	Hands employed	Yearly wages ($)
1871	37,874,010	87,281	21,415,710
1881	80,950,847	118,308	30,604,031
1891	175,972,021	166,326	49,733,359
1901	214,972,275	151,081	44,656,032
1911	595,394,608	216,362	95,674,743

Year	Value raw material ($)	Value product ($)	Value added ($)
1871	65,114,804	114,706,799	49,591,995
1881	91,164,156	157,889,870	66,825,714
1891	128,142,371	231,781,926	111,639,555
1901	138,230,400	241,533,486	103,303,086
1911	297,580,125	579,810,225	282,230,100

SOURCE: Canada, *Census*, 1871–1891. Note that the 1901 and 1911 figures are unadjusted in light of the changing criterion employed by the census in enumerating manufacturing establishments. All firms were considered for 1871–91, while on those firms employing five or more hands were considered in 1901 and 1911. The capital invested figures for 1901 and 1911 are computed by adding together the figures for fixed and working capital. There had been no distinction between these realms in the earlier period.

Table 8.2
Trends Within the Aggregate Ontario Data, 1871–1911

Year	Capital as % of value added	Wages as % of value added	Capital as % of product value	Wages as % of product value	Per capita yearly wages ($)	Capital invested yearly per worker ($)	Yearly national growth rates in manufacturing output (%)
1871	76	43	33	18	245	433	
							4.4
1881	121	45	51	19	257	684	
							4.8
1891	157	44	73	18	287	1,057	
							2.4
1901	208	43	89	18	295	1,422	
							6.0
1911	210	33	102	16	441	2,751	

SOURCES: Our calculations from census data. Same reservations as in source note to Table 8.1.
Yearly national growth rates in manufacturing output are taken from Gordon W. Bertram,
"Historical Statistics on Growth and Structure of Manufacturing Canada, 1870–1957," in
C.P.S.A. Conference on Statistics, 1962 and 1963, eds: J. Henripin and A. Asimakopulos (Toronto:
University of Toronto Press 1964)· 93–146

important shifts and developments. If, for instance, we take capital invested as a percentage of value added, we note a steady increase over the years 1871–1901, with the decadal rate of that increase dropping precipitously in the opening years of the twentieth century. Wages, however, exhibit a different trend, and as a percentage of value added were relatively stable until they fell dramatically in the 1901–11 years. When we take capital invested and wages as a percentage of the total product value other trends emerge: capital as a percentage of product value rises steadily over the entire period, while wages as a percentage of value decline only in those years of most pronounced economic growth, the 1880s and 1900s.

Such rough calculations gesture toward essential processes in the sphere of social and productive relations. First, we note that wages declined as a percentage of product value precisely in those years – 1881–91 and 1901–11 – that the growth rates in national manufacturing output soared. This suggests a growing intensification of labour; that these periods, then, saw increasing organization among Ontario workers – first, in the Knights of Labor, and second in the craft unions during the upheaval of 1898–1904 – should cause no surprise. But to study the character of exploitation we must probe the relationship of wages to value added, considering the capital output. This leads us to our second speculative hypothesis: it would appear that the social cost of labour was relatively high throughout the late nineteenth century, years which pre-dated Taylorism, broadly conceived. It is not until the turn of the century that wages as a percentage of value added plunged, even in the face of soaring per capita yearly wages (largely a consequence of inflation, for real wages declined).[23] These turn-of-the-century years also witness a virtual doubling of the capital invested yearly per worker, and leave behind the more modest decadal increases in this relationship characteristic of the 1871–1901 years. And yet, even given this mammoth dose of capital in the years associated with the beginnings of Canada's century, capital as a percentage of value added makes only a marginal, clearly insignificant, gain. Thus, although both the 1880s and 1900s are years of economic growth and increasing intensification of labour, it is not until the 1901–11 years that one sees the actual rationalization of productive relations, a shift in the character of exploitation, and the probable degradation of labour. Before that the social costs of labour remained high.[24] What gains in output that did occur late in the century were probably more a consequence of capital input than of extraction of surplus from the hide of labour, although these spheres are ultimately impossible to separate analytically.

If this was indeed the trend then it becomes important to ask what forces kept the social cost of labour high in this period. The lack of a managerial strategy at the workplace, "scientifically" conceived, was no doubt one aspect, as was the technological foundation of production, weak in the 1880s compared to the post-1900 years. However, the mass character of the Knights of Labor, as a movement aimed at uniting all workers, probably played a considerable role in resisting capital's quest to increase output and reduce labour costs through wage reductions or increasing the pace of work. Looking at the yearly per capita wage figures confirms this picture. While yearly wages rose only $12 in the 1870s and only $8 throughout the 1890s, the increase for the 1881–91 years was at least two-and-one-half times as great, or $30. Even granting all the ambiguities in this admittedly speculative and tentative argument, much of the data points towards the high social cost of labour in the late nineteenth century; labour seemed relatively better off in these years, in terms of its capacity to extract a larger portion of its product, than it would in later times, when capitalistic appropriation was undoubtedly more refined and effective. The social relations of production, in which worker stood counterposed to employer and in which the nature and extent of organization was of vital importance, must have contributed to this outcome.

There is no mistaking the tremendous expansion in the manufacturing sector. An analysis of county data shows impressive quantitative gains in workers employed in manufacturing between 1871 and 1891. This growth displayed tangible regional patterns – the dominance of Toronto-Hamilton, the underdeveloped but nevertheless significant economic activity along the St Lawrence and Ottawa Rivers, the manufacturing importance of various small towns. More than fifty per cent of the manufacturing of the 1880s was located in small Canadian communities, where the population never climbed above 10,000.[25] The regional economy of Ontario, then, was a far from homogenous entity, even as late as the 1880s. The closing years of the century were something of a struggle for industrial hegemony, in which the small manufacturing unit servicing a local market gave way to the larger productive concern, often contributing towards the decline of the small town and a shift in the location of industry to the population centre of a larger city. Thus the value added in all manufacturing activity in York County (Toronto) rose from 27.44 per cent in 1870 to 32 per cent in 1890. Toronto and Hamilton each accounted for 20 per cent of industrial employment in southern Ontario in 1881, although they contained only 6.5 per cent of the region's population. But even given this increasing specialization, localization, and gross expansion in the manufacturing sector the 1880s were still a decade of contrasts: handicraft forms of production still co-existed with thoroughly mechanized processes; the large factory still occupied minority status given the number of small shops.[26]

How did this process of advancing but uneven development stamp itself upon the character of specific Ontario locales, where the Knights of Labor would come to prominence in the later years of the nineteenth century? As we have already seen, the industrial cities of Toronto and Hamilton led the way. (We have commented briefly on the experience of these major centres in other works.[27]) Beyond the boundaries of these reasonably well-studied industrial cities lies a virtual no man's land, where our knowledge of economic activity is severely restricted. Yet it is clear that in countless Ontario communities capitalist development touched the lives of many workers and employers. Linked closely to this process was the importance of railways, which served as a connecting link, integrating a developing home market. This revolution in transportation was perhaps the key element in the shifting location and expansion of manufacturing in these years from 1870–90.[28]

Most of the railways built in southern Ontario after 1881 radiated out from Toronto, further contributing to that city's metropolitan dominance. Of great significance was the increasing importance of the old established lines in western Ontario – the Grand Trunk, Great Western, and Canada Southern – which received great stimulus as the CPR and GTR battled for control of the country's rail lines. In this struggle for hegemony local traffic was actively sought, mileage was expanded, and efforts were made to capture a greater share of the American through traffic. Centres such as St Thomas and Stratford became links in a chain of economic development, and their wage-earning class was often tied directly to the shops that served the railways or the rail systems themselves. St Thomas, for instance, grew rapidly in the 1870s, being transformed from a modest pre-industrial service town to a dynamic railway centre linked to the major Ontario metropolitan markets. Major shops of the American-owned Canada Southern Railway located there, employing about 700 men by the mid-1880s, and the Great Western established a repair shop in the city. By 1885 the New York Central had also commenced similar operations. Because of this rapid growth the city's class boundaries were rigid and geographically specific.[29]

The railways, through declining freight rates and economies of scale, helped to concentrate economic activity in a number of diversified manufacturing centres, whose growth took place at the expense of the smaller towns where factories were insufficiently developed to capitalize on transport costs compared to their larger, better situated rivals. London was just such a place. Its strength seemed to reside disproportionately in the food-processing sector, with concentrations of capital in bakeries, breweries, and tobacco-related works. But this city also gained prominence as a marketing and distributing centre for the dairy belt of western Ontario's Middlesex, Oxford, Elgin, Lambton, Perth, and Huron counties. In the textile sphere, the city's garment industry grew on the basis of its proximity to the Niagara Peninsula's cotton mills. Finally, in the wood-processing sector concerns like the London Furniture Company employed fifty men, while in metal fabricating the city's McClary Manufacturing Company, Ontario Car Works, and E. Leonard & Sons produced stoves, engines, and other goods. These latter firms employed between 80 and 450 hands throughout the decade of the 1880s.[30]

Other western Ontario towns also exhibited indications of the importance of industrial activity. Brantford's economic place in late nineteenth-century Ontario was dominated by the Harris, Wisner, and Cockshutt agricultural implements companies, and a hosiery factory. Harris & Son, taken together with the Massey works of Toronto (and with which it would merge in 1891), accounted for sixty per cent of all agricultural implement sales in the Dominion by the mid-1880s. Guelph, Galt, Berlin, Hespeler, and even Collingwood to the north all housed similar, if much smaller, manufacturing concerns, producing for local, even regional, markets. In Guelph a hosiery factory employing over one hundred workers, the Raymond Sewing Machine Company, the Guelph Sewing Machine Company, and the Crowe Iron Works dominated the industrial landscape.

Further to the north and to the east industrial production was less well established, particularly in the area of secondary manufacturing. By the 1880s the Ottawa-Hull and Muskoka regions had established hegemony over the production of wood products, and a number of mills engaged in the preparation of sawn lumber, shingles, and matches. The dominance of lumber was even more pronounced in the Ottawa Valley, where the five largest producers in Canada had congregated by 1874. Over 2,500 men were employed in the production of lumber in 1891 in the city of Ottawa alone, and the industry found market outlets in both Britain and the United States.

East of Toronto, along the St Lawrence River and Lake Ontario, small-scale processing industries and metal-fabricating plants attempted to capture a share of a largely local market. In the larger regional towns, however, there was room for some consolidation. Gananoque, Brockville, Cobourg, Belleville, Smiths Falls, Oshawa, and Kingston all had the ubiquitous foundries, machine shops, and agricultural implements works of the period. G.M. Cossitt & Brothers and Frost & Wood Company established significant agricultural factories in Smiths Falls, the latter company employing over 150 skilled hands, producing goods valued at $150,000 destined for the farms of Canada, Australia, and South Africa. Kingston's large engine works employed over 350 workers in the early 1880s, and a cotton mill with approximately 200 hands opened in 1882. In the southern section of Ontario County, Oshawa-Cedardale was dominated by the Joseph Hall Works. Concentrating on the production of threshing machines, mowers, and ploughs for the Canadian market the works employed 250 men as early as 1867. By the 1880s other important shops had long-established histories: the McLaughlin carriage works, Masson's seed-drill plant, A.S. Whiting Agricultural Implements, Oshawa Stove Company, W.E. Dingle's Fanning Mills and Seeders, and the Robson & Lauchland Tanneries.[31]

But the most dramatic expression of industrial growth in eastern Ontario was Cornwall's cotton mills. Here was one city where the National Policy tariff of thirty to thirty-five per cent was never challenged. In 1876 Cornwall's Canada Company cotton mills were the largest in the nation, the value of the plant hovering near the half-million dollar mark, the annual product valued at $400,000. Approximately 350 workers (100 males and 250 females) toiled over 20,000 spindles to earn yearly wages of $75,000. Five years later, protected by the newly-revised tariff and stimulated by the return to prosperity, Cornwall's three cotton mills – one was a relatively small firm – employed 133 men, 277 women, 186 boys, and 190 girls. Their yearly wages totalled $179,900 and $456,000 worth of material was used to produced cotton goods and cloth valued at $833,000. By the time another half-decade had passed, Cornwall's two major textile producers – the Canada Company and the Stormont – had made impressive expansionary strides.[32]

Across the province, then, in spite of the increasing dominance of Toronto and Hamilton, of underdevelopment, uneven growth, and reliance upon primary production of the old timber staple in some areas, capitalist production was a force to reckon with by the 1880s. It transformed social and productive relations in the large cities as well as in the tiny rural hamlets. In this changed context class came to the fore as a clearly perceived reality; a culture premised upon this historic relationship of antagonism emerged more forcefully than it had in the past, and old distinctions appeared to fade in the face of a common experience and a recognition of the unity of life and work within a generalized system of appropriation. Railroads began the process of integrating a large regional unit, and linked the province to national if not international markets. Town and country increasingly found themselves enmeshed in a setting in which their pronounced differences began to pale before significant similarities. Social costs were many and varied, from the growing impersonalization of the wage relationship to the sooty environment of iron-and-steel-dominated Hamilton to the stark landscape of the milltown. Workers, of course, did not passively accept such developments, which had necessarily been part of a protracted process, and years well before the 1880s witnessed the first stirrings of Ontario's working-class movement. In that decade, however, came the essential changes, as class arrived on the scene, forcefully and unambiguously, for the first time. This class, which had been more than fifty years in the making, and had at its back a culture of ambiguity and diversity, became unmistakably entwined with the rise of the Knights of Labor, a body which took the ambivalence of the past cultural context of working-class life and forged it into a movement culture of opposition. In the expanding economic context of the 1880s Ontario workers made strides towards unifying their lives as productive men and women and their lives as citizens, family members, neighbours, and advocates of change. A whole series of cultural expressions thus linked up with a class content, and the fragmented and sectional concerns of the past gave way to a broader demand that encompassed fundamental challenges to the established order of capitalist society. In whatever area one wants to consider – economic, social, political, cultural – the Noble and Holy Order of the Knights of Labor voiced the need to go beyond the social relations of production as then constituted. An alternative hegemony was finally on the agenda, finally in the process of formation. The significance of the 1880s, as this moment of reaching out, was further confirmed by the gains in organization among workers not necessarily affiliated with the Knights. But this growth, however significant, paled in comparison, quantitatively and qualitatively, to the upsurge of the Knights of Labor.

WARP, WOOF, AND WEB: THE STRUCTURAL
CONTEXT OF THE KNIGHTS OF LABOR IN
ONTARIO

"To write the history of the Knights of Labor is an impossibility," warned Terence V. Powderly. "Its history was the history of the day in which it moved and did its work." The much-maligned leader of the Order was aware that "some young men fresh from college have tried to write the history of the organization," but he argued that they had failed: "They applied logic and scientific research; they divided the emotions, the passions, and feelings of the members into groups, they dissected and vivisected the groups; they used logarithms, algebraic formulas, and everything known to the young ambitious graduate of a university." Given this, Powderly felt that it was not advisable to take "the historian too seriously; at best he but weaves the warp of fancy into the woof of fact and gives us the web called history." Powderly's words of warning are worth remembering. Yet, in spite of our recognition of the importance of his sceptical assessment of a history premised on impersonal data and mere quantities, we commence with plenty of numbers. They, too, were part of the day in which the Noble and Holy Order moved and did its work.[33]

Organizationally, the Knights drew workers into their ranks through a relatively simple procedure and institutional apparatus. Individual members joined local assemblies, either in mixed (diverse occupational affiliations) or trade (adhering more rigidly to specific craft categories) assemblies. Normally those who were part of a specific trade assembly followed a particular skilled calling, but occasionally the trade assembly was merely an organization of all workers employed in the same plant, shop or factory. For a local assembly to be organized formally a minimum of ten members was required, and once established local assemblies were known to swell in membership to over a thousand. If a specific geographical region or trade contained five or more assemblies a district assembly could be formed. District assemblies were of two types: the national trade district, representing the interests of all assemblies of a specific craft, such as the window glass workers or the telegraph operatives; or the mixed district assembly, in which diverse interests of many mixed and trade assemblies were represented. In Canada it was this latter mixed district assembly that was pre-eminent, and in Ontario the various district assemblies were always mixed in form and representative of specific geographical/territorial units. Local assemblies were allowed one delegate in the district assembly for each hundred members they had enrolled, and one for each additional hundred or fraction thereof. Presiding over all these bodies were a series of leading elected officials: the master workman of the local assembly; the district master workman; and many lesser figures. Each district elected delegates to the annual convention of the Order, the general assembly, and at this gathering, in turn, were elected the national officers and the general executive board. The Order, then, was a highly centralized body, with a well-defined hierarchy and structure; yet it was also egalitarian, and the local assemblies had a large measure of autonomy, with their own courts to prosecute those who transgressed the discipline and regulations of knighthood.

How many of these local assemblies were there, where were they, and what type of assembly prevailed in specific places?[34] Although strongest in Ontario's rapidly expanding industrial cities like Toronto and Hamilton, the Knights also penetrated the province's towns, villages, and tiny hamlets. In its approximately thirty-year lifespan (1875–1907), the Order organized locals in eighty-two towns from Amherstburg in the west to Cornwall in the east, and from Port Colborne in the south to Sudbury in the north. These eighty-two towns contained a total of at least 249 local assemblies, which in turn formed ten district assemblies. Toronto, Hamilton, and Ottawa led the way with fifty-eight, thirty, and twelve local assemblies respectively, but the Knights were also active in eight communities of less than 1,000 people, and there were thirty-one local assemblies in places with populations of under 3,000. Ontario's five largest cities in the 1880s (Toronto, Hamilton, Ottawa, London, and Kingston) contained forty-six per cent of all Knights of Labor assemblies, but it was the range and dispersal of the Order that was perhaps most significant: of the forty-seven Ontario towns with a population of at least 3,000 in the 1880s, fully thirty-eight, or eighty-one per cent, witnessed the formation of a local assembly. Maps 8.1 and 8.2 detail this impressive organizational achievement, with Map 8.1 indicating those centres where the Knights were present and Map 8.2 portraying graphically the relative strength of the Order in specific locales which contained two or more local assemblies.

In Ontario there was an almost even division between trade and mixed locals, but if we consider the size of the town where the assembly was located a discernible pattern emerges. Mixed assemblies were far more popular in smaller places while trade assemblies were most often found in the cities. As always there were exceptions to this general pattern. St Thomas and London, for example, although large and important Knights' centres, possessed almost no trade assemblies. But on the whole the large manufacturing cities contained sufficient numbers of skilled workers to form trade assemblies, while in the smaller towns the mixed local assembly proved a more flexible organizing device. Since many of these less populous centres were not large enough to support sufficiently numerous groups of tradesmen to give rise to craft unions, the mixed assembly fit their needs well. Thus in towns under 5,000 the mixed assembly was dominant with fifty-eight per cent of all local assemblies, while trade assemblies and locals of unknown character each provided twenty-one per cent of all local assemblies. Cities with a population in excess of 30,000, however, were the more likely home of the trade assembly; fifty-seven per cent of all local assemblies were of this type and thirty per cent were mixed, with thirteen per cent of unknown character.

Map 8.1
Distribution of Knights of Labor Local Assemblies in Southern Ontario

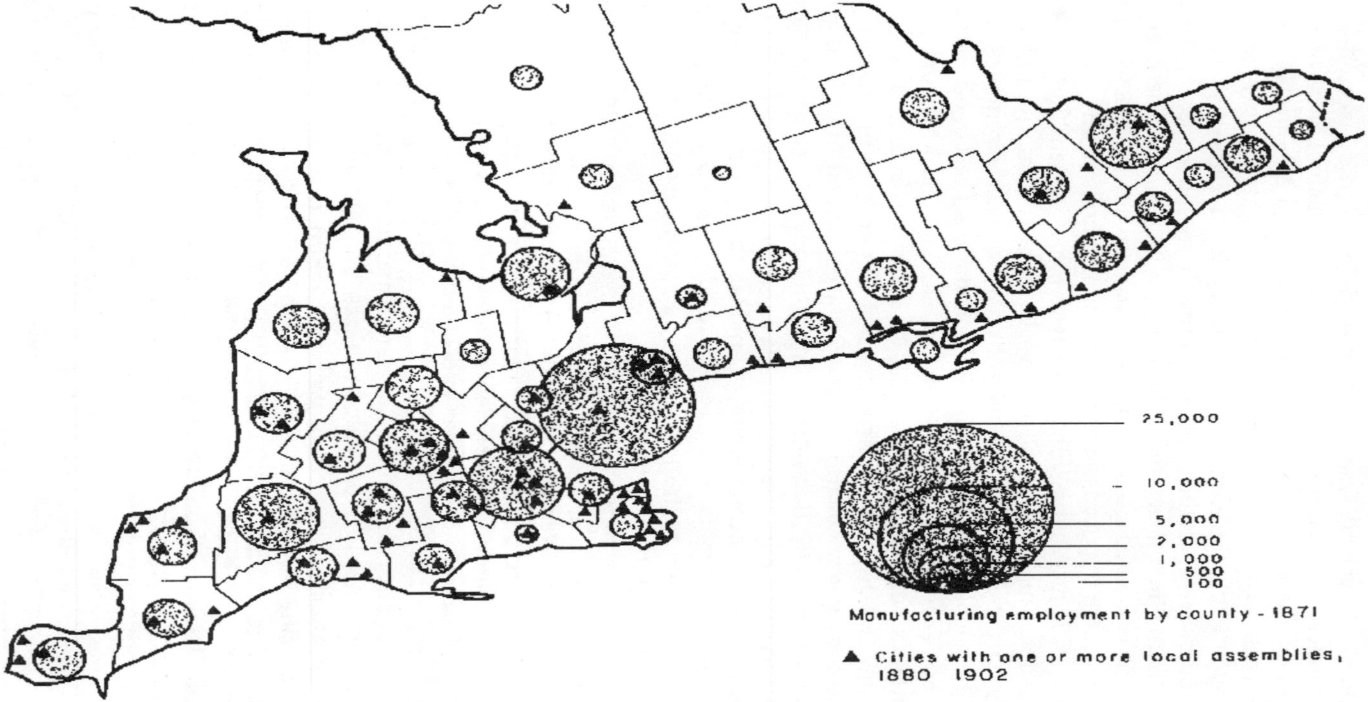

25,000

10,000

5,000
2,000
1,000
500
100

Manufacturing employment by county - 1871

▲ Cities with one or more local assemblies,
    1880   1902

Map 8.2
Distribution of Knights of Labor Local Assemblies in Southern Ontario, 1880–1902

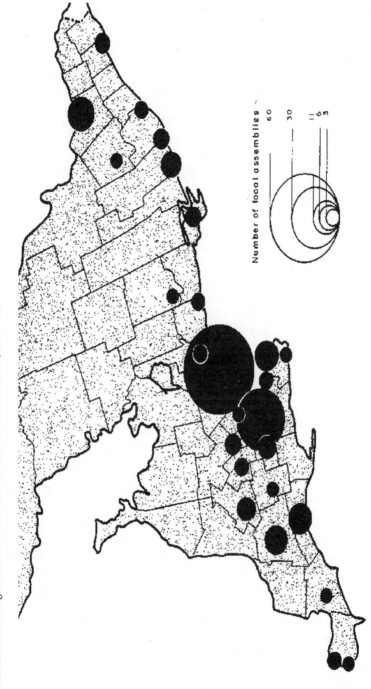

Number of local assemblies

How many members were drawn into the ranks of the Knights of Labor? This is a difficult question. In the u.s. at their peak, the Knights were said to have enrolled between 700,000 and 1,000,000 members, but this is a static count taken in the spring months of 1886. The data are questionable and tend to underestimate the membership. Moreover, the central problem is the timing of influx into the Order, for the Knights peaked at different moments in different regions. Thus, Jonathan Garlock has estimated that if one looks beyond peak membership the American Order may well have enrolled over 3,000,000 workers in its assemblies over the course of its history. We are plagued with problems of comparable, if not greater, magnitude in the case of Ontario, for membership data after 1885 are shaky at best, and official estimates seldom reliable. As in the United States, the Ontario Knights did not peak until 1886, a year which saw the founding of ninety-nine local assemblies, and even then the dating of the upsurge varied from region to region within Ontario. Thus, across south-central Ontario the Knights of Labor climbed to their highest membership point in 1886 and then deteriorated, rapidly in some places, more slowly in others. Towns close to the American border (Brockville and Hamilton, for instance) experienced the Order's impact earliest. But in the northwest, in the timber country of the Muskoka region, the Order achieved prominence later, as it did in some eastern Ontario towns like Kingston, where the Knights had 1,500 supporters in 1887. In Ottawa the Order's successes came, not in the 1880s, but in 1891. All this is further complicated by the fact that even *within* industrial cities like Toronto and Hamilton, which followed the classic pattern of cresting in 1886, there were some working-class sectors – letter carriers, longshoremen, and labourers – who joined the ranks of the Knights after the Order was in obvious retreat. Thus, any attempt to address the numerical significance of the Order will founder if it is reduced to a count of peak membership at any given point.

We can, nevertheless, start with peak official membership at single points in time for some specific locals. Toronto DA 125's forty-one local assemblies and 5,000 members in 1886, while Hamilton DA 61's 2,200 workers were organized in thirty local assemblies. District Assembly 6, of Ottawa, had 2,000 affiliated in 1892. The London-St Thomas DA 138 reported a membership of 4,435 in 1886–87, enrolled in thirty-six assemblies in western Ontario towns like Aylmer, Ingersoll, Listowel, and Wyoming. St Catharines DA 207 encompassed some 2,000 advocates in twenty-two local assemblies. Other district assembly peaks were Windsor DA 174's 616, Belleville DA 235's 1,548, Uxbridge DA 236's 523, and Berlin DA 241's 348. Perhaps more strik-

ing still are some of the individual town reports: Brockville's Franklin
LA 2311 with 430 members in November 1883; Gananoque's 700–800
members in 1887; Gravenhurst LA 10669's 300 lumber workers in
June 1888; the 500 cotton workers in Merritton's Maple Leaf LA 5933
in 1886; Petrolia's Reliable LA 4570 with 500 members in 1886; LA
6722's 20 workers at the Frost and Woods agricultural implements
works in Smiths Falls in August 1887; and the 500 workers of Woodstock's Unity and Concord LAS 3151 and 4922 in 1886. If we recall our
earlier discussion of the localized nature of manufacturing activity in
various Ontario cities and towns, in fact, we see that the Knights were
strong wherever a particular industrial activity predominated: among
Cornwall's cotton workers, Hamilton's iron and steel workers, or St
Thomas's railway workers the Order had many advocates.

Available data do not allow us to make any firm calculations on the
percentage of the workforce organized by the Order, nor would the
official membership figures necessarily reveal the true impact: the
tendency is always to under-represent the strength, and the volatility
of the rank and file further compounds this problem of undercount-
ing. Thus in five selected Toronto local assemblies the membership
fluctuated greatly between the date of their initial report and 1 July
1885. In these assemblies ninety-six members were enrolled on the
books at the time of the first membership report to Philadelphia.
Between 1882 and 1885 these assemblies added 666 members but
they also deleted 573, and so on 1 July 1885 reported a total membership of only 189. Their peak strength, then, would hardly address the
question of the masses of workers who passed through specific assembly halls. The case is made strongly in the instance of Toronto's
LA 2305, which reported a mere twenty-nine members in July 1885,
swelled to 550 in the following months, and then fell back to forty-five
within a year. To appreciate fully the numerical significance of the
Order we need to understand, not a static cross-sectional profile, but
a process and flow, determined, in part, by the movement's vitality
and particular events, developments in the economic realm, and social
relations. But the figures do not readily allow this, and we are forced
to consider the Knights in the context of peak membership figures
that defy all this, a problem further exacerbated by the problems of
reliance on census data that correspond only to decadal points and
that mask local situations in larger county calculations.

We can begin with the larger picture. If we take the total peak
memberships (at specific points in time with no account taken of
volatility) across the province and add them together we see that over
the course of their history the Knights organized a minimum of
21,800 workers. (A figure double this might not overstate the num-

bers actually enrolled.) This represented 18.4 per cent of the hands employed in manufacturing in 1881 and 13.1 per cent of those so employed in 1891. If we add to these figures the percentages of workers enrolled in trade unions but not members of the Knights of Labor (and we have no accurate statistics on this phenomenon, although it is estimated that in the United States approximately one-half of the Knights' members were trade unionists) it is apparent that at a very minimum the 1880s saw twenty to twenty-five per cent of the total non-agricultural work-force drawn to the ranks of organized labour. This, we need remember, is a higher percentage than any period prior to the post-World War II upsurge, and it is only with the increasing unionization of the public sector in recent decades that we have seen the figure climb to thirty-five per cent and over. For much of the early twentieth century, especially prior to World War I, no more than ten per cent of the work-force was organized.[35]

These aggregate data, of course, distort the facts dramatically, for they include all workers with no regard for region, sex, or age. Some, but not all this distortion can be eliminated by looking at particular places, presented in Table 8.3. The limitations of the census impose themselves here, for in attempting to focus on the percentage of the total work-force organized we are handcuffed to the 1881 and 1891 figures: the former are problematic because the Knights were not even on the scene at that early date, while the latter are equally flawed because the Order was, by that time, in the throes of decline. Moreover, such data are often available only on a county basis. Locales like St Thomas get buried in the total county employment figures. Nevertheless, the figures are an indication of the impressive numbers of workers drawn to the Order, and in places like St Thomas, Kingston, and the Lincoln, Niagara, and Welland region there is no doubt that the Knights of Labor organized an absolute majority of the people employed in manufacturing.

The census, moreover, did not report on the hands employed in such small towns as Merritton, Chatham, or Gananoque. Yet we know from many sources that the Order was actively engaged in such places. To attempt a crude estimate of the percentage of the work-force organized we have taken our figures on membership and compared them to a rough calculation of the number of hands employed. This latter figure was obtained by taking the total population for 1881. In no case would the work-force have been more than forty per cent of the population, and it is unlikely that it would have even reached twenty per cent in these years, but we have taken these poles as our gauge. (Note that if we took twenty per cent of the populations of Toronto, Hamilton, and Kingston for 1881, we would

Table 8.3
Knights of Labor Membership as Percentage of Hands Employed, 1881 and 1891

City or county	1881	1891
Essex (Windsor)	30.0	22.2
London	29.3	22.5
Elgin East (St Thomas)	80.0	58.6
Hamilton	33.8	22.8
Toronto	39.3	20.4
Brockville	44.9	31.9
Kingston	101.8	56.0
Cornwall	32.3	14.8
Lanark South (Perth, Smiths Falls, Carleton Place)	21.1	18.1
Ottawa	–	31.7
Lincoln, Niagara and Welland (St Catharines, Welland, Merritton, Thorold)	–	50.5
Perth North (Stratford, Listowell)	36.0	30.5

SOURCES: Canada, *Census*, 1881 and 1891: Knights of Labor, General Assembly, *Proceedings*: Ontario Bureau of Industry, *Annual Reports*

expect work-forces of 17,283, 7,192, and 2,818. The census recorded 1881 work-forces of 12,708, 6,493, and 1,473, so in no case have we underrepresented the work-force. Our method, then, can only understate the impact of the Order. Since the small towns considered here did not expand greatly in the 1880s, using the 1881 population figures does not pose a great problem.) Table 8.4 reveals how thoroughly the Order penetrated these small Ontario manufacturing towns, organizing an extremely high percentage of the work-force.

What all this means, we would argue, is that the Knights of Labor represented the most important moment in the history of Ontario labour until the coming of the Congress of Industrial Organizations in the late 1930s. More workers were drawn to the cause of the Order in more Ontario communities and in greater numbers than most of us can actually believe. Across the province between ten and eighty per cent of all workers in particular cities, and we stress once more that these are minimum estimates, became Knights of Labor. That structural context was a large part of warp, woof, and web of the history of the 1880s. We have, against Powderly's advice, divided this out from the passions, emotions, and feelings of the membership, and it is now time to turn to another aspect of the history of the Order. For if the Knights of Labor represented a quantitative breakthrough for Ontario's workers, they also represented a crucial qualitative shift in the orientation of the working class. The Order took the raw material of a class culture – ambiguous, fragmented, and unfocused – and moulded it into a movement culture of opposition and alternative.

Table 8.4
Knights of Labor Membership as Percentage of Workforce (Estimated at between
Twenty and Forty Per cent of 1881 Population)

Town	20% of 1881 population	40% of 1881 population
Chatham	25.4	12.7
Woodstock	46.5	23.2
Petrolia	72.0	36.0
Merritton	139.0	69.5
St Catharines	51.8	25.9
Guelph	17.6	8.8
Hespeler	71.4	35.7
Oshawa	52.0	26.0
Gananoque	87.0	43.5
Smiths Falls	47.9	23.9

SOURCES: Same as in Table 8.3.

SPREADING THE LIGHT: THE EMERGENCE
OF A MOVEMENT CULTURE

There is no such historical phenomenon as an alternative hegemony
attained. At the moment that it is realized, an alternative hegemony
passes into hegemony and assumes its place as arbitrator of social,
economic, political, and cultural values, expressed through the control
of state power, the majesty of the law and a wide range of formal
institutions and informal sanctions. A subordinate class can thus only
reach towards an alternative hegemony but it cannot "dominate the
ethos of a society."[36] Alternative hegemonies can, historically, pass
into new hegemonic cultures, although this necessarily involves the
rise to power of new classes and the dissolution of old ways of life.
The revolutions of 1789 and 1917 were just such epoch-shaking moments of transformation, although it is questionable if North America
has ever witnessed upheavals of such magnitude: certainly Canada
has not.

In the Ontario of the 1880s, however, there was an alternative
hegemony in formation. It did not win the day, although it raised a
series of challenges and oppositions that remain with us yet; its
lifespan was indeed short, although the issues it addressed seem
timeless. We refer to this creative moment as a movement culture, a
recognition that the Knights of Labor built upon a culture of class
experience that had little direction and unity to consolidate a class
effort that sought to transform the very nature of the society in which
workers found themselves.

The movement culture was formed in the process of daily life,
both on and off the job, and it was tempered in the political and

workplace struggles that we will examine shortly. It began with the worker's initiation into the Knights of Labor assembly, where a whole series of symbolic and ritualistic practices rooted the member in the movement, reinforcing traditions of collectivity and solidarity in an age of hostile, individualistic pieties. Each new initiate vowed to defend the interest and reputation of all true members of the Order, be they employed or unemployed, fortunate or distressed, and was instructed that "Labor is noble and holy." To defend it from degradation, to divest it of the evils to body, mind, and estate, which ignorance and greed have imposed; to rescue the toiler from the grasp of the selfish is a work worthy of the noblest and best of our race." Upon admission to the Order, the recently christened Knight was informed that "open and public associations have failed, after a struggle of centuries, to protect or advance the interest of labor," and that the Knights of Labor merely imitated "the example of capital," endeavouring "to secure the just rewards of our toil." "In all of the multifarious branches of trade," the convert was told, "capital has its combinations, and whether intended or not, it crushes the manly hopes of labor and tramples poor humanity in the dust." To counteract this distressing tendency of the modern age, the Order asserted: "We mean to uphold the dignity of labor, to affirm the nobility of all who earn their bread by the sweat of their brow." In these ritualized incantations, which resounded in local assembly halls across south-central Canada, lay much of the promise and potential of the Knights of Labor.[37]

That promise and potential reared its head in many cultural events: in the many picnics, parades, demonstrations, dances, hops, and balls that the Knights organized across the province in the heady days of the upheaval of the 1880s. These occasions were no doubt moments of recreations, diversions which moved people away from the everyday concerns of the next day's work, the next week's groceries, and the next month's rent – the range of insecurities the next year could bring. But they were also exhilarating reminders of self-worth and class strength. They were prominent in Toronto and Hamilton, as we would expect, but places like London, Woodstock, Ingersoll, Chatham, Thorold, Gananoque, and Belleville were also the sites of such cultural activities, and the Order was capable of drawing anywhere from 1,000 to 5,000 people to these "monster" gatherings. After an 1887 Gananoque Knights of Labor picnic, the local newspaper commented: "Probably no gathering anywhere near the size ever took place here, where there was such good order ... They have shown that they are a power in the community, able to command respect."[38]

In all this, from the pounding footsteps of workers marching by the thousands in Toronto, Hamilton, or Ottawa, through a day of sports and frolicking in Ingersoll, Belleville, or Kingston, to a mammoth picnic and long-winded speeches on an island in the St Lawrence near Gananoque, we catch mere glimpses of a self-generating culture of collectivity, mutuality, and solidarity. An understanding of class place and pride stood at the core of this culture, as well as individual longing for a better world. Forging a multitude of diverse, often contradictory, ideals into a collective assertion was the movement itself. As a strikingly creative effort, the Knights of Labor was the very embodiment of human striving that evolved out of residual components of a class culture, nudged towards new, or emergent, purpose by those who embraced the causes of labour's rights, men and women who, in advocating reform, did much to create a culture of "democratic promise." The difficulty we ourselves experience in comprehending their vision and their striving is a measure of significant failures – theirs *and* ours.[39]

But in the 1880s that failure was not a settled fact, embedded in the historical record in indisputable concreteness; the sharp clarity of defeat was not yet there for all to see. Thousands of Ontario workers took Richard Trevellick's words to heart when he promised that the Knights of Labor would "make Labor respectable by having men and women respect themselves, and while courteous and kind, refuse to bow and cringe to others because they possess wealth and social position." Certainly Thomas J. O'Neill, of Napanee's Courage Assembly (LA 9216), regarded such proclamations with appropriate seriousness, writing to Powderly that, "this section of the country is sadly in need of organization, but fear of the money kings [The Rathbuns] keep the working class in slavery." Railroad men, organized in Headlight Assembly (LA 4069) of St Thomas, acted upon Trevellick's words in 1885. They conducted their own statistical survey of their town of 11,000 with the intention of using "all lawful means of obtaining their rights, also to educate those of our members who heretofore have permitted others to do their thinking, thereby allowing themselves to be used as mere machines in the hands of unscrupulous men." The *Labor Union* proclaimed its mission in mid-January 1883: "To Spread the Light; to expose the inequalities of distribution by which the few are enriched at the expense of the many. To call things by their right names, and to point out to workingmen how these inequities could be redressed and the workingman secure the full reward of his toil." Employers found much to dislike in the words of Trevellick, O'Neill, LA 4069, and the *Labor Union*. Their actions throughout the 1880s spoke loudly of their fears and antagonisms. They regarded the increasing consciousness of class, and threat of active opposition, as a dangerous development. By 1891 the business community was convinced that "the spirit of trades unionism is strangling honest endeavour, and the hard-working, fearless thorough artisan of ten years ago is degenerating into the shiftless, lazy, half-hearted fellow who, with unconscious irony, styles himself a knight of labor." The culture had, as well as advocates, staunch opponents.[40]

It was in the midst of a virtual war between these contending forces (in which battles were both practical and intellectual) that the labour reform cause gained hard-won adherents. And it was in this context that the "educational" thrust so prominent in the Order's own priorities consolidated. Local assemblies became, in the parlance of the 1880s, "schools of instruction" in which the lessons learned turned on the principles of labour reform, reaching a mass audience in literally hundreds of reading rooms, Knights of Labor libraries, and assembly halls. In the words of Trevellick, it was in the "schoolroom" of the local assembly where members first learned "their duties and their rights."[41]

Providing much of the text of instruction was a handful of committed publishers/editors. Often themselves practical printers, these men struggled through the 1880s and 1890s, working into the early morning hours to put out their weekly journals, devoted, as in the case of the *Palladium of Labor*, "to the Interests of the Workingmen and Workingwomen." Always on the brink of financial ruin, such newspapers kept afloat during these years only by dint of extraordinary effort, personal perseverance, and occasional support from a long-established trade union. Smothered by their dependence on advertising revenue, limited by their subscribers' inability to contribute financially, with circulation often hovering around the 1,000 mark, seldom over 5,000, these papers occupied an unenviable position in the often gloomy world of the nineteenth-century press. Small wonder that the men who kept them going were often ill-tempered, and indiscriminately combative, as with Hamilton's William H. Rowe or St Thomas' George Wrigley, or constantly manoeuvring to attain economic ends, like the notorious but resourceful A.W. Wright. But whatever their personal idiosyncrasies these men attempted to move the class beyond economism, striving "to take a broader and more comprehensive view of the entire subject of Labor Reform than is embodied in mere unionism, and to grasp and apply those great underlying principles of equity and justice between men which alone can permanently and satisfactorily solve the issues between Labor and Capital." This was an important component of what Frank Watt has referred to as the "freely germinating" radicalism of the 1880s, a phenomenon spawned by the presence of the Knights of Labor.[42]

This radicalism was popularized by a group of brainworkers and local advocates: men like Toronto's Phillips Thompson, as well as more obscure, but highly talented and committed local figures. Among these were Joseph Marks of London, who began as a Knight, organized the Industrial Brotherhood in the 1890s, and edited the *Industrial Banner* well into the twentieth century; Galt's J.L. Blain, a lecturer who described himself to Powderly as a well-educated "rat from the sinking ship of aristocracy"; a Hamilton coppersmith, George Collis, who boomed the Order under the nickname "Sandy the Tinker," travelling to Oshawa, London, and other southern Ontario towns; poets like the carpenter Thomas Towers and Listowel's blind and deaf Walter A. Ratcliffe; or anonymous supporters – St Thomas' "Knight of the Brush" and "True Reformer"; Brantford's "Drawbar"; or "Pete Rolea" from the oil-producing community of western Ontario. Individuals like these helped the Order to establish itself in countless communities, and made the cause of reform a popular and lasting one. "Lignum Vitae" reported to the *Journal of United Labor* on the progress of Guelph LAS 2980 and 4703: "The masses are beginning to believe us when we tell them this endless toil for a miserable existence was never intended by an all wise creator. I wish I had only more time that I could go out to these people and invite them into an Order whose object is the complete emancipation of all mankind, and lift from off their necks the yoke of subjection, and often tyranny of a few." From virtually every corner of the province anonymous correspondents informed labour newspapers of the local state of reform agitation.[43]

This agitation contributed much to the attainment of class cohesion, strengthening the bonds of unity. The old sectarian quarrels between Orange and Green were, for the most part, left behind; the Order itself assumed the place and role of a religion of reform, labour sermons being preached in local assembly halls; the Irish, once despised by all respectable workers, were at the centre of the Knights of Labor activity. Education became, not the responsibility of the schools, the press, and the élite, but the duty of all. "L.C.S." of Gananoque argued that the Knights were "engaged in solving the greatest problem of the age," urging all wage labourers to drink at the fountain of labour reform, rather than from the cesspool of the "capitalistic press," which consistently suppressed facts, failed to consider just causes, and aligned itself with "upper anarchy," money, and monopoly. "Educate yourself and you will be in a position to enlighten others," he wrote. That accomplished, working people had only to "obey the laws of knighthood, be loyal to self and manhood, defend the interest of the Order, and labor for the new era until it dawns upon the toilers of our country, until the weary men and women chained by the wage-system can see justice enthroned, and this, the land of the free," As Albert V. Cross reported to Powderly from Hamilton's LA 2481 in 1887:

When we entered the Order we were taught that in the home of labor there would be no distinctions of Country, Creed & Color because all were of the Earth and with equal rights to Earth, when we understood this great truth that all men are brothers we rejoiced, and we solomly [sic] resolved that we would do all in our power to strengthen the bonds of unity between the workers of the world.[44]

Perhaps the most significant aspect of this strengthening of the bonds of unity was the Order's role in overcoming past deficiencies of workers' organizations. Nowhere was this more visible than in the Knights of Labor effort to draw *all* workers into one large movement. Across the province skilled and unskilled workers, craftsmen, factory operatives, and labourers, united in local assemblies to oppose a common enemy and to cultivate common ties. Unlike virtually every previous chapter in the history of Ontario workers' rebellion, the Knights of Labor stamped these pages of the 1880s with concern for those whose status in the working-class community ill-suited them to wear the badge of respectability, a consensual cultural norm that the Order recast to express class antagonisms. Premised on the fundamental rejection of exclusion (tarnished only by the Order's stand on the Chinese), the Knights of Labor, most often led by skilled workers, offered their ideals and their strengths as a force protecting and speaking for all of those "below" them. As Leon Fink has argued in the case of the United States, masses of workers who had never experienced the fruits of full citizenship joined the skilled leadership sector of the Order, forging an alliance of the "privileged" working class and a younger thoroughly proletarianized group, composed of male and female factory operatives and unskilled labourers.[45]

Indeed, the introduction of women into the mass struggles of the 1880s shattered decades of complacency and effected a fundamental shift in attitude. To be sure, the Knights acted out of chivalrous intent, and did not abandon age-old conceptions of hearth and home, domesticity and place. But they could turn all this to new purpose, and strike out at forces which they felt to be undermining all that was good and proper in such traditional practices. Thus, at a London speech by the popular and well-travelled Knight, Richard Trevellick, members of the Order raised "their hands to heaven and pledged themselves that wherever women were employed, they would demand equal pay for equal work without regard to sex whatsoever." It is difficult to see in such action only a retrogressive glance over one's shoulder to a pre-industrial arcadia: the language is unmistakably that of an industrial society, and the problem has yet to be resolved. Finally, the Knights did not stop and settle comfortably in this economistic niche, but attacked those who would define women's rights in some circumscribed way. In Knights of Labor centres like Belleville, Brantford, London, Stratford, St Thomas, Thorold, Hamilton, and Toronto, where "the ladies" joined the Order in assemblies named "Advance" and "Hope," and attended musical and literary entertainments as "Goddesses of Liberty," the possibility forged in the 1880s was on many women workers' lips. With the passing of the Knights of Labor those lips were sealed for a time, but the possibility itself could not be written out of the past.[46]

It is this notion of possibility, this movement towards alternative hegemony, that is central to an understanding of the Knights of Labor in the 1880s. To rescue that moment, and to realize that its insights and social practice were achievements of considerable stature is part of our purpose in presenting this analysis of the Knights of Labor. With the vision of a more humane social order always before it, the culture forged by the Knights of Labor is worth knowing today. In the words of Phillips Thompson, member of Toronto's Victor Hugo LA 7814, that culture taught men and women to "dream of what might be." By doing their part in "spreading the light," Thompson argued, labour reformers were bringing close to realization the "beautiful ideal of universal democracy and co-operation." Far from a utopian fantasy, the promise of a better society was merely "a faint presentation of what might be – what cannot be at present solely because of the blindness, ignorance, and want of union among workingmen – but what I trust yet will be when the scales of error, of misleading education and of temporary self-interest have fallen from their eyes – so they can see the light."[47] To explore both the strengths and weaknesses of this reform crusade we now turn to the political and workplace struggles in which the Knights of Labor both thrived and foundered.

THE KNIGHTS IN POLITICS

The Knights articulated this new "movement culture" in the realm of Ontario politics. On all levels, municipal, provincial, and federal, the Order expressed the class interests of Ontario workers in new ways. This unprecedented upsurge of labour involvement menaced both old-line parties' control over their respective electorates. In Ontario this represented a significant danger to Macdonald and the Tory party, while Blake regarded it as the key to potential political success, especially given Oliver Mowat's Ontario record.[48]

To those of us familiar with the older Canadian political history, the role of the Order in the politics of the 1880s may come as a considerable surprise. Yet it was no secret to the political partisans of the day. Not only in Toronto and Hamilton but throughout the southwestern Ontario manufacturing belt and even penetrating into eastern Ontario, the Knights created a political movement that demanded attention. Macdonald in assessing the political climate in the summer of 1886 worried that the Conservative party was "not in a flourishing state." The "rocks ahead" which threatened the Tory "ship" were "Riel, Home Rule, the Knights of Labor and the Scott Act."[49] The Knights thus specifically merited "the old chieftain's" close attention and two of the three other threatening reefs were movements intimately tied to the Order and its ideals, namely the Irish question and temperance.[50]

From the moment of their entrance into Canada the Knights actively engaged in politics. December 1882 saw the first stirrings of these activities when in Hamilton labour helped elect two aldermen[51] and meanwhile in Toronto the Labour Council played a prominent role in defeating a candidate identified as particularly anti-labour.[52] Those initial successes propelled labour reformers in both cities into independent campaigns in the 1883 provincial election. In Hamilton locomotive engineer and prominent Knight Ed Williams, an English immigrant and the epitome of the respectable working man, ran and won a slid 23.4 per cent of the vote in a three-way race.[53] In Toronto, where partisan politics had flared during the nominating process, the campaign results were more mixed. Painter John Carter, a labour leader of the 1870s and a member of Toronto's Excelsior LA 2305, ran in Toronto West and won forty-eight per cent of the vote. His candidacy, however, had gained the unstated support of the Reform Party which ran no candidate against him. In Toronto East, carpenter Samuel R. Heakes faced nominees from both old-line parties and finished a distant third with only seven per cent of the vote.[54]

Despite the relative success of these campaigns, partisan recriminations followed and were to re-emerge in subsequent campaigns. In both cities disgruntled Tory workingmen accused the Grits of double-dealing.[55] In Hamilton these charges died down, however, and labour reformers created the Hamilton Labor Political Association to continue the thrust for an independent working-class party. In subsequent municipal elections in 1883 and 1884, the association under the leadership of Knights' activist Robert Coulter enjoyed some success in electing Knights as aldermen. The best-known of these figures was Irish carter Thomas Brick who provided Hamilton workers with a colourful and bombastic leader.[56]

In Toronto Excelsior LA 2305's leadership core of old labour reformers, led by Daniel J. O'Donoghue with the able support of Charles March and Alfred Jury, consolidated the position of the Knights of Labor first in the newly-created Trades and Labor Congress of Canada (which first met in 1883) and subsequently in the Toronto Trades and Labour Council (TTLC). Once entrenched there they proceeded to make good use of both bodies as effective lobbying agencies, especially against the federal Tory government.[57] Their success in attracting political attention was evident on T.V. Powderly's 1884 Toronto visit. The stage at his major address was graced by the presence of Edward Blake, Timothy Anglin, Toronto Tory Mayor Boswell, and numerous Tory aldermen.[58] In the ensuing 1884 municipal election Toronto workers threw a considerable scare into the Tory machine although it held the mayoralty by a slim margin.[59] In 1885, however, this hold was broken with the sweeping victory of W.H. Howland who enjoyed the united support of the Toronto reform community, including the extremely active support of both the Knights of Labor and TTLC.[60] His victory led to considerable soul-searching on the part of the Tories both in Toronto and in Ottawa. The results of this re-evaluation manifested themselves in a remarkable labour settlement at the *Mail* newspaper, where an iron-clad contract had caused many former Tory workingmen to defect,[61] and later in the equally striking creation of the Royal Commission on the Relations of Labor and Capital.[62]

These quite considerable concessions to the political strength of the working-class movement did not prevent it from contesting the December 1886 Ontario provincial election and the February 1887 federal election. In December seven labour candidates took the field. One could be described as Lib-Lab, two as Tory-Labour, and the other four were independents who faced candidates from the other two parties. St Thomas brakeman and leading Knight Andy Ingram won West Elgin,[63] while in Lincoln Lib-Lab candidate William Garson succeeded.[64] In Lambton A.W. Wright, running as a Conservative-Labour candidate, caused considerable controversy when many of the Knights repudiated him. Not surprisingly he did not run strongly.[65] In London, however, cabinet marker and Knight Samuel Peddle, running with temperance support, gave Tory Opposition Leader W.R. Meredith a considerable scare before going down to a narrow defeat. In the previous election Meredith had gained his seat by acclamation.[66]

Toronto witnessed a confused race owing to the extraordinary gerrymandering of Oliver Mowat. Toronto had gained a third seat in a redistribution, but the three MPPs were to be elected at large for a city-wide riding, *and* each voter would be allowed to vote for only two candidates. The logic of this tactic was, of course, to ensure that at least one Grit would be returned from Tory Toronto. The strategy eventually paid off, but the race saw two Tory, one Grit, and two Labour candidates. Knights' organizer Charles March finished fourth overall, while his Knight running mate, temperance advocate and evangelical Christian John Roney finished fifth. Statistical calculations in this anomalous electoral situation are complex but March did win over 4,000 votes and Roney some 3,400. (Tory E.F. Clarke, an Orange printer, topped the poll with 7,000.)[67]

In Hamilton complications also arose when the Tories nominated a leading moulder John Burns as their candidate and then called on Labour to endorse him. The Labour convention refused, however, roundly condemning Burns and the Tories. Instead they nominated Grand Trunk machinist and Knight Hamilton Racey. In the bitter three-way race that followed Racey finished third with 17.2 per cent of the vote, a total which fell short of Ed Williams' 1883 vote.[68] This result did not prevent Hamilton workers from trying again in the federal election in which moulder Fred Walters ran as a Lib-Lab candidate in the two-seat constituency. He outpolled his Liberal running-mate but nevertheless trailed the two victorious Tories, although his 48.8 per cent was a respectable showing.[69]

In Toronto E.E. Sheppard, the controversial editor of the *News*, campaigned in West Toronto for labour, which in East Toronto Knights' leader Alfred Jury ran. Neither was opposed by a Liberal although Sheppard's previous ties were Tory, if anything. Sheppard won forty-seven per cent and Jury thirty-five per cent, but expectations of victory had been so high that this was viewed as a significant setback.[70] Fierce factional fighting ensued which pitted D.J. O'Donoghue and his *Labor Record* against A.W. Wright and the *Canadian Labor Reformer*. The charges back and forth only confirmed for many the growing fear that independent labour politics was a diversion from the Knights' major tasks.[71]

Workers had entered politics with considerable scepticism and their failure to make a quick and decisive breakthrough led to much discouragement, especially since it appeared that their leaders were still intriguing in partisan politics. Nevertheless throughout the late 1880s municipal politics continued to gain much attention from the Order and victories were recorded which ranged from Brantford and Chatham to Brockville and Ottawa.[72] In Cornwall, for example, the Knights helped defeat a municipal railroad bonus in the 1888 municipal election and two years later were reported to have elected nine of thirteen aldermen and the mayor and reeve.[73] Moreover the Order was particularly prominent in lobbying activities in Ottawa after the creation of a Canadian Knights of Labor Legislative Committee.[74]

The Knights then made significant political efforts and enjoyed some success, but they certainly did not overcome all the tensions in the working-class world. Partisan politics had established a deep hold on Canadian workers and the battle to create an independent working-class party was sharp and difficult. Yet on the local level tangible gains were made – early closing, union wages and jobs in corporation work, just assessment rates, more responsible public transit. Nevertheless the Knights had never regarded the political arena as their major battlefield. It was only one campaign in a war on many fronts. This war was perhaps sharpest at the workplace.

THE PEOPLE'S STRIKE

Much of the previous literature on the Knights of Labor has focused on their dislike of strikes. Frequent citation of major Knights' leaders such as T.V. Powderly and lengthy consideration of splits within the Order, such as the expulsion of the general executive board member T.B. Barry in 1888, lead to the image of an organization committed to class co-operation through the vehicle of arbitration. Like most long-propounded views, these arguments contain a kernel of truth but they also disguise much that is central to an understanding of the Knights of Labor. In Ontario the Knights either led or were involved in almost all the major strikes of the 1880s and early 1890s. This should not surprise us since, as we have already argued, the Order should not be viewed as one contending force within the working-class world, but rather as the embodiment of that class in these years. Thus in the period of the Order's growth in Ontario from 1882 to 1886, the Order came to represent a solid working-class presence united behind its eclectic but critical aims.

In the Order's earliest years in Canada it grew owing to its willingness to organize the larger class forces on behalf of localized trade or industrial struggles. Thus in Toronto the Order emerged from the coalition of forces knit together by experienced trade-union militants to support the striking female boot and shoe operatives in the spring of 1882.[75] This was apparent again the following summer when DA 45 (Brotherhood of Telegraphers) engaged in a continent-wide strike against the monopolistic telegraph companies. Although DA 45 had done little preparatory work within the Order before their epic struggle, as a bitter Powderly would argue again and again, it did appear to have established sufficient local contacts so that organized labour, and especially the Knights, rallied to its cause.[76] In Hamilton and Toronto, for example, support came from union contributions to the strike fund, benefit concerts, lectures, and theatricals.[77] Meanwhile the first wave of massive Labour Day demonstrations organized by the Knights, but involving all organized labour, took place in Toronto, Hamilton, and Oshawa.[78] In each case, support for the telegraphers played a prominent role in the speeches and provided a compelling symbol for the necessity of labour solidarity. The ultimate failure of the telegraphers' strike and its bitter aftermath, which saw DA 45 withdraw from the Knights of Labor, appear to have been less important than the solidarity expressed in its course. As the *Palladium of Labor* declared: "The telegraphers' strike is over. The People's Strike is now in order."[79]

"The People's Strike" took many forms in the following few years. At its most dramatic it involved mass strikes which crippled whole industries or communities. Examples of struggles of this magnitude included the two Toronto Street Railway strikes of the spring and summer of 1886, a Chatham town-wide strike of December 1886, the cotton strikes in Merritton (1886 and 1889) and Cornwall (1887, 1888, and 1889), and the massive lumber strikes in Gravenhurst in 1888 and in Ottawa-Hull in 1891.[80] Each of these struggles rocked their communities with previously unmatched levels of class conflict and involved workers previously untouched by trade-union organization. Yet the Knights of Labor also led or took part in conflicts far less riveting. In the early 1880s this often meant coming to the support of striking craftsmen as with Toronto female shoe operatives in 1882 and their Hamilton sisters in 1884, or Toronto printers in 1884.[81] In these cases and in countless others, the Order proved its mettle by practising what it preached and aiding all workers' struggles. It was this type of activity which initially helped to break down entrenched conservative craft suspicions of the Order. Then, as craft unionists and craft unions flooded into the Order in 1885–86, the Order continued to fight their battles. These struggles, often involving issues of control, represent the second major type of Knights' strike activity.

It would be impossible to chronicle all these strikes here. Toronto Knights alone, for example, fought nineteen strikes between 1883 and 1889, and this number does not include the large number of strikes which they actively supported or in which some Knights were involved. Let us turn instead first to a perusal of strike activity among one important group of craft workers, the moulders, and then turn to an analysis of a few of the mass strikes.

Moulders had their own international craft union which dated from the late 1850s in Ontario. The Iron Molders International Union (IMIU) had very strong locals in Hamilton (No. 26) and Toronto (No.

28) and after 1887 had an Ontario-wide district organization.[82] The relationship between the IMIU and the Knights cannot be plotted with mathematical certainty but in Brantford (Standard LA 3811), Hamilton (Library LA 1864), Kingston (Frontenac LA 10539), and Oshawa (Tylers LA 4279) there existed trade assemblies identified as moulders. In addition, however, we know from scattered sources that Toronto (Maple Leaf LA 2622), Brockville (Franklin LA 2311), Smiths Falls (LA 6772), Lindsay (LA 5402), and Oshawa (Aetna LA 2355 and LA 4428) all contained moulders and other metal workers as well. Finally we have considerable reason to suspect that Cobourg (LA 2598), Toronto (LAS 5254 and 5650), Woodstock (LAS 3151 and 4992), Galt (LA 6112), and Peterborough (LA 6952) might also have had moulder members.[83] The lines between the craft unions and the Knights were never drawn as sharply in reality as they have been by historians subsequently.

Organized throughout Ontario in stove foundries and in the agricultural implements industry, the moulders played a significant role in one of Ontario's most successful industries. This prominence and their skill, which resisted mechanical innovation throughout this period, gave them a high degree of workplace control which they fought vigorously to maintain.[84] These issues led to at least twenty-five strikes between 1880 and 1895.[85] The major strikes in 1887, 1890, and 1892 in Toronto and Hamilton have already received historical attention,[86] but much smaller Ontario centres such as Brockville, Oshawa, and London also saw frequent struggles in their foundries throughout the 1880s. These smaller centres demonstrate well the interrelationship of IMIU members and Knights.

Brockville, a railroad and manufacturing centre on the St Lawrence in eastern Ontario, illustrates these themes. The James Smart Manufacturing Co. (est. 1854) dominated the local economy of the 1880s and employed by 1890 two hundred workers in the production of stoves and lawn mowers.[87] The IMIU first organized in Brockville in 1868 or 1869 and had a spasmodic existence there throughout the 1870s, which included work stoppages in 1875, 1879, 1880, and 1881 – the last three of which appear to have resulted in union victories.[88] The last two struggles took place after Robert Gill replaced James Smart as the manager of the works and tried to break the union by demanding the workers abandon it. After this failed, there was a single year of peace at the foundry – a year in which the Knights strongly established themselves in Brockville. In August 1882, Ogdensburg Knights' leader Archer Baker organized Franklin LA 2311 which grew rapidly. By the following summer the assembly numbered in the hundreds and contained many of the most prominent moulders' leaders in town including Samuel Miller, a former IMIU international convention delegate and a perennial member of the moulders' local executive.[89] The year of peace ended in June 1883 when Gill refused the moulders' demand for a wage increase. The ensuing eleven-week strike was eventually lost but the polarization of the community continued to increase. During the strike Brockville's working class demonstrated its solidarity when the corpse of twenty-eight year old moulder William Hutcheson, murdered by a scab in a strike in Troy, New York, was returned to his native town for burial.[90] The delegation of Troy Knights and moulders which accompanied the body joined with the Brockville Knights in commemorating his death with "one of the largest funerals" ever seen in Brockville.[91] Building on this solidarity, the Knights grew rapidly that summer enrolling over one hundred members in one week shortly after Hutcheson's funeral. The town also had a telegraphers' LA 2335 with about forty members which struck solidly and with "manifest public sympathy" during the continent-wide strike.[92] In the early fall Franklin Assembly held a picnic which attracted 500 to 800 and by November the assembly reported a membership of 430.[93]

The stage was set for the next bitter conflict between Gill and his moulders which began in January 1884. Seven months later in late July the moulders returned to work, their union crushed and their vestiges of craft control destroyed, at least for the moment. This time the Gills ignored community sentiment and engaged in active union-smashing. They recruited scabs from Connecticut, housed them in the foundry, and ignored the public discontent which labelled the company managers, "the enemies of Brockville." When forced to defend his position, Gill explained simply:

The question at issue is simply one of "control." It is a fact, however humiliating the acknowledgement, that during the past three years of the company's existence, the business has been practically controlled by the Moulder's Union. ... If the conditions are such that "control" cannot be gained by the proprietors, then Brockville will lose the industry which we are trying to carry on.[94]

In Brockville the owners won back their control but only after a long history of struggle in which the Knights helped to provide the opposition. The intimacy of Knights and moulders in Brockville was evident in the latter stages of the 1884 strike when Franklin Assembly selected moulders' leader Sam Miller as its general assembly delegate and when John S. McClelland of the general executive board arrived in Brockville to investigate the strike. McClelland's visit resulted in a $500 grant from the Order's assistance fund.[95]

Oshawa, west of Brockville on Lake Ontario, witnessed an analogous set of struggles in the 1880s and a very similar organic relationship between IMIU Local No. 136 and the Knights. The IMIU which dated from 1866 was joined in Oshawa by the Knights on 12 August 1882 when Aetna LA 2355 was organized by a Buffalo Knight.[96] This large assembly with nearly 300 members in 1883 was entrenched in the local iron and agricultural implements industry. Co-operating closely with the IMIU, the Oshawa Knights hosted nearly 2,000 workers at their August 1883 labour demonstration. IMIU Local 136 marched in a uniform of "gray shirts, black hats and black neckties" and were joined by their brother moulders from Toronto (Nos 28 and 140) and Cobourg (No. 189) and over 1,500 Knights of Labor. Local 136 provided the "main feature of our procession," "the moulding, melting, and casting of iron in the line of march," reported LA 2355 and IMIU No. 36 Recording Secretary Joseph Brockman. The commemorative coins they struck during the procession were distributed to the participants.[97] Two months later the labourers at the Malleable Iron Works, members of Aetna LA 2355, struck against a wage reduction. The moulders, out in support of the labourers and facing a similar wage cut, were warned that if they did not return, the shop would "be permanently closed against them." Six weeks into the strike the Oshawa Stove Works and the Masson Agricultural Implements Works locked out their moulders to create a slid employer block against the workers. Even then it was only after the Oshawa moulders' sister union in Hamilton (No. 26) and Toronto (No. 28) accepted ten per cent wage cuts in December without striking, that Oshawa No. 136 felt compelled to concede defeat. Earlier in December the labourers had returned on the advice of the LA 2355 executive which argued that "it would have broke Jay Gould with his seventy-three millions of stolen money to have kept labourers and immigrants away from here."[98]

By the next fall, however, the union had reasserted itself and another of its leaders (and a charter member of LA 2355), Lewis Allchin, wrote Powderly seeking his support for a profit-sharing plan at the Oshawa Stove Works. He also mentioned that they had "affected every Reform obtained in the shop, one for instance, piece workers used to work almost all noonhour, and not later than last spring, we managed to institute a rigid observance of noonhour, we also limited the wages to $2.50 per day."[99] The new success of the moulders probably made another struggle almost inevitable and it came two years later in late January 1886 when the Malleable Iron Works again tried to force the union out of its foundry. This time the issue was simply the question of a closed shop. John Cowan, the manager of the works, insisted on continuing to employ two non-union moulders; IMIU No. 36 and Tylers LA 4279 (Moulders) refused to work with them. After a bitter two-month strike in the depths of a severe winter which witnessed alleged incendiarism, a "surprise party" (charivari?), a widespread sending to Coventry of the non-union moulders, and considerable public support for the men, the company finally caved in and recognized the closed shop. The concession came at the end of March when the union and LA 4279 began to call for a total boycott of the foundry's goods.[100]

Similar events involving moulders and Knights occurred in Lindsay in 1886,[101] in Kingston in 1887,[102] in London in 1882 and 1886,[103] and in Ayr, Galt, and Smiths Falls later in the decade.[104] Success varied dramatically, but in all these cases the principles of the Knights, of craft control and of labour reform were carried on. Lewis Allchin, Oshawa moulder-Knight and the author of "Sketches of our Organization" (a serialized history of the IMIU from its founding to 1890 published in the *Iron Molders Journal*), summed up the close intertwining of these themes: "The object, in brief, is the *complete emancipation of labor*, and the inauguration of a higher and nobler industrial system than this of the present, under which one human being is dependent upon another for the means of living." Denying at the outset later historians' views of the Knights, he emphasized: "We cannot turn back if we would; we cannot return to a primitive system of working, however much we might desire it." Trusts and syndicates, he viewed as "an inevitable phase" of "an excessive and pernicious competitive system," but they would not "be the *finale* of the whole question." They "contained within themselves the germs of their own dissolution," since "selfishness and greed were but foundations of sand to build upon." The future he would not predict, but he hazarded one final conclusion:

That no system which does not recognize the right of labor to a first and just share of its products, which refuses each and every toiler a voice in the business transactions of the enterprise, that does not establish a just and relative measure or standard of value for all services rendered, labor performed, products manufactured, and commodities exchanged, will ever be a just or permanent one.[105]

Here, quite clearly, we can see that the values and ideas of the late nineteenth-century working-class world were shared by its articulate leadership, be they Knights or craft unionists, and, as was so often the case, the very personnel overlapped. For our chosen group of skilled workers, the moulders, this unity demonstrated itself most clearly in the streets of London in the late summer of 1886 when the IMIU held its seventeenth convention. The city's first labour demonstration "of 4000 unionists in line" was held to honour the assembled moulders and was witnessed by crowds estimated at between 8,000 and 10,000.[106] Addressed by Captain Richard Trevellick, the Knights' chief itinerant lecturer, the convention also considered at length a motion to amalgamate the IMIU with the Knights of Labor. After a full day of debate the resolution was soundly defeated but it did win support from militant moulders' strongholds such as Albany and Troy, New York. In registering his opposition, the IMIU president made clear his support "for always remaining on the most friendly terms with the Knights of Labor, and rendering them all the assistance that our organization can possibly give them in all legitimate undertakings in the interest of labour."[107] This solidarity began to disintegrate the following year during the vicious war between the Founders Association and the moulders in the Bridge and Beach strike.[108]

The solidarity so evident in the London streets in July 1886 had also spread far beyond the moulders and their other skilled worker brethren. The Knights also successfully organized the unskilled – women factory workers, male operatives, and large numbers of labourers both in Ontario's cities and towns, and in her resource hinterland. These workers, organized for the first time under the banners of the Knights of Labor, also engaged in militant struggles in the 1880s and early 1890s. Strikes to gain either the right to organize or to win modest economic advances occurred in these sectors as opposed to the control struggles of the skilled workers. Ranging in size from minor affairs to massive, almost general, strikes which polarized single-industry communities, these struggles were most prominent in the mill towns of eastern and western Ontario.

Cotton mill struggles hit Merritton in 1886 and 1889 and Cornwall in three successive years, 1887, 1888, and 1889. The Merritton mill, which remained totally organized as late as 1892, witnessed numerous work stoppages led by the Knights in 1886.[109] Three years later a week-long strike over a wage reduction won a compromise settlement.[110] None of these represented major victories but in an industry known for its exploitation and anti-unionism Maple Leaf LA 5933's 500 workers were more successful than most. Their achievement may well have been one of the factors that led Canadian Coloured Cottons to shut down the plant after the merger of 1892.[111]

Cornwall's cotton workers joined the Knights of Labor in 1886 in LAS 6582 and 6583. The first test of the Order came in the summer of 1887 when eighteen dyers demanded that their hours be reduced from ten to nine. Although the Order provided $400 in financial assistance to its striking members, they still lost the strike.[112] In February 1888 wage reductions at both the Canada and Stormont mills precipitated strikes involving from 1,300 to 1,500 employees. After a few weeks the workers returned with a compromise settlement. The wages were still cut but by an estimated ten per cent instead of the alleged twenty to twenty-three per cent originally imposed. This settlement held at the Stormont mill, but the Canada mill was struck again when workers accused the company of not living up to the agreement. After another month these workers again returned.[113] One year later in the spring of 1889 the Stormont mill workers struck once again. After five weeks the 600 operatives returned when the company agreed to honour the weavers' demands.[114]

The lumber industry, another long hold-out against trade unionism, also experienced two major strikes led by the Knights of Labor. Gravenhurst LA 10669 was organized in 1887 under the leadership of Uxbridge DA 236 after a short lumber strike in which the hours of work in the mills on Muskoka Bay had been reduced from eleven to ten-and-a-half with a promise that in 1888 they would be further shortened to ten. In 1888, however, a province-wide agreement was signed by the Muskoka, Georgian Bay, and Ottawa River lumber barons which prevented a further reduction of hours under pain of forfeiting a bond. The angry workers of LA 10669 consulted the DA 236 leadership which counselled caution and urged the assembly to strengthen its ranks. By June 300 of the 375 workers had joined the Order and they then appointed a committee to meet with the mill owners. This met with a blanket refusal from the employers and the workers again sought aid from DA 236. Although reluctant, the district assembly had no choice but to sanction a strike which began on 3 July 1888. A few mills acceded but the majority held out. Aylesworth of the Knights' general executive board responded to an emergency call from DA 236, but his efforts were unsuccessful and by September the men had returned to work with no gains.[115]

In the Chaudière region of the Ottawa-Hull area, another lumber workers' strike erupted in September 1891.[116] As in Muskoka, the Ottawa Valley was ruled by a closely-knit group of entrepreneurs which had made fortunes and consolidated power on profits from sawn lumber and lumber by-products. Nine firms were involved in the 1891 strike and they were headed by a distinguished group of Canadian capitalists, notably J.R. Booth, E.H. Bronson, and E.B. Eddy. While they prospered, their mill-hands eked out a marginal existence on wages of $7.00 to $9.50 for a sixty-hour week. The Knights' success in the Ottawa Valley came late and it was only in the fall of 1890 that they had gained a foothold in the mills with the creation of Chaudière LA 2966.

As three years earlier in Gravenhurst, a particularly harsh winter created the situation which would lead to that fall's huge mill strike. Already late returning to work because of the weather, the workers were informed of a fifty-cents-a-week wage cut. In return for the reduction, the owners offered the ten-hour day but soon violated their own concession. With hours again extended to eleven and twelve the workers sought the aid of the Knights of Labor in May. When informed that the Order would not sanction a strike until they had been in the organization for at least six months, the workers remained on the job. By fall, however, their tempers had worn thin and on Saturday, 12 September 1891 the outside workers at Perley and Pattee demanded that their wages be reinstated to the 1890 rate. Denied this on Saturday, the workers met on the Sunday and agreed to repeat their demand the next day. Again rebuffed, they proceeded to march from mill to mill pulling all the workers out. Over 2,400 workers left their jobs and the Knights quickly took over the strike leadership. The mill workers were subsequently enrolled in Chaudière LA 2966 and Hull's Canadienne LA 2676.

Over the next few weeks some of the smaller mills conceded to the workers' demands of the previous year's rate and a ten-hour day, but the larger mills stood firm. As community support for the workers stiffened, massive meetings of 3,000 to 10,000 people were held. Meanwhile incidents of violence occurred, the militia was mobilized, and workers responded with a charivari and with their own security force. Over $1,500 was raised by the Order and an extensive relief system was established. By the end of September, however, strike leaders urged their followers to seek employment elsewhere and by early October the relief system began to break down. By 12 October the workers were back with their 1890 wage but with the same long hours of work. Two hundred of Bronson's workers promptly struck again on 14 October when they claimed he had reneged on his agreement. by the end of the month, however, work was back to normal. Although not an unmitigated success, the Order had won a limited victory and the millmen stayed with the Knights. The next year Ottawa DA 6 was created with an impressive 2,000 workers, largely from the lumber industry. These workers finally won the ten-hour day in 1895.

Turbulence, strikes, and class conflict thus played an important role in the history of the Knights of Labor in Ontario. The oft-invoked image of an organization interested in avoiding strikes at all cost and the implicit projection of a class-co-operative, if not collaborationist, body begins to dissipate under more careful scrutiny.

CONCLUSION

The 1880s were a critical decade in Canadian history – a decade which witnessed the fulfilment of the National Policy industrial strategy with a rapid expansion in Canadian manufacturing, especially in textiles. Yet these years also saw the breakdown of the previous consensus on industrial development, as Canadian workers, especially in the country's industrial heartland, began to raise their voices in an unfamiliar, concerted fashion to join the growing debate about the nation's future. Ontario's mainly British and Canadian workers, many with previous trade union and industrial experience, provided leadership to the emerging working-class movement which found its most articulate expression in the Knights of Labor. The challenge which this movement mounted in all realms of Ontario society – the cultural, intellectual, and political as well as the economic – engendered in turn a class response from employers and from the state. The employers engaged in a virulent, open warfare with their worker-Knights, especially in the period of economic decline after 1886. In the 1890s they began as well to turn to the ever-increasing concentration and centralization of capital and later to the modern management devices of a rampant Taylorism in their battle with labour. Meanwhile the state and the political parties responded in a more conciliatory fashion. Mowat and, to a lesser degree, Macdonald interceded to provide workers with many of the protections they demanded – factory acts, bureaux of labour statistics, arbitration measures, suffrage extension, employers' liability acts, and improved mechanics' lien acts. The political parties proved even more flexible and managed through patronage and promises to contain much of the oppositional sentiment which flared in the 1880s. Thus the Canadian political system functioned effectively to mediate the fiery class conflict of the 1880s.

In the following decade, with the exception of eastern Ontario, the Knights were moribund. Their precipitous decline was halted by a slight resurgence in the late 1890s, but the 1902 Berlin decision delivered the final *coup de grâce*. Yet as we suggested earlier, the heritage of the Order lived on. Its major contributions to working-class memory centred on its oppositional success as a movement which for the first time provided *all* workers with an organizational vehicle and, further, which, for a moment at least, overcame the splintering forces which so often divided the working class.

NOTES

We would like to thank Russell Hann, Debbi Wells, Dale Chisamore, and Peter DeLottinville for research assistance and sharing their own research with us. This paper was written as a summary of a larger project on the Knights of Labor in Ontario funded by the Social Sciences and Humanities Research Council of Canada. The larger project was published in 1982 by Cambridge University Press as *"Dreaming of What Might Be": The Knights of Labor in Ontario.*

1 See Saul Alinsky, *John L. Lewis* (New York: Vintage 1970), 15, and Melvyn Dubofsky and Warren van Tine, *John L. Lewis: A Biography* (Chicago: Quandrangle 1976), 9–11.

2 Thomas R. Brooks, *Clint: A Biography of a Labor Intellectual – Clinton S. Golden* (New York: Atheneum 1978), 17–18.

3 Hamilton Public Library, Hamilton Collection, "Recollections of John Peebles, mayor of Hamilton, 1930–1933," 7 February 1946.

4 Gordon Bishop, "Recollections of the Amalgamated," unpublished typescript, Gananoque, in possession of authors.

5 *Citizen and Country* (Toronto) 4 May 1900.

6 Melvyn Dubofsky, "The Origins of Western Working Class Radicalism, 1890–1905," in *Workers in the Industrial Revolution: Recent Studies of Labor in the United States and Europe*, eds, Peter N. Stearns and Daniel J. Walkowitz (New Brunswick, NJ: Transaction 1974), 383.

7 University of Toronto, Kenny Papers, *The Knights of Labor, the American Federation of Labor and the One Big Union*, One Big Union Leaflet No. 2 (Winnipeg nd [c. 1920]).

8 David J. Bercuson, *Fools and Wise Men: The Rise and Fall of the One Big Union* (Toronto: McGraw-Hill Ryerson 1978), 120.

9 Irving Bernstein, *The Lean Years: A History of the American Workers, 1920–1933* (Boston: Houghton Mifflin 1960), 34.

10 Norman J. Ware, *Labor in Modern Industrial Society* (New York: Russell and Russell 1968), 258.

11 Gerald N. Grob, *Workers and Utopia: A Study of Ideological Conflict in the American Labor Movement, 1865–1900* (Chicago: Quadrangle 1961), esp. 34–59, 79–80.

12 Leon R. Fink, "The Uses of Political Power: Towards a Theory of the Labor Movement in the Era of the Knights of Labor," Paper presented to the Knights of Labor Centennial Symposium, Chicago, 17–19 May 1979, and "Workingmen's Democracy: The Knights of Labor in Local Politics, 1886–1896" (PHD diss., University of Rochester 1977). The Ware argument is stated most concisely in Norman J. Ware, *The Labor Movement in the United States, 1860–1890: A Study in Democracy* (New York: Vintage 1964), xi–xiii, 350–70.

13 Previous Canadian work on the Knights of Labor in Ontario includes
Victor Oscar Chan, "The Canadian Knights of Labor with special
reference to the 1880s" (MA thesis, McGill University 1949); Douglas
Kennedy, *The Knights of Labor in Canada* (London: University of Western Ontario Press 1956); Eugene Forsey, "The Telegraphers' Strike of
1883," *Transactions of the Royal Society of Canada* Series 4, 9 (1971):
245–59; Bernard Ostry, "Conservatives, Liberals, and Labour in the
1880s," *Canadian Journal of Economics and Political Science* 27 (May
1961): 141–61; F.W. Watt, "The National Policy, the Workingman and
Proletarian Ideas in Victorian Canada," *Canadian Historical Review* 40
(March 1959): 1–26. Cf., given the above, Fred Landon, "The Knights
of Labor: predecessors of the CIO," *Quarterly Review of Commerce* 1
(Autumn 1937): 1–7. While all this work provides valuable empirical
detail it has been dated by the availability of new sources and lacks a
firm grounding in local contexts. Interpretatively, it presents us with
few bench-marks in understanding the Knights of Labor. We have
drawn upon Raymond Williams, "Base and Superstructure in Marxist
Cultural Theory," *New Left Review* 82 (November–December 1973):
1–16; Lawrence Goodwyn, *Democratic Promise: The Populist Movement in
America* (New York: Oxford University Press 1976).

14 Joseph R. Buchanan, *The Story of a Labor Agitator* (Westport, Conn.:
Greenwood Press 1970), vii.

15 H.V. Nelles, *The Politics of Development: Forests, Mines & Hydro-Electric
Power in Ontario, 1849–1941* (Toronto: Macmillan 1974), 48–107.

16 *Journal of Commerce* (Toronto), 7 September 1888, cited in Michael
Bliss, *A Living Profit: Studies in the Social History of Canadian Business,
1883–1911* (Toronto: McClelland and Stewart 1974), 120.

17 See Greg Kealey, ed., *Canada Investigates Industrialism: The Royal
Commission on the Relations of Labor and Capital 1889* (Toronto: University of Toronto Press 1973), esp. ix–xxvii; Fernand Harvey, *Révolution
industrielle et travailleurs: Une enquête sur les rapports entre le capital et le
travail au Québec à la fin du 19e siècle* (Montréal: Boréal Express 1978).

18 R.J.K., "The Dynamic Year of 1886," *One Big Union Monthly*, 23 September 1927, courtesy Allen Seager, is one good example of this.

19 Gustavus Myers, *A History of Canadian Wealth* (Toronto: James
Lorimer 1972); H.C. Pentland, "The Development of a Capitalistic
Labour Market in Canada," *Canadian Journal of Economics and Political
Science*, 25 (November 1959): 450–61, and "Labor and the Development
of Industrial Capitalism in Canada" (PHD diss., University of Toronto
1960); Stanley B. Ryerson, *Unequal Union: Roots of Crisis in the Can-
adas, 1815–1873* (Toronto: Progress Books 1968); Gordon W. Bertram,
"Historical Statistics on Growth and Structure of Manufacturing in
Canada, 1870–1957," in C.P.S.A. *Conference on Statistics, 1962 and 1963,*

eds, J. Henripin and A. Asimakopulos (Toronto: University of Toronto Press 1964), 93–146; Bryan D. Palmer, *A Culture in Conflict: Skilled Workers and Industrial Capitalism in Hamilton, Ontario 1860–1914* (Montreal: McGill-Queen's University Press 1979), 3–31; Gregory S. Kealey, *Toronto Workers Respond to Industrial Capitalism, 1867–1892* (Toronto: University of Toronto Press 1980), 1–34.

20 *People's Journal* (Hamilton), 1 April 1871, cited in Steven Langdon, *The Emergence of the Canadian Working Class Movement* (Toronto: New Hogtown Press 1975), 3; *Journal of the Board of Arts and Manufactures for Upper Canada* 7 (1867): 220.

21 Bertram, "Historical Statistics," 93–146; Warren Bland, "The Location of Manufacturing in Southern Ontario in 1881," *Ontario Geography* 8 (1974): 8–39; T.W. Acheson, "The Social Origins of the Canadian Industrial Elite, 1880–1885," in *Canadian Business History: Selected Studies, 1947–1971*, ed. David S. Macmillan (Toronto: McClelland and Stewart 1972), 144; Peter Warrian, "The Challenge of the One Big Union Movement in Canada, 1919–1921" (MA thesis, University of Waterloo 1971), 11.

22 Bertram, "Historical Statistics," 133. On the importance of this period of price deflation in the United States see Harold G. Vatter, *The Drive to Industrial Maturity: The U.S. Economy, 1860–1914* (Westport, Conn.: Greenwood 1975), and on the twentieth century, Harry Braverman, *Labor and Monopoly Capital: The Degradation of Work in the Twentieth Century* (New York: Monthly Review 1974).

23 See, for instance, Terry Copp, *The Anatomy of Poverty: The Condition of the Working Class in Montreal, 1897–1929* (Toronto: McClelland and Stewart 1974); Michael J. Piva, *The Condition of the Working Class in Toronto, 1900–1921* (Ottawa: University of Ottawa Press 1979); David Millar, "A Study of Real Wages: The Construction, Use and Accuracy Check of a Constant-Dollar Plotter," unpublished research paper, University of Winnipeg 1980.

24 Jacques Ferland, "The Problem of Change in the Rate of Surplus Value Studied Through the Evolution of the 'Social Cost of Labour' in Canada, 1870–1910," unpublished MA thesis research paper, McGill University 1980.

25 Acheson, "Social Origins of Elite," 162; see maps on "Manufacturing Employment by County," in *Economic Atlas of Ontario*, ed. W.G. Dean (Toronto: University of Toronto Press 1969).

26 Jacob Spell, *Urban Development in South-Central Ontario* (Toronto: McClelland and Stewart 1972), 101–86; Edward J. Chambers and Gordon Bertram, "Urbanization and Manufacturing in Central Canada, 1870–1890," in *C.P.S.A. Conference on Statistics, 1966*, ed. Sylvia Ostry (Toronto: University of Toronto Press 1966), 225–55; Bland, "Location

of Manufacturing," 8–39. See the important statement in Raphael
Samuel, "The Workshop of the World: Steam Power and Hand Technology in Mid-Victorian Britain," *History Workshop Journal* 3 (Spring
1977): 6–72.

27 On Hamilton see Palmer, *A Culture in Conflict*, 3–31, and on Toronto
Kealey, *Toronto Workers*, 1–34.

28 Note V.I. Lenin, *The Development of Capitalism in Russia* (Moscow:
Progress 1964), 551.

29 G.P. de T. Glazebrook, *A History of Transportation in Canada*, 2 vols
(Toronto: McClelland and Stewart 1964), II: 91–118; Kenneth Lloyd
Clerk, "Social Relations and the Urban Change in a Late Nineteenth
Century Southwestern Ontario Railroad City: St. Thomas, 1868–1890"
(MA thesis, York University 1976).

30 Richard A. Trumper, "The History of E. Leonard & Sons, Boilermakers
and Ironfounders, London, Ontario" (MA thesis, University of Western
Ontario 1937); Benjamin S. Scott, "The Economic and Industrial History of the City of London, Canada from the Building of the First
Railway, 1855 to the Present, 1930" (MA thesis, University of Western
Ontario 1930), 56–65, 169–70; Carrol J. Grimwood, "The Cigar Manufacturing Industry in London, Ontario" (MA thesis, University of Western Ontario 1934), 3.

31 Leo A. Johnson, *History of the County of Ontario, 1615–1875* (Whitby:
Corporation of Whitby 1973), 250-2; "The Canadian Locomotive Com-
pany Limited: History of the Works at Kingston," *Queen's Quarterly* 10
(April 1903): 455–65; information on Smiths Falls courtesy Peter de
Lottinville.

32 *Report of the Select Committee on the Causes of the Present Depression of
the Manufacturing, Mining, Commercial, Shipping, Lumber and Fishing
Interests* (Ottawa 1876), 142–8; Kealey, *Canada Investigates Industrialism*,
179–92; Chambers and Bertram, "Urbanization and Manufacturing,"
242–55.

33 Terence V. Powderly, *The Path I Trod: The Autobiography of Terence V.
Powderly* (New York: Columbia University Press 1940), 3–4, 102.

34 All organizational data throughout are based on our own calculations.
We should note, however, a debt of gratitude to two pieces of pioneer-
ing research on the Knights which were of inestimable value to us.
Eugene Forsey's massive compilation of materials on organized labour
in Canada before 1902 includes much on the Knights and a helpful
attempt at a local-by-local reconstruction. See Eugene Forsey, *History of
Canadian Trade Unionism* (Toronto: University of Toronto Press 1982).
Jonathan Garlock, *Knights of Labor Data Bank* (Ann Arbor, Mich.: Inter
University Consortium 1973), and "A Structural Analysis of the Knights
of Labor" (PHD diss., University of Rochester 1974) have been of con-

siderable help. For a description of the data bank, see Jonathan Garlock, "The Knights of Labor Data Bank," *Historical Methods Newsletter* 6
(1973): 149–60. Our corrections to the data bank will be incorporated
into the computer file at Ann Arbor. These corrections are based on
the labour and local press of Ontario, on the Ontario Bureau of Industry, *Annual Reports*, on various trade-union minutes and proceedings,
and on the extensive Ontario correspondence scattered throughout the
Powderly Papers, recently indexed at the National Archives of Canada
(hereafter NA) by Russell Hann. The population data are from the 1881
and 1891 censuses.

35 J. Smucker, *Industrialization in Canada* (Scarborough: Prentice Hall
1980), 209; H.C. Pentland, "A Study of the Changing Social, Economic, and Political Background of the Canadian System of Industrial
Relations," draft study for the Task Force on Labour Relations, Ottawa
1968, 70–1.

36 E.P. Thompson, "The Peculiarities of the English," in *The Poverty of
Theory and Other Essays* (London: Merlin Press 1978), 74.

37 Ezra Cook, ed., *Knights of Labor Illustrated: Adelphon Kruptos: The Full
Illustrated Ritual Including the "Unwritten Work" and an Historical Sketch
of the Order* (Chicago 1886); Catholic University of America,
Washington, DC, Powderly Papers (hereafter PP), "The Great Seal of
Knighthood" and "Secret Circular: Explanation of the Signs and Sym-
bols of the Order"; Carrol D. Wright, "An Historical Sketch of the
Knights of Labor," *Quarterly Journal of Economics* 1 (January 1887):
142–3; Powderly, *Path I Trod*, 434–5.

38 *Gananoque Reporter*, 25 August 1887.

39 Note the comments in Russell Hann, "Brainworkers and the Knights of
Labor: E.E. Sheppard, Phillips Thompson, and the Toronto *News,*
1883–1887," in *Essays in Canadian Working Class History*, eds Gregory
S. Kealey and Peter Warrian (Toronto: McClelland and Stewart 1976),
57; Goodwyn, *Democratic Promise*, 540–3.

40 *Palladium of Labor* (Hamilton), 5 September 1885; PP, O'Neill to Powderly, 13 January 1885; *Statistics as Collected by Headlight Assembly No.
4069, K. of L. for Its Exclusive Use* (St Thomas 1885), 3; *Journal of Commerce*, 13 March 1891, as cited in Bliss, *A Living Profit*, 78; *Labor Union*
(Hamilton), 13 January 1883.

41 Ontario Bureau of Industry, *Annual Report* (Toronto 1888), Part 4, 18;
Palladium of Labor, 21 February 1885; *St. Thomas Times*, 21 April 1886;
Journal of United Labor (Philadelphia), March 1883, quoted in Fink,
"Workingmen's Democracy," 399.

42 G. Weston Wrigley, "Socialism in Canada," *International Socialist
Review* 1 (1 May 1901): 686; Watt, "The National Policy, the Workingman and Proletarian Ideas."

43 *Journal of United Labor*, 25 March 1886.

44 PP, Cross to Powderly and G.E.B., 9 July 1887; *Gananoque Reporter*, 3 December 1887.

45 See, especially, Fink, "Workingmen's Democracy."

46 *Brantford Expositor*, 16 July 1886; *London Advertiser*, 29–30 October 1886; Susan Levine, "The Best Men in the Order: Women in the Knights of Labor," unpublished paper presented to the Canadian Historical Association, London, 1978, and "The Knights of Labor and Romantic Ideology," paper presented to the Centennial Conference, Newberry Library, Chicago, 17–19 May 1979.

47 *Palladium of Labor*, 26 December 1885.

48 On Mowat and Labour see Margaret Evans, "Oliver Mowat and Ontario: a Study in Political Success" (PHD diss., University of Toronto 1967), esp. chap. 3.

49 Sir John A. Macdonald to Sir Charles Tupper, 21 June 1886, in Sir Joseph Pope, ed., *The Correspondence of Sir John A. Macdonald* (Toronto: Oxford University Press 1921), 382.

50 On the Knights and the Irish see Eric Foner, "Class, Ethnicity, and Radicalism in the Gilded Age: The Land League and Irish America," *Marxist Perspectives* I (Summer 1978): 6–55; on Home Rule see Kealey, *Toronto Workers*, chap. 14.

51 PP, George Havens to Powderly, 4 January 1883.

52 Kealey, *Toronto Workers*, chap. 11.

53 *Labor Union*, 3, 10 February, 3 March 1883; PP, Gibson to Powderly, 7 February 1883, and Powderly to Gibson, 9 February 1883.

54 *Trade Union Advocate* (Toronto), 11, 18, 25 January, 1, 8, 15 February 1883; NA, Toronto Trades and Labor Council, Minutes, 19 January, 2 February 1883; *Globe* (Toronto), 5, 8 February 1883.

55 PP, D.B. Skelly to Powderly, 15 December 1884; NA, Macdonald Papers, Small to Macdonald, 10 April 1883.

56 *Palladium of Labor*, 25 August, 28 September, 13, 20 October, 24 November 1883; 12 January, 31 May, 5 December 1884; 15 May, 4 July, 28 November, 5 December 1885.

57 Kealey, *Toronto Workers*, chap. 11.

58 *Globe*, 14 October 1884.

59 NA, Macdonald Papers, Boultbee to Macdonald, 12 September, 29, 30 December 1884; Macpherson to Macdonald, 27 December 1884.

60 NA, Toronto Trades and Labor Council, Minutes, 4, 14, 18, 29 December 1885; *News* (Toronto), 4 January 1886; *Palladium of Labor*, 5 December 1885; PP, O'Donoghue to Powderly, 7 January 1886.

61 NA, Macdonald Papers, Piper to Macdonald, 2, 3 February 1886; *Toronto World*, 13, 16 March 1886; Kealey, *Toronto Workers*, chaps 6, 11; PP, O'Donoghue to Powderly, 29 March 1886.

62 Kealey, *Canada Investigates Industrialism*, ix–xxvii, and Harvey, *Révolution industrielle et travailleurs*.

63 *St. Thomas Daily Times*, February–December 1886; *Canada Labor Courier* (St Thomas), 29 July, 30 December 1886. See also Barbara A. McKenna, "The Decline of the Liberal Party in Elgin County," unpublished paper presented to the Canadian Historical Association, London 1978.

64 PP, William Garson to Powderly, 21 March 1884 and 22 October 1885.

65 *London Advertiser*, 21 December 1886; *Sarnia Observer*, 10 September 1886, 7 January 1887; *Canadian Labor Reformer* (Toronto), 18 December 1886; *Toronto World*, 2 December 1886; *Globe*, 8 December 1886; *News*, 22 December 1886.

66 *London Advertiser*, 24 November, 7, 9, 10, 11, 16, 17, 18, 29, 30 December 1886, 7, 11 January 1887; *Palladium of Labor*, 27 November, 11 December 1886; *Canada Labor Courier*, 20 December 1886; PP, Hewit to Powderly, 13 December 1886.

67 Kealey, *Toronto Workers*, chap. 12.

68 PP, Freed to Powderly, 2 December 1886; *Palladium of Labor*, 4, 7, 11, 18 December 1886; *Hamilton Spectator*, 4, 7, 8, 14, 22 December 1886.

69 Ibid., 13 January, 24 February 1887.

70 Kealey, *Toronto Workers*, chap. 12.

71 Ibid., chaps 12–13.

72 *Courier* (Brantford), 4 January, 15 April, 28 December 1886; *Brantford Expositor*, 16 April, 20 August, 24 September, 17, 31 December 1886; *Canada Labor Courier*, 30 December 1886, 13 January 1887; *Brockville Recorder*, 1887–88; *Ottawa Citizen*, 1890–91.

73 *Brockville Recorder*, 4 January 1888, *Cornwall Freeholder*, 3, 10 January, 7 February 1890. These newspaper discussions are somewhat confusing as various candidates denied formal connections with the Order. Yet in the aftermath the *Cornwall Freeholder*, 7 February 1890, argued that one loser "had arranged against him the workingmen, which is no mean factor in election contests in Cornwall these days."

74 Kealey, *Toronto Workers*, chap. 12.

75 Ibid., chaps 3 and 10.

76 Ibid., chap. 10; Palmer, *A Culture in Conflict*, chap. 6; and Forsey, "The Telegraphers' Strike of 1883."

77 Kealey, *Toronto Workers*, chap. 10; Palmer, *A Culture in Conflict*, chap. 6.

78 *Iron Molders Journal* (Cincinnati) (hereafter *IMJ*), 31 August 1883; *Palladium of Labor*, 18 August 1883.

79 *Palladium of Labor*, 25 August 1883.

80 For Tornto see Kealey, *Toronto Workers*, chap. 10; for Chatham see *Canada Labor Courier*, 30 December 1886, 13 January 1887; for cotton and lumber see below.

81 Kealey, *Toronto Workers*, chap. 10; Palmer, *A Culture in Conflict*, chap. 6.

82 For background on the Iron Moulders see C.B. Williams, "Canadian-American Trade Union Relations: A Case Study of the Development of Bi-National Unionism" (PHD diss., Cornell University 1964); Palmer, *A Culture in Conflict*, passim; and Kealey, *Toronto Workers*, chap. 5. The following is also based on the *IMJ* and the International's convention proceedings.

83 Organizational data are drawn from Garlock data bank; Forsey, *History of Canadian Trade Unionism*; and Kealey and Palmer, *"Dreaming of What Might Be,"* chap. 1.

84 David Montgomery, *Workers' Control in America* (New York: Cambridge University Press 1979), chap. 1 and passim; Kealey, *Toronto Workers*, chap. 5; Palmer, *A Culture in Conflict*, chap. 3; Wayne Roberts, "Studies in the Toronto Labour Movement, 1896–1914" (PHD diss., University of Toronto 1978), chap. 3.

85 Strike data are drawn from *IMJ*; Iron Molders International Union (hereafter IMIU), *Proceedings*, 1860–1895; and Ontario Bureau of Industry, *Annual Reports*.

86 Kealey, *Toronto Workers*, chap. 5; Palmer, *A Culture in Conflict*, chap. 3.

87 Dale Chisamore et al., *Brockville: A Social History* (Brockville: Waterway Press 1975), chap. 4.

88 Ibid., chap. 5; *IMJ*, 1868–92; IMIU, *Proceedings*.

89 Chisamore, *Brockville*, chap. 5.

90 Daniel Walkowitz, *Worker, City, Company Town* (Champaign, Ill.: University of Illinois Press 1978), 211, 213, 239–40; and a review of Walkowitz by Bryan Palmer, *Labour/Le Travailleur* 4 (1979): 261–7.

91 *Brockville Recorder*, 12, 13, 14 June 1883.

92 Ibid., 25 July 1883.

93 Ibid., 17 November 1883.

94 Ibid., 5, 6, 10 March 1884.

95 Knights of Labor, General Assembly, *Proceedings*, 1884, 652.

96 PP, James R. Brown to Powderly, 29 September 1882; Johnson, *History of the County of Ontario*.

97 *Palladium of Labor*, 18, 25 August 1883; *IMJ*, 31 August 1883; Nancy Stunden, "Oshawa Knights of Labor Demonstration Medal," *Canadian Labour History, Newsletter of the Committee on Canadian Labour History* 4 (1974): 1–2.

98 *Palladium of Labor*, 20 October, 8, 15, 22 December 1883; *IMJ*, 31 August 1890.

99 PP, Lewis Allchin to Powderly, 20, 25 October 1884.

100 *News*, 23 February, 6, 9, 15 March 1886; *IMJ*, 30 September 1890.

101 *Labor Record* (Toronto), 14 May 1886; Trent University Archives, Gainey Collection, IMIU Local 191, Minutes, 1886.

102 *British Daily Whig* (Kingston), 13, 14, 16, 18, 19, 23 May 1887; *Gananoque Reporter*, 21 May 1887; and Ontario Bureau of Industry, *Annual Report* (Toronto 1887), 42.
103 IMIU, *Proceedings*, 1882 and 1886; *IMJ*, 31 May 1890.
104 IMIU, *Proceedings*, 1890 and 1895; *IMJ*, August 1889.
105 Ibid., 31 January 1891.
106 Bryan Palmer, "'Give us the road and we will run it': The Social and Cultural Matrix of an Emerging Labour Movement," in *Essays in Canadian Working Class History*, eds Kealey and Warrian, 106–24; *IMJ*, 31 October 1890, 31 July 1886.
107 IMIU, *Proceedings*, 1886; *IMJ*, 31 October 1890.
108 IMIU, *Proceedings*, 1888; Richard Oestreicher, "Solidarity and Fragmentation: Working People and Class Consciousness in Detroit, 1877–1895" (PHD diss., Michigan State University 1979), chap. 7.
109 Ontario Bureau of Industry, *Annual Reports* (Toronto 1886, 1889, and 1890).
110 Ibid.
111 Peter DeLottinville, "The St. Croix Manufacturing Company and its influence on the St. Croix Community, 1880–1892" (MA thesis, Dalhousie University 1979).
112 Ontario Bureau of Industry, *Annual Report* (Toronto 1887); *Brockville Recorder*, 12 July 1887.
113 Ontario Bureau of Industry, *Annual Report* (Toronto 1888); *Cornwall Standard*, 28 January, 2 February 1888; *Montreal Gazette*, 14 February 1888. Our thanks to Peter DeLottinville for these newspaper references. See also *Gananoque Reporter*, 4, 11, 18 February 1888.
114 Ontario Bureau of Industry, *Annual Report* (Toronto 1889); *Gananoque Reporter*, 16 March 1889.
115 This draws on: PP, R.R. Elliot to Powderly, 12, 19 July 1888; William Hogan to Powderly, 21 September, 8 November 1888; Archy Sloan to Powderly, 3 September 1888; Powderly to William Sloan, 10 September 1888. *Journal of United Labor*, 12 July 1888. See also PP, D.J. O'Donoghue to Powderly, 9 August 1888; *Globe*, 25 July, 10 August 1888.
116 The following draws on: Edward McKenna, "Unorganized Labour versus Management: The Strike at the Chaudière Lumber Mills, 1891," *Histoire sociale/Social History* 10 (1972): 186–211; Forsey, *History of Canadian Trade Unionism*, chap. 7; Peter Gillis, "E.H. Bronson and Corporate Capitalism" (MA thesis, Queen's University 1975), esp 72–81; Ontario Bureau of Industry, *Annual Report* (Toronto 1892); and *Ottawa Citizen* and *Ottawa Journal*, September–October 1891.

9 1919: The Canadian Labour Revolt

In late March 1919 a worried Union government appointed a Royal Commission to "enquire into Industrial Relations in Canada." From 26 April to 13 June, the Commissioners toured industrial Canada visiting 28 cities from Victoria to Sydney and examining a total of 486 witnesses. Their travels coincided with the greatest period of industrial unrest in Canadian history. Their report, published in July 1919, and the subsequent September National Industrial conference held to discuss their recommendations, appear now only as minor footnotes to the turbulence of the year. Like many Royal Commissions, the Mathers investigation proved far more important than the lack of tangible results.

The Royal Commission on Industrial Relations had two recent and prominent predecessors in its field of inquiry: the 1914 United States Commission on Industrial Relations and the 1917 British Whitely Committee on Industrial Conciliation. It also had one earlier Canadian predecessor, although one suspects it was but dimly remember in 1919. The Royal Commission on the Relations of Capital and Labor had been appointed by a previous Conservative prime minister, Sir John A. Macdonald, at a similar moment of crisis in class relations in 1886. That inquiry had also included trade unionists as commissioners, had toured the industrial sections of the nation, and had interviewed hundreds of Canadian workers. Its report also received little attention and resulted only in the establishment of Labour Day as a national holiday – a considerable accomplishment compared to the complete legislative failure of the Mathers Commission.

The Royal Commission on the Relations of Capital and Labor, a testament to the turmoil of the "Great Upheaval," has been extensively studied by historians interested in the social history of Canadian workers in the late nineteenth century. The Industrial Relations Commission, however, has received far less attention. Yet the evidence it heard is an equally rich source for the post-war upsurge of working-class militancy. The very titles of the two Royal Commissions convey much about the transformation which had taken place in Canadian industrial capitalist society in the approximately thirty intervening years. The rather quaint, Victorian "Relations between Labor and Capital" with its echo of classical political economy gives way to the modern sounding "Industrial Relations," hinting now not at conflicting classes but at a system of mutual interests. If the titles suggest something of transformed bourgeois and state attitudes, then the contents of the two collections of testimony tell us much about the development of the Canadian working class. The specific material complaints enumerated by Canadian workers vary little from 1886 to 1919 – unemployment, low wages, high prices, long hours, unsafe and unsanitary working conditions, abysmal housing, the super-exploitation of women workers, employer blacklists, non-recognition of unions, refusal of collective bargaining – all remain a constant in the working-class bill of grievances. What differs, however, is the workers' attitude. The cautious note of respectability and, in some cases, of near deference present in 1886 was transformed into a clarion cry for change. From Victoria to Sydney, Canadian workers appeared before the 1919 commission and defiantly challenged it. From Socialist Party of Canada (SPC) soap-boxer Charles Lestor in Vancouver to the Nova Scotia leaders of newly-organized District 26, United Mine Workers of America (UMWA), the message the Commission received was the same across the country. The capitalist system could not be reformed, it must be transformed. Production for profit must cease; production for use must begin.

British Columbia MLA J.H. Hawthornthwaite, a former SPC stalwart and then Federated Labour Party leader, asserted in his appearance before the Commission:

Working men today understand these matters ... and if you go into any socialistic bodies and listen to the discussion you would understand the grasp that these men have. I do not know any college man or university man who can for ten minutes hold their own in an argument among these people.[1]

Workers across the country more than lived up to Hawthorthwaite's boast. In city after city, the Commissioners were regaled with Marxist-influenced histories of the development of industrial capitalism. A few of these lectures came from middle-class proponents of the workers' movement such as Edmonton Mayor Joseph Clarke or social gospel ministers William Irvine, A.E. Smith, William Ivens, Ernest Thomas, and Salem Bland. But more impressive were the many workers – some well-known leaders, but many not – who appeared to explain patiently to the Commissioners, in the words of Edmonton Grand Trunk Railway machinist E.J. Thompson, "We are the producers and we are not getting what we produce." Like most other workers who appeared, Thompson was uninterested in the Commission's extensive plans for Industrial Councils; only "complete ownership of the machines of production by the working class" would suffice, he asserted. When pushed by hostile Commissioners who claimed that the new Canadian National Railway represented the nationalization he sought, Thompson responded in kind, reminding the Commissioners that workers saw their investigation as nothing but "a talkfest" and as "camouflage" for the anti-labour Union government.[2]

Thompson's evidence is of interest for two reasons: first, he was not a front-line leader of western labour; second, he came directly out of the railway machine shops. In city after city, metal trades workers from the shipyards, from the railway shops, and from the more diversified contract shops came forward and talked socialism. Even James Somerville, the International Association of Machinists' (IAM) Western representative, who predictably chose to distinguish himself from the radicals in his testimony, and who worried about the workers having "gone so far that they do not recognize the authority even in their own organization," explained:

One of the things they want first is nothing short of a transfer of the means of production, wealth production, from that of private control to that of collective ownership, for they know that is the only solution.[3]

Lest there be any notion that this was a regional manifestation of class unrest, let us travel east to Sudbury, Ontario. There Frederick Eldridge, a machinist and secretary of the local Trades and Labour Council, received "considerable handclapping, stamping of feet, and vocal enthusiasm" from the Commission's working-class audience, when he asserted:

The workers do not get enough of that which they produce ... I advocate government ownership of everything: mills, mines, factories, smelters, railroads, etc. That is the only solution of the problem and I am only one of hundreds of workmen in Sudbury that think the same thing.[4]

In Toronto, machinist James Ballantyne called for the nationalization of all industry.[5] In Hamilton, IAM District 24 representative Richard Riley more cautiously noted that "although a great many workers have not given the matter much thought, they are beginning to think that there must be a change of the system, that is to say the present competitive system."[6] When the Commission reached Montreal, John D. Houston of IAM District 82 presented a prepared brief on the economic system, arguing in part:

I believe that in the system of ownership lies all our social problems ... For 300 years or over, while the businessman was consolidating his position as captain of industry, the institutions of autocracy provided, through the law, the machinery of force and fraud which was rigorously applied, to make the workers a proletarian with no means of livelihood except for work for wages or a salary ...

He closed with the familiar call for production for use, not for profit.[7]

By the time the Commission arrived in the Maritimes, the Commissioners' impatience was showing, no doubt increased by the mounting industrial crisis which was sweeping the nation. While the evidence of their sessions in Amherst, Nova Scotia, at the height of the General Strike there, has unfortunately been lost, evidence from New Glasgow and Sydney demonstrates the eastern manifestation of the workers' revolt.[8] While UMWA District 26 leaders such as Dan Livingstone, Robert Baxter, and Silby Barrett provided much of the fire, Alex T. Mackay, representing carmen and steelworkers, infuriated the Commissioners by warning of an intensification of the struggle:

The way the fight in Winnipeg will be terminated, will very largely influence the attitude throughout Canada. I think if matters are allowed to run their course there will be no interference in this part of Canada, but if there is any attempt at coercion, the first shot fired in Winnipeg, will hit every labouring man in eastern and western Canada, and the result will be confusion from the Atlantic to the Pacific.[9]

A day earlier, in Halifax, Nova Scotia Federation of Labour organizer C.C. Dane had threatened a province-wide General Strike for the eight-hour day and had added almost gratuitously: "Industrial unrest? Why, gentlemen, we have none to what we are going to have. I am a Bolshevist and I will warn these two governments that trouble is coming and the men will have what belongs to them."[10] Dane, a boilermaker from Australia, had played a major role in the March 1919 establishment of the Federation.

Machinists were not the only group of workers who testified in these terms. Indeed most workers who appeared made similar points, although not always couched in a socialist framework. An additional important group of witnesses who echoed much of the above but who also added a new dimension to the workers' revolt were women witnesses. Unlike the young women workers paraded before the 1886 Commission, who testified only to oppressive conditions and often answering in monosyllables, the women appearing in 1919 included representatives of retail clerks' unions, women's labour leagues, local councils of women, and consumer groups. Among them were then-prominent figures such as Montreal's Rose Henderson or later leading Communist militant Bella Hall, but also many women who enjoy no such historical fame. These women universally complained of bad housing, runaway inflation, high food prices, and the low wages paid to working women. Calgary's Mrs Jean MacWilliams, who had organized laundry workers, asked rhetorically, "Are we in favour of a bloody revolution?" and answered, "Why any kind of revolution would be better than conditions as they are now."[11] In Saskatoon, Miss Francis, representing the local TLC, demanded that "plundering must cease, profiteering must go, commercialized industries and institutions must give way to the larger hopes of the people" and "production for use" must replace "production for profit."[12] Mrs Resina Asals of the Regina Women's Labour League told the Commission:

There is only one thing that the workers have to thank the capitalists for, and that is that they have tightened the screw up so much that they are awakening the worker up to the fact that he is the most important factor and that until we produce for use instead of profit this unrest will still prevail. Let the workingman, the one who produced, have control and then we shall see the light of a new dawn.[13]

Rose Henderson simply advanced the proposition that "the real revolutionist is the mother – not the man. She says openly that there is nothing but Revolution."[14] Working-class women, both wage workers and unpaid domestic workers, also had started to view the world in new ways in 1919.

These examples are intended simply to demonstrate that the revolt was national in character and that its seeds were not rooted in any unique regional fermentation. The "radical" west and the conservative east have become sorry shibboleths of Canadian historiography. The foundation of our understanding of 1919 must be built on national and international conjunctures. While the local and regional pictures are not identical, as we come to know the history of eastern and central Canadian workers as well as we know that of western workers, the similarities of struggle begin to outweigh the initial impression of regional particularism. World War 1, a profoundly national experience for Canadians, helped provide part of the cement for this nascent national working-class response.[15] Moreover, we should also remind ourselves at the outset that, as David Montgomery has argued, "Strikes can only be understood in the context of the changing totality of class conflicts, of which they are a part."[16] In 1919 Canada, that totality was increasingly national in scope.

Yet World War 1, while providing specific sparks to light the flame of working-class struggle in 1919, should not be viewed as its cause. Underlying structural changes in capitalist organization, both on a national and international scale, must be viewed as providing the necessary fuel for this fire. Indeed, although the early war years 1914 to 1916 had seen little overt class conflict in Canada, the changes in the capitalist organization of production and the consequent "remaking" or reconstitution of the working class was well advanced before the outbreak of war. The years 1912 and 1913 should be seen as a prelude to the 1917 to 1920 conflagration. Table 9.1 demonstrates this continuity with pre-war class conflict.[17] This argument is not unique to this paper as various community studies, including Bercuson's on Winnipeg and Reilly's on Amherst, have perceived the continuity of class struggle between the pre- and post-war period.[18] This continuity extended, however, throughout the entire country. Craig Heron and Bryan Palmer's perceptive study of strikes in southern Ontario from 1901 to 1914 demonstrates a pattern that held for the other cities whose labour history has been chronicled, including Winnipeg.[19] Lest there be any doubt about this, note the provincial distribution figures in Table 9.2 for the pre- and post-war peak strike years. The one striking anomaly on Table 9.2, namely the especially high British Columbia figures, are largely accounted for by loggers' strikes as shown in Table 9.3. When we turn from regional variation to the industrial pattern for these years, some other important common ingredients emerge, especially the ongoing importance of mining and the metal trades. Yet our attention is also drawn to new developments apparent only in the later period such as the importance of wartime shipbuilding, and the rise of logging and "service strikes."

A more specific look at 1919 and especially at the months of May, June, and July helps to clarify some of these points. While these months generally figure high in the calendar of industrial conflict, clearly summer 1919 was not simply any year. Table 9.4 shows both the geographic and industrial range of the strikes and Table 9.5 highlights the central role of coal, the metal trades, shipbuilding, and, of course, the general strikes themselves in the wave of unrest.

The summer strike wave consisted of three main types of strikes: first, local strikes contesting the normal range of issues; second, general strikes called in support of such local strikes as Winnipeg, Amherst, and Toronto; and, third, general sympathy strikes called either in support of the Winnipeg General Strike or to protest its re-

Table 9.1
Strike Activity in Canada, 1912–1922

Year	Number of strikes	Number of workers involved	Striker days lost
1912	242	43,104	1,136,345
1913	234	4,004	1,037,254
1914	99	9,911	491,358
1915	86	11,480	95,242
1916	168	26,971	241,306
1917	222	50,327	1,123,916
1918	305	82,573	657,152
1919	428	149,309	3,401,843
1920	459	76,624	814,457
1921	208	28,398	1,049,719

Significant increase

Table 9.2
Number of Disputes by Province

	1912	1913	1917	1918	1919	1920
Nova Scotia	9	12	8	18	19	39
Prince Edward Island	1	–	2	–	–	1
New Brunswick	21	20	5	11	19	15
Quebec	32	31	31	28	100	79
Ontario	100	114	68	112	158	122
Manitoba	13	6	18	20	16	5
Saskatchewan	19	10	6	10	13	4
Alberta	23	15	24	53	29	39
British Columbia	22	25	55	46	73	24
Interprovincial	2	1	5	7	2	1
Total	242	234	222	305	428	459

Table 9.3
Number of Disputes by Selected Industry

	1912	1913	1917	1918	1919	1920
Logging	1	–	1	–	32	66
Coal mining	6	5	22	49	22	48
Other mining	6	6	6	3	10	14
Metal manufacturing	27	30	44	43	46	61
Shipbuilding	2	3	13	16	25	12
Steam Railway	16	8	12	16	6	2
Electric Railway	2	7	5	11	12	5
Service	12	18	11	30	39	38
General	–	–	–	1	12	–
Total	72	77	114	169	204	246
N	242	234	222	305	428	459
% Total	29.8	32.9	51.4	55.4	47.7	53.4

Figure 9.1
Striker Days: May, June, July 1919

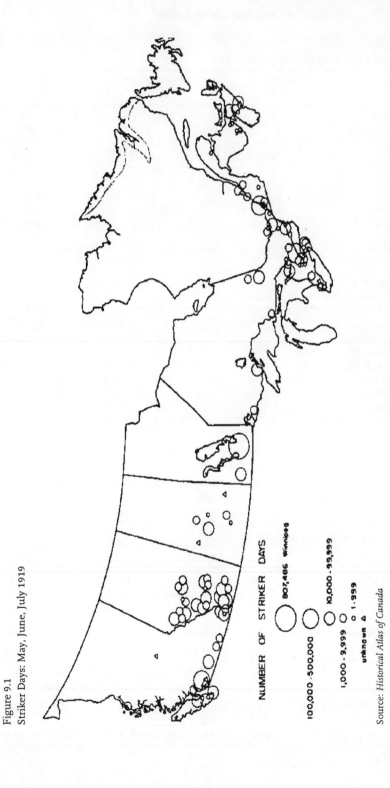

NUMBER OF STRIKER DAYS

807,486 Winnipeg

100,000 - 500,000

10,000 - 99,999

1,000 - 9,999

unknown

Source: *Historical Atlas of Canada*

Table 9.4
Strikes: May, June and July 1919[a]

	Number of strikes (total)	Number of strikes (complete data)	Number of workers involved[b]	Duration in worker days[c]
A. BY MONTH				
May	110	96	68,606	742,506
June	101	89	84,054	1,274,998
July	84	75	71,121	555,802
Total	210[d]	178[d]	114,423[d]	2,573,306
B. BY PROVINCE				
Nova Scotia	11	9	3,461	85,135
New Brunswick	6	6	128	631
Quebec	57	50	25,988	395,285
Ontario	90	78	34,544	632,409
Manitoba	6	5	21,756	817,686
Saskatchewan	9	7	2,041	31,833
Alberta	9	8	9,271[e]	304,967[e]
British Columbia	23	16	17,234[e]	305,360[e]
Total	210[f]	178[f]	114,423	2,573,306

a Strikes in progress.

b Figures for strikes beginning before May or extending beyond the end of a month are not adjusted to account for strikers returning to work.

c Figures are adjusted to account for strikers returning to work.

d Totals are for strikes in progress over the three month period.

e Include provincial estimates for the District 18 coal mining strike.

f District 18, UMWA strike counted once.

pression. Variants two and three have received some attention, although even here the focus on Winnipeg has tended to obscure these less well-known struggles. Local strikes, however, have received little study.

Table 9.5, while describing all industrial action in these three months of 1919, suggests how important the local or category one conflicts were to the strike wave. Clearly these strikes cannot be described in this paper in any detail but I will highlight a few to suggest the range of activity. Let us reverse the historiographic trend and travel across the country from east to west.[20] In Moncton, NB, and Amherst, NS, moulders won victories over iron founders. A lockout of 350 quarry workers in Sweet's Corner, NS, lasted 55 working days and resulted in higher wages. Brief walkouts on the street railway systems in Halifax and Moncton also occurred. The most significant story in the Maritimes, however, focused on Amherst and we will return to it in our discussion of general strikes.

Quebec's 57 strikes were highly concentrated in Montreal which

Figure 9.2
General Strikes, 1919

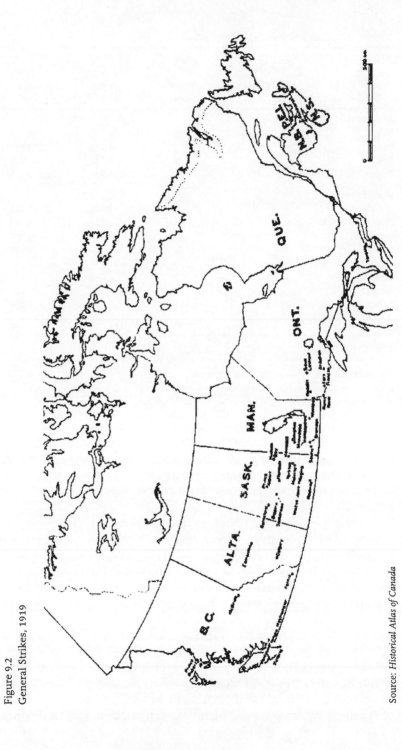

Source: *Historical Atlas of Canada*

Table 9.5
Strikes: May–July 1919, by Industry

	Number	%	Number workers involved	%	Duration in strikes days	%
Mining	11	5.2	10,216	8.9	340,216	13.2
Manufacturing total	101	48.1	43,495	38.0	922,117	35.8
Manufacturing leather and textile	(20)	(9.5)	(9,505)	(8.3)	(204,897)	(8.0)
Manufacturing metal and shipbuilding	(43)	(20.5)	(24,590)	(21.5)	(623,577)	(24.2)
Construction	32	15.2	9,829	8.6	185,488	7.2
Transportation and public utilities	21	10.0	4,772	4.2	68,964	2.7
Service and public administration	19	9.1	1,137	1.0	4,799	.2
Other industries	14	6.7	607	.5	18,036	.7
General	12	5.7	44,367	38.8	1,033,686	40.2
Total	210	100.0	114,423	100.0	2,573,306	100.0

accounted for 47 of them (82 per cent). Outside Montreal, the major strikes occurred in the shipbuilding industry at Lauzon and Trois Rivières, and in the metal trades at Lachine and Sherbrooke. The brief metal strikes were both successful for the workers, and the Trois Rivières shipyard strike won union recognition for the strikers. Montreal, however, was the centre of activity in Quebec. Indeed, the Borden government was sufficiently alarmed about the conflicts in Montreal that the city was included on their emergency daily briefing list. Over 22,000 workers in Montreal struck during the three-month period, logging nearly 380,000 striker days lost. Again the metal trades and shipbuilding figured prominently. A metal trades strike at Canadian Car and Foundry in early May involving 4,000 workers ended in victory after only three days. In the shipyards, however, it took a one-day strike to force negotiations and then a five-week strike before the employers conceded to some of the demands of their 3,500 workers. This strike was led by a General Strike Committee, not by the union officials of the Marine Trades Federation. A major strike of 2,000 wire workers failed after three weeks. A series of skirmishes in the garment trades led to a number of worker victories, and a major battle involving over 3,500 workers at Dominion Textiles gained some employer concessions after nearly three months of struggle. This strike was marked by a successful sympathetic strike at Montmorency Falls where 1,100 workers stayed out for ten days in support of their Montreal comrades and returned to work with a wage increase. Other industrial workers showed a new ability to organize as well. Over 1,400 rubber workers, for example, won a compromise settlement after a strike of three weeks, as did 350 sugar refinery employees, while 700 meat packers won a quick victory to match a settlement won earlier by Toronto workers. This militant activity on the part of industrial workers represented a new departure for Montreal's working class, as did the willingness of Montmorency textile workers to resort to a sympathy strike.[21] While the majority of the Montreal Trades and Labour Council (MTLC) opposed a general sympathetic strike, the tactic has proponents in Montreal. The machinists (IAM) and the engineers (ASE), true to national form, held a massive support rally in late May which was addressed by Winnipeg strike leader R.J. Johns, who was in Montreal representing Division No. 4, railroad shop craft workers, at Railroad Board arbitration meetings. Those attending, identified as workers from the Canadian Vickers Shipyard, heard speeches from A.H. McNamee, president of the ASE, and radical machinists Richard Kerrigan and William Turnbull, as well as from Montreal "reds" such as Beckie Buhay and Albert St Martin.[22] In early June the MTLC endorsed the 44-hour week and called for the reinstatement of the postal workers who had been dismissed in Winnipeg.[23] At their subsequent meeting in mid-June the arrests of the Winnipeg strike leaders were roundly condemned and Richard Kerrigan led a debate in which the Canadian Vickers General Strike Committee sought to gain the endorsation of the Council for a general sympathetic strike. In this, they failed.[24]

Ontario's 90 strikes involving 34,122 workers were not as concentrated as Quebec's, although Toronto did account for 22 (24 per cent) in addition to its General Sympathetic Strike, which I will deal with later. Ottawa had eleven strikes, London seven, Hamilton six, St Catharines and Windsor, five each. Major mining strikes took place in Cobalt and Kirkland Lake where 2,200 and 525 miners respectively struck for eight and 21 weeks. In both cases the miners were defeated by intransigent mining companies, although not before there had been discussions of a Northern Ontario-wide general strike.[25]

In Toronto, newly-organized workers in the meat packing industry, organized on an industrial basis, took on the giants of the industry, including Swift Canada, as over 3,000 workers struck in the stockyards area after the companies refused to negotiate with the union. In addition to union recognition, they sought the eight-hour day and 44-hour week, and guaranteed minimum levels of employment. After just over a week on the picket line in early May, an IDIA board was agreed to by both sides and reported unanimously on 29 May mainly in favour of the workers, granting a 48-hour week, a weekly guarantee

of 40 hours, overtime pay, a formal grievance procedure, and seniority provisions. this settlement became the model for the industry and
workers in Montreal, Ottawa, Hamilton, and Peterborough fought for
it in summer 1919 and spring 1920.[26] Beginning in July almost 2,00
Toronto garment workers led by the International Ladies Garment
Workers Union (ILGWU) struck over 40 shops for twelve weeks before
winning wage and hour concessions. Both of these industries
involved high proportions of ethnic workers and their successful
strikes suggest the expansion of both trade union organization and
class struggle to new and difficult terrain.

Ontario's shipyard workers, who in 1918 had organized a Marine
Trades and Labour Federation of Canada, engaged in a series of seven
strikes covering almost all the province's shipbuilding centres.
Bridgeburg, Collingwood, Fort William–Port Arthur, Midland, Welland, and Toronto each witnessed strikes involving workforces ranging from 100 to 1,300. Most of these strikes were fought for wage
increases and the 44-hour week, and resulted in significant worker
gains. In Collingwood, however, 900 workers failed in a three-week
strike in July demanding the rehiring of Orange fellow-workers who
had been fired for refusing to work on the glorious twelfth.

In the metal trades, which included many of the same trades as
shipbuilding, 1919 saw the machinists attempt to gain Ontario-wide
uniformity of wages and conditions. The first provincial convention of
Ontario machinists held in Toronto in July 1918 had decided to force
this issue. Their major aim was to gain the eight-hour day and 44-
hour week and in spring 1919 metal trades meetings were organized
province-wide to prepare for that struggle. IAM Vice-President John
McClelland reported that "the largest halls in many of the towns"
were "too small to accommodate the crowds." Moving beyond IAM
exclusivism, McClelland worked for "complete affiliation of the metal
trades," and "in the meantime" organized metal trades councils as the
basis for a strike which would "completely close down the industry
until a settlement is reached."

The Toronto campaign became the central battle for the war for
recognition of the metal trades councils as bargaining agents and for
the eight-hour day. The demands were sent to the employers on 1
April and tools were dropped on 1 May by some 5,000 metal trades
workers. Meanwhile in Peterborough, approximately 100 moulders
struck on 1 May and were followed by their fellow workers in Brampton (thirty) and Hamilton (250 on 5 May). Four days later the Kingston Metal Trades Council struck the Canadian Locomotive Company,
pulling out 650 workers. On 12 May the Ottawa Metal Trades Council
called some 200 machinists and patternmakers out of fifteen small

shops. The following day Brantford moulders struck. St Catharines moulders and machinists left work on 23 May.[27]

The results of these strikes varied but by and large they were defeated. In Toronto the metal trades council ended its strike on 28 July, although 750 moulders refused to end their strike which was still continuing at year's end. In Peterborough the moulders won a victory after a 22-week strike. Their fellow craftsworkers in Brampton returned after eight weeks but 250 striking moulders in Hamilton remained out for the rest of the year. In Kingston a compromise ended the metal trades strike after almost 26 weeks, while Ottawa machinists and patternmakers admitted defeat after almost thirteen weeks on the lines. Brantford moulders remained out the entire year. Clearly the metal trades workers' optimism as they approached May Day 1919 had turned out to be illusory.

In the west, Manitoba's strikes revolved totally around the epic struggle in Winnipeg and the General Sympathy Strike in Brandon which we will turn to later. In Saskatchewan, the pattern was similar involving primarily sympathetic strikes. In Alberta, however, a successful Calgary metal trades strike in April and May won shorter hours and higher wages for machinists, moulders, and other metalworkers. In addition, UMWA District 18's over 6,200 coal miners left the pits at the end of May and stayed out until 1 September when they returned on the advice of OBU leaders.[28] This General Strike was exceptional in that as a "100 per cent" strike involving the maintenance people, it transgressed UMWA custom and in the fact that some of the firebosses, the foremen in the mines, also took part. By July what had started partially as a sympathy strike with Winnipeg had been transformed into a major struggle for recognition of the OBU which would play itself out over the next few years.

In British Columbia the District 18 strike spread into the southeastern coal field and a series of small logging strikes under the leadership of the new, later OBU, BC Loggers Union took place. the major activity in BC, however, also revolved around the June sympathy strikes.

The three General Sympathetic Strikes generated by local industrial struggles were in Amherst, NS, Toronto, and Winnipeg. The sensitive work of Nolan Reilly has provided us with a model study of the community background to the Amherst General Strike, an event which had gone almost unnoticed. In Amherst, the local Federation of Labour, under the rubric of One Big Union, led a general strike which spread out from the Canadian Car and Foundry workers' demands that they receive pay equal to that which their 4,000 Montreal co-workers had won in a three-day strike in early May. The company's intransigence led to a city-wide walkout involving all of Amherst's

major employers. While proceeding from local causes and representing the culmination of a decade of industrial conflict in Amherst, the
strikers identified themselves with the national struggle, as their
enthusiastic correspondence with the OBU suggest.[29]

Events in Toronto in 1919, while less dramatic than those in
Amherst, nevertheless caused Prime Minister Borden and his government considerable consternation.[30] As elsewhere, the metal trades
were central in the crisis. Toronto's extensive foundries, machine
shops, and metal factories had been at the core of war production.
The city's metal trades workers, who had organized a joint council in
1901 and who had endorsed a call for industrial unionism in 1913, led
the battle to enforce collective bargaining and a "fair-wage schedule"
on the Imperial Munitions Board (IMB).[31] This struggle first came to
a head in spring 1916 when Toronto machinists tried to extend gains
they had made in some shops in December 1915 to the entire city. In
addition, Hamilton machinists also demanded parity with their
Toronto comrades. The joint threat of a general metal trades strike in
Toronto issued by IAM District 46 in March, and a machinists' strike
in Hamilton, combined with McClelland's public worry that he could
no longer retain control of his people, led to the appointment of a
three-member government commission to investigate the munitions
plants in Toronto and Hamilton and the general extension of the
Industrial Disputes Investigation Act (IDIA) to all war industry. This
commission, however, which the Trades and Labour Congress (TLC)
regarded as a victory, eventually proved meaningless when Hamilton
employers refused to abide by its recommendation of the nine-hour
day and wage increases. The subsequent Hamilton-wide strike of
some 2,000 workers which included a coalition of machinists (IAM),
engineers (ASE), and unorganized, unskilled workers ended in a major
defeat for Hamilton workers at the hands of Canadian Westinghouse,
National Steel Car, the Steel Company of Canada, Otis Elevators, and
Dominion Steel Foundry. Although Toronto IAM members, for the
second time in only a few months, threatened a general strike in
sympathy with the Hamilton workers, the IAM international leadership managed to prevent it. The Metal Trades Council did manage,
however, to help move the Toronto Trades and Labour Council (TTLC)
significantly to the left during these developments. In March and
April TTLC condemnation of the Borden government and of the IMB
for failure to implement a fair-wage schedule had been shelved by a
worried TLC executive in Ottawa. Both Secretary Draper and President
Watters apparently hoped their cap-in-hand lobbying would result in a
breakthrough. In this they were to be sadly disappointed. The late
March extension of the IDIA to cover shipbuilding and munitions led

to a furious response from the TTLC which "emphatically denounced this uncalled for and unwarranted action" and accused the TLC executive of "not fulfilling their obligation to the workers of Canada."[32] Thus Toronto and Hamilton metal trades workers as early as summer 1916 found themselves moving in opposition to state labour policy and already identifying their differences with both the TLC leadership and to some degree with their own international officers such as McClelland and James Somerville, all of whom were continually promoting patience and industrial peace. These latter strategies looked increasingly problematic. Thus, as Myer Siemiatycki has noted with considerable irony, "the war-induced epidemic of general strikes, which one prominent unionist subsequently dubbed 'Winnipegitis,' found its earliest germination in Toronto."[33]

By the time of the next major metal trades struggle which came in May 1919, the metal workers exercised considerable control over the TTLC. In a May Day meeting, the TTLC voted to contact all Canadian Trades and Labour Councils to get support fro the metal trades fight for the eight-hour day. Moreover,they "requested sympathetic action to bring about the result desired." A 13 May meeting demanded that metal trades employers negotiate and then issued a call for a general strike convention for one week hence. While this motion noted western strikes in Winnipeg and Calgary and other Ontario strikes, its major interest was in the Toronto Strike.[34]

The vote in favour of a general strike by 44 unions representing 12,000 workers led to hurried correspondence between Toronto politicians and Ottawa. Newton Rowell, president of the Privy Council, sought permission from his cabinet colleagues to pressure the employers to concede to the demand for collective bargaining. If they refused, he proposed to embarrass them publicly. Not surprisingly, a hurried negative response came from Minister of Finance Thomas White who had consulted Minister of Labour Gideon Robertson.[35] The following day Toronto Mayor Tommy Church wrote directly to Prime Minister Borden seeking government legislation on shorter hours, explaining that his offer of mediation had won a brief delay in the planned walkout, and seeking Borden's personal intervention in the talks if necessary. Borden's agreement provided Church with an important talking point in a 27 May conference at City Hall which brought together the strike leaders and some of the major metal employers such as Findlay of Massey-Harris and White of Canadian Allis-Chalmers. Although the employers made no major concessions, the workers were placed in an embarrassing situation and finally agreed to Church's proposal that a joint delegation visit Ottawa and talk to Borden. Subsequently the union "convention" authorized this trip, while reaffirming that the General Strike would commence on Friday, 30 May, unless the right of collective bargaining and the 44-hour week were granted to the Metal Trades Council.[36]

Borden's intervention led only to an offer of arbitration, which the workers scornfully declined, but again the employers scored a minor publicity coup by offering a compromise 48-hour week, although not agreeing to Metal Trades Council recognition.[37]

The sympathetic strike commenced on 30 May and from 5–15,000 workers left their jobs. The strike's strength predictably lay in the metal trades in shipbuilding, among some groups of building trades workers, especially carpenters, and among garment workers. Its major failing was the decision by civic employees and especially the street railway workers to stay on the job until their contract expired on 16 June. The strike lasted until 4 June when it was called off by the Central Strike Committee at the request of the Metal Trades Council. The Committee of fifteen which ran the strike included nine metal trades workers, four building trades workers, and two garment trades workers.[38]

Although the left in Toronto had suffered a defeat in this struggle, they were not repudiated. Instead they took control of the TTLC in its subsequent July election. Left-wing revelations that prominent right-wingers on the Council's executive had received $5,000 from the Toronto Employers' Association to support a new labour paper in Toronto which had worked to divide metal trades workers during the strike, helped them gain control. Thee charges were sustained by a Council investigation.[39]

The Winnipeg General Strike we will simply pass over in order to discuss the rather less well-known wave of general sympathy strikes. Compilation of these is somewhat risky since the Department of Labour's official version and even their manuscript materials do not necessarily conform to all strikes mentioned in the labour press or even in the various security reports which crop up in the Borden Papers and elsewhere. Table 9.6 lists those identified in Department of Labour data (A) and then adds a list compiled from other sources (B).[40]

In Manitoba many small railroad junction towns such as Dauphin supported Winnipeg as did workers in Brandon. The strike in Brandon, the longest of all the sympathy strikes, was extremely solid and orderly. It eventually involved civic workers who had fought and won their own strike in April but who still came out in solidarity as repression mounted in Winnipeg. Controlled throughout by the Brandon Trades and Labour Council, the strike extended to unorganized workers who were guaranteed "full protection" from the labour council.[41]

Table 9.6
General Strikes in Sympathy with Winnipeg, May–July 1919

Location	Dates	Number workers involved	Duration in strike days
A			
Brandon	20 May–2 July	450	10,200
Calgary	26 May–25 June	1,500	31,700
Edmonton	26 May–25 June	2,000	24,000
Saskatoon	27 May–26 June	1,200	24,000
Prince Albert	28 May–23 June	300	5,000
Regina	29 May–26 June	350	1,500
Vancouver	3 June–4 July	8,000	160,000
New Westminster	13–23 June	537	3,400
Victoria	23 June–7 July	5,000	28,000
B			
Atikokan, Ont.	Neepawa, Man.	Melville, Sask.	
Fort Frances, Ont.	Souris, Man.	Moose Jaw, Sask.	
Rainy Rier, Ont.	Battleford, Sask.	Radville, Sask.	
Redditt, Ont.	Biggar, Sask.	Yorkton, Sask.	
Sioux Lookout, Ont.	Hudson Bay Jct., Sask.	Prince Rupert, BC	
Dauphin, Man.	Humboldt, Sask.	McBride, BC	
Minnedosa, Man.	Kamsack, Sask.	Fernie, BC	

The list of small Saskatchewan railway junction towns makes clear the support of railroad shop workers and of some running trades workers, although the Brotherhoods exerted all the pressure they were capable of to prevent this. Prince Albert's sympathy strike involved mainly Canadian Northern workers.[42] In Saskatchewan's larger urban centres a similar pattern prevailed. Regina workers initially supported a general strike but only a minority eventually struck, mainly from the railroad shops. In Moose Jaw, shopcraft workers, street railway workers, civic employees, and some building trades workers provided the strike's backbone. Saskatoon's sympathy strike was the most successful in the province and included the Sutherland CPR shop workers, street railway workers, freight handlers, postal workers, teamsters, and at least eleven other local unions.

In Alberta, as elsewhere in the west, both Edmonton and Calgary workers had flirted with general strikes earlier. In Edmonton, the Trades and Labour Council had endorsed a general sympathy strike in October 1918 to aid the Canadian Brotherhood of Railway Employees. Events in 1919 led to a vigorous left-right struggle for control of the Edmonton TLC which culminated in late April in the expulsion of the Carpenters, led by SPC militant Joe Knight, Federated Labour Union, No. 49, which included Carl Berg and Sarah Johnson Knight, and the UMWA, Local 4070. As a result of the expulsions, the machinists and street railway workers also left the council. Despite this serious split, a successful sympathy strike was organized. The Federated Railway Trades (shop workers) introduced a motion in the ETLC calling for a meeting of all Edmonton trade unionists to plan for a strike. At that meeting the machinists successfully moved for a strike vote of all unions to report to a Central Strike Committee composed of represen- tatives from both sides of the previous split. This vote resulted in a 1,676–506 vote for a strike with 34 of the 38 unions voting casting pro-strike ballots; eleven locals, however, failed to vote. Major strike support came from railway carmen, machinists, railroad shop workers, street railway workers, coal miners, building trades workers, and civic employees. The strike held until the Committee called it off and was marked by a minimum of disorder of any kind. This partially resulted from the tacit support the strike received from pro-labour Edmonton Mayor Joe Clarke, who RCMP security regarded as less than trustworthy.[43]

In Calgary the huge CPR shops were central both to the city's economy and to its trade union movement. Carmen, machinists, and all the other Railroad Shops Federated Trades exercised a considerable thrust for and experience of amalgamation. During the war years, the machinists came to dominate the CTLC and, as Taraska has argued, forged "a new working-class solidarity which led to class conscious action."[44] Militance and political lobbying on the part of munitions workers led to a Provincial Munitions Commission ruling that war contracts should go only to union shops. Thus by the end of 1915 the war shops were fully unionized. Skilled machinists' leaders such as Socialist and Labour Alderman A. Broach, R.J. Tallon, and H.H. Sharples came to dominate the local council and to push it success- fully into local politics. Tallon became president of Division 4 of the Railway Employees department of the American Federation of Labor in 1917 which represented over 50,000 shopcraft workers on the Canadian railways. The Division, created to negotiate directly with the Railway War Board, entered negotiations with the CPR in April 1918. After heated negotiations the Board offered parity with the United States McAdoo Award which was rejected by an overwhelming Divi- sion 4 vote. Armed with this rejection, Division 4 leaders threatened a nation-wide rail strike. A series of walkouts led to dire threats from the government and the active intervention of the AFL which ordered Division 4 to accept the Board's offer. In September reluctant railway shop workers did so but in Calgary trouble flared up quickly when the CPR victimized from freight handlers who had not been formally allowed to enter Division 4. The freight handlers struck demanding the McAdoo award. Calgary Labour Council unions voted in favour of a general strike in support of the freight handlers and a shopcraft workers' strike began on 11 October 1918. Street railway workers and civic employees also struck in sympathy. The threat to prosecute under Privy Council Order 2525 banning all strikes proved futile when Alberta courts refused to uphold it. A compromise, arranged by Senator Gideon Robertson, ended the affair in late October but general strike tactics had definitely been sustained. This set the scene for the following year's city-wide metal trades strike in April and the subsequent sympathy strike in May and June. Predictably the major support during the general strike came from the CPR Ogden shops and the Metal Trades Council. One outstanding feature of this strike was the creation of an extremely active Women's Labor Council.[45]

In British Columbia, the SPC-controlled Vancouver Trades and Labour Council (VTLC) responded more slowly and deliberately to events in Winnipeg. In mid-May VTLC President Harold Winch of the longshoremen and Secretary Victor Midgley wired Winnipeg congratulating the workers for their "cohesion" which "augured well for the future."[46] The following week they warned the Borden government that any military interference in Winnipeg would force them to call a general strike and simultaneously requested that all Vancouver trade unions take a vote on the question.[47] One week later they issued the following demands:

Realizing that while there are many problems that face the workers that cannot be solved under capitalism, and that the end of the system is not yet; also realizing that the present situation is a political one, due to the action of the Dominion Government in the Winnipeg strike, and that as taking care of the soldiers ... are working class problems, the majority of the soldiers being members of the working class, therefore be it resolved that the following be the policy of the workers in Canada now on strike, or about to come on strike in support of the Winnipeg workers:

1 The reinstatement of the postal workers ...
2 The immediate settlement of the postal workers' grievances.
3 The right of collective bargaining through any organization that the workers deem most suited to their needs.
4 Pensions for soldiers and their dependents.
5 A $2,000 gratuity for all those who served overseas.
6 Nationalization of all cold storage plants, abattoirs, elevators ...
7 A six-hour day.

They closed by calling for the strike to continue until either the demands were granted for the government resigned and called new elections.[48]

The strike, which commenced on 3 June, initially saw 37 unions out but this actually increased in the first few days of the strike. As elsewhere, it found its major support among the metal trades, in the shipyards, and on the street railway. Unique to Vancouver as a major port, however, was the militant support of longshoremen, sailors, and other marine workers. As in Calgary, a series of women's meetings met with enthusiastic support.[49]

While the SPC provided leadership and intellectual sustenance, their reluctance and fears were manifest. Even at the final preparation meeting on 2 June, William Pritchard posed the question less than enthusiastically:

Their comrades were in the fight, and it was now a question of standing by them, and, if necessary, going down with them – or, later, going down by themselves. His advice was: "If you are going to drown – drown splashing!"[50]

Two weeks later at an SPC educational, W.W. Lefeaux explained that party policy did not include promoting strikes, only analyzing and explaining them.[51]

The strike ended in confusion a week after Winnipeg's return to work. A recommendation from the strike committee to go back earlier had been voted down by rank-and-file militants.[52] The strike committee's final report to the VTLC indicated that 45 unions had struck over the course of the strike, but admitted the initial vote had been a narrow 3,305–2,499 victory. Although 57 per cent of those voting favoured the strike, the under 6,000 votes represented only 40 per cent of VTLC members.[53]

In Prince Rupert a sympathy strike had commenced earlier on 29 May when railroad workers left their jobs, while in Victoria the sympathy strike developed very slowly with considerable reluctance being shown by Victoria TLC leaders. Nevertheless almost 5,000 workers left their jobs on 23 June, following the lead of the Metal Trades Council, and remained out until early July.[54] A smaller sympathy strike also took place in New Westminster.

These Canadian events captured the attention of European militants. On 14 June 1919, in Turin, Italy, Antonio Gramsci described "The Revolutionary Tide" which had brought "the struggle on a world scale." "The revolution can no longer be exorcized by democratic swindlers, nor crushed by mercenaries without a conscience," the Italian revolutionary argued. Gramsci's youthful optimism stemmed partially from his view of current world struggles and specifically of those in Canada where, he argued, "industrial strikes have taken on the overt character of a bid to install a soviet regime." Meanwhile, in

Glasgow, John MacLean enthused about "the great Canadian strike," which, he argued, had stimulated American labour's "general rank-and-file strike which terrorized the union leaders."[55] While these claims appear exaggerated in retrospect, the important point here is that 1919 was an international event, or as MacLean termed it: "class war on an international scale." It was no more limited to Canada than it was to Winnipeg within Canada. In the years from 1917 to 1920, a working-class movement whose internationalism had been destroyed in 1914, ironically responded with an international surge of class militancy which knew no national limits and few, if any, historical precedents.

One little-known example of the international nature of the uprising can be drawn from Newfoundland, then a self-governing British colony in the North Atlantic. The story of Newfoundland's working class largely remains to be written but in the years 1917 to 1920 at least it resembled closely the Canadian and international pattern of revolt. In the immediate pre-war years Newfoundland fishermen and loggers had commenced to organize. The meteoric rise of the Fishermen's Protective Union, representing both groups of workers, led not only to industrial gains but to great political success and legislative reforms. In the later war years, an economic crisis which revolved around profiteering and rampant inflation led to an investigation which found that the St John's merchants had indeed engaged in rapacious price gouging. In 1917, St John's workers created the Newfoundland Industrial Workers' Association (NIWA), an avowedly industrial unionist organization which immediately proceeded to organize workers across the island. Thus, Newfoundland workers conformed to the international wave of industrial unionist unrest. Equally the NIWA found its leadership in the railway shops of the Reid Newfoundland Company and among local socialists and drew its membership from St John's metal shops and the foundry. Its major industrial battle gainst Reid Newfoundland involved a three-week strike of 500 railway workers in spring 1918 which involved threats of an island-wide walkout and extensive sympathetic activities in St John's.[56]

The international literature on the post-war upsurge has blossomed of late and important articles by Larry Peterson and James Cronin have chronicled these red years in rich international comparison.[57] As has often been the case, the comparative insights offered by international labour and working-class history open some interesting avenues for investigation. First, however, let us eliminate a few dead ends of previous Canadian investigation. In the aftermath of the strike, the BC *Federationist* concluded: 'The first lesson that workers must learn is

that only by organization and cohesion, not only in each centre, but
throughout the country, can they resist the encroachments of capital."[58] Similar statements have often been used to buttress a "western
revolt" notion of 1919, arguing that only workers west of the Lakehead behaved "radically." The lesson, however, surely lay not in a
regional understanding of the revolt but rather in the reverse –
namely, the necessity of perfecting nation-wide organization. The
defection of the AFL, the TLC, and much of the international union
leadership had left the working-class movement fragmented and,
although the SPC leadership tried valiantly to fill the gap, the consequent breakdown in communications and lack of a national focus
proved costly. While the established weekly labour press and the
emergent daily strike bulletins were remarkably vibrant and blanketed
the country with an extraordinary and rich range of labour opinion,
they carried little national coverage. Thus workers in Vancouver knew
little of Amherst,and District 18 miners lacked direct contact with
their Nova Scotia District 26 comrades. The revolt was not western,
however, it was national; but the size and regional fragmentation of
the country proved a major impediment to systematic national
organization and co-ordination.

Second, there is no doubt that the AFL and TLC leadership, not to
speak of the railroad running trades leadership, played reprehensible
roles. They undoubtedly exploited their image as respectable labour
leaders who believed in the sanctity of contracts. We must add, however, that this ideological and political battleground existed within the
North American labour movement everywhere, not only on both sides
of the border but also at both ends of each country. The struggle
within the TLC so often depicted as east/west was not so simple. At
the 1917 TLC convention in Ottawa the debate on the executive's collapse on the issue of conscription and their decision not to resist the
law once enacted revealed no simple regional vote. In a lengthy debate 28 delegates spoke with only nine fully supporting the executive
of which only two actually supported conscription. The nineteen
speakers who opposed the executive included eleven eastern delegates
and eight westerners.[59] Eastern opponents included moderate Toronto
socialists John Bruce and Jimmy Simpson and Montreal radical machinists Tom Cassidy and Dick Kerrigan. Cassidy engaged in the debate's major rhetorical flight, albeit prescient in light of events in
1919:

When the machine guns are placed on the streets of Winnipeg to shoot down
strikers, also in Montreal, Vancouver Island, and other places, it shows that
these organized soldiers are willing to shoot their fellow workingmen. I am

not afraid to die ... The masters of the world must be whipped ... We have only one enemy and that is the international capitalist class.

When the vote finally came the major amendment, introduced by Alberta leaders Farmilo and Ross, failed narrowly 101 to 111. Since there were only 44 western delegates present, it should be clear that there was considerable eastern opposition to conscription as well. Indeed when a conciliatory division on conscription itself was taken only ten delegates voted in favour of the calling-up of manpower.

At the 1918 TLC convention in Quebec where seething western discontent eventually led to plans for the Calgary Conference of March 1919 similar non-regional divisions were evident. Westerners represented only 45 of 440 delegates. While radical motions were consistently lost and elections to executive positions saw moderates emerge victorious, nevertheless there were far more votes for radical positions than simply those of the west. For example, the one roll call vote on a Winnipeg motion to release all conscientious objectors from prison was narrowly defeated 99 to 90. The minority radical vote was composed of 58 eastern delegates and 32 western, while the conservative vote included two westerners and 97 easterners. The clear lesson to be learned was that the west should send more delegates.[60]

When the TLC met in Hamilton in fall 1919 the battle between craft unionism and the OBU for control of the labour movement was raging. In that context and with OBU members and sympathizers either departed or expelled, it should not surprise us that the Convention witnessed much red-bashing. yet there was also an undercurrent of support for industrial unionism and disgust for the TLC's failure to support Winnipeg workers. There was vociferous eastern criticism of the TLC leadership. Toronto delegate Birks denounced "organized officialdom within the trade union movement as something opposed to the spirit and mind of the rank and file."[61] District 26 leader J.B. McLachlan introduced a motion for a general strike demanding the restoration of freedom of speech and of the press and the repeal of the Criminal Code amendments passed during the Winnipeg General Strike.[62] Toronto carpenter McCallum, speaking "as a member of the working-class movement," argued that craft unions were outmoded and asked "Why ban men who demand change?"[63] St Catharines' delegate Grant "advocated the adoption of the shop steward as the most effective form of organization."[64] Later Ottawa stonecutters introduced a motion for broad joint strikes and denounced their international for ordering them back to work during a general building trades strike in May 1919. As one delegate argued, "the boss beat us because we were divided into small locals." Winnipeg's George

Armstrong availed himself of this opportunity to condemn "the machinery of the AFL which made massed action impossible."[65]

Similar battles went on within the international unions as well. For example, the 1920 convention of the IAM saw bitter debate about the expulsion of OBU supporters. Montreal and Toronto machinists led a losing but fiery effort to defend their comrades.[66]

The fight in the Canadian labour movement thus rested on different views of labour's future organization. The western SPC leaders looked to the OBU as the way forward. Despite much historical debate about the intellectual orientation of the OBU, which I will not detail here, the OBU was certainly not syndicalist. An organization led by the SPC could never have been anti-political and thus the supposed "turn" to politics after Winnipeg is nonsense. The political aims of the SPC never varied.[67]

The strike wave, of course, gained SPC leadership only begrudgingly for that very reason. The SPC doubted the wisdom of the industrial actions but had no choice but to lend its leadership skills to the working-class militancy which engulfed the nation. They never, however, viewed 1919 as a nascent revolution. They were politically too experienced for that. While Joe Knight and Carl Berg in Edmonton allowed their rhetoric to exceed the SPC line in the heady days of June 1919, the leading Vancouver comrades never lost sight of the limitations of the situation. Thus, *The Soviet* could argue, displaying the syndicalist tendencies of Knight and Berg:

In Winnipeg and Toronto today the same condition is observable. The General Strike by paralyzing industry, paralyzes government. The Strike Committees are forced to rule the cities, to "exempt" certain industries and services in order to provide for elementary human needs; they must police the cities themselves. Willy-nilly "this production for use and not for profit" is undertaken for the benefit of the workers. It displaces the capitalist government which operated for the benefit of the bourgeoisie ...[68]

Vancouver's *Red Flag*, on the other hand, was consistent and cautious. The OBU, it noted, simply represented:

... a decided urge towards industrial unionism which has lately become very insistent. We have referred to this movement several times and have criticized it and analyzed it. That is our function. We don't initiate movements, we seek to understand them. We realize that beyond a very transitory influence, great movements are not caused by individuals, they are the result of conditions.[69]

Later, after the Winnipeg General Strike had commenced, they warned:

It may be that some half-baked socialist is voicing Revolutionary phrases in Winnipeg. We doubt it. We know that a bunch of workers who are able to keep their heads in spite of the extreme provocation to which they are being subjected will not allow any muddle head from their own ranks to precipitate trouble.[70]

Simultaneously, the *B.C. Federationist* editorialized:

Neither the Seattle nor the Winnipeg strikes were revolutionary upheavals. They were strikes in the one instance for higher wages, and in the later case, for the recognition of the right to collective bargaining. Is that a revolutionary strike?

In that same editorial they cautioned against violence and promoted discipline "because the ruling class have the guns, and if blood is shed, it will be the blood of the working class." In a revolution, they continued, it was necessary to "control the means of coercion," and there was no such opportunity in Canada.[71] A week later they again emphasized, "The strike is not a revolutionary strike," and argued instead: "The issue is political. The workers must take the matter up on those lines, and wring political concessions from the master class, and beat them at their own game."[72] All of this fits well with William Pritchard's now famous aphorism: "Only fools try to make revolutions, wise men conform to them."[73]

Ironically, Aaron Mosher, the president of the Canadian Brotherhood of Railroad Employees, shared the SPC perspective to the degree that he recognized that radical leaders could not be held responsible for the labour revolt. In a letter volunteering his services to Prime Minister Borden, he noted:

Numerous telegrams we are receiving from our local branches throughout the entire west asking authority to strike and the fact that some of our members have gone on strike after authorization was denied them, leads me to believe that it is not just a few labour agitators at Winnipeg who are causing the unrest. In most cases, I am sure the rank and file in the labour movement are forcing the leaders to take the stand they have taken, and it would be well to look into this phase of the situation.[74]

Commissioner Perry of the Royal North West Mounted Police argued similarly in his "Memorandum on Revolutionary Tendencies in Western Canada:"

At the foundation of all this agitation is the general restlessness and dissatisfaction. The greater number of labour men, and probably of the community
as a whole, are in an uncertain, apprehensive, nervous and irritable temper.
Perhaps these agitators are but the foam on the wave.[75]

Let us take Mosher's advice and Perry's metaphor and close this
chapter with a consideration of the causes of the "wave" of unrest.
　　Eric Hobsbawm, some 20 years ago, suggested that:

The habit of industrial solidarity must be learned ... so must the common
sense of demanding concessions when conditions are favourable, not when
hunger suggests it. There is thus a natural time lag, before workers become
an "effective labour movement."[76]

Writing ten years later, Michelle Perrot argued: "The strike is a
weapon of conquest, the major instrument of a working class more
and more desirous and capable of improving its lot, more and more
fascinated by the possibilities of the strike."[77] By 1919, Canadian
workers had certainly become an "effective labour movement" and
they also had developed in wartime conditions a considerable fascination with "the possibilities of the strike." Indeed, as this paper argued
earlier, the 1919 revolt represents a return, albeit at a higher level of
intensity, to the pre-war pattern of conflict. This intensification was
fuelled by the addition of new groups of workers to the struggle.
These new groups included public service workers, west coast loggers,
and previously unorganized or at best partially organized groups of
industrial workers such as those in Toronto's and Montreal's packing
houses and garment shops. Among these last group of workers, as
also in Winnipeg and certainly as in the coal mines of District 18,
another crucial new ingredient was present – ethnic solidarity. In
1919, momentarily at least, the divisiveness of ethnicity was surpassed
in the struggle. A Canadian working-class movement which had been
swamped with new immigrants from eastern and southern Europe in
the pre-war years had matured, coalesced, and to some degree at least,
commenced the process of incorporating the new workers into the
movement. These "new" Canadian workers, as we are only now coming to realize, often were not "new" to the working class. Indeed
Finns, Jews, and Ukrainians often arrived with a more extensive
socialist background than their much celebrated English and Scot
immigrant comrades. A brief Winnipeg example demonstrates this
point poignantly. In the aftermath of the strike a number of "aliens"
were transported to Kapuskasing, Ontario to await deportation. All
had been arrested in the riot on Bloody Saturday. The *Strikers' Defense*

Bulletin provided short biographies of thirteen ethnic workers. One German sheet metal worker joined twelve east Europeans hailing from Galicia (seven), Bukovina (two), "Austrian Poland," the Ukraine, and Russia. Occupationally, they included two boilermakers' helpers, a carpenter, a teamster, and eight labourers. Of the labourers,three were unemployed and the others worked for the city, on the railroad, in a restaurant, in the railway shops, and for Swift's. This state-selected group of foreign-born Winnipeg workers demonstrates graphically the ethnic presence in the Winnipeg strike. This presence was not unique to Winnipeg.[78]

In addition to the new ethnic component of the labour movement there was also a more pronounced presence of women workers. The new involvement of public sector workers brought groups of telephone operators and civic employees, while organization also spread to department store clerks and waitresses, and, of course, into the heavily female garment trades. In Winnipeg, Toronto, Calgary, Vancouver, and elsewhere women workers played important roles in the 1919 strikes, both as strikers and as members of Women's Labour Leagues and Councils which, in some cases, emerged during the general strikes.[79]

Thus the structural transformation of the working class generated by the Second Industrial Revolution and by the ongoing process of the concentration and centralization of capital, which on some levels weakened the working-class movement, simultaneously stimulated an enhanced capacity for collective resistance at the workplace. Thus, scientific management and other managerial innovations, which attacked what Robert Morris has usefully termed the "moral economy of the skilled man," began the process of generating an industrial union response.[80]

The rapid urban expansion generated by monopoly capitalist growth also played its role in the revolt. The working-class neighbourhoods of Toronto's and Montreal's garment districts or those associated with the huge metal plants and railroad shops in those cities and in the west became centres of workers' lives and slowly began to generate working-class community institutions. North-end Winnipeg is perhaps the most celebrated example, but all Canadian cities developed equivalent districts. While sometimes ethnically segregated, these areas often took on instead occupational associations as in Toronto's stockyard area or even Toronto's Junction district. In this period before the automobile's dispersal of the working class, a relationship continued to exist between domicile and workplace. We need to know much more about these communities and their role in sustaining working-class opposition. Neighbourhood may have played another role as well.

Witness after witness before the Mathers Commission complained of poor and expensive housing in Canadian towns and cities. This near-universal complaint also undoubtedly contributed to the working-class revolt of 1919 and helped to widen it beyond simple workplace issues. Thus the general and sympathetic strikes extended beyond organized workers to embrace many workers outside the unions.

Also helping to widen the conflict in a similar fashion were the inter-related issues of inflation, the cost of living, and war profiteering. Recent econometric work on real wages in the first three decades of the twentieth century confirms that "real wage rates declined significantly during the First World War."[81] The new national index compiled by Bertram and Percy shows a low of 85.5 in 1917 (1913 equals 100), while Eleanor Bartlett's work on Vancouver shows the low point as either 1917 or 1918, depending on the choice of indices. What is clear in these studies and in earlier studies of Montreal, Toronto, and Winnipeg is that workers suffered a real decline on a national basis during the second half of the war. These econometric data provide the hard conformation, for those who still need it, of the testimony of hundreds of workers before the Mathers Commission. They complained continuously of high food prices, of blatant profit-eering, and of bureaucratic ineptitude, as well as of inflationary rents and inadequate housing. These complaints united all workers in ways that the more limited workplace battles sometimes failed to. Moreover the political dynamite in this situation was the clear dichotomy between a government which refused "fair wages" and conscripted manpower, and a government which allowed blatant profiteering and refused to conscript wealth. The transparency of the relationship between capital and the state in the war years allowed socialist propaganda to reach a growing and increasingly sympathetic audience. Demands for nationalization of abattoirs, cold storage plants, and elevators, which might at first seem surprising, must be viewed in this context. As Cronin has argued in the European context, the coincidence of these consumer demands with intense struggles at the point of production helped to deepen class conflict into something approaching conscious class struggle.[82]

The violent repression in Winnipeg, the strike trials and the mar-tyrdom of the leaders, the creation of the Royal Canadian Mounted Police, the conscious victimization of thousands of strikers, the TLC's retreat into craft exclusivism, all suggest a bleak aftermath and a story of defeat.[83] Yet as late as September 1919, Commissioner A.B. Perry of the new RCMP, an acute observer of labour radicalism, warned of the continuing "general state of unrest" which he found "far from satisfactory." Further, he cautioned:

The leaders of the recent movement are determined, resourceful men; that
their aims and objects are revolutionary in character has been clearly established. They have sustained a temporary setback, but to think we have heard
the last of them is only resting in a false sense of security.[84]

The war on the labour left did continue and proved successful in the
short term.

Yet the seeds of industrial unionism would survive to sprout later.
Moreover, if the 1920s and early 1930s appear as a period of relative
national labour quiescence, the phenomenon is far from unique. The
working-class movement in other advanced industrial countries also
slipped into what Yves Lequin has recently termed "the great silence,"
a period which stretched from the end of the great revolt until the
resurgence of industrial unionism in the mid to late Depression
years.[85] The fascination with industrial councils and various other
welfare capitalist schemes which was so evident in the Mathers Commission and in the National Industrial conference also had ambiguous results. The seemingly tame industrial councils often provided
the basis for the new thrust to real industrial unions when the time
was again propitious for working-class struggle.[86]

Defeats should not be confused with failure and perhaps the spc
leaders should be allowed to write their own epitaph. In Winnipeg,
F.W. derived the following "Lessons of the Strike:"

This is only a local momentary defeat on a world-wide battlefront. Remember
that permanently we cannot lose. Every struggle is a lesson in class solidarity.
every brutal act of suppression brings capitalism nearer to its inevitable doom
... Courage, fellow workers. Study your class position and you cannot lose.[87]

Meanwhile in Vancouver, Comrade C.K. addressed "The Burning
Question of Trade Unionism," echoing a Daniel DeLeon pamphlet
title. Developing a "dialectical" position against the old "philosophy of
misery" school, he argued that trade unions must be viewed not
simply as they are but rather as they might develop. The events of
1919, he wrote, led inexorably to the workers' recognition of the need
for political action. He closed on an optimistic note which, although
too reminiscent of Second International evolutionism, nevertheless
might be a message for all of us in this period of renewed attacks on
labour:

There is a benevolent appearing old gentleman wearing long white whiskers
clad in a nightshirt and carrying a scythe. He is known as "father time." The
fact is not generally known but he is a socialist of the most pronounced

revolutionary type. He is very busy among the trade unions these days. He is working for us.[88]

NOTES

This paper draws on various ongoing research projects. In each of these, I owe a debt of gratitude for research assistance. The revised strike statistics are drawn from work for volume three of the *Historical Atlas of Canada* and Douglas Cruikshank has performed yeoman service in gathering the data. Ontario materials are drawn from work for the Ontario Historical Studies series. Data on the Maritimes owe much to the mutuality and exceptional research and publications of my former Dalhousie colleagues and students. My friends at the National Archives (NA), archivists Danny Moore and Peter DeLottinville, have come up with emergency aid, as usual, far beyond the call of duty. Finally, Linda Kealey has discussed much of this paper with me and I am grateful for her insights and support.

1 Royal Commission on Industrial Relations, Evidence, Victoria, BC, 26 April 1919, 243–3. (Henceforth cited as Mathers Commission.) One SPC view of the Commission is *Causes of Industrial Unrest* (Winnipeg 1919), a pamphlet published by SPC Local No. 3.
2 Mathers Commission, Evidence, Edmonton, 6 May 1919, 987–90.
3 Ibid., Moose Jaw, 9 May 1919, 1330–42.
4 Ibid, Sudbury, Ont., 17 May 1919, 1968–72.
5 Ibid., Toronto, 28 May 1919, 2940–4.
6 Ibid., Hamilton, 21 May 1919, 2261–81.
7 Ibid., Montreal, 29 May 1919.
8 For a partial reconstruction of this evidence from newspaper sources, see Nolan Reilly, "The General Strike in Amherst, Nova Scotia, 1919," *Acadiensis* 9 (1980): 56–77; see also *Eastern Federationist* 14 June 1919.
9 Mathers Commission, Evidence, New Glasgow, NS, 5 June 1919, 3533–55.
10 Ibid., Halifax, 4 June 1919, 4355–9. On Dane, see Clifford Rose, *Four Years with the Demon Rum* (Fredericton 1980), 5–9, 83.
11 Ibid., Calgary, 3 May 1919, 786.
12 Ibid., Saskatoon, 7 May 1919, 1036.
13 Ibid., Regina, 8 May 1919, 1191.
14 Ibid., Montreal, 29 May 1919, 3163.
15 See Russell Hann's excellent introduction to Daphne Read, comp., *The Great War and Canadian Society* (Toronto 1978), 9–38.
16 David Montgomery, "Strikes in Nineteenth-Century America," *Social Science History* 4 (1980): 100.
17 All strike data in this paper are drawn from recalculations for the *Historical Atlas of Canada*, volume III. These recalculations are based

on the addition of Maritime provinces material compiled from local
sources by Ian McKay of Dalhousie University and on a careful re-
examination of all the "incomplete" files available in the NA, Department of Labour, Strikes and Lockouts files. This work commenced by
Peter DeLottinville has been carried through to completion by Douglas
Cruikshank. These data currently being compiled for publication in the
Atlas provides an entirely new data series for Canadian strike activity.
For a report on McKay's work, see his "Strikes in the Maritimes,
1900–1914," *Acadiensis* 13 (1983): 3–46.

18 David Bercuson, *Confrontation at Winnipeg: Labour Industrial Relations,
and the General Strike* (Montreal 1974) and Reilly, "The General Strike."
19 Craig Heron and Bryan D. Palmer, "Through the Prism of the Strike:
Industrial Conflict in Southern Ontario, 1901–14," *Canadian Historical
Review* 58 (1977): 423–58.
20 Unless other sources are cited this account draws on NA, Department
of Labour, Strikes and Lockouts files as well as on the original published version, *Labour Gazette*, 20 (1920): 267–94.
21 For a brief account, see Terry Copp, *Anatomy of Poverty* (Toronto 1974),
134–5.
22 *Gazette* (Montreal), 28 May 1919.
23 Ibid., 6 June 1919.
24 Ibid., 20 June 1919. For a brief reminiscence of the emerging Montreal
red world, see Catherine Vance, *Not by Gods, But by People: The Story of
Bella Hall Gauld* (Toronto 1968), 19–44. On the Vickers strike see,
Ontario Labor News (Toronto), 1 July 1919.
25 On Cobalt, see Brian F. Hogan, *Cobalt: Year of the Strike, 1919* (Cobalt
1978); on Kirkland Lake, see Laurel Sefton MacDowell, "Remember
Kirkland Lake": The Gold Miners' Strike of 1941–42 (Toronto 1983),
58–60, and Wayne Roberts, ed., *Miner's Life: Bob Miner and Union
Organizing in Timmins, Kirkland Lake and Sudbury* (Hamilton 1979),
1–2.
26 J.T. Montague, "Trade Unionism in the Canadian Meat Packing Indus-
try," unpublished PHD diss., University of Toronto, 1950, 31–8 and
George Sayers Bain, "The United Packinghouse, Food and Allied
Workers," MA diss., University of Manitoba, 1964, 35–67.
27 *Machinists Monthly Journal* 31 (April 1919): 330, cited in Donald Wright,
"Belshazzar, the Medes, and the Persians: The Rise and Fall of the
Metal Trades Strike in Toronto, 1919," unpublished paper, Dalhousie
University, 1979. Planning for 1919 took place at the second Provincial
Convention of the IAM in late November 1918. See *Labour Gazette* 19
(1919): 51–2. See also *Ontario Labor News* 1 May–1 July 1919.
28 For details see David Jay Bercuson, ed., *Alberta's Coal Industry 1919*
(Calgary 1978); Bercuson, *Fools and Wise Men: The Rise and Fall of the*

One Big Union (Toronto 1978), 196–214; Allen Seager, "Socialists and Workingmen: The Western Canadian Coal Miners' Movement, 1900–1920," paper presented at American Historical Association Meetings, December 1982.

29 Nolan Reilly, "The General Strike," his "Notes on the Amherst General Strike and the One Big Union," *Bulletin of the Committee on Canadian Labour History* 3 (Spring 1977): 5–8, and his "The Emergence of Class Consciousness in Industrial Nova Scotia: A Study of Amherst, 1891–1925," PHD diss., Dalhousie University, 1982. See also *Eastern Federationist*, 24 May–21 June 1919.

30 Borden Papers, NA, MG 26 H vol. 13 pt. 1 and pt. 2, file OC 546 (henceforth Borden Papers). See, for example, N.W. Rowell to White, Toronto, 26 May 1919; White to Rowell, Ottawa, 26 May 1919; T.L. Church to Borden, Toronto, 27 May 1919; Church to Borden, 31 May 1919; Church to Borden, 2 June 1919.

31 The literature on the munitions industry, the IMB, and labour unrest is growing, but for contrasting views, see: D.J. Bercuson, "Organized Labour and the Imperial Munitions Board," *Relations Industrielles* 28 (1974): 602–16; Peter Rider, "The Imperial Munitions Board and its Relationship to Government, Business, and Labour, 1914–1920," PHD diss., University of Toronto, 1974, esp. chap. 9; Michael Bliss, *A Canadian Millionaire: The Life and Business Times of Sir Joseph Flavelle, Bart., 1858–1939* (Toronto 1978), esp. 270–2, 280–4, 320–5, 378–81; Myer Siemiatycki, "Munitions and Labour Militancy: The 1916 Hamilton Machinists' Strike," *Labour/Le Travailleur* 3 (1978): 131–51; Craig Heron, "The Crisis of the Craftsman: Hamilton's Metal Workers in the Early Twentieth Century," *Labour/Le Travailleur* 6 (1980): 7–48; and, for Toronto metal trades background, Wayne Roberts, "Toronto Metal Workers and the second Industrial Revolution, 1889–1914," *Labour/Le Travailleur* 6 (1980): 49–72.

32 TTLC, Minutes, 2, 16 March, 6, 20 April 1916, including correspondence from Draper and Watters of the TLC.

33 Siemiatycki, "Munitions and Labour Militancy," 141.

34 TTLC, Minutes, 1, 13, 15 May 1919; *Ontario Labor News*, 15 May 1919.

35 Borden Papers, Rowell to White, 26 May 1919 and White to Rowell, 26 May 1919. Statistics from *Ontario Labor News*, 1 June 1919.

36 Ibid., Church to Borden, 27 May 1919 and "Minutes of Toronto Meeting."

37 Ibid., Borden to R.O. Hawtrey, 2 June 1919.

38 Low estimate is Department of Labour; high estimate is given by Mayor Church in letter to Borden, 2 June 1919. The *Globe* decided on 8000. See *Globe*, 30 May–7 June 1919.

39 TTLC, Minutes, 7, 21 August, 3 October, 6 November, 4, 18 December

1919, 22 January, 19 February 1920; Michael J. Piva, "The Toronto District Labour Council and Independent Political Action, 1900–21," *Labour/Le Travailleur* 4 (1979): 126–8. See also *The New Democracy* (Hamilton), 31 July, 7 August 1919.

40 Data on additional Saskatchewan locations from W.J.C. Cherwinski, "Organized Labour in Saskatchewan: The TLC Years, 1905–45," unpublished PHD diss., University of Alberta, 1972, chap. 2, and his "Saskatchewan Organized Labour and the Winnipeg General Strike, 1919," unpublished paper, Memorial University of Newfoundland, 1976; for Prince Rupert, see *BC Federationist*, 30 May 1919; for Radville through Souris, see Walter Scott Ryder, "Canada's Industrial Crisis of 1919," unpublished MA thesis, University of British Columbia, 2910, 36. How reliable this last list of whistle stops (literally) is, is not clear. Ryder, however, was writing in the immediate aftermath of the event and most of these are railway junction towns where there were probably significant groups of shopcraft workers.

41 On Brandon, see A.E. Smith, *All My Life* (Toronto 1949), chaps 3–6; Kathleen O'Gorman Wormsbecker, "The Rise and Fall of the Labour Political Movement in Manitoba, 1919–1927," MA thesis, Queen's University, 1977, esp. chap. 2; Brandon Trades and Labor Council, *Strike Bulletin*, 21–31 May 1919; *Western Labor News* (Winnipeg): 7, 9 June 1919. On the earlier Brandon strike, see *Confederate* (Brandon), 4 April 1919 and *Western Labor News*, 25 April, 7 May 1919.

42 On Saskatchewan see Cherwinski, "Organized Labour," chap. 2 and his "Organized Labour and the Winnipeg General Strike."

43 For the Edmonton strike, see William R. Askin, "Labour Unrest in Edmonton and District and its Coverage by the Edmonton Press, 1918–19," unpublished MA thesis, University of Alberta, 1973 and Carl Betke, "Influence and Community: The Ambiguity of Labour Organization in Edmonton, 1906–1921," unpublished paper presented at the Canadian-American Urban Development Conference, University of Guelph, August 1982. See also *The One Big Union Bulletin* (Edmonton), 25 March 1919; *Edmonton Strike* Bulletin, 5, 11 June 1919; and *Edmonton Free Press*, 12 April–12 July 1919.

44 For Calgary, see Elizabeth Ann Taraska, "The Calgary Craft Union Movement, 1900–20," unpublished MA thesis, University of Calgary, 1975, quotation at 46 and *Calgary Strike Bulletin*, 30 May–24 June 1919.

45 Ibid., chap. 5 and *Labour Gazette* 18 (1918): 615, 759, 857, 1005, and 820, 974–5.

46 *BC Federationist*, 16 May 1919 and Vancouver Trades and Labor Council, Executive Minutes, 15 May 1919 and Vancouver Trades and Labor Council, Executive Minutes,15 May 1919. See also Paul Phillips, *No*

Power Greater (Vancouver 1967), 80–1; *Strike Bulletin* (Vancouver), 9–26 June 1919; *The Camp Worker* (Vancouver), 2 June 1919; *The Vancouver Citizen*, 16 June–3 July 1919; and *The Critic*, 26 April–12 July 1919.

47 Ibid., 23 May 1919; Borden Papers, G.H. Deane to Borden, Vancouver, 27 May 1919. J. Kavanagh, Secretary VTLC, to Borden, 27 May 1919; and VTLC, Executive Minutes, 22, 27, 28 May 1919.

48 *BC Federationist*, 30 May 1919.

49 For list of unions supporting the strike, see ibid., 6 June 1919. On women, see *Strike Bulletin*, 16 June 1919. It is worth noting the *Citizen*, the viciously anti-union publication of the Citizens' Committee, propagandized actively for women's support. See, for only two examples, "To the Women," 20 June 1919 and "Women! With Whom?" 21 June 1919.

50 *BC Federationist*, 6 June 1919.

51 Ibid., 20 June 1919.

52 Ibid., 27 June, 4 July 1919.

53 Ibid., 4 July 1919. For another brief account of the Vancouver Strike, see Elaine Bernard, "Vancouver 1919," *Democrat* 20 (June–July 1980).

54 Phillips, *No Power Greater*, 80–1. See also the short memoir by machinist Arthur J. Turner, *Somewhere – A Perfect Place* (Vancouver 1981), 22–6, for a brief memory of the Victoria Sympathy Strike. See also *Semi-Weekly Tribune* (Victoria), 14 April–30 June 1919 and Victoria Trades and Labor Council, Minutes, esp. 9 June 1919.

55 Antonio Gramsci, *Selections from Political Writings (1910–1920)* (New York 1977), 61; Nan Milton., ed., *John MacLean: In the Rapids of Revolution* (London 1978), 137, 190

56 On Newfoundland,see Melvin Baker, Robert Cuff, Bill Gillespie, *Workingmen's St. John's: Aspects of Social History in the Early 1900s* (St John's 1982). Also Robert Cuff, "The Quill and the Hammer: Labour Activism in Newfoundland and Nova Scotia, 1917–1925," Honours BA thesis, Department of History, Memorial University of Newfoundland, 1980; Bill Gillespie, "A History of the Newfoundland Federation of Labour, 1936–63," unpublished MA thesis, Memorial University of Newfoundland, 1980; John Joy, "The Growth and Development of Trades and Manufacturing in St. John's, 1870–1914," unpublished MA thesis, Memorial University of Newfoundland, 1977; and Ian McDonald, "W.F. Coaker and the Fishermen's Protective Union in Newfoundland Politics, 1909–1925," unpublished PHD diss., University of London, 1971.

57 Larry Peterson, "The One Big Union in International Perspective: Revolutionary Industrial Unionism 1900–1925," *Labour/Le Travailleur* 7 (1981): 41–66; James E. Cronin, "Labor Insurgency and Class Formation: Comparative Perspectives on the Crisis of 1917–1920 in Europe," *Social Science History* 4 (1980). 125–52.

58 *BC Federationist*, 4 July 1919.

59 Trades and Labour Congress of Canada, *Proceedings*, 1917, 141–55. For a good example of similar fights in the US, see Cecelia F. Bucki, "Dilution and Craft Tradition: Bridgeport, Connecticut, Munition Workers, 1915–1919," *Social Science History* 4 (1980): 105–24. Also see John Laslett, *Labor and the Left* (New York 1970), passim.

60 Ibid., 1918, 138–9. Note that my count is slightly at variance with Gerald Friesen, "'Yours in Revolt': Regionalism, Socialism, and the Western Canadian Labour Movement," *Labour/Le Travailleur* 1 (1976): 141. The point, of course, remains the same. His count, however, is 29 west and 51 east vs 3 west and 81 east.

61 Ibid., 1919, 165.

62 TLC, *Proceedings*, 1919, 156–7. See David Frank, "The Cape Breton Coal Miners, 1917–1926," unpublished PHD diss., Dalhousie University, 1979, 315–19.

63 Ibid., 166.

64 Ibid.

65 Ibid., 190–2.

66 On the IAM, see *Proceedings*, 1920, esp.129–40,559–62, 248–56, 187–98, 380. See also *Bulletin* (Winnipeg), April–August 1919.

67 The syndicalist "accusation" has come ironically from both ends of the ideological spectrum over time. Gideon Robertson, for example, simply, and I believe sincerely, equated the OBU with the IWW. Later communist historians, refusing to forgive Bob Russell's refusal to join the CPC, have made the same charge. More recently some historians have repeated the error, while not necessarily sharing either Robertson's or the CPC's political position. See, for example, *Canada's Party of Socialism* (Toronto: Progress 1982), 32–3; James Foy, "Gideon Robertson: Conservative Minister of Labour, 1917–1921," unpublished MA thesis, University of Ottawa, 1972; Bercuson, *Confrontation at Winnipeg*, 89; Bercuson, *Fools and Wise Men*, passim; A. Ross McCormack, *Reformers, Rebels, and Revolutionaries: The Western Canadian Radical Movement 1899–1919* (Toronto 1977), 98, 112–13, 143 ff.; Martin Robin, *Radical Politics and Canadian Labour 1809–1930* (Kingston 1968), 150–1, 171–7, 275. this argument is not unique to this paper, of course. See Peterson, "One Big Union," 53–8 and Friesen, "'Yours in Revolt,'" 139–40 for similar interpretations.

68 The *Soviet* (Edmonton), 1, 13 (20 June 1919).

69 *Red Flag* (Vancouver), 1, 9 (22 March 1919).

70 Ibid., 1 18 (24 May 1919).

71 *BC Federationist*, 23 May 1919.

72 Ibid., 30 May 1919.

73 Gloria Montero, *We Stood Together: First Hand Accounts of Dramatic*

Events in Canada's Labour Past (Toronto 1979), 14. Also, of course, the source of Bercuson's title.

74 Borden Papers, A.R. Mosher to Borden, 29 May 1919.

75 Department of National Defence, RG 24, vol. 3985, N-S-C 1055-2-21, *Secret*, "Memorandum on Revolutionary Tendencies in Western Canada," prepared by Assistant Comptroller, RNWMP.

76 E.J. Hobsbawm, *Labouring Men* (London 1964), 144.

77 Michelle Perrot, *Les Ouvriers en grève, France 1871–90*, tome 1 (Paris 1974), 64.

78 The new literature on ethnic workers is already too voluminous to list, but note especially Varpu Lindstrom-Best's work on the Finns and Orest T. Martynowych's essays on Ukrainian socialism. See, also, the special issue of *Canadian Ethnic Studies* 10 (1978) on ethnic radicalism. For the Winnipeg data, see *Strikers' Defense Bulletin* 1, 4 (27 August 1919). For additional Winnipeg evidence see Donald Avery, "The Radical Alien and the Winnipeg General Strike of 1919," in Carl Berger and Ramsay Cook, eds, *The West and the Nation* (Toronto 1976), 209–31 and his "Ethic Loyalties and the Proletarian Revolution," in Jorgen Dahlie and Tissa Fernando, eds, *Ethnicity, Power and Politics in Canada* (Toronto 1981), 68–93.

79 On Vancouver telephone operators and the General Strike see Elaine Bernard, *The Long Distance Feeling: A History of the Telecommunications Workers Union* (Vancouver 1982), 50–65.

80 Robert Morris, "Skilled Workers and the Politics of the 'Red' Clyde," unpublished paper, University of Edinburgh, 1981. As Morris notes, his echo of Edward Thompson's "moral economy" is intentional.

81 On the war economy in general see R.T. Naylor, "The Canadian State, the Accumulation of Capital, and the Great War," *Revue d'études cana-diennes* 16, 3 and 4 (1981): 26–55. On inflation specifically see: Terry Copp, *Anatomy of Poverty*, for Montreal; Michael J. Piva, *The Condition of the Working Class in Toronto*; Harry Sutcliffe and Paul Phillips, "Real Wages and the Winnipeg General Strike: An Empirical Investigation," unpublished paper, University of Manitoba, 1973; Gordon Bertram and Michael Percy, "Real Wage Trends in Canada 1900–26," *Canadian Journal of Economics* 12 (1979): 299–312; and Eleanor Bartlett, "Real Wages and the Standard of Living in Vancouver, 1901–1929," *BC Studies* 51 (1981): 3–62. For a slightly later period, see Michael J. Piva, "Urban Working-Class Incomes and Real Incomes in 1921: A Comparative Analysis," *Histoire sociale/Social History* 31 (1983): 143–65. See also for a US comparison, Frank Stricker, "The Wages of Inflation: Workers' Earnings in the World War One Era," *Mid-America* 63 (1981): 93–105. For the general US economic context, see David M. Gordon, Richard Edwards, Michael Reich, *Segmented Work, Divided Workers: The*

Historical Transformation of Labor in the United States (New York 1982), 127–64.

82 Cronin, "Labour Insurgency and Class Conflict," passim. See also his *Industrial Conflict in Modern Britain* (London 1979), 109–20.

83 Much of this has been chronicled elsewhere. For an apologetic but detailed description of the creation of the RCMP see S.W. Horrall, "The Royal North-West Mounted Police and Labour Unrest in Western Canada, 1919," *Canadian Historical Review* 61 (1980): 169–90. On victimization, especially of postal workers, see Borden Papers, various letters June to September 1919, pp. 62179–257. On one particularly unseemly aspect of TLC behaviour, see Tom Traves, "'The Story that Couldn't Be Told': Big Business Buys the TLC," *Ontario Report* 1, 6 (September 1976): 27–9.

84 A.B. Perry, "Draft Memorandum," 1 September 1919, Royal Canadian Mounted Police Papers, volume 1003, NA.

85 Yves Lequin, "Social Structures and Shared Beliefs: Four Worker Communities in the Second Industrialization," *International Labor and Working-Class History* 22 (1982): 1–17.

86 On Councils in Canada, see Bruce Scott, "'A Place in the Sun': The Industrial Council at Massey-Harris, 1919–1929," *Labour/Le Travailleur* 1 (1976): 158–92; Tom Traves, *The State and Enterprise: Canadian Manufacturers and the Federal Government 1917–1931* (Toronto 1979), 86–94; and Foy, "Gideon Robertson." For U.S. comparisons see Stuart D. Brandes, *American Welfare Capitalism, 1880–1940* (Chicago 1976), passim, but esp. 119–48.

87 *Socialist Bulletin* (Winnipeg), 1, 7 (July 1919).

88 *Red Flag*, 1, 22 (21 June 1919). For an academic echo of labour's educational gains from the strike, see D.G. Cook, "Western Radicalism and the Winnipeg Strike," MA thesis, McMaster University, 1921, which argues, on the basis of interviews with Winnipeg strikers, that: "The gains of the strike were many for the labour group. The six-week's strike was like a college course in Economics. Papers were read, issues discussed, and many addresses were given by the leaders. Many of the labour men became enlightened as to the real struggle. There grew a strong spirit of solidarity in the rank and file of labour" (62).

PART FOUR

Overviews

10 The Structure of Canadian Working-Class History

In this paper I want to accomplish a rather large, perhaps impossible, task – namely to offer you an overview of Canadian working-class history. The nature of this overview may at first seem strange, even to those readers familiar with the general history of Canadian labour. Strange, because what I want to offer is an interpretation that does more than simply present the history of working people as an interesting addition to our general knowledge of Canadian history. Instead I want to argue that Canadian workers have been central to Canadian historical development and that Canadian history cannot be understood without their inclusion. Much previous Canadian historical writing has simply ignored the presence of working-class people, just as it has ignored the existence of women, of native people, and of other oppressed groups. More recently, with the rise to acceptable status of social history, it has become commonplace to find workers and women simply added to the general contours of the old view of historical development. In this version workers are now present but – and this is a rather large but – their presence makes little discernible difference. This essay will argue that if class and gender are added to the historical record, then that record must of necessity be transformed.

Canadian labour and working-class history and indeed the broader critical social thought of which it is a part, have made remarkable strides in the last fifteen to twenty years. These years have witnessed the blossoming of critical Canadian scholarship, built to a large degree on the various social struggles of the 1960s wherein renewed class conflict was a significant element. Given the all-too-frequent recent attempts to belittle the experiences of the late 1960s both inside and outside the universities, I think this is an important fact to assert at the outset.

The focus of the recent work in Canadian labour and working-class history has changed significantly. Rather than simply considering the labour movement – even in its broadest sense involving economic struggles and political activities as well as trade union organization – most of the recent work in the field has taken a still wider field of vision which encompasses the totality of the working class, a totality which has always, unfortunately, transcended the labour movement. The new labour and working-class history argues that the larger issue of the entire working class must be the focus of our analysis because of the structural tensions which often surround the relationship between organized and unorganized. Indeed, the simple fact that the history of the Canadian labour movement and the history of the Canadian working class are not identical represents one of the major questions on which our historical analysis must focus. While this totality must go beyond economic and political factors, and most of the new literature does this quite successfully, I will focus my attention here primarily on the workplace. This is a disservice in general, especially to women whose work has often been outside the paid labour force. Moreover, the whole sphere of reproduction is analytically cut off from production only at great cost. Unfortunately, however, the realm of reproduction is only now beginning to be studied by social historians in relation to class.

I suspect that no one will be surprised if I suggest that the Canadian economy, and the world capitalist order of which it is part, are in profound crisis – a crisis unmatched since the 1930s. The crisis surrounds us, pervades our everyday lives, and shows little sign of abating despite recent political assurances of recovery. The official national unemployment rate remains above 11 per cent, and even the most optimistic prophets of recovery hold out little hope for improvement in the near future. Material recently published by the Social Planning Council of Metropolitan Toronto estimates that the official unemployment figures hide another 9–10 per cent who simply have stopped looking for jobs. In British Columbia, the virulent offensive launched against working people by the Socred government and their Fraser Institute advisors continues. On all sides there is further news of shutdowns and layoffs. For those still at work, wage gains at best match inflation. Meanwhile, of course, the social wage – the hard-won social security net of the post-war accord between labour and capital – declines everywhere, not only in British Columbia. Attacks on the social wage are matched by equally vicious offensives against collective bargaining rights, especially in the public sector. The Anti-Inflation Board, "6 & 5," back-to-work legislation, the jailing of labour leaders, and ever-increasing designation of public-sector jobs as "essential" services all reflect the depth and extent of the crisis.

Yet it is useful to remind ourselves that this is not Canadian capitalism's first major crisis. The depression of the 1930s, broken only by the advent of World War II, the significant depression of the 1890s, and the massive dislocations of the 1840s, all represent equivalent economic crises in the development of Canadian capitalism and major moments in the making and remaking of the Canadian working class. An understanding of these past crises can provide us with historical perspective on the current crisis and perhaps even suggest some paths to be taken in the fight to resist the current onslaught against Canadian workers. For while crisis is a dangerous time, it is also a time of opportunity – a time when structural change is on the agenda, a time when the way forward is up for grabs, and thus a time which occurs only periodically in history.

I want to argue here in favour of a five-period construction of Canadian working-class history. First is the period before 1850 about which we have known little until recently. The old Staples, Laurentian, and Metropolitan approaches to Canadian history remained silent about the nature of class formation under what has sometimes been termed as "pre-industrial capitalism," but which might be better described as a period of primitive accumulation, as Bryan Palmer has persuasively argued. In this period, under the general hegemony of merchant's capital, two conflicting methods of appropriating economic surplus co-existed side by side. In the country an agrarian petty capitalism rooted in household production held sway, while in the towns and villages of the British American colonies an early inhibited manufacturing emerged. Both forms of appropriation held within them the seeds of transformation. In the country the productive household was premised on expansion without which the large numbers of progeny demanded to work the land would find themselves facing a bleak future. Equally, expansion led to an ever-increasing commercialization which in turn fuelled proto-industrial manufacturing of agricultural implements, milling, and food processing. The relationship of town and country in this period demands further historical attention.

Meanwhile, a form of metropolitan industrialization developed in the towns, which would eventually displace such rural proto-industrial production. In cities like Montreal, Quebec, Saint John, Halifax, and Toronto, manufacturing engendered a bewildering number of forms – early factories, manufactories, artisan shops, sweatshops, and outwork. Women, we should note, were especially prevalent in outwork and early factory work. Such an extraordinary mix of work sites combined with the different interests of town and country might suggest a society in which merchants' hegemony would go unchallenged, but such was not the case. Both in country and city, resistance was offered by their respective producers, although it took quite different forms. In the country the major aim was to resist the proletarianization which became increasingly evident as the once favourable land-to-labour ratio started to reverse itself. In town and city the plebeian orders engaged in a wide array of riotous behaviour (over 400 riots before 1855); they also began to form the more familiar trade societies and unions which in the Canadas alone would conduct some forty-five strikes before 1850.

The second period, which has been studied far more extensively, covered the years from the late 1840s to the 1890s and included Canada's industrial revolution and might be termed the period of initial "proletarianization." During this time workers actively participated in the destruction of the old colonial system and helped to build a new nation oriented to American trade and increasingly to industrial development behind protective tariffs and a boosterish promotional climate. These new economic directions also led to Confederation and the creation of a national economic entity out of the previously disparate British American colonies. The inspiration for this creation came from Toronto and Montreal capitalists and their British allies who saw a brave future in the economic exploitation of the west and the integration of the Atlantic colonies into a national system. It should be added, however, that the Atlantic colonies had their share of industrial capitalist visionaries as well, although they were less powerful in their local bailiwicks than their central Canadian counterparts.

The first twenty-five years of the nation's existence were troubled ones, but beneath the pessimism associated with population loss and economic recession a steady industrial growth was achieved which especially accelerated during the early 1880s after the inauguration of the National Policy tariffs. The CPR was not the only economic achievement of these years since rapid growth also took place in both consumer goods and producer goods segments of the new manufacturing sector. Moreover, while the CPR tied the slowly developing west into the new state, the completion of the Intercolonial also integrated the Maritimes into the new national economy.

During these years competitive capitalism was at its height. Despite recent capitalist rhetoric, the state played an active role in economic development. Laissez faire was a myth that applied only in the social realm of government activity. Canadian tariff policy was only one example where the models of German and American industrial development helped offset the ideological claims of Manchester liberalism. The state, then, was a particularly active partner in Canadian industrial development.

In these years the capitalist mode of production triumphed and large numbers of Canadians were proletarianized. Canadian capitalists overcame significant impediments to the development of a waged labour force such as the availability of land. They were helped in this immensely by the massive famine migration of the Irish in the late 1840s and early 1850s. In addition to immigrants, however, waged labour was also recruited from the native farm population, especially in Quebec, from the ranks of women and children, and from craftsmen's shops. Thus Canadian workers continued to be segmented along various lines – craft versus unskilled, male versus female, and native versus Irish and other immigrant groups.

In this second period capitalist production was based on the new proletariat, but the new industrialists failed to achieve much control over the labour process. Traditional techniques of production prevailed in most sectors of the economy and even in the largest factories skilled workers retained considerable control over production. Thus while skilled workers lost much independence and control of their means of production, they still retained a power based on their skill and knowledge. Accordingly skilled workers through their craft unions fought bitterly to resist attempts to disrupt traditional methods of production. Economic growth in this second period continued to be "extensive" not "intensive," and was based largely on expansion.

By the 1870s and 1880s the very success of capital in creating the new industrial nation had begun to create the contradictions which would only be resolved in the crisis of the 1890s through the final arrival of what Marx termed modern industry. Capital's success in creating a an increasingly national market led to intensive competition which in turn caused price declines. Owing to lack of control over the labour process, industrialists could not intensify production in the face of craft workers' intransigence. Even in industries where crafts had not existed, the managerial wherewithal to control large bodies of workers through intermediaries had not yet been established. Instead industrialists turned to wage cutting and to intrusions into the labour process, both of which helped to engender the massive labour revolt of the Great Upheaval of 1885–87. Only with the eventual defeat of labour's first significant challenge was capital able to commence transforming the labour process to eliminate the bottleneck of craft control.

In the Great Upheaval, for a time, labour overcame many of its structural weaknesses through the all-inclusive organizational strategy of the Knights of Labor. The Knights tried to organize all workers regardless of skill, gender, race, or ethnicity. The Knights also entered the political arena in a significant manner, running independent labour candidates and influencing the politics of the young nation. Their potential power was underlined by the appointment of the Royal Commission on the Relations of Labour and Capital in 1886 and by the creation of various provincial bureaus of labour.

Perhaps the Knights' greatest contribution was their willingness to address the question of women's work. While preferring the model of the family wage and thus of an idealized proletarian family in which the male head-of-household could support his wife and family through the achievement of wage rates high enough to sustain that goal, the Knights recognized the necessity of organizing women workers as part of that struggle. With women in their ranks, they were pushed to discuss organizing domestic workers as well, and even on occasion to consider the collectivization of elements of the reproductive sphere. The Knights' insights in this realm, like many of their other aims, would be partially eclipsed in the 1890s. Pure-and-simple trade unionism would make fewer efforts in this direction.

The importance of the Knights' aim of organizing all workers is especially evident when we consider in more detail the three separate worlds of these nineteenth-century workers. Women factory operatives, skilled male workers, and labourers occupied different spaces within the working class, as David Montgomery has argued. Much of the most mechanized factory work, for example in textiles and boot and shoe manufacturing, became women's work. Meanwhile men were sharply divided between the craftsmen and the labourers. Craftsmen, even in the new factories, continued to control much of their work and that of their helpers. While seeing themselves as socially superior to their helpers (often apprentices or youth) and to labourers, they nevertheless led the trade union and socialist movement. Their socialist ideas were based on their primacy in production. As the real creators of the world's wealth, they deserved to control not only production but also society. Production for use not profit would insure social equality.

Nineteenth-century labourers worked as surrogate brutes. They constituted a high proportion of the male labour force, perhaps one-third, but they simply supplied the craftsmen in industry. In construction and on the public works they carried and excavated. In their work world there was little price. Their major goal was to prevent being overworked and to gain wages adequate for their families' survival.

While often rebellious, as on Canada's canal and railroad building projects, they seldom formed permanent unions.

Simply tracing these themes into the next major period – the third period stretched from the 1890s to the crisis of the Great Depression and World War II – suggests the major transformation of the labour process and massive reconstitution of the working class which occurred in the following forty years, years which might be typified by the phrase "homogenization," following again on the usage suggested by Gordon, Reich, and Edwards.

The "Second Industrial Revolution" which swept North America at the turn of the century ended the nineteenth-century relationship of craftsman to labourer by universalizing the factory operative. The new techniques of Frederick Winslow Taylor and Henry Ford systematized the mental labour involved in production. The beneficiary of this process was the engineer; the loser was the craftsman. Scientific management did not eliminate skilled workers, but instead shifted them out of production. The unskilled operatives became the producers; the skilled craftsmen took over jobs such as set-up, inspection, toolmaking, and maintenance. They also created a vast array of new clerical and related white-collar jobs, increasingly filled by women. For example, Imperial Oil in Canada employed 11 white collar workers in 1898 but over 6,000 by 1919. Public service employment also grew rapidly with 17,000 in 1901, 77,000 in 1911, and 108,000 in 1931. Put in different terms, in 1911 there were 8.6 administrative workers for each 100 production workers; by 1931 there were 16.9 per 100.

These changes in the nature of production led factory workers towards industrial unionism and away from themes stressing workers' control of production. But first they fought an extended struggle against capital's attempt to transform production. Typified by the uniform organization of production in which work tasks were reduced to detailed, atomized, semi-skilled operations, capital aimed to destroy all remnants of the old workers' control and replace it with enhanced managerial power which would expand the corporations' ability to extract labour. Here we find the switch from "extensive" to "intensive" growth and control. Key to all of this were the massive merger movement of the late nineteenth and early twentieth century, the Second Industrial Revolution, and the massive influx of American capital and corporations into Canada. The merger movement was, of course, based on the creation of national markets, the arrival of the stock market, and the transformation of the law to allow for corporate consolidation. In turn the new massive factories were based on far more extensive mechanization, but here we should remind ourselves that these machines were not simply part of some neutral progress, representing scientific advance and more efficient production, but rather the specific machines were often intended simply to displace the skills, and thus the power, of the skilled worker.

The managerial system that accompanied homogenization is described by Gordon, Reich, and Edwards as "the drive system." While there were many experiments with scientific management, most often associated with Taylor and termed Taylorism, these probably can best be taken as symbolic of the new emphasis on "science" and "efficiency." In most industry, "drive" was enough, and the complexity of Taylorism found relatively few advocates. Equally symbolic was Ford's assembly line, which had been predated by similar processes in meat packing and in the development of interchangeable parts in the sewing machine, clock and watch, and small arms industries. Nevertheless, Fordism like Taylorism has become a symbol of the twentieth-century transformation of capitalism.

The "drive" system of production was based on three interrelated factors: 1) the reorganization of work through mechanization and job restructuring; 2) the rapid increase in plant size and the subsequent impersonality of labour relations; 3) the continuous expansion of the foreman's role. It might be defined as the policy of achieving efficiency by putting pressure on workers to work hard, with the pressure being sustained by keeping the workers in permanent fear of management.

Predictably the working class did not respond well to these innovations and the history of the labour movement in this period is one of accelerating militancy which culminated in the labour revolt of 1917–21. The extent of this working-class resistance demanded a corporate response and capitalist strategy aimed directly at the suppression of this working-class threat. Two broad strategic aims can be detected: 1) the attempt to increase the threat of the reserve army of labour (massive immigration); 2) efforts to divide and fragment working-class solidarity on the job. There is not space available to examine the specifics of this strategy but let me suggest a few of its components: centralized personnel offices concerned with hiring and transfers – specifically aimed at activists; artificial job ladders; decentralization of factories (industrial suburbs); fragmentation of plant design; wage incentive schemes; welfare plans; racial and ethnic manipulation; militant antiunionism; the "open shop"; the American plan; use of the courts; and cooptation of AFL/TLC as "responsible" labour.

Monopoly capitalism replaced the older form of competitive capitalism during those decades and successfully initiated a national labour market to match the new national product market. In addition, capitalists recruited labour from a vast international pool and continuously extended the concentration and cartelization of capital which had begun to emerge in the 1890s. Overseeing all of these developments, capital had a more mature partner – a state that was willing to conciliate and to moderate between capital and labour through new agencies such as the Department of Labour and new legislation such as the Industrial Disputes Investigation Act. If these allegedly neutral activities failed, then capital's partner was also willingly to play a harsher role. Staggering demonstrations of force, unprecedented in the nineteenth century, were used to intimidate workers in the coal fields of Nova Scotia and British Columbia and in industrial centres such as Winnipeg and Sydney.

An understanding of working-class history in Canada must seriously face the differences which confronted the working-class movement as capital changed its nineteenth-century face into its modern twentieth-century countenance. For too long Canadian history has viewed this transformation only in quantitative terms. The rapid growth of the Canadian industrial economy and the arrival of American capital have been appreciated, but the complete revision of the "rules" under which capital and labour operated has been underestimated. Capital in its new phase did not play according to the old rules and it took the labour movement some time to learn the nature of the new contest. Moreover, workers faced an entirely new set of problems created by the vast resources that capital now had in its service. Labour faced a new enemy and the proven nineteenth-century tactics of class struggle had to be modified accordingly. The new strategies were evident in the level of class conflict which prevailed in Canadian society throughout these years; that they failed was also quite evident by the 1920s. The strength of capital had been too great. Moreover, labour's ability to resist in a concerted, country-wide fashion was weakened by the relatively late national consolidation of the labour movement itself. Institutionally the Trades and Labor Congress only became nation-wide at the turn of the century and even this centralization led to the loss of certain national and Quebec unions, as well as the remnants of the Knights of Labor.

One example of all these trends must suffice. Let us consider the case of the Canadian steel industry. Until the construction of the Algoma and Disco plants in the early twentieth century, the Canadian steel industry fit well our model of the previous period where skilled workers exercised considerable workplace control. With the coming of massive American capital to build the plants in the Sault and Sydney, and then with the merger magic of Max Aitken to create Hamilton's Stelco, Canada had three world-class modern steel plants before World War I. The effects on production well illustrate the new system:

1901	4,110 workers	245,000 T. pig iron
		26,000 T. steel
1929	10,500 workers	1.1 m. T. pig iron
		1.3 m. T. steel

Production in these steel plants was definitely based on the drive system. The twelve-hour day, seven-day week existed in Hamilton at Stelco until 1930 and did not end in the Sault and Sydney until 1935. Piece rates and tyrannical foremen prevailed and workers were drawn from diverse ethnic and racial roots. Labour relations were authoritarian and based on fear and resentment. In the aftermath of labour's defeat in steel – the old skilled craft union, the Amalgamated Association of Iron, Tin and Steel Workers, was totally gone by 1923 – there was some softening, partially because of the commonly perceived problem of high turnover rates. This brought increased internal recruitment, job ladders, welfare programs, and industrial councils of various types.

The choice of steel, of course, suggests that this system too would end in crisis and that the workers would eventually mount an effective assault. The major contradictions which had emerged in the drive period revolved around the extraordinary turnover rates and later around the subterranean revolt of informal work groups in which workers devised effective methods of restricting output. Other contradictions of a different order also existed. These resulted in the crash of 1929 and a decade of depression which ended only with the outbreak of World War II. Relatively untrammeled capitalist growth in the 1920s unleashed the Great Depression. Out of this major crisis and the class conflict it engendered grew yet a fourth major stage of capitalist development which saw the creation and elaboration of a welfare state as its major symbol. The establishment and later sophistication of a different structure of legal constraints surrounding the entire realm of class relations was another major innovation of this period. The creation of a new administrative system of labour law entrenched in federal and provincial labour boards once again transformed industrial relations and provided both capital and labour with another set of new rules intended to regulate and delimit their struggles. This fourth period which stretched from the 1940s to the 1970s we might term the period of "segmentation."

The intense struggles of the 1930s and 1940s, which saw the arrival of the CIO and industrial unionism in Canada, forced another major restructuring on capital. Unable to solve the crisis of the depression until the outbreak of World War II resolved the question, capital and the state slowly responded to the demands of an increasingly assertive and militant labour movement. From the miners of Kirkland Lake through the steelworkers of the industrial heartland to shipyard and aircraft workers, a national strike wave of previously unprecedented heights forced the King government to guarantee the right to bargain collectively. While PC 1003 finally brought this right to Canadian workers in February 1944, it would take the further post-war struggles of 1945–46 to confirm the gains. The massive Ford Windsor strike and the equally important Stelco strike led to the final confirmation of a new legal status for Canadian workers. This was entrenched in the Industrial Relations and Disputes Investigation Act of 1948 and in a series of equivalent provincial acts.

While representing a major gain for Canadian workers, and one which should never be denigrated, it is nevertheless clear that the effects of this legislation and the subsequent elaboration of yet more complex legal and quasi-legal systems of labour relations in this country were undoubtedly not what CIO and CCL activists had envisioned. The intricate complexity of the legal structures are themselves based on two elaborate myths: first, that the two parties involved – capital and labour – meet as equal parties in so-called "free" collective bargaining ("industrial pluralism"); and second, that the state role is simply that of a neutral umpire, aiding the two parties in their deliberations and protecting the interests of the public. The first, of course, perpetuates the commonly-held myth of the equal power of capital and labour, while the second disguises the pro-capitalist role of the state and especially of its potential for coercion. Meanwhile the IRDIA which is often compared with the American Wagner Act, contained within it a series of important limitations on labour's power which continued the earlier Canadian tradition enshrined in King's original IDIA of 1907. The major example, of course, was the fencing-in of labour's ability to resort to strike action during negotiations or during the life of a collective agreement. In addition, various unfair union practices were named and proscribed and the underlying assumption of the state's role to assist the two negotiating parties remained. Restrictions on the nature of picketing and on secondary boycotts were further limitations. All this then was ironically also part of Canadian labour's supposed Magna Carta.

The Canadian state also delivered a second concession to working-class militancy in this period. In a complex series of decisions, the King government assumed some element of responsibility for insuring "a high and stable level of employment" and for offering security provisions for those who were unable to find work. Note that these levels of employment were, of course, never defined as "full." Moreover, while the King government moved to implement some elements of the social security program discussed by its various advisory committees, it stopped well short of the full vision of the 1943 Marsh report.

The choice of C.D. Howe as the minister ultimately in charge of the reconstruction package demonstrates how free enterprise notions still prevailed and that social reform remained subject to the dictates of the capital accumulation process. Thus elements of the social wage were won, notably family allowances and unemployment insurance, but the grandiose plans for extensive pension and national health schemes would wait some twenty years. In addition, investment decisions were left entirely up to capital.

Thus the vaunted post-war accord brought circumscribed welfare state reforms, new labour legislation, and a limited commitment to reducing unemployment. These were undoubtedly gains for Canadian workers, but they were intended, as Justice Rand actually said in his important, precedent-making decision in the Ford strike of 1946, to help maintain capitals' "long-run dominant position." The rule of law had come to prevail in labour relations. In the process the ideology of "industrial pluralism" has dictated that workers "fight their daily workplace struggles out in an invisible, privatized forum where each dispute is framed in an individuated, minute, economistic forum."

Ironically given women's significant contribution to the war effort, they were nevertheless largely forced out of industrial work after the men came home, as Ruth Pierson has convincingly demonstrated. Nevertheless the trend towards higher female participation in the work force continued, and increased dramatically in the 1950s and 1960s. Changes in the family also meant that increasing numbers of married women began to join their single sisters in the paid labour force. The labour movement made some efforts to organize women workers in the post-war period, the most famous being the huge drive to organize Eaton's, an effort which eventually failed.

While the dust of the post-war accord was settling, capital got on with the business of accumulation. In return for various collective bargaining concessions to the CIO which included grievance procedures, seniority provisions, and productivity-related gains in real wages – clearly attempts by labour to disrupt the authoritarian elements of the old drive system – capital gained an important concession, namely management's rights clauses. These clauses, in effect, conceded all residual areas to management and allowed capital to get on with its restructuring. In the propitious climate of the post-war world with American capital dominant and the Cold War raging, the multinational corporations developed systematic collective bargaining strategies and restructured work by increasing technical control through technological change but also through the creation of new forms of control termed "bureaucratic" by Richard Edwards. In corporations such as Polaroid and IBM, internal labour markets were created on the basis of elaborate job systems and rules. Here too one finds finely divided jobs situated within detailed job ladders and internal promotion systems. Technology is used not simply to regulate the pace of work but also to serve broader managerial aims. Hiring, promotion, and firing are all regularized, and collective bargaining tends to focus on wages and fringes, leaving the organization of work to engineers and labour relations experts. Corporations have fully developed systems of rules and procedures which leave little to the haphazard nature of arbitrary supervisory intervention. This system is termed "segmentation" by Gordon, Edwards, and Reich.

They further argue that this system is most fully elaborated only at the heights of the economy in the largest firms in the monopoly sector. Thus the working class comes to be further split between this *primary* segment and a *secondary* segment typified by peripheral firms which have never gained this kind of labour control and indeed still function in the drive stage typical of the 1920s and 1930s. Clothing and textiles would probably be the best example of the secondary segment. Moreover, even in the primary sector they see a further division between what they term *independent* jobs and those they describe as *subordinate*. Independent jobs are typically of professional, managerial, and technical kinds, and provide considerable autonomy and independence. Subordinate jobs are those which are routinized, repetitive, more heavily supervised, and based on extensive formal rules. These significantly divided areas of labour fractured the unity of the working class severely and limited its ability to resist the reorganizations of capital.

The period of "segmentation" prevailed from the 1940s through the late 1960s, but has been in crisis since. The fifth period – the current crisis – is what we are living through now and the nature of its resolution is far from clear. It seems that the post-war accord had ended. Labour began to demonstrate its impatience in the 1960s when the management prerogative to organize production came under increasing challenge even while workers were still receiving real wage increases. Typified by wild cats and refusals to ratify collective agreements in the 1960s, revolt in this area led to extensive governmental concern, evidenced in the Woods Task Force on Labour Relations on the federal level and various similar efforts by provincial governments, such as Ontario's Rand Report. With the demise in the inflation-plagued 1970s of those gains, with the further erosion of employment security, and with deteriorating working conditions, the crisis in the subordinate primary sector had fully arrived.

The current crisis of "deindustrialization" is being fought on this terrain as corporations seek to solve the crisis by various means – increasing supervision and speedups; shutdowns and new plants in labour-weak areas; extensive anti-union activities; and demands for concessions and give-backs. Further ahead, corporations seem to be looking to more technological solutions involving robotics and micro-electronics, various worker-participation schemes (representation on boards, QWL), and interest in Japanese corporate labour relations schemes, and, of course, as in the 1970s, wage determination through the state.

Even in the independent primary sector the erosion of wage differentials, the lessening of autonomy, the decline of stable employment, and the erosion of advancement chances have also resulted in rising dissatisfaction and further unionization. Among teachers, nurses, health care workers, and college and university professors, increased militancy from the 1960s on has been the order of the day.

In the secondary segment improvements had been limited anyway, even in the post-war period, but now real wages are falling rapidly and job insecurity prevails. It is here that the growing International Division of Labour has made itself most deeply felt with the export of vast numbers of jobs. Here in what is sometimes termed "peripheral Fordism" we see one major effort by capital to create a new strategy of accumulation. Capital, which formerly imported foreign labour now hires cheap labour in Third World countries to manufacture for metropolitan markets. The Third world's vast potential reserve army of labour is being exploited. While initially limited to the secondary segment, in the late 1970s and early 1980s, this process is spreading to subordinate primary jobs as is only too evident in automobile and steel manufacturing. Desperate economic straits apparently are to be depended on to discipline recalcitrant workers in the private sector.

Meanwhile in the public sector, the state continues its assault on workers who only joined the post-war accord in time to see it disintegrate. Public sector workers in Canada only gained collective bargaining rights and, in some jurisdictions, the right to strike, in the 1960s and early 1970s. From its beginnings public sector collective bargaining legislation was heavily restrictive, nowhere fully approximating the rights of workers in the private sector. For example, the scope of bargaining is limited dramatically by the legislation itself. Moreover, the right to strike is forbidden in many jurisdictions including Ontario and Nova Scotia. In addition far more public servants are eliminated from collective bargaining by extensive definitions of confidentiality – up to 27 per cent in Ontario. Nevertheless, even with all these restrictions, this is the group of workers currently facing strident governmental attacks.

This current attack on public sector unions and wages is related to the more extended attack on the "social wage." Some estimates place the total Canadian social wage at fully 21 per cent of wages and salaries in 1982. If attacks such as the Bennett government's 1983 autumn offensive are allowed to gain ground, all workers, not only those in the public sector, stand to lose.

The expansion of public sector employment commensurate with increased levels of state intervention and welfarism has come under ideological assault of late. For structural reasons, especially the holes in our allegedly "progressive" tax system, many of these arguments have proven persuasive with some workers. The cost of state efforts have been increasingly transferred to individual Canadian taxpayers. The general split in the Canadian labour movement between the industrial unions and the new, rapidly growing public sector unions has also played into this divide. Just as racial, ethnic, and sexual divisions have hindered working-class unity in the past, the public/ private rift sometimes does the same now. Divisions based on the too easily perceived white collar/blue collar differentiation between public and private sector and the fact that public sector strikes often directly inconvenience private sector workers because they too are dependent on government services, should no longer divide workers, BC's Operation Solidarity, while highly suggestive of what is possible, faltered partially on this divide.

The increased participation of women in the labour force and the rising prominence of public sector and service sector employment which involve high concentrations of women workers has contributed a renewed vibrancy to the labour movement of late. While labour has often carried progressive positions on women's issues, for example, equal pay for work of equal value, their actual performance often left much to be desired. Women workers have increasingly made their voices heard and the most recent organizational gains are coming in precisely those areas where women work such as data processing at the banks and in retail trade. Given the generally dismal record of late this represents one of the few bright spots on labour's horizon.

In conclusion I would like to reiterate that Canadian historical de-velopment to date has been based on the combined effect of capital-ists' and workers' activities within the broader context of the contours of capital accumulation. We have identified five major periods: up to the 1840s, the 1840s–90s, the 1890s–1940s, the 1940s–70s, and from the 1970s one, which we have described in terms of primitive accumulation, proletarianization, homogenization, segmentation, and the current crisis. Since the late 1960s then, we have entered into what appears to be another major capitalist crisis which will only be resolved by the creation of a new social structure of accumulation. In each of the previous crises the working-class role had significant import. In the late nineteenth century the skilled workers' control of production and increasing militancy in the 1880s set the limits on the productivity of initial proletarianization. In the post-war revolt of 1919, labour defiantly challenged the new system of homogenization but failed; it renewed that challenge through industrial unionism, and the organization of the mass production industries in the 1930s and 1940s, ending the homogenization phase. Since the late 1960s the increased economic and political power of labour has played a role in the destabilization of the institutional arrangements of the post-war accord. Solutions to the crises of the 1890s and the 1930s both demanded major structural transformations. The resolution of the current crisis can be expected to as well. In this process labour must struggle to prevent that solution from emerging from the New Right coalition which aims to reestablish the conditions which predated the post-war accord. The Bennett program in British Columbia attempts to revive the boom by rolling back the last forty years of working-class gains. It is the task of the labour movement today to pose a socialist alternative either to that or to other forms of capitalist restructuring. It certainly should be clear again that capitalism simply does not deliver the goods.

11 Strikes in Canada, 1891–1950

WITH DOUGLAS CRUIKSHANK

ANALYSIS

The birth, life and death of a strike could be said to be a classic piece of urban theatre, but it would be a bare stage without the actors. The strikers' actions and cries bring the stage alive; sometimes they even obscure the mechanism and architecture that their great numbers reveal to our dazzled eyes. The strikers do not move at random, however; their playing obeys rules whose code it is up to us to recover.

Michelle Perrot[1]

In the years 1891–1950, some 2,600,000 Canadian workers engaged in almost 9,700 strikes which absorbed a total of over 42,000,000 person days. Not surprisingly, these strikes did not occur in any simple pattern of linear growth. Instead, like strikes elsewhere, they came in bursts or waves that initially drew on workers' sense of opportunities to be seized and subsequently fed on initial successes. Disaggregated by decade, the war decades 1911–20 and 1941–50 emerge as the most active with 4,886 of the strikes (50 per cent), 1,654,000 of the strikers (64 per cent), and almost 25,000,000 person days of duration (59 per cent). (See Table 11.1 and Figure 11.A.)*

Indeed, if we move beyond the decadal data, we can discern a series of strike waves, similar to those described by Shorter and Tilly, Cronin, and Edwards in their respective studies of France, Britain,

*Tables and figures with alphabetic designations appear in the last section of this chapter. Those with numeric designations are placed in the text.

Table 11.1
National Strike Estimates by Decade, 1891–50

	Number of strikes	Number of workers involved (000)[a]	Duration in person days (000)
1891–1900	511	78	1,742
1901–10	1,548	230	5,492
1911–20	2,349	521	10,821
1921–30	989	261	6,626
1931–40	1,760	376	3,444
1941–50	2,537	1,133	14,142
Total	9,694	2,599	42,267

a Workers involved in strikes extending beyond 31 December are counted twice in these totals.

and the United States.[2] After some introductory discussion of the general shape of the findings, this paper will look more intensively at the strike waves of this sixty-year period. The paper will close with some brief and preliminary reflections on international comparisons of strike activity in this period.

This three-part report presents the results of a major research project undertaken in the early 1980s. The project aimed to establish a new statistical time series for strikes in Canada. The final results of this work appeared in 1990 in volume three of the *Historical Atlas of Canada* which will contain a series of four plates on Canadian labour in the years 1891–1961. In this report we shall focus on the data concerning the years 1891–1950. An essay on method and sources is published here as Part II of this report and the data set is presented fully in Part III. In addition, we want to state at the outset that the more we work on this data, the more fully we agree with David Montgomery's assertion that "any attempt to formulate a positivistic 'natural history of strikes' is doomed to failure. Strikes can only be understood in the context of the changing totality of class conflicts, of which they are a part."[3]

I

A brief review of Bryan Palmer's research report on nineteenth-century strikes suggests that in the years prior to our study, Canadian workers also struck in cyclical waves. The early 1850s and 1870s and the mid 1880s represent years of intense strike activity well beyond the levels of the surrounding years. Thus, Palmer's work appears to lend considerable support to Tilly/Shorter's and Cronin's arguments concerning the nature of industrial conflict, which emphasize bursts of activity.[4] If we continue simply to look at the absolute frequency of strikes in Canada, we can discern an overall pattern in the first half of the twentieth century as well. Strikes grew in absolute numbers in the 1890s, 1900s, and especially the 1910s but fell in the 1920s well below the level established in the 1900s. The number climbed above that level again in the 1930s and reached a peak in the 1940s higher even than the World War I decade (see Figure 11.A). This decadal data, of course, disguises the peaks and troughs within the decades which can be more clearly seen on Figure 11.B. Here the important national strike waves, as defined by Charles Tilly,[5] of 1899–1903, 1912–13, 1917–20, 1934, 1937, and 1941–43 stand out. Especially arresting is the pronounced importance of the war-time strike waves, 1917–20 and 1941–43. We shall return to these waves later.

Another way to consider the frequency of strikes is to control for the size of the labour force and measure strikes per 1,000,000 non-agricultural employees. (For details on methodology see Part II.) When this statistic is calculated the strike-prone first two decades of the twentieth century led the way with the 1930s and 1940s following (see Table 11.2).

In addition to frequency, of course, there are other important measures of strike activity. The number of strikers and the duration of strikes are the two other most-cited strike variables. On a national level, strikes declined in size in the 1900s, increased in the 1910s, fell slightly in the 1920s and more rapidly in the 1930s, and then exploded in the 1940s. Meanwhile, duration fell constantly with the exception of the 1920s when it increased to its highest point in the decades under study. The decline in duration in the 1930s and 1940s was especially sharp.

In this paper we must assume the general contours of the national economic picture as we currently understand them. Let me describe them briefly, however, so there is no confusion.[6] Canada burst out of the 1890s depression into a period of rapid and sustained economic growth before World War I. Massive immigration, western settlement, the construction of two new transcontinental railroad systems, metal mining booms in the west and in northern Ontario, all figured in this major surge. In addition, immense imports of American capital in the form of branch plants brought to Canada all the advances in United States corporate strategies. A Canadian "second" industrial revolution took place simultaneously with the American and transformed Canadian workplaces in all the same ways. Scientific managers, multi-plant organization, assembly line production, all arrived in the two decades before World War I. The war experience simply intensified these changes. After an initial post-war depression the national economy

Table 11.2
National Strike Dimensions, 1891–1950

	Frequency (strikes/1m. non-agricultural employees)	Size (workers involved/ strike)	Duration (working days/ strike)
1891–1900	55	218	25
1901–10	115	180	23
1911–20	123	286	20
1921–30	43	270	30
1931–40	61	218	11
1941–50	70	452	9

recovered in the 1920s and received another major infusion of American capital in the late 1920s. As in the earlier wave, this set off a merger movement of significant proportions. In general, Canadian economic development closely parallelled the American in this period and the better-known generalizations of Brody, Montgomery, and Gordon, Reich and Edwards on the interaction of economic change and the working-class movement are broadly applicable.[7] The 1930s, of course, were a decade of depression, ended only by the outbreak of World War II. As in World War I the working class mobilized strongly and made major strides in the later war years which they fought to maintain the war's aftermath.

In Canadian historical writing since the 1960s region has received considerable attention. This regional influence has also been evident in the historiography of the working class. Heavily influenced by the work of Herbert Gutman, much recent work in the field has consisted of community studies either of towns or cities or coal-mining districts.[8] Even specific studies of strike activity have tended to be regional in focus such as McKay's work on the Maritimes from 1901–14, Heron and Palmer's on southern Ontario in the same period, and Jacques Rouillard and James Thwaite's studies of Quebec.[9] On occasion this regional interpretation had almost degenerated into cheerleading for the militancy of a regions' workers, often at the expense of some other regions' putative lack of radicalism. This problem is most evident in David Bercuson's attempt to retain a "western exceptionalist" argument in the face of compelling contrary evidence.[10] Indeed, to a large degree, the assertiveness of the western historian's claims has led to a distorted debate.[11]

Our data has been disaggregated by province which allows a consideration of Canadian strike activity in terms of regional variation (see Tables 11.3, 11.D, and 11.E). Table 11.3 shows the results of this regional tabulation. As can be seen, there has been significant variation over

Table 11.3
Canadian Strikes by Region, 1891–1950

	British Columbia and Alberta		Saskatchewan and Manitoba		*Percentage of total strikes*[a] Ontario		Quebec		Maritimes	
	% strikes	% workers involved	% strikes	% workers involved	% strikes	% workers involved	% strikes	% workers involved	% strikes	% workers involved
1891–1900	15	28	5	2	49	21	19	30	10	10
1901–10	14	19	7	5	43	24	19	26	17	18
1911–20	26	32	8	9	39	24	16	20	10	14
1921–30	24	21	6	1	35	15	19	20	15	39
1931–40	17	13	8	2	41	28	14	22	19	32
1941–50	16	18	4	1	36	32	23	24	20	25

a Totals do not equal 100 because Yukon, Northwest Territories, Newfoundland, and itnerprovincial (except coal mining) strikes have been omitted.

time, although central Canada has never fallen below 54 per cent of the total strikes. The western strike scene has been dominated by Alberta and British Columbia and peaked in the 1910s and 1920s, whereas in eastern Canada, equally dominated by Nova Scotia, the peaks came in the 1920s, 1930s, and 1940s. Quebec, too, enjoyed later prominence, while Ontario's highest figures occurred before World War I and during the Great Depression.

One rough method of measuring leadership in provincial strike activity, which incorporates the three measures (frequency, size, and duration), is simply to rank each province by decade on all three measures. When this is done using the data presented in Table 11.G, we achieve an ordering which shows Alberta, Nova Scotia, and British Columbia leading in strike frequency; Nova Scotia, Quebec, and British Columbia ahead in strike size; and British Columbia, Manitoba, and Ontario at the top in the length of strikes. Running the three measures together for an even rougher proxy for strike leadership, we find British Columbia, Nova Scotia, Alberta, Ontario, and Quebec in the lead.[12]

A more intensive look at the 1891–50 data allows further comment on provincial variation (see Figure 11.D and Tables 11.D and 11.E). Prince Edward Island, primarily an agricultural province, trailed national statistics on almost all measures for each decade. New Brunswick and Nova Scotia, however, calling into further question their putative image of conservatism, often exceeded the national levels. Nova Scotia, for example, exceeded national figures for strike frequency in the 1900s and 1920s and for size in all six decades, leading the nation in five of the six. In each case, coal and steel help to explain the higher numbers. New Brunswick exceeded national frequency in the 1900s and 1910s, and again in the 1940s, largely owing to the militancy of Saint John workers, but, lacking Nova Scotia's industrial concentration, was consistently beneath national size figures except in the 1930s. In duration, Nova Scotia saw longer than national average strikes in the 1900s, largely owing to the tri-partite Great Strike of 1909–11 in the coal fields of Springhill, Inverness, and Glace Bay. In general, the old accepted wisdom of Atlantic provinces' labour quiescence is badly damaged by this data. Moreover, it is not simply a phenomenon of the pre-World War I period as studied by McKay or the 1920s insurrection in Cape Breton. Indeed Nova Scotia's national prominence reached its peak in the 1930s and 1940s when the province was the scene not only for the most frequent strikes in the nation but also the largest. Meanwhile New Brunswick saw the nations' third largest strikes in the Depression and third most frequent in the 1940s, both above the national average.

In central Canada, Quebec was consistently beneath the national figures for frequency but consistently above them for size, partially owing to large strikes in textiles and boot and shoe in the early years especially. In duration it was lower in all decades except the 1920s when it led the nation. Ontario simply reversed that pattern. Often higher in frequency, owing to the preponderance of small manufacturing and building trades strikes, it trailed the national figures for size in each decade. While Ontario strikes exceeded the national duration figures in the 1890s, thereafter they were almost identical to the national average.

In the west, largely agricultural Saskatchewan behaved like Prince Edward Island in the east, falling below national figures on all measures except duration in the 1930s and 1940s. Manitoba on the other hand, had more frequent strikes in the 1890s, 1900s, and 1930s. Only in the World War I decade were Manitoba strikes larger than the national average, primarily because of the general strikes of 1918 and 1919, while throughout the first 40 years they were always shorter, although this reversed itself in the 1930s and 1940s. Alberta and British Columbia, on the other hand, exceeded national figures for frequency for all decades (except for BC in the 1940s), and with the exception of BC in the 1920s and Alberta in the 1940s did the same for duration. In size Alberta strikes in the 1910s and 1920s exceeded national figures as did BC strikes in all but the 1920s and 1930s (see Table 11.G).

Extremely important in contributing to the provincial and regional patterns of Canadian strike activity has been the geographic distribution in the country of manufacturing and of resource extraction. The shifting regional balance of strike activity was related not only to the opening of the west but also to the nation's resource/industrial mix. The literature on strike propensity is by now huge and cannot be reviewed here. The Canadian data contain few surprises. Data problems limit these discussions to the years after 1911 (see Table 11.F and Figure 11.D.) The massive importance of mining in terms of frequency and size, far exceeding national figures in every decade, makes clear why it dominates the industrial side of Figure 11.D and in the process also helps to explain the graphic dominance of British Columbia, Alberta, and Nova Scotia on the provincial side. In frequency, construction with many small local building trades strikes held second place in the 1910s and 1920s with manufacturing replacing it in second in the 1930s and 1940s, with the rise of industrial unionism, and exceeding the national average throughout. Meanwhile transportation and service trailed behind throughout the period with transportation exceeding the national level only once in the 1910s. In size, however, transportation, owing to a number of massive railroad strikes, switched places with construction and surpassed manufacturing as well in the 1910s and 1940s. The service and public administration sectors with few organized workers, were last on both measures and never exceeded the national figures. In duration manufacturing struggles led with the longest average strikes followed by mining and construction in the 1910s, by transportation in the 1920s, and by service in the 1930s and 1940s.

The discussion of strike issues is fraught with ambiguity. Needless to say, wages almost always figure prominently, both in times of union strength and weakness. What changes, of course, is whether the strike aims to increase workers' earnings or to prevent employers' incursions against the wage packet. Thus one anticipates struggles for higher wages in period of boom accompanied by tight labour markets and battles to maintain wage levels in periods of economic decline and high unemployment. Table 11.4 demonstrates this hypothesis rather well with 15 years in which strikes for wage increases exceeded 40 per cent. Of these 15, fully 10 were associated with the strike waves that we identified earlier. In the 11 years in which strikes against wage cuts surpassed 20 per cent, all were in periods of economic distress. The multiplicity of issues involved in almost every strike makes generalizations about other elements in each dispute hard to sustain, but Table 11.4 minimally demonstrates the pervasiveness of work-related struggles and battles concerning union rights.

Similarly, methods of dispute settlement throw only limited light at this gross aggregate level, especially given the high number for which the method was unknown. Yet in the years of the strike waves we can detect increases in settlements by negotiation and third-party intervention combined and, more obviously, decreases in resolutions involving the return or replacement of the striking workers. In contrast, years of economic trauma for workers led to the disastrous strike records (see Table 11.5.)

A perusal of strike results in Table 11.6 shows some interesting patterns. Until the early 1920s generally 20 to 30 per cent of strike results were either indefinite or undetermined. In that period, the strike wave years of 1902–3, 1912, and 1917–19 were the only years in which strikers won more strikes than employers in the box scores (with the sole exception of 1916). Similarly, if we add workers' victories and compromises together, it is only in the strike wave years of 1900–2, 1912, and 1917–19 that workers exceeded a success rate of 50 per cent (again with the exception of 1916). On the employers' side the depression years of 1893–94, 1896, 1908, and 1921–24 all saw bosses' victories rocket above 40 per cent. In the period from the mid

Table 11.4
Strike Issues, 1891–1950[a]

	Issues					
	Earnings		Working conditions			Other and indefinite
	For change	Against change	Hours	Other	Unionism	
			Percentage of Total Issues			
1891	26	3	16	24	18	13
1892	25	20	15	20	15	5
1893	24	22	–	38	8	8
1894	17	40	2	27	6	8
1895	27	18	9	32	7	7
1896	18	21	5	21	23	13
1897	36	15	13	21	8	8
1898	30	8	8	25	25	5
1899	42	9	3	23	18	6
1900	40	6	8	19	22	6
1901	39	8	13	25	11	5
1902	39	3	15	13	20	10
1903	40	3	12	16	20	8
1904	35	6	11	26	18	3
1905	35	5	11	26	16	7
1906	38	2	15	17	21	8
1907	44	4	12	16	20	5
1908	25	3	10	23	10	9
1909	44	8	5	18	21	4
1910	38	5	9	23	15	10
1911	40	5	11	16	22	7
1912	41	3	16	18	16	6
1913	44	6	13	13	15	10
1914	23	24	4	19	23	8
1915	30	15	4	26	20	6
1916	50	6	9	16	16	3
1917	46	4	14	13	17	5
1918	44	3	13	15	16	10
1919	39	3	26	10	14	8
1920	45	3	15	16	16	5
1921	12	41	16	13	15	3
1922	18	38	7	12	21	4
1923	37	8	9	19	20	7
1924	29	16	11	22	18	3
1925	23	20	9	19	27	2
1926	32	8	12	21	23	4
1927	32	4	11	23	23	6
1928	33	9	5	23	25	6
1929	41	3	6	31	16	3
1930	32	15	8	17	25	2
1931	13	29	3	23	26	6

Table 11.4 (continued)

	Earnings		Working conditions			Other and indefinite
			Issues			
	For change	Against change	Hours	Other	Unionism	
			Percentage of Total Issues			
1932	14	31	5	27	20	4
1933	33	10	11	19	24	3
1934	35	6	15	15	26	3
1935	36	2	10	24	25	3
1936	35	3	10	19	30	3
1937	42	1	9	18	28	3
1938	28	8	10	21	30	3
1939	29	5	8	34	20	4
1940	33	3	6	36	16	5
1941	45	1	4	23	21	5
1942	47	2	4	28	16	3
1943	39	1	3	36	18	3
1944	28	2	3	43	16	7
1945	29	1	2	39	19	9
1946	33	1	14	20	21	12
1947	37	1	8	12	28	15
1948	38	2	5	13	30	13
1949	34	1	7	16	30	11
1950	30	3	8	20	31	10

a Issues articulated at the beginning of each strike. More than one issue for some strikes.

1920s to 1950 the undetermined or indefinite category almost always fell well below 20 per cent. In these years workers' victories exceeded employers' in 1925, and, perhaps surprisingly, in 1933–38. The combination of victories and compromises exceeded 60 per cent in 1933–38, 1941, and 1947. Meanwhile, employers' successes topped 40 per cent in 1930, 1932, and 1943–45. thus, the pattern of the first three decades which clearly related the strike waves and high success rates is less apparent during the Great Depression and World War II. Workers in the 1930s enjoyed high rates of success in both the strike wave years of 1934 and 1937 and in 1933, 1935–36, and 1938. On the other hand, the militancy of workers during World War II was rewarded with far lower rates of success, even in one of the three years of the 1941–43 strike wave. It seems likely that the extremely high rate of third party settlements of 1941–45 (Table 11.5) is related to the lower rate of success. During World War II state involvement in labour relations reached unprecedented heights with the advent of PC 1003 in 1944, which was later entrenched as the Industrial Relations and Labour Disputes Investigation Act of 1948.[13]

Table 11.5
Methods of Strike Settlement, 1891–1950

	Methods				
Year	Negotiations	Third party	Return of workers	Replacement of workers	Indefinite
	Percentage of total strikes				
1891	23	5	15	18	38
1892	35	8	13	13	33
1893	30	5	23	18	25
1894	26	3	28	10	33
1895	23	10	36	5	26
1896	32	3	19	19	26
1897	24	9	15	18	35
1898	38	2	14	18	28
1899	38	3	3	22	30
1900	35	10	20	11	25
1901	40	12	12	17	19
1902	38	12	9	11	29
1903	37	10	13	11	29
1904	40	8	17	13	22
1905	43	2	10	24	21
1906	46	4	14	22	15
1907	44	7	12	15	23
1908	28	5	27	24	16
1809	29	7	15	22	27
1910	38	6	15	16	24
1911	33	7	14	16	31
1912	47	6	10	15	23
1913	38	7	14	15	28
1914	28	10	12	22	27
1915	40	13	12	20	16
1916	43	13	13	11	20
1917	43	18	11	7	21
1918	41	23	13	6	17
1919	49	13	13	8	17
1920	38	12	13	13	24
1921	37	10	14	18	21
1922	39	6	16	19	10
1923	40	13	20	14	12
1924	41	15	25	15	4
1925	57	9	6	16	11
1926	46	7	12	23	12
1927	49	9	20	12	9
1928	47	12	18	16	7
1929	41	14	17	18	10
1930	41	14	19	20	7
1931	40	13	19	19	9
1932	44	12	18	21	4
1933	56	12	14	11	8

Table 11.5 (continued)

Year	Negotiations	Third party	Return of workers	Replacement of workers	Indefinite
			Methods		
			Percentage of total strikes		
1934	55	12	14	16	4
1935	49	21	8	14	6
1936	51	20	9	13	8
1937	49	24	11	11	5
1938	37	34	14	9	6
1939	32	25	30	7	6
1940	35	23	28	9	5
1941	30	37	23	7	3
1942	23	50	19	5	3
1943	26	54	17	2	2
1944	17	56	20	3	4
1945	17	49	31	1	3
1946	24	46	22	5	4
1947	36	32	17	8	7
1948	37	30	20	4	8
1949	45	26	16	4	9
1950	32	23	20	7	18

Table 11.6
Strike Results, 1891–1950

Year	Workers' favour	Compromise	Employers' favour	Indefinite
		Results		
		Percentage of total strikes		
1891	18	10	33	38
1892	28	8	30	35
1893	16	9	52	23
1894	13	10	44	33
1895	8	18	38	36
1896	19	16	42	23
1897	6	21	38	35
1898	8	22	38	32
1899	23	12	32	34
1900	23	16	31	29
1901	27	23	30	20
1902	35	21	19	25
1903	34	21	23	22
1904	28	20	31	21
1905	25	14	36	25
1906	24	21	37	18

Table 11.6 (continued)

Year	Workers' favour	Compromise	Employers' favour	Indefinite
		Results		
	Percentage of total strikes			
1907	21	26	31	23
1908	20	10	53	18
1909	19	18	39	24
1910	19	16	37	28
1911	15	17	33	35
1912	29	23	27	21
1913	21	21	29	29
1914	16	16	34	33
1915	21	21	35	23
1916	26	30	25	19
1917	40	20	19	21
1918	34	26	16	24
1919	30	24	28	18
1920	18	23	32	27
1921	16	13	47	24
1922	14	22	43	20
1923	26	19	42	13
1924	16	23	47	15
1925	36	23	28	13
1926	26	22	36	15
1927	31	21	37	11
1928	28	26	37	9
1929	30	24	35	11
1930	27	24	43	5
1931	27	24	37	13
1932	29	20	46	5
1933	34	27	32	6
1934	37	26	33	4
1935	41	27	25	7
1936	41	24	24	11
1937	29	37	25	9
1938	29	35	26	11
1939	26	31	35	8
1940	16	41	35	7
1941	22	38	30	10
1942	27	23	39	11
1943	34	20	40	6
1944	28	22	43	7
1945	19	25	48	8
1946	24	33	32	10
1947	25	35	25	14
1948	22	37	25	16
1949	15	36	23	26
1950	18	33	29	20

While the state's role as conciliator, mediator, and "umpire" in class conflict has received considerable attention in Canadian labour historiography recently, the state's coercive function was also extremely important throughout this period as can be seen in Tables 11.7–9.[14] Despite the state's enthusiastic recourse to coercion, violence of a serious kind was rare in Canadian strikes. Workers remained aware of the state's potential for violence and behaved in a generally disciplined fashion. As can be seen in Table 11.7 strikes involving collective violence fluctuated in number over our period reaching a peak during the Great Depression. On the other hand, military intervention all but disappeared by the 1930s suggesting that it was not closely related to labour "violence." Its disappearance arose from an increasing public sentiment that sending in the troops was not an acceptable response to a labour dispute. The removal of the army, however, should not be equated with any decline in coercion. Police forces – national, provincial, and municipal – quickly filled any gap left by the changes in legislation governing military aid to the civil power.[15] Table 11.8 shows the pattern of collective violence in strikes on an industrial basis and demonstrates the significant shift that occurred in the 1930s with the spread of strike "violence" into the manufacturing sector and the invention of the sit-down strike as a weapon in labour's arsenal. Coal mining maintained its position throughout the period. Without doubt the 1930s witnessed the most "intense" strikes, to use Stuart Jamieson's phrase to describe strikes involving violence and illegality.[16] Over 40 per cent of all "violent" strikes occurred in that decade with Ontario leading the way with 47 incidents of strike-related collective violence, followed by Quebec (18), British Columbia (10), and Nova Scotia (8). Over the 40 years for which we collected this information those same four provinces led all others with 95, 59, 26, and 26 "violent" strikes respectively.

II

Let us now turn to the six strike waves of the period 1891–50 – 1899–1903, 1912–13, 1917–20, 1934, 1937, and 1942–43 (see Table 11.10). In many ways the first three waves are closely related. Certainly it can be argued that the 1917–20 wave was simply a continuation of the struggles of 1912–13 which came to an abrupt halt owing both to a depressed economy and to the outbreak of World War I. Yet, as we shall see, there were also key differences in these first three waves, shifts in both geographic and industrial focus which imbued the third wave, 1917–20, with a more menacing and insurgent character.

Table 11.7
Strikes with Collective Violence[a] and Military Intervention,[b] 1891–1940[c]

Decade	Percentage of total strikes with collective violence	Percentage of total strikes with military intervention
1891–1900	4.5	1.0
1901–10	2.6	1.0
1911–20	2.1	.7
1921–30	2.9	.5
1931–40	5.6	.2
1891–1940	3.3	.6

a These statistics were not intended originally to provide a measure of violence, but rather of an alternative form of collective action which, in this instance, happened to be strike-related. They count strikes in which a group of 50 or more acted together and attempted to seize or damage persons or objects not belonging to itself. This defiition was adapted from C., L., and R. Tilly, *The Rebellious Century, 1830–1930* (Cambridge, MA 1975), Appendix D, 313.

b Military aid to the civil power. Our work here was aided immensely by the work of Major J.J.B. Pariseau. See n. 15.

c Totals for 1930s exclude sitdowns which did not involve the use of force.

The 1899–1903 and 1912–13 strike waves were heavily dominated by the combination of manufacturing, construction, and transportation strikes both in terms of number of strikes and number of strikers (see Table 11.11). Geographically the 1899–1903 wave was concentrated in Ontario, while the 1912–13 wave found a more national focus. The greater contrast, however, comes in the 1917–20 wave in which the strikes spread themselves somewhat more evenly through the entire working class in terms of both occupational and geographic mix. The labour revolt of 1917–20 represented an insurgency involving almost all elements of the working class and covering the entire nation.

In the first wave of this period, 1899–1903, the 726 strikes involved roughly 120,000 workers. Manufacturing figured prominently averaging 49 per cent of the strikes in progress each year and 34 per cent of the strikers. Construction workers accounted for 23 per cent of the strikes but only 13 per cent of the strikers, while transportation workers' strikes made up 17 per cent of the total but involved 22 per cent of all strikers. The final major industrial actor, mining, accounted for 5 per cent of the strikes and 13 per cent of the strikers.

As the above figures suggest transportation and mining strikes tended to be much larger than manufacturing and especially construction strikes. Transportation and mining strikes, because of their size, militancy, and often national character, frequently seized the attention

Table 11.8
Strikes with Collective Violence and Military Intervention by Industry, 1891–1940

	1891–1930		1931–1940[a]		
Industry	Percentage of total strikes with collective violence	Percentage of total strikes with military intervention	percentage of total strikes with collective violence	Percentage of total strikes with sitdowns[b]	Percentage of total strikes with collective violence or sitdowns
Logging	–	–	10.0	1.4	11.4
Fishing and trapping	9.8	2.4	–	–	–
Mining	4.5	1.1	4.5	1.2	5.7
Manufacturing: total	1.7	.4	7.8	2.5	10.0
Manufacturing: leather and textile	2.4	.4	8.9	1.0	9.9
Manufacturing: wood	2.9	1.1	7.0	.8	7.8
Manufacturing: metal and ships	1.5	.4	6.3	7.3	11.5
Construction	1.4	.2	1.2	2.9	3.5
Transportation and public utilities: total	6.7	1.7	5.0	2.5	7.5
T. & P.U.: steam railway	6.3	1.0			
T. & P.U.: electric railway	20.7	8.1			
T. & P.U.: water	7.2	1.4			
Trade	1.7	–	8.3	–	
Service	1.2	.9	–	3.9	–
General	15.4	7.7	–	–	–
All industries	2.6	.6	5.6	2.3	8.0

a The military only intervened in four strikes in the 1930s (.3 per cent of mining and .4 per cent of manufacturing).
b Strikes in which workers occupied the workplace against the wishes of the employer and in which observers or participants termed this action a "sitdown" or "staydown."

Table 11.9
Strikes with Collective Violence, Military Intervention, and Sitdowns by Province and Decade, 1891–1940[a]

	1891–1900		1901–10		1911–20		1921–30		1931–40			Total		
	CV	MI	CV	MI	CV	MI	CV	MI	CV	MI	SD	CV	MI	SD
Nova Scotia	3	0	5	4	4	1	6	3	8	0	2	26	8	2
New Brunswick	0	0	1	0	2	2	2	1	3	0	0	8	3	0
Quebec	7	2	12	2	13	3	9	1	18	0	1	59	8	1
Ontario	12	2	18	8	16	6	2	0	47	2	24	95	18	24
Manitoba	0	0	3	1	2	1	1	0	8	0	0	14	2	0
Saskatchewan	0	0	1	0	0	0	0	0	2	2	1	3	2	1
Alberta	0	0	0	0	1	0	7	0	2	0	6	10	0	6
British Columbia	1	1	3	0	10	4	2	0	10	0	3	26	5	3
Total[b]	23	5	41	15	48	17	29	5	98	4	37	239	46	37

a Includes strikes in which the military was put on alert. Collective violence occurred in 36 of the 46 case of military intervention.

b Two railway strikes (CPR in 1908 and GTR in 1910) which featured collective violence in more than one province, are counted only once in the totals.

of the public and the state in this period. National strikes by Grand Trunk Railway trackmen in 1899, Canadian Pacific Railway (CPR) trackmen in 1901, and non-running trades CPR workers, organized into the United Brotherhood of Railway Employees (UBRE), an American Labor Union (ALU) affiliate, in 1903, all gained a national audience. Equally prominent were the struggles of Western Federation of Miners (WFM), metal miners in the BC interior, in 1899, 1900, and 1901, and especially the Vancouver Island and Crows Nest Pass coal mining strikes of 1903. The 1903 struggles led to the appointment of a Royal Commission to investigate Labour Unrest in British Columbia, to the passage of the Railway Labour Disputes Act, the state's first major effort to create a role for itself in "harmonizing" class relations, and to the virulent denunciation of all unions, initially only the so-called revolutionary unions such as the UBRE and the WFM, but later broadened to include an attack on all international unions.[17]

The state's fear of the ALU unions invokes no surprise, but the state attack on the American Federation of Labour (AFL), disdainfully termed the American "separation of labor" by syndicalists, demands further explanation. The strikes in the manufacturing and construction sectors provide part of the answer, although dramatic strikes on the Quebec, Vancouver, Montreal, and Halifax waterfronts in 1901, 1902, and 1903,[18] led by AFL-affiliated unions, and violence-laden strikes on the street railway systems of London, Toronto, and Montreal

Table 11.10
National Strike Waves, 1891–1950

	Given measure as a percentage of its mean over the previous five years[a]	
Year	Number of strikes (N)	Number of workers involved (W)
I		
1899	264	382
1900	219	448
1901	198	219
1902	199	98
1903	205	224
II		
1912	158	164
1913	150	147
III		
1917	132	190
1918	190	296
1919	244	412
1920	190	119
IV		
1934	204	266
V		
1937	203	221
VI		
1941	128	187
1942	182	202
1943	183	333

a The above list includes years for which N or W is above 150 if they are contiguous to years in which both N and W exceed 150. This is a slight modification on the Tilly and Shorter useage but is in line with Edwards, Strikes, 258. In the stricter useage 1902, 1913, 1917, 1920, and 1941 would be deleted.

in 1899, 1902, and 1903 which culminated in the use of the military against the striking AFL members of the Amalgamated Street Railway Workers Union, also played a role.[19]

A closer look at the manufacturing and construction sector reveals national patterns which closely resemble the detailed city and craft studies we have of this period. In manufacturing the strikes clustered in three major areas – the metal trades and shipbuilding, boot and shoe, and clothing and textiles. Over the five-year period these three groups accounted for 55 per cent of the strikers. The metal trades and shipbuilding accounted for 32 per cent of the manufacturing strikes and almost 20 per cent of the sector's strikers; clothing and textiles 16 per cent of strikes and 33 per cent of strikers; and boot and shoe 7

Table 11.11
National Strike Waves by Region and Industry

	Waves											
	1899–1903		1912–13		1917–20		1934		1937		1941–43	
	% strikes	% workers involved	% strikes	% workers involved	% strikes	% workers involved	% strikes	% workers involved	% strikes	% workers involved	% strikes	% workers involved
REGION												
East[a]	12	9	13	6	10	16	13	24	18	25	24	31
Quebec	19	33	13	18	17	19	17	28	15	34	28	31
Ontario	50	21	45	31	35	23	49	34	49	35	31	22
West	18	30	28	43	38	39	20	14	18	7	17	15
INDUSTRY												
Mining[b]	5	13	5	13	12	25	13	28	15	24	21	26
Manufacturing	49	34	35	26	41	36	59	55	48	64	58	59
Construction	23	13	36	38	15	8	4	1	11	2	7	2
Transportation	17	22	15	14	12	13	6	1	7	2	5	3
Trade and service	4	–	8	1	11	4	9	2	13	2	7	3

a Totals do not equal 100 because territorial and interprovincial (except coal mining) strikes have been excluded.
b Totals to not equal 100 because agricultural, fishing, logging, miscellaneous, and interinudstrial strikes have been excluded.

per cent of the strikes but 25 per cent of the strikers. Clearly the shape of strikes in these three manufacturing areas was quite different. In the metal trades strikes were small but frequent, while in clothing and textile, and in boot and shoe they tended to be less frequent but much larger.

Metal workers' strikes primarily revolved around shop floor struggles concerning control issues. Moulders and machinists fought the largest number of such battles but boiler, core, and pattern makers also participated. While active in most major Canadian cities, Ontario metal workers were the most prominent in these strikes. One particularly bitter struggle in Toronto involved almost 300 moulders against the city's major foundries. The moulders sought the nine-hour day and over eight months found themselves facing scabs, injunctions, and even *agents provocateurs*. The strike ultimately failed.[20]

Quebec workers, however, played the major role in the other strike-prone manufacturing sectors of boot and shoe and clothing and textiles. Major conflicts in boot and shoe came in Quebec City in 1900 and 1903 when industry-wide strikes occurred involving 4,000 and 5,000 workers respectively in lengthy struggles. Similarly, the major textile strikes occurred in Quebec. The troops were sent in to Magog to quell a strike of 900 unorganized workers against Dominion Cotton in early August 1900. Dominion Cotton defeated its workers and rid its mill of a union in Montmorency where it simply outlasted 600 Knights of Labor strikers who were forced to concede after two months on the picket line. In Valleyfield, however, 1,500 workers at Montreal Cotton walked out in late January for six days but returned pending an increase. They struck again on 21 February in even larger numbers (2,500), after rejecting the company's offer. They subsequently compromised and again returned, but struck again in July for four days against company employment policy. In October, when the militia was called in to break a strike by 200 construction workers building a new cotton mill, 3,000 cotton workers walked out in sympathy and returned only after the troops were withdrawn.[21]

Construction strikes in this period were dominated by the building trades which constitute 81 per cent of the 174 strikes and 91 per cent of the approximately 16,000 strikers. The other construction strikes were on nine railroad, seven canal, and five highway or bridge projects. Although ubiquitous in Canadian towns and cities in these years and while generally short in duration and small in number of workers involved, there were exceptions. Some 700 Sydney, Nova Scotia, bricklayers, stonemasons, and plasterers, for example, struck for seven months in 1901 before gaining a wage increase and shorter hours. That same summer almost 400 Ottawa carpenters were off the job for about six weeks to win wage increases and changes in work rules. Later that year 400 Winnipeg carpenters failed in their almost two-month-long strike to gain higher wages and shorter hours. In 1903, however, Toronto was the site for a city-wide building trades strike which involved almost 1,000 carpenters, over 3,000 building labourers, 250 painters, and over 100 structural iron workers in a 10-week strike which the employers ultimately won.[22] The issues for Canadian building trades workers in these years were identical to those faced by their English comrades. *The Ragged Trousered Philanthropists* described the experience of North American building trades workers.

Despite defeats such as those mentioned above, strikers did well in the years 1899–1903. Strikes were largely offensive and the success rate (victories plus compromises) ranged from an 1899 low of 35 per cent to a 1902 high of 56 per cent. In 1902 and 1903 clear-cut victories outnumbered defeats (see Table 11.6).

Similarly during the second strike wave, 1912–13, the primarily offensive strikes led to a 52 per cent success rate in 1912 and 42 per cent in 1913, although in the latter year employers' clear-cut victories rose above full workers' victories. As we noted earlier the dominance of manufacturing, construction, and transportation and of BC, Ontario, and Quebec still prevailed in this pre-World War I strike wave but some broadening in geographic and industrial mix is evident compared to 1899–1903 (see Table 11.11). This widening is more apparent geographically and can be explained by the much greater presence of the west. The admittedly less clear spread in industrial mix stems from a rise in strikes in the trade and service sector. Numerous small trade and service sector strikes composed 8 per cent of the strike total but only 1 per cent of strikers. Nevertheless, union incursions into trades and services indicates a broadening of the labour movement in this pre-war period.

A dissection of the statistics for the three largest industrial groups also shows some changes from the previous strike wave. Construction displaced manufacturing as the leader in both strikes and strikers with 36 per cent and 38 per cent compared to manufacturing's 35 and 26 per cent. Transportation trailed each with 15 per cent of strikes and 14 per cent of strikers, perhaps indicating at least one minor area of success for the IDIA.

The primacy of construction strikes is based not only on the 141 building trades strikes in the two years but on significant strike actions among construction workers on railroad, canal, and road projects who added 28 strikes which accounted for 45 per cent of total construction strikers. By far the most dramatic of these was the Industrial Workers of the World (iww) strike in British Columbia on the construction of the Canadian Northern Railway. Some 6,000–7,000 railway navvies, almost all immigrants, struck for five months in the face of severe state repression and overt co-operation between the construction companies and the provincial government. At least 250 Wobblies were jailed, receiving sentences of up to 12 months for offences such as vagrancy and infractions of the Public Health Act. Not surprisingly, in the face of such repression the strike was broken. Needless to says its memory lived on, commemorated in Joe Hill's "Where the Fraser River Flows."[23]

Among the urban building trade strikes of these two years one of the largest involved 2,000 Winnipeg carpenters for almost six weeks in the summer of 1912. Their strike to win recognition, wage increases, and shorter hours was eventually successful.[24] Similarly, some 300 Halifax carpenters left work on 1 April 1913 and returned about a month later with a settlement largely in their favour. The historian of these carpenters notes that this strike "marked a new level of militancy and a significant broadening of perspective on the part of Local 83." He further argues, and our Winnipeg example would support his claim, that their pre-war apprenticeship in the "new rules" of monopoly capitalist society lay the groundwork for "their post-war radicalism."[25]

Interestingly, not all urban construction strikes involved skilled craftsmen and craft unions. In Ottawa in 1912 and in Hamilton in 1913 large groups of unskilled labourers, the urban equivalents of the railway navvies, struck for higher wages. In Ottawa about 1,100 labourers employed on sewer projects succeeded in increasing their wages after three days of marching and demonstrating. The next year 250 Hamilton labourers, largely immigrant, working on electrical transmission lines struck for a wage increase but failed after three days which included a battle with strikebreakers.[26] Again in this case the importance lies in the suggestion that resort to strike action was spreading to workers previously uninvolved in labour activities.

In manufacturing a disaggregation of the general data suggests an intensification of the 1899–1903 pattern. In 1912 and 1913, metal trades strikes accounted for 37 per cent of all manufacturing strikes and 20 per cent of that sector's strikes; clothing and textile 25 per cent of strikes and a remarkable 50 per cent of strikers; and boot and shoe 7 and 16 per cent. The three together then represent 69 per cent of all manufacturing strikes and 86 per cent of all manufacturing strikers. One major development hidden in these statistics is the emergence of garments strikes as a major component of the textile and clothing category. Major garment strikes were fought by the United Garment Workers of America (UGWA) in Montreal in 1912 and 1913, the first involving 4,500 workers in the men's clothing industry for six weeks. The industry-wide 1912 strike succeeded in increasing wages, shortening hours, and changing pay systems and shop rules. The following year, a strike against a wage reduction at one shop involving 450 workers dragged on for five months before failing. In Hamilton in April 1913, 2,000 garment workers led by the UGWA struck the city's four major clothing factories and within two weeks had won a victory. The solidarity of women workers was crucial in this victory as in the 1912 Montreal case.[27] The other major garment strike took place in Toronto in 1912 against Eaton's, the city's major department store. The strike, led by the International Ladies Garment Workers Union (ILGWU), quickly became a *cause célèbre* because of the national prominence of the firm and its Methodist owners. originating with male sewing machine operators who refused to perform women's work (finishing) for no increase in pay, the strike was fought avowedly to save women's jobs and its Yiddish slogan translates as "We will not take morsels of bread from our sisters' mouths." Over 1,000 garment workers, about one-third women, struck in support of the 65 men. The strikers gained wide support from the labour movement and a national boycott against Eaton's enjoyed some limited success. In Montreal ILGWU workers in Eaton's shops struck in sympathy with their Toronto counterparts. Nevertheless the strike was broken after four months and the ILGWU took some four years to recover in Toronto.[28] Here again the important point to note is the spread of unionism and militancy among previously unorganized sectors and specifically among immigrants and women. Also important was the concerted turn to industrial unionism by many of the craft unions, particularly in the metal trades.[29]

This process is evident as well in some of the transportation-related strikes of the period. Coal handlers on the Port Arthur docks, primarily southern European, struck in 1919. The 250 workers won their strike but only at considerable cost because two of their Italian members received ten-year jail terms for assaulting the Chief of Police in a violent picket line altercation which left several strikers wounded and resulted in the militia being called out.[30]

Similarly street railway strikes in Port Arthur and Halifax in 1913 led to violent encounters between crowds and strikebreakers. In the Lakehead the workers lost after a month-long war with scabs and the ubiquitous Thiel detectives; the major battle in this campaign came in mid-May when a crowd overturned a street car and then attacked a police station in an attempt to free an arrested comrade. In the foray against the police station a striker was killed. In Halifax, the strike lasted only one week before a compromise settlement was reached.

Major mining struggles in Canada have played a major part in the national strike waves, and indeed miners have maintained high levels of struggle even in periods outside of the national waves. The Vancouver Island coal strike of 1912–14 which lasted from 16 September 1912 to 19 August 1914, was a major struggle of this wave. Military metaphors seem only too appropriate for the strike because it was actually closer to war than any other strike in this period. Violence incited by strikebreakers, special police, and the Canadian army was endemic and the two-year experience could only be described as a state invasion of the coal towns. The miners finally returned to the mines in late summer 1914 when the outbreak of war ended the possibility of proposed BC Federation of Labour-led general strike.[31] Lest BC coal miners be thought to have received special treatment at the hands of the Canadian state, let us consider the parallel case of northern Ontario gold miners who endured a seven-month struggle from mid-November 1912 to mid-June 1913 in an attempt to gain an increase in wages and shorter hours. These South Porcupine members of the Western Federation of Miners faced strikebreakers, Thiel detectives, and changes and convictions under the Industrial Disputes Investigation Act.[32]

The most dramatic strike wave consisted of the labour revolt of 1917–20. In those four years workers struck more frequently and in larger numbers than ever before in Canadian history. From 1917–20 there were 1,384 strikes involving almost 360,000 workers which expressed as percentages means those four years accounted for just over 14 per cent of all Canadian strikes between 1891 and 1950 and about 14 per cent of all strikers. As Table 11.11 shows this strike wave, more than its predecessors, was national in scope. The previous dominance of Ontario here gives way to a more balanced nation-wide effort, although with a very heavy western presence. Most evident, however, is the sectoral balance. Mining struggles played a much more significant role in the 1917–20 strike wave, as did the impressive increase in trade and service strikes, many of them, as we shall see, involving public sector workers. Equally important is the vast increase in the "other" category which includes general strikes and also the spread of trade unionism and strike activity among loggers.

As in most strike waves, success fed on success. In 1917 outright workers' victories hit their highest level in the 60-year period (except for 1935 and 1936) and when combined with compromises totalled 60 per cent. The same held true for 1918, when employers' victories reached their 60 year low. In 1919 employers' victories began to climb back up, however, reaching 28 per cent, although worker gains stayed high at 54 per cent. By 1920, the wave was breaking and employers won 32 per cent outright, while workers' victories and compromises fell to 41 per cent (see Table 11.6).

The literature on the events of 1917 to 1920 and especially of 1919 is huge; and, one of us has been adding to it recently.[33] Here we would simply like to emphasize some points made in these earlier articles and amplify on some other which we feel were not adequately emphasized.

First, the 1917–20 events in Canada were part of the same international working-class insurgency that engulfed all industrial nations in those years. The new international literature on the working-class revolt at war's end focuses on issues reflected in Canadian events. Thus James Cronin's comments about the movements' "similarity and simultaneity" applies to Canada, indeed to North America, as well as to Europe.[34] In addition, as Cronin argues for Europe, the labour revolt should be seen as continuous from the pre-war crisis. While much that was new occurred in 1917–20, the general patterns had been amply prefigured in 1912–13. The war contributed an intensity and a breadth to the later struggles but it did not create them.

A disaggregation of Canadian manufacturing strike data for these years demonstrates these continuities and a few discontinuities. Using the same categories as before, we discover that boot and shoe almost disappeared from the strike statistics. Over the four years the industry contained only 2 per cent of the manufacturing strikes and less than 1 per cent of the strikers. Clothing and textiles, on the other hand, while nowhere near as prominent as in 1912–13, accounted for 16 per cent of both strikes and strikers. In both industries a renewed militancy struggled for industrial unionism. Our third category, metal and shipbuilding, provides the most significant story. For here the continuities of struggle and their particular intensification owing to the war experience become clearest. The metal trades constitute 33 per cent of manufacturing strikes and 30 per cent of strikers, while its cognate industry shipbuilding added 11 per cent of strikes and 24 per cent of strikers. Workers in other manufacturing sectors who begin to show up in the data for the first time included pulp and paper (5 per cent of manufacturing strikes and strikers), rubber (2 and 3 per cent) and meat packing (2 and 4 per cent). In meat packing successful industry-wide strikes in Toronto and Montreal in 1919 set a pattern for the industry which workers in other meat packing centres fought to gain in the next two years. Here again it was new industrial unionism that won the day.[35]

In addition to the new industrial unions, which were primarily sanctioned by the AFL, trade unionism spread into other new areas. The spread of organization to increased numbers of women workers we shall not pursue here and the great importance of immigrant workers one of us has discussed elsewhere. We would note here, however, the crucial and innovative rise of public sector unionism especially at the municipal level but also among some provincial and federal workers.

Two major strikes represent two distinct manifestations of this process. The first was the month-long Winnipeg civic workers' strike of May 1918 which ended only when Borden's Minister of Labour, Senator Gideon Robertson, hurried to Winnipeg to prevent the expansion of sympathy strikes into a threatened city-wide general sympathetic strike.[36] Such discussions were led by the Winnipeg Trade and Labour Council (TLC) but were not confined to it. The Jewish immigrant left, for example, organized a late May Help the Strikers Conference which brought together all radical elements of the Jewish community – revolutionary Marxist, Socialist-Zionist, and anarchist.[37] To end the crisis and avoid a general strike, Robertson capitulated to almost all of the civic workers' demands. In the process, he helped to cement in Winnipeg and Canadian workers' minds the efficacy of the general strike tactic. But Robertson's concession was not singular, a similar threat by the Edmonton TLC led to the recognition of the firemen's union in that city. In general, there was a massive expansion throughout the country of civil employees' unionism usually organized into Federal Labour Unions directly chartered by the TLC.

Federal employees also expressed massive dissatisfaction with wartime conditions. For example, the Civil Service Federation of Canada enjoyed major growth, which unfortunately remains unstudied.[38] Instead let us consider the major public sector strike of 1918, namely the 1918 national postal strike led by the Federal Association of Letter Carriers.[39] Commencing in Toronto on 22 July 1918, with at best half-hearted support from the union's national leader Alex McMordie, the strike spread across the country involving over 20 cities and led to sympathetic walkouts by other postal workers. Supposedly settled on 15 July by McMordie, who ordered his workers back in return for a promise of a cabinet investigation, the strike continued across the country as many rank-and-file letter carriers angrily rejected the settlement. A week later Borden Cabinet Ministers Crothers and Meighen arrived in Winnipeg to negotiate a new agreement with an ad hoc Joint Strike Committee again in the face of a series of threatened general strikes in a number of western cities, including Winnipeg, Vancouver, and Victoria, and, significantly, by UMWA District 18. The terms of settlement included guarantees of non-discrimination against the strikers, the dismissal of all scab labour, and, amazingly, pay for the strikers for the period of the walkout.

But perhaps most alarming of all to the Canadian bourgeoisie in 1918 was the emergence of police unionism. In ten major Canadian cities TLC-affiliated police activists organized unions that year. In Ontario the provincial government set up a Royal Commission to consider the question of police unionism.[40] Only in Ottawa did civic officials quell the dissent by firing almost one-third of the force. In Toronto, Victoria, Vancouver, Edmonton, Calgary, Winnipeg, Saint John, Montreal, and Quebec, serious struggles over the question of police unionism occurred, but trade union rights won out. In Toronto, for example, Police Magistrate Dennison remembered that during the 1886 street railway strike law and order prevailed only because "Our police force was able to keep them down." "If they had been in a union," he concluded, "I don't suppose they would have been able to do such good work."[41] Nevertheless, Toronto Police FLU No. 68 gained initial recognition after a successful strike to protest the firing of 11 union leaders. Meanwhile, in Montreal a common front of some 1,500 firemen and policemen struck in December. They gained victory in the aftermath of a night of rioting in which volunteer strikebreakers were beaten and fire stations were occupied by crowds supporting the strikers.[42] In Vancouver the threat of a general strike after the firing of four police union leaders led to an ignominious surrender by the Chief Constable. But it was in Saint John, New Brunswick, that the degree of labour solidarity with these efforts found its most profound expression. The firing of half the force for joining a union led to a city-wide campaign organized by the labour movement to recall the police commissioners guilty of the victimization of the police unionists. The success of the recall campaign resulted in a new election in which the anti-union commissioners were defeated. These 1918 public sector successes did much to set the terms for the 1919 struggles. The extent of working-class support for public sector workers stemmed from a combination of factors – a recognition of the generally blue-collar workers as labour, the strong World War I notions that the state was greatly indebted to the working class and should be model employers, and finally the pervasiveness for all workers of the issues at stake in these strikes – the living wage and the recognition of the right to organize.

The brief story of the national postal strike suggests another theme which needs to be emphasized. By and large the 1917–20, and especially 1919, insurgency was a rank-and-file revolt. In many cases, as with the letter carriers, workers simply ignored their leaders. In some cases old leaders unsympathetic to the new militancy were unceremoniously dumped. For example, Arthur Puttee, a long-time Winnipeg labour leader, former lib-lab MP, and labour alderman, was removed from the editorship of *The Voice* in 1918 because of his refusal as alderman to support fully the striking civic workers. In many cities the left won control of TLCS which, of course, became the vehicle for orchestrating general and sympathetic strikes. Even where the left held control, however, leaders found themselves following rank-and-file actions in directions with which they were not always in total sympathy. This tension was especially evident among some of the Socialist Party of Canada leaders who felt the masses were not ready for actions the authorities increasingly deemed "revolutionary."

Much historical discussion of strikes, as David Montgomery has reminded us, has revolved around Eric Hobsbawm's notion of workers' "learning the rules of the game" and Michelle Perrot's idea about workers' fascination "with the possibilities of the strike."[43] By 1919 Canadian workers clearly had learned the new rules that accompanied monopoly capitalism and indeed they had come to recognize that such economic organization presented them with considerable possibilities for action. They exercised those options and found themselves facing a newly united front of capital and state, both of whom, like labour, saw the outcome of the struggles of 1919–20 as setting the pattern for the post-war world. Despite labour's new solidarities and extraordinary militancy capital triumphed. For many Canadian historians this defeat for labour has led either to liberal criticism of a state over-response or a conservative dismissal of labour's struggle as a naïve and utopian "children's crusade."[44] Even the often astute Clare Pentland missed the point badly when he attributed, albeit only partially, the failure to a generation "decimated by war, exhausted by struggle, and diluted by barely literate immigrants from Europe." His argument that the "gap in capacity between bosses and workers had widened again" contains hidden assumptions almost as questionable as the ethnic chauvinism of the previous quotation.[45] But, more important, was his further and main argument that the decline of western capital in the 1920s and 1930s decimated the possibilities of working-class advance. His point about the west applies even more to the Canadian east where a process of deindustrialization evident even before the war would quicken over the next two decades. Thus, while workers had begun during World War I to act on a vision of a national labour market with national wage rates, the regional realities of Canadian capitalist development in the interwar years would rob them of the possibility of realizing such goals. Such labour aims would reemerge during World War II. The relative quiescence of Canadian labour between the wars, of course, to some degree parallels the experience of other western nations – what Yves Lequin has termed "the great silence."[46]

But "the great silence" should not blind us to the achievements and especially the possibilities of 1919. When Sir Robert Borden, the Canadian Prime Minister of the day, composed his *Memoirs*, almost 20 years later, he noted that "In some cities there was a deliberate attempt to overthrow the existing organization of the Government and to supersede it by crude, fantastic methods with a stern hand and from this I did not shrink."[47] Borden's words should be read in the same way his government's actions must be understood; they reflect the fears of a militant working class in motion and represent the harsh and rational response of the bourgeois state.[48]

The Depression strike waves of 1934 and 1937 are the only one-year "waves" in this sixty-year period. Geographically these waves are notable for the increased eastern strike activity in the country. The Maritimes with 13 and 18 per cent of the strikes in 1934 and 1937 respectively and about 25 per cent of the strikers played a more prominent role than in any previous wave (see Table 11.11). Similarly Quebec with 17 and 15 per cent of the strikes and almost one-third of the strikers achieved its highest rates since the wave of 1899–1903. Ontario played about the same role as in previous waves, while the west fell to its lowest levels, perhaps for the reasons Pentland asserted.

Industrially both waves were dominated by manufacturing at 59 and 48 per cent of strikes and 55 and 64 per cent of strikers. Mining with 11 and 15 per cent of strikes and 28 and 24 per cent of strikers finished a distant second. More interestingly, service sector strikes rose to third place in each year with 9 and 14 per cent of strikes and 2 per cent of strikers. Construction and transportation strikes continued to play less prominent roles than they had earlier in the century.

In terms of strike issues in these depression years 1934 and 1937 are notable for their high number of offensive strikes for changes in wages and conditions and especially for the very high number of recognition strikes (see Table 11.4). Equally notable was the increase in third party intervention to bring settlements, especially in 1937 (see Table 11.5). This pattern, of course, would increase noticeably during World War II with the extension of the IDIA under wartime emergency measures legislation and with the advent of PC1003. Finally, as in earlier waves workers in 934 and 1937 enjoyed considerable success with 63 and 66 per cent of combined strike victories or compromises.

Provincially Ontario and Quebec dominated in strikes and strikers in 1934 and 1937 owing to the prominence of the manufacturing sector. This was equally true with regards to intensity. Ontario accounted for eight of the 14 "violent" strikes in 1934 and 11 of 17 in 1937 while Quebec added three and five. Manufacturing was the site of eight in 1934 and 13 in 1937. Initially under Workers Unity League leadership and subsequently, after the move to the United Front, under CIO leadership, the drive to industrial unionism in the mass production industries was the major story of 1934 and 1937. In many ways these struggles were a reenactment in numerous industries of the aborted victories of the labour revolt of 1917 to 1920. Moreover, in manufacturing at least, 1934 was something of a dress rehearsal for the larger struggles of 1937. Thus, for example, 1934 and 1937 saw major struggles in the forests of Ontario and British Columbia as loggers again organized, this time under the banners of the Workers Unity League's Lumber Workers Industrial Union.[49] Over 2,300 Vancouver Island loggers struck for some four months in early 1934 and won a partial victory, although later that fall their Ontario comrades were defeated in major struggles in the Iroquois Falls and Sault Ste Marie areas. Similarly in January 1937 some 2,300 Flander, Ontario loggers fought and gained a partial victory. All three of these Ontario lumber strikes involved incidents of picket line violence.

Mining struggles played an important role in both years but especially in 1937. In 1934, 1,300 Stellarton, NS coal miners struck for almost three months to prevent wage cuts and then went out again for almost two weeks in late July and early August to protect a union activist. Perhaps the most famous mining struggle of 1934, however, was the Flin Flon, Manitoba, metal mining strike led by the Mine Workers Union of Canada, an affiliate of the Communist Party's trade-union wing, the Workers Unity League. While the Hudson Bay Mining and Smelting Company won a short-term victory after a two-month struggle involving nearly 1,100 miners, the CPC further strengthened its position as the militant, fighting arm of Canadian labour.[50] In 1937, however, numerous struggles in the Maritimes, including major struggles in Florence, Stellarton, and Springhill, Nova Scotia and in Minto, New Brunswick, made mining an even more pronounced factor in the strike wave. In Minto, where there had been almost continuous labour strife since 1919, a major struggle broke out in October 1937 and lasted into the New Year involving 1,200 members of the UMWA.[51] Third-party intervention in the form of an IDIA conciliation board proved ineffectual and the workers suffered a serious setback. In 1937 Nova Scotia coal miners left the pits on some 30 occasions to back demands. These mining strikes played a large role in the east's new prominence in the national labour scene.

In central Canada, however, manufacturing dominated the strike scene. In 1934 the action was primarily in boot and shoe and in clothing and textiles which together accounted for 53 per cent of the manufacturing strikes and a remarkable 83 per cent of strikers. In the former, of 19 strikes, involving some 2,300 workers, 15 were in Ontario, primarily in Toronto and most were struggles for union recognition. In the latter there were some 56 strikes in the clothing industry where major struggles occurred in Toronto (2,000 workers in January and another 2,000 in July–August), and in Montreal (1,500 Millinery Workers in March, some 3,000 dressmakers in August–September, and 4,000 workers in the men's clothing industry in July–August). A number of these struggles too were led by a WUL affiliate, in this case the Industrial Union of Needle Trades Workers which battled with the ILGWU and the Amalgamated Clothing workers for union control of the sector.[52] As was too often the case in the 1930s and 1940s, much energy was expended on internecine political struggle between communist and labourist union leaders.

In 1937 the manufacturing sector saw battles spread far beyond the clothing industry, which itself saw a massive April–May work stoppage of 5,000 Montreal women's clothing workers led to victory by the newly unified ILGWU.[53] Major textile struggles broke out in Ontario at Welland (765 workers for three months), Cornwall (1,700 in July–August and 1,600 in August–September), and in Quebec at Montreal (9,000 in August) and Louiseville (900 in September). Nevertheless clothing and textile and boot and shoe accounted for only 40 per cent of the manufacturing strikes and 35 per cent of the strikers down considerably from 1934. Among the new areas where organization spread were meatpacking in which major strikes were fought in Montreal, Edmonton, and Vancouver, rubber (Kitchener, 550 in March–April and 700 in September–November);[54] and furniture (1,500 in March throughout western Ontario). Perhaps the most significant strike of 1937, however, was that by 4,200 Oshawa General Motors workers for three weeks in April. This struggle became a major battle between the emerging CIO forces, in this case led by the United Auto Workers (UAW), and the Hepburn government of Ontario which was desperate to barricade the border against the spread of industrial unionism, at least partially in a vain attempt to protect northern Ontario mining magnates. Unfortunately for Hepburn, the industrial union bug was indigenous to Canadian workers and his vigorous attempts to defeat the UAW and the CIO proved futile.[55]

The World War II strike wave of 1941–43 came closest to matching the prominence of the 1917–20 labour revolt. Its 1,106 strikes and nearly 425,000 strikers represent slightly over 11 per cent and 16 per cent respectively of all Canadian strikes and strikers in the 60-year period. These figures exceed those of 1917–20 for strikers but fall short in strikes. Rough annual averages for frequency and size suggest similar conclusions. The World War I wave's index numbers averages 130 for frequency, while the World War II wave averages are higher. Given the vast growth of the nation's labour force in the years between 1920 and 1940 it remains evident that the four-year long labour revolt of 1917–20 must be seen as the major strike wave of the period to 1950.

The trends evident in the strike waves of the 1930s toward an increased prominence of the eastern provinces continued in World War II. The Maritimes increased their share of Canadian strikes during strike waves to its highest level with 24 per cent of strikes and 31 per cent of strikers (see Table 11.11). Meanwhile, Quebec did the same and raised its proportion of strikes to a century high 28 per cent with 31 per cent of strikers only slightly behind its high of 34 per cent in 1937. Growth in the Maritimes and Quebec was largely at Ontario's expense which fell to 31 per cent of strikes and 22 per cent of strikers, while the west stayed approximately at its Depression strike wave levels of 18 and 15 per cent, far lower, of course, than its role in the earlier waves. Industrially, manufacturing continued to dominate with 58 and 59 per cent, while mining contributed 21 per cent of strikes and 26 per cent of strikers. Construction, service, and transport failed far behind.

Strikes appear to have been fought primarily for improvements in wages and conditions and recognition struggles declined when compared to the 1930s (see Table 11.4). Given the existence of the war, the rapid rise in third party settlements to its century high is not surprising (see Table 11.5). Indeed the struggles of 1941–43 would force the state to implement its most interventionist labour relations policy in the century. PC1003 of 1944 and its later entrenchment in 1948 as the Industrial Relations and Labour Disputes Investigation Act brought an entirely new legal regime to bear in Canadian labour relations. Perhaps not coincidentally, the 1941–43 strike wave witnessed not only the most third-party settlements but also an unusually large number of workers' losses for a strike wave. Employers actually won 30, 39, and 40 per cent of the struggles with clear workers' victories at 23, 22, and 34 per cent respectively. the combination of worker victories and compromises led to 61, 50, and 54 per cent in the three years (see Table 11.6). Nevertheless, the higher level of employer victories seems quite suggestive and is quite out of step with the pattern of the previous strike waves.

Indeed the strike wave of 1941–43 was typified by a new pattern of quick, mass walkouts which under the pressure of war conditions often led to short, sharp workers' victories. If strikes did not finish

quickly, workers' chances were much worse.[56] The strike wave consisted primarily of short, often effective mining strikes, especially in
Nova Scotia, the continuation of efforts to organize the mass production industries, especially in Ontario and Quebec, and huge strikes in
war production industries, especially shipbuilding. Manufacturing and
mining dominated this strike wave more totally than in any of the
previous five waves in percentage of strikes with 79 and its 85 per
cent of strikers was second only to 1937's 88 per cent (see Table
11.11).

In coal mining the struggles built through the wave with 47, 57,
and 112 strikes in the three years. The 112 strikes of 1943 was the
highest in the 60-year period. Nova Scotia dominated with numerous
strikes in both the mainland and Cape Breton coal fields. Only in
November 1943, when there was a UMWA District 18-wide shutdown
involving almost 10,000 miners in BC and Alberta for two weeks, did
the west figure prominently in coal strikes in these years.

Similarly, in auto and steel and in shipbuilding and aircraft, the
struggles built to a peak in 1943. A three-week strike of 3,700 St
Catharines auto parts workers in 1941 was followed in 1942 by a
Windsor strike of over 14,000 autoworkers fighting for equal pay for
equal work. In 1943, some 15,000 Windsor autoworkers fought speedups. The final showdown in auto would come in 1945.[57] The pattern
in steel showed like developments. Various strikes in steel fabrication
in 1941 in Hamilton, Toronto, Montreal, and Trenton were followed
by 1942 struggles in Trenton and Vancouver, but in 1943 an almost
nation-wide strike in basic steel by nearly 13,000 steelworkers at
Sydney, Trenton, and Sault Ste Marie brought the industry to an
abrupt halt.[58]

The pattern in shipbuilding and aircraft, relatively unstudied to
date, looks almost identical. A brief aircraft strike in Toronto in 1942
was followed the next year by a Vancouver strike of almost 7,000
workers and by a massive Montreal walkout of or 21,000 workers for
nearly two weeks. In shipbuilding strikes were huge and generally
short as workers struck over control issues. These strikes were
especially prominent in 1942 and 1943 and took place in virtually all
Canadian shipyards in the east, on the St Lawrence and Great Lakes,
and on the west coast. The largest stoppages took place in Lauzon,
Sorel, and Montreal, Quebec, and in Vancouver. East coast strikes
were smaller but no less frequent.[59]

Manufacturing's 58 per cent of strikes and 59 per cent of strikers
was almost totally dominated by metals and shipbuilding with 51 per
cent of strikes and 78 per cent of strikers. Clothing and textile added
17 per cent of strikes and 6 per cent of strikers. Outside of manufac-

turing and mining, the largest strikes occurred in 1943 in Montreal where 3,000 transit workers struck and where a series of strikes by civic workers foreshadowed much later developments elsewhere in the country.[60] Again, as in 1919, Montreal policemen and firemen organized as well.

The events of the strike wave of 1941–43 led eventually, after much delay, to a new industrial relations system, which we have mentioned briefly earlier in this paper. The clear aim of the King Liberal government in labour and in general social policy was to move to the left as quickly as possible in an attempt to maintain power in the post-war world and to prevent the massive upheaval of 1919. The key strikes of 1945–46 at Hamilton Stelco, Ford Windsor, and in the British Columbia woods made 1946 the sixty-year leader in person days lost, but unlike 1919 it did not bring the country to the brink of political crisis.

III

Let us return briefly to our aggregate data simply to suggest the possibilities of a more rigorous international comparison of working-class formation. As is often the case varying methods of presenting data limits us here to two rather simplistic comparisons but from each interesting contrasts appear.

Table 11.12 compares the number of strikes and strikers in Britain, France, and Canada from 1891–1950. The magnitude of the struggles in Britain and France are, of course, far larger than in Canada but when expressed simply in percentages of strikes and strikers in the 60-year period significant patterns emerge. Strikes in Britain in the 1890s played a far more prominent role relative to the entire period than in Canada or France, while in the latter countries the 1901–10 decade figured more prominently. Canada's World War I and immediate post-war experience, on the other hand, resembled British experience, although Canada's strike statistics relative to the entire period are the highest of the three nations, although Britain led in strikers. Canadian strikes in the 1920s resembled British proportions in number of strikes but fell behind in strikers, no doubt owing to the 1926 British General Strike. Both Canada and Britain trailed France in strike proportions. France, with the extraordinary experience of the Popular Front, led in the 1930s, trailed by Canada and Britain, while the British dominated in number of strikes in the 1940s while Canada led in strikers. Of course, we should remember again that we are only comparing patterns here not actual experiences. If we look at the real numbers in Table 11.12 we should note

Table 11.12
Number and Percentage of Strikes and Workers Involved in Great Britain, France, and Canada, 1891–1950[a]

	Number of Strikes and Workers					
	Great Britain[b]		France[c]		Canada	
	Strikes	Workers involved (000)	Strikes	Workers involved (000)	Strikes	Workers involved (000)
1891–1900	7,930	2,476	4,890	1,020	511	78
1901–10	4,636	1,484	10,050	2,112	1,548	230
1911–20	9,187	9,220	9,891	3,852	2,349	521
1921–30	5,066	7,256	9,421	3,130	989	261
1931–40	6,874	2,525	22,463[d]	4,504[d]	1,760	376
1941–50	17,276	4,063	6,908[d]	14,069[d]	2,537	1,133

	Percentage of Strikes and Workers					
	Great Britain[b]		France[c]		Canada	
	Strikes	Workers involved	Strikes	Workers involved	Strikes	Workers involved
1891–1900	16	9	8	4	5	3
1901–10	9	6	16	7	16	9
1911–20	18	34	16	13	24	20
1921–30	10	27	15	11	10	10
1931–40	13	9	35[d]	16[d]	18	14
1941–50	34	15	11[d]	49[d]	26	44

a It should be noted that the operative definition of a "strike" used by these authors varies. In Britain small strikes were not counted which biases frequency down and size up.
b The French statistical series is not strictly comparable for either decade owing to the World War II occupation experience.
c Cronin, *Industrial Conflict*, 206–7, 109–11.
d Shorter and Tilly, *Strikes in France*, 360–3.

that while France had by far the most strikes of the three countries, Britain had the largest until the 1940s. We should also remember that the data sets are not perfectly comparable.

Table 11.13 presents evidence on Canadian/American comparisons over the period, 1891–50. As can be readily seen, Canada trailed in frequency in every decade except the 1920s and in size in every decade except the 1900s. Canada's low figures in the 1890s for frequency in comparison to the U.S. match the similar contrast with Britain and France and emphasize, we think, the relative immaturity of the national Canadian working-class experience of the 1890s. In subsequent decades, however, that gap was closed and Canadian strike

Table 11.13
Frequency and Size of Strikes, Canada, and the United States, 1891[a]

	Frequency[b]		Size[c]	
	United States[d]	Canada	United States[d]	Canada
1891–1900	113	55	274	218
1901–10	162	115	179	180
1911–20	143	123	397	286
1921–30	41	43	521	270
1931–40	80	61	432	218
1941–50	99	70	604	452

a American data tends to eliminate small strikes thus biasing frequency down and size up.
b Total number of strikes per 1,000,000 non-agricultural employees.
c Number of workers involved per strike.
d u.s. data from Edwards, *Strikes*, 13.

frequency never fell below two-thirds of the American. In size Canadian strikes in the 1920s and 1930s ran about one-half of the American compared to four-fifths in the 1890s and about three-quarters in the 1910s and 1940s.

The Canadian case, then, while showing broad similarities with the American (although we should add that those similarities have been breaking down since 1960), provides further support for the notion that questions of national "exceptionalism" are incorrectly posed.[61] Each national labour movement must be studied historically and understood in light of working-class experience, not held up against a reified model, which existed only in the minds of Second International theorists.

METHODS AND SOURCES

Now that the strikes and lockouts files of the Department of Labour have been microfilmed, they are likely to be consulted more than ever by labour historians and other researchers. If these records and the statistics derived from them are to be used effectively, it is important to know how they were compiled.

Soon after it was founded in 1900, the Department of Labour established a procedure for systematically gathering information on Canadian labour disputes, a procedure that was to remain essentially the same throughout the period covered in this report. When the department first received news of a strike, either from the correspondents of the *Labour Gazette* or through the regular press, it sent strike inquiry forms to representatives of the employers and employees involved in the dispute. Initially, a single form was mailed asking for the beginning and end dates of the dispute, the "cause or object" and "result," and the number of establishments and number of male and female workers directly and indirectly involved. In 1918 the department began sending two forms – one to be returned immediately and the other after settlement – which requested more detailed information regarding the usual working day and week. The department also asked for monthly reports from participants in longer strikes. These questionnaires sometimes provided all of the data needed to complete the various lists and statistical series, but because they were often not returned or contained conflicting responses, the department also relied on newspaper coverage and supplementary reports from fair wage and conciliation officers, *Labour Gazette* correspondents, Royal Canadian Mounted Police informants, and Employment Service of Canada/Unemployment Insurance Commission officials.

Once all of the documents relating to a strike were gathered into a single file and given a separate reference number, estimates of the number of establishments and workers involved, duration in working days, and duration in "man days lost" were made, and the causes, methods of settlement, and results were classified.[62] These data, as well as basic qualitative information, were then entered into a Trade Dispute Record register (1904–16),[63] onto a separate Trade Dispute Record sheet (1917?–44),[64] or onto a sheet of paper at the beginning of the file (1945–50). In turn, the sheets provided the data base for annual reviews of strike activity which were published in the *Labour Gazette* beginning (for 1901 and 1902) in January 1903.[65] In 1913 the department published a separate report which included statistics for two five-year periods, 1901–5 and 1906–10, and a complete list of known strikes from 1901 to 1912.[66] A similar report dealing with the period up to 1916 was published in 1918.[67] The department began preparing a third report early in the 1920s but never published it.[68]

The third report was not published partly because of changes occurring in the system used to classify strikes by industry. In 1917 the department stopped categorizing strikes according to the occupation or trade of the majority of workers involved and instead began classifying them according to the product of the industry affected. This new system was still undergoing changes and was revised again in 1922. Thus, while it appears from the records that the department began to reclassify pre-1917 strikes according to the 1917 system, its efforts were soon made redundant.

By the early 1920s it was also clear that the strikes and lockouts series was in need of much more fundamental revisions. Despite the claim in the 1913 report that regarding the stated number of strikes "the margin of uncertainty is practically nil," the department had simply missed a large number of disputes.[69] When comprehensive revisions were finally undertaken in the last 1920s, 455 more strikes were discovered and incorporated into a new series covering the period between 1901 and 1929. The vast majority of these new strikes occurred before 1921.

Some of the additional disputes had been intentionally omitted from the original statistics because of a policy of removing "minor" strikes from the record. Although the department maintained this policy in preparing the revisions, a number of strikes originally deleted were inserted because of various changes in the definition of minor strikes. In 1900 strikes "affecting less than ten work people, and those lasting less than one day" were to be excluded;[70] beginning in 1903 "disputes involving less than six employees or of less duration than 24 hours" were to be omitted;[71] between 1919 and 1921 strikes were to be left off unless they involved "six or more employees and were of not less than forty-eight hours duration";[72] and finally, after returning to the six workers/one day rule until 1923, a proviso was added which stated that such strikes were to be included if they involved a time loss of ten person days or more.[73] This last rule was adopted for the revisions completed in 1930 and remained in effect through 1950.

Small and short strikes involving ten or more person days lost, however, made up a very small percentage of the new strikes included in the revised totals. A larger portion had been left off the original record either because they had been incorrectly combined with other strikes or because sufficient information about them was lacking. And the majority were strikes that had, for various reasons, including censorship during the war, simply escaped the attention of the department. New evidence about these kinds of strikes, as well as about those already recorded, was discovered by means of a thorough search of all of the major labour newspapers published between 1901 and 1929.[74]

This evidence was used in preparing new Trade Dispute Record sheets for all of the strikes. In many instances the original estimates of workers involved duration, and person days lost were amended to make them more consistent over the 29-year period.[75] Causation was reclassified to conform with a more detailed system first used in the 1924 annual report. Methods of settlement and results were classified using the same system as before, but many strikes were reinterpreted. The amended Trade Dispute Record sheets were filed by year and industry, along with the original sheets and the notes from the survey of labour newspapers.[76] Researchers interested in compiling local strike statistics should refer to these files as well as to the published record for 1901–29.

Summary tables showing the revised number of strikes, workers involved, and person days lost by major industrial classes and by result were published in the *Labour Gazette* in 1931.[77] A similar industrial table, with minor revisions, more detailed breakdowns, and statistics for 1931–50, was published in 1951.[78] Draft tables showing the annual totals by province, cause, method of settlement, and by revised orders of magnitude of workers involved, duration, and time loss were never published, but are still available in manuscript form.[79] Together, the published and manuscript tables make the revised estimates for 1901–29 completely compatible with those published annually between 1930–50. And because it is so complete, this series remains very useful for researchers interested in national trends over extended periods. Nevertheless, it still has a number of serious deficiencies.

Some of the problems are evident in the three basic units of measurement: the number of strikes, the number of workers involved, and the duration in person days lost.[80] In determining the number of strikes, both definition and coverage are important. Generally, the department adhered to the definitions contained in the Industrial Disputes Investigation Act, 1907 (IDI Act).[81] A strike was deemed a "cessation of work by a body of employees acting in combination, or a concerted refusal or a refusal under a common understanding of any number of employees to continue to work for an employer, in consequence of a dispute, done as a means of compelling their employer, or to aid other employees in compelling their employer, to accept terms of employment," and a lockout "a closing of a place of employment, or a suspension of work, or a refusal by an employer to continue to employ any number of his employees in consequence of a dispute, done with a view to compelling his employees, or to aid another employer in compelling his employees, to accept terms of employment."[82] Since strikes were often impossible to distinguish from lockouts, the two terms were either used interchangeably or the phrases "trade dispute," "industrial dispute," or "work stoppage" were used instead.

The definition was open to interpretation in at least three areas. The department interpreted the meaning of "cessation" or "suspension" of work fairly uniformly. Although sitdowns were counted, slowdowns and other actions involving less than a complete stoppage of work were not. Group desertions by workers who did not want to return to work, and plant closures by owners who did not intend to start up again were also excluded. For the most part, each stoppage in a rotating or recurring strike was counted separately, provided it ended before the next one began. Although the department began to bend this rule in 1939, the regularity of the statistics was not seriously affected until the 1950s when rotating strikes gained greater popularity.[83] In 1951, for example, eighty-two stoppages at the Sydney steel works, many of which did not overlap, were counted as a single strike. Finally, strikes occurring simultaneously at more than one establishment were combined if they were centrally directed and the issues were the same. Sympathy strikes were counted separately because this last criterion did not apply.

The department also interpreted the phrase "terms of employment" consistently. Grievances did not have to be expressed specifically in terms of a particular employment relationship, but they did have to affect such a relationship. Strikes over union jurisdiction, for example, were included. Some political strikes, such as two work "holidays" held in Nova Scotia in 1943 to protest closures at the Trenton Steel Works, were counted, while others, such as one held in British Columbia in 1918 to protest the shooting of Albert Goodwin, were not. The line between political strikes that were related to employment and those that were not must have been difficult to draw, but since these kinds of strikes were relatively rare in Canada, any mistakes in this area would not have altered the record significantly.

Arbitrary readings of the words "employee" and "employer" had a greater impact. In the revised statistics for 1901–29, for example, strikes by independent teamsters were counted, but in subsequent statistics disputes involving truck driver-owners were omitted. In the late 1940s, the department also considered excluding strikes by most fishers because, like truck driver-owners, they were note considered to be employees.[84] After including relief worker strikes in the reports for 1931–33, the department began excluding them because relief agencies were not thought of as employers. Strikes by teachers, nurses, and other "professional" occupations were omitted from both the 1901–29 revisions and subsequent annual reports. Finally, strikes involving part-time workers, mostly women and children, were excluded from the record.

The second element in determining the accuracy of the strike count is the coverage provided by the statistics. Although in this respect the revised totals for 1901–29 are definitely better than the originals, they still underestimate the actual number of strikes. It is difficult to judge the severity of this problem, but in a recent survey of newspapers and other sources, Ian McKay found reference to 411 strikes in the Maritime provinces between 1901 and 1914.[85] This is more than twice as many as the department included in the revised statistics. The Maritimes might be an exceptional case because of the relatively poor coverage provided there by labour newspapers, but since McKay's statistics are the only comprehensive independent test available, there is no way of assessing this.

Some of the difference between the official and McKay's totals can be attributed to the department's exclusion of strikes involving less than ten person days lost. Those who favoured this practice argued that since a large number of small strikes were inevitably going to escape the attention of the department anyway, it was better to admit this weakness in the statistics beforehand. Moreover, given that the immediate purpose of the official statistics was to measure the economic impact of strikes, these minor strikes were not really of much consequence. But for more recent analysts, who are often concerned about the social implications of strike activity, these minor, often spontaneous strikes are just as critical as the longer, well-orchestrated ones. Present researchers might also be more interested in obtaining a representative sample of the strikes occurring in a particular occupation, location, or period than in ensuring that they have all of the strikes involving more than some arbitrary number of person days lost. Although the department might have increased the accuracy of the statistics by limiting their coverage, at the same time it distorted the story that they told.

In any event, only a few of the strikes added by McKay were excluded by the department because they were considered to be too small. The rest were either missed entirely or ignored because of insufficient information. While these kinds of omissions probably did not affect the national trends significantly, McKay's statistics show that they do matter at the provincial and regional levels. The logging industry in 1919 and 1920 provides a good example of why they also matter at the level of individual industries. For these two years the department left as many as (50) logging strikes off the revised record as it recorded (47) because it lacked complete information. Again, this might be an exceptional case, since logging strikes are difficult to track down, but even so, our research shows that trends in the number of strikes in nearly every industry were at one time or another affected by the exclusion of minor and incomplete disputes.[86] Until further research is completed at the industrial and provincial levels, we can only guess at how much more the trends would be changed by the addition of strikes that were missed altogether.

The main problem in calculating the second major unit of measurement, the number of workers involved, was conflicting information. The department attempted to gauge the total number of workers directly involved in the strike. Whenever possible, the number indirectly involved was also estimated and published as a footnote to the annual list of strikes. Because strike leaders and employers often disputed the number of workers who were active participants, it was usually necessary to consult a number of independent sources before making final estimates. In doing so the department made many mistakes but does not appear to have exhibited any clear bias toward reports submitted by either employers or strikers.

Some bias, however, was evident in enumerating person days lost, the third principal unit of measurement.[87] In theory the calculation of person days lost was simple enough: the number of workers involved was multiplied by the duration of the strike in working days. But, in practice, since many strikes were effectively resolved by the full replacement of strikers and since many strikers often returned to work before strikes were officially declared over, applying the definition was difficult. Early in the original record, the department decided to consider strikes terminated once production was no longer affected.[88] This policy was also suggested in a report on strike statistics published by the International Labour Office in 1926, the arguments being that the calculation of persons days lost from the workers' perspective (or "striker days") was impractical.[89] But for obvious political reasons, it was even more impractical to ignore completely the viewpoint of workers. This would have meant considering strikes over once a full complement of strikebreakers had been hired, even though the strikers might still be actively pursuing their objectives or state conciliation proceedings might still be underway.

Therefore, in the revised and subsequent statistics, the department would have preferred to compute a hybrid person days lost/striker days statistic. Ideally, when production was resumed through some combination of returning strikers and strikebreakers,strikes would be considered finished only after the vast majority of strikers had stopped actively participating (by removing pickets, cancelling strike benefits, and obtaining work elsewhere). Some strikes would remain on the record long after the employer had considered them over, while others would be removed well before the strikers (despite working elsewhere, etc.) had surrendered. The problem with this approach, however, was that the data needed to calculate such a statistic was rarely available. And since it was generally easier to obtain information about production than about picketing, strike pay, and the employment status of long-time strikers, it was usually the workers' perspective that was sacrificed. When forced to choose between the date that strikers were replaced and the date that strikers officially surrendered, the department most often selected the former.

One final difficulty in estimating person days lost was encountered when some but not all workers returned during a strike or when a strike was settled at some but not all of the establishments involved.

In these cases the department multiplied the maximum number of workers involved during each month by the duration in working days. If the normal working day and week were unknown, they were estimated on the basis of an eight to nine hour day and a five-and-a-half to six day week. The department also tried to subtract days when the establishment would not normally be in operation. This explains why the revised persons days lost totals for many longshoring and coal mining strikes occurring before 1919 were so much lower than the original estimates.

At the provincial and industrial levels, the person days lost statistics suffer from the same deficiency as the estimates showing the number of strikes: they often fail to incorporate enough of the strikes that actually occurred. In determining whether or not this is the case, tables 11.c and 11.e should be of some assistance. Prepared for volume 3 of the *Historical Atlas of Canada*, these statistics include estimates for 1,581 strikes that came to the attention of the department but were not included in the official statistics for one of the reasons discussed earlier. They also include estimates for 114 of the additional strikes found by McKay.[90] Also on table 11.c, interprovincial coal mining strikes have been disaggregated by province in order to reflect activity in Alberta, British Columbia, New Brunswick, and Nova Scotia more accurately. Ideally, the same should have been done for all interprovincial strikes, but the necessary data was simply unavailable. Finally, we have corrected a number of mistakes made by the department in tabulating the official statistics. The majority of these errors were made in the statistics covering the period before 1929. A couple of metal mining strikes occurring in 1919 and 1920, for example, were incorrectly added to the coal mining totals. Of the many more mistakes in the unpublished provincial statistics, the most serious occurred in the table for 1911 when a huge BC construction strike was incorrectly attributed to Alberta. In a few instances, we were unable to determine why the tabulated statistics did not exactly match the sum of the data on the Trade Dispute Record sheets.

It should be emphasized that tables 11.c and 11.e are not intended to replace the official statistics. Rather, they are meant to provide as large a sample as possible with which to gauge both the accuracy of the official statistics and the actual amount and character of strike activity at the provincial and industrial levels. It is hope that they will provide a sound starting point for further research.

Tables 11.b and 11.d show our estimates of strike activity in the 1890s. In compiling these statistics, a preliminary list of strikes was prepared after surveying *The Globe* (1891–1900), Ian McKay's notes from the *Acadian Recorder* (1891–1900), labour newspapers, union proceedings, and all relevant secondary literature, including Hamelin, Larocque, and Rouillard's report on strikes in Quebec.[91] Local newspapers were then checked in an attempt to round out the data and new strikes encountered during this second search were added to the list.

We have tried to calculate the statistics in a way that would make them comparable with those available for the years after 1901. But since our database was often smaller than the department's, we have resorted to estimates much more frequently. The person days lost statistics do not accurately account for reductions in the number of workers involved during the course of strikes and, consequently, are probably too high. Because of the sources used, the statistics are clearly biased toward central Canada.[92] Nevertheless, if considered as a sample, the annual totals for the entire country and the ten year totals by industry and province should be useful.

In portraying the strikes graphically, we have adopted a method used by Shorter and Tilly in their work on strikes in France.[93] The graphs are three dimensional and show the average annual "shape" of strikes by province and major industrial classes over a ten-year period. The height of each cube represents the average size of strikes (that is, the average number of workers involved); the width represents the mean duration; and the depth is a measure of the frequency of strikes (the number of strikes per million non-agricultural employees). In determining size and duration, we have only included strikes for which complete information was available, but for frequency we have included all strikes (see Tables 11.F and 11.G and Figure 11.A).

The methods used to calculate these dimensions are all, of course, debatable.[94] It might be argued, for example, that the frequency of strikes would be better measured against union membership than non-agricultural workforce. To respond that this would be inappropriate for Canada because of the large number of "unorganized" strikes is not to suggest that non-agricultural workforce provides a perfect base. It ignores the fact that farm labourers occasionally went on strike and, more important, that the workforce statistics themselves are very incomplete. While Marvin McInnis has provided us with standardized estimates by industry and province for the census years 1911–51, we have been forced to assume constant growth between these years.[95] This, of course, was not always or even usually the case. The comparative depths of the cubes, therefore, should be assessed cautiously not only because of the problems with the strike statistics but because of the absence of a fully compatible common denominator. Despite these qualifications, however, the cubes are still a useful device for showing a number of longer-term trends that might otherwise be overlooked.

THE DATA*

Table 11.A
Number of Strikes Commencing, 1891–1950

Year	Number	Year	Number
1891	32	1921	196
1892	35	1922	103
1893	43	1923	88
1894	39	1924	69
1895	39	1925	95
1896	31	1926	83
1897	34	1927	73
1898	50	1928	105
1899	101	1929	103
1900	107	1930	74
Total 1891–1900	511	Total 1921–30	989
1901	124	1931	91
1902	169	1932	125
1903	225	1933	143
1904	144	1934	222
1905	131	1935	154
1906	188	1936	185
1907	223	1937	337
1908	90	1938	166
1909	110	1939	146
1910	144	1940	191
Total 1901–10	1,548	1931–40	1,760
1911	159	1941	265
1912	239	1942	407
1913	224	1943	434
1914	95	1944	214
1915	85	1945	211
1916	163	1946	240
1917	216	1947	269
1918	303	1948	164
1919	420	1949	144
1920	445	1950	189
Total 1911–20	2,349	Total 1941–50	2,537
		Total 1891–1950	9,694

* For a list of Tables and Figures, see pp. ix–xi.

Table 11.B
Strike Estimates by Industry, 1891–1900

| | Fishing and trapping | | | | Mining | | | | | | | | Manufacturing | | | |
| | | | | | Coal | | | | Other | | | | | | | |
	A	B	C	D	A	B	C	D	A	B	C	D	A	B	C	D
1891	1				1	1	400	100					17	12	3,291	75
1892					1	1	1,000	5					25	16	1,122	64
1893	1	1	1,600	8	5	5	1,650	24					21	13	853	20
1894	1				4	3	2,300	12					23	17	1,420	41
1895					3	1	1,000	2	2				15	10	791	10
1896	2	2	2,500	30	1	1	250	14	2				13	7	646	26
1897	2				1	1	800	22					11	7	179	2
1898													33	21	2,419	34
1899	1	1	2,500	18	1	1	100		4	4	2,730	295	54	36	4,908	95
1900	2	1	6,000	120	6	3	380	7	1	1	2,000	168	57	44	15,276	269

A = Number of strikes in progress
B = Number of strikes in progress with complete data
C = Number of workers involved
D = Duration in person days (000)
a Includes one logging strike (1900) which involved 19 workers for a total of 19 person days.

Table 11.C
Strike Estimates by Industry, 1901–50

| | Logging | | | | Fishing | | | | Coal mining | | | |
	A	B	C	D	A	B	C	D	A	B	C	D
1901	2	1	100	1	2	1	8,000	130	4	2	1,760	7
1902	1	1	30	1	1	1	30	1	5	4	2,010	12
1903					1	1	4,100	49	9	7	5,410	173
1904					2	2	870	4	8	6	2,424	18
1905									11	10	5,564	102
1906									15	13	4,549	147
1907					2	2	375	10	14	13	8,990	103
1908									8	7	3,541	14
1909					3	3	1,171	7	17	15	9,143	723
1910									5	3	2,950	485
1911									7	6	9,890	1,513
1912	1	1	33		1	1	620	31	6	3	2,258	107
1913					3	2	6,220	54	5	4	4,837	562
1914					1				3	3	2,500	281
1915									9	9	2,753	12
1916					1				10	8	11,270	72
1917	1								22	21	17,379	585
1918									49	49	23,623	138
1919	32	19	2,741	62	1	1	11		22	19	10,070	383
1920	66	28	3,012	52	1				48	38	28,136	142

Table 11.B (continued)

	Construction				Transportation and public utilities				Service				Total[a]			
	A	B	C	D	A	B	C	D	A	B	C	D	A	B	C	D
1891	15	10	246	12	5	2	60						39	25	3,997	187
1892	9	3	1,066	12	3	3	670	5	2	2	22		40	25	3,880	85
1893	9	3	177	1	7	6	850	2	1	1	7		44	29	5,137	56
1894	4	3	2,100	25	5	3	380	4	2	1	31		39	27	6,231	82
1895	13	7	630	2	3	2	808	7	3	3	112		39	23	3341	21
1896	7	3	1,018	11	6	6	1,121	8					31	19	5,535	89
1897	14	8	531	2	4	3	555	1	2	2	32	1	34	21	2,097	28
1898	5	2	160	1	9	8	1,128	6	3	2	63		50	33	3,770	42
1899	16	9	1,395	17	24	18	4,372	55	2	2	12		102	71	16,017	480
1900	27	19	1,449	14	14	11	2,342	94	4	3	85	1	112	83	27,551	673

	Other mining				Manufacturing				Construction			
	A	B	C	D	A	B	C	D	A	B	C	D
1901	4	3	1,125	91	73	59	4,919	158	20	17	2,596	49
1902					79	66	3,875	120	43	37	3,479	35
1903	3	2	299	8	102	82	12,219	281	68	51	7,275	147
1904	2	1	360	5	74	67	5,412	130	32	22	3,529	46
1905	5	4	281	1	61	51	2,431	49	33	22	1,803	30
1906	4	2	215	2	92	82	8,163	145	46	34	8,273	66
1907	5	4	3,119	79	98	85	9,338	169	63	58	5,876	125
1908	3	3	408	2	43	36	10,304	213	26	23	3,269	33
1909	2	2	490	6	41	32	2,851	90	31	28	3,241	48
1910	4	4	439	7	64	49	6,889	70	51	35	7,473	115
1911	3	3	104	2	65	40	5,345	60	52	35	8,655	200
1912	6	5	2,085	45	78	62	9,553	351	94	78	20,875	509
1913	6	6	2,008	59	88	65	12,427	214	76	51	10,792	109
1914	2	1	75		39	27	4,887	177	37	26	2,069	29
1915	3	2	2,700	8	42	37	4,307	38	10	7	241	11
1916	3	3	2,500	25	71	62	7,539	97	24	17	1,632	12
1917	6	4	2,310	62	100	74	17,899	368	36	25	2,456	42
1918	3	2	1,663	17	122	95	29,130	294	30	18	1,556	12
1919	10	7	3,498	105	185	162	58,073	1,315	70	56	14,708	354
1920	14	11	2,080	38	176	148	24,291	406	73	51	10,109	94

Table 11.c (continued)

	Logging				Fishing				Coal mining			
	A	B	C	D	A	B	C	D	A	B	C	D
1921	7	4	435	11	1	1	100	1	10	10	1,456	31
1922	3	2	250	3	3	2	985	16	26	21	26,475	799
1923	2	2	437	7					24	24	20,844	300
1924	1	1	1,800	38	1	1	573	5	16	15	21,201	1,089
1925					2	2	980	5	17	17	18,672	1,040
1926	5	4	1,750	52					16	16	8,445	35
1927	2	2	770	4	1	1	300		20	20	16,653	54
1928	5	5	1,006	13	1	1	1,500	5	15	14	5,033	88
1929	3	3	1,075	26	1				10	9	3,049	7
1930	2	2	170	1	2	2	700	12	15	15	6,228	24
1931	3	3	236	2	3	3	1,000	11	9	9	2,129	12
1932	11	11	1,435	10	2	2	3,200	30	33	33	8,540	133
1933	16	15	5,392	105	1	1	250	7	22	21	3,028	33
1934	17	17	5,889	194	1	1	50		26	26	11,461	91
1935	3	2	2,132	35	4	4	1,330	15	17	17	6,131	66
1936	6	6	2,605	31	3	3	2,840	41	21	20	8,581	56
1937	9	9	3,030	27	1	1	80	2	46	44	15,477	113
1938	6	5	910	2	8	8	1,848	23	26	26	5,204	22
1939	1	1	70		1	1	15		53	52	33,702	111
1940	1	1	50		6	5	1,855	12	66	66	31,552	69
1941	2	1	300	4					47	47	38,161	109
1942	5	5	604	1	1	1	3,260	10	57	55	19,716	66
1943	7	7	641	7					112	112	46,745	193
1944	2	2	90						46	46	11,180	29
1945									39	39	27,422	183
1946	2	2	19,000	450	3	3	800	8	42	42	21,414	44
1947	1	1	50		5	3	775	31	12	11	45,467	1,314
1948	6	6	1,495	10	3		4,570	27	11	11	14,695	304
1949					3	2	70	2	7	7	1,558	3
1950	1	1	130	1	1	1		2	11	11	4348	15

Table 11.c (continued)

	Other mining				Manufacturing				Construction			
	A	B	C	D	A	B	C	D	A	B	C	D
1921	5	4	189	2	116	99	19,728	799	44	34	3,990	135
1922					38	36	10,397	572	26	26	1,870	40
1923	5	5	1,906	4	35	34	7,698	280	15	12	1,002	7
1924					30	28	6,818	129	16	16	1,049	8
1925	1	1	11		48	44	7,648	136	17	17	1,499	11
1926	1	1	35		40	39	11,872	163	16	13	1,208	13
1927					19	19	930	38	25	25	3,242	55
1928					48	48	5,557	40	31	31	4,334	75
1929	2	2	70	9	45	43	2,912	49	33	33	5,689	56
1930					25	25	5,497	40	20	20	1,367	12
1931					49	48	5,582	150	16	15	616	3
1932					60	60	8,938	77	10	10	390	4
1933	1	1	400	14	75	75	15,712	151	13	12	272	3
1934	2	2	1,373	27	132	127	25,583	254	10	10	478	2
1935	3	3	638	8	66	62	14,638	82	13	10	425	1
1936	2	2	74	1	86	86	15,192	126	17	17	786	1
1937	6	5	2,060	27	165	160	47,049	688	38	38	1,406	7
1938	1	1	12		76	76	7,510	81	18	17	949	1
1939	2	2	231	11	51	50	8,304	82	14	13	558	1
1940	5	5	600	8	67	66	17,185	151	22	22	1,289	2
1941	3	3	3,340	83	155	151	38,413	207	23	23	4,781	13
1942	10	9	2,756	63	256	248	81,947	297	36	35	3,998	4
1943	9	9	496	3	234	234	129,484	767	15	15	1,015	2
1944	3	3	864	1	128	128	53,481	401	6	6	427	1
1945	3	3	470		136	136	63,073	1,239	8	8	505	3
1946	9	9	5,727	186	128	128	86,921	3,760	16	15	994	7
1947	5	5	1,799	45	142	141	42,070	878	38	35	6,131	44
1948	1	1	2,000	5	85	84	18,862	488	21	20	3,352	40
1949	8	8	7,179	505	94	94	31,906	433	14	14	3,620	41
1950	4	4	2,910	33	107	104	49,113	246	20	15	2,370	29

	Transportation and public utilities				Trade and service				Total[a]			
	A	B	C	D	A	B	C	D	A	B	C	D
1901	19	15	5,576	301	6	4	48		130	102	24,124	738
1902	30	22	4,816	36	11	6	119	2	170	137	14,359	206
1903	40	31	8,893	196	8	7	324	5	231	181	38,520	860
1904	14	6	1,295	6	12	7	116	1	144	111	14,006	211
1905	15	12	1,843	63	6	3	164	1	133	104	12,936	247
1906	28	21	2,554	20	5	3	58	1	190	155	23,812	380
1907	33	28	6,441	37	12	11	538	7	229	202	34,683	529
1908	13	8	8,560	442	4	1	10		97	78	26,092	704
1909	19	14	1,750	10	3	1	40		116	95	18,686	884
1910	20	14	4,545	56	11	3	67		156	108	22,363	733
1911	30	20	4,974	39	10	6	491	7	167	110	29,459	1,822

Table 11.c (continued)

	Transportation and public utilities				Trade and service				Total[a]			
	A	B	C	D	A	B	C	D	A	B	C	D
1912	39	28	7,012	88	17	12	668	5	242	190	43,104	1,136
1913	34	24	4,468	36	22	12	252	3	234	164	41,004	1,037
1914	8	4	253	2	9	6	127	2	99	67	9,911	491
1915	10	5	1,340	25	12	9	139	1	86	69	11,480	95
1916	43	31	3183	29	14	10	847	6	166	131	26,971	241
1917	39	32	9,470	60	14	7	813	6	218	163	50,327	1,124
1918	58	48	18,248	129	39	25	8,196	66	305	239	82,573	657
1919	40	32	12,634	130	52	40	3,175	19	427	350	149,309	3,402
1920	34	27	6,727	55	43	31	2,150	22	457	335	76,624	814
1921	11	9	1,172	66	12	9	738	3	208	172	28,398	1,050
1922	12	10	3,640	94	10	10	175	5	118	107	43,792	1,529
1923	12	11	2,572	73	4	4	79	1	97	92	34,538	672
1924	3	3	133	1	8	7	2,742	24	75	71	34,316	1,295
1925	5	5	131		6	4	86		96	90	29,027	1,193
1926	4	4	515	2	3	3	24	1	85	80	23,849	267
1927	4	4	326	1	4	4	82	1	75	75	22,303	153
1928	3	3	132	3	4	4	153	1	107	106	17,715	224
1929	5	4	247	4	5	5	67	1	105	100	13,120	152
1930	4	4	296	1	6	6	109	2	74	74	14,367	92
1931	5	5	607	22	8	8	133	1	93	91	10,303	201
1932					15	14	150		131	130	22,653	253
1933	5	5	384	1	12	10	137	3	146	141	26,775	318
1934	14	13	511	1	21	19	983	8	224	216	46,421	577
1935	24	20	6,060	75	18	17	370	1	154	140	33,899	289
1936	19	19	3,413	12	29	28	954	5	186	184	35,571	278
1937	25	24	1,684	15	46	42	1,567	9	341	327	73,221	887
1938	15	14	2,770	10	19	19	1,796	11	171	168	21,019	150
1939	5	5	415		20	17	929	20	148	142	44,233	225
1940	10	9	6,834	15	15	13	2,184	10	193	187	61,549	267
1941	19	19	1,747	4	18	18	1,195	14	267	262	87,937	434
1942	16	15	2,233	5	25	24	1,056	6	409	395	116,220	454
1943	25	25	8,842	19	30	29	9,069	27	435	434	220,102	1,042
1944	16	15	7,699	46	16	11	2,187	13	217	211	75,928	491
1945	13	12	4,322	28	12	11	694	4	212	210	96,499	1,458
1946	22	20	3,645	52	22	21	1,172	9	243	239	139,673	4,516
1947	26	25	4,869	75	43	42	4,352	11	272	263	105,513	2,399
1948	15	15	1,312	26	31	30	1,571	14	171	168	43,397	886
1949	10	10	2,305	46	13	13	2,355	18	149	148	53,493	1,072
1950	15	14	132,608	1,008	33	26	2,365	57	192	176	193,914	1,390

A = Number of strikes in progress.
B = Number of strikes in progress with complete data.
C = Number of workers involved.
D = Duration in person days (000).

a Includes 56 miscellaneous and interindustry strikes, 48 of which involved 57,816 workers for a total of 1,081,116 person days. A 1946 strike was divided between logging and wood manufacturing but counted only once in the total.

Table 11.D

Strike Estimates by Province, 1891–1900

	British Columbia				Manitoba				Ontario				Quebec				New Brunswick				Nova Scotia				Interprovincial				Total			
	A	B	C	D	A	B	C	D	A	B	C	D	A	B	C	D	A	B	C	D	A	B	C	D	A	B	C	D	A	B	C	D
1891	7	3	448	100	2	1	60	1	15	10	205	15	4	3	562	7	1				8	6	172	6	2	2	2,550	58	39	25	3,997	187
1892	6	3	1,030	2	1				24	16	995	63	3	2	175	4					4	3	1,230	14	1	1	450	2	40	25	3,880	85
1893	11	9	3,303	33	2	2	305	5	20	12	902	17	7	4	542	2	4	2	85										44	29	5,137	56
1894	6	3	156	1	4	3	345	4	11	7	543	6	8	7	2,617	56	6	4	270	3	4	3	2,300	12					39	27	6,231	82
1895	2				1	1	20		19	11	1,130	8	8	6	946	8	6	4	245	3	3	1	1,000	2					39	23	3,341	21
1896	5	2	2,500	30	2	1	10		17	10	1,690	37	2	1	160		3	3	125		1	1	250	14	1	1	800	7	31	19	5,535	89
1897	4				1				16	11	831	2	8	6	430	3					3	3	826	22					34	21	2,097	28
1898	5	3	145	1	2	1	8		26	21	3,327	29	16	7	268	8					1	1	22	3					50	33	3,770	42
1899	12	9	5,442	315	9	7	841	11	49	35	3,291	80	23	12	2,899	33	1				5	5	544	4	3	3	3,000	36	102	71	16,017	480
1900	19	10	8,636	309	1	1	7		65	51	3,356	89	17	17	14,397	241					3	3	355	4	1	1	800	30	112	83	27,551	673

A = Number of strikes in progress

B = Number of strikes in progress with complete data

C = Number of workers involved

D = Duration in person days (000)

a Includes three strikes in the Northwest Territories (1892 and two in 1897), one of which involved 10 workers for a total of 10 person days. Prince Edward Island apparently was strike free in the 1890s.

Table 11.E
Strike Estimates by Province, 1901–50

	British Columbia				Alberta				Saskatchewan			
	A	B	C	D	A	B	C	D	A	B	C	D
1901	13	6	9,394	223								
1902	16	9	598	10	1	1	90	1				
1903	30	20	8,874	259	7	5	303	5				
1904	4	4	899	5	2	1	28					
1905	15	12	3,266	63	3	2	400	13	1	1	20	
1906	20	13	2,039	67	15	13	1,559	84	1	1	4	
1907	22	19	3,747	81	12	11	2,883	32	3	3	98	
1908	7	7	3,122	12	4	3	554	4	6	1	200	1
1909	12	11	1,465	45	11	10	2,763	176	4	3	218	
1910	15	8	964	19	12	8	911	15	6	4	344	12
1911	17	13	9,304	612	16	11	6,275	932	2			
1912	22	10	12,173	542	23	17	3,274	27	19	15	2,310	12
1913	25	16	13,000	667	15	10	987	13	10	6	258	4
1914	14	8	2,252	277	8	7	860	9	4	2	53	
1915	13	8	1,587	22	8	8	851	6	3	1	12	
1916	21	16	6,381	44	8	7	6,125	26	8	7	455	2
1917	55	35	15,075	335	24	20	12,013	388	6	4	201	1
1918	46	32	16,371	200	53	47	7,812	66	10	8	456	9
1919	73	46	22,008	516	29	26	12,534	299	13	10	2,351	42
1920	124	67	10,456	141	39	35	6,323	78	4	2	100	1
1921	37	25	2,849	58	11	10	786	12	11	8	234	3
1922	15	11	3,104	144	29	27	9,669	446	3	3	73	2
1923	8	8	2,947	80	16	15	4,291	47	2	2	24	
1924	9	9	4,400	185	10	9	7,118	652	1	1	38	
1925	15	15	2,918	20	19	18	6,181	126				
1926	16	15	1,350	23	3	3	445	8	1			
1927	9	9	815	12	5	5	765	8	3	3	94	1
1928	10	10	2,671	30	11	11	2,147	86	2	2	115	1
1929	15	12	691	10	4	4	324	10	1	1	56	
1930	8	8	266	3	5	5	174	2	2	2	95	1
1931	19	19	3,037	82	9	9	632	6	6	6	748	7
1932	22	22	4,500	38	20	20	3,294	112	9	9	369	4
1933	18	16	2,412	27	11	11	1,235	14				
1934	23	23	4,271	141	10	10	524	6	1	1	6	
1935	33	25	6,898	118	13	12	1,870	20				
1936	17	17	5,740	75	15	14	2,783	21	2	2	6	
1937	28	25	1,774	46	18	18	2,421	15	5	5	130	1
1938	11	11	791	20	13	11	1,721	10	3	3	481	3
1939	5	5	922	16	10	10	1,574	19	4	2	520	14
1940	8	7	1,862	16	8	8	892	8				
1941	14	13	1,751	9	10	10	1,478	10				
1942	52	49	18,590	50	20	20	4,571	9	3	3	229	2
1943	29	29	21,581	78	43	43	14,800	98	4	4	158	2
1944	15	15	6,379	5	21	21	2,543	8	1	1	48	

Table 11.ε (continued)

	Manitoba				Ontario				Quebec			
	A	B	C	D	A	B	C	D	A	B	C	D
1901	7	4	512	18	62	54	3,467	49	29	27	3,273	124
1902	11	8	400	16	79	73	5,397	82	30	24	4,243	66
1903	8	4	857	11	115	91	9,587	229	39	38	14,852	285
1904	8	5	151	1	64	54	3,923	60	35	32	3,312	56
1905	13	10	497	7	45	34	1,919	39	23	22	1,797	30
1906	10	10	4,445	38	78	64	6,371	93	33	31	6,146	77
1907	12	10	1,177	17	98	90	11,594	265	46	40	7,957	61
1908	1	1	16		35	29	2,567	34	26	23	9,784	178
1909	9	8	1,572	27	45	35	2,833	47	16	15	3,057	50
1910	16	12	1,231	16	64	47	6,416	77	26	21	6,344	70
1911	10	8	644	3	71	49	4,898	60	30	21	6,515	38
1912	13	12	2,972	31	100	88	13,157	286	32	28	6,996	170
1913	6	5	1,138	20	114	79	13,128	187	31	27	7,810	94
1914	5	2	168	4	44	31	1,957	45	15	11	4,165	145
1915	7	5	121	1	31	27	1,864	18	14	10	2,965	27
1916	16	12	1,130	11	75	63	6,300	70	28	21	4,415	50
1917	18	12	2,264	46	68	53	8,295	53	31	26	9,246	272
1918	20	17	9,062	84	112	85	11,813	115	28	18	4,782	44
1919	16	13	22,530	820	158	139	41,260	846	100	86	39,530	753
1920	5	3	392	1	152	130	20,341	242	79	59	15,324	201
1921	10	7	868	55	79	67	11,745	471	29	24	4,993	184
1922	6	6	464	64	34	32	3,615	349	19	18	10,904	208
1923	1	1	23	1	27	24	2,327	152	25	25	4,641	75
1924	1	1	60		18	15	1,287	46	25	25	5,850	80
1925	4	4	124		29	27	1,621	17	24	21	4,059	100
1926	4	3	278	3	27	25	2,643	68	17	17	10,924	137
1927	2	2	75	1	25	25	3,511	45	13	13	1,022	40
1928	4	4	862	11	55	55	3,773	41	12	12	3,531	25
1929	5	5	144	2	47	45	5,596	91	16	16	3,233	33
1930					24	24	4,036	28	13	13	2,560	16
1931	8	8	408	7	27	26	2,905	66	17	16	1,221	8
1932	6	5	82	1	40	40	3,580	35	23	23	6,014	44
1933	21	21	448	1	55	54	11,246	187	26	25	9,615	69
1934	11	11	1,640	40	109	105	15,631	173	39	36	13,182	132
1935	19	18	717	9	59	55	10,785	78	15	15	8,590	33
1936	13	13	2,094	20	103	102	11,776	89	21	21	5,926	33
1937	11	11	734	16	166	159	25,393	320	51	50	24,530	358
1938	10	10	459	1	77	77	8,631	73	19	19	2,191	11
1939	6	6	159	1	44	42	5,385	60	21	20	2,549	16
1940	5	5	133		61	60	10,379	42	24	23	8,653	107
1941	2	2	163	1	127	124	28,483	239	44	43	12,020	52
1942	9	9	476		103	99	27,508	172	154	149	41,942	156
1943	9	9	1,158	2	109	108	36,730	191	114	114	78,126	457
1944	4	4	220	1	70	69	32,342	261	48	46	18,822	113

Table 11.E (continued)

	British Columbia				Alberta				Saskatchewan			
	A	B	C	D	A	B	C	D	A	B	C	D
1945	14	13	6,749	68	20	19	9,576	123	3	3	83	
1946	20	20	41,998	1,292	24	24	9,320	28	4	4	103	2
1947	29	28	6,314	128	14	14	1,273	15	9	9	734	9
1948	12	12	4,260	111	6	6	7,059	200	9	9	598	11
1949	17	16	5,487	40	8	8	687	5	6	6	425	5
1950	25	21	3,801	32	12	12	1,963	14	4	3	199	1

	New Brunswick				Prince Edward Island				Nova Scotia			
	A	B	C	D	A	B	C	D	A	B	C	D
1901	7	3	124	1					11	7	2,354	23
1902	18	10	408	15	2	2	47	1	13	10	3,176	16
1903	18	14	930	10					13	8	2,717	23
1904	12	2	16	1					17	11	4,477	84
1905	13	11	1,414	6	1				18	11	3,123	32
1906	13	11	601	4	2				18	12	2,647	16
1907	21	15	1,653	19					15	14	5,474	52
1908	11	10	1,472	30					6	3	377	5
1909	7	3	105	2					13	11	6,673	537
1910	6	1	150	1					9	5	2,903	478
1911	14	5	188	8					7	3	1,335	152
1912	21	10	903	8	1	1	26		9	7	243	3
1913	20	12	1,170	22					12	8	2,763	18
1914	3	2	230	3					5	3	196	7
1915	3	3	135	1					7	7	3,945	20
1916	6	3	325	4					5	3	1,274	19
1917	5	3	97	2	2	2	270	1	8	7	1,415	12
1918	11	9	3,324	16					18	16	23,635	68
1919	19	18	4,068	28					19	12	3,778	90
1920	15	12	1,448	30	1	1	7		39	27	21,133	112
1921	13	13	1,629	48	1	1	9		13	13	1,041	66
1922	3	3	88	1	1	1	50	2	9	7	15,825	313
1923	2	2	287	2					17	16	19,998	315
1924	1	1	57	1					9	9	12,778	306
1925									4	4	11,574	910
1926	4	4	705	8	1	1	75		11	11	7,379	20
1927	1	1	25	1	1	1	100		16	16	15,896	46
1928									12	11	3,866	12
1929	1	1	5						13	13	2,990	7
1930	4	4	186	1					18	18	7,050	40
1931	2	2	44						4	4	1,186	5
1932									11	11	4,814	18
1933	5	5	123	1					10	9	1,696	18

Table 11.E (continued)

	Manitoba				Ontario				Quebec			
	A	B	C	D	A	B	C	D	A	B	C	D
1945	12	12	402	6	74	74	44,480	1,175	43	43	11,086	29
1946	6	6	380	22	84	80	40,383	1,885	46	46	15,982	430
1947	10	9	875	23	117	113	14,662	166	53	53	20,090	237
1948	4	4	243	3	78	76	14,172	283	34	34	8,925	234
1949	5	5	1,124	19	68	68	28,993	307	24	24	10,006	540
1950	3	3	402	2	93	86	42,923	198	35	33	8,196	97

	Interprovincial (except coal)				Total			
	A	B	C	D	A	B	C	D
1901	1	1	5,000	300	130	102	24,124	738
1902					170	137	14,359	206
19031	1	1	400	38	231	181	38,520	859
1904	2	2	1,200	5	144	111	14,006	211
1905	1	1	500	58	133	104	12,936	247
1906					190	155	23,812	380
1907	1	1	100	1	229	202	34,683	529
1908	1	1	8,000	440	97	78	26,092	704
1909					116	95	18,686	884
1910	2	2	3,100	46	156	108	22,363	733
1911	1	1	300	17	167	110	29,459	1,822
1912	2	2	1,050	57	242	190	43,104	1,136
1913	1	1	750	14	234	164	41,004	1,037
1914	1	1	30	1	99	67	9,911	491
1915					86	69	11,480	95
1916	1	1	566	16	166	131	26,971	241
1917	3	3	1,451	13	218	163	50,327	1,124
1918	7	7	5,318	55	305	239	82,573	657
1919	1	1	1,250	8	427	350	149,309	3,402
1920	1	1	1,100	8	457	335	76,624	814
1921	3	3	4,224	152	208	172	28,398	1,050
1922					118	107	43,792	1,529
1923					97	92	34,538	672
1924	2	2	2,728	25	75	71	34,316	1,295
1925	1	1	2,550	20	96	90	29,027	1,193
1926	1	1	50	1	85	80	23,849	267
1927					75	75	22,303	153
1928	1	1	750	19	107	106	17,715	224
1929	1	1	11		105	100	13,120	152
1930					74	74	14,367	92
1931	1	1	122	20	93	91	10,303	201
1932					131	130	22,653	253
1933					146	141	26,775	318

Table 11.E (continued)

	New Brunswick				Prince Edward Island				Nova Scotia			
	A	B	C	D	A	B	C	D	A	B	C	D
1934	6	6	1,484	15	1	1	15		22	22	9,468	67
1935	1	1	125		2	2	51		11	11	4,713	29
1936					1	1	20		13	13	7,154	39
1937	11	11	3,723	79					50	47	14,366	51
1938	5	5	920	4	1	1	67		31	30	4,658	25
1939	7	7	847	1	2	2	150		49	48	32,127	97
1940	5	4	1,763	17	2	2	75		79	77	31,792	66
1941	18	18	3,877	16	1	1	30		49	49	39,475	101
1942	9	9	2,848	5	1	1	10		58	56	20,046	60
1943	23	23	2,456	5	1	1	9		102	102	64,038	206
1944	11	10	1,007	3					47	45	14,567	101
1945	10	10	582	4					35	35	17,994	35
1946	10	10	1,172	11					43	43	13,936	45
1947	12	12	2,824	73	2	2	164		25	22	44,663	1,285
1948	8	8	517	8					17	16	6,889	10
1949	2	2	22						9	9	1,592	6
1950	4	4	421	5					7	5	2,877	7

Table 11.E (continued)

	Interprovincial (except coal)				Total			
	A	B	C	D	A	B	C	D
1934	1	1	200	3	224	216	46,421	577
1935	1	1	150		154	140	33,899	289
1936	1	1	72		186	184	35,571	278
1937					341	327	73,221	887
1938	1	1	1,100	3	171	168	21,019	150
1939					148	142	44,233	225
1940	1	1	6,000	10	193	187	61,549	267
1941	1	1	150	1	267	262	87,937	434
1942					409	395	116,220	454
1943	2	2	1,046	4	435	434	220,102	1,042
1944					217	211	75,928	491
1945	1	1	5,527	18	212	210	96,499	1,458
1946	5	5	16,319	801	243	239	139,673	4,516
1947	3	3	13,914	464	272	263	105,513	2,399
1948	4	4	734	27	171	168	43,397	886
1949	2	2	2,359	127	149	148	53,493	1,072
1950	2	2	130,483	1,001	192	176	193,914	1,390

A = Number of strikes in progress.
B = Number of strikes in progress with complete data.
C = Number of workers involved.
D = Duration in person days (000).
a Eighteen interprovincial coal mining strikes have been disaggregated by province.
.b Includes eight strikes in the Northwest Territories and Yukon (1921, two in 1929, 1934, 1937, 1941, 1945, 1946), seven of which involved 850 workers for a total of 5,910 person days, and 15 strikes in Newfoundland (eight in 1949 and seven in 1950) which involved 5,447 workers for a total of 56,343 person days.

Table 11.F
Strike Dimensions by Industry, 1911–50[a]

Industry and decade	Frequency (depth)[c]	Size[b] (height)[d]	Duration[b] (width)[e]
Mining			
1910s	479	646	20
1920s	301	749	15
1930s	419	392	9
1940s	448	1,163	5
Manufacturing			
1910s	193	225	24
1920s	75	191	45
1930s	106	205	14
1940s	134	411	10
Construction			
1910s	262	201	29
1920s	114	111	17
1930s	72	44	5
1940s	71	146	6
Transportation and public utilities			
1910s	151	272	11
1920s	23	161	23
1930s	41	199	9
1940s	49	998	7
Service, Finance, and public administration			
1910s	41	109	14
1920s	10	78	22
1930s	20	34	10
1940s	18	144	10

a Average annual frequency, size, and duration of strikes in progress, 1911–20, 1921–30, 1931–40, 1941–50.
b Estimates of average size and duration are based only on strikes for which data on duration and the number of workers involved was obtained.
c Total number of strikes per million non-agricultural employees.
d Number of workers involved per strike.
e Mean duration in working days.

Table 11.G
Strike Dimensions by Province, 1891–1950[a]

Province and decade	Frequency (depth)[c]	Dimensions Size[b] (height)[d]	Duration[b] (width)[e]
Nova Scotia			
1890s	32	258	25
1900s	119	369	25
1910s	99	642	19
1920s	89	834	26
1930s	194	412	5
1940s	226	592	4
Prince Edward Island			
1890s	–	–	–
1900s	41	25	15
1910s	32	75	3
1920s	30	58	15
1930s	64	42	3
1940s	29	42	2
New Brunswick			
1890s	35	56	8
1900s	186	86	21
1910s	147	154	23
1920s	32	103	24
1930s	43	220	6
1940s	88	148	6
Quebec			
1890s	36	354	12
1900s	81	223	18
1910s	77	331	20
1920s	29	281	40
1930s	30	333	10
1940s	55	385	8
Ontario			
1890s	63	88	33
1900s	124	95	23
1910s	124	165	21
1920s	40	118	30
1930s	67	147	12
1940s	65	346	9
Manitoba			
1890s	87	94	17
1900s	136	151	23
1910s	98	454	14
1920s	24	88	32
1930s	63	64	14
1940s	33	86	10

Table 11.G continued

Province and decade	Frequency (depth)[c]	Dimensions Size[b] (height)[d]	Duration[b] (width)[e]
Saskatchewan			
1890s	–	–	–
1900s	55	68	13
1910s	94	113	13
1920s	23	33	19
1930s	23	81	14
1940s	31	61	12
Alberta			
1890s	–	–	–
1900s	161	176	20
1910s	244	303	14
1920s	94	298	25
1930s	89	138	16
1940s	94	301	8
British Columbia			
1890s	143	516	26
1900s	127	315	31
1910s	223	433	24
1920s	64	180	27
1930s	69	189	17
1940s	67	541	12
Canada			
1890s	55	218	25
1900s	115	180	23
1910s	123	286	20
1920s	43	270	30
1930s	61	218	11
1940s	70	452	9

a Average annual frequency, size, and duration of strikes in progress, 1891–1900, 1901–10, 1911–20, 1921–30, 1931–40, 1941–50.

b Estimates of average size and duration are based only on strikes for which data on duration and the number of workers involved was obtained.

c Total number of strikes per million non-agricultural employees.

d Number of workers involved per strike.

e Mean duration in working days.

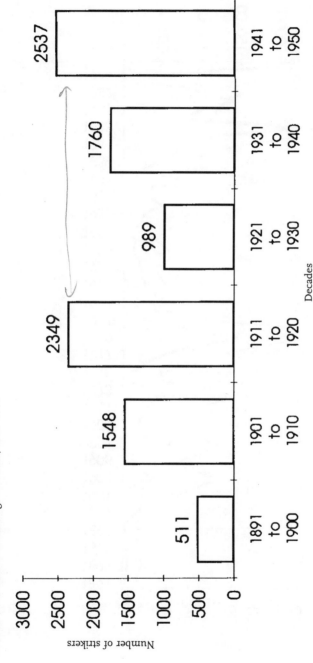

Figure 11.A
Number of Strikes Commencing in Canada, 1891–1950

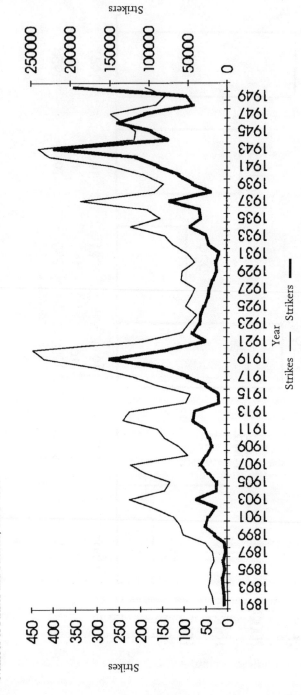

Figure 11.B
Number of Strikes and Strikers, 1891–1950

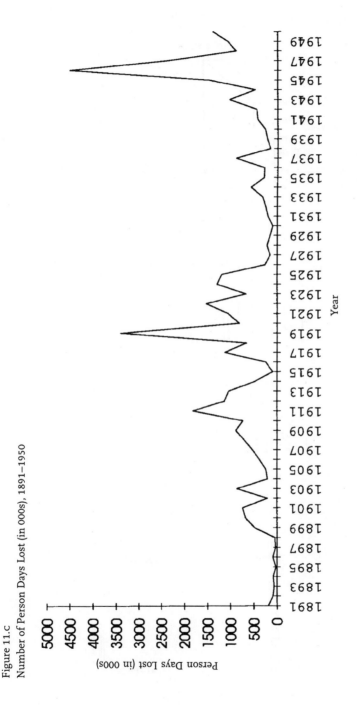

Figure 11.c
Number of Person Days Lost (in 000s), 1891–1950

Figure 11.D
Strike Shapes by Industry and Province, 1891–1950

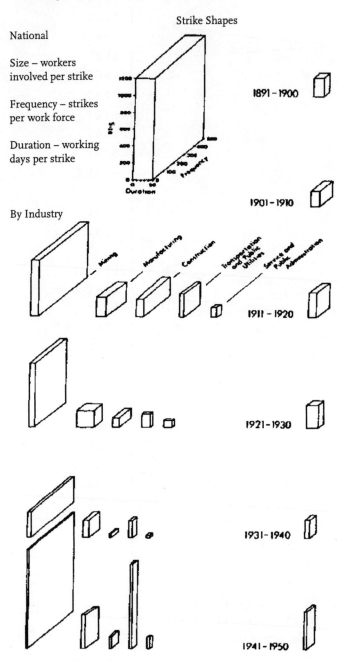

Strike Shapes

National

Size – workers
involved per strike

Frequency – strikes
per work force

Duration – working
days per strike

By Industry

Figure 11.D (continued)

By Province

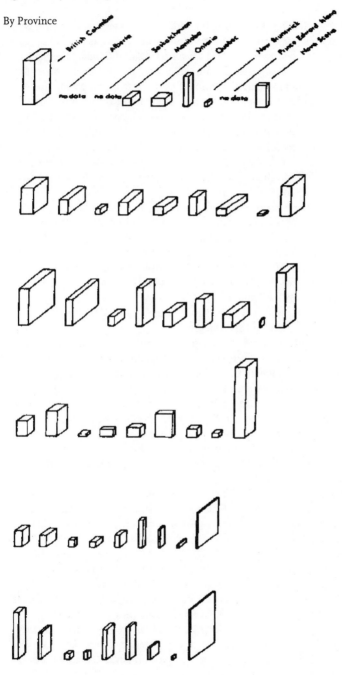

NOTES

We would like to thank Robert Hong for additional research aid. For aid with graphs and figures our thanks to Robert Hong and Susan Laskin. This project has been supported by funds from the *Historical Atlas of Canada*, the Social Sciences and Humanities Research Council of Canada, and the Institute for Social and Economic Research at Memorial University. In preparing these statistics we would like to acknowledge the assistance of Peter DeLottinville who began the research, and Ian McKay, who gave us complete access to his notes on strikes in the Maritimes. We would also like to thank our *Historical Atlas* colleagues for useful comments, statistical help, and design aid.

1 Michelle Perrot, *Workers on Strike: France 1871–1890* (New Haven 1987), 12. For the full, original, magisterial work see her *Les Ouvriers en Grève, France, 1871–1890* (Paris 1974), 2 vols.

2 To cite only their major strike monographs: Edward Shorter and Charles Tilly, *Strikes in France, 1830–1968* (Cambridge 1974); James Cronin, *Industrial Conflict in Modern Britain* (London 1979); and P.K. Edwards, *Strikes in the United States, 1881–1974* (Oxford 1981). Indeed this entire project is indebted to their stimulating and innovative reconstructions of their respective national strike stories, especially to their methods and techniques.

3 David Montgomery, "Strikes in Nineteenth-Century America," *Social Science History* 4 (1980): 81–104.

4 Cronin, *Industrial Conflict*, esp. chap. 3–5, but passim; Shorter and Tilly, *Strikes in France*, chap. 5. Moreover, the general timing of the waves from 1870–1920 run parallel to those discussed in Friedhelm Boll, "International Strike Waves: A Critical Assessment," in Wolfgang J. Mommsen and Hans-Gerhard Husung, eds, *The Development of Trade Unionism in Great Britain and Germany, 1880–1914* (London 1985), 78–99.

5 For Tilly a strike wave occurs "when both the number of strikes and the number of strikers in a given year exceed the means of the previous five years by more than 50 per cent." Shorter and Tilly, *Strikes in France*, 106–7.

6 What follows draws on G.S. Kealey, "The Structure of Canadian Working-Class History" in W.J.C. Cherwinski and G.S. Kealey, eds, *Lectures in Canadian Labour and Working-Class History* (St John's 1985) and Craig Heron and Robert Storey, "On the Job in Canada" in their *On the Job* (Montreal 1986).

7 David Montgomery, *Workers Control in America* (New York 1979) David Brody, *Workers in Industrial America* (New York 1980); and David M. Gordon, Richard Edwards, and Michael Reich, *Segmented Work, Divided Workers: The Historical Transformation of Labor in the United States* (New York 1982). Finally for sceptics who like their economic history undiluted, see M.C. Urquhart, "New Estimates of Gross National Product, Canada, 1870–1926: Some Implications for Canadian Development," Queen's University Institute for Economic Research, Discussion Paper, No. 586.

8 Bryan D. Palmer, *A Culture in Conflict: Skilled Workers and Industrial Capitalism in Hamilton, Ontario* (Montreal 1979); Gregory S. Kealey, *Toronto Workers Respond to Industrial Capitalism* (Toronto 1980); David Frank, "The Cape Breton Coal Miners, 1917–1926' (PHD diss., Dalhousie University 1979); Nolan Reilly, "Emergence of Class Consciousness in Industrial Nova Scotia: Amherst, 1891–1925" (PHD diss., Dalhousie University 1983); Allen Seager, "The Proletariat in Wild Rose Country: The Alberta Coal Miners, 1905–1945" (PHD diss., York University 1982); Craig Heron, "Working-Class Hamilton, 1895–1930" (PHD diss., Dalhousie University 1981); Wayne Roberts, "Studies in the Toronto Labour Movement" (PHD diss., University of Toronto 1978); Robert Storey, "Workers, Unions, and Steel: The Shaping of the Hamilton Working Class, 1935–1948" (PHD diss., University of Toronto 1982).

9 Ian McKay, "Strikes in the Maritimes, 1901–1914," *Acadiensis* 13 (1983); Craig Heron and Bryan Palmer, "Through the Prism of the Strike: Industrial Conflict in Southern Ontario, 1901–1914," *Canadian Historical Review* 57 (1977): 423–58; Jacques Rouillard, "Le militantisme des travailleurs au Québec et en Ontario niveau de syndicalisation et mouvement des grèves (1900–1980)," *Revue d'histoire de l'Amérique française* 37 (1983): 201–25; and James Thwaites, "La grève au Québec: Une analyse quantitative exploratoire portant sur la période 1896–1915," *Labour/Le Travail* 14 (1984): 183–204.

10 David Jay Bercuson, "Labour Radicalism and the Western Industrial frontier," *Canadian Historical Review* 58 (1977): 154–75.

11 In addition to the above, see also his *Confrontation at Winnipeg* (Montreal 1974) and *Fools and Wise Men* (Toronto 1978). Other similar claims are made in Ross McCormack, *Reformers, Rebels and Revolutionaries* (Toronto 1977) and, more carefully, in H.C. Pentland, "The Western Canadian Labour Movement, 1847–1919," *Canadian Journal of Political and Social Theory* 3 (1979): 53–78.

12 These rank orderings were calculated simply by assigning a ranking of one to nine to each province on each of the three measures for each decade and then summing the scores for each measure and for the three measures together. The 1890s were excluded owing to the lack of comparability in the data. The resultant rankings:

	Total	Frequency	Size	Duration
British Columbia	39	16	15	8
Nova Scotia	48	15	5	28
Alberta	55	8	22	25
Ontario	66	22	26	18
Quebec	74	36	15	23
New Brunswick	76	19	29	28
Manitoba	76	30	29	17
Saskatchewan	110	41	40	29
Prince Edward Island	126	38	44	44

13 Laurel Sefton MacDowell, "The Formation of the Canadian Industrial Relations System During World War II," *Labour/Le Travailleur* 3 (1978): 175–96.

14 Paul Craven, *"An Impartial Umpire": Industrial Relations and the Canadian State, 1900–1911* (Toronto 1980) and Leo Panitch and Don Swartz, "Towards Permanent Exceptionalism: Coercion and Consent in Canadian Labour Relations," *Labour/Le Travail* 13 (1984): 133–57.

15 On military aid to the civil power see Desmond Morton, "Aid to the Civil Power: The Canadian Militia in Support of Social Order," *Canadian Historical Review* 51 (1970): 407–25; Don Macgillivray, "Military Aid to the Civil Power: The Cape Breton Experience in the 1920s," *Acadiensis* 3 (1974): 45–64; Major J.J.B. Pariseau, *Disorders, Strikes, and Disasters: Military Aid to the Civil Power in Canada, 1867–1933* (Ottawa 1973); and his "Forces armées et maintien de l'ordre au Canada 1867–1967: un siècle d'aide au pouvoir civil" (thèse présentée pour obtenir le doctorat 3è cycle, Université Paul Valéry III, Montpelier 1981).

16 Stuart Jamieson, "Militancy and Violence in Canadian Labour Relations: 1900–1975," University of British Columbia, Department of Economics, Discussion Paper No. 79-17, April 1979. Jamieson's measure of violence is different than ours. His statistics show:

1900–13	125	1930–39	125
1914–19	12	1940–49	24
1920–29	15		

17 For more detailed accounts of these strikes see: Allen Seager, "Socialists and Workers: The Western Canadian Coal Miners, 1900–21," *Labour/Le Travail* 16 (1985): 23–59; Paul Phillips, *No Power Greater: A Century of Labour in BC* (Vancouver 1967); Stuart Jamieson, *Time of Trouble: Labour Unrest and Industrial Conflict in Canada, 1900–66* (Ottawa 1968); J. Hugh Tuck, "The United Brotherhood of Railway Employees in Western Canada, 1898–1905," *Labour/Le Travail* 11 (1983): 63–88. For the broader national response, see Robert Babcock, *Gompers in Canada* (Toronto 1974) and Craven, *An Impartial Umpire.*

18 On the Halifax Waterfront, see Ian McKay, "Class Struggle and Merchant Capital: Labourers on the Halifax Waterfront, 1850–1902" in Bryan Palmer, ed., *The Character of Class Struggle* (Toronto 1986).

19 For a study of the London street railway strike, see Bryan Palmer, "'Give Us the Road and We Will Run It': The Social and Cultural Matrix of an Emerging Labour Movement," in G.S. Kealey and Peter Warrian, eds, *Essays in Canadian Working-Class History* (Toronto 1976). See also Peter D. Lambly, "Working Conditions and Industrial Relations on Canada's Street Railways, 1900–1920" (MA thesis, Dalhousie University 1983) and Christopher Armstrong and H.V. Nelles, *Monopoly's Moment: The Organization and Regulation of Canadian Utilities, 1830–1930* (Philadelphia 1986), 213–48.

20 Craig Heron, "The Crisis of the Craftsman: Hamilton Metal Workers in the Early Twentieth Century" and Wayne Roberts, "Toronto Metal Workers and the Second Industrial Revolution, 1889–914," *Labour/Le Travail* 6 (1980): 7–48, 49–72.

21 *Globe* (Toronto), 21 February, 1 March, 18 July, 26, 27, 29, 30, 31 October 1900; *Gazette* (Montreal), 25, 26, 27 October 1900; and *Star* (Montreal), 22, 23 February and 14, 16 July 1900. See also Jacques Rouillard, *Les travailleurs du coton au Québec, 1900–1915* (Montreal 1974), 107–29.

22 For discussions of building trade workers see Wayne Roberts, "Artisans, Aristocrats and Handymen: Politics and Trade Unionism among Toronto Skilled Building Trades Workers, 1896–1914," *Labour/Le Travail* 1 (1976): 92–121 and Ian McKay, *The Craft Transformed: An Essay on the Carpenters of Halifax, 1885–1985* (Halifax 1985).

23 On this strike, see A. Ross McCormack, "Wobblies and Blanket-stiffs: The Constituency of the IWW in Western Canada" in Cherwinski and Kealey, eds, *Lectures* and his "The Industrial Workers of the World in Western Canada, 1905–1914," *Historical Papers* (1975): 167–90. See also James Mark Leier, "Through the Lens of Syndicalism: Fragmentation on the Vancouver and British Columbia Left before the Great War" (MA thesis, Simon Fraser University 1987), esp. 37–46.

24 *Voice* (Winnipeg), 5, 12 July 1912; National Archives of Canada (hereafter NA), RG37, vol. 300, file 3531.

25 McKay, *The Craft Transformed*, 54–63.

26 *Ottawa Citizen*, 13 July 1912; *Ottawa Journal*, 10 July 1912; *Stratford Herald*, 20 September 1913.

27 Mercedes Steedman, "Skill and Gender in the Canadian Clothing Industry, 1890–1940" in Heron and Storey, eds, *On the Job*, 152–76.

28 Ruth Frager, "Sewing Solidarity: The Eaton's Strike of 1912," *Canadian Woman Studies* 7 (1986): 96–8.

29 Roberts, "Toronto Metal Workers," 71–2.

30 Jean Morrison, "Ethnicity and Violence: The Lakehead Freight Handlers before World War 1" in Kealey and Warrian, *Essays*, 143–60.

31 P.G. Silverman, "Aid of the Civil Power: The Nanaimo Coal Miners' Strike, 1912–1914," *Canadian Defence Quarterly* 4 (1974): 16–52; Lynn Bowen, *Boss Whistle: The Coal Miners of Vancouver Island Remember* (Lantzville, BC 1982), 131–98.

32 NA, RG27, vol. 300, file 3618 and vol. 302, file 13 (90) A.

33 Gregory S. Kealey, "1919: The Canadian Labour Revolt," *Labour/Le Travail* 13 (1984): 11–44 and "The State, the Foreign-Language Press, and the Canadian Labour Revolt of 1917–1920," in Christiane Harzig and Dirk Hoerder, eds, *The Press of Labour Migrants in Europe and North America, 1880s–1930s* (Bremen 1985).

34 James Cronin, "Labor Insurgency and Class Formation: Comparative Perspectives on the Crisis of 1917–1920 in Europe," *Social Science History* 4 (1980): 125–52. see also James Cronin and Carmen Sirianni,

eds, *Work, Community and Power: The Experience of Labor in Europe and North America, 190–1925* (Philadelphia 1983). For a third North American case see Peter McInnis, "Newfoundland Labour and World War 1: The Emergence of the Newfoundland Industrial Workers Association" (MA thesis, Memorial University of Newfoundland 1987).

35 J.T. Montague, "Trade Unionism in the Canadian Meat Packing Industry" (PHD diss., University of Toronto 1950), 31–8 and George Sayers Bain, "The United Packinghouse, Food and Allied Workers" (MA thesis, University of Manitoba 1964), 35–67.

36 A.E. Johnson, "The Strikes in Winnipeg in May 1918: The Prelude to 1919?" (MA thesis, University of Manitoba 1978).

37 R. Usiskin, "Toward a Theoretical Reformulation of the Relationship Between Political Ideology, Social Class, & Ethnicity: A Case Study of the Winnipeg Jewish Radical Community, 1905–1920" (MA thesis, University of Winnipeg 1978), esp. chap. 5, and her "The Winnipeg Jewish Radical Community: Its Early Formation, 1905–1918," in *Jewish Life and Times: A Collection of Essays* (Winnipeg 1983), 155–68.

38 William Doherty, "Slaves of the Lamp: A History of the Staff Association Movement in the Canadian Civil Service, 1860–1924," unpublished ms, is a promising beginning. See also Anthony Thomson, "'The Large and Generous View': The Debate on Labour Affiliation in the Canadian Civil Service, 1918–1928," *Labour/Le Travailleur* 2 (1977): 108–36.

39 William Doherty, "Slaves of the Lamp," esp. chap. 9. See also NA, Post Office Papers, RG3, vol. 646, file 96853, "List of Offices Affected by the 1918 Postal Strike." See also Anthony Thomson, "'The Large and Generous View,'" 108–36.

40 Ontario, Royal Commission on Police Matters, *Report*, 1919.

41 Jim Naylor, "Toronto, 1919," *Historical Papers* (1986): 33–55.

42 G. Ewen, "La contestation à Montréal en 1919," *Histoire des travailleurs québécois. Bulletin RCHTQ*, 36 (1986): 37–62.

43 Montgomery, "Nineteenth-Century Strikes"; for Hobsbawm, see his "Economic Fluctuations and Some Social Movements" and "Customs, Wages and Workload" in *Labouring Men* (London 1964); for Perrot, see her magisterial *Les ouvriers en grève: France 1871–1890*.

44 D.C. Master, *The Winnipeg General Strike* (Toronto 1950); David Bercuson, *Confrontation at Winnipeg*, 188.

45 H. Clare Pentland, "The Western Canadian Labour Movement, 1897–1919," *Canadian Journal of Political and Social Theory* 3 (1979): 53–78.

46 Yves Lequin, "Social Structures and Shared Beliefs: Four Worker Communities in the Second Industrialization," *International Labor and Working-Class History* 22 (1982): 1–17.

47 Sir Robert Borden, *Memoirs* (Toronto 1938), II: 972.

48 On state repression and the creation of a new security branch see Kealey, "1919" and "The State" and S.W. Horral, "The Royal Northwest

Mounted Police and Labour Unrest in Western Canada, 1919," *Canadian Historical Review* 61 (1980): 169–90.

49 For events in BC see Myrtle Bergren, *Tough Timber* (Toronto 1966) and Jerry Lembcke and William M. Tattam, *One Union in Wood: A Political History of the International Woodworkers of America* (Madiera Park, BC 1984).

50 For a detailed analysis of this strike, see Robert S. Robson, "Strike in the Single Enterprise Community: Flin Flon, Manitoba: 1934," *Labour/Le Travailleur* 12 (1983): 63–86. The best study of the Workers Unity League by far is John Manley, "Communism and the Canadian Working Class during the Great Depression: The Workers' Unity League, 1930–1936" (PHD diss., Dalhousie University 1984). See also Ian Angus, *Canadian Bolsheviks: The Early Years of the Communist Party of Canada* (Montreal 1981), 273–88.

51 Allen Seager, "Minto, New Brunswick: A Study in Canadian Class Relations between the Wars," *Labour/Le Travailleur* 5 (1980): 81–132.

52 Rose Pesotta, *Bread upon the Waters* (New York 1941), 253–77, provides a first-person account by an ILGWU organizer. See also C. McLeod, "Women in Production: The Toronto Dressmakers' Strike of 1931" in J. Acton, et al., eds, *Women at Work* (Toronto 1974), 309–29; Evelyn Dumas, *The Bitter Thirties in Quebec* (Montreal 1975), 43–69; and Irving Abella, ed., "Portrait of a Jewish Professional Revolutionary: The recollections of Joshua Gershman," *Labour/Le travailleur* 2 (1977): 184–213; perhaps most useful of all is Manley, "Communism and the Canadian Working Class," 464–534. In addition see Terry Copp, "The Rise of Industrial Unions in Montreal, 1935–1945," *Relations industrielles* 37 (1982): 843–75.

53 Pesotta, *Bread*, 253–77 and Dumas, *Bitter Thirties*, 43–69.

54 For the struggles in rubber, see Terry Copp, ed., *Industrial Unionism in Kitchener, 1937–47* (Elora, ON 1976), esp. 1–29.

55 Irving Abella, "Oshawa 1937" in his *On Strike* (Toronto 1974), 93–128, and Eric Havelock, "Forty-five Years Ago: The Oshawa Strike," *Labour/Le Travailleur* 11 (1983): 119–24.

56 One prime example was Kirkland Lake. See Laurel Sefton MacDowell, "Remember Kirkland Lake": The Gold Miners' Strike of 1941–42 (Toronto 983). This strike involved almost 3,000 workers for three months from 18 November 1941–12 February 1942.

57 David Moulton, "Ford Windsor 1945," in Abella, ed., *On Strike*, 129–61.

58 See Laurel Sefton MacDowell, "The 1943 Steel Strike Against Wartime Wage Controls," *Labour/Le Travailleur* 10 (1982): 65–85 and Craig Heron and Robert Storey, "Work and Struggle in the Canadian Steel Industry, 1900–1950," in their *On the Job*, 210–44.

59 Douglas Cruickshank, "Dominion Wartime Labour Policy and the Politics of Unionism, 1939–1945: The Experience of the canadian Congress of Labour's Eastern Canadian Shipyard Unions" (MA thesis, Dalhousie

University 1984). For first-hand accounts, see David Frank and Donald MacGillivray, eds, *George MacEachern: An Autobiography* (Sydney 1987), esp. chap. 6 and Howard White, *A Hard Man to Beat* (Vancouver 1983).

60 Dumas, *Bitter Thirties*, 78–100 and 101–27.

61 Ira Katznelson and Aristide R. Zolberg, eds, *Working-Class Formation: Nineteenth-Century Patterns in Western Europe and the United States* (Princeton 1986), esp. 3–41, 397–455. See also Sean Wilenz, "Against Exceptionalism: Class Consciousness and the American Labour Movement," *International Labour and Working-Class History* 26 (1984): 1–24, and responses in 26 (1984): 25–36; 27 (1985): 35–8; and 28 (1985): 46–55.

62 The surviving strikes and lockouts files date from March 1907 which is the same month that the Industrial Disputes Investigation Act was passed. It is unclear how the records were kept before this.

63 NA, Records of the Department of Labour, RG 27, vol.599.

64 It appears that Trade Dispute Record sheets were subsequently prepared for the period 1901–16 according to the industrial classification system adopted in 1917. All of the sheets completed before 1927 were then revised in the late 1920s. The original and revised sheets are filed together in NA, RG 27, vols 2332–42, microfilm reels T6212–7 and T6663–6.

65 *The Labour Gazette* 3 (January 1903): 533–45.

66 Canada, Department of Labour, *Reports on Strikes and Lockouts in Canada from 1901 to 1912* (Ottawa 1913).

67 Canada, Department of Labour, *Reports on Strikes and Lockouts in Canada 1901–1916* (Ottawa 1918).

68 Parts of the draft report are located in NA, RG 27, vol. 2342, microfilm reel T6666.

69 *Report on Strikes and Lockouts 1901–1912*, 9.

70 This rule was not followed for very long: in the monthly report for December 1900 a strike involving three bakers was included. *The Labour Gazette* 1 (November 1900): 117; 1 (January 1901): 250.

71 *The Labour Gazette* 3 (March 1903): 709.

72 *The Labour Gazette* 20 (March 1920): 267.

73 *The Labour Gazette* 24 (February 1924): 109.

74 From the notes contained in the Trade Dispute Record sheet files, it appears that almost all of the newspapers held by the department were surveyed.

75 The total number of workers involved, 1901–29, was increased by 29,262 and the time loss was reduced by 2,944,064 person days.

76 NA, RG 27, vols 2332–42, microfilm reels T6212–7 and T6663–6.

77 *The Labour Gazette* 31 (February 1931): 133–41.

78 Canada, Department of Labour, *Strikes and Lockouts in Canada During 1950*, supplement to *The Labour Gazette* 51 (April 1951): 8–23.

79 NA, RG 27, vols 2342–3, microfilm reel T6666–7.

80 Arguments about the reliability of official strike statistics are almost as old and as plentiful as the statistics themselves. For an excellent summary of the principal points of view concerning these three measurements and also the systems used to classify issues and settlement, see P.K. Edwards, *Strikes in the United States, 1881–1974* (Oxford 1981), 284–301.

81 Although the department did not explicitly define the terms "strike" or "lockout" in any of its published reports until 1957, there are frequent references to the IDI Act in the strikes and lockouts files. See, for example, William Edgar's arguments in favour of counting a 1909 strike of survey workers in Prince Rupert, NA, RG 27, vol. 296, file 3110, microfilm reel T2685, memorandum for Mr. Acland, 19 March 1909. In 1957 a strike was defined as "a stoppage of work by a group of employees to press for a settlement of a demand or a grievance," and a lockout "a suspension of work initiated by an employer or a group of employers as a result of failure to reach agreement in the course of a dispute over terms of employment." Canada, Department of Labour, *Strikes and Lockouts in Canada 1957* (Ottawa 1958), 26.

82 *Statutes of Canada*, 2907, 6–7 Edward VIII, c. 20.

83 Between 1939 and 1950, fourteen stoppages which did not overlap were counted as five strikes.

84 The department eventually decided to continue counting fishing strikes. See NA, RG 27, vol. 2275, microfilm reel T6183.

85 Ian McKay, "Strikes in the Maritimes, 1901–1914," *Acadiensis* 13 (Autumn 1983): 3–46.

86 This shows up most clearly in our detailed industrial tables, which for reasons of space we are unable to publish here.

87 For reasons why the term itself might be a loaded one, see H.A. Turner, G. Clack, and G. Roberts, *Labour Relations in the Motor Industry* (London 1967), 54.

88 *The Labour Gazette* 3 (February 1903), 626. This principle was not applied religiously.

89 International Labour Office, *Methods of Compiling Statistics of Industrial Disputes*, Studies and Reports, Series N (Statistics), No. 10 (Geneva 1926), 33–4.

90 Our research was completed before McKay had found all 181 of the extra strikes included in his published statistics.

91 Jean Hamelin, Paul Larocque, and Jacques Rouillard, *Répertoire des grèves dans la province de Québec au XIXe siècle* (Montreal 1970).

92 The sources were not considered adequate to include estimates for the North West Territories. It also appears from ongoing research that at least twice as many strikes occurred in British Columbia. Most of the strikes missed in the *Atlas* survey, however, tend to emphasize rather than alter the general pattern of strike activity over the decade. Certainly, they extend British Columbia's lead as the most strike prone province of the 1890s.

93 Edward Shorter and Charles Tilly, "The Shape of Strikes in France, 1830–1960," *Comparative Studies in Society and History* 13 (1971): 60–86.
94 See Robert N. Stern, "Methodological Issues in Quantitative Strike Analysis," *Industrial Relations* 17 (February 1978): 32–42.
95 We are grateful to Marvin McInnis for allowing us to use his revised work force estimates. Provincial work force estimates for 1891 and 1901 were taken from the 1891 census and 1951 census.

12 The Canadian State's Attempt to Manage Class Conflict, 1900–48

It if very often asserted that those political laboratories, the Colonies of Great Britain, shrink from no experiment the object of which is to regulate and improve the condition of the labourer. This assertion is but partly true ... Two of the knottiest questions which humanitarian social reformers have endeavoured in our time to solve, are confessedly the conflict of organised capital with organised labour, and the necessity of securing a minimum of comfort for the humbler class of workers. Among 11 self-governing British colonies two only have made any serious attempt to cope with the second of these problems, and only one has made any determined effort to grapple with the first.   (William Pember Reeves, London, 1900)[1]

I

Canada was certainly not one of the self-governing British colonies credited by Pember Reeves in 1900 with "any serious attempt" or "determined effort." Yet within the following decade the Dominion government would implement a labour relations policy which received almost as much international study and acclaim as had Pember Reeves's own pioneering efforts. The Industrial Disputes Investigation Act (IDIA) of 1907 and, to a lesser degree, its predecessors, the Conciliation Act of 1900 and the Railway Labor Disputes Act of 1903, constitute Canada's major contribution to the international discussion of "the labour problem" so popular with social reformers at the turn of the century.[2] More importantly in terms of national history, the IDIA laid the foundation for the particular industrial relations system which still exists in Canada. Although modified by important Second

World War and post-war labour legislation, the specific innovations of
the IDIA were retained in both the emergency war legislation of 1944
(PC 1003) and its permanent embodiment, the 1948 Industrial Relations and Disputes Investigation Act (IRDIA).[3] Today the IRDIA and its
provincial equivalents remain the basis of Canada's industrial relations system, although this system has recently reexperienced heavy
assaults in both provincial and federal jurisdictions.[4]

This paper will study the emergence and development of the Canadian industrial relations system in the context of class conflict, while
also trying to suggest some international comparisons. The Canadian
industrial relations system is situated towards the middle of a continuum which places Australia and New Zealand on an interventionist
pole and Great Britain on an opposite, voluntarist extremity. The
significant question is why these English-speaking industrial capitalist
nations evolved such distinctive legal structures for governing class
relations at the workplace. This chapter can only begin that discussion
by providing an historical description of the development of the
Canadian industrial relations system.

There have been three major periods of Canadian state activity in
the realm of industrial relations – the 1870s, the 1900s, and 1937–48.
Each of these decades saw major state initiative coinciding with
crucial shifts in the development of Canadian capitalism and respond-
ing to major surges of class conflict. Let us consider each in turn.

II

Canadian state consideration of a labour relations policy appropriate
for an industrial nation commenced cautiously in the early 1870s.
Trade unions had established themselves in the previous decade as an
increasingly potent force likely to play a permanent role in Canadian
society. The turmoil of the Nine Hours' movement of 1872, and
specifically the conspiracy prosecution of Toronto printers, led the
Conservative government of Sir John A. Macdonald to pass a Trade
Unions Act and a Criminal Law Amendment Act, both of which imitated Gladstone's British legislation of 1871. The new, legal status of
trade unions clarified current confusions about the standing of laws
on combination and conspiracy, and paved the way to further amendments in the mid-1870s which purported to grant labour equal standing in law with capital. "Free" labour now clearly implied the legal
right to combine, but nothing more.[5]

The first central organization of Canadian workers, the short-lived
Canadian Labor Union (CLU, 1873–8), lobbied effectively for subsequent changes in the Criminal Law Amendment Act and especially

pushed for amendment of outmoded Masters and Servants Acts which harkened back to a pre-industrial capitalist labour market. In this latter case constitutional confusion about jurisdiction slowed progress, but the CLU finally prevailed upon Alexander Mackenzie's federal Liberal government to pass a new Breaches of Contract Act in 1877 that was more to labour's liking, although far from completely satisfactory.[6]

Ontario's Liberal government of Oliver Mowat also courted working-class support in the 1870s. In 1873 it passed a Trades Arbitration Act in imitation of the 1867 and 1872 British legislation.[7] The fact that wage disputes were excluded from its terms rendered this Act totally inoperative, and even its amendment in 1890 to correct this lacuna changed little. While throughout the 1870s the CLU continued to promote arbitration, the precise meaning of that phrase remained unclear.

The rise to prominence of the Knights of Labor in the 1880s gave arbitration high priority among the articulated demands of Canadian organized labour.[8] Point 10 of the Knight's Declaration of Principles, however, suffered from ambiguous phrasing: "The substitution of arbitration for strikes, whenever and wherever employers and employees are willing to meet on equitable ground."[9] Before the Royal Commission on the Relations of Labor and Capital, Knights and trade unionists enthusiastically promoted arbitration. Appointed as an election device in December 1886 by the Macdonald Conservative government, the Commission was charged to enquire into and report on "the practical operations of Courts of Arbitration and Conciliation in the settlement of disputes between employers and employees, and on the best mode of settling such disputes."[10] The two reports which eventually emerged in 1889 both endorsed arbitration, although the majority report, signed by the trade union commissioners, called for "a system of local and voluntary boards, together with a permanent board," while the minority employers' report sought "courts of arbitration, conciliation and the settlement of minor differences."[11] What either group or, for that matter, what most of the working-class witnesses who endorsed arbitration, actually meant by the phrase remains obscure.

In that same decade the Provincial Workmen's Association (PWA), a Knightslike Nova Scotia organization predominantly composed of coal-miners, also heartily endorsed arbitration. At the PWA's behest the Fielding Liberal Nova Scotia government introduced into the legislature a compulsory arbitration Bill to cover coal -mining in 1887. Bitter opposition from the mine owners led to the Bill's failure in the Upper House after it had passed in the Assembly. Although successfully enacted the following year, this Act and its 1890 successor were also used infrequently.[12]

In the 1890s both British Columbia and Ontario introduced additional interventionist measures modelled directly on the New South Wales Trades Disputes Conciliation and Arbitration Act of 1892. Pember Reeves described this Act in the following terms:

Much was expected of it, and indeed it was an amiable and nicely-drafted measure, which, appealing as it did to pure reason and the good sense of disputants, had just the success always met with by conciliation laws dependent on the willingness of capital and labour to use them ... Employers treated them with contempt.[13]

Similar experiences in Ontario and British Columbia resulted in the legislation being used only once or twice.

Nevertheless, the Canadian Knights and their trade unionist allies continued to use the platform of the Trades and Labour Congress (1883, 1886 onwards) to endorse arbitration schemes. Beginning at the first convention in 1883, the new Congress had gone on record as approving "the appointment of a Board of Arbitration to which all disputes between workmen and their employers shall be submitted." In 1886 this had become much more explicit, with the addition that the Congress "petitions the various Governments to pass a law giving legal and binding effect to the decision of any Board of Arbitrators mutually agreed upon by both parties to any labour dispute." In subsequent congresses the TLC alternated almost annually between approval of voluntary and compulsory arbitration schemes. By the end of the century, however, the Congress appeared to move firmly behind compulsory arbitration, incorporating it as a plank in its platform in 1898 and calling on "the Dominion Government to establish a Board of Arbitration to adjust all disputes between employers and Employees."[14]

Some Canadian scholars have argued that the "copy-cat" nature of this legislation demonstrated an embarrassing national immaturity. Perhaps, but what surely is of more historical consequence is the preference of Canadian legislators for the New South Wales and English voluntarist models. Other Australasian examples were available: the 1890 South Australia "Act to Encourage the Formation of Industrial Unions and Associations and to Facilitate the Settlement of Industrial Disputes," and the more famous 1984 New Zealand Act of the same name introduced by Liberal Labour Minister, William Pember Reeves.[15] The New Zealand compulsory arbitration legislation became world famous at the turn of the century and was endorsed by disparate social reformers, especially the American Henry Demarest Lloyd. Lloyd's *A Country Without Strikes* (1900) apparently helped persuade Pember Reeves to produce his important chronicle of the Australasian experience, *State Experiments in Australia and New Zealand* (1902). The major point, however, remains that Canadian parliamentarians opted for the British and American voluntary principle.

III

Economic recovery after 1896 provided the labour movement with new room to manoeuvre, and rapid trade union growth ensued. In addition, labour militancy spread and Canadian strike indices began to move in an upward direction (see Tables 12.1 and 12.2). The Laurier Liberal government consequently passed a Conciliation Act in 1900 modelled on the equivalent British legislation of 1896. This Act created a Department of Labour to provide voluntary *ad hoc* conciliation services and to publish information. To aid in this last enterprise a monthly publication, *Labour Gazette*, was established, and an editor, William Lyon Mackenzie King, was hired.[16] The Dominion government had finally moved beyond Royal Commissions and had commenced to legislate in the realm of disputes resolution, no matter how haltingly.

King, probably Canada's most written-about historical figure, set about his new tasks enthusiastically. Trained at the universities of Toronto and Chicago, and later at Harvard, King epitomized the new social reform "expert." He was a "professional" social scientist who specialized in the new realm of labour economics, which was well on its way to becoming labour relations. He quickly turned this expert status to his advantage. In only ten years he created an impressive departmental edifice, first as civil servant (Deputy Minister) and later, after his 1908 entry into electoral politics, as Minister. From the first days of his arrival in Ottawa, King worked to expand the Department and, not coincidentally, his own career. After launching the *Labour Gazette* and slowly but surely increasing the size of the Department, King turned his attention to what he later would term one of his "children," namely conciliation. For King, as a socially committed Christian activist, the realm of disputes resolution offered the greatest rewards, no matter how fraught with political dangers. Thus, while it might be argued that the Laurier government's initial conception of the Department had been little more than political window-dressing aimed at winning the labour vote. King transformed it into a vastly more important undertaking. For example, he personally made the

Table 12.1
Strikes in Canada, 1891–1950

1891–1900	511
1901–10	1,548
1911–20	2,349
1921–30	989
1931–40	1,760
1941–50	2,537

SOURCE: Douglas Cruikshank and Gregory S. Kealey,
Historical Atlas of Canada, Vol. 3 (Toronto:
University of Toronto Press 1990).

Table 12.2
Canadian Strikes: Frequency, Size, and Duration, 1891–1950

	Frequency[a]	Size[b]	Duration[c]
1891–1900	55	218	25
1901–10	115	180	23
1911–20	123	286	20
1921–30	43	270	30
1931–40	61	218	11
1941–50	70	452	9

a Frequency = *Strikes*/Workers x 1,000,000
b Size = *Workers involved*/Strikes
c Duration = *Duration in worker days*/Workers involved
SOURCE: Same as Table 12.1.

weak legislation of the Conciliation Act work. Quite possibly, without King's zeal, the 1900 Act would have been as totally ineffectual as its provincial predecessors in Ontario, British Columbia, and Nova Scotia.[17]

An individual evaluation of King's role in acting under the Conciliation Act (1900) is less rewarding than an overall examination of the effect of this new state role on Canadian workers. The relationship of King's evolving practice as a mediator in the legislative solutions, offered later in the Railways Labour Disputes Act (RLDA 1903) and the Industrial Disputes Investigation Act (1907), must also be considered. Between 1900 and 1907 the Department of Labour intervened in forty-three disputes; in forty-two of those cases they acted under the Conciliation Act and on one occasion under the RLDA (given this infrequent invocation of the RLDA, the two Acts were actually consolidated in 1906). While the Conciliation Act offered a series of possible options for the Minister, including unilateral action to bring about a conference between the disputants, conciliation on the request of at least one party to the dispute, and arbitration if requested by both parties, all forty-two interventions in fact came upon request. While refusing to appear to be acting unilaterally, in a number of these cases the request for intervention came only after not very subtle suggestions were received from Ottawa (see Tables 12.3 and 12.4).[18]

Paul Craven's description of King's behaviour in these disputes, which emphasizes his role as an active mediator, is most apt.[19] In all cases King's major aim was to get the workers back on the job. His customary procedure on arrival was to interview both sides, try to discover grounds for a compromise, and then gain mutual agreement to some compromise. These compromises seldom reflected his own personal judgment of the justice of either side's case. Indeed, they often contradicted his initial assessments. Equally, the information he carried between the parties did not always convey an accurate version of the other side's position. Ending strikes took complete priority over any other consideration, and the Department of Labour's own assessments of success or failure reflected only that fact. In seven cases, for example, the Department simply reported that because the employer had already filled the strikers' job, nothing could be done. In another five cases the terms of settlement were not made public despite the clause in the Act that called for public disclosure. In at least one of these cases it is clear that this non-disclosure caused the union to return to work with the minimum of face-saving. Twelve cases, even as reported officially by the Department of Labour, simply regained the workers' jobs with no resolution of any of the original strike demands. Of the remaining eighteen cases where workers made some gains, all were compromise settlements, and in some of these the companies later repudiated the agreement.[20]

One example must suffice. In late October 200 construction labourers at the Montreal Cotton Company mill in Valleyfield, Quebec, struck for a wage increase from $1 per day to $1.25. The company refused to negotiate, and when strikers picketed the cotton mill itself, the company appealed to the civil authorities, who called in the militia from Montreal. The arrival of the military backfired, and the cotton workers walked out *en masse* in sympathy with the labourers. The cotton workers' union applied for conciliation, and King arrived on the scene. After discussions with both sides, he convinced the mill workers to return to their jobs in return for the withdrawal of the militia. The original labourers' strike demands simply disappeared in the shuffle. Perhaps more importantly, but not commented on by the Department publicly, was that in the following October the mill workers again applied for conciliation after the company fired a union leader. King gained the worker's reappointment, but only after

Table 12.3

Proceedings under the Conciliation Act (1900) and the Railway Labour Disputes Act (1903)

		Result[a]		
Year	No. of interventions	Workers' victory	Compromise	Loss
1900	2	1	0	1
1901	8	1	3	4
1902	7	0	2	5
1903	16	3	4	9
1904	2	0	0	2
1905	3	0	1	2
1906	3	1	1	1
1907	2	1	1	0
Total	43	7	12	24

a Results are, of course, highly subjective. This is my reading of the outcome in each case.

SOURCE: Canada, Department of Labour, *Annual Reports*, 1900–9.

Table 12.4

Proceedings under the Conciliation Act (1900) and the Railway Labour Disputes Act (1903) by Industry

Industry	Number
Manufacturing	21
Mining	7
Coal	(5)
Metal	(2)
Transportation and communication	11
Railroad	(6)
Street railway	(1)
Shipping	(2)
Telephone	(1)
Telegraph	(1)
Construction	4
Total	43

the union agreed to apologize. Only two years later, however, the company fired five union leaders for seeking a wage increase, and the Department was once more asked to intervene by the workers. Again Departmental intervention won little. This time four of the five regained their jobs, but no wage increase was granted. In the light of this experience the disappearance of union organization from Valleyfield in 1903 is not very surprising.[21]

The mention of the presence of the militia at Valleyfield should remind us that not all labour relations in these years involved peaceful conciliation. Indeed, on at least two other occasions the Conciliation Act was invoked with the military already present. Thus the new interventionism of the state in a conciliatory fashion must be understood in the context not only of the long history of coercive interventions by militia and police but as a continuing simultaneous ingredient. The first two decades of the twentieth century witnessed both the innovation of a liberal rule of law in labour relations and the largest number of military interventions of any period in Canadian history. Moreover, the recourse to coercion increasingly focused on the elements of the Canadian working class that resisted most strenuously the implementation of the new rule of law, namely the British Columbia and Nova Scotia coalminers.

Two further points should be made about the performance of King and his Department under the conciliation Act. First, the Act provided no mechanism for resolving recognition struggles; indeed, in every case where recognition was an issue the mediated settlement abandoned it. Second, the Act, perhaps surprisingly, was mainly used in manufacturing disputes. Of the forty-two interventions, precisely half occurred in manufacturing; the other twenty-one were split between transportation (ten), mining (seven), and construction (four). This raises some interesting questions about both the interpretation of the interventionist Canadian state and the subsequent disputes resolution legislation, given that it did not cover manufacturing under normal circumstances.

In April 1902, perhaps carried away by the early successes of the Conciliation Act and allegedly in response to the 1901 Canadian Pacific Railway (CPR) strike, the Minister of Labour introduced a compulsory arbitration Bill to cover the railways. The origins of this Bill remain obscure. The *Labour Gazette* officially attributed it to the CPR's summer-long trackmen's strike of 1901, but given the timing this seems somewhat questionable. Craven implies Australian influence from Minister of Labour Mulock's visit there, but King reported in his diary immediately after his first interview with the Minister on his return that he had been unimpressed with New Zealand's compulsory arbitration. King, too, was unenthusiastic about compulsory arbitration. He had opposed former British Columbia Minister of Mines, Smith Curtis's, attempts to promote compulsion throughout 1901. Nevertheless it would appear that such a scheme, probably promoted mainly by Lib-Lab MP Ralph Smith, won the day in early 1902. The problem was that Smith, President of the Trades and Labour Congress (TLC) had misread the attitude of the Canadian labour movement. The Railway Brotherhoods intransigently opposed the Bill, and their permanent Dominion lobbyist worked hard to undercut it.

Meanwhile, south of the border, Samuel Gompers (President of the American Federation of Labor) was furious, and demanded that the TLC reject the Bill. Not too surprisingly, given this constellation of forces, Ralph Smith and compulsory arbitration both went down to smashing defeats at the Berlin convention of the TLC. In autumn 1902, John Flett, the AFL's Canadian organizer, replaced Smith as President of the Congress, and compulsory arbitration was denounced as the TLC committed itself "to use every effort in their power ... to defeat this measure." On the following day the Congress amended its platform, substituting "voluntary" for "compulsory" in its arbitration plank. While often dismissed in the literature as simply another example of baneful AFL domination of the Canadian labour movement, labour's pervasive and continuing confusion about conciliation and arbitration prevents any such simple national categorization.[22]

In the wake of the Berlin Congress, the Laurier government decided to rethink its compulsory arbitration measure. Deputy Minister King spent part of his New Year's Day in 1903 working on a new draft Bill. His reflections on that occasion captured his attitude:

My present feelings are against the appointment of a permanent Board, as increasing machinery which is at this stage not necessary, and as less likely to be competent than the board chosen with view to a particular pursuit. I would rather make the whole an addition to conciliation, thereby strengthening the power of the former and minimizing the need of arbitration. Machinery is nothing, personality is everything.

Only a paragraph earlier he had reflected:

Personality lies at the root of it all. This being so, to talk of the "solution" to the labour problem, apart from the "solution" of "restoring humanity" is to speak of an impossible thing. People mean only a solution of some of the present-day difficulties which appear incidental to relationships between employers and employees as they frequently are.

The next day, as though preparing arguments for his later legislation, he wrote:

I think a measure of this kind should be brief and with as little machinery about it as possible; its aims should be to afford a means of the public getting an intelligent view of the situation and of bringing an enlightened public opinion to bear. In this connection I'd like to make the LG give even greater service.[23]

Approximately two weeks later Mulock arranged an all-day session with a deputation of railwaymen led by their lobbyist, J. Harvey Hall. King first read the Bill aloud, and a free discussion of each point followed.[24] When this Bill went to the legislature later that session, it received labour support and was passed. Ironically, given this complicated history, the Bill was used only one. On that occasion, after the breakdown of negotiations with the Grand Trunk in April 1904, the Telegraphers applied for a board under the RLDA. Conciliation failed in July, and the dispute went to arbitration before the same tripartite Board in August. In February 1905 the Board finally reported, with the chairman siding with the labour representative. the company representative filed a minority report opposing the recommended settlement. Under the terms of the Act, the settlement was not compulsory, and the company refused to accept it. Thus, after almost a year of delay, the telegraphers had gained nothing from this elaborate procedure. Again, perhaps it is not too surprising that no further use was made of the Act.

Nevertheless, despite infrequent use, the Act laid the groundwork for later legislation. It pioneered the tripartite Board structure, initiated compulsory investigation, and continued a tradition of voluntarism through its non-enforceable award. In addition, while it represented an expansion of intervention beyond the Conciliation Act, it implicitly opened the way for a retreat by introducing special measures for particularly sensitive components of the national economy. While this might have derived from constitutional sensitivity to the Dominion government's limited standing in labour matters, this was not the case. Indeed, the provinces appeared quite happy to leave this domain to central government, although both Ontario and Quebec did pass seldom-used conciliation Acts modelled on the federal legislation. Nova Scotia's compulsory arbitration legislation in mining was used only once after the turn of the century, with disastrous results for the workers involved.

Throughout this period King's aims and underlying assumptions expressed themselves most clearly when he could not find his bearings because his legitimacy was not accepted. His pervasive conviction that he was fulfilling a humanitarian mission to bring industrial "peace" (by which he meant order) led him to react self-righteously when faced with individuals who denied his (and the state's) right to intervene. On occasion this anger played itself out against particularly neanderthal capitalists, but it primarily applied to socialists, especially those of a revolutionary syndicalist hue. Thus British Columbia's militant miners and railway workers provoked King's anger more than any other workers. On his first encounter with them at Rossland late in 1901, King seemed truly shocked:

All of Canada can learn from BC; the province speaks a note of warning in strongest terms against the dangers of labour democracy. Industry will be fettered and the source of wages and wealth left undeveloped, if change does not come. Where men without a stake rule those who have everything to lose, or at least to risk, the alarm is great.[25]

So spoke the workingman's friend on his first encounter with British Columbia labour. On returning to Ottawa he acted on these insights and condemned the Rossland miners: "I have at least been fearless and honest in this exposé of Rossland proceedings," he confided in his diary; "It is the first time I have had to come out against the workingman and it pained me to do it, but if their cause is to prosper honesty must characterize it." His final reflection on the affair, however, prefigured his next visit to British Columbia: "The report was not really against the workingmen – in fact it was a strong defence of the men who acted uprightly and fearlessly and returned to work, it was a condemnation of selfish and irresponsible leaders."[26]

In 1903 King returned to British Columbia as Secretary of a Royal Commission to investigate labour unrest, especially the strikes of the United Brotherhood of Railway Employees (UBRE) and Western Federation of Miners (WFM). He disliked Dunsmuir, the Vancouver Island coal magnate, intensely, describing him as "a selfish millionaire who has become something of a tyrannical autocrat." King further claimed that "to satisfy a prejudice or greed he [Dunsmuir] has undertaken to make serfs of a lot of free men."[27] Yet in the long run, while blaming Dunsmuir for much of what had occurred, King preferred him to the revolutionary socialists. Indeed, he saw tyrannical capital and revolutionary socialism existing in a sycophantic relationship:

Two things impressed me during the day. The tremendous nature of the organized movement among workingmen, gradually uniting all workingmen into one great brotherhood, banded together for mutual support. The danger is of this whole body being converted to socialism if employers fail to take them into a sort of partnership through agreements with recognized unions.[28]

As the days passed, King's notion of this responsible partnership clarified:

The solution of the problem of strikes seems to me to lie along the business partnership arrived at by long term agreements between responsible leaders of organized capital on the one side and organized labour on the other. The trade unions must be incorporated and limits put on the right to strike without compliance and with safeguards in the constitution, as, for example, three months' notice, vote of two-thirds majority of men over 21, who've been members of union for at least six months ... Conciliation, compulsory investigation, and then compulsory arbitration seem the steps absolutely necessary in view of the interdependence and interrelation of individuals and public welfare.[29]

The Report issued by the Commission followed many of these ideas and went further in a repressive direction than any other written by King in this period. While piously calling on employers to remember that they were dealing with "sentient human beings," the report had more to say about labour. It "condemned the sympathy strike, the boycott, intimidation, the blacklist, and picketing as it is commonly practised." It argued that strikes for a closed shop should be outlawed, and further that "sympathy strikes ought to be rigidly repressed, as they are opposed to public opinion as well as natural justice and reason." Recognition strikes, it thought, were a difficult question, but facing the challenge squarely the Report ingenuously recommended to workers that "the surest and best way" to gain recognition was by "showing the employer by experience that it is to their advantage to deal with unions as such." After a lengthy assault on the socialist UBRE, WFM and the American Railway Union (ARU), it concluded that they should all be outlawed from Canadian soil and that no foreign unionists of any kind should operate in Canada. Following King's earlier musings, the Report then recommended (shades of Taff Vale) the incorporation of unions which, it acknowledged, would make them legally liable; however, to comfort the unions, it offered to insure union benefit funds from such liability. as a model constitution for these newly incorporated unions, the Report suggested the following clauses: no strikes without thirty days' notice; two-thirds majority in any strike vote; a secret ballot for strike votes; and no strikes in violation of contract. Finally, it recommended state compulsory investigation and publicity of strikes, and conciliation prior to any strike. Anticipating the IDIA, the Report also suggested that "special cases" such as public services might be singled out for particular consideration, and specifically proposed compulsory arbitration in such areas. In closing, the Report reiterated King's insights about incorporation and contracts:

We would therefore suggest that the courts be clothed with power to disincorporate any incorporated union ... which is shown to have violated any contract, or to have gone out on sympathy strike.[30]

Many of these measures were non-starters politically. Certainly the opposition to all international unionism was soon dropped, especially when the Lougheed Bill, having successfully passed the Senate, made no progress in the House of Commons. This Bill, which aimed to ban international unions from Canada, found only limited political support.[31] Nevertheless, the coincidental timing of these attempts to sever Canadian unionists from their international connections with the United States suggests an orchestrated attack.

Four years later, with the Conciliation Act declining dramatically in use, King proposed a new Act to Prime Minister Laurier and Minister of Labour Lemieux. By 1907 King's status was such that neither the minister responsible nor any other cabinet minister even saw the draft legislation before it was introduced in Parliament. This final, and most important, piece of legislation of the period was the Industrial Disputes Investigation Act (1907). This Act created great foreign interest and brought international attention to Canadian industrial relations for perhaps the first and last time. A series of foreign investigators studied the Act and its workings, commencing with Victor S. Clark in 1908 ad again in 1909, and including among others Lord Askwith, Ben Selekman, and J.R. Commons. In the tradition that had led Henry Demarest Lloyd to Australasia at the turn of the century and Clark in 1903–4, these investigators came to consider the possible applicability of the Canadian system to their own emerging industrial relations systems. While none manifested Lloyd's fervour for "A Country Without Strikes," all seemed marginally impressed with King's innovative compulsory investigation combined with a cooling-off period.

The IDIA passed Parliament in the aftermath of a serious coal strike at Lethbridge, Alberta, late in 1906. In most accounts this strike is given credit for producing the IDIA. While in no way denying that it undoubtedly eased the IDIA's passage through Parliament, the strike should not be given such prominence as a causative factor. Indeed, it might be argued that King took the opportunity offered by the strike to introduce legislation that he had been formulating out of his extensive experiences as a conciliator. To a large degree those practices, combined with the RLDA, prefigure the key components of the IDIA. Of the four major elements of the IDIA only one was not present in the RLDA, namely the cooling-off period. The IDIA prevented strikes and lockouts during the period of compulsory investigation. Thus it accomplished what the Conciliation act had seldom been able to achieve by bringing government intervention before the cessation of work. The cooling-off period immediately became the focus of labour opposition, especially from the railway brotherhoods. On this occasion, however, their lobbying won them nothing but an ineffectual amendment that offered them their choice of either the IDIA or the RLDA – ineffectual because the RLD was amended to include a cooling-off period as well.

The IDIA, if judged by the Department of Labour's claims, was a great success. Tables 12.5 and 12.6 demonstrate that it prevented strikes in most cases where it was invoked. Yet, simultaneously, Canadian class conflict reached previously unprecedented heights, especially in the period between 1917 and 1920. But the avoidance of strikes was never the major aim of the IDIA, or of any of the rest of this legislation. Its chief objective, which was also shared by social reformers in other countries, was to delimit rather than to end industrial warfare. The creation of limits involved a subtle process of establishing contact with the labour movement and of creating a legal structure that established parameters for class conflict. King and his kind knew only too well that strikes would not disappear; these social engineers were not utopians. They aimed instead at implementing a rational and efficient system to ensure that class conflict became a series of individual trade disputes. The process of the bureacratization of the labour movement had commenced.

While King would not necessarily accept this interpretation of his achievements, he certainly would never have undervalued their importance. In his diary, where he described his feverish work on the legislation over the Christmas season, he took care to establish the uniqueness of his contribution. "The measure is my own," he wrote; "The ideas embodied in it were mine before I knew they had found expression in legislation elsewhere ... So far as Canada is concerned it does not owe its origin to other countries, their methods or ideas." But lest King seem immodest, let us allow him to close this section with his final word on that triumphant day. King, it seems, did have a co-author after all: "God has given me the opportunity, has used me as his instrument to frame the measure, and I have done it along lines and in a manner which I believe will further His Will among men."[32]

IV

By leaping ahead three decades to the late Depression and the early years of the Second World War, one might expect to leave William Lyon Mackenzie King behind. Instead we now find him installed as Prime Minister of Canada. We also find a labour relations system that had remained almost totally unchanged. Trade unions were still legal, and the IDIA and its provincial enabling Acts still provided the framework for industrial relations. yet, commencing in 1937, rapid changes ensued that transformed the Canadian labour relations system from

Table 12.5
Proceedings under the Industrial Disputes Investigation Act, 1907–24

Year	No. of applications	No. of boards granted	No. of disputes where strike not averted
1907	25	22	1
1908	27	25	1
1909	22	21	4
1910	28	23	4
1911	21	16	4
1912	16	16	3
1913	18	15	1
1914	18	18	1
1915	15	12	1
1916	29	16	1
1917	53	37	1
1918	93	59	2
1919	70	47	3
1920	61	41	5
1921	54	26	2
1922	42	29	2
1923	22	17	1
1924	5[a]	1	0
Total	619	441	37

a First three months only.

SOURCE: Department of Labour (Canada), *Judicial Proceedings Respecting Constitutional Validity of the Industrial Disputes Investigation Act 1907* (Ottawa 1925): 281.

one which combined *ad hoc* coercion and conciliation in an unpredictable mixture to one which endorsed compulsory collective bargaining, but did so through an extraordinary complex of administrative boards and a mystifying maze of what soon thereafter would become "labour law."

The circumstances of this transformation can only be sketched here. Basically they involved the final arrival in Canada of successful industrial unionism, and the rise, especially in wartime, of a significant electoral threat from the left. These two factors, combined with massive workplace militancy in 1942 and 1943, brought about the Wartime Labour Relations Regulations or, as they are more commonly known, PC 1003. The dramatic change of heart of the King government in 1943, as it redirected its attentions to labour reform and social welfare innovations for the post-war world, have been well-established in recent revisionist Canadian historical writing and need not detain us here. Instead let us turn to one provincial case study which demonstrates the important shift from the better-known federal focus to the complex world of provincial variation.[33]

Table 12.6
Proceedings under the Industrial Disputes Investigation Act, by Industry, 1907–24

Year	No. of applications	No. of disputes where strike not averted
Mining		
Coal	68	10
Metal	21	5
Transportation and communication		
Railroad	188	7
Street railway	102	7
Express	11	1
Shipping	32	0
Telegraph	17	1
Telephone	7	0
Miscellaneous		
Light and power	22	3
Elevators	1	0
War work	30	1
Other not clearly within scope of Act	120	2
Total	619	37

SOURCE: Same as Table 12.5.

In 1937 Nova Scotia became the first Canadian jurisdiction to pass labour legislation that followed the American Wagner Act in compelling employers to engage in collective bargaining with duly organized workers. While Canadian labour had been pressing for such legislation for years, it took the combination of strong pressure from Nova Scotia steelworkers and coalminers and the particular conjuncture in provincial politics to allow for this significant breakthrough. This Act, in addition to forcing employers to bargain collectively, also gave union action the force of law; it contained (by later standards) almost no restrictions on the right to strike; most importantly, perhaps, it failed to impose compulsory conciliation. Ignored by labour relations scholars as unimportant because it was Nova Scotian, it was also seen to give too much discretionary power to the provincial Department of Labour, and criticized for failing to set up specific administrative machinery for enforcement. Nevertheless, this Act in many ways set better precedents for labour than PC 1003.

With the outbreak of the Second World War, the federal government took jurisdiction over almost all labour relations in the country through the invocation of wartime emergency powers. The rusty machinery of the IDIA, however, even when aided by various privy council orders, failed to deal adequately with the massive surge of labour organization and the wave of working-class militancy which spread across the country in the early years of the war. Again largely related to local political scenarios, the provinces moved faster than the federal government in meeting the strongly articulated demands of the now-menacing labour movement. In both British Columbia and Ontario, the threat of massive social democratic electoral gains led to new collective bargaining acts which added administrative machinery to the two provinces' late-Depression legislation to compel collective bargaining.

In the face of such examples the King government finally, in February 1944, introduced the Wartime Labour Relations Regulation, PC 1003. These regulations allowed all employees to join unions (with relatively few exceptions); called for the certification of bargaining agents in appropriate units; introduced compulsory collective bargaining which mandated the obligation to bargain in good faith and to attempt to reach an agreement; maintained a combination of conciliation officer and conciliation board mechanisms; introduced the demand that all collective agreements contain a clause creating mechanisms for the handling of disputes during the life of the contract; prevented strikes until after the failure of conciliation mechanisms in situations where there was no previous collective agreement in force; and set up a Wartime Labour Relations Board to administer the Act and to enforce its numerous punitive clauses. Often regarded as Canadian labour's Magna Carta, PC 1003 certainly introduced important new rights to labour, but its maintenance of King's earlier innovations circumscribed these important rights with a labyrinth of law.

PC 1003 succeeded in helping to lower the Canadian strike rate in the last years of the war, primarily by eliminating the need for labour to fight recognition strikes. In the aftermath of the war, however, industrial relations and everything else remained an open question. Again industrial militancy – especially the Ford strike of late 1945 and the Stelco strike of 1946 – helped to ensure that rights won in wartime would not be lost during reconstruction.[34] Thus, in October 1946, a Federal-Provincial Conference on Labour Relations empowered the Federal Department of Labour to draft legislation for the federal jurisdiction and then to submit it to the provinces for their consideration and advice, all on the understanding that both levels of government would attempt to legislate uniformly in the realm of collective bargaining. On the federal level this agreement resulted in the Industrial Relations and Disputes Investigations Act of 1948 (IRDIA).

The IRDIA basically combined the measures of the old IDIA with many of the provisions of PC 1003. The provinces, however, did not live up to their commitment to uniformity, and the result has been a patchwork of labour legislation across the country which shares many of the major provisions of the IDIA and PC 1003 but which varies significantly from jurisdiction to jurisdiction, adding a nightmare of local idiosyncrasy to the maze of regulation. Again to use Nova Scotia as one example, its 1947 Trade Union Act failed to extend union security rights equivalent to those in the federal draft legislation and introduced a series of putative limitations on labour's rights. Among these provisions were significant fines for illegal strikes and the assumption that the union was liable for the enforcement of the contract,employers' rights clauses including an employers' right to freedom of speech, the refusal to allow any organizational efforts at the workplace, the innovative notion that the results of the mandatory strike vote were to be based on a majority of all employees (not simply those voting), and an enlarged role for the newly created Labour Relations Board which gave it the power to define appropriate bargaining units in terms of the employees' "community of interest."

While undoubtedly representing a major gain for Canadian workers, the effects of the IRDIA and its subsequent elaboration into yet more complex legalities, varying from jurisdiction to jurisdiction, certainly did not represent what Canadian Congress of Labour and Congress of Industrial Organization activists had envisioned in their fight for industrial justice and equality. Aside from the uncertainty for labour of the rule of law itself, the complex labour relations system finds its rationale in two pervasive myths: first, that the two parties involved – capital and labour – meet as equals in so-called "free" collective bargaining (what liberal theory terms "industrial pluralism"); and second, that the role of the state is simply that of a neutral umpire, aiding the two hostile leviathans to make peace and thus protecting the interests of the unprotected public.

In the years after 1948 the labour relations system evolved along the lines of the IRDIA. The only significant change came with the granting of collective bargaining rights to civil servants and other public sector employees, commencing with Quebec in 1965, the federal government in 1967, and the other provinces soon thereafter. Interestingly, the extension of trade union rights in this sector did not take place under the old legislative blanket. Instead, a new series of laws for public sector collective bargaining was passed, all of which seriously restricted public servants' rights compared with those of workers in the private sector. This last point is of special significance in Canada today because, in all jurisdictions, public sector workers find themselves singled out for governmental hostility and for further legislative encroachment on their limited and recently gained rights. Indeed, the entire liberal edifice so carefully constructed over the last 100 years appears to be in grave danger of collapse.

V

The Canadian industrial relations system has evolved through three distinct phases, each of which coincided with significant transition points in the development of Canadian capitalism. The phases can also be shown to have emerged as partial answers to crucial moments of class conflict. The first step in this process came with the Canadian state's formal recognition of the legal existence of trade unions as labour's institutional embodiment. A second and more critical period came in the first decade of the twentieth century when, in the face of labour militancy and the regional development of strong socialist movements, William Lyon Mackenzie King stepped forward and applied the newly developing international expertise of labour reform to create a peculiarly Canadian system of industrial relations which lay halfway between British and Australasian experience. The uniqueness of his creation led foreign observers, especially Americans, to study the Canadian IDIA intensively for the following twenty years. Finally, in the face of the Depression crisis ad the biggest strike wave in Canadian history, Canadian provincial governments and eventually the federal government passed compulsory collective bargaining legislation and created an administrative tribunal system to enforce the law.

The underlying logic of the system lies in three areas. First,the aim was seldom simply to repress conflict, although, as we have seen, that too was occasionally indulged in, especially during the 1900–20 crisis. Instead the aim from early on was to institutionalize and confine conflict. Strikes of a legitimate type were acceptable, albeit not desirable, but strikes that went beyond the acceptable aims of collective bargaining (narrowly defined) were to be eliminated. Thus sympathetic strikes, secondary boycotts, politically motivated stoppages, wildcats, strikes in "key" sectors, and many public sector strikes, all lay outside the state-imposed definition of "acceptable." A similar way of thinking forced all issues into a highly formalized and institutionalized legal structure. If strikes during the life of the collective agreement were proscribed, then another method of disputes resolution was necessary; here lay the origin of the extensive system of grievance arbitration.

Second, labour's long-range aim of industrial democracy, and indeed an avowed aim of liberal industrial relations theorists such as King, came to be defined in ways that limited employee participation in workplace management. Participation was restricted to the narrow aims of the collective agreement, and larger issues were declared off-limits by the pervasive management rights clauses that became an entrenched part of Canadian collective agreements in the post-war period. Here again the focus became procedure, not substance.

Third, the union by necessity became responsible. King's original distinction between responsible and irresponsible unions gained an increasingly legal definition. Unions became legally responsible for disciplining their members in various ways, most obviously so in their legal mandate to prevent wildcats and ensure enforcement of the terms of the collective agreement. Some unions have gone further and often appear to share in responsibility for the efficient operation of the business. Thus unions become structurally separated from their membership, and leaders lose touch with the reality of the workers' world. The reign of the "responsible" union leader has been accelerated by the complexities of the industrial relations system itself.

Neither King nor anyone else fully understood the logic of the industrial relations system that they had created, but King's quest for a system typified as "a business partnership arrived at by long term agreements between responsible leaders of organized capital on the one side and organized labour on the other" certainly became part of the system's accomplishment.[35] That it was something less than totally successful became increasingly evident from the mid-1960s. A new crisis of accumulation and a new surge of working-class militancy has again raised far-reaching questions about the nature of the Canadian industrial relations system.

NOTES

1 William Pember Reeves, *State Experiments in Australia and New Zealand* (London 1901).
2 Henry Demarest Lloyd, *Newest England: Notes of a Democratic Traveller in New Zealand with Some Australian Comparisons* (New York 1900).
3 Laurel Sefton MacDowell, *"Remember Kirkland Lake": The Gold Miners' Strike of 1941–42* (Toronto 1983), and "The Formation of the Canadian Industrial Relations System during World War II," *Labour/Le Travailleur* 3 (1978): 175–96; H. Clare Pentland, "The Canadian Industrial Relations System: Some Formative Factors," *Labour/Le Travailleur* 4 (1979): 9–23; and Jeremy Webber, "The Malaise of Compulsory Conciliation: Strike Prevention in Canada during World War II," *Labour/Le Travail* 15 (1985): 57–88.
4 Leo Panitch and Donald Swartz, *From Consent to Coercion: The Assault on Trade Union Freedoms* (Toronto 1985).
5 Gregory S. Kealey, *Toronto Workers Respond to Industrial Capitalism, 1867–92* (Toronto 1980), chap. 8.
6 Ibid.
7 Ibid., chaps 8 and 9, and Leslie Wismer, ed., *Proceedings of the Canadian Labour Union, 1873–77* (Montreal 1951), passim.

8 Gregory S. Kealey and Bryan D. Palmer, *Dreaming of What Might Be: The Knights of Labor in Ontario, 1880–1902* (New York 1982), chap. 9.
9 Ibid., 399–400.
10 Gregory S. Kealey, ed., *Canada Investigates Industrialism* (Toronto 1973), 3.
11 Ibid., 8–58.
12 Ian McKay, "By Wisdom, Wile or War: The Provincial Workmen's Association and the Struggle for Working-Class Independence in Nova Scotia, 1879–1897," *Labour/Le Travail* 18 (Fall 1986).
13 Reeves, *State Experiment*.
14 Eugene Forsey, *Trade Unions in Canada, 1812–1902* (Toronto 1982), chap. 16.
15 Reeves, *State Experiments*.
16 R. McGregor Dawson, *William Lyon Mackenzie King, 1874–1923* (Toronto 1980).
17 Ibid. For a more critical approach see H.S. Ferns and B. Ostry, *The Age of Mackenzie King* (London 1955) and Paul Craven, *"An Impartial Umpire"": Industrial Relations and the Canadian State, 1900–1911* (Toronto 1980).
18 Department of Labour (Canada), *Annual Reports*, 1900–7.
19 Craven, *"An Impartial Umpire,"* passim.
20 Department of Labour (Canada), *Annual Reports*, 1900–7.
21 Ibid., 1901–3.
22 Forsey, *Trade Unions*, chap. 16. See also Robert Babcock, *Gompers in Canada* (Toronto 1974).
23 King, William Lyon Mackenzie, *Diary*, 2 and 3 January 1903.
24 Ibid., 17 January 1903.
25 Ibid., 19 November 1901.
26 Ibid., 10 January 1902.
27 Ibid., 10 May 1903.
28 Ibid., 6 May 1903.
29 Ibid., 15 May 1903.
30 "Report of the Royal Commission on Industrial Disputes in the Province of British Columbia," Department of Labour (Canada), *Annual Report*, 1903.
31 Babcock, *Gompers in Canada*.
32 King, *Diary*, 1–3 January 1907.
33 MacDowell, *"Remember Kirkland Lake."*
34 For the Ford strike see David Moulton, "Fort Windsor 1945," in Irving Abella, "On Strike (Toronto 1974); on Hamilton, see Craig Heron and Robert Storey, "Work and Struggle in the Canadian Steel Industry, 1900–1950," in their *On the Job: Confronting the Labour Process in Canada* (Montreal 1986).
35 King, *Diary*, 15 May 1903.

Index

Manitoba, 33, 40–1, 75, 302, 305, 350–1
manufacturing, 351–2, 359, 365–6, 373–4, 376–7, 427
manufacturing condition, 243
March, Charles, 268–9
Marine Trades and Labour Federation of Canada, 301
Marine Trades Federation, 298
marine workers, 309
Maritimes, 112, 348, 373, 376, 384
Marks, Joseph, 263
Marsh, Leonard, 10–11, 340
Martin, William, 13
Marx, Karl, 42, 64, 72–3, 77, 109, 125, 149, 240, 333
Marxism Today, 64
Marxist, 34, 37 290
Marxist Quarterly, 12, 64–7, 69
Marxist Review, 63–4
Marxist Studies Centre, 64
Marxist-Christian dialogue, 66
Masons, 174
Massachusetts, 34
Masses, The, 49, 51
Massey, 249
Massey-Harris, 14, 304
Masson Agricultural Implements Works, 250, 274
Master Employers' Association, 218
Master Printers, 219
Masters and Servants Acts, 421
matrix law, 220, 222
Mavor, James, 24
Mayo, Elton, 13, 26
meat packers, 300
meat packing industry, 13, 300, 336, 369, 375

mechanics' institutes, 38
Medcalf, Francis H., 167, 177, 185, 194–6, 198–9
Meighen, Arthur, 41, 370
Memorial University of Newfoundland, xiv–xv, 410
men's clothing industry, 375
Meredith, W.R., 268
Mergenthaler, Otto, 224
merger movement, 335
Merritton, 257–8, 271, 276
metal and shipbuilding, 369
metal mining, 347
metal trades, 294, 298, 301, 303, 309, 362, 364, 369
Metal Trades Council, 301–2, 305, 308–9
metal trades strikes, 308, 366
metal trades workers, 122, 291, 304
Metcalfe, Lord, 174–5, 183, 200
Methodist, 367
methods of dispute settlement, 352
Metropolitan Police of England, 194
micro-electronics, 342
Midgley, Victor, 308
Midland, 301
military aid to the civil power, 358–9
militia, 425–7
Miller, Samuel, 272–3
Millinery Workers, 375
Mine Workers Union of Canada, 374
Miners' Magazine, 239
mining, 351, 359, 373–4, 376–7, 427
Mining and Smelting Company, 374
mining strikes, 377
Minto, 374
Moncton, 297

Monière, Denis, 78
Montague, J.T., 13
Montgomery, David, 18, 22, 103, 116, 127, 140, 149, 151, 294, 334, 348, 372
Montgomery, John, 179
Montmorency, 300, 364
Montmorency Falls, 298
Montreal, xvii, 10, 15, 21, 51, 59, 70, 77, 84, 106, 111, 140, 179, 187, 212, 216–17, 221–2, 291–2, 297–8, 300–2, 311, 313, 315, 316, 317, 331–2, 361, 367, 369, 371, 375, 377–8
Montreal Cotton Company, 364, 425
Montreal Star, 215
Montreal Trades and Labour Council (MTLC), 300
Moodie, Captain Bob, 188
Moore, Tom, 41
Moose Jaw, 306
Morley, Terry, 103
Morris, Leslie, 55–6, 58, 61, 64, 66, 69, 91
Morris, Robert, 316
Morris, William, 117–18
Morrison, Dr. Thomas David, 171
Morton, Desmond, 18–20, 124
Moscow, 55, 59, 61
Mosher, Aaron, 314–5
moulders, 297, 364
movement culture, 241, 260, 266
Mowat, Oliver, 266, 268, 279, 421
Mulock, William, 427, 429
Multicultural History Society of Ontario, 147
multiculturalism, 147
Municipal Act, 178
Municipal Corporations Act, 178, 190
Municipal Loan Fund Act, 184